JUST THE PLANT NAME

Yvonne de La Paix

Avery Publishing Group
Garden City Park, New York

Cover Design: William Gonzalez
In-House Editor: Lisa James
Typesetting: Phaedra Mastrocola
Illustrator: John Wincek
Printer: Paragon Press, Honesdale, PA

ISBN 0-89529-723-X (mass market)

Printed in the United States of America

10 9 8 7 6 5 4 3 2 1

ontents

Acknowledgments

Introduction, 1

The Girls' Names, 7
  Changing Female Names to Male Names, 17
  Prefixes: Bat-/Bath-, Ben-, 21
  Southern Colonial Girls' Names, 31
  Suffixes: -esha, -isha, 35
  Prefixes: De, Di, Da, 38
  Prefixes: De, De la, Del, De las, De los, 40
  Suffix: -el, 45
  Surnames as First Names, 50
  Suffix: -kin, 55
  Hyphenated Names, 62
  America Loves Its Soaps, 64
  Prefix: Les, 68
  Prefix/suffix: Kill-, -kill, 76
  Suffix: -ko, 78
  Prefix: La, 81
  Deep South Girls' Names, 82

New England Girls' Names, 102
Prefix: No- , 104
Suffixes: -ova, -ovna, 106
Prefix: O-, 107
Great Plains Girls' Names, 111
A Soapy Sampler (of girls' names), 114
Homes on the Range Girls' Names, 118
Southwest Girls' Names, 125
Suffix: -sten, 128
Tribal Traditions, 135
Suffixes: -lin, -lyn, 137
Prefix/suffixes: Vel-, -veld, -vel(d)t, 140
Northwest Girls' Names, 144
Pairing Surnames, 148

The Boys' Names, 153
Prefix: Abd al, 154
Changing Male Names to Female Names, 161
Prefixes: Bar-, Ben-, 169
Southern Colonial Boys' Names, 180
Prefixes: de, d', de la, de l', du, des, 190
Prefix: El, 196
Prefixes: Al, El, 197
Prefix: Fitz-, 202
Saint Names, 208
Suffix: -holm, 216
Prefix: Il, 220
"Junior" or "Il," 226
No More Saints & Prophets, Now It's Sports & Stars, 233
Deep South Boys' Names, 239
Prefix: Le, 241
Prefixes: Mac-, Mc-, 245
Prefixes: Ap, Map, 246
New England Boys' Names, 256

Suffixes: -ovich, -vich, 260
Great Plains Boys' Names, 263
A Soapy Sampler (of boys' names), 267
Homes on the Range Boys' Names, 276
Suffix: -son, 283
Prefix/suffixes: Sen, -sen, -sin, 285
Twins or More, 291
Suffixes: -on, -won, -quon, 295
Prefixes: Von, Van, 297
Puritan Virtue Names, 298
Northwest Boys' Names, 302
Southwest Boys' Names, 307

Afterword, 311

acknowledgments

Thanks to my father, Leo Charles, and my mother, Karen Sue for saying, "We don't know what it means, honey, we just liked the way it sounded" (well, for that and a lot of other things); to my friend Rhonda Lisette, whose first name never appeared in any name book as a separate and unique name, which it is, till now; to my friend Kendra Jo, who thought her name had only one meaning; to Penelope Lela for the long weekends at work; to the publisher, who gave a novice writer a shot after one clever letter; and to my editor, Lisa James, for being brave enough to stand in the line of fire.

*To the memory of Ken Bond, because he
made me promise I would.*

Introduction

Congratulations! You're having a baby! There's *so* much to do—and that includes choosing a name. You want a name that not only sounds good to you, you want a name that means something to you. In America today, many of us are returning to our roots and seeking ways to express our heritage or beliefs. *Just the Perfect Name* provides you with a comprehensive list of names from a wide variety of cultures and religious traditions. Literature, sacred writings, plays, poems, hymns, legends, histories, dictionaries, encyclopedias, concordances . . . these are the resources I used in putting this book together. Whether your tribe came from Asia, Africa, Europe, India, the Americas, or the tropics, you will find a large choice of suitable names.

Of course, a name is no less a name if you made it up. Quite a few names were pulled out of the blue by writers and have since been used as proudly as names with long, long histories—Pamela, Wendy, and Geraldine are but three examples. If anybody asks about the name's meaning, just use the old, trusty "origin uncertain" line! There are a number of names in this collection that are so old or so accepted in many cultures that their true origins may never be determined.

There are also many new names that are popping up and spreading like wildfire. I have tried to keep you up to date with the latest trends, such as the use of surnames as first names (see page 50). You can also pull a name from TV, movies, books, music, and sports (see pages 64 and 233). As long as the name means something to you, that's all that matters. You may, after all this information, just choose a name or sequence of names because it "just sounds good." Ask my parents about that one.

You can customize a name by spelling it differently or by combining two names. Combination names are quite common. For instance, the number of names that contain Mary is amazing. There are also a number of African Yoruba combination names that include Ade or Arabic names that include Abd al, so putting two names together is common throughout the world.

While I do encourage individualism in the naming of a child, it is possible to go too far. You don't want to condemn your child to a lifetime of teasing. Therefore, I offer the following advice:

- *Please,* say the full name aloud a few times. Does it make a sentence or describe something amusing—"Jay Walker," "Paige Turner," "Jack Daniels"? Try not to use it.

- Write the initials of the name. Do they spell something negative—"Andrew Steven Smith," "Bethany Ann Dunn," "Samuel Nicholas Miller"? Try not to use it.

- If you are foreign-born and selecting a name from your homeland, please ask your American friends if the name has a negative meaning here in the States. The Vietnamese name "Phuc," the Asian names "Bong" or "Dong," and the African name "Dudu" are among the names that will cause more hard times for your child than necessary. Try not to use them.

Let's go through a sample name entry:

YVON,[1] "ee-VON" and "ee-VAWN"[2]—*French version of John*[3]: *"God's gracious gift"*[4]*; Greek: "tranquility" and "flower."* **IBAN** (ee-bahn), **IBON** (ee-bohn)—Basque; **YVAN** (ee-VAN), **YVAIN**—Bretagne.[5] In the Arthurian lore of Bretagne, Sir Yvain was a Knight of the Round Table driven mad by love. He wanders, wild and troubled, in the woods, and encounters a lion. The lion and he take a liking to one another, and they calm and restore one another.[6] VON, VONNY.[7] See also EVAN, IVAN, JOHN. F[8]

1. A frequent version of the name.
2. Suggested pronunciation for American English speakers.
3. Language, country, or culture of origin or common use.
4. Translation. If no translation is clear, other notes.
5. Variations on the name.
6. Further notes, if any.
7. Diminutives or nicknames.
8. Sign that there is an opposite-sex counterpart, which may provide more ideas or information. (By the way, the female counterpart of YVON happens to be YVONNE.)

Best wishes for your family, and blessings for your soon-to-be-born baby.

THE GARYS NAMES

THE TOP FIVE

ASHLEY
AMBER
AMANDA
ANN(E)/ANITA
ANDREA

If the name you're looking for isn't here, see the other vowels.

ABBEY. See ABIGAIL.

ABDIELLE, "ahb-dee-EHL"—*Hebrew: "servant of God."* M

ABELIA, "ah-BEH-lee-ah" or "ay/ah-beh-LEE-yah"—*Hebrew: "breath" or "meadow"; Assyrian: "daughter."* Abelia is a semievergreen shrub which produces lightly fragrant pink or white flowers. M

ABEY, "ah-BAY"—*Native American Omaha: "a leaf."* ABEYTU (ah-bay-TOO, "green leaf").

ABIA, "ah-BEE-ah"—*Arabic: "powerful."*

ABIGAIL, "AB-ih-gale"—*Hebrew: "father's strength" or "father's delight."* ABAIGEAL (ah-BYE-gahl or AH-bye-gahl)—*Irish Gaelic;* ABICHAYIL (ahbih-KHA-eel—"KHA" like you're clearing everything out of your throat), AVICHAYIL (ahbih-KHA-eel—"KHA" like you're clearing everything out of your throat)—*Israeli.* In the Old Testament/Tanakh, Abigail became King David's wife. ABBI(E), ABBEY, ABBY; GAEL, GAIL, GALE, GAYLE.

ABIRA, "ah-BEER-ah"—*Hebrew: "strong"; Arabic: "fragrant."*

ABRA, "AH-brah"—*Arabic: "example,"* *Hebrew: "earth mother."* In the Old Testament/Tanakh, a woman named Abra was one of King Solomon's favorite wives. Abra is also a character in *Armadis of Gaul,* a sixteenth-century English romance.

ACADIA, "ah-KAY-dee-ah" or "ah-KAYD-yah"—*French.* ACCADIA. This is the name of a region, originally settled by the French, in Nova Scotia, New Brunswick, and Prince Edward Island in Canada. When the Acadian settlers moved down into the southern United States, the word "Acadian" got shortened and slurred to "Cajun."

ACELINE, "ahs-LEEN"—*French from Teutonic: "noble."*

ADA, "AY-dah" or "ah-DAH"—*Hebrew: "ornament"; German: "noble"; Teutonic: "joyous."* ADAH—*Hebrew.* Adah was one of the daughters of Adam and Eve. Ada has been a name used in literature, appearing in Charles Dickens's *Bleak House,* Vladimir Nabokov's *Ada,* and Lord Byron's *Childe Harold's Pilgrimage.* ADDA, ADDI(E), ADDY. See also ADABELLE.

ADABELLE, "AH-dah-behl" or "AY-dah-behl"—*Teutonic/French: "joyous and comely."* This is an example of the limitless possibilities of combining two names—in this case, Ada and Belle.

ADALIA, "ah-DAHL-yah" or "ah-DAY-lee-ah"—*German: "noble."* **ATHALIA** (ah-TAH-lee-ah)—French. **ADDI(E), ADDY.**

ADAMA, "ah-DAHM-ah"—*Hebrew: "of the Earth" or "red earth."* **ADAMINA.** M

ADARA, "ah-DAHR-ah"—*Hebrew: "dark noble"; Arabic: "virginal" or "pure"; Greek: "beauty."* **ADIRA, DARA.** M

ADDI(E). See ADA, ADELAIDE, ADELINE.

ADELAIDE, "AD-uh-layd"—*German: "of noble birth"; English: "propserous" or "happy."* **ADALAIDA** (ah-deh-LAYD-ah), **ADALINE, ADDALA, ADELAYDA**—Italian; **ADELA; ADELAJDA** (ah-deh-LAH-ee-yah)—Polish; **ADELENA** (ah-deh-LEH-nah), **ALINA, ALITA** (ah-LEE-tah)—Portuguese and Basque; **ADELHEID** (AD-ehl-hayd or AD-ehl-hyde), **ADELHEIDE, ADELIN**—German; **ADELINDA, ADELINE** (ah-deh-LEEN), **ADELIZ** (ah-deh-LEEZ)—Spanish; **ALINE, ALYNE** (ah-LEEN), **ATHELINE** (ah-teh-LEEN), **ATHELYNE**—French; **AZALAID** (AHZ-ah-layd), **AZALAIS**—Slavic. Queen Adelaide was the wife of England's William IV. Not only was her name given to the capital of the province of South Australia, it became a popular name for girls in Britian. **ADDI(E), ADDY; DEL, DELLA; HEIDE, HEIDI.**

ADELEKE, "ah-DEH-leh-keh"—*African Yoruba: "crown of joy."*

ADELINE, "AD-eh-line," or rarely "ad-eh-LEEN"—*German: "of noble birth."* **ADALINE; ADELINA** (ah-deh-LEE-nah)—French; **ADELINDA** (ah-deh-LEEN-dah)—Spanish. In Lord Byron's *Don Juan*, Adeline is one of the main character's objects of desire. From this work comes the bud of the idea that became "Sweet Adeline," a perennial barbershop-quartet favorite; from this song

title comes the name of a women's close-harmony vocal group. **ADA, ADDI(E), ADDY; LINDA.** See also ADELAIDE, ADELLE.

ADELLE, "ah-DELL"—*German: "of good cheer."* **ADALIA, ADDALA, ADELA, ADELINA, ADELINDA, ADELINE** (ah-deh-LEEN or ah-deh-LINE), **ADELLA; ADÈLE, ADETTE**—French. Saint Adella was the abbess of Pfalzel, a convent in Germany, and a daughter of King Dagobart II. **DEL, DELLA.**

ADENA, "ah-DAY-nah" or rarely "ah-day-NAH"—*Hebrew: "adornment."* **ADENE.** An Adeni is someone who lives near the Gulf of Aden in the western Arabian Sea, where the countries of Yemen and Somalia are. **DENA.** See also ADINA.

ADERETTE, "ah-dehr-EHT"—*Hebrew: "crown."*

ADESINA, "ah-deh-SEE-nah"—*African: "she has unlocked the path."* The path referred to is the path for other babies to follow. It is a name given to first-born daughters in the Nigerian group of tribes. **SINA.**

ADIELLE, "ah-dee-EHL"—*Hebrew: "ornament of God."* M

ADILA(H), "ah-DEE-lah" or "AH-dee-lah"—*Arabic: "equal" or "just."* M

ADINA, "ah-dee-NAH" or "ah-DEE-nah"—*Hebrew: "voluptuous," "sensual," or "pliant."* **ADINE, DINA.** See also ADENA.

ADITI, "ah-DEE-tee"—*Sanskrit: "boundless"; Hindu: "free."* In Hinduism, Aditi is a primordial goddess from whom sprang the Adityas, or sovereign deities. Her children number from six to twelve, depending upon which source you consult. The number twelve seems to fit nicely with the twelve astrological signs, one for each month of the year.

ADIVA, "AH-deev-ah"—*Arabic and Hebrew: "pleasant" or "gentle."* **DIVA.**

ADONA, "ah-DOHN-ah" or "ah-DAWN-ah"—*Phoenician: "lady."* M

ADONIA, "ah-DOHN-yah" or "uh-DAWN-ee-ah"—*Greek: "beautiful young one."* This name is lifted from the earlier Phoenician words for gods and goddesses. M

ADRIANNE, "AY-dree-un" or "ay-dree-ANN"—*Greek: "rich" or "of the (Adriatic) sea"; Latin: "of the Adriatic" or "dark-haired."* **ADREA, ADREANA, ADRIANE, ADRIANNA, ADRIENNE; ADRIANA** (ah-dree-AH-nah)—Italian; **AIDRIAN** (eye-dree-AHN)—Irish Gaelic. **ADREE, ADRIA, ADRI(E), ADRY.** M

ADRIELLE, "AH-dree-ehl" or "ah-dree-EHL"—*Hebrew: "God's majesty" or "of God's congregation."* **ADRIELLA.** M

AFINA, "ah-FEE-nah"—*Rumanian: "blueberry."*

AFIYA, "ah-FEE-yah"—*Swahili: "healthy."* **FIYA.**

AFRA, "AH-frah"—*Arabic: "fawn-colored" or "earth-colored"; Hebrew: "young doe."* **APHRA, APHRAH; OPHRA, OPHRAH.** Seventeenth-century Aphrah Behn was the first woman to make a living as a writer *using her own name.* Thanks, from all of us.

AGATHA, "AH-gah-thah" or "AG-ah-thah"—*Greek: "good"; French: "precious stone."* **AGACE** (ah-GAHSS), **AGATHE** (ah-GAHT), **AGIDIA** (ah-ZHEE-dee-ah)—French; **AGACIA** (ah-GAH-see-ah)—Italian; **AGAFIA**—Russian; **AGATA**—Polish; **AGATA, AGATON**—Swedish; **AGATE; AGATHI** (ah-YAH-tee)—Greek; **AGI, ÁGOTA, ÁGOTHA**—Hungarian. Saint Agatha, who lived in the third century, was martyred for refusing the advances of a Roman consul. The veil of

Saint Agatha is said to have protected a city in Sicily from the eruption of Mount Etna, and so she is a saint called upon for protection from fire and burning. Agate stone was used for carving figurines at the French court in the sixteenth century. Both the stone and the name were believed to impart to the owner eloquence and independence. **AGGI(E), AGGY.**

AGAVE, "ah-GAH-veh"—*Greek: "noble."*

AGGI(E). See AGATHA, AGNES.

AGNES, "AG-ness" or "AG-nez"—*Greek: "chaste" or "pure"; Latin: "lamb."* **AGNE, AGNEK, AGNETA**—Swedish; **AGNEDA, AGNELLA, AGNESE** (ah-NYEH-seh)—Italian; **ÁGNES** (AHG-nyesh)—Eastern European; **AIGNÉIS** (eygh-NAYS[H])—Irish Gaelic; **INES** (ee-NEHS), **INEZ** (ee-NEHZ), **YNES** (ee-NEHS), **YNEZ** (ee-NEHZ)—Spanish and Portuguese. Saint Agnes was thirteen when she was martyred in Rome for refusing to worship the Roman goddess Minerva. Because of her youth, Agnes is the patron saint of teenagers. **AGGI(E), AGGY; NESS, NESSA, NESSI(E), NESSY.**

AGNI, "AHG-nee"—*Sanskrit: "fire."* In Hinduism, Agni is the god of fire, and is notable for being born three different times in three different ways. Thus, he is comfortable on all three levels: earth, in-between, and heaven.

AHURA, "ah-HOO-rah"—*Avesta/Ancient Persian: "lord" (as in "god" or "deity").* See also UHURA.

AIDA, "ah-EE-dah"—*Italian: "happy"; Arabic: "reward" or "present."* **AÏDA.** In *Aida*, the famous 1871 opera by Verdi, Aida is a slave in Egypt who turns out to be the daughter of an African king.

AIKO, "ah-EE-koh"—*Japanese: "little loved one."*

AILEEN, "AY-leen" or "EYE-leen"—*Scottish version of Helen: "light" or "luminous."* **AILA, AILENE, ALEEN** (ah-LEEN or AY-leen), **ALINE, AYLA, AYLEEN, AYLENE.** See also HELEN.

AISHA, "ah-EE-shah"—*Arabic: "living" or "lively"; Swahili: "life."* **AYISHA, AYESHA.** This name is incorrectly used interchangeably with A'isha.

A'ISHA, "AH ee-SHAH"—*Arabic: "prosperous."* A'isha was the third wife of the prophet Mohammed. She was seven years old at the time, and when she moved into his home, she brought along her toys and games. Later, A'isha opposed the successors to Mohammed.

AISLINN, "EYES-lihn"—*Gaelic: "vision" or "dream."* **AISLEEN, AISLINE, ISLEEN.**

AJA, "AH-jah"—*Hindu: "nanny goat."*

AJANTA, "ah-JAHN-tah"—*Sanskrit: "realm of the mountain goat(?)."* Ajanta is a place name for the twenty-nine caves in western India that were cut into the cliffs to create temples and monasteries in early Buddhism. They still house some astounding works of art and engineering.

AKA, "AH-kuh"—*Hawaiian: "laughter."* M

AKELA, "ah-KAY-luh"—*Polynesian: "noblewoman."*

AKI, "ah-KEE"—*Japanese: "born in the autumn."* M

AKILA, "ah-KEEL(-ah)"—*Moroccan: "one who reasons well" or "thoughtful."* **AKILAH.** See also AQUILA. M

AKINA, "ah-KEE-nah"—*Japanese: "bright flower."*

AKIVA, "ah-KEEV-ah"—*Hebrew: "to protect."* **AKIBA, KIBA, KIVA**—Israeli. See also JACOBA. M

AKUBA, "ah-KOOB-ah"—*Israeli version of Jacoba: "the supplanter."* **AKIBA**—Armenian; **AKKUBA.** See also JACOBA.

ALA, ALE, "AH-lah" or "AH-leh"—*African Ibo: a mother goddess.* One prays to Ala for fertility of one's family and lands.

ALAMEA, "ah-lah-MAY-ah"—*Hawaiian: "precious."*

ALAMEDA, "ah-lah-MEE-dah"—*Native American: "a grove of cottonwoods."*

ALAN(N)A, ALANAH, "ah-LAHN-ah"—*Irish: "noble"; Celtic: "harmony"; Irish Gaelic: "O, child!"; Polynesian: "offering."* **ALEANBH** (ah-LAWN-eh)—Irish Gaelic; **AILÍN** (EYE-leen)—Irish Gaelic. M

ALAULA, "ah-LAH-ooh-lah"—*Hawaiian: "glow of dawn" or "glow of sunset."*

ALBERICE, "AHL-beh-reese"—*Nordic: "powerful elf."* **ALBERIKA; AUBERICE.**

ALBERTA, "al-BUR-tah" or "ahl-BEAR-tah"—*German: "noble and bright."* **ALBERTINA**—Swedish; **ALBERTKA**—Slavic. **ALLI(E), ALLY; BERTI(E), BERTY.** M

ALBINA, "ahl-BEE-nah"—*Latin: "white" or "blonde."* **ALBANY, ALBENA, ALBINIA; ALBINKA**—Polish. M

ALBION, "AHL-bee-awn"—*Greek and Roman: "whiteness."* This is the ancient name for the British Isles.

ALCANDRA, "al-KAH-drah" or "ahl-KAHN-drah"—*Greek: "strong-minded."* **ALCANNA.** M

ALCEA, "ahl-SAY-ah" or "al-SEE-ah"—*Latin: "hollyhock."*

ALCINA, "ahl-SEE-nah"—*Greek: "strong-willed."* **ALSINA. CINA. SINA.**

ALCYONE. See HALCYONE/ALCYONE.

ALDORA, "ahl-DOH-rah"—*Greek: "winged gift."* **ALDORIA, ALDORIE, ALDORYA. DORI(E), DORY.**

ALEEZA, "ah-LEE-zah"—*Hebrew: "joy."* **ALEEZAH, ALIZA, ALIZAH, ALITZAH; LEEZA(H).**

ALETHEA, "ah-LEE-thee-ah"—*Greek: "truth."* **ALETHIA, ALITHEA, ALITHIA.**

ALEX(IS). See ALEXANDRA.

ALEXANDRA, "al-ex-AN-dra" or "ah-lehk-ZAHN-dra"—*Greek: "defender or protector of humankind."* Okay, here we go: **ALEJANDRA** (ah-leh-HAHN-drah)—Spanish; **ALEKSANDRA, ALEKSY**—Polish; **ALESSANDRA**—Italian; **ALEXA, ALEXANDRIA, ALEXIS; ALEXANDRINA**—Portuguese; **ALEXANDRINE** (ah-lehk-ZAHN-dreen), **ALEXINE, ALIX**—French; **ALEXIA**—Greek; **ELEKSA** (eh-LECK-shah), **ELEKSANDRIKA** (eh-leck-SHAHN-dree-kah), **LEKSZI** (leck-SHEE)—Eastern European; **ZINDELLE** (ZEEN-dehl or zeen-DEHL), **ZINDILA, ZUNDA**—Yiddish. Several Christian saints' names can be found in this list. Alexandra has long been associated with rulers: it was the name of several Russian queens and a queen of Judea in the first century B.C. **ALEKA, ALEX; LEXI(E), LEXINE, LEXY; SASHA.** See also SANDRA. M

ALFONSA, "ahl-FAWN-sah"—*Teutonic: "eager or ready soldier."* **ALFONZA; ALONSA, ALONZA; ALPHONSA, ALPHONSINE.** M

ALFRE, "AHL-freh"—*Nordic: "queen of the elves."* M

ALICE, "AL-iss" or "AH-leese"—*German: "noble" or "kind"; Greek: "truth."* **AILÍSE** (eye-LEES[H])—Irish Gaelic; **ALICIA, ALLY-CIA, ALYCIA; ALISA, ALISSA, ALYSSA; ALISZ** (AH-leezh)—Hungarian; **ALIZA, ALIZIA; ALLYCE, ALYCE; ALLYS, ALYS.** A famous fictional Alice is the central character in several books by Lewis Carroll. **ALI, ALLI(E), ALLY.**

ALICIA. See ALICE.

ALIDA, "ah-LEE-dah"—*German: "kind"; Greek: "dressed in finery"; Latin: "little winged one."* **ALEDA, ALEIDA, ALETA.**

ALIKA, "ah-LEE-kah"—*African: "her beauty outshines all."*

ALIMA(H), "ah-LEEM-ah"—*Arabic: "all-knowing" or "skilled in the arts."*

ALIYA(H), "ah-LEE-yah"—*Hebrew: "to ascend."*

ALLEGRA, "ah-LEG-rah"—*Italian: "lively."*

ALLI(E). See ALBERTA, ALICE, ALLISON.

ALLISON, "AL-ih-sun"—*Scandinavian: "child of Alice," that is, "child of nobility," "child of kindness," or "child of truth."* **ALISEN, ALISON, ALYSON; ALLISEN, ALLYSON. ALLEE, ALLI(E)** (AL-ee), **ALLEY** (Scottish). See also ALICE.

ALMA, "AHL-mah"—*Celtic: "goodness"; Italian: "cherishing" or "loving"; Arabic: "learned"; Russian and Spanish: name of a river; Hebrew: "maiden."* This is quite a multiple choice of meanings.

ALMIRA, "ahl-MY-rah" or "ahl-MEE-rah"—*Arabic: "princess."*

ALMITA, "ahl-MEE-tah"—*Latin: "kindly."*

ALOHA, "uh-LOW-hah"—*Hawaiian: "love."*

ALOHI, "uh-LOW-hee"—*Polynesian: "bright" or "shining."*

ALONA, "ah-LOHN-nah"—*Hebrew: "oak*

tree." **ALLONA, ALLONIA**—Israeli. M

ALPHONSA. See ALFONSA.

ALTA, "AWL-tah"—Latin: "tall."

ALTHEA, "ahl-THEE-ah"—Greek: "wholesome" or "healing." **ALTHEE, ALTHETA. THEA.**

ALVARA, "ahl-VAH-rah"—Portuguese: "white." M

ALYSSA, "ah-LIHS-sah"—Greek: "sensible." **ALISSA; LISA, LISSA, LYSA, LYSSA.** See also ALICE.

AMADEA, "ah-mah-DAY-ah"—Latin: "loving God" or "God-loving." **AMADIS** (ah-MAH-dees)—Spanish; **AMÉDÉE** (ah-may-DAY)—French. Several saints have had this name, or variations of it.

AMADI, "ah-MAH-dee"—African Ibo: "rejoicing."

AMALIA, "ah-MAH-lee-ah"—German: "worker" or "industrious"; Hebrew: "labor of the Lord." **AMALIE; AMALIJA** (ah-mah-LEE-yah)—Russian; **MALCSI** (MAHL-tchee), **MALIKA**—Hungarian. See also AMELIA, EMILY.

AMANDA, "ah-MAN-dah"—English via Latin: "worthy of love." **AMANDINE** (ah-mahn-DEEN)—French; **MENDI** (mehn-dee)—Basque. This name first appears in a 1694 play by Colly Cibber called Love's Last Shift. It is one of the most popular names for a girl in the United States. **MANDI(E), MANDY.**

AMANY, "ah-MAHN-ee"—Arabic: "aspiration."

AMARIS, "ah-MAH-rihss"—Hebrew: "God has promised." **MARIS.**

AMBER, "AHM-bur"—Persian: a semiprecious stone. Amber is actually formed from tree resin that has been fossilized, so it is an ancient reminder of a living thing. The movie Forever Amber (1947) popularized the name.

AMBROSIA, "ahm-BROH-zhah"—Greek: "immortal." Ambrosia was a nectar on which the gods and goddesses were nourished. See also AMRITA.

AMELIA, "ah-MEE-lee-ah"—Latin: "industrious." **AMÉLIE** (AH-may-lee), **AMELINE** (ah-meh-LEEN)—French; **AMELINA, AMELITA**—Spanish and Portuguese. Amelia Earhart was an aviation pioneer, the first woman to cross the Atlantic by air (in 1928). During a trip in which she was to circumnavigate the globe in 1937, her plane vanished somewhere in the South Pacific. **AMEE, AMI(E), AMY.** See also AMALIA, EMILY.

AMENA, "ah-MAY-nah"—Celtic: "honest."

AMESHA, "ah-MAY-shah"—Avesta/Ancient Persian: "immortal."

AMETHYST, "am-eh-THIHST"—Greek: "intoxicating." Amethyst is also the violet stone that is the birthstone for February.

AMIDA, "ah-MEE-dah"—Sanskrit: "infinite light" or "infinite life." Amida is an incarnation of the Buddha worshipped in Central Asian regions.

AMIELLE, "ah-mee-EHL"—Hebrew: "the God of my people." M

AMIRA, "ah-MEER-ah"—Arabic: "princess"; Yiddish: "grain." **AMEERAH**—Afghani; **MEERAH, MIRA(H).** M

AMITY, "AM-ih-tee"—Latin: "friendly" or "friendship." See also AMY.

AMMI, "AH-mee"—Hebrew: "my people." **AMI.**

AMORETTE, "ah-moh-REHT"—Latin:

"little sweetheart." This name was invented by Edmund Spenser in 1590 for a character in *The Faerie Queen*.

AMRITA, "ahm-ree-TAH" or "ahm-REE-tah"—*Sanskrit: "immortality."* Amrita was the nectar of immortality that was drunk by the gods. **RITA.** See also AMBROSIA.

AMY, "AY-mee" or "ay-MEE"—*French: "friend"; Latin: "loved one."* **AIMÉE** (ay-MAY)—French; **AMI(E), AMITY.** This name was probably popularized by Louisa May Alcott's *Little Women* (1869). See also AMELIA.

ANAELLE, "AH-nah-ehl" and "ah-nah-EHL"—*Hebrew: "pure fire of heaven" or "pure light of heaven."* **ANA-EL.** Ana-el is often considered chief of the Principalities, an order of the heavenly hierarchy of angels. Ana-el is one of the "seven angels of creation," and is associated with human sexuality and the Moon (and is therefore, probably female). The Essenes, a Jewish sect, call Anael the Angel of Air, with rulership over Friday.

ANAHITA, "ah-nah-HEE-tah"—*Persian: "spotless."* Anahita was a goddess of the waters in ancient Persia. **ANAÏS.**

ANALA, "ah-NAH-lah"—*Hindu: "fire."*

ANANDA, "ah-NAHND-ah"—*Pali: "bliss"; Sanskrit: "rejoicing."* Ananda was a cousin of the Buddha, Siddhartha Gautama; a founder of an order of Buddhist nuns; and the editor and writer or translator of the Pali Canon, sacred writings important to Ceylon, Laos, Thailand, Burma and that general region.

ANASTASIA, "ahn-ah-STAH-see-ah" or "ahn-ah-STAY-see-ah," or "ahn-ah-STAH-syah" or "ahn-ah-STAY-syah"—*Latin: "resurrection."* **ANASTASSIA, NASTYA, STASYA,** **TASENKA, TASYA**—Russian; **ANASZTAIZIA**—Hungarian; **ANATAZJA** (ah-nah-STAH-zyah)—Polish; **NASTASSIA.** Anastasia is one of the Christian saints. When the last czar of Russia and his family were rounded up in the night and shot by the instigators of the Communist Revolution, Princess Anastasia was the only female child to escape. A couple of different women claimed, in their later years, to be the princess. **STACEY, STACI(E), STACY, STASSI(E).** M

ANATTA, "ah-NAH-tah"—*Pali: "selflessness."* See also HANATA.

ANDI(E). See ANDREA.

ANDRA, "AHN-drah"—*Norse: "breath."* M

ANDREA, "AN-dree-uh" or "ahn-DRAY-uh"—*Greek: "strong and womanly."* **AINDRÉA**—Irish Gaelic; **ANDRASHA, ANDRIKA**—Eastern European; **ANDREANA** (ahn-dray-AH-nah)—Italian; **ANDRÉE** (AWN-dray—"r" deep in your throat)—French; **ANDRI(A); ANDRIANNE**—Greek; **ANNDRA, ANNDREE**—Scottish. Several Christian saints' names can be found in this list. **ANDEE, ANDI(E), ANDY.** M

ANDROMEDA, "an-DRAW-meh-dah"—*Greek: "unsurpassed by mere mortals(?)"* or traditionally, *"more beautiful than a goddess."* Actually, Ethiopian Queen Cassiopeia declared that her daughter, Princess Andromeda, was more beautiful than the Nereids, or sea nymphs, who were the daughters of Poseidon, Greek god of the seas. Needless to say, this brought down the wrath of Poseidon, who sent a sea monster to ravage the African kingdom. The beast needed to be appeased with human sacrifices and eventually, Andromeda was one of the virgins tied to the rock, but was rescued by Perseus. The constellation Andromeda can be seen chasing the Sun at dusk in late November or early December. The Sun is "in" Andromeda from late February to mid-March.

ANGELA, "AN-jeh-lah"—*Latin: "messenger"; Greek: "an angel."* **AINGEAL** (EYE-nghal)—Irish Gaelic; **ANGE, ANGELE** (anh-YEH-leh)—Greek; **ANGE** (ONZHE), **ANGÈLE** (on-ZHEHL), **ANGELINE** (onzhe-LEEN)—French; **ANGELINA**—Italian; **ANGELINHA**—Portuguese; **ANGIA, ANGIOLETTA, ANGIOLETTE, ANJELA, ANJI(E), ANJILETTE, ANJY.** Saint Angela founded the first order of female teachers, the Ursulines, in the late fifteenth century. **ANGEL, ANGI(E); GELI.** M

ANGELICA, ANJELICA, "ahn-JEHL-ih-kah" or "an-JEHL-ih-kah"—*Latin: "like an angel."* **ANGELIKA, ANJELIKA; ANGELIKI** (ahn-yeh-LEE-kee)—Greek; **ANGELIQUE** (onzhe-LEEK)—French; **ANGYALKA** (AHN-dthahl-kuh)—Hungarian; **ENGELTJE** (ehn-GHELT-yuh)—Dutch. Angelica is a literary name, figuring prominently in William Congreve's *Love for Love!,* William Thackeray's *The Rose and the Ring,* and John Milton's *Paradise Regained.* The spicy herb angelica is used in herbal and folk medicine. **ANGI(E), ANJI(E).**

ANGENI, "ahn-JAY-nee"—*Native American: "spirit."* **ANJENI. ANGE, ANGIE, ANJE, ANJI, JENI.** See ANGELICA—interesting, isn't it, how so many cultures have similar names for similar things?

ANGI(E). See ANGELA, ANGELICA/ ANJELICA.

ANILA, "ah-NEE-lah"—*Hindu: "goddess of wind."*

ANISA(H), "ah-NEE-sah" or "ah-NIH-sah"—*Arabic: "good company."* **ANISE, ANISSA; NISSA.** Spicy anise or aniseed is used in herbal and folk medicine. See also ANNISA.

ANITA, "ah-NEE-tah"—*traditionally, diminuative of Ann: "grace," but how about Gaelic: "joy"; Native American Choctaw: "bear"; Sanskrit: "ephemeral"; or Persian: "the great mother goddess."* **ANAHITA** (ah-nah-HEE-tah)—Ancient Persian/Avestan; **ANITRA; ANITYA** (ah-NEET-yah)—Sanskrit. **NEET, NEETA, NEETAH; NITA(H), NITRA.** See also ANN(E).

ANJANETTE, "ann-jah-NET"—*French combination name: Ange + Anne, or Ange + Janet, thus "graceful little angel" or "God's gracious angel."* **ANGEAN(N)ETTE, ANJAN(N)ETTA, ANJANNETTE.**

ANN(E), "ANN"—*Hebrew: "grace," "gracious," or "God has favored"; Gaelic: "joy."* **ANA**—Israeli; **ANA, ANNA**—Spanish; **ANAÏS** (ahn-nah-EESE), **ANNELLE** (ah-NEHL), **ANNETTE** (ah-NET), **ANOUCHE** (ah-NOOSH), **ANOUK** (ah-NOOK)—French; **ANCI, ANNUS(H)KA, ANYU**—Hungarian; **ANE** (ah-neh)—Basque; **ANECHKA, ANYA, ASYA**—Russian; **ANETTE**—Norwegian; **ANIA, ANIELI, ANKA**—Polish; **ANICA, ANNICA**—Danish; **ANNIKA, ANNIKE** (AHN-ih-keh)—Swedish; **ANTJE** (AHN-tyeh)—Dutch; **AYN, AYNA**—Eastern European; **NINA; ONA**—Hebrew; **VANIA** (VAHN-yah), **VANYA**—Russian. This is a very old and much honored name, borne by rulers, lovers, and saints, and by heroines real and fictional. Traditionally, Anne is supposed to be the mother of the Virgin Mary, and there are a couple of Christian saint names on this list as well. *Anne of Green Gables,* written by L.M. Montgomery, was published in 1908. Anaïs Nin was a writer of erotic fiction. **ANNI(E), ANNY.** See also NANCY, ROS(E)ANNE.

ANNABEL, "AN-uh-bell" or "AH-nah-bell"—*Scottish, Anne + Belle: "grace and beauty."* **ANNABELLA, ANNABELLE; ANNA-BLÁ** (AH-nah-blaw)—*Irish Gaelic. Annabel Lee is a poem by Edgar Allan Poe.* See also ANN(E), BELLE.

ANNETTE. See ANN(E).

ANNIKA, ANIKKA, "AHN-ih-kah"—*Scandinavian version of Ann(e): "grace"; Pali: "ephemeral."* **ANICCA, ANNICA.** See also ANN(E).

ANNISA, ANISSA, "ahn-nee-SAH" or "ah-NEE-sah"—*Arabic: "womankind."* See also ANISA(H).

ANSARA, "ahn-SAHR-ah"—*Arabic: "helper."* M

ANTHEA, "AHN-thee-ah"—*Greek: "flowerlike."* **ANTHIA.**

ANTONIA, "an/ahn-TOHN-ee-ah"—*Latin: "of infinite value" or "inestimable"; Greek: "beyond praise."* **ANDONA, ANDONIÑE** (ahn-do-nee-nyeh)—*Basque;* **ANDONIA**—*Greek;* **ANTA, TOLA, TOSIA**—*Polish;* **ANTALIA** (ahn-TALL-yah), **ANTALYA**—*Eastern European;* **ANTINKA, TONECHKA** (toh-NETCH-kah), **TONYA** (TOHN-yah)—*Russian;* **ANTOINETTE** (ahn-twa-NET) *French;* **ANTONETTA**—*Swedish;* **ANTONINA.** *Several Christian saints' names can be found on this list.* **TONEE, TONI(E).** M

AOLANI, "AY-oh-lah-nee"—*Polynesian: "heavenly cloud."*

APHRODITE, "ah-froh-DYE-tee"—*Greek: "born from the foam."* Born of the ocean waves, Aphrodite was the Greek goddess of love and beauty, and of the feminine in nature. Some sources say she is the daughter of Zeus by Dione, not by the oceans. An aphrodite is also a type of brilliantly colored butterfly.

APOLLONIA, "ah-pah-LOW-nee-ah"—*Greek: "from the God of the Sun."* **APPOLINE, APOLLONA; APOLONA, APOLONIA.** M

APONI, "ah-POH-nee"—*Native American Apache: "butterfly alighting."* **PONI.**

APRIL, "AY-prihl"—*Latin: "open to the sun"; Celtic: "boar warrior"; and of course, the month April.* **ABRIL** (AH-breel)—*Spanish, Portuguese, and Arabic;* **APRILLE, APRILLETE; APRYEL** (ah-pree-EHL)—*Russian;* **AVRIL** (ahv-REEL), **AVRILLE**—*French;* **SHIGWATSU**—*Japanese. The images of pastoral Spring and of a vicious, tenacious warrior just seem too strange to come together like this! The traditional flower of April is the sweet pea, and the traditional birthstone is the diamond.*

APSARA, "ahp-SAH-rah"—*Sanskrit: "moving through water."* In Hinduism, the Apsaras were celestial nymphs.

AQUARELLE, "ah-kah-REHL"—*French: "watercolor" or "pastels."*

AQUILA, "ah-KEE-lah"—*Latin: "eagle."* The constellation Aquila can be seen flying after the Sun at dusk from the last week of August through about September 20. The Sun is "in" the Eagle from November through most of December. See also AKILA.

ARABELLA, "ah-rah-BEHL-lah"—*Latin(?): "able to be moved"; Hebrew: "beautiful altar"; German: "beautiful eagle."* **ARABEL(LE).**

ARANYA, "ah-RAHN-yah"—*Sanskrit: "of the forest."*

ARDIS, "AHR-dihss"—*Latin: "fervent."* **ARDEEN, ARDENE, ARDINA, ARDINE; ARDELLA, ARDELLE; ARDELIS; ARDITH.**

ARENE, "ah-reh-neh"—*Basque: "holy one."*

ARETHA, "ah-REE-thah"—*Greek: "nymph," "orchid,"* or *"excellence."* **ARETHUSA, ORETHA.** In Greek mythology, Arethusa was a nymph who was transformed into either a stream or an orchid by either Artemis or Aphrodite—it depends on which source you consult—as she begged to be saved from the advances of the river god Alpheus. Singer/songwriter Aretha Franklin certainly lives up to the "excellence" definition.

ARIA, "AH-ree-ah"—*Latin: "melody."* M

ARIELLA, "ah-ree-EHL-ah" or "air-ee-EHL-ah"—*Hebrew: "lioness of God."* **ARIELLE** (ah-ree-EHL)—French. Ariel is the brightest moon of Uranus. M

ARINNA, "ah-RIH-nah"—*Hittite: "goddess of the Sun."* Arinna was the Hittites' chief female goddess. Her symbols, the dove and the lioness, metaphorically embody the extremes of feminine nature. **RINNA.**

ARISTA, "ah-RIHS-tah"—*Greek: "the best."* M

ARLEEN. See ARLENE.

ARLENE, "ahr-LEEN"—*Celtic: "pledge"* or *"promise"; German: "girl."* **ARLAYNE, ARLEEN, ARLENA, ARLEYNE, ARLINA, ARLINE; ARLETA, ARLETTA, ARLETTE.**

ARMIDA, "ahr-MEE-dah"—*Latin: "little warrior."* **ARMINA, ARMITA.**

ARMILLA, "ahr-MIHL-ah"—*Latin: "bracelet."*

ARNA, "ARE-nah"—*Teutonic/German: "eagle."* M

ARNETTE, "ahr-NEHT"—*German/French: "little eagle."* M

ARTEMIS, "AHR-teh-mihs"—*Greek.*

ARTEMISIA (ahr-teh-MIHZ-yah). Artemis was the Greek goddess of the Moon, the hunt, animals, and related matters. She was the daughter of Zeus. Artemisia Gentileschi (1593-1653) was the first female painter to be widely known and appreciated. She turned her own story—rape and a miscarriage of justice—into a source of power and creativity, instead of letting it destroy her. The plant artemisia, also called the sagebrush, produces silver, aromatic foliage. M

ARUNA, "ah-ROON-ah"—*Hindu: "radiant as the sun."* **ARUNI.** M

ARUNDELLE, "AIR-un-dehl" or "air-un-DEHL"—*English: "the eagle dell."* M

ARVA, "AHR-vah"—*Latin: "countryside"* or *"pasturelands."*

ASAHELLE, "AH-sah-hehl"—*Hebrew: "made of God."*

ASENKA, "ah-SEHN-kah"—*Russian: "graceful."*

ASHA, "AH-shah"—*Swahili: "lively."*

ASHIRA, "ah-SHEE-rah"—*Hebrew: "wealthy."*

ASHLEY, "ASH-lee"—*Irish: "vision"* or *"dream"; English: "from the ash-tree meadow."* **AISLING** (ICE-leengh), **AISLINN** (ICE-leen)—Irish Gaelic; **ASHLEIGH** (ASH-lee/lay)—English; **ASHLING.** This name's first surge in popularity in the twentieth century came from the book and film *Gone With the Wind* because one of the characters, a male, bore this name. What has caused its unbounded rise as a female name towards the end of the century is not clear.

ASHURA, "ah-SHOO-rah"—*Swahili: "born in Ashur."* Ashur is one of the Islamic holy months.

CHANGING FEMALE NAMES TO MALE NAMES

If you like a particular female name, but are expecting a boy, *no problem!* Many female names are acceptable for males, many names are gender-shared, and many are used as is, especially in Europe, as middle names. If, however, you want to masculinize a selection, it's as easy as removing the final vowels until you reach a consonant, and/or adding any one of these endings: "ad(o)," "al(o)," "am(o)," "an(o)," "ar(o)," "at(o)"; "d," "l," "n"; "io," "ion," "ius"; "o," "ol," "ol(l)o," "om," "on," "on(n)o," "or," "or(r)o," "os," "os(s)o," "ot," "ot(t)o"; "s," "t"; "u," "ud," "uk," "ul," "ul(l)o," "um," "um(m)o," "un," "un(n)o," "ur," "ur(r)o," "us," "us(s)o," "ux," "uxo," to mention a few. Anything that hardens the sound is a good bet.

Demetra—DEMETRIUS	Maria—MARIO
Sabine—SABINO	Brooke—BROOK
Lisa—LISADO	Darla—DARLAN

ASIMA, "ah-SEEM-ah"—*Arabic: "protector" or "guardian."*

ASPHODEL, "AS-foh-dehl"—*Greek: "lily."*

ASTA, "AH-stah"—*Greek: "star."* **ASTRA.**

ASTER, "AS-tur"—*Greek: "star,"* or the aster flower.

ASTLEY, "AST-lee"—*Greek/Celtic: "starlit meadow."* **ASTLEE, ASTLEIGH, ASTLIE, ASTLY.** M

ASTOR, "AS-tohr"—*Irish Gaelic: "loved one."* **ASTHORA, ASTHOR** (as-TORE)—French and Nordic; **ASTORA, ASTORIA; ASTOIRE** (ah-STOW-eer)—*Irish Gaelic.* M

ASTRID(E), "AHS-treed" or "AZ-trihd"—*Scandinavian: "divine strength" or "beautiful strength."* Eleventh-century zealot Saint Astrid was martyred for her beliefs.

ASVINA, "ahs-VEE-nah"—*Hindu: equivalent of Libra.*

ATA, "ah-TAH"—*Arabic: "a gift."*

ATALIA, "ah-TAHL-yah"—*Hebrew: "the Lord is mighty."* **TALIA.**

ATHENA, "ah-THEE-nah"—*Greek.* **ATHENE, ATHINA.** Athena was the Greek goddess of wisdom and justice. She was also in charge of battle—obviously the strategy part, and not the mind-numbing violence. Athena was the patron goddess of the city of Athens. The entire ancient Greek civilization, seeking to glorify her, left its impression on individuals and governments seeking knowledge, reason, and justice.

ATIRA, "ah-TEE-rah"—*Hebrew: "prayer."* **TIRA.**

ATIYA, "AH-tee-yah"—*Arabic: "gift."* **ATYA.**

AUDNY, "AWD-nee"—*Norwegian: "newfound prosperity."*

AUDREY, "AWD-ree"—*English: "noble strength."* **AUDRA, AUDRIE.** Saint Audrey was a Saxon in the seventh century. Audrey Hepburn was a classic beauty, award-winning actress, and world-renowned humanitarian. **AUDI(E)**.

AUGUSTA, "aw-GUS-tah"—*Latin: "venerable," "majestic,"* or *"born in August."* **AGOSTINA** (ah-goh-STEE-nah)—*Portuguese, Italian, and Spanish;* **AOÛT** (AHOO or AHOOT—like one syllable), **AUGUSTINE** (aw-goo-STEEN)—*French;* **AUGUSTYN(E)**—*Slavic;* **AVGUSTA** (AHV-goost-ah)—*Russian;* **HACHIGWATSU**—*Japanese.* The traditional flower of August is the gladiolus, and the traditional birthstone is the peridot. **AUGGI(E), AUGI(E); GUS, GUSSI(E)**. M

AURELIA, "oh-RAY-lee-ah"—*Latin: "golden."* **ARANKA**—*Hungarian;* **AURELIAN(E), AURELIANNE, AURELIE; AURÈLIE** (aw-REHL-ee)—*French.* M

AURORA, "ah-ROAR-ah"—*Latin: "dawn."* **AURORE**. Aurora was the Roman goddess of the dawn. **RORA, RORY**.

AUTUMN, "AWT-um"—*Latin: "autumn!"* **AKI**—*Japanese;* **AUTOMNE** (aw-TUN)—*French;* **AUTONNE**—*French;* **AUTUNNA** (aw-TOO-nah)—*Italian;* **CHARIF** (KHAH-reef—the "KH" in your throat)—*Arabic;* **HERBST**—*German;* **HØST** (HAWST), **HÖST**—*Scandinavian;* **JESIEN** (yeh-see-EHN)—*Polish;* **OSEN** (OH-sehn)—*Russian;* **OTOÑNA** (oh-TOHN-yah)—*Spanish;* **SONBAHAR** (SAWN-bah-hahr or sawn-BAH-hahr)—*Turkish.* M

AVA, "AY-vah"—*Latin: "bird."* **AVIS**. Actress Ava Gardner has given this name its twentieth-century popularity.

AVASA, "ah-VAH-sah"—*Hindu: "independent."*

AVESTA, "ah-VEHS-tah"—*Ancient Persian: "knowledge"* or *"scriptures."* The Avesta is the sacred text of the Zoroastrian religion.

AVIELLE, "ah-vee-EHL"—*Hebrew: "God is my father."* M

AVISHA, "AH-vee-sha"—*Hebrew: "God's gift."* **AVISHAI**.

AVIVA, "ah-VEEV-ah"—*Hebrew: "springtime"* or *"fresh."* **AVIVI, AVIVIT**. M

AVOCETTE, "AH-voh-seht" or "ah-voh-SEHT"—*French.* The avocet is a long-legged shore bird with a slightly upturned beak. **AVOCETTA** (ah-voh-CHEH-tah)—*Italian.* M

AYA, "ah-YAH"—*Hebrew: "bird."*

AYAME, "ah-YAH-may"—*Japanese: "iris."* The flower.

AYASHE, "ah-YAH-sheh"—*Native American Chippewa: "little one."*

AYITA, "ah-YEE-tuh"—*Native American: "a good worker"; Cherokee: "first for the dances."*

AYOMI, "ah-yoh-MEE"—*African Yoruba: "gift for me"* or *"my joy."*

AZAMI, "ah-ZAH-mee"—*Japanese: "thistle."*

AZIZA, "ah-ZEE-zah"—*Swahili: "precious"; Persian: "cherished."* **AZIZAH**.

AZURE, "ah-ZOOR" or "AZ-yoor"—*Persian: "lapis-lazuli stone."* Lapis lazuli was ground up to make deep blue dyes the color of the sky, thus leading to the meaning most of us know: "clear blue." **AZURA**. M

THE TOP FIVE

BRITTANY
BRETT
BARBARA
BRENDA
BERNADETTE

If the name you're looking for isn't here, see "V."

BABETTE. See BARBARA.

BACCIATA, "bah-chee-AH-tah"—*Italian: "kissed."* Kissed, presumably, by God or the gods.

BAKA, "BAH-kah"—*Hindu: "crane."* The crane is a symbol of good luck and long life.

BALI, "BAH-lee"—*Sanskrit: "strength."* **VALI.** The mythical Bali of Hindu and Pali tradition is a great monkey king who was off fighting demons while his brother usurped the throne. Bali returned, though, and regained his place. This myth parallels the later real-life situation of England's King Richard the Lion-Hearted and his brother, Prince John. Bali is also the name of an island paradise in the Pacific.

BAMBI, "BAHM-bee" or "BAM-bee"—*Arabic: "pink."*

BAMI, "BAH-mee"—*African Yoruba: "blessing."*

BARAKA, "bah-RAH-kah" or "BAH-rah-kah"—*Arabic: "white one"; Hebrew: "blessing" or "lightning."* In the Old Testament/Tanakh, Barak was a warrior who fought under the direction of the Hebrew queen Deborah. See also BURAQ. M

BARBARA, "BAHR-bah-rah"—*Latin: "foreigner" or "stranger."* **BABETTE** (bah-BEHT), **BARBETTA, BARBETTE**—French; **BAIRBRE** (BEAR-breh)—Irish Gaelic; **BARBARELLA, BARBARELLE**—Italian; **BARBERA, BARBRA; BARBICA** (bahr-BIH-kah), **BARBIKA**—Nordic; **BASHA**—Polish; **BORA, BORBÁLA, BORKA, BORSALA**—Hungarian; **VARINA** (vah-REE-nah)—Slavic; **VARVARA** (VAHR-vah-rah), **VARENKA** (vah-REHN-kah), **VARINKA, VARYA, VARYUSHA** (vahr-YOOSH-kah)—Russian. Barbara was one of the Christian saints, a second- or third-century convert martyred by her father, who wanted her to renounce Christianity. Saint Barbara is the patron saint of gunners and miners, and provides protection against storms. One Barbra is no "stranger" to entertainment: Barbra Streisand is an award-winning actress, singer, arranger, director, producer, and activist. Ruth and Elliott Handler, founders of the Mattel Corporation, had a daughter named Barbara, whence comes the name for the Barbie doll. **BAB, BABS; BARB, BARBI(E), BARBY.**

BARBI(E). See BARBARA.

BARCAROLE, "BAHR-kah-roll" or "bahr-kah-ROLL"—*Anglo-Saxon: "boats-*

man's song." **BARCAROLLE**—French; **BAR-CARUOLA**—Italian.

BARDIELLE, "BAHR-dee-ehl" and "bahr-dee-EHL"—*?: angel of hail.* **BARDI-EL.**

BARIELLE, "BAH-ree-ehl" and "bah-ree-EHL"—*?, probably Hebrew: "excellence of the Lord."* **BARI-EL.** Barielle is one of the Virtues in the heavenly hierarchy of angels.

BARIKA, "BAH-ree-kuh"—*Swahili: "successful."* **RIK, RIKA, RIKKI.**

BARRIE, "BARE-ee"—*Irish and Welsh: "spear."* M

BASHA. See BARBARA.

BASILIA, "bah-ZIHL-yah" or "bah-SIHL-ee-ah"—*Greek: "royal" or "regal."* **BASILLE** (bah-SEEL or bah-ZEEL)—French; **BAZYLI**—Polish. The herb basil is used in many cuisines around the world. The plant bears white flowers. M

BATYA, "BAHT-yah"—*Hebrew: "daughter of God."* **BITHIA, BYTHIA**—Egyptian; **BITYA**—Israeli. In the Old Testament/Tanakh, Bithia is the Pharaoh's daughter, the one who rescued the baby Moses from the water and raised him as her own. When Moses was allowed to take the Hebrews out of Egypt, Bithia went with him.

BAY, "BAY"—*Vietnamese: "seventh child or "seventh month (July)"; a body of water.* **BAHIA** (bay-YAH), **ESTERA** (EH-steh-rah)—Spanish; **BAIE, BAYE**—French; **BANDAR** (bawn-DAHR)—Persian; **BODDEN** (BOW-dehn), **BUSEN** (BOO-sehn), **BUCHT** (BOO-kht—"kh" is guttural)—German; **BOKA** (boh-KAH or BOH-kah)—Serbo-Croatian; **BUGT, BUK**—Scandinavian; **FLOI**—Icelandic; **GHUBBAT** (goo-BAWT), **KHALIJ** (khah-LEEJ), **SAWQIRAH** (saw-KEE-rah or SAW-kee-rah)—Arabic; **GUBA** (GOO-bah),

LIMAN (LEE-mawn), **ZALIV** (zah-LEEV)—Russian; **HAVE** (HAH-veh)—Swedish; **KENET** (keh-NEHT)—Albanian; **KOLPOS, ORMOS**—Greek; **KORFEZI** (kohr-feh-ZEE or kohr-FEH-zee)—Turkish; **OKI** (OH-kee)—Japanese; **SELKA**—Finnish; **TELUK** (teh-LOOK)—Indonesian; **VINH**—Vietnamese; **WAN**—Chinese; **ZALEW** (zah-LEHV), **ZATO-KA** (ZAH-toh-kah)—Polish. M

BAYO, "BAH-yoh"—*African Yoruba: "joy has found us."*

BEATRICE, "BEE-uh-triss"—*Latin: "bringer of joy" or "blessed."* **BEATA**—Swedish; **BEATE** (BAY-ah-teh)—Norwegian; **BEATRICE** (bay-ah-TREE-cheh)—Italian; **BEATRISS; BEATRIX**—Dutch. Saint Beatrice's brothers were all murdered by a greedy neighboring landowner with the excuse that they were closet Christians. Beatrice was executed when she tried to retrieve her brothers' bodies for proper burial—a tale similar to the Greek story of Antigone.

BEATRIX. See BEATRICE.

BECKY. See REBECCA.

BEDA, "BAY-dah" or "BEH-dah"—*English: "warrior maiden."* **BEDDA, BETTA.**

BEL, "BAYL"—*Hindu: "apple tree."*

BELINDA, "beh-LIHN-dah" or "bay-LEEN-dah"—*German: "dragon"; Italian: "wise immortal"; Spanish: "pretty one" or "serpent."* **BELENDA, BELINA; VELINDA, VELINA.** The reptilian connotations of this name in some European cultures are not negative, but rather symbolize wisdom and immortality. Belinda is one of the moons of Uranus.

BELLANCA, "beh-LAHN-kah"—*Italian: "blonde."*

BELLE, "BELL"—*French: "beautiful."* **BELA, BELLA.** See also ADABELLE, CHRISTA-BELLE.

Bat-/Bath-, Ben-

These are Hebrew prefixes that mean "daughter of" and "the family of." You may add them to any name you choose.

BELLONA, "beh-LOW-nah"—*Latin: "war goddess, warrior."* **BELLONE** (beh-LOAN or beh-LAWN), **BELLONIA** (beh-LOAN-yah, beh-LOAN-ee-ah, beh-LAWN-yah, beh-LAWN-ee-ah), **BELLONYA.** In Roman mythology, Bellona is the sister (or sometimes, the wife) of Mars. If you like this name, you may want to try one of the diminutives or variants, to avoid having a child people think you named after your favorite luncheon meat.

BELVA, "BEHL-vah"—*Italian: "beautiful to look at."*

BEN(N)A, "BEH-nuh"—*Native American: "the pheasant"; Hebrew: "wise."* **BENAY.**

BENEDETTA, "beh-neh-DEHT-ah"—*Italian: "she blesses" or "blessings."* **BENITA.** M

BENEDICTA, "beh-neh-DIHK-tah"—*Latin: "blessed."* **BENCE** (BEN-tseh), **BENCI**—Hungarian; **BENEDEKA, BENEDIKA, BENKE**—Eastern European; **BÉNÉDICTE** (bay-nay-DEEKT)—French; **BENTE** (BEHN-teh)—Norwegian; **VENEDICTA** (veh-neh-DEEK-tah)—Greek. **BEN, BENE, BENNI(E), BENNY, DIXIE.** M

BENJAMINA, "behn-jah-MEE-nah" or "behn-yah-MEE-nah"—*Hebrew: "daughter of the right hand" or "daughter of the south."* **BANNERJEE**—Gaelic; **VENIAMINA** (vehn-yah-MEE-nah or vehn-YAH-mee-nah), **VERNAMINA**—Greek. Benjamina is one of the Christian saints. **BEN, BENNI(E), BENNY; BENJI(E), BENJY.** M

BENNI(E). See BENEDICTA, BENJAMINA.

BERNADETTE. See BERNARDA.

BERNARDA, "BUR-nahrd-ah" or "BEAR-nahrd-ah"—*Old German: "heart of a bear" or "courage of a bear."* **BERNADETTE, BERNALDETTE, BERNARDETTE, BERNARDINE** (bear-nahr-DEEN)—French; **BERNARDINA** (bear-nahr-DEE-nah)—Spanish; **BERNÁTA**—Eastern European; **BERNHARDA**—German and Austrian; **VERNADA** (vare-NAH-dah)—Greek. Several Christian saints have names on this list. One, Saint Bernadette, was a young girl in 1858 when she claimed to have seen and spoken to the Virgin Mary at a spring near Lourdes. Since then, it has been claimed that many miracles have taken place there. **BERN, BERNA, BERNI(E).** M

BERNI(E). See BERNARDA, BERNIA, BERNICE.

BERNIA, "BARE-nee-ah"—*Anglo-Saxon: "she-bear."* **BERNEE, BERNÉE, BERNI(E).**

BERNICE, "bur-NEESE" but rarely "BUR-niss"—*Greek: "bright victory" or "glorious victory."* **BERENICE** (bare-eh-NYE-chee), **BERENIKE** (bare-eh-NYE-kee)—Greek; **BERENICIA** (bare-eh-NEE-see-ah), **BERNELLE** (bare-NEHL)—French; **BERNESS, BERNESSA, BERNISE**—German; **BERNIECE**—American; **BERONIA** (beh-ROH-nee-ah)—Italian. The full name of the Greek goddess of wisdom, justice, and battle (among other things) is Athena Berenike, especially when she is called upon to assist or intercede in a fight that is more a moral struggle than a material one. Coma Berenices, "the hair of Athena Berenike," is a constellation which seems to be following the Sun at dusk from late May through the first week of June. The Sun is actually "in" Coma Berenices during September. **BERN, BERNE, BERNI(E).**

BERTA, "BURT-ah"—*German: "bright" or "glorious."* **BERIT** (BARE-it)—*Swedish;* **BERTE** (BARE-teh)—*Norwegian;* **BERTHA; BERTICE** (bear-TEESE—"r" in your throat)— **BERTILLE** (bear-TEEL—"r" in your throat)— *French;* **BERTILDE** (bur-TEELD), **BERTINA** (bur-TEE-nah), **BETTINA** (beh-TEE-nah)— *German.* Saint Bertha built several churches in the early days of Christianity. M

BERTHA. See BERTA.

BERTI(E). See ALBERTA, ROBERTA.

BERTRADE, "bear-TRAHD"—*English: "brilliant counsellor."* **BERTRA, BERTRIE, BERTRY; BERTRADIA, BERTRADYA.**

BERYL, "BARE-ihl," occasionally slurred to "BURL"—*Arabic: "crystal"; Greek: "sea-green jewel"; Sanskrit: "precious stone."* Any way you look at it, Beryl is a gem of a name.

BESS, "BEHSS"—*diminutive of Elisabeth: "consecrated"; Egyptian: deity of fun and music, and also childbirth.* The Egyptian meaning is kind of a diverse job description, but hey, that's life in the pantheon. See also ELISABETH/ELIZABETH.

BETH, "BEHTH"—*Hebrew: "the house of" or "the home of"; diminutive of Elizabeth: "consecrated to (the house of) the Lord."* See also BETHANY, ELISABETH/ELIZABETH.

BETHANY, "BEHTH-ah-nee"—*Hebrew: "daughter of the Lord"; Scottish: "life."* **BETTINA** (beh-TEE-nah), **BETTINE** (beh-TEEN). **BETH.**

BETSY, BETTY, "BEHT-see" or "BEHT-ee"—*diminutives of Elizabeth: "consecrated to God."* **BETTE** (BEHT-ee or BEHT); **BITSY.** Bette Davis was an award-winning actress, known for playing the parts of (and for truly being) a tough, smart, independent woman, which broke the mold of cultural expectations in the 1930s, 1940s, and 1950s. Bette Midler is an energetic singer, actress, and entertainer. See also ELISABETH/ELIZA-BETH.

BETTINA. See BETHANY.

BETTY. See BETSY/BETTY.

BEVERLY, "BEH-vur-lee"—*English: "beaver meadow."* **BEVERELY, BEVERLEE, BEVERLEIGH** (BEH-vur-lee). **BEV, BUFFY.**

BEVIN, "BEH-vihn"—*Gaelic: "sweet lady."* **BÉBHINN** (bay-VEEN)—*Irish Gaelic.* The name Bébhinn first appears in print in James MacPherson's *Ossianic Poems (1765).* See also VEVINA.

BIANCA, "bee-AWN-kah"—*Italian: "white."* Bianca is one of the moons of Uranus.

BIBI, "BEE-bee"—*French: "toy" or "delight."* **BEBE.** See also BIBIANA, KEBIBI, KIBIBI.

BIBIANA, "bee-bee-AHN-ah"—*Portuguese version of Vivian: "lively."* **BIBIANE, BIBIANNA, BIBIANNE; BIBIÑE** (bee-bee-nyeh)—*Basque.* **BIBI.** See also VIVIAN.

BIJOU, "BEE-zhoo"—*French: "jewel"; English: "ring."* **BIJOUX** (BEE-zhoo), **BIZOU.**

BILLIE, "BIL-ee"—*diminutive of Wilhelmina, Teutonic: "resolute protector"; German: "strong-willed."*

BINAH, "BEE-nah"—*Hebrew: "understanding" and "wisdom."*

BINNIE, "BIH-nee"—*Welsh: "crib" or "wicker basket"; German: "kettle-shaped hollow."* M

BITTATTI, "bih-TAH-tee"—*Sumerian: "daughter-gift(?)."* Bittatti is the first feminist in recorded history. She was a wealthy Sumerian woman who sought a divorce from her husband. Since she had helped in the amassing of their wealth, she demanded her fair share. She got it, too, and her children had first rights to any inheritance from their father, even if he had more children. (Go on, girl!)

BITTORE. See VICTORIA.

BLAINE, "BLAYN"—*Celtic: "slender"; English: "fire."* **BLAAN, BLAIN, BLANE, BLAYNE.** A Scottish saint bears the name Blane. M

BLAIR, "BLARE"—*Celtic: "place" or "plains"; German: "field of battle."* M

BLAISE, "BLAZE"—*Celtic: "firebrand."* **BLAZE, BLEISE.** M

BLANCA, "BLAWN-kah"—*Spanish: "white."* **BELLANCA.**

BLANCHE, properly "BLAWNCH," but also "BLANCH"—*French: "white."* M

BLESSING, "BLEH-sing"—*English: "consecration."*

BLIMA, "BLEE-mah"—*Yiddish: "blossom."*

BLOSSOM, "BLAW-sum"—*English: "flower."*

BLYTHE, "BLITH" (long "I" sound)—*English: "happy, carefree."* **BLISS.**

BO, "BOH"—*Chinese: "precious"; Vietnamese: "black."* See also BOTAN. M

BOBBI(E). See ROBERTA.

BONITA, "boh-NEE-tah"—*Spanish: "pretty."* **BONNIE, BONNY; BUNNIE, BUNNY.**

BONNIE, "BAW-nee"—*Scottish: "sweet and beautiful"; Latin: "sword" or "fire."* **BONNE, BONNEY, BONNI, BONNY; BUNNIE, BUNNY.** See also BONITA.

BORGNY, "BORG-nee"—*Norse: "from the new castle."* **BORGNINA.**

BOTAN, "bow-TAHN"—*Japanese: "peony."* In Japan, this name is given to a child born in June. **BO.** M

BOUDICA, "BOH-dih-kah"—*Celtic: "conqueror."* **BOADICA, BOADICCA, BOADICCA; BOADICEA** (boh-dih-SEE-ah)—*Latin;* **BOADICIA** (boh-ah-dee-SEE-ah)—*Nordic;* **BONDICA, BONDUCA, BONDUGA**—*Gaelic;* **BONDIGA, BOUDIGA**—*Cymric/Welsh.* Boudica was the queen of the Iceni Celtic tribe who almost succeeded where the kings before her had failed, namely, in ridding Britain of the Romans. She led an uprising against the intruders in A.D. 60, and though she was finally defeated late the next year, her stand against the Roman Empire resulted in the Britons being treated liberally and with tolerance for the native culture. Because of her, much of the Celtic heritage remains in our British—and American—ideas and traditions.

BRANDY, "BRAN-dee"—*English: "flaming torch"; Irish: "raven."* **BRANDEE, BRANDEY, BRANDI, BRANDIE.** M

BREE, "BREE"—*Gaelic: "a hill."* **BRAE, BRAY, BRI.**

BREENA, "BREEN-ah"—*Irish: "an elf/fairy palace."*

BRENDA, "BREHN-dah"—*English: "firebrand"; Norwegian: "flame"; Scottish: "sword."* This old name from the Shetland Islands was given new life by Sir Walter Scott in *The Pirate* (1821), and remains a popular name. **BRINDA.**

BRENNA, "BREH-nah"—*Celtic: "dark-maned maiden."*

BRET(T)(E), "BREHT"—*Celtic: "from Bretagne" or "from Brittany."* This is a very popular name for both boys and girls. See also BRITTANY. **M**

BRIANNE, "bree-AWN" or "bree-AN"—*Celtic: "from the hills"; Greek: "strong."* **BRIANNA; BRIENNA; BRYANNA, BRYANNE. M**

BRIDGET, "BRIH-jet"—*Gaelic: "the high one"; Teutonic: "mountain's protector"; Celtic: "strong"* and *"goddess of moving waters."* **BÉRGHETTA** (BARE-yeh-tah or bare-YEH-tah), **BRÍD** (BREED), **BRIGIT** (BREE-gheet)—Gaelic; **BERIT** (BEH-riht/reet), **BIRGIT** (beer-GHEET), **BIRGITTE** (beer-GHEET-eh), **BIRTE** (BEERT)—Norwegian; **BIRGET** (BUR-zhet), **BIRGITTA** (BUR-zhee-tah), **BRIGITTA**—Swedish; **BIRKITA** (beer-kee-tah)—Basque; **BRIDGETTE; BRIGITTA** (brih-ZHEE-tah)—Scandinavian; **BRIGITTE** (bree-ZHEET)—French; **BRITES** (BREE-tes)—Portuguese; **BRYGID**—Polish. Water, as in "goddess of moving waters," has always had associations with emotion and subconscious. In Bretagne, the goddess was called Brigindu, in Britain she was Brigantia, a patron deity of tribal leadership. The name was also associated with an ancient tribe of people in Northern England called the Brigantes. Bridget in its many variations is also a name belonging to several Christian saints, one of which is the patroness of Ireland.

BRITTANY, "BRIH-tah-nee"—*Celtic: "from Bretagne."* Bretagne is a northern province of France that has influenced, and been influenced by, the British Isles from very early times. Brittany is currently a very popular name. **BRITT.** See also BRET(T)(E).

BROOKE, "BRUK"—*English: "a brook or small stream."* **BAHR**—Arabic; **BROOK, BROOKES, BROOKS; CAYI** (KAH-yee)—Turkish; **LAM** (LAWM)—Thai. Brooke Shields is an actress. **M**

BRUNA, "BROO-nah"—*German: "brown."* **BRUNELLA. M**

BUFFY. See BEVERLY.

BUNMI, "BOON-mee"—*African Yoruba: "gift."*

BUNNIE. See BONITA, BONNIE.

BURAQA, "boo-RAHK-ah"—*Arabic: "white one"; Hebrew: "lightning."* There are two stories that go with this name. Either *Buraq* is the mountain upon which Mohammed is said to have begun his Night Journey from Mecca, through Jerusalem, and then through the Seven Heavens, or *Buraq* is the creature upon which Mohammed is supposed to have made his Night Journey, a winged mare with a peacock's tail and a woman's head. See also BARAKA. **M**

BUTTERFLY, "BUH-tur-fly"—*English: "the butterfly."* **BABOCHKA** (BAH-boch-kah)—Russian; **BORBOLETA** (bohr-boh-LAY-tah)—Portuguese; **CHOO**—Japanese; **FARASHA** (fah-RAH-shah)—Arabic; **FARFALLA** (fahr-FAH-lah)—Italian; **FJÄRIL** (FYA-rihl)—Swedish; **FLUTURE** (FLOO-toor[-eh])—Rumanian; **KELEBEK** (KEH-leh-behk or keh-LEH-behk)—Turkish; **KIPEPEO** (kee-peh-PEH-oh or kee-PEH-peh-oh)—Swahili; **KUPU-KUPU**—Indonesian; **LEPKE** (LEHP-keh)—Hungarian; **MOTYL** (MOH-teel)—Czech and Polish; **PARPAR** (PAHR-pahr)—Hebrew; **PAPILLON** (pah-pee-

YAWN)—French; **PERHONEN** (pare-HOH-nehn)—Finnish; **SCHMETTERLING** (SHME-HT-ur-leeng)—German; **SOMMERFUGL** (zaw-mehr-FYOO-gul)—Norwegian and Danish; **VLINDER** (VLIHN-dur)—Dutch. The butterfly is a lot like a baby—it starts life as a caterpillar, a little creepy-crawly, and metamorphoses into a wondrous, delightful creature.

THE TOP FIVE

COURTNEY
CHELSEA
CATHERINE
CANDICE
CHERYL

If the name you're looking for isn't here, see "K" or "S."

CABIRI, "kah-BEE-ree—*Greek: "deity."*

CADY, "KAY-dee—*Irish: "hillock."* **KEADY.** M

CAITLIN, "KATE-lihn—*Welsh version of Catherine: "pure."* **KAITLIN; CATELYN, KATE-LYN.** See also CATHERINE.

CALA, "KAH-lah—*Arabic: "castle."*

CALABARA, "kal-ah-BAHR-ah—*Russian: "gray squirrel."*

CALANDRA, "kah-LAHN-drah—*Greek: "the lark."* **CALANDREA, CALANDRIA.**

CALEDONNE, CALEDONIA, "KAL-uh-dawn" and "kal-eh-DOHN-yah—*Scottish.* Caledonia is the old name for Scotland. **CALLIE; DONIA, DONNA.** M

CALISTA, "kah-LIHS-tah—*Greek: "most beautiful one."* **CALISTO, CALLISTO; CALLIA**—*French;* **CALLISTA; KALLISTA**—Greek. In Greek mythology, Calista was a lovely nymph who caught the god Zeus's roving eye. She was turned into a bear by Zeus's jealous wife and set into the sky as the constellation Ursa Major, or Great Bear. Callisto is the largest of Jupiter's moons.

CALLAN, "KAL-un—*Greek: "beautiful"; German: "to chatter"; Scottish: "child."*

CAILEAN (KYE-lawn)—*Scottish Gaelic.* **CALLEE, CALLI(E), CALLY.**

CALLIOPE, "kah-LYE-oh-pee—*Greek: "beautiful voice."* **KALLIOPE**—Greek. In Greek mythology, Calliope is one of the nine Muses; her special interest is epic poetry. Another Calliope is one of the Christian saints. Calliopsis plants bear loads of daisy-like flowers in a variety of colors.

CALLULA, "kah-LOO-lah—*Latin: "little beauty."* **CALLIE.**

CALYPSO, "kah-LIHP-soh—*Greek: "concealer."* **CALLIPSO, CHALLIPSO.** Calypso was a sea nymph who enchanted the Greek adventurer Odysseus, and kept him on her island for seven years. Calypso is also one of Saturn's moons, an orchid, and a type of loosely constructed, catchy music originating in Trinidad.

CAM, "KAHM—*Vietnamese: "orange fruit"* or *"sweet."* See also CAMERON.

CAMBRIA, "KAME-bree-ah—*Latin.* Cambria is the ancient Roman name for Wales.

CAMELLIA, "kah-MEEL-yah—*Latin: the camellia bush or flower.* Camellias can be grown as either trees or shrubs. They must be cultivated carefully if they are to produce their large, striking flowers in abundance.

CAMERON, "KAM-eh-rawn"—*Celtic: "crooked nose"; Latin: "from Cameris."* **CAMEREN, CAMERIN.** Cameris was a Sabine region of ancient Rome, in what is now central Italy. **CAM, CAMMI(E), CAMMY.** M

CAMILLE, "kah-MEEL"—*French from Latin: a type of ceremonial attendant.* **CAMILLA** (kah-MIHL-ah or kah-MEEL-ah); **KAMILKA**—Polish; **KAMILLA, KAMILLE.** In Europe, Camille is also a masculine name. Saint Camillus was a sixteenth-century gambler who straightened out and took on the task of improving nursing standards in homes or hospitals for the sick or wounded in Naples, Italy. He founded a Catholic order of nuns and monks who cared for the ill and incapacitated, and was the first to send nurses into battle zones. Thus, he is patron saint of the sick and the nurses who care for them.

CAMPANA, "kam-PAN-ah"—*Latin: "bell."*

CANA, "KANE-ah"—*Hebrew.* This is the name of a city in Canaan where Jesus performed his first recorded miracle—turning water into wine at a wedding.

CANDACE, CANDICE, "KAN-dass"—*Greek: "shimmering light" or "shimmering white."* **CANDIS.** Kandis or Candace was the title of Ethiopian queens. **CANDI(E), CANDY.** See also KANDIS.

CANDIDE, "kahn-DEED"—*French from Latin: "glowing white."* **CANDIDA**—Italian. Voltaire's 1759 play was entitled *Candide*, and interest in the name surged again with George Bernard Shaw's 1898 play *Candida*.

CANDY, "KAN-dee"—*Sanskrit: "sweet."* **CANDEE, CANDI, CANDIE; KANDEE, KANDI, KANDIE, KANDY.** See also CANDACE/ CANDICE.

CANNA, "KAN-ah"—*Greek: "white" or "light."* Canna lilies have sturdy, long leaves and large flowers in a variety of colors.

CANTARA, "kahn-TAH-rah"—*Arabic: "small bridge."*

CAPRI, "kah-PREE"—*Latin: "goat."* The island of Capri, a popular resort off of southern Italy, got its name from the goats the first settlers found there.

CAPRICE, "kah-PREESE"—*Italian: "fancy, whim."* **CAPPIE.**

CARA, "KAH-rah"—*Irish: "pillar stone"; Celtic: "friend"; Vietnamese: "diamond"; Italian: "dear."* **CARINA** (kah-REE-nah)— Italian. See also KARA.

CARILLA, "kah-RIH-lah" or "kah-REE-lah"—*German: "farmer."*

CARINA, "kah-REE-nah"—*Latin: "keel."* **CARINE.** The constellation Carina is following the Sun at dusk from late February to early April. It is best seen in the Southern Hemisphere. The Sun is "in" Carina from June through the end of July. **CARI.** See also CARA.

CARISSA, "kah-RIH-sah"—*Latin: "dear little one."* **CARISA, CHARISSA** (chah-RIH-sah or kah-RIH-sah).

CARITA, "kah-REE-tah"—*Latin: "beloved one."* **CARRIE; RITA.** See also CHARITY.

CARLA, "KAHRL-ah"—*Teutonic: "strong and womanly,"* one of the many versions of *Charlotte; Scottish: "precocious."* **CARLEE, CARLIE, CARLY**—Scottish and English; **CARLITA** (kahr-LEE-tah)—Spanish and Portuguese. See also CHARLOTTE, KARLA. M

CARMELA, "KAHR-meh-lah" or "kahr-MEH-lah"—*Hebrew: "garden or vineyard of the Lord"; Basque: "song."* **CARMELITA**

(kahr-meh-LEE-tah)—Spanish; **CARMEL-LA**—Italian; **KARMELE** (kahr-meh-leh)—Basque.

CARMEN, "KAHR-mehn"—*Latin: "song."* **CARME** (KAHR-meh or KAHR-mee)—Greek; **CARMELINA**—Spanish; **CARMIN, CARMINE**—Italian; **CHARMIAN, CHARMION.** *Carmen* is a very well-known opera by Georges Bizet. Carme is one of the moons of Jupiter. See also CHARMAIN/CHARMIAN.

CAROL(E), "KARE-ohl" or "KAH-rohl"—*French: "to sing" or "joyous song"; Gaelic: "champion."* **CAROLIA, CAROLLIA, CARROL(L), CARROLIA; CAROLINA, CAROLINE, CAROLYN; KAROLA.** Carol and Carole came into vogue during the 1930s, thanks to actress Carole Lombard. Carolyn Jones was an actress in many good films of the 1950s and 1960s, but we will never forget her two-year stint as dark Morticia on TV's *The Addams Family.* M

CAROLINE, CAROLYN. See CAROL.

CARRIE, "KARE-ee"—*Latin: "loved"; English: "castle"; Welsh: "stony island"; Irish: "Kerry," a place name.* **CARRI; KARRI(E), KERRI(E), KERRY.** See also CARITA. M

CASHLIN, "KAHSH-lihn/leen" or "CASH-lihn/leen"—*Irish: "little castle."* **CAISLÍN** (KYE-sleen)—Irish Gaelic.

CASSANDRA, "kah-SAWN-drah" or "kah-SAN-drah"—*Greek: "the prophetess."* **CASSANDRE.** In Greek mythology, Cassandra was the oracle at Delphi, the prophetess and psychic in the temple of Apollo, the sun god. She was given the gift of prophecy, but when she wouldn't yield to Apollo's desires, he cursed her gift by declaring that no one would believe her visions. **CASS, CASSI(E); SANDRA** (SAWN-drah or SAN-drah), **SAUNDRA, SONDRA.**

CASSIOPEIA, "kah-see-OH-pee-ah" or "kah-see-oh-PEE-ah"—*Greek: "praised voice" or "voice of praise."* In Greek mythology, Cassiopeia was a queen of the Ethiopians, the mother of Andromeda. She boasted that her daughter was more beautiful than the Nereids, or sea nymphs, and Poseidon—Greek god of the sea and father of the Nereids—sent a sea monster to ravage the kingdom. The constellation Cassiopeia can be seen chasing the Sun at dusk in late November and early December. The Sun is "in" Cassiopeia in late February and early March.

CATHERINE, "KATH-eh-rihn," "KAT-eh-reen," or "kat-eh-REEN"—*Greek: "pure."* **CAITLIN** (KATE-lihn)—Welsh; **CAITROÍNA** (kye-tree-OH-nah), **CATRAOINE** (kah-trah-oh-EEN)—Irish Gaelic; **CATERINA**—Italian; **CATHARINA**—Dutch; **CATHIRIN(E)**—Norwegian; **CATHRYN**—English; **CATIA** (KAHT-yah)—Portuguese; **CATIA** (kah-TEE-ah)—French; **CATRINA, CATRINE, CATRINJA** (kah-TREEN-yah)—Scandinavian; **CATRIONA** (kah-tree-OH-nah)—Scottish; **CATRÍONA** (kah-TREE-oh-nah)—Scottish Gaelic. Many saints have had names on this list, including Saint Catherine of Alexandria, who refused to worship idols and was placed on a spiked wheel. The wheel shattered, and 200 witnesses were immediately converted, so they say. Catherine has also been the name of Russian, French, English, and Spanish queens. **CAT, CATHEE, CATHEY, CATHI(E), CATHY.** See also KATHARINE/KATHERINE, KIT(TY).

CATHLEEN, "cath-LEEN"—*Irish version of Katherine: "pure."* **CAITLIN** (KAYT-lihn), **CATHLYN; CAITLÍN** (KITE-leen or kite-LEEN)—Irish Gaelic; **CATALIN(A)** (cah-tah-leen[-ah])—Basque; **CATHELLE** (kah-TEHL)—French. **CAT, CATHEE, CATHEY,**

CATHI(E), CATHY. See also CATHERINE, KATHLEEN.

CATHY. See CATHERINE, CATHLEEN.

CAVATINA, "kah-vah-TEE-nah"—*Italian: a short, simple aria.*

CECILE, "seh-SEEL"—*Latin: traditionally "gray-eyed" or "blind," but also "hearthstone" and "of the god Vulcan," the Roman god of fire and craftsmen.* CECELIA, CECILIA (seh-SEEL-yah), CECILY (SEH-sih-lee), CELIA (SEEL-yah), CELIE (SEEL-ee), CICELY (SIHS-eh-lee), CILI (TSEE-lih), CSILLA (CHEE-lah)—Hungarian; SILJE (SEEL-yah)—Dutch; SISILE (she-SHEEL)—Irish Gaelic; SISSELJE (sih-SEHL-yah)—Norwegian. Saint Cecilia is the patron saint of music and poetry, and her story appears in Geoffrey Chaucer's *The Canterbury Tales.* CECE, CIS, CISSY.

CEIBA, "SAY-bah" or "SYE-bah"—*Native South American: a silk-cotton tree.*

CELADONNE, "SEH-lah-dawn"—*Bretagne(?).* Celadon is a soft or grayed green. M

CELANDINE, "SEHL-an-deen," "seh-LAHN-deen," or "sehl-an-DEEN"—*Greek: "a swallow."* Celandine is an herb used in folk medicine.

CELENA, "seh-LEE-nah"—*Greek: "of the moon goddess."* In Greek myth, Celena is one of the daughters of Atlas. There were seven, and they are represented in the constellation called the Pleiades. See also CELINE, SELENA.

CELESTE, "seh-LEHST"—*Latin: "the heavens."* CELESTINA, CELESTINE, CELESTYNE. M

CELINE, "seh-LEEN"—*French, from Latin: "hammer."* CELINA; CESIA—Polish. Singer Celine Dion's popularity has nudged this old-fashioned name back onto the popular name charts. See also CELENA, SELENA.

CEPHORAH, "SEH-foh-rah"—*Hebrew: "bird."* CEPHIRAH, CEPORAH; ZIPPORAH. In the Old Testament/Tanakh, Cephorah was the long-suffering wife of Moses.

CERES, "SEE-reez"—*Latin: Roman goddess of grains or of corn.* CERELIA (see-REEL-yah). Ceres is a symbol of the bounty of Spring—thank her when you eat your breakfast "cereal." Ceres is also the largest of the minor planets of the asteroid belt between Mars and Jupiter.

CETA, "SEE-tah"—*Latin: "the whale" or "the porpoise."* M

CH'AN, "ch'AHN"—*Chinese: "Zen."* M

CHANDRA, "CHAHN-drah"—*Hindu: "goddess of the moon."* M

CHANSONNE, "shahn-SAWNN"—*French: "song."* CHANTAL. M

CHARIS, "KARE-iss" or "KAHR-iss"—*Greek: "love" or "grace."* CARESS(E), CARESSA; CHARISSA.

CHARITY, "CHARE-ih-tee"—*Latin: "charity or kindness."* CARITA (kah-REE-tah)—Spanish and Italian. This is one of the Puritan virtue names.

CHARLENE. See CHARLOTTE.

CHARLOTTE, "SHAR-lawt," rarely "CHAR-luht"—*Teutonic: "womanly"; Germanic: "free woman."* CARLA; CARLOTA (kahr-LOH-tah)—Spanish and Portuguese; CARLOTTA (kahr-LOH-tah)—Italian; CHARLENE, CHARLEEN—American; CHARLOTTA (shahr-LOH-tah)—Swedish; KARLA; LOTJE (LOH-tyeh)—Dutch; SÉARLAIT (SHARE-lah-eet)—Irish Gaelic. Charlotte Brönte was one of the trio of talented Brönte sisters, each an excellent writer. Lady Charlotte Guest translated eleven medieval Welsh romances to produce the classic *Mabinogion* in the early nineteenth century. **CHARLEY, CHARLI(E), CHARLY, LOTTA, LOTTE** (LOH-teh or LAW-teh), **LOTTI(E).** M

CHARMAIN, CHARMIAN, "shahr-MAYN" or "CHAR-mee-ahn"—*French version of Carmen: "song"; Greek: "drop of joy."* **CHARMAINE, CHARMAYNE.** See also CARMEN.

CHAUSIKA, "chow-SEE-kah"—*Swahili: "born in the night."* **CHAUSA, CHAUSI; SEKA, SIKU.**

CHELSEA, "CHEHL-see"—*Cymric: "dweller in the woods by the sea"; German: "from the sea" or "near the sea."* **CHELSEY.** After Bill and Hillary Rodham Clinton moved to the White House in 1992, the name of their daughter, Chelsea, skyrocketed in popularity. Her name, in turn, was taken from a Joan Baez song, *"Chelsea Morning,"* indicating a place called Chelsea—there's one in Britian, for example. See also KELSEY.

CHEN, "CHEHN"—*Chinese: "orange" or "tangerine," or "vast" or "great."* M

CHENETTE, "cheh-NEHT"—*Greek: "goose"; French: "oak tree."* **CHENETTA; KENETTA, KENETTE.** M

CHENILLE, "sheh-NEEL"—*French: "caterpillar."* The word refers to the fuzzy kind of catepillar, after which the fabric chenille was named. Remember that cute, creepy-crawly caterpillars turn into beautiful, bewinged butterflies.

CHENOAH, "cheh-NOH-uh"—*Native American Sioux: "the dove."* **CHENNA; NOAH.**

CHERI, CHERYL, "sheh-REE" and "SHARE-ihl"—*French: "cherished one."* **CHÈRE (SHARE), CHEREE, CHERIE, CHERILL, CHERILYN.** Cher—born Cherilyn Sarkesian—is an award-winning actress, singer, and entertainer. **CHER.** See also SHERRIL(L).

CHEROKEE, "CHEH-roh-kee"—*Native American Cherokee: "my people, our people, us."* This is a tribe name for a democratic, progressive group of people originating in the Great Lakes area. By the mid-eighteenth century, they ended up in what is now Tennessee and Virginia, and North and South Carolina. They created well-organized towns, and this quiet orderliness was a part of their basic nature. The Cherokee attempted repeatedly to deal fairly with other tribes and the colonists, and, later, the Americans.

CHERRY, "CHAYR-ee"—*Greek: "cherry tree"* or its fruit. **CEREJA** (seh-RAY-hah)—Portuguese; **CEREZA** (seh-RAY-zah)—Spanish; **CERISE** (seh-REEZ)—French; **CHERRI(E); CIREASHA** (sih-RAY-shah)—Rumanian; **CSERESZNYE** (tseh-REZH-nyeh)—Hungarian; **KARAZ** (KAH-rahz)—Arabic; **KERSEN** (KUR-sehn)—Indonesian; **KIRAZ** (KEE-rahz)—Turkish; **KIRSCH(E)** (KEERSH)—German; **KIRSIKKA** (KEER-see-kah)—Finnish; **SAKURA, SAKURANBU** (sah-KOOR-ahn-boo)—Japanese; **TRES-NYE** (TREHZ-nyeh)—Slavic; **VISHNYA** (VEESH-nyah)—Russian; **WISNIA** (VEEZ-nyah)—Polish. Wild cherry bark is used in herbal and folk medicine. "Cherry" also has a slang meaning of newness, beauty, and excellence.

CHESNA, "CHEZ-nah"—*Slavic: "peaceful."*

CHEYENNE, "shy-EN" or "shy-AN"—*French/Sioux: "people of a different lan-*

guage." **CHEYENNA**. This is a tribe name for a group of people originally from what is now Minnesota. The Sioux forced the Cheyenne out onto the Great Plains by the mid-eighteenth century, where they became the typical Plains Indians—nomadic hunters. The Cheyenne were among the most deeply religious of the Native American tribes. In addition to publicly practicing the Sun Dance and other ceremonies, prayers were a part of every person's daily private life, and personal, supernatural visions were expected. M

CHI, "CHEE"—*African: "guardian angel" or "guardian spirit."* M

CH'I, "CHEE"—*Chinese: "breath" or "vapor."* Ch'i is one of the fundamental elements of the cosmos in Taoist and Confucianist thought. In Confucianism, ch'i brings order and focus to matter and energy. M

CHIMENA, "chih-MAY-nah" or "shih-MAY-nah"—*Greek: "hospitable."* **CHIMENE**, **XIMENA** (shih-MAY-nah), **XIMENE**, **XIMENIA**.

CHINA, "CHY-nah"—*the Asian country.* **CHINE (SHEEN)**—French; **CHYNA**. See also KACHINA.

CHLOÉ, CHLOË, "KLOH-ee"—*Greek: "blossom" or "green" as in healthy plants and springtime.* **CLOË**. Chloë is associated with the various goddesses of the Earth.

CHO, "CHOH"—*Japanese: "born at dawn" or "butterfly"; Korean: "beautiful."*

CHRIS. See CHRISTIAN(E), CHRISTIN(E).

CHRISTABELLE, "KRIHS-tah-bell"—*concocted from Greek: "beautiful or handsome Christ" or "beautiful Christian,"* although the root words can be taken to mean "bright and attractive," "luminous beauty," or "golden beauty." In 1816, Samuel Taylor Coleridge published *Christabel*, which is largely responsible for the popularity of the name. **BELLA, BELLE; CHRISTA, CHRISTI(E)**.

CHRISTI(E). See CHRISTABELLE, CHRISTIAN(E), CHRISTIN(E).

CHRISTIAN(E), "KRIHS-tyahn"—*Greek: "of the (golden) Light."* **CHRÉSTIEN**, **CHRÉTIENNE** (kreh-TYEN—"r" in the back of your throat)—French; **CHRISTIAAN**—Dutch; **CHRISTIANNA, CHRISTIANNE; CHRISTION, CHRISTIONA**—Irish Gaelic. The light referred to is Jesus of Nazareth. There are several Christian saints' names on this list.

SOUTHERN COLONIAL GIRLS' NAMES

Girls born in Southern states along the Atlantic coast are most likely to have the following names:

1. Ashley	6. Amber	11. Lauren	16. Amanda
2. Jessica	7. Jasmine	12. Hannah	17. Victoria
3. Brittany	8. Jordan	13. Elizabeth	18. Morgan
4. Sarah	9. Kayla	14. Megan	19. Chelsea
5. Emily	10. Courtney	15. Rachel	20. Anita

CHRIS, CHRISSI(E), CHRISSY, CHRISTI(E), CHRISTY. See also CHRISTIN(E), KIRSTEN, KRISTA, KRISTIN(E). M

CHRISTIN(E), "krihs-TEEN" and "KRIHS-tihn"—*Greek: "a Christian."* **CAIRISTIÓNA** (kayrz-tee-OH-nah)—Scottish; **CARSTEN**—Dutch; **CHRISTINA; CRISTIN, CRISTINA**—Italian; **KIRSTEN. CHRIS, CHRISSI(E), CHRISSY, CHRISTI(E), CHRISTY.** See also CHRIST-IAN(E), KRISTA, KRISTIN(E).

CIAN, "KYAHN" or "KEE-ahn"—*Irish Gaelic: "ancient."* M

CIARAN, "KYAH-rahn"—*Irish: "little dark one."* Ciaran is the name of two Irish saints. See also KAREN.

CICELY, "SIH-seh-lee" or "SYE-seh-lee"—*Latin/Greek: a type of sweet herb.* See also CECILE.

CINDY. See CYNTHIA.

CINNABAR, "SIHN-eh-bahr"—*Persian: "red," "reddish," or "vermilion."* **KINNIBAR**—Greek; **ZINIFAR, ZINIFRAH**—Persian. Natural cinnabar is a crystalline red substance.

CINNAMON, "SIHN-eh-mawn"—*Hebrew.* **KINNAMON**—Greek; **QINNAMON**—Hebrew. This can refer to either the spice, or to the reddish-brown color.

CIRINE, "kee-REEN"—*Irish Gaelic: "exalted."* **CIRINEEN.**

CISSY. See CECILE.

CLARA, "CLARE-ah" or "KLAH-rah"—*Anglo-Saxon: "illustrious"; Latin: "clear"; Yiddish: "clean."* **CLAIRE, CLARE**—French; **CLARICE** (KLAH-reese), **CLARISSA** (klah-RIHS-sah). Several saint names are on this list. M

CLA(I)RE. See CLARA.

CLARISSA, "klah-RIH-sah" or "klah-REE-sah"—*Anglo-Saxon: "she will be famous."* **CLARICE, CLARISE, CLARISSE.** *Clarissa* is an eighteenth-century novel about a willful English heiress, written by Samuel Richardson. See also CLARA.

CLAUDETTE. See CLAUDIA.

CLAUDIA, "KLAWD-yah"—*Latin: "lame."* **CLAUDETTE, CLAUDINE**—French. There are several Christian saints' names on this list. **CLAUDI(E).** M

CLEMATIS, "kleh-MAH-tihss"—*Greek: "climbing rose."* Clematis is a woody vine with flowers in all colors except for yellow.

CLEMENTA, "kleh-MEHN-tah"—*Latin: "merciful."* **CLEMENTINA, CLEMENTINE.** M

CLEOPATRA, "klee-oh-PAH-trah"—*Greek: "glory of her father."* **KLEOPATRA**—Eastern European. The much-sung Cleopatra most associated with this name, the one who seduced Mark Antony, was actually Cleopatra the Seventh. **CLEA, CLEO; KLEA, KLEO.** See also CLIO.

CLETA, "KLEET-ah"—*Greek: "summoned."* **CLETIA, CLETIS.** M

CLIO, "KLEE-oh"—*Greek: "celebrate," "praise," or "the proclaimer."* **CLEA, CLEO.** Clio is one of the nine Muses, and is especially interested in history and writing. See also CLEOPATRA.

CLORIS, "KLOH-rihs"—*Greek: "pale" and "goddess of flowers."* **CHLORIS.**

CLOVER, "KLOH-vur"—*English: "clinging."* Clover is a generally three-lobed, lusciously green plant that is sometimes used in making honey.

CLYTIE, "KLY-tee"—*Greek: "splendid."* In Greek mythology, Clytie is a maiden who felt unrequited love for Helios, the sun god. She was transformed into the heliotrope, a plant whose flowers always follow the sun.

COCHA, "KOH-chah"—*Inca: "sea."* Mamacocha is the great Inca goddess of the sea and its bounty.

COCHAVA, "koh-KHAH-vah" ("KHA" is guttural)—*Hebrew: "starlight."*

COCOPA, "koh-KOH-puh"—*Native American Hokan: "where the river flows."* This is a tribe name for a lowland clan of the numerous Yuma tribes. Their cultural nonchalance and their carelessness about personal possessions surprised some, until it was realized that they inhabited a region of the Colorado River that was prone to flooding, which often wiped out their belongings. How do you say "Que sera, sera" in Hokan?

COL(L)ETTE, "koh-LET"—*French diminutive of Nicola: "victory of the people."* **KOLETE** (koh-leh-teh)—Basque. Colette Sidonie was a forward-looking French novelist, perhaps best known for her 1944 novel *Gigi.*

COLLEEN, "KAW-leen" or "kaw-LEEN"—*Irish: "girl."* **CAILÍN** (KYE-leen, kye-LEEN)—Irish Gaelic.

COLOMBIA, "koh-LUHM-bah"—*Latin: "dove" or the columbine plant.* **COLOMBA**—Spanish; **COLUMBANA, COLUMB(I)A; COLUMBINE.** The columbine plant's flowers resemble a gathering of doves, thus the name. The constellation Columba flies in Southern skies behind the Sun at dusk through the month of February. The Dove flies with the Sun from mid-May to mid-June. M

CONCHETTA, "kawn-CHEH-tah"—*Italian: "conception."* **CONCEISAO** (kohn-shay-sah-oo)—Portuguese; **CONCETTA; CONCHATA, CONCHATTA.** The conception referred to is the Immaculate Conception of Jesus Christ.

CONNY. See CONSTANTINA.

CONRADA, "kawn-RAD-ah"—*German: "bold counsellor."* **CONRADINA, CONRADINE; KONRADINA, KONRADINE**—Eastern European. M

CONSTANCE. See CONSTANTINA.

CONSTANTINA, "kawn-stan-TEE-nah" —*Latin: "constant or steadfast."* **CONSTANCE, CONSTANT; CONSTANTIA**—Greek; **CONSTANTINE; CONSTANZA** (kawn-STAHN-zah)—Italian; **KONSTANCJI** (kawn-STAHN-chee), **KONSTANTY**—Polish; **KOSTYA, KOSTYUSHKA**—Russian. Several Christian saints have names on this list. **CON, CONNI(E), CONNY.** See also KONSTANTINA. M

CONSUELA, "kawn-SWAY-lah"—*Spanish from Latin: "consolation."*

CORA, "KOH-rah"—*Greek: "maiden"; Irish: "spear."* **COREN, CORETTA, CORETTE; KORA, KOREN.** In Greek mythology, Cora was a daughter of Zeus and Aphrodite. **CORI(E).**

CORAL, "KOH-rul"—*Greek: "coral."* **CORALEE, CORALIE, CORI(E), CORY.**

CORDELIA, "kohr-DEE-lee-ah"—*Celtic: "daughter of the sea" or "jewel of the sea."* **CORDELIE, CORDELLA, CORDELLE.** The original word for Cordelia in Celtic is *Creiddylad,* which is the name of the sea nymph daughter of the great ocean god Llyr. Cordelia was the only daughter in Shakespeare's *King Lear* who was actually faithful to the king—but the old guy was so paranoid, it didn't matter. Cordelia is also one of the moons of Uranus.

CORI(E). See CORA, CORAL.

CORINA, "koh-REE-nah"—*Greek: "maiden."* **CORINE, CORRINA, CORRINE.** Corinna was a fifth century B.C. Greek poet, a beautiful and talented woman who was recognized for her mind by being awarded major prizes for poetry several times.

CORNELIA, "kore-NEEL-yah"—*Latin: "horn" and "cornell tree."* **KEES** (KAYS)— Dutch; **KORNELIA; KORNELIKA.** This is one of the Christian saints. M

CORONA, "koh-ROH-nah"—*Spanish: "crown."* **COURONNE.** The Corona Australis, the Southern Crown, is a constellation that appears to chase the Sun at dusk from mid-August to mid-September. The Sun is "in" Corona Australis in December. The Corona Borealis, the Northern Crown, is a constellation that appears to chase the Sun at dusk in the month of July. The Sun is "in" Corona Borealis in November.

COSMA, "KAWS-mah"—*Greek: "the universe" or "order."* **COSIMA, KOSIMA, KOSMA.** Cosmos is also a plant that bears feathery flowers in various shades of red, pink, yellow, orange, and white.

COURTNEY, "KOHRT-nee"—*French: "one who lives at court."* **COURTENAY, COURTENEY.**

CRESSIDA, "KREH-sih-dah"—*Greek.* Cressida is one of the moons of Uranus, named after one of the title characters in Shakespeare's *Troilus and Cressida.* The story of the Trojan pair and their broken love affair first appears in literature with Geoffrey Chaucer's *Troilus and Criseyde.*

CRYSTAL, "KRIHS-tahl"—*Greek: "clear ice" or "purity."* **CHRISTEL(LE)**—French; **CHRYSTAL**—Irish; **CRIOSTAL**—Irish Gaelic; **CRYSTEL(LE); KRISTAL(LE), KRISTEL(LE)**— Swedish; **KRYSTALLE**—German; **KRYSTEL(LE)**—Norwegian, Danish, and Dutch; **KRYSTAL** . . . And any other way you can imagine spelling this word, which describes the shape taken by a variety of minerals.

CULLEY, "KUH-lee"—*Irish: "the holly meadow."* M

CYBELE, "SEE-bell-eh" or "see-BELL"— *French version of Sybil: "prophetess" or "wise woman"; more accurately, Greek: a goddess of fertility, nature, and health.* **CYBELLE, CYBIL, CYBILLE.** Cybele was first worshipped as the great mother-goddess in Asia Minor, but her cult also transferred to Greece and Rome. She is associated with fertility, untamed nature, and mountains, and her festivals were almost as rowdy as the Bacchanalia in honor of Bacchus, the Greek god of wine. See also SYBIL.

CYGNA, "SIHG-nah" or "SEEN-yah"— *Latin: "the swan."* **CIGNA, CIGNET, CIGNETTE; CYGNE, CYGNET, CYGNETTE.** The constellation Cygnus can be seen flying after the Sun at dusk from September throughout the first half of October. The Sun is "in" Cygnus from Thanksgiving through Christmas.

CYMA, SYMA, "SEE-mah"—*Greek: "flourishing."* **XEMA.**

CYMRY, "SIHM-ree" or "KIHM-ree"— *Celtic.* **CYMRIC, CYMRICA.** Cymry is the name for the ancient Celtic tribes of Wales, Cornwall, and Bretagne (in northwestern France).

CYNARA, "see-NAH-rah"—*Greek: "thistle."* **CYNA, CYNARETTE.** Cynara is another name for the artichoke.

CYNTHIA, "SIHN-thee-ah"—*Greek:*

another name for the Greek goddess Artemis or the Roman goddess Diana; Sanskrit: "of the Indus river." **CYNTHA, CYNTHEE, CYNTHIE; KYNTHIA, KYNTHIOS; SINDHI**—Sanskrit. This Greek goddess ruled over the Moon, the feminine principle, and the animals, among other things. As with most heavenly beings, the praises sung to Diana were sung so much and were so numerous that people had to come up with alternate names. **CINDI, CINDIE, CINDY; CYNDEE, CYNDI(E), CYNDY.**

CYRILLA, *"see-RIHL-ah"—Greek: "lordly" or masterly."* **CYRILLIA; KIRILLA.** M

-esha, -isha

These are African-American suffixes often found in the names of urban girls. They were invented after World War II as the African-American community began to assert its own identity. There was precious little native African scholarly work available to the average American, so a unique *sound* was created. Urban African-American names take the first syllable or two of a more traditional name and add the suffix that the parents think looks best when written, since both versions are pronounced "EE-shah," the "EE" being the most stressed syllable of the entire name.

> Monica—Monesha
> Laurie—Laurisha

Also rising in popularity for girls is the suffix "-ika," and to a lesser extent, "-eka." Both are pronounced "EE-kah," with the "EE" being the most stressed syllable of the entire name.

> Monica—Moneka
> Laurie—Laurika

THE TOP FIVE

DANIELLE
DIANA
DAKOTA(H)
DESTINY
DREW

If the name you're looking for isn't here, perhaps it is a variant or a diminutive of another primary name.

DAFFODIL, "DAF-oh-dihl"—*English.* This spring-blooming flower is a member of the amaryllis family.

DAGNY, *"DAHG-nee"—Norwegian: "day"; Norse: "bright," as in daylight.* This is not to say that the name's bearer can't be bright as in brainpower, as well. M

DAHLIA, "DAHL-yah"—*Latin: the dahlia plant; Norse: "from the valley."* Dahlias are flowers that come in many, many colors and color combinations. They like to spread out equally in all directions.

DAI, "DAH-ee"—*Japanese: "great."* M

DAIREEN, "dye-REEN"—*Irish(?).* This is, perhaps, the feminized version of Dahy. This name first appears in 1893 as the heroine's name in F.F. Moore's *Daireen.*

DAISY, "DAY-see" or "DAY-zee"—*English: "the day's eye,"* the Sun, and also the flower. *Daisy Miller* is the unconventional title character in a book by Henry James (1879). The book struck such a nerve that it generated the phrase "Daisy Millerism," applied to any unconventional behavior by women.

DAKOTA(H), "dah-KOH-tah"—*Native American Sioux: "friendly one(s)."* This is one of the three tribes of the Great Sioux Nation. M

DALE, "DAIL"—*English: "valley"; Norse: "hollow," as in the topographical feature.* **DAEL, DAILE, DAYLE.** M

DALILA, "dah-LEE-lah"—*Swahili: "gentle."* **LEELA.**

DALILI, "DAH-lee-lee"—*Swahili: "a sign from the gods" or "an omen."* **LEELI, LILIE.**

DAMARA, *"dah-MAH-rah" or "DAH-mah-rah"—Greek: "gentle girl."* This is also the name of a group of people who live in central southwest Africa, in Damaraland.

DAMARIS, "dah-MAH-rihs"—*Greek: "sweet heifer."* **MARIS.**

DAMIA, "dah-MEE-ah" or "DAH-mee-ah"—*Greek.* This is a Greek nature goddess.

DAMIANE, "DAY-mee-ann" or "dah-mee-AHN"—*Greek: "to tame," "to domesticate," or "to calm."* **DAMIAN(N)A; DAMIENNE.** The damiana plant's spicy leaves are used in herbal and folk medicine. M

DAMITA, "dah-MEE-tah"—*Spanish: "little noblewoman."*

DANICA, "DAN-ih-kah"—*Norse: "Morning Star (the planet Venus)."* **DANIKA. DANNI(E), DANNY.**

DANIELLE, "dah-NYELLE"—*Hebrew: "God is my judge."* **DANEILA** (dah-NEEL-ah)—Eastern European; **DANELE** (dah-neh-leh)—Basque; **DANELLA, DANETTE, DANICE**—French; **DANIEL(L)A, DANIEL(L)I**—Italian; **DANIYELLE**—Israeli. **DANNA, DANNI(E), DANNY, DANYA.** M

DANISHA. See TANISHA.

DANNI(E). See DANICA, DANIELLE.

DANTELLE, "dahn-TEHL"—*Italian: "lasting" or "patience."* M

DANU, "DAH-noo"—*Celtic.* This is the Celtic mother goddess.

DANYA, "DAHN-yah"—*Ukrainian, from Bogdana: "God's gift."*

DAPHNE, "DAFF-nee"—*Greek: "the laurel."* **DAPHNAH** (DAHF-nah)—Italian. Daphne was a river nymph whose beauty enchanted the Greek god Apollo. When he tried to forcibly express his desire, Daphne broke away into the woods, pleading with the goddess Artemis (in some tellings) to help her maintain her virginity. Always a little extreme in their problem solving, the Olympian deities turned Daphne into a laurel tree. Apollo then took the laurel tree as one of his symbols, and laurel continues to be a symbol of honor and greatness. Daphne shrubs bear fragrant flowers in pinks and purples amidst lush foliage.

DARA, "DAHR-ah"—*Hebrew: "pearl"; Irish: "oak tree."* See also ADARA, MANDARA. M

DARBY, "DAHR-bee"—*Gaelic: "free man."* Like many other female names nowadays, this started out as a male name, so the name would be more meaningful if you thought of it as "free woman." M

DARCY, "DAHR-see"—*French: "from the fortress"; Celtic: "dark one."* **DARCEY, DARCI, DARCIE.**

DARIA, "DARE-ee-ah"—*Persian: "many possessions"; Latin: "dark queen."* **DARICE; DARIE.** M

DARLA. See DARLENE.

DARLENE, "DAHR-leen" or "dahr-LEEN"—*English: "darling."* **DARLEEN, DARLINE, DARLYN. DARLA.** This is an example of how a term of endearment—"darling"—becomes a name in itself.

DARRYL, "DARE-ihl"—*English: "dear" or "darling."* **DARRELLE, DARYL.** The fame of actress Daryl Hannah has popularized the use of this traditionally male name for girls. M

DARSANA, "DAHR-sah-nah"—*Sanskrit: "to see."* **DARSIE, DARSY.**

DASHA, "DAH-shah"—*Russian: "gift of the Lord."*

DAUPHINE, "doh-FEEN"—*French: "princess" or "dolphin."* **DAUPHINÉE**—French. Dauphiné is also a region in the south of France. See also DELBINE, DELPHINA, DELVINA. M

DAVIDA, "DAY-vihd-ah," "dah-VEE-dah," or "DAH-vee-dah"—*traditionally, Hebrew: "beloved" or "adored"; but also Scandinavian: "two rivers."* **DABIDA** (dah-bee-dah)—Basque; **DAIBHIDHA** (DYE-VYAH)—Scottish Gaelic; **DAVEN**—Scandinavian; **DAVITA**—Israeli; **TAFFY**—Welsh. M

DAVINA, "DAH-vihn-ah" or "dah-VEE-nah"—*Norse: "Finnish."* M

DAWN, "DON"—*English: "daybreak."*

De, Di, Da

These are Italian prefixes. "De" ("day") means "of" or "from." "Di" ("dee") means "of the" or "from the," and is followed by a singular noun—generally one that ends in "a" or "o." "Da" ("daw") means "of the" or "from the," and is followed by a plural noun—generally one that ends in "i" or "s." You may add these yourself to any name.

DAYA, "DAY-ah" or "DAH-yah"—*Hebrew: "bird."* **DAYAH.**

DEANA, "DEEN-ah" or "dee-AN-ah"—*English: "from the forest."* **DEANNA; DINA** (DEE-nah)—Italian. Deanna Durbin was a child star of the 1930s and 1940s with an unquestionably soprano singing voice. The name again became popular when a character named Deana appeared on *Star Trek: The Next Generation.* See also DENA, DIANA, MANDEANA/MANDA. M

DEBBY. See DEBORAH.

DEBORAH, "DEHB-oh-rah" or "deh-BOH-rah"—*Hebrew: "a bee"* or *"eloquence."* **DEBORA**—Dutch; **DEVORA** (deh-VORE-ah), **DEVORE**—Russian; **DEBRA**—Portuguese; **DOBEH** (DOH-beh or doh-BEH), **DOBRA**—Yiddish. In the Old Testament/Tanakh, Deborah was a judge and a prophetess who led an uprising against the Canaanites. The *Song of Deborah* is one of the oldest portions of these sacred writings. **DEBBI(E), DEBI, DEBBY.**

DEE, "DEE"—*Welsh: "holy one" or "black."* See also DEIRDRE. M

DEIRDRE, "DEER-drah"—*Gaelic(?): "broken-hearted(?)."* **DEIDRA, DEIDRE, DEIRDRA.** In Irish folklore, the king of Ulster had arranged to marry the maiden Deirdre against her will. She did not love him, but rather, one of three brothers. The king got rid of all three brothers to eliminate any competition. The legend is related in William Butler Yeats's *Deidre* (1907) and in J.M. Synge's *Deirdre of the Sorrows* (1910). **DEE, DEEDEE.**

DELBINE, "del-been" or "del-bee-neh"—*Basque: "dolphin."* See also DAUPHINE, DELPHINA, DELVINA. M

DELIA, "deh-LEE-ah" or "DEE-lee-ah"—*Greek: "she from Delos," a Greek island.* This is another name for the goddess Artemis or Diana. As with most heavenly beings, the praises were sung so often and were so numerous that people had to come up with alternate names.

DELILAH, "deh-LYE-lah" or "deh-LEE-lah"—*Hebrew: "gentle, tender" or "temptress"; Arabic: "guide" or "leader."* **DELILA.** In the Old Testament/Tanakh, Delilah's guile and beauty led her husband, Sampson, to tell her the secret of his great strength. To find out the rest of the story, rent the video. **LILA(H).**

DELLA, "DEHL-ah"—*Italian(?): "of good cheer,"* or the Italian version of Adele: *"of noble birth."* See also ADELAIDE, ADELLE.

DELMA, "DEHL-mah"—*Latin: "from the sea."* M

DELPHI, "DEHL-fye"—*Greek: "sacred"*

and "love." Delphi is the site of sacred temples of the Greek gods of Olympus, a place where mortals could learn the will of the gods. It is located on Mount Parnassus at the Gulf of Corinth. The most famous structure here is the temple of Apollo, where his oracles, always women, would prophesy. A sacred stone is at Delphi, the Omphalos or "navel stone," said to mark the center of the Earth. As the center of the Earth, this place was a gathering spot for governments, and was an important place to sack if you were taking over Greece. There is even a shrine to John the Baptist at the sacred stream of Delphi. M

DELPHINA, "dehl-FEE-nah"—*Greek: "a dolphin" or "serenity"; or it can refer to the flower: "delphinium."* **DELFA, DELFINA, DELFINE** (dehl-FEEN); **DELPHA, DELPHINE** (dehl-FEEN); **DELPINA.** The constellation Delphinus can be seen chasing the Sun at dusk in the last half of September. The Sun is "in" the Little Dolphin at Christmastime. Delphinium are tall, sturdy plants with cones of cascading flowers that come in all colors. See also DAUPHINE, DELBINE, DELVINA. M

DELTA, "DEHL-tah"—*Greek: "river delta" or "four."* Deltas—the triangle-shaped islands that form where a river joins a larger body of water—look like "delta," the fourth letter of the Greek alphabet.

DELVINA, "dehl-VEE-nah"—*English from Greek: "dolphin."* **DELFINA.** See also DAUPHINE, DELBINE, DELPHINA. M

DEMBE, "DEHM-beh"—*African Luganda: "peace."* M

DEMI, "DEH-me" or "deh-ME"—*diminutive of Demitra, Greek: "earth mother."* **DEMETER; DEMETRA, DEMETRIA, DEMI-**TRA; **DIMITIRA, DIMITRA.** Demi Moore is an actress.

DENA, "DAY-nuh" or "DEE-nah"—*Native American: "the valley"; diminutive of Adena, Hebrew: "adornment."* **DINA.** See also ADENA, DEANA.

DENISE, "deh-NEESE" or "duh-NEEZE"—*French: "Dionysius, god of wine" or "from Nîce"; Greek: "of Nysa," a Greek mountain.* **DENISKA**—Russian; **DENYSE** (deh-NEESE)—English; **DINISIA** (dee-NEE-see-ah)—Portuguese. M

DEOLINDA, "DAY-oh-LEEN-dah"—*Latin/Portuguese: "beautiful God" or "beautiful goddess"; Germanic: "dragon goddess."*

DERORA, "deh-ROH-rah"—*Hebrew: "freedom."* **DERORIT** (deh-roh-REET), **DERORICE.**

DERRY, "DARE-ee"—*Irish: "oak grove."* **DERRI(E).** M

DÉSIRÉE, "day-see-RAY" or "DEH-zih-ray"—*French via Latin: "desire" or "desired."* **DESIDERIA** (deh-see-DEH-ree-ah)—Spanish. M

DESMA, "DEHZ-mah"—*Latin: "a part of all creation"; Greek: "a bond or pledge."* M

DESTINE, "DEHSS-tihn" or "dehss-TEEN"—*French: "destiny," "fate," or "luck."* **DESTINY** (DESS-tih-nee).

DEVA, "DAY-vah"—*Sanskrit: "divine," "shining one," or "to gleam."* **DIVA.**

DEVADATTA, "day-vah-DAH-tah"—*Hindu: "god-given."*

DEVIN, "DEHV-ihn"—*Celtic: "poet."* M

DHANIE, "d'HAH-nee"—*Sanskrit: "wealthy."* M

DIAMOND, "DYE-uh-mund" or "DYE-mund"—*French: "diamond" or "glittering"; English: "bright protector."*

DIANA, "dye-AN-ah," "dye-AH-nah," or "dee-AH-nah"—*Latin: "bright one"; Sanskrit: "reflection, meditation"; Native American: "a deer."* **DEANN, DEANNA, DEANNIE; DIANE, DIANNA, DIANNE; DYAN, DYANNA, DYANNE; DEINA** (day-ee-nah)—Basque; **DHYANA**—Sanskrit; **DIANDRA, DIANDRE.** Diana was the Roman goddess of the Moon and the feminine principle. She held rulership over forests, animals, and children. The former Lady Diana Spencer, who married the heir to the British throne and became the object of everyone's fancy as Princess Diana, is now a very wealthy goodwill ambassador. **DI.** See also DEANA, DIANTHA, MANDEANA/MANDA.

DIANDRA, "dee-AHN-drah" or "dye-AN-drah"—*Greek: "twice a man" or "two men."* **DIANDRE.** One daughter worth two sons, or one heck of a woman.

DIANE. See DIANA.

DIANTHA, "dye-AN-thah"—*Greek: "heavenly flower."* **DIANTHE.**

DIEGA. See JACOBA, JAMIE.

DILLIAN, "DIHL-ee-an"—*Latin: "image of worship."* **DILLA; DILLIANNA, DILLIANNE. DILLI(E), DILLY.** M

DIMITRA. See DEMI.

DINA. See ADINA, DEANA, DENA, DINAH, UNDINE.

DINAH, "DEE-nah" or "DYE-nah"—*Hebrew: "vindicated"; Greek: "power."* **DEENA(H), DINA, DYNA(H).** The Dinah of the Old Testament/Tanakh is a beautiful daughter of Jacob and Leah.

DIONE, "dee-OHN" or "dee-AWN"—*Greek: "child of heaven and earth" or "sky goddess."* **DEONNE; DIONA, DIONNA, DIONNE.** Dione was an ancient Greek deity who, when the newer group of gods moved in, became associated with Aphrodite, the goddess of love, beauty, art, and femininity. Dione is one of the moons of Saturn. M

DISA, "DEE-sah"—*Norse: "active."*

DIVA. See ADIVA, DEVA.

DIXIE, "DIHKS-ee"—*Latin: "tenth"; Norse: "busy sprite."* "Dixie," in reference to the

De, De la, Del, De las, De los

These are Spanish prefixes. "De" ("day") means "of" or "from"; "de la" ("day-lah") means "of the" or "from the." "De" must be followed by a name that is a singular noun, while "de la" must be followed by a name considered to be a singular, feminine noun—add an "a" to anything, if in doubt, and avoid a final "o." "Del" means "of the" or "from the" and must be followed by a name considered to be a singular, masculine noun. "De las" ("day-lahs") means "of the" or "from the" and must be followed by a plural, feminine noun. "De los" ("day-lohs") means "of the" or "from the" and must be followed by a plural, masculine noun—when in doubt, add "os" to a word. You may add these yourself to any name.

American South, comes from the Confederate ten-dollar note, on which the Latin and French word for ten—"dix"—was printed. See also BENEDICTA. M

DOANNE, "DOH-ahn" or "doh-AN"—*Celtic: "sand dunes."* M

DODI, "DOH-dee"—*Hebrew: "beloved," "friend," or "aunt."* **DODA, DODIE, DODY.** If you're lucky, you have one person who's all three.

DODONA, "doh-DOH-nah"—*Greek: "god-given(?)."* This is a place name for the oracle of the Greek god Zeus, where his priests would commune with him and give guidance to mortals. Dodona is associated with oak trees and doves, since both the trees and the birds spoke to mortals and ordered a temple be built to this greatest of Greek gods.

DOE, "DOH"—*English: "(a deer, a) female deer."*

DOLI, "DOH-lee"—*Native American Navajo: "blue bird."* See also DOLLY.

DOLLY, "DAWL-ee"—*English: "doll."* **DOLL, DOLLEY, DOLLIE.** Dolley Madison, First Lady from 1809 to 1816, is best remembered for being an excellent hostess who threw the hottest parties in town. The name became popular again with the rise to fame of singer/actress Dolly Parton. See also DOLI.

DOLORES, "doh-LOH-rehz"—*Spanish from Latin: "lady of sorrows."* **DALORA, DELORA; DALORES, DALORIS, DELORES, DELORIS; DOLORITA** (doh-loh-REE-tah), **DOLOURS.** The "lady" in question is usually the Virgin Mary.

DOMINA, "doh-MEE-nah"—*Italian: "lady."*

DOMINICA, "doh-MIHN-ih-kah"—*Latin:*

"of the Lord." **DOMENICA; DOMENIKA** (doh-MEHN-ee-kah)—*Greek;* **DOMINGA** (doh-MEEN-gah)—*Spanish;* **DOMINICIA** (doh-MEE-nee-kah)—*Italian;* **DOMINIKA**—*Eastern European;* **DOMINIQUE** (doh-mee-NEEK)—*French.* M

DOMINIQUE. See DOMINICA.

DO(N)NA, "DAWN-ah" and "DOHN-ah"—*Latin: "lady."* **DOÑA.** See also CALEDONNE/CALEDONIA.

DONOMA, "doh-NOH-mah"—*Native American Omaha: "the first or last visible sun."*

DORA, "DOH-rah"—*Greek: "gift"; French: "golden."* **DORETTA, DORETTE. DORI(E), DORY.** See also DORIANNE, ENDORA, THEODORA. M

DORCIA, "DOHR-see-ah" or "DOHR-syah"—*Greek: "gazelle."* **DORCAS** (DOHR-kahss).

DOREEN, "doh-REEN"—*Irish: "sullen"; French: "golden girl."* **DORENE; DOIREANN** (doh-ee-RAHN)—*Irish Gaelic;* **DORINE**—*French.* The Irish usage of this name is older than the French usage.

DORI(E). See ALDORA, DORA, DORINDA, DORIS, THEODORA.

DORIANNE, "doh-ree-AN"—*Greek: "gift"; Latin/French: "golden."* **DORIENNE; DORIJÁNKA** (dor-YAHN-kah)—*Hungarian.* **DORA.** M

DORINDA, "doh-RIHN-dah"—*Greek: "bountiful gift."* **DRINDA, DURINDA. DORI(E), DORIN, DORY.**

DORIS, "DOHR-ihss"—*Greek: "wealth of the sea," and the name of a mermaid.* **DORIA, DORICE, DORIKA, DORITA, DORRIS, DORRIT.** In Greek mythology, Doris was the daughter of Oceanus and the wife of

Nereus; she bore all fifty of the golden-haired Nereids (sea nymphs) on her wedding day. Whew! Actress Doris Day was a singer for big bands before becoming America's sweetheart, the plucky girl next door, in the late 1950s and 1960s. **DORI(E), DORRI(E), DOR(R)Y.**

DORIT, "doh-REET"—*Hebrew: "the new generation."* **DORRITT.**

DOROTHY, "DOHR-oh-thee" or "dohr-oh-TEE"—*Greek: "gift of God."* **DÍORBHAIL** (DYOR-vail—resist the temptation to say "Doorbell"!)—Scottish Gaelic; **DOORTJE** (DORT-tyeh)—Dutch; **DORDEI** (dohr-DAY), **DORDI, DORTE, DORTEA** (dohr-TAY-uh), **TEA**—Norwegian; **DORIKA, DOROTTYA** (doh-ROW-tyeh)—Hungarian; **DOROTA** (DOH-roh-tah)—Polish; **DOROTEA** (doh-roh-TAY-ah and doh-roh-TEE-ah)—Swedish and Italian; **DOROTEYA, DOSYA**—Russian; **DOROTHÉE** (doh-roh-TAY)—French. Saint Dorothea was martyred for refusing to worship idols. Dorothy is the main character in L. Frank Baum's Oz tales. **DOT, DOTTI(E), DOTTY.**

DOT(TY). See DOROTHY.

DRAIGHEAN, "DRAH-een"—*Gaelic: "the blackthorn."*

DREW, "DROO"—*Greek, diminutive of Andrew: "strong"; German: "carry" or "trust."* Actress Drew Barrymore has popularized the use of this traditionally male name for females. She was named after her famous forebears—the Drew and Barrymore clans of actors. **DRU.** M

DRISANA, "dree-SAH-nah"—*Sanskrit: "daughter of the sun."*

DRUCILLA, "droo-SIHL-ah"—*Celtic: "capable."* See also DRUSILLA. M

DRUELLA, "droo-EHL-ah"—*German: "elfin vision."* **DRUELLE. DRU.**

DUANA, "doo-AHN-ah"—*Irish: "little dark one"; Celtic: "singing."* See also DUENA. M

DUENA, "DWAYN-ah"—*Spanish: "chaperone."* See also DUANA.

DULCIE, "DUL-see"—*Latin: "sweet" or "gentle."* **DULCEA, DULCIA, DULCINEA** (dul-sih-NAY-ah)—Spanish and Italian; **DULCET(TE)** (duhl-SEHT)—French; **DULCY, DULSIE, DULSY**—English, Nordic, and German. In Cervantes's *Don Quixote*, the name of the woman the title character imagines to be his maiden in distress—the one for whom he, Don Quixote, is champion!—is Dulcinea.

DURGA, "DUR-gah"—*Sanskrit: "inaccessible one."* Durga is a Hindu goddess known for slaying demons and riding a lion. She is also called the Queen of the Cosmos.

DUVESSA, "doo-VAY-sah"—*Irish: "dark beauty."*

DYANI, "dee-YAH-nee" or "dye-AH-nee"—*Native American: "a deer."* **DYAN.** M

DYSIS, "DY-sihss"—*Greek: "musical interlude" or "sunset."* **DIESIS, DYESIS. DICE, DIES, DYS.** M

THE TOP FIVE

EMILY
ELIZABETH
ELLEN
ERICA
EDEN

If the name you're looking for isn't here, see "Y" and the other vowels.

EARTHA, "UR-thah"—*German: "the earth"* *or "land."* **ERDA, ERTHA, HERTHA.** Eartha Kitt is a sultry singer and actress whose personal story—her rise from humble beginnings and her antiwar activism—is quite dramatic.

EBONY, "EH-boh-nee"—*English: "the ebony tree" or "black"; French: "dark."* **HEBNI** (HEHB-nee)—Egyptian. Ebony wood is very hard, heavy, and durable, and can be polished to a very bright shine.

EBUN, "eh-BOON"—*African: "a gift."*

EDA, "EE-dah"—*English: "blessed."*

EDANA, "ee-DAHN-ah"—*Irish Gaelic: "little fiery one."* **M**

EDDA, "EHD-ah"—*Norse: "poetry."* The *Edda* is a collection of Old Nordic mythological poems and prose. It was probably written in Iceland as early as the ninth century.

EDEN, "EE-dehn"—*Hebrew: "delight."* The legendary Garden of Eden was a paradise on Earth until Adam and Eve goofed. **M**

EDIE, "EE-dee" and also "EH-dee"—*Swedish: "unresting"; Norse: "whirlpool."* See also EDITH, EDWARDA, EDWINA.

EDINA, "eh-DEE-nah"—*Scottish: "girl from Edinburgh."*

EDITH, "EE-dihth" or "ay-DEET"—*Teutonic: "rich gift"; English: "bountiful."* **DUCI** (DOO-tsee)—Hungarian; **EDIT**—Scandinavian; **EDIT-TA** (ay-DEE-tah)—Italian; **EDYTA**—Polish. Two saints and two queens have borne this name. **EDIE, EDDIE.**

EDURNE, "eh-door-neh"—*Basque: "snow."*

EDWARDA, "ehd-WAHR-dah"—*English: "happy or wealthy guardian."* **DUARTA** (doo-AHR-tah)—Portuguese; **EDOARDA** (eh-doh-WAHR-dah)—Italian; **EDUARDA** (eh-doo-AHR-dah)—Spanish; **EDVARDE** (ehd-VAHR-deh)—Swedish; **EDVARDKA**—Eastern European. **ED, EDIE, EDDI(E), EDDY. M**

EDWINA, "ehd-WEE-nah"—*English: "happy or wealthy friend."* **EDUINA**—Spanish and Portuguese; **EDVINA**—Eastern European; **EDWYNNA** (ehd-WIHN-ah), **EDWYNNE** (ehd-WIHN)—Welsh. **ED, EDIE, EDDI(E), EDDY. M**

EFFIE, "EHF-ee"—*Greek: "famed and fair."* This is the modernized version of the ancient Greek name Iphigenia. See also IPHIGENIA.

EGERIA, "ee-JEER-ee-ah" or "ay-JEER-ee-ah"—*Greek: "wise advisor."* **EGERJA, EGERYA.** The Roman demigoddess of water, Egeria, was associated with the goddess Diana and had some connections to pregnancy.

EGRETTE, "EE-greht"—*English: the egret bird.* **AIGRETTA, AIGRETTE** (ay-GREHT)—French, Italian, and Spanish; **EGRETTA.** The egret is a type of heron, usually with long, white feathers.

EILEEN, "EYE-leen" or "eye-LEEN"—*version of Helen: "light" or "luminous"; Greek: "twist" or "roll."* **ILENE.** See also HELEN.

ELAINE, ELAYNE, "ee-LAYN"—*European version of Helen: "luminous" or "illustrious."* **ELAIN, ELAYN; ELENA** (eh-LAY-nah)—Spanish and Italian; **ELI** (EH-lee), **ELIN, ELINE**—Scandinavian. In Arthurian legend, the Lady Elaine—also known as the Lady of Shalott—was a lover of Sir Lancelot, having come across him as he wandered the British Isles during one of his spells of madness. See also HELEN.

ELANA, "ay-LAHN-ah"—*Latin: "spirited"; French: "ardor" or "vivaciousness"; Hebrew: "tree" (ay-LAH-nah).* **ELA, ELAH, ELAI, ELON, ELONA, ILANA.** M

ELARA, "ee-LAH-rah"—*Latin/Greek: "shining" or "famous."* Elara is one of the moons of Jupiter, named after a little lady with whom the Greek god Zeus had an affair.

ELDORA, "ehl-DOH-rah"—*Spanish: "golden one."*

ELEANOR, "EHL-ah-nohr" or "eh-LAY-ah-nohr"—*version of Helen: "luminous" or "illustrious."* **EALANOR** (AY-lah-nohr), **EILEANÓIR** (AY-lah-nohr), **EILÍONÓRA** (ay-lee-oh-NOH-rah)—Gaelic; **ELEANORE, ELINOR, ELINORE; ÉLÉNORA** (ay-lay-NOH-rah)—French; **ELEONORA** (ay-lay-oh-NOH-rah)—Italian and Swedish. Eleanor has a long and grand history of belonging to powerful women. The first, and probably the most powerful, was Eleanore of Aquitaine, a French queen who was taken as a bride by Henry II of England—some say just to get his hands on the vast holdings of his queen. But they had eight children together, including King Richard the Lion-Hearted and King John. American Anna Eleanor Roosevelt, a niece of President Theodore and First Lady to President Franklin from 1933 to 1945, set quite a standard of service, compassion, and intelligence, and also made a public relations splash. **ELLA, ELLE, ELLI(E), ELLY.**

ELECTRA, "ee-LEK-trah"—*Greek: "bright" and "amber-haired."* **ELEKTRA, ELLEKTRA; ELETRA, ELLETRA.** There were two Electras in Greek legend. One was a lover of the god Zeus, and mother to the hero Perseus; she is represented by one of the stars in the Seven Sisters star cluster near the constellation Taurus.

ELELE, "eh-LAY-leh"—*Hawaiian: "angel."*

ELENA. SEE ELAINE/ELAYNE.

ELIA, "EE-lyah" or "EHL-yah," or "EE-lee-ah" or "ee-LYE-ah"—*Hebrew: "Jehovah is my God."* **ELI, ELYE.** M

ELIORA, "eh-lee-OH-rah"—*Hebrew: "God is my light."* **ELEORA; LEORA, LIORA.**

ELISABETH, ELIZABETH, "ay-LEES-ah-beht" or "ee-LIHSS-ah-beth" and "ay-LEEZ-ah-beht" or "ee-LIHZ-ah-beth"—*Hebrew: traditionally, "consecrated to God," but also "the Lord's oath."* **BETI, BOSKE** (BOH-skeh), **BÖZSI** (BAWZ-shee), **ELIZ, ERSSIKE** (EHR-shih-keh), **ERZSÉBET** (EHR-zheh-beht), **ERZSI** (EHR-zhee), **ERZSOK, ORZSÉBET** (ohr-ZHAY-beht or OHR-zheh-beht)—Hungarian; **BETJE** (BEH-tyeh), **ELIZA** (eh-LEEZ-ah), **ELS, LIJSBET** (LEEyez-beht)—Dutch; **BETTI, ELIZAVETA** (eh-lee-zah-VAY-tah), **LIZABETA, YELISAVETA**—Russian; **EILÍS** (EYE-leese)—Irish Gaelic; **ELISABET, ELSA**—Swedish; **ELISABETTA** (ay-LEE-sah-BAY-tah)—Italian; **ELISE** (ell-LEE-seh), **ELLISIF** (eh-LEE-sihf or EHL-ehs-ihf), **ELSE** (EHL-seh), **LISBET** (LEES-beht)—Scandinavian; **ELISE** (ee-LEESE), **ELSIE, ELYSE, LILIBET** (LIH-lih-beht), **LILIBETH**—English; **ELISHEBA, ELISHEVA** (eh-LEE-sheh-vah)—Israeli; **ELIZABETE** (eh-lee-zah-beh-teh)—Basque; **ELSBETH, ELSPETH, ELZBETH**—German; **ELZBIETA** (ehlz-bee-EH-tah)—Polish; **LISBET** (LEES-beht)—Danish; **LIZETE**—Portuguese. Quite a few saints have names on this list—one Saint Elisabeth is the mother of John the Baptist. There have also been many queens with this name. In Britian, the first Queen Elizabeth gave her name to the age best known for producing William Shakespeare, while the second has seen the world change drastically in the last half of the twentieth century. **BESS, BESSI(E), BESSY; BETH, BETTE** (BEHT or BEH-tee), **BETTI(E), BETTY; BETSY; LISA, LISETTA, LISETTE, LISSA, LISSETTA, LISSETTE, LISSI(E), LISSY; LIZ, LIZA** (LIH-zah or LYE-zah), **LIZETTA, LIZETTE, LIZZETTE, LIZZI(E), LIZZY.** See also ISABELLA.

ELKA, "EHL-kah"—*Yiddish: "swear by/to God."* **ELKE; ILKA**—Scandinavian.

ELKE, "EL-keh"—*Teutonic: "elk."* **ELKA.** Elke Somers is an model turned actress.

ELLA, "EHL-ah"—*English: "fairy maiden"; German: "all."* This can also be used as a suffix that turns a masculine name into a feminine name. **ELLIE, ELLY.** See also ELEANOR.

ELLEN, "EH-lehn"—*version of Helen: "luminous" or "illustrious."* **EILIDH** (EYE-lee)—Gaelic; **ELLYN, ELLENE, ELLI(E), ELLY; LENE** (LEH-neh), **LINE** (LEE-neh)—Norwegian. See also HELEN.

ELLIE, "EHL-ee"—*Hebrew: "the Lord is God."* **ELLY.** See also ELLA, ELLEN. M

ELOISE, "eh-loh-EEZ" or "EH-loh-eez"—*German: "battle maiden."* See also HELOISE, LOIS, LOUISE.

ELSA, "EHL-sah"—*Swedish from Greek: "truthful"; Celtic: "noble"; Anglo-Saxon: "swan."* **ELSIE, ILSA; ELSJE** (EHL-syeh)—Dutch. See also AILSA, ELISABETH/ELIZABETH.

ELVA, "EHL-vah"—*Gaelic: "leader of the elves"; Nordic: "wise elf."* M

-el

As a suffix, this has an ancient history, going as far back as Assyrian times. It is an adjective that describes a luminous, supernatural being. Originally, it was exclusively an angel, but it has carried over into the European mind as "elf," another glowing, magical being. The four Archangels of the three great monotheistic religions—Judaism, Christianity, and Islam—are Micha-el, Gabri-el, Rapha-el, and Uri-el. "-el" can be tagged onto any name of either gender, though it is generally changed to "-elle" for females.

ELVIRA, "ehl-VYE/VEE-rah"—*Spanish: "white or fair"; German: "wise advisor."* **ALBIRA** (ahl-BEE-rah), **ALVIRA**—Spanish; **ALVIRIA, ALVIRUM** (ahl-VEE-ruhm)—German; **ELVERA**—Italian; **ELVÉRA** (ehl-VAY-rah), **ELVIRE**—French; **ELWIRA** (ehl-VEE-rah)—Polish.

ELYSIA, "ee-LEE-zhah"—*Greek: "blissful."* **ELISE, ELYSE; ELYSIAN, ELYSIANNE.** In Greece, the Elysian Fields were the sections of the afterworld in which those who were good got their reward of paradise.

EMERALD, "EHM-eh-rahld"—*Latin: "the emerald."* **EMERAUDE** (eh-meh-ROAD)—French. **EM, EMMI(E), EMMY.**

EMILY, "EH/AY-mih-lee"— *Latin: "industrious"; Teutonic: "energetic."* **ÉMÈLINE** (ay-meh-LEEN), **ÉMILIE** (AY-mee-lee)—French; **EMELINHA** (ay-may-LEEN-hah), **EMILINHA** (ay-mee-LEEN-hah)—Portuguese; **EMILIA**—Spanish and Scandinavian; **EMILIANA** (ay-mee-lee-AH-nah)—Spanish, Portuguese, and Italian; **EMMALINA, EMMELINA**—Italian; **EMMELINE** (EH-mih-leen)—English; **MILA** (MY-lah or MEE-lah), **MILLA**—Latin. Emily is a name used often in European writings, including those of Geoffrey Chaucer, Jane Austen, and Giovanni Boccaccio. **EM, EMMIE, EMMA, EMMY; MIL, MILLI(E), MILLY.** See also AMALIA, AMELIA. M

EMMA, "EH-mah"—*German: "universal"; Teutonic: "one who heals."* **EM, EMMI(E), EMMY.**

EMMANUELLE, "ay-MAHN-yoo-ehl" and "e-mahn-yoo-EHL"—*Hebrew: "God is with us."* **EMANUELA, EMANUELLA; MANUELLA. EMAN.** See also IMMANUELLE. M

EMMY. See EMERALD, EMILY, EMMA.

ENA, "EE-nah"—*Irish: "fire."* **ENOLA.**

ENCINA, "en-SEE-nah"—*Spanish: "live oak."*

ENDORA, "ehn-DOH-rah"—*Aramaic: "fountain."* **DORA, ENDA.**

ENID, "EE-nid"—*Welsh: "pure" or "flawless"; Celtic: "soul."* In Arthurian legend, Enid, the wife of Prince Geraint, a Knight of the Round Table, had to deal with her husband's rampaging jealousy. She was faithful, true, and patient; assertiveness was one of her traits, too.

ENRICA, "ehn-REE-kah"—*Spanish version of Henriette: "lady of the estate."* **ENRIQUETA** (ehn-REE-keh-tah)—Portuguese. **RICA.** See also HENRIETTE. M

ENYE, "EHN-yeh"—*Yiddish version of Ann(e): "grace"; Greek: "goddess of war."* **ENYA, ENYO.** See also ANN(E).

EOS, "AY-awss"—*Greek: "dawn goddess."* The Greek goddess Eos is said to have driven a chariot across the sky, pulled by two horses, Shining and Bright. She was also a woman who went after the men she wanted, sometimes even kidnapping them. This included the god of war, Ares, who kind of liked it, which made his usual mate, Aphrodite, jealous.

ERANTHE, "air-ANTH(-eh)"—*Greek: "spring flower."*

EREKY, "EH-rehk-ee"—*Polish: "lovable."* M

ERELAH, "eh-REH-lah"—*Hebrew: "angel" or "messenger."*

ERIANTHE, "air-ee-ANTH(-eh)"—*Greek: "sweet as a field of flowers."* **ARIANTHE.**

ERICA, "EH-rik-ah"—*traditionally Teutonic: "queen" or Norse: "ever powerful"; but try on Turkish: "plum" or Russian: "appointed by God."* **ERICHA** (AIR-ihk-ah)—German; **ERIKA**—Scandinavian; **ERYKA**—Polish.

RICKI(E), RICKY; RIK, RIKI(E), RIKKI, RIKKY. M

ERIN, "AYR-ihn"—*Irish: "Ireland" or "peace."* **ERIN(N)A.** An ancient Irish queen was named Erin.

ERLINE, "ur-LEEN"—*English: "elf."* **LERLINE, LURLINE** ("the elf"); **MERLINE, MURLINE** ("my elf").

ERMA. See IRMA.

ERNESTINE, "ur-nehs-TEEN"—*German: "vigor"; Teutonic: "intense."* **ERNESTA** (urNEHS-tah)—Spanish and Italian; **ERNESZTINA**—Hungarian. M

ESHE, "AY-sheh"—*Swahili: "life."*

ESME, "EHZ-may"—*Persian: "emerald"; Latin: "adorned"; Scottish: "beloved."* **ESMÉE**—French. See also ESMERALDA.

ESMERALDA, "ehz-meh-RAHL-dah"—*Latin: "adorned"; Greek: "emerald."* **ESMERELDA.** Esmeralda is the heroine in Victor Hugo's *The Hunchback of Notre Dame* (1831), and in the 1996 Disney movie of the same name. ESME.

ESPE, "es-peh"—*Basque: "hope."*

ESPERANZA, "eh-speh-RAHN-zah"—*Spanish: "hope."* **SPERANZA**—Italian.

ESTA, "EHS-tah"—*Italian: "from the East"; Latin: "of a famous ruling house."* M

ESTELLE, "ehs-TEHL"—*Latin: "star."* **ESTELLA; ESTRELA** (ehs-TRAY-lah)—Italian and Scandinavian; **ESTRELINHA** (ehs-trehLEEN-hah)—Portuguese; **ÉTOILE** (ayTWAHL)—French. **STELA, STELLA, STELLE.** See also STAR(R).

ESTHER, "EHS-ter"—*Hebrew: "the planet Venus (the Morning Star)"; Phoenician: "goddess of the moon"; Babylonian: "goddess of love and desire."* **EISTIR** (EYEsteer)—Irish Gaelic; **ESTÉE** (ehs-TAY)—French; **ESTER; ESZTER, ESZTI**—Hungarian. In the Old Testament/Tanakh, Esther was a Hebrew queen of Persia who saved her people from death by thwarting a plot to destroy the Hebrews. This feat is celebrated at Purim.

ETENIA, "eh-teh-NEE-uh"—*Native American: "wealth."*

ETTA, "EH-tah"—*Yiddish: "light"; German: "little one."* **ETTE** (EH-teh); **ITTA** (EE-tah), **ITTE; YETTA, YETTE.**

ETTARE, ETTORE, "eh-TAHR(-eh)" or "eh-TORE(-eh)"—*Greek: "steadfast."* **ETTARA, ETTORA. TARA, TORI(E).**

EUDORA, "yoo-DOH-rah"—*Greek: "generous" or "good gift."*

EUDOSIA, "yoo-DOH-zyah/syah"—*Greek: "esteemed" or "gifted."* **EUDOCIA.** This is one of the Christian saints.

EUGENIA, "yoo-JEEN-ee-ah" or "yooHAY-nee-ah"—*Greek: "nobly born" or "wellborn."* **EUGENIE** (yoo-JEHN-ee)—Swedish; **EUGÉNIE** (yoo-ZHAY-nee), **GÉNIE**—French; **EVGENIA** (ehv-GAY-nyah), **YEVGENIA, ZENECHKA** (zeh-NETCH-kah or ZEH-netchkah), **ZENYA**—Russian. Several saints and popes have had names on this list. Eugénie was one of Napoleon's lovers, but at least this one was given some executive power; she acted as regent of France when N.B. was out of town. **GINA, GENI(E).** M

EUI, "UH-ee"—*Korean: "meaningful."*

EULAILE, "yoo-LAY-leh"—*Greek: "wellspoken" or "sweet-tongued."* **EULAILEE, EULAILI(E), EULAILY; EULALIE** (yoo-LAHlee)—French. Saint Eulalia was martyred in the fourth century for trying to retain her virginity. **EULA.**

EUN, "UH-un" or "AY-un" as if one syllable—*Korean: "silver."*

EUNICE, "YOO-nihss"—*Greek: "good victory."* In the New Testament, Eunice is the mother of the disciple Timothy.

EUPHEMIA, "yoo-FAY-mee-ah"—*Greek: "well-spoken."* **EADAOINE** (yah-DAO-ween or ay-DAO-ween)—Gaelic; **EUFEMIA; EUPHÈME** (ooh-FEHM or ooh-FEHM-eh)—French. **EFFI(E), EFFY; EPPI(E), EPPY.**

EUROPA, "yoo-ROPE-uh"—*Greek: "well-formed(?)" or "beautifully formed(?)."* Europa was a legendary Phoenician princess who caught the perpetually wandering eye of the Greek god Zeus. He appeared to her as a magical white bull and carried her away to the north. Her encounters with Zeus began a new race, the Europeans. Europa is one of the moons of Jupiter.

EUSTACIA, "yoo-STAY-see-ah"—*Greek: "plentiful" or "fruitful"; Latin: "tranquil."* **ESTACIA** (eh-STAH-see-ah)—Portuguese; **EUSTAQUIA** (yoo-STAH-kee-ah)—Spanish; **EUSTAZIA** (yoo-STAHZ-ee-ah)—Italian. **STACIA, STACEY, STACI(E), STACY.**

EVADNE, "ee-VAD-nee"—*Greek: "fortunate."* **EVA.**

EVANDRA, "eh-VAN-drah"—*Greek: "good woman."* Evandra was a nymph who founded a city at the base of Palatine Hill in Greece. M

EVANGELIA, "eh-vahn-JEH/JAY-lee-ah" or "eh-vahn-heh-LEE-ah"—*Greek: "brings good news."* **EVANGELINA, EVANGELINE, EVANGELISTA, EVANGELISTE.** The name Evangeline, which started this whole thing in the nineteenth century, was made up by Henry Longfellow for his poem of the same name. **EVANA, LIA, LITSA.** M

EVANIA, "eh-VAHN-yah"—*Greek: "tranquil(ity)."* **IVANYA, YVONYA.** See also YVONNE.

EVANTHE, "eh-VAHN-theh"—*Greek: "flower."* **IVANYA, YVONYA.** See also YVONNE.

EVE, EVA, "EEVE" and "EE-vah" or "AY-vah"—*traditionally, Hebrew: "life," but also Gaelic and Celtic: "pleasant"; German/French: "hazelnut," seen as symbolic of wisdom.* **AOIFFE** (ah-oh-EEF-eh—the "ah-oh" like one syllable), **EEVE** (AYV-eh), **EIBHLIN** (ive-LEEN), **EUBHA** (OO-vah)—Gaelic; **EEFJE** (EEF-yeh)—Dutch; **ÉVA, EVACSKA** (eh-VATCH-kah), **EVIKE**—Hungarian; **EVALINA**—Russian; **EVALYN, EVALYNN(E), EVELYN, EVELYNN(E); EVELINA**—Swedish; **EVETTA, EVETTE** (ee-VEHT)—French; **EWA** (AY-vah)—Polish. In the Old Testament/Tanakh and the Qur'an, Eve is the mother of all humankind, the first woman. See also EVADNE.

EVELYN, "EHV-eh-lihn," rarely "EEV-eh-lihn"—*Anglo-Saxon: "dear youth."* See also EVE/EVA.

THE TOP FIVE

FRANCI
FRANCES
FLORENCE
FALLON
FATIMAH

If the name you're looking for isn't here, see "P" and "V."

FABANA, "fay-BAH-nah"—*African Zulu: "chief"* or *"leader."*

FABIANA, "fay-bee-AH-nah" or "fah-bee-AN-nah"—*Latin: literally, "bean grower," but traditionally translated as "prosperous farmer."* **FABIA, FABIENNE** (fah-bee-ENN)—French; **FABIOLA** (fah-bee-OH-lah)—Italian; **FABIYANA.** This is a Christian saint name. **FAB, FABBIE, FABBY, FABI.** M

FABRETTE, "fah-BREHT" ("R" in the back of your throat)—*French: "blacksmith"* or *"metal worker."* **FAB, FABBIE, FABBY; FABRA, FABRAY, FABRIE, FABRY.** M

FABRICE, "fah-BREESE" or "fah-BREE-cheh"—*Latin: "skilled crafter."* **FABRETTA; FABRICA; FABRIZIA**—Italian. **FAB, FABBIE, FABBY.**

FAIR, "FARE"—*English: "attractive," "light-colored,"* or *"equitable."* **FAIRE.** Pick a definition (or two or three). M

FAITH, "FAYTH"—*Latin: "trust"* or *"belief."* **FAITHE, FAYTH, FAYTHE.** This is a Puritan virtue name. **FAE, FAY, FAYE.**

FALA, "FAH-lah"—*Native American Choctaw: "clever crow."*

FALASHA, "fah-LAH-shah"—*Ethiopian: "stranger"* or *"foreigner."* The Falasha Jews are an Ethiopian group who claim lineage back to King Solomon and the queen of Sheba.

FALCHIONNE, "fawl-CHAWN"—*French.* This was a sword used in the Middle Ages that had a slightly curved blade. M

FALINE, "fah-LEEN"—*Latin: "catlike."* **FALINA; FALLON; FELINA, FELINE, FELINI, FELLINA, FELLINI.**

FALLON, "FAH-lun" or "FAL-un"—*Gaelic: "she-wolf."* **FALON(E).** The Gaelic word "phe-lan" denotes a charmed wolf, not just your plain old generic wolf. This name has been popularized by the TV show *Dynasty.* See also FALINE.

FALLOW, "FAL-oh"—*Old English: "tawny"; Modern English: "pale yellow"* or *"pale red"; both: "the fallow deer."* The fallow deer is a small deer that develops a white-spotted coat in the summer. M

FANCHONNE, "fan-CHAWN"—*French: "liberated."* **FANCHE; FANN, FANNIE, FANNY.** M

FAR(R)AH, "FAH-rah" or "FARE-ah"—*Arabic: "happiness"; English: "pleasant"* or *"fair."* **FAR(R)RA.** Actress Farrah Fawcett popularized this traditional old name, which has seen a rise in popularity since the 1970s.

FARAJI, "fah-RAH-jee"—*Swahili: "consolation, comfort."* **FARA, FARIJI, RAJEE.**

FARANDA, "FARE-an-dah"—*Bretagne: "spinning" or "whirling."* **FARANDOLIA** (FARE-an-doh-LEE-ah). This comes from a type of fast dance called a farandole, in which partners spin one another in and out around the edge of a circle of dancers. M

FARIDA(H), "fah-REED-ah"—*Arabic: "unique."* M

FATIMA(H), "fah-TEE-mah" or "FAH-tee-mah"—*Arabic: "charming."* Fatima was the daughter of Mohammed by his first wife, Khadija. There is not much written about her in the Qur'an, but the Shi'ite Muslims have elevated her in importance, holding her up as a model of womanhood in her devotion to father and husband. A woman named Fatima was the only one of notorious pirate Bluebeard's wives to out-fox him—she lived and he died.

FATINAH, "fah-TEE-nah"—*Arabic: "captivating."* **FATINHA**—Portuguese. **TINA.**

FAVIA, "FAY-vee-ah"—*Latin: "woman of understanding."* **FAVIANNE; FAVIEN, FAVIENNE. FAVE.** M

FAWN, "FAWN"—*Latin: "young deer."* **FAWNA, FAWNE, FAWNIA.**

FAY, FAE, "FAY"—*French: "faith"; Anglo Saxon: "to fit closely, join closely"; Gaelic "fairy" or sometimes "raven," a magical raven.* **FAYE, FAYETTE.** Faye Dunaway is an actress best known for playing the icy blonde. See also FAITH.

FELDA, "FEHL-dah"—*German: "from the fields."*

FELICE, "feh-LEESE" or "feh-LEE-cheh"—*Latin: "happy" or "lucky."* **FELCIA** (FEHL-chyah)—Polish; **FELICIA** (feh-LEE chee-ah or feh-LEE-see-ah)—Spanish and Italian; **FÉLICITÉE** (fay-LEE-see-tay)—French; **FELICITY** (feh-LIHS-ih-tee)—English; **FELICJA** (feh-LEETS-yah)—Slavic **FELIZA** (fay-LEEZ-ah), **FELIZIA**—Spanish and Portuguese. Felicia was the Roman goddess of good luck and happy events. A ton of Christian saints have had these names. M

FELICIA. See FELICE.

FELIPITA, "feh-lee-PEE-tah"—*Spanish version of Philipa: "lover of horses."* **FILIP-PA**—Italian. **LIPPA; PIP, PIPPA.** See also PHIL(L)IP(P)A. M

FEMI, "FEH-mee"—*African Yoruba "love me."*

FEODORA, "FAY-uh-dohr-ah"—*from Theodora, Greek: "gift of God."* **PHEODORA.** See also THEODORA. M

SURNAMES AS FIRST NAMES

The use of surnames as first names is quite popular now, both for boys and girls. Witness the rise of Taylor, Tyler, Cooper, and many other "trade" names. This is also a way for the child's mother to give it her family name if a hyphenated last name would be too long.

FERN, "FURN"—English: "the fern"; Greek: "feathery." **FERNE.**

FIDELIA, "fee-DEHL-yah"—Latin: "faithful." **FIDÈLE** (fee-DEHL)—French; **FIDELIA** (fee-DAY-lee-ah)—Italian; **FIDELLA.** M

FILIA, "FEE-lee-ah"—Greek: "friendship."

FINOLA, "fih-NOH-lah"—Irish: "fairskinned." **FENELLA, FINELLA**—Scottish; **FIONUALA** (fee-oh-NOO-lah), **NUALA**—Irish Gaelic.

FION(N)A, "fee-OWN-ah"—Scottish invention from Irish, "Finn" or "fair-haired"; Cymric: "ivory-skinned."

FIORENZA, "fee-oh-REHN-zah"—Italian: "flower." See also FLORENCE.

FLEUR, "FLUR"—French: "flower." **FLEUR-ETTE.**

FLORA, "FLOH-rah"—Latin: "flower." **FLEUR** (FLUR); **FLORELLA, FLORELLE, FLORETTE; FLORIDA, FLORITA.** Flora was the Roman goddess of fruits, flowers, and berries.

FLORENCE, "floh-RENTS" or "FLOH-rents"—Latin: "flowering" or "blooming." **FIORENZA** (fee-oh-REHN-zah), **FIORENZIA**—old-fashioned Italian; **FLORENCIA** (floh-REHN-see-ah or floh-REHN-chah), **FLOREN-ZIA**—Italian; **FLORENTINE; FLORENTYNA** (floh-rehn-TEE-nah)—Polish; **FLORETTA, FLORETTE, FLORIANE**—French. A few Christian saint names are listed here. Florence Nightingale (d. 1910) was a nurse who pushed for medical reform and improvement. She went into war zones to provide care and assistance to the injured and depressed, and she was one of the pioneering female health-care professionals. **FLO.** M

FOLA, "FOH-lah"—African Yoruba: "honor."

FOLADE, "fohl-ah-DEH" or "fohl-AH-deh"—African Yoruba: "honor is my crown." M

FOMORIA, "foh-MOH-ree-ah"—Celtic: "sea gods"; Irish: "pirate." **FOMHOIRE** (foh-HOYR or FOHM-oh-eer)—Irish. The ancient sea gods were worshipped in the British Isles long before the Celts arrived on the scene. Most are associated with emotion and fertility. **MOIRA.**

FONDA, "FAWN-dah"—English: "tender"; French: "to melt"; Latin: "deep." "Deep," in the Latin meaning, as in psychological depth and complexity.

FORTUNA, "for-TYOO-nah"—Latin: "good luck." **FORTUNATA, FORTUNE.** The Roman goddess Fortunata held rulership over good fortune and fertility. Yes, luck really is a lady.

FRANCES, "FRANT-sehz"—Teutonic: "free woman" or "a Frank." **FERI, FERKE**—Eastern European; **FRANCESCA** (frahn-CHEHS-kah); **FRANCI(E)** (FRANT-see, FRAWNT-see)—Italian; **FRANCINE** (fran-SEEN, frawn-SEEN)—Italian and French; **FRAN-CISCA** (frahn-SEES-kah)—Spanish; **FRAN-ÇOISE** (frawn-SWAHZ)—French: **PROINSÉAS** (PROYN-shahs)—Irish Gaelic. The Franks were a European tribe who occupied Gaul, which is known today as France. **FRANKI(E).**

FRANCESCA, "frahn-CHEHS-kah"—version of Frances: "free" or "a Frank." **FRANCESKA, FRANCISKA**—Eastern European; **FRANCISCA** (frahn-SEES-kah)—Spanish and Portuguese; **FRANCISQUE** (frawn-SEESK)—French; **FRANCISZKA** (frahn-TSEESH-kah), **FRANIA, FRAKA**—Polish. See also FRANCES. M

FRANCI, "FRAN-tsee" or "FRAWN-tzee"—

Teutonic: "free" or *"Frankish (French)."* **FRANCIE; FERIKE** (feh-REE-keh or FEH-ree-keh)—Eastern European. The popularity of Franci as a name unto itself, rather than as a diminutive of other "Fran-" names, came in the 1960s after the series of books and movies, and a television show, with a title character named Franci Lawrence—aka Gidget ("girl" + "midget")—a petite, plucky teenaged surfer girl.

FRANCINE. See FRANCES.

FREDERICA, "FREHD-eh-rihk-ah" or "frehd-eh-REE-kah"—*Teutonic: "peaceful ruler."* **FEDERICA** (fehh-deh-REE-kah)—Italian; **FREDEKA**—Eastern European; **FREDERICKA; FREDERIKA**—Nordic; **FRÉDÉRIQUE** (fray-day-REEK)—French; **FREDRICA**—Swiss; **FREDRIKA**—German; **FRICI** (FREE-tsee)—Hungarian; **FRYDERYKA** (FRIHD-eh-rihk-ah)—Polish. Many empresses, queens, and saints have borne this name. **FREDA, FREDDA, FREDDI(E), FREDDY, FREDI(E); RICK, RICKA, RICKI(E), RICKY; RIK, RIKA, RIKKA, RIKKI(E), RIKKY.** M

FREYA, "FRAY-ah"—*Scandinavian: "lady."* **FREYJA, FREYYA.** Freya was one of the supreme beings of the Nordic pantheon. She was the feather-clothed goddess of love, beauty, and fertility, and was said to have had a chariot drawn by magical cats.

FRIDA, "FREE-dah" or "FRIH-dah"—*Teutonic: "peaceful."* **FRIDDA, FRYDA, FRYDDA.** See also FRIEDA.

FRIEDA, "FREE-dah"—*Yiddish: "peace."* See also FRIDA.

FULANI, "foo-LAH-nee"—*African Ibo: "my people, our people, us."* **FALANI. FALA(H), FULA(H).** M

THE TOP FIVE

GABRIELLE
GINGER
GLORIA
GEORGIA
GINA

If the name you're looking for isn't here, see "J" and "Q."

GABRIELLE, "GAH-bree-ehl" or "gah-bree-EHL"—*Hebrew: traditionally "God is my strength," but also "servant of God."* **GABIRELE** (gah-bih-rel-eh)—Basque; **GABRIEL**—Hebrew and Persian; **GABRIELLA**—European; **GAVEE, GAVI, GAVRIELLA, GAVRILA** (GAHV-rih-lah)—Hebrew. Many "angelologists" and religious scholars think that Gabriel is probably a female angel. She, or he—we'll say "she" from now on—is an Archangel, and one of the great Seraphim in the angelic hierarchy in direct contact with God/Allah. Gabriel is extraordinary in that she may also leave God's/Allah's side to be in direct contact with humans, the only member of the heavenly host so directly intimate with both God/Allah and humans. Communication, intuition, prediction, and go-between are all traditionally feminine assignations of supernatural beings; Gabriel sits at the left hand of God, and the left is also traditionally associated the female aspect of spiritual matter. Gabriel is said to be the ruler of the cherubim—in the modern sense, the little angels—and also supervises guardian angels. In Middle Eastern folklore, Gabriel is said to pluck a soul from paradise and place it in the mother's womb while instructing it for the nine months of gestation. **GABBI(E), GABBY; GABI(E).** M

GAEA, "GAY-ah"—*Greek: "earth mother" or "steadfast."* **GAIA, GAYA.** Gaea is one of the Old Ones, the mother of all the members of the pre-Olympian Greek pantheon and the inhabitants of Olympus. She mated with Chaos and created the world, and many of the things in and above it.

GAEL, "GALE"—*Welsh: "wild"; Scottish: "a highlander."* This is the collective term for Gaelic speakers in Scotland, Ireland, and the Isle of Man. See also ABIGAIL, GAIL, GALE. M

GAETANA, "guy-TAHN-ah"—*Italian: "from central Italy."* M

GAIL, "GAYL"—*diminutive of Abigail, the part meaning "joy"; Gaelic: "courageous"; Celtic: "lively."* **GAL** (GAHL), **GAILE, GALE, GALI, GALY, GAYLE.** See also ABIGAIL, GAEL.

GALATEA, "gah-lah-TEE-ah" or, rarely, "gah-LAH-tee-ah"—*Greek: "milky white."* **GALATÉE** (gah-lah-TAY)—French. In Greek mythology, a sculptor named Pygmalion was given a beautiful, milky white stone in which he carved an image of a woman. It came so easily and turned out so beautifully that he began to have fantasies about it. He prayed to the goddess of love, Aphrodite, to make the woman real. Aphrodite, always the soft touch, did so, and Pygmalion lived happily ever after with his perfectly perfect wife, Galatea. Another Galatea is one of the Nereids, or sea nymphs; from this Galatea comes the name of one of Neptune's moons.

GALATI(A), "gah-LAY-tee" and "gah-LAY-shah" or "gah-LAH-tee" and "gah-LAH-shah"—*Greek: "milk."* The similarity of this name to Galatea lies in the fact that Galatia was the name of a Roman province in Turkey where there were great, milky white stones. Nowadays, "Milky Way" is a friendlier way of saying "galaxy."

GALE, "GAYL"—*Norse: "to sing"; Danish: "crow"; Icelandic: "fury" or "furious"; Irish: "vapor"; French: "gallant" or "brave."* **GAIL, GAYLE.** See also ABIGAIL, GAEL. M

GALIA, "gah-LEE-ah" or "GAH-lyah"—*Hebrew: "God has redeemed."* **GALENKA, GALINA, GALOCHKA, GALYA**—*Russian.*

GALILAH, "GAH-lee-lah," "gah-LEE-lah," or "gah-lee-LAH" (did I miss one?)—*Hebrew: "the gentle redemption of God" or "lilac fountain."* **GALILEA, GALILEE.** Galilee was one of the places where Jesus spent his time.

GALILAHI, "gah-lee-LAH-hee"—*Native American Cherokee: "likeable" or "attractive."* **GALIL, GALILA.**

GALLINA, "GAL-lih-nah," or rarely, "gah-LEE-nah"—*Latin: "hen."*

GANESHA, "gah-NAY-shah"—*Hindu: "leader."* This is the Hindu goddess of good luck and wisdom. She helps people overcome obstacles.

GARNET, "GAHR-neht" or "gahr-NEHT"—*Latin: "grain"; French: "pomegranate."* The French derivation explains the name of the semiprecious stone garnet, which looks like a pomegranate seed.

GAYORA, "gah-YOH-rah"—*Hebrew: "valley of light."*

GAZARA, "GAH-zahr-ah"—*Palestinian: "sparkling silk."* **GAZARRA, GAZZARA, GAZZARRA.** Gazar is a transparent, silken fabric bedecked with metallic beads or shining gemstones.

GAZELLE, "gah-ZEHL"—*Arabic: "a gazelle."* **GAZELLA.**

GECHINA, "geh-chee-nah"—*Basque: "grace."*

GEDALYA, "geh-DAHL-yah"—*Hebrew: "God has made good."* **GEDALIAH.**

GEFJON, "GEHF-yohn"—*Norse: goddess of agriculture, protector of virgins.* **GEFFEN, GEFFIN, GEFFON.**

GELLA, "GHEH-lah"—*Yiddish: "yellow."* **GELLE.**

GEMARA, "gheh-MAH-rah" or "jeh-MAH-rah"—*Aramaic: "completion."*

GEMINI, "JEH-mih-nye"—*Latin: "twins."* The Geminid is the annual meteor shower visible over several nights in mid-December, so named because the bodies seem to stream from the constellation Gemini. The constellation Gemini can be seen chasing the Sun at dusk from February through the end of March. The Sun is "in" Gemini from late May through June. To the Assyrians, it was the sign of YAV, the Future. To the early Christians, it was the sign of JAMES. To the Egyptians, it was the sign of ATUM the Double Crown. To the Greeks and Romans, it was the sign of APOLLO the Lyre. To the early Hebrews, it was the sign of SIMEON-LEVI the Sword and Pitcher. To the Norse peoples, it was TYR, the Sword. The Aztecs called this the sign of QUETZALCOATL the

-kin

"-kin" ("kihn") is the German and Central European suffix that means "little" or "little one." It can be added to any name you choose.

Hero. To the Babylonians, it was TUAME RABUTI the Great Twins (combining Gemini and Orion as two brothers). Earthly rulers at this time are the HAWTHORN TREE and OAK TREE for Celts and Druids, and the WISTERIA for the Japanese.

GEMMA, "JEH-mah"—*French: "precious stone" or "bud of a plant."* **JEMMA.**

GENA. See EUGENIA.

GENEVA, "jeh-NEE-vah" or "JEH-neh-vah"—*French: place name for the city in Switzerland and "juniper bush."* **GENÈVE** (jeh-NEHV)—French; **GENEVIA** (jeh-neh-VEE-ah or jeh-NEE-vee-ah), **JANEVA, JANEVIA; GENEVRA** (jeh-NEHV-rah)—Italian. **GENNA, JENNA.**

GENEVIEVE, "JEHN-eh-veev"—*Bretagne from Celtic: "white wave"; German: "woman-kind."* **GENEVIÈVE** (zhehn-vee-EV)—French; **GENOBEBA** (jehn-oh-BAY-bah)—Spanish; **GENOVEFFA** (jehn-oh-VEH-fah), **GENOVEVA** (jehn-oh-VEE-vah)—Italian; **JANUVEVA** (jah-noo-VAY-vah)—Slavic; **ZENEVIEVA** (zehn-eh-VYEH-vah)—Hungarian and Polish. **GEN, GENNI(E), GENNY.**

GENNIFER. See JENNIFER.

GEORGETTE. See GEORGIA.

GEORGIA, "JOR-jah"—*Greek: "farmer."* **GEORGEANNE, GEORGIANA, GEORGIANNA,** GEORGINE; GEORGETTE (zhor-ZHEHT), GEORGINA—French; GIORGIA (JYOHR-jee-ah)—Italian; GYÖRGIKE (DTHOR-ghee-keh or DTHOR-dthee-keh), GYURI (DTHY-OO-ree)—Hungarian; JOJIKO—Japanese; SEOIRSHIENN (SHORE-sheen)—Irish Gaelic. GEORGIE. M

GERALDINE, "jeh-rahl-DEEN" or "gheh-rahl-DEEN"—*Teutonic: "mighty with the spear."* **GEARÓIDIN** (gare-oy-DEEN)—Irish Gaelic; **GERALDA** (heh-RAHL-dah)—Spanish; **GERROLDINA.** The aristocratic Fitz-Geralds, earls of Kildare in Ireland, were, as a group, referred to as the Geraldines. Samuel Taylor Coleridge's 1816 work *Christabel* had a character named Geraldine, which revived the name's popularity. See also JERALDINE. M

GERDA, "GEHRD-ah"—*German: "protection" or Teutonic: "fighter."*

GERMAINE, JERMAINE, "jur-MAYN" or "jare-MAYN"—*Latin: "full of buds"; Celtic: "of (the area of and around present-day) Germany."* **GERMAIN, JERMAIN.** Saint Germaine of Pibra was a sickly little French girl with harsh parents. She would give bread to persons worse off than her herself, and this angered her stepmother. Apparently, one day the woman caught Germaine redhanded, and demanded that she unfold her apron or frock, expecting to find a loaf of bread there. Instead, witnesses reported, Germaine's apron held spring flower buds. She is the patron saint of young people blossoming into adulthood. M

GIGI, "JEE-jee" or "ZHEE-zhee." See GILLIAN, GINGER, GIOVANNA, GISELLE.

GIJS, "GEESE"—*Dutch: "bright."*

GILDA, "GHIHL-dah" or "ZHEEL-dah"—*English: "gilded" or "golden"; Celtic: "God's servant."* This name was first popularized by the 1946 movie *Gilda*, which starred Rita Hayworth. It became popular again when Gilda Radner, a much-beloved actress and comedienne in the early years of TV's *Saturday Night Live,* came to prominence.

GILLIAN, "GIHL-ee-un" or "gihl-ee-AN," rarely "JIHL-ee-an"—*Anglo-Saxon: "laughter, happiness"; Gypsy: "song" or "singer."* **GILLIANNE.** Gillian Anderson plays smart, strong, sexy FBI Special Agent Dana Scully on the TV series *The X Files.* **GIGI; GIL, GILLEY, GILLI(E), GILLY.** See also JILLIAN.

GINA, "JEE-nah"—*Hebrew: "garden."* **GINAT.** See also EUGENIA.

GINGER, "JIHN-jur"—*Latin: "ginger spice."* **AWAPUHI** (ah-WAH-poo-hee)—Hawaiian; **XI XIN** (ZEE ZEEN or ZHEE ZHEEN)—Chinese. Ginger is a popular spice used in a variety of cuisines. Ginger root is used cosmetically to enhance the red in one's hair, and in herbal and folk medicine. **GIGI, GINNI(E), GINNY.** See also VIRGINIA.

GIORA, "JOHR-ah"—*Aramaic: "a convert."*

GIOVANNA, "joh-VAH-nah"—*Italian version of Roman Jovita: "of the god Jupiter."* Jupiter was the supreme god, ruler over learning, good fortune, increase, propserity, etc. **GIGI.** See also JOVITA. M

GISELLE, "jih-ZEHL" or "zhee-ZEHL"—*French from Teutonic: "pledge or promise"; Anglo-Saxon: "sword."* **GHISLAINE** (gheez-LEHN)—French and Swiss; **GISELA, GISELLA** (jih/zhee-ZEHL-ah or GHEE-zeh-lah); **GISELDA** (ghee-SEHL-dah)—German; **GISÈLE** (zhee-ZEHL)—French; **GIZELA** (ghih-ZEHL-ah)—Polish. **GIGI.**

GIZA, "ghee-ZAH" or "GHEE-zah"—*Egyptian: "hewn stone."* **GISA, GISALA; GIZAL.** The trio of Great Pyramids in Egypt is located at Giza.

GIZANE, "gee-zah-neh"—*Basque: "like Christ."*

GLEN(N), GLENNA, "GLEHN" or "GLEH-nah"—*Scottish: "a glen or small valley."* **GLAN, GLANNA; GLENDA, GLENNIS; GLIN, GLINDA; GLYN, GLYNIS, GLYNNIS.** Glenn Close is an award-winning actress. M

GLENDA. See GLEN(N)/GLENNA.

GLORIA, "GLOH-ree-ah"—*Latin: "glory."* **GLORIANNA, GLORIANNE. GLORI(E), GLORY.**

GOLDA, "GOHL-dah"— *English: "like gold."* **GOLDIA, GOLDYA.** This was a popular Jewish name, but the fame of Golda Meir made it more familiar to a wider audience. Meir was one of the prime movers and shakers who put the nation of Israel back onto the map. She served as prime minister for a long time, paving the way with her powerful leadership for other women in similar positions. **GOLDI(E), GOLDY.**

GORANE, "goh-rah-neh"—*Basque: "holy cross."*

GRACE, "GRAYSS"—*Latin: "thanks," "gracefulness," or "graciousness."* **ENGRACIA** (ehn-GRAH-syah)—Spanish; **GRACA** (grah-kah), **GRACINHA** (grah-SEE-nah)—Portuguese; **GRACIA, GRACIELLA, GRACIELLE, GRACYE; GRAINNE** (GRAYN or GREHN); **GRANIA**—Gaelic and Nordic; **GRAZIA** (GRAHT-see-ah), **GRAZIEL(L)A, GRAZINA**—Italian; **GRAZYNA** (grah-ZEE-nah)—Polish. This is a Puritan virtue name. Grace was a princess of Monaco, but prior to that, she was Grace Kelly, an American actress of the 1950s, famed for her cool, aristocratic good looks and demeanor. **GRACIE.**

GREER, "GREER"—*Greek: "the watchful one."* **GRIER.**

GRETA, "GREH-tah"—*from Margaret: "a pearl."* **GHITA** (GHEE-tah)—Italian; **GRETE** (GREH-teh), **GRETL**—Eastern European; **GRETEL** (GREH-tehl), **GRETHA** (GREH-tah), **GRETHE**—Scandinavian; **GRETTA, GRETTE**—German; **GRIETJE** (GREE-tyeh)—Dutch; **GRYTA**—Slavic. Timeless beauty Greta Garbo popularized this already popular European name in the United States. She was a Swedish actress who made the transition from silent to sound films—with a huge success!—whose mystique continues today. Clare Booth Luce once said of Garbo: "She is a deer in the body of a woman, living resentfully in the Hollywood Zoo." See also MARGARET.

GRETCHEN. See MARGARET.

GRETEL. See GRETA.

GRISELDA, "grih-SEHL-dah"—*German: "gray battle-maiden."* **GRISELDIS**—Dutch; **GRISELLA, GRISELLE**—Spanish and French; **GRISHILDA, GRISSEL** (grih-SEHL)—German; **GRISILDA**—Nordic; **GRIZEL** (grih-ZEHL), **GRIZELDA**—Polish. In Geoffrey Chaucer's *The Canterbury Tales,* the heroine of the Clerk's Tale is named Griselda. This German name is popular in the Hispanic community. SELDA, ZELDA.

GUADALUPE, "GWAH-dah-loo-peh" or "gwah-dah-LOO-peh"—*Mexican/Mayan from Latin: "curved sword of the wolf."* The name is often given to Catholic girls to honor Our Lady of Guadalupe, a vision of the Virgin Mary that is said to have appeared in Guadalupe, Mexico. GUADELUPE. LUPE.

GUENEVERE, GUINEVERE, "GWEN-uh-veer"—*Old Welsh: "white shadow," "white phantom," or sometimes "white or fair lady."* **GUENEVER, GUENIVERE, GUINEVER; WINLOGEE** (van-low-ZHEE)—Bretagne, rare. In Arthurian legend, Queen Guinevere was the wife of King Arthur and the lover of his beloved, troubled friend, Sir Lancelot.

GURI, "GOO-ree"—*Norse: "lovely goddess"; Hindu: "goddess of abundance."*

GUSSI(E). See AUGUSTA.

GUTA, "GOO-tah"—*Yiddish: "good."* GUTE.

GWEN. See GWENDOLYN, GWYNETH.

GWENDOLYN, "GWEHN-doh-lihn"—*Welsh: "fair-haired"; Gaelic: "white circle"; Celtic: "white-browed."* **GWENDA, GWENDOLEN, GWENDOLINE; GWYNETH** (GWIH-nehth), **GWYNETTE, GWYNNE**—Welsh. GWEN; WINNI(E), WYNNE.

GWYNETH, "GWIH-nehth"—*Celtic: "blessed."* **GWENDA, GWENITH, GWINETH; GWYNEDD** (GWIH-nehth)—Welsh. Actress Gwyneth Paltrow has made people aware of this old name. GWEN, GWIN, GWYN. See also GWENDOLYN. M

GYPSY, "JIHP-see"—*English: "wanderer."*

THE TOP FIVE

HANNAH
HEIDI
HEATHER
HELEN
HOLLY

If the name you're looking for isn't here, see the vowels and "J."

HADAR, "hah-DAHR"—*Hebrew: "ornament" or "glory."* M

HADARA, "hah-DAHR-ah"—*Hebrew: "splendor."*

HADIYA(H), "HAH-dyah" or "hah-DEE-yuh"—*Arabic: "guide to righteousness"; Swahili: "a gift."* M

HALCYONE, ALCYONE, properly "hahl-SY-oh-nee" and "ahl-SY-oh-nee," but often "HAL-see-awn" and "AL-see-own"—*Greek: "the halcyon bird" or "kingfisher bird."* **ALCIONE, ALCYONNE; HALCIONE, HALCYONNE.** The halcyon bird—later identified with the kingfisher—was said to make its nest on the winter seas, at which time the oceans were calm. Therefore, halcyon days are the seven days before the winter solstice and the seven days after. Alcyone is the Greek demigoddess (one of the Pleiades, or daughters of Atlas) who began the myth by being turned into the halcyon bird: in mourning for her husband, Ceyx, she threw herself into the sea to die, and moved by this show of love and devotion, the goddess Aphrodite turned Alcyone into a bird that could live on the waters. Alcyone is one of the fixed stars used for centuries by navigators and astrologers because of their apparent constance. Alcyone is found in Taurus, near Gemini, and is one of the star cluster called the Seven Sisters, or Pleiades.

HALESIA, "hah-LEE-see-ah" or "hah-LEHSH-ah"—*?: the silverbell plant.*

HALEY, "HAY-lee"—*Irish Gaelic: "ingenious."*

HALI, "HAH-lee"—*Greek: "the sea."* **HALLI(E), HALLY.**

HALIMA(H), "hah-LEEM-ah"—*Arabic: "gentle" or "patient"; Swahili: "tender."* M

HALIMEDA, "hah-lee-MAY-dah"—*Greek: "thoughts of the sea."* **HALLI(E), HALLY.**

HALINA, "hah-LEE-nah"—*Hawaiian: "likeness."*

HALLI(E), HALLEY, "HAH-lee" or "HAL-ee"—*Norse: "heroic"; English: "covered" or "the meadow by the manor."* Halle Berry is an actress. **HALLE, HALLEA, HALLEIGH, HALLI, HALLY.** See also HALI, HALIMEDA. M

HALOKE, "hah-LOW-keh"—*Native American Navajo: "shimmering salmon."* M

HALONA, "hah-LOW-nuh"—*Native American: "happy" or "fortunate."* **LONA.**

HAMIDA(H), "hah-MEED-ah"—*Arabic: "praiseworthy."* M

HAMMALEA, "hah-MAH-lee-ah"— *Greek: "fruit tree nymph."* **HAMALIA, HIMALIA, HIMMALEA.** Himalia was one of the loves of the Greek god Zeus, and is one of the moons of Jupiter.

HANA(E), "huh-NAH" or "huh-NAH-ay"— *Japanese: "flower" or "blossom."* **HANAKO.**

HANAN, "HAH-nahn" or "hah-NAHN"— *Hebrew: "grace"; Arabic: "mercy."*

HANANELLE, "hah-nah-NEHL"— *Hebrew: "God is gracious."* M

HANATA, "hah-NAHT-ah"—*Semitic: "Evening Star."* See also ANATTA.

HANIFA(H), "hah-NEEF-ah"—*Moroccan: "true believer."* In the Arab world, this refers to one who believes in the God of Ibrahim and Ismail, even if that person is not a Muslim. M

HANNAH, "HAH-nah"—*Hebrew: traditionally, "the Lord has favored me," but also "happiness" or "full of grace."* **HAJNA** (HAH-ee-nah)—Hungarian; **HANA, HANNA; HANIYAH**—Moroccan; **HANIYYAH** (HAH-nee-yah)—Tunisian; **HANNE** (HAH-neh)— Nordic; **HANNELE** (HAH-nehl)—German. The prophetess Hannah was the mother of the Old Testament/Tanakh prophet Samuel. **HANNI(E), HANNY.**

HARA, "HAH-rah"—*Hindu: "to seize."*

HARI, "HAH-ree"—*Hindu: "dark" or "tawny."*

HARLEE, "HAR-lee"—*English: "hare's meadow"; German: "field of flax or hemp."* **HARLAN, HARLEA, HARLEIGH.** M

HARMONY, "HAHR-moh-nee"—*Greek: "agreement, concord."* **HARMONIA.** In Greek mythology, Harmony was a goddess who was married to Cadmus, the founder of the city of Thebes. M

HARRIET, "HAIR-ee-eht"—*Norse: "war chief"; Anglo-Saxon: "army commander."* **HARIETTA, HARIETT(E), HARRIETTA, HARRIETT(E); HERALDA** (heh-RAHL-dah)— Portuguese. All in all, a Harriet is a take-charge type. M

HASIA, "HAH-syah"—*Hebrew: "protected by the Lord."* **HASYA.**

HASINA, "hah-SEE-nah"—*Swahili: "good."* **SINA.**

HASNA, "HAHS-nah"—*Arabic: "beautiful."* **HOSNA.** M

HAWA, "HAH-wah"—*Swahili: "longed for"; Arabic and Hebrew: "breath of life."*

HAYA, "hah-YAH"—*Japanese: "quick."*

HAYFA, "hah-EE-fah" or "hah-ee-FAH"— *Arabic: "slender" or "beautiful body."* **HAIFA.**

HAYLEY, "HAY-lee"—*Norse: "heroine"; English: "hay meadow."* **HAYLEA, HAYLEE, HAYLEIGH, HALEY.**

HAZEL, "HAY-zehl"—*English: "the hazel tree."*

HEA, "HEH-ah"—*Korean: "graceful."*

HEATHER, "HEH-thur"—*Scottish: the heather flower or heather plant.* **HESTER.** M

HEDDA, "HEH-dah"—*German: "vigorous fighter."* **HEDDE, HEDDI(E), HEDDY, HEDI(E), HEDY.** In early Hollywood, gossip columnist Hedda Hopper was a force to be reckoned with by everyone in the industry.

HEDIA, "heh-DEE-ah"—*Greek: "pleasing."* **HEDILA, HEDYLA. HEDI(E).**

HEDY, "HEHD-ee"—*diminutive of Hedwig, Teutonic: "refuge in battle"; German: "storm."*

HEDWIG (HEHD-vihg); **JADWIGA** (YAHD-vee-gah or yahd-VEE-gah)—Polish. Hedy Lamarr was an Austrian actress who was brought to Hollywood after appearing nude in the 1933 Austrian release *Extase*. However, she took a practical view of things, having said: "Any girl can look glamorous; all she has to do is stand still and look stupid." **HEDDI(E), HEDDY, HEDI(E).** See also HEDDA.

HEIDE, HEIDI, "HYE-dee"—*German diminutive of Adelaide: "of noble birth."* See also ADELAIDE.

HELEN, "HEH-lehn"—*Greek: "light," "fair,"* or *"luminous."* **AILEEN** (ay-LEEN or EYE-leen)—Scottish; **EILEEN** (EYE-leen)—Irish; **HALINA** (hah-LEE-nah)—Polish; **ELAINE** (ee-LAYN)—European; **ELEANOR** (EHL-ah-nohr or eh-LAY-ah-nohr), **ELLEN** (EH-lehn); **HELAINE, HELLAE** (heh-LAY), **HELLAIS**—Greek and Latin; **HELENA** (heh-LAY-nah or HEH-leh-nah), **HELENE** (heh-LEEN), **HELLEN; HÉLÈNE** (eh-LAYN or heh-LAYN)—French; **HELENKA**—Hungarian; **ILONA** (ih-LOH-nah or ee-LOH-nah)—Eastern European; **LÉAN** (LAY-on), **LÉANA**—Irish Gaelic; **NELL**—Scotch-Irish; **NORA; OLENA, OLENKA**—Russian. Helen of Troy, the "face that launched a thousand ships," was the wife of the Greek king Menelaus. She was spirited away by Paris, a prince of Troy, and her abduction caused the Trojan War and all the legends connected with it. Helena is one of the Christian saints, and a mother of Emperor Constantine. Helen Keller (d. 1968) was born blind and deaf, but overcame those handicaps and became an eloquent writer and speaker. Helene is one of the moons of Saturn. **LENA, LINA.** See also LENORA.

HELENE. See HELEN.

HELOISE, "HEH-loh-eez" or "AY-loh-eez"—*French: "famous warrior."* **ELOISE.** The affair between twelfth-century lovers Heloise and Peter Abelard is well-documented by their letters to one another. Peter was a philosopher and teacher who fell in love with one of his students, Heloise. The two married in secret, but her family forced them apart. So husband and wife both took religious vows, and as monk and nun, continued to write each other until death did them part. See also LOUISE.

HELSA, "HEHL-sah"—*Scandinavian, from Elizabeth: "consecrated to God."* **HÅLSA** (HEHL-sah).

HEMA, "HEE-mah" or "HEH-mah"—*Hindu: "daughter of the mountains."*

HENRIETTE, "HEHN-ree-eht"—*Teutonic: "owner of the estate" or "lady of the estate."* **ENRICA** (ehn-REE-kah)—Italian and Spanish; **HEINRICKA** (HINE-rih-kah)—German; **HEINRIKKA** (HINE-rih-kah); **HEN-DRIKA** (HEHN-drih-kah), **RIKA**—Dutch; **HENERIKA** (HEH-neh-rih-kah)—Danish; **HENKA**—Polish; **HENRIETTA; JETJE** (YEHT-yeh)—Dutch. **HENNI(E), HENNY.** M

HENTSHE, "HEHNT-sheh"—*Yiddish: "grace."* **HENYE.**

HERA, "HARE-ah"—*Greek: "womanly"* or *"goddess above all women."* In Greek mythology, Hera was the wife of the supreme god Zeus, and held rulership over marriage, childbirth, and all manner of female expression.

HERMOSA, "air-MOH-sah" or "her-MOH-sah"—*Spanish/Basque: "lovely."*

HESPER, "HEHS-purr"—*Greek: "Evening Star"* or *"western star."* **HESPERIA** (heh-SPARE-yah). Hesper was the name the ancient Greeks had for Italy. The Hesperides, or nymphs of the west, had quite the green thumbs: they were able to grow golden apples. M

HEST(I)A, "HEHS-tah" and "HEHS-tyah"—*Greek: alternate names for Vesta, goddess of home and hearth.* See also VESTA.

HESTER, "HEHS-tur"—*Persian: "Evening Star."* **HETTI(E), HETTY.** See also HEATHER.

HILDA. See HILDE.

HILDE, "HIHL-deh"—*Norse: "battle maid," one of the Valkyries.* **HILDA.** This is a Christian saint name, and the name of the leader of the Valkyries in Norse mythology. The Valkyries rode through the battlefield and took fallen heroes to their reward in Valhalla **HILDI(E), HILDY.**

HILLAIRE, HILLARY, "hih-LARE" or "ee-LARE" and "HIH-lah-ree"—*Latin: "cheerful."* **HILAIRE, HILARI(E), HILARY, HILLARI(E); ILARI** (ee-lah-ree)—Basque. Hillary Rodham Clinton began serving as First Lady in 1993. She is noted for her assertiveness and activism. M

HINA, HINE, "HEE-nah/nay"—*Tahitian: "girl" or "maiden."*

HIRANY, "hee-RAH-nee"—*Sanskrit: "golden."* **RANY(A).** M

HIROKO, "hee-ROH-koh"—*Japanese: "generous" or "fair."*

HISA(E), "hee-SAH" or "hee-SAH-ay"—*Japanese: "long-lasting."* **HISAKO, HISAYO.**

HISOKA, "hee-SOH-kah"—*Japanese: "reserved."*

HOKU, "HOH-koo"—*Hawaiian: "star."* See also STAR(R). M

HOLLY, "HAW-lee"—*English: "holly tree" or "holly shrub."* **HOLLEE, HOLLEY, HOLLI, HOLLIE.** Holly, one of the few green things in the dead and dark of winter, is a symbol of hope in the midst of a cold and bitter season, and was used for sacred winter solstice festivals by the Druids and early Britons. When Christian festivals were being introduced, the birth of Jesus was equated with hope in the dark, cold world, and so holly continues to have its place in December celebrations. M

HONONAH, "hoh-NOH-nah"—*Native American Miwok: "bear."* M

HONOR, "AWN-er"—*Latin: "honor" (what'd ya think?).* **HONORA** (aw-NOHR-ah), **HONOREA** (aw-NOH-ree-ah), **HONORIA** (aw-NOH-ree-ah); **HONORATA** (aw-noh-RAH-tah)—Polish; **HONORINE** (aw-noh-REEN)—French. This name refers to honor either in the sense of personal integrity or in the sense of a reward or recognition. It is another one of those Puritan virtue names. Honor Blackman was a proper British actress until she broke that mold (and how) as the first female lead on TV's *The Avengers.* M

HONOVI, "hoh-NOH-vee"—*Native American Hopi: "the strong deer."* M

HOPE, "HOPE"—*English: "hope."* Hope is one of the three cardinal virtues of Christianity, and is a Puritan virtue name.

HOPI, "HOH-pee"—*Native American Ute/Aztec: "peaceful."* This is a tribe name for an ancient group of people who live in adobe pueblos on high mesas in the American Southwest. They have a very rich, ancestor-based religious culture. They are known for their snake dances and kachina (carved doll) icons, and for their excellence in silverworking.

HYPHENATED NAMES

These are great for the indecisive! Hyphenated names can be used as a first name (like explorer/environmentalist Jacques-Yves Cousteau), a middle name (like the author of this book), or a surname (like actress Joanne Whalley-Kilmer). The hyphenated surnames arose as a result of power plays in aristocratic Europe and among the wealthy in America—if one was descended from parents who were both from noteworthy families, then both surnames were used. More recently, hyphenated names have been used in a desire to declare equality within marriage, so that the wife's identity is no longer eliminated.

HOSHI, "HOH-shee"—*Japanese: "star."* **HOSHIKO.** See also STAR(R). M

HUA, "HOO-uh"—*Tahitian: "beautiful."*

HUAHINE, "HOO-uh-HEE-nay"—*Tahitian: "beautiful girl."* This is also a place name in the Tahitian island chain.

HUYANA, "hoo-YAH-nah"—*Native American Miwok: "falling rain."*

HYACINTH, "hye-ah-SIHNTH" or "HYE-ah-sihnth"—*Greek: "purple" and the hyacinth flower.* **HYACINTHE, HYACYNTHE; JACINDA, JACINTA** (yah-SIHN-tah)—Spanish; **JAKINDA** (yah-keen-dah)—Basque. In Greek myth, Hyacinthus was a beautiful young man. He was slain, and wherever his blood dropped, the hyacinth flower bloomed.

HYE, "h'YEH"—*Korean: "gracefulness."*

HYLA, "HI-lah"—*Hebrew: ?.*

HYUN, "HYUHN"—*Korean: "wisdom."*

THE TOP FIVE

ISABELLE/A
INGA
INGRID
IRIS
IRENE

If the name you're looking for isn't here, see "Y" and the other vowels.

IANTHE, "ee-AHNTH-ee"—*Greek: a purple flower.* The Ianthe in Greek mythology was a sea nymph.

IBERIA, "ee-BAY-ree-ah" or "eye-BEER-ee-ah"—*Latin: "Spain."*

IBIS, "IH-bihs" or "EYE-bihs"—*Egyptian: "ibis bird."* The ibis was a consort of the Egyptian god Thoth, and was associated with knowledge.

IDA, "EYE-dah" or "EE-dah"—*German: "vital"; English: "protection" or "possession"; Norse: "womanly."* An operetta by Gilbert and Sullivan is called *Princess Ida*, which was, in turn, based on a poem by Alfred, Lord Tennyson.

IDUNA, "ee-DOO-nah"—*Norse: "lover."*

IFAMA, "ee-FAH-mah"—*African Ibo: "everything is fine."*

IGNATIA, "ihg-NAHT-yah," "eeg-NAHT-yah," or "ee-NYAHT-yah"—*Latin: "fiery"; Irish Gaelic: "forceful person."* **IGNAZIA** (ee-NYAH-tsee-ah)—*Italian.* M

IKERNE, "ee-kehr-neh"—*Basque: "visitation (by an angel)."* M

IKU, "EE-koo"—*Japanese: "nourishing."* M

ILA, "ee-LAH"—*Old English: "the insulated"; Old French: "isle."* See also ILONA.

ILANA, "ee-LAH-nah"—*Hebrew: "tree."* **ILANIT** (ee-LAH-neet or eel-lah-NEET).

ILENE. See EILEEN.

ILITHYA, "ih-LIHTH-yah"—*Greek.* Ilithya was the Greek goddess who protected pregnant women.

ILKA, "EEL-kah"—*Teutonic: "light"; Celtic: "hard worker."* **ILKE.**

ILONA, "ih-LOH-nah" or "ee-LOH-nah"—*Eastern European version of Helen: "luminous"; Hungarian: "beauty."* **ICA** (EE-tsah), **ILONKA** (ee-LAWN-kah)—*Hungarian;* **ILON, ILONE, ILU; ILUS(H)KA, LENCI** (LEHN-tsee)—*Russian.* **ILA, ILI.** See also HELEN.

IMALA, "ee-MAH-lah"—*Native American: "disciplined" or "she who brings discipline."*

IMAN, "ee-MAHN"—*Arabic: "faith" or "belief."*

IMMANUELLE, "ee-man-yoo-EHL" or "ee-man-WELL"—*Hebrew: "God is with us."* **IMMANUELLA, MANUELLA, MANUELLE; IMANOLE** (ee-mah-nohl-eh)—*Basque.* See also EMANUELLE. M

IMOGENE, "IH-moh-jeen" or "ih-moh-JEEN"—*Latin: "image" or "imagine."* **IMAGINA, IMAGINE, IMOGEN, IMOGINE, IMOJEAN.**

AMERICA LOVES ITS SOAPS

This is another observation as to how complete the devotion to soap operas runs: the popular rise and fall of names. Erica Kane's character on *One Life to Live* is a villainess you love to hate, and the rise of the name ERICA has paralleled the questings of the actress. KAYLA was half of a wildly popular tragic-romantic duo on the soap opera *Days of Our Lives,* and the frequency of this name being given to newborns rose as the storyline peaked and has fallen off since the character was written out. LUKE was half of a popular love match on *General Hospital,* and the use of Luke as a given name has followed the character's fortunes. Prime-time soaps pushed ALEXIS to the top, and got a respectable ranking for the previously almost unknown FALLON. The explosion of popularity for the names BRANDON and DYLAN parallels those characters' popularity on *Beverly Hills 90210.*

INA, "EYE-nah" or "EE-nah"—*Greek: "pure."*

INANNA, "ee-NAH-nah"—*Sumerian: goddess of love and war.* This is a passionate name, to be sure. Many temples were built to Inanna in ancient Sumerian cities.

INAS, "ee-NAHS"—*Arabic: "sociable."*

INDA, "EEN-dah" or "een-DAH"—*Yiddish: "pleasure."* **INDE.**

INDIRA, "ihn-DEE-rah"—*Hindu: "India."* Indira was a common Hindu name that became known in wider circles because of Indira Gandhi. She was prime minister of India, one of the first women to be so politically powerful.

INES, "EE-ness/nez" or "ee-NESS/NEZ"—*Spanish from Greek: "gentle" or "pure."* **INESSA, INEZ.** See also AGNES.

INEZ. See AGNES, INES.

INGA, "ING-ah" (softened "G" like in "singer," not like in "finger")—*Norse: "daughter."* **INGE** (ING-eh).

INGEN, "ING-en" (softened "G")—*Norse: "child of love" or "love child."* **INGUNN**—Norwegian.

INGRID, "ING-rihd" (softened "G")—*Norse: "beautiful daughter."* **INGER.** Beautiful Swede Ingrid Bergman was an award-winning actress in some of the absolute classics of the golden age of Hollywood, such as *Casablanca* and *Gaslight.*

IOLA, "eye-OH-lah" or "ee-OH-lah"—*Greek: "violet cloud."*

IOLANTHE, "ee-oh-LANTH"—*Greek: "violet flower."*

IONA, "eye-OWN-ah" or "ee-OWN-ah"—*Greek: "a purple jewel."* **IONE, IONIA.** The island of Iona is in the Hebrides chain off of Scotland, while Ionia is off of Greece.

IPHIGENIA, "if-ih-jeh-NEE-ah," "if-ih-jeh-NYE-ah," "if-ih-heh-NEE-ah," or "if-ih-HAY-nee-ah"—*Greek: "famed and fair daughter."* The Greek goddess Artemis demanded that King Agamemnon sacrifice his daughter, Princess Iphigenia, if he wanted to be victorious in the Trojan War. But the goddess was merely testing his resolve, and spared Iphigenia at the last moment. **EFFIE, EFFY; IDGIE, IDGY.**

IRENE, "eye-REEN," "ee-REEN," or "ee-REH-neh"—*Greek: "peace."* **EIRENE** (eye-REE-nee)—Greek; **IRÉN** (ee-RAYN), **IRENKE** (ee-RAYN-keh)—Hungarian; **IRENA** (ee-RAY-nah)—Polish; **IRINA** (ee-REE-nah)—Russian. Eirene was the Greek goddess of peace. A Christian saint, several Greek and Russian queens, and a Byzantine empress have all borne this name.

IRIS, "EYE-rihs" or "EE-reese"—*Greek: "rainbow" or "colorful."* **IRISA** (ee-REE-sah)—Russian; **IRITA** (ee-REE-tah)—Spanish, Portuguese, and Italian; **IRYS.** Iris was the Greek goddess of the rainbow, which was considered to be a bridge between the gods and mortals. The iris is also a very dramatic, showy flower.

IRMA, "UR-mah"—*Teutonic: "soldier."* **ERMA, ERME, IRME; IRMUS, IRMUS(H)KA**—Eastern European.

ISA, "EE-sah"—*German: "iron-willed"; Arabic: "Jesus."*

ISABELLE, "IZ-ah-bell," "iz-ah-BELL," "EEZ-ah-bell," or "eez-ah-BELL"—*Hebrew: "consecrated to God"; Teutonic/French: "strong-willed and beautiful."* **BELLA, IZABEL, IZABELLA, IZBEL**—Eastern European; **ISABEAU** (EE-zah-bow)—French; **ISABEL, ISABELLA; ISEABAIL** (EE-shah-bile/bail)—Scottish; **ISIBÉAL** (ih-shee-BAYL)—Irish Gaelic; **ISOBEL**—Scottish, German, and Austrian; **ISOBELLA, ISOBELLE**—German and Austrian; **YSABEL, YSABELLA, YSABELLE**—Portuguese and Spanish. Several European queens have borne this name. One, Queen Isabella of Castile, had enough faith in Christopher Columbus to hock her jewelry for the money to send him and his three ships on the voyage that changed the world. See also ELISABETH/ELIZABETH.

ISI, "EE-see"—*Native American Choctaw: "deer."* M

ISIDORA, "ihz-ih-DOH-rah" or "eez-ee-DOH-rah"—*Greek: "a gift of ideas"; Latin: "gift of Isis."* **ISADORA; ISDRELLA** (ees-DREH-lah)—Portuguese; **IXIDORE** (ee-shee-dohr-eh)—Basque; **IZIDORA**—Eastern European. This is the name of a Christian saint. The dancer Isadora Duncan shocked early twentieth-century society with her carefree behavior. M

ISIS, "EYE-sis"—*Egyptian: "the throne" or "queen goddess."* When the world was new, Isis was the Egyptian goddess who ruled in tandem with her brother-husband, Osiris.

ISOKE, "ee-SOH-keh"—*African: "gift from God."*

ISOLDE, "ee-SAWLD"—*Welsh: "beautiful to see"; Celtic: "fair maid"; German: "ice."* **HISOLDE, ISEULT, ISEULTE, ISOLD, ISOLDA, YSEULT, YSOLTE.** In Arthurian legend, Princess Isolde was the lover of Sir Tristram, even though she was promised to King Mark of Cornwall. Operas, books, poems, and songs have been written about Isolde and Tristram's ill-fated love.

ITHUNE, "ee-THOON(-eh)" (go easy on the "TH")—*Norse: goddess of youth.* In Norse mythology, Ithune was the keeper of the golden apples of youth.

ITHURIELLE, "ih-THYOO-ree-ehl"—*Hebrew: "the superiority of God."*

ITUHA, "ee-TOO-hah"—*Native American: "a sturdy oak."* M

IVANA, "ee-VAHN-ah"—*Eastern European version of Johnna: "God's gracious gift."* **EYVANA** (EYE-vahn-ah)—Gaelic; **IVAH; VANYUSHA**—Russian; **YVANA** (ee-VAHN-ah)—Bretagne. See also JOHNNA. M

IVARA, "ee-VAH-rah"—*Teutonic: "yew tree"* or *"archer"; Welsh: "noble lady."* **IVORA.** The Teutonic derivations may seem unrelated, but the yew tree produces a wood that is desirable for bowmaking. M

IVORY, "EYE-vree" or "EYE-vah-ree"—*Old French from Latin: "white"* or *"white horn."* An elephant's tusks and a rhino's horns are made of ivory. A west African nation, the Ivory Coast, got its wealth from trade in ivory, which was used to make, among other things, jewelry and piano keys. Fortunately, most nations now refuse to use ivory.

IVY, "EYE-vee"—*English: "ivy."* The ivy was a sacred plant to the ancient Romans and Druids. Because the ivy vine clings to whatever is supporting it, ivy is sometimes used as a symbol of faithfulness.

IWA, "EE-wuh"—*Polynesian: "bird."*

IZARRA, "ee-zar-ah"—*Basque: "star."* See also STAR(R). M

IZEGBE, "ee-ZEG-beh"—*African: "long-awaited one."*

IZUSA, "ee-ZOO-sah"—*Native American Iroquois: "a white stone."*

THE TOP FIVE

JESSICA
JASMINE
JORDAN
JADE/JADA
JACQUELINE

If the name you're looking for isn't here, see "G," "H," or "Y," or the vowels.

JACANA, "zhah-sah-NAH" or "jah-KAH-nah"—*Native American Tupi-Guarani: "bird who walks on water."* **JAÇANA** (jah-sah-NAH). A jacana is an aquatic bird that can walk on top of floating aquatic plants.

JACKIE, "JAK-ee"—*diminutive of Jacoba or Jacqueline, but also: "assistant," "a fish," "to increase," "to advance," "breadfruit tree," or "blonde wood."* **CHAK(K)A**—Polynesian and Malaysian; **JACA**—Portuguese; **JACQUI(E)** (zhaw-KEE)—French. See also JACOBA, JACQUELINE. M

JACOBA, "JAY-koh-bah" or "jah-KOH-bah"—*Hebrew: traditionally "the supplanter," but more likely "protector" or "guardian."* **AKIBA** (ah-KEE-bah), **AKIVA**—Persian and Arabic; **AKOOBJEE** (ah-KOOB-jee)—Hindu; **DIEGA** (dee-AY-gah), **TIAGA** (tee-AH-gah)—Spanish; **GIACOBBE** (JAH-koh-beh)—Italian; **JACOBINA, JACOBINE; JAKOBE** (yah-KOH-beh)—Scandinavian; **JAKUBA** (YAH-koob-ah)—Polish. **JACKI(E), JACKY.** See also JAMIE, JACQUELINE. M

JACQUELINE, "zhahk-LEEN" or "JAK-weh-lihn"—*French version of Jacoba: "the supplanter."* **JACKLYN, JACLYN, JACQUETTA, JACQUI(E)**—French; **JACKOLIN** (YAH-koh-lihn or JAH-koh-lihn), **JAKOLINA**—Eastern European; **JACQUENETTA**—Swiss; **JAQUETTA**—Italian. Jacqueline Kennedy (d. 1994) was First Lady from 1961 to 1963—a young, lovely, gracious, intelligent trendsetter. For the next three decades, she was always news wherever she appeared. **JACKIE.** See also JACOBA. M

JACY, "JAH-see" or "JAY-see"—*Native American Kiowa: "the powers of the moon."* **JACE.** M

JADA, "JAH-dah" or "ZHAH-dah"—*Hebrew: "wise."*

JADE, "JAYD"—*French: "jade stone."*

JAELLA, "yah-EHL-ah" or "YALE-ah"—*Hebrew: "mountain goat" or "climber."* The Biblical heroine Jael was a woman who killed an enemy of Israel. See also YAEL. M

JALA, "jah-LAH"—*Arabic: "clarity."*

JAMIE, "JAY-mee"—*popular American variation on Jacoba: traditionally "the supplanter" but more likely "protector" or "guardian."* **DIEGA** (dee-AY-gah)—Spanish; **JAIME, JAIMEY, JAMEY, JAMI; SHANE** (SHAYN)—Scotch-Irish. **JIM, JIMI, JIMMI(E).** See also JACOBA. M

JAMILA, "jah-MEEL-ah"—*Swahili: "beautiful."* **JAMILAH.**

Les

"Les"—pronounced "lay" when followed by a consonant, "layz" when followed by a vowel—is the French version of the article "the." It accompanies a plural noun, which means that the noun which follows must end in an "-s" or "-aux." You may add this yourself to any plural name.

JAN. See JANE.

JANAN, "jah-NAHN"—*Arabic: "heart" or "soul."*

JANE, "JAYN"—*British Isles version of Johanna: "God's gracious gift" or version of Sha(i)na: "beautiful."* JAN, JAYNE; JANET, JANETTA, JANETTE, JANNETTE; JANEEN, JANINE, JANINA; JANICE, JANIS, JANISE, JENNICE; SEÓNAID (SHOH-nayd)—Scottish Gaelic; SINÉAD (she-NAYD), SINÉIDIN (she-NAYD-een)—Irish Gaelic. Two English queens and one saint have had this name. The name appears in the literary world, from characters, such as Jane Eyre, to authors, such as Jane Austen. But Janes have made their mark in other worlds, too, from Jane Addams (d. 1935), a social reformer and suffragette, to Janet Guthrie, the first woman to compete in the Indianapolis 500. See also JOHANNA, SHA(I)NA.

JANET. See JANE.

JANIS, "JAN-ihs"—*variation on Jane.* JANES (YAH-nehss)—Dutch, Danish, Swedish, Norwegian, and Finnish; JANUSZY (YAH-noo-zhee or yah-NOOZH-ee)—Polish and Slavic. Rhythm and blues singer Janis Joplin lived a torrid life, and her wailing, tortured voice has been much imitated, but never duplicated. See also JANE.

JANNA, "JAH-nah"—*Arabic: "Garden of Eden."*

JASMINE, "JAZZ-mihn"—*Persian: "jasmine vine."* GELSOMINA (jehl-soh-MEE-nah)—Italian; JASMIN, JASMINA; JESSAMINE, JES SAMYN—English; YASIMAN (YAH-see-mahn)—Hindu; YASMIN (YAHS-mihn), YASMINA, YASMINE (yahs-MEEN)—Arabic. JAZZ, JAZZI(E); YAZZ, YAZZI(E).

JAY(E), "JAY"—*Latin: "rejoice"; Anglo-Saxon: "little crow," "lively," or the blue jay.* M

JAYNE, "JANE"—*Hindu: "victorious."* JAINE, JAYA. Jayne Mansfield made several movies in the 1950s and 1960s, but public reaction to her killer proportions frustrated her yearning to do serious roles. See also JANE.

JEAN(NE), "JEEN" for both or "ZHEEN" for Jeanne—*French version of Johnna: "God's gracious gift."* JEANETTA, JEANETTE, JEANINE, JEANNETTE; SINA, SINE (SHEEN)—Irish Gaelic. JEANIE, JEANNIE. See also JOHANNA.

JENNA. See GENEVA, JENNIFER.

JENNET, "JEH-neht"—*Spanish: a small horse.*

JENNIFER, "JEHN-ih-fur" or "YEHN-ih-fur"—*Celtic: "white wave."* GENIFER, GENNIFER, GINEVRA (jee-NAY-vrah)—Italian; JENEFER, JENIFER, JENNEFER. This name is another form of Guinevere, the name of King Arthur's queen, and was popular in this country early in this century, thanks mainly to singer Jenny Lind. It became popular again in the 1970s when the book (and the movie) *Love Story* appeared, in which the heroine was named Jenny. **GEN, GENNI(E), GENNY; JEN, JENNA, JENNI(E), JENNY.**

JENNY. See JENNIFER.

JENSINE, "yehn-SEEN(-eh)"—*Scandinavian: "God is gracious."* **JENSINA.** M

JERALDINE, "jeh-rahl-DEEN" or "yeh-rahl-DEEN"—*Teutonic: "mighty with the spear."* **JERROLDINA.** See also GERALDINE. M

JESSANTE, "JEHS-ant"—*Bretagne: "shooting forth" or "springing forth."* In heraldry, a design—usually a plant or an animal—that is coming from the center of another design is said to be jessant. **JESS, JESSE, JESSI(E), JESSY.** See also JESSICA.

JESSICA, "JEHS-ih-kah"—*Hebrew: "God is kind," "riches," or "wealthy."* **JESSALINE, JESSALYN, JESSLYN.** Thanks to Academy Award winner Jessica Lange and the character Jessica on the TV show *Soap*, this name began a meteoric rise in popularity in the early 1980s that shows no sign of stopping. **JESSI, JESSIE, JESSY.** See also JESSANTE. M

JESUSA, "JEE-zuh-sah," "jeh-SOOS-ah," or "heh-SOOS-ah"—*Egyptian/Arabic feminine of Jesus, which is itself a version of Jason, from Hebrew: "the healer"; a variation on Joshua: "God is salvation."* **JESITA, JESUSITA**—Spanish; **JESUSINA, JESUSINE**—Portuguese and Italian. M

JETTE, "JEHT," "YEH-teh," or "JEH-teh"—*Danish: "coal black"; Greek: "black stone."* The Greek derivation refers specifically to the Great Stone of Gagai in ancient Lycia, which was like a black diamond. M

JEWEL, "JOOL"—*French: "jewel."* **JEWELL, JEWELLE.**

JILLIAN, "JILL-ee-un"—*Scottish version of Julie: "youthful," "sportive," or "flirt."* **GILLET, JILLET; GILLETTE, JILLETTE.** One's jill is also one's sweetheart or girlfriend to the Scots. The much-loved character of Jill on the TV series *Home Improvement* has probably contributed to the return of this old favorite to the lists of popular names. **GILLI(E), GILLY; JILL, JILLI(E), JILLY.** See also GILLIAN, JULIE, JYLLAND.

JINA, "JIHN-ah" or "JEE-nah"—*Sanskrit: "conqueror."* **JINNA.**

JINNA, "JIHN-ah"—*Arabic: "spirits," usually associated with air or fire.* This is another version of the English word "genie." M

JIVANTA, "jee-VAHN-tah"—*Hindu: "giver of life."* **JIBBILA, JIVILA.** M

JOAN, "JONE"—*from Johnna: "God's gracious gift"; from Jonah: "dove."* **JOANI(E), JONEE, JONETTE; JONE** (yoh-neh)—Basque; **SEONAG** (SHOH-nahg)—Scottish Gaelic; **SIOBHÁN** (SHOH-vahn or shoh-VAHN)—Irish Gaelic; **SION** (SHONE)—Welsh. Saint Joan, Joan of Arc, is the patron saint of France. She was burned at the stake in 1431 by the English, against whom she rode into battle. An early eighteenth-century ballad about a John Darby and his wife Joan was a very popular story-song: "Darby and Joan" refers to married bliss and the types of happiness couples share. Actress Joan Crawford was born Lucille Le Sueur, and got her stage name as a result of a contest her studio sponsored to "name the rising starlet." Joni Mitchell is a folksinger. **JONI, JONI(E)**. See also JOHNNA.

JOANN(E), "joh-ANN"—*from Johnna: "God's gracious gift."* See also JOHANNA.

JOCELYN, "JOHSS-eh-lihn" or "JAW-seh-lihn"—*German: "of the Goths"; Celtic: "winner"; Latin: "the fair."* **JOCELIN, JOCE-LINE, JOICE, JOICELYN, JOSLINE, JOSLYN; JOYCE, JOYCELIN, JOYCELYN.**

JOCHEBEL, JOCHEVEL, "YOH-sheh-bell" or " YOH-kheh-bell" and "YOH-sheh-vehl" or "YOH-kheh-vehl" ("kh" like you're clearing your throat)—*Hebrew: "God is glorious."* Amram and Jochebel were the natural parents of the Moses of Judeo-Christian and Islamic tradition. After the Egyptian ruler Ramses ordered that all Hebrew boys under three years of age be put to death, Jochebel set Moses on the river in a basket and hoped some Egyptian woman would find him and call him her own. That woman happened to be a princess, and Moses was raised as a prince.

JOELLE, "joh-EHL" or "yoh-EHL"—*Hebrew: "Jehovah is God."* **JOELENE, JOELLA, JOELY; JOLENE, JOLINE. M**

JOHANNA, "yoh-HAHN-ah" or rarely "joh-HAHN-ah"—*Hebrew: "the grace of God."* **IOANNA** (yoh-AH-nna)—Greek; **JANKA** (YAHN-kah)—Eastern European; **JOANKA** (yoh-AWNK-ah)—Polish; **JOHANA** (yoh-HAH-nah)—Dutch; **JOHANNE** (yoh-HAHN-eh)—German and Scandinavian; **YOCHAN-NA** (yoh-KHAHN-ah—"KH" in the throat)—Hebrew. Several Christian saint names can be found on this list. See also JOHNNA. M

JOHNNA, "JAWN-ah"—*Hebrew: there are several translations: "God's gracious gift," "God has favored," "the Lord is favored," "the Lord is gracious," "the Lord is merciful," and "God is kind."* Here are a few versions,

but by no means all, I'm sure! **EOINA** (ay-OYN-ah), **SÉANA** (SHAWN-ah)—Irish Gaelic; *GIANNA* (JYAHN-ah); **HANSA** (HANZ-ah or HAHNIS-ah)—German; **IOANNA** (yoh-AH-nah), **YANNIA** (YAH-nyah)—Greek; **IVANA** (ee-VAHN-ah), **JANI** (YAH-nee), **JANIKA**—Eastern European; **JANA** (YAN-ah), **JANECS-KA** (yah-NESH-kah), **ZANA, ZANNA** (ZAH-nah)—Polish; **JANA** (JAN-uh), **JANNA**—Scotch/Irish; **JANCSI** (YAHN-tsee)—Hungarian; **JANE** (YAH-neh), **JENE** (YEH-neh)—Swedish; **JANITA** (yah-NEE-tah), **JANSJE** (YAHN-syeh)—Finnish; **JANTJE** (YAWN-tyeh)—Dutch; **JEAN** (JEEN), **JEANNE** (JEEN or ZHEEN)—French; **JENSJE** (YEHNS-yeh)—Norwegian; **JONNA; JUANA** (HWAHN-ah), **JUANITA** (HWAH-nee-tah or hwah-NEE-tah)—Spanish; **SEANA** (SHAWN-ah), **SHAW-NA**—Scottish; **SEONA** (SHONE-ah)—Scottish Gaelic; **SHAUNA**—Irish; **SIANA**—Welsh. The names of many saints are on this list. **JOHN-NI(E), JONNI(E)**. See also JOANN(E), JOHAN-NA. M

JOLANTA, "yol-LAHN-tah"—*Polish, from Greek: "violet blossoms."* **JOLANDA. JOLA.**

JOLI(E), "JOH-lee" or "ZHOH-lee"—*French: "pretty"; English: "spirited."* **JOLENE, JOLINE.**

JOLINE. See JOELLE, JOLI(E).

JONATHA, "JON-uh-thuh"—*Hebrew: feminized combination of John and Nathan, "beloved gift" or "God has graciously given."* **JONATHELLE. M**

JONI. See JOAN.

JONQUIL, "JAWN-kwihl," "JAWN-kihl," or "zhawn-KEEL"—*French: "the rushes" or "jonquil."* **JONQUILLE** (zhawn-KEEL)—French. Jonquils, such as narcissus and daffodils, are fragrant, lovely flowers.

JORA, "YOH-rah" or "JOH-rah"—*Hebrew: "autumn rain," and the sign Scorpio.*

JORDAN, "JORE-den" or "YORE-den"—*Hebrew: name of a river in the Middle East, meaning "to flow down" or "to descend."* **GIORDANA**—Italian; **JARDENA** (YAR-deh-nah)—Hebrew; **JORDAAN** (yore-DAHN)—Dutch; **JORDÃO** (YAHR-da-oh)—Portuguese. The River Jordan plays a major role in the religion and folklore of the Middle East. The superstardom of basketball player Michael Jordan has made this a popular name for daughters of hoop fans. M

JOREN, "YOH-rehn"—*Scandinavian: "love of the chief."* **JORUNN**—Norwegian. M

JOSEPHA, "JOH-sehf-ah" or "YOH-sehf-ah"—*Hebrew: "God will add" or "she will add."* **CHE** (CHAY)—Spanish and Portuguese; **FIFI, JOSÉE** (zhoh-ZAY), **JOSETTE**—French; **GIUSEPPINA** (joo-seh-PEE-nah)—Italian; **JOSEFINA, JOSEFINE**—German and Scandinavian; **JOSEPHINA, JOSEPHINE; JOSKA** (YOHSH-kah), **JOXEPE** (yoh-shep-eh), **YOSEBE** (yoh-seb-eh)—Basque; **JOZSA** (ZHOH-zah), **JOZSI, JOZSKA**—Eastern European; **JOZSI** (YOH-zhee)—Hungarian; **PEPITA**—Spanish, Portuguese, Basque, and Italian; **SEOSAIMHÍN** (shoh-sah-VEEN)—Irish Gaelic. Josepha was the real name of Empress Josephine, wife of Napoleon. **JO, JOÉE, JOEY, JO-JO, JOSIE.** M

JOSEPHINE. See JOSEPHA.

JOSIE. See JOSEPHA.

JOVITA, "joh-VEE-tah"—*Roman: "of Jupiter," the Roman supreme male god.* **GIOVANNA** (joh-VAH-nah)—Italian; **JOVANNA, JOVANNE.** Jupiter is a planet associated with happiness, good fortune, and learning. M

JOY, "JOY"—*English: "great happiness"* or "merriment." **JOI, JOIA, JOYA.** See also JOYCE.

JOYCE, "JOYSS"—*French: "merry"; Celtic: "winner" or "champion."* **JOICE, JOY.** Joyce was a seventh-century prince of Bretagne who became a saint. As in the case of many other names, what started out as a male name wound up as a name for girls. See also JOCELYN.

JUANITA, "wah-NEE-tah" or "hwah-NEE-tah"—*Spanish: "little Johnna"; Native American: "doe" or "fawn."* **JUANA; WENITA(H)** (weh-NEE-tah)—Native American Cherokee and Sioux. See also JOHNNA. M

JUBA, "JOO-bah"—*African: "lion's mane."* The juba is also a lively dance.

JUDITH, "JOO-dihth" or "yoo-DEET"—*Hebrew: "praised."* **GIUDITTA** (joo-DEE-tah)—Italian; **JUDIT** (YOO-deet). In the apocryphal books of the Old Testament, Judith is a brave, beautiful, wealthy Hebrew widow who does what she has to do to protect her people. Judy Holliday is the definitive ditzy blonde in movies of the late 1940s to the early 1960s; she's at her best in *Adam's Rib, Born Yesterday,* and *Bells Are Ringing.* **JUDI(E), JUDY.** M

JUDY. See JUDITH.

JULIE, "JOO-lee" or "YOO-lee"—*Latin: "youthful," Greek: "soft" or "downy."* **GIULIA** (JOO-lee-ah), **GIULIETTA** (joo-lee-EHT-ah), **GIULIETTE** (joo-lee-EHT)—Italian; **GYALA** (DTHAH-lah), **GYULA** (DTHOO-lah), **GYUSZI** (DTHOO-shee), **JULCSA** (YOOL-chah), **JULI** (YOO-lee), **JULINKA**—Hungarian; **JILLIAN** (JILL-ee-un)—Scottish; **JOLIET, JULIA, JULIANNA, JULIANNE, JULIET, JULIETTA, JULIETTE; JULIA** (ZHOOL-yah)—Portuguese; **JULITA** (yoo-LEE-tah)—Polish. There are several saints' and queens' names on this list. Saint Julianna rejected the advances of a nobleman. She was tossed into a fire as punishment, and the fire went out; thus, she is the patroness of firefighters. Shakespeare's version of the Hatfields and the McCoys, *Romeo and Juliet*, boosted the popularity of Juliet as a name. Juliet is one of the moons of Uranus. M

JULY, "joo-LYE"—*Latin: "youthful."* DJUI (JOO-ee)—Indonesian; JUILLET (zhwee-YAY)—French; JULHA (HOOL-hah)—Portuguese; JULIA (HOO-lee-ah)—Spanish; SHICHIGWATSU (SHEE-cheeg-waht-soo)—Japanese; YULA (YOOL-ah)—Russian. The traditional flower for July is the larkspur, the traditional birthstone is the ruby. The month of July was named after Julius Caesar, the great Roman emperor who was born in this month.

JUNE, "JOON"—*Latin: "young," and the month of June.* DJUNI—Indonesian; GIUGNIA (JOON-yah)—Italian; JUIN (ZHWAN)—French; JUNHA (JOON-hah)—Portuguese; JUNI (YOO-nee)—German and Scandinavian; JUNIA (YOO-nee-ah)—Greek; JUNIA (JOON-yah)—Spanish; ROKUGWATSU (ROH-koog-waht-soo)—Japanese; YUNA (YOON-ah)—Russian; YUNI—Hebrew and Arabic. The traditional flower for this month is the rose, while the traditional birthstone is the pearl. The Roman goddess Juno celebrated by this name is the supreme female deity, wife of Jupiter, and the mother of the god Mars. June is one of the Christian saints.

JUNIPER, "JOON-ih-pur"—*Latin.* Spicy-sweet blue juniper berries are used in herbal and folk medicine for their antiseptic and stimulant properties. They are also used to make a type of gin.

JUNO, "JOO-noh"—*Latin: "queen of the gods."* In Roman mythology, Juno was the wife of Jupiter, and the supreme female deity.

JUSTINE, "juss-TEEN"—*Latin: "the just."* GIUSTINA (joo-STEE-nah)—Italian; JUSTINA (yoo-STEEN-ah)—Greek; JUSTYNA (yoo-STEEN-ah)—Polish. Several saints have names on this list. TINA. M

JYLLAND, "JILL-end" or rarely "YIHL-end"—*Danish: "land of the Jutes" or "land of the lindens."* The Jutes were an early Germanic tribe. JUTLAND. See also JILLIAN.

THE TOP FIVE

KAYLA
KATHERINE
KAREN
KELSEY
KHADIJAH

If the name you're looking for isn't here, see "C" and "Q."

KACHINA, "kah-CHEE-nah"—*Native American Shoshone: "the sacred dancer."* **CHINA.**

KAEDE, "kah-EH-day"—*Japanese: "maple leaf."*

KAGA, "KAH-gah"—*Native American: "writer" or "chronicler."* M

KAGAMI, "kah-GAH-mee"—*Japanese: "mirror."*

KAI, "kah-EE"—*Polynesian: "sea."* M

KAILI, "kah-EE-lee"—*Hawaiian: "goddess of the waters."*

KAIRA, "KAY-rah"—*Irish: "sheep."* **KEERA, KEERAGH.**

KAITLIN. See CAITLIN.

KAJ, "KAH-ee"—*Danish: "earth."* **KAIA, KAJA.**

KALA, "KAH-lah"—*Hindu: "time" or "black."*

KALANI, "kuh-LAW-nee"—*Hawaiian: "the heavens."* M

KALILA, "kah-LEEL-ah"—*Arabic: "good friend" or "beloved friend"; Greek: "beautiful."* **KAHILA, KAHILLE, KAHLILAH, KHALILA.** M

KALINDA, "kah-LEEN-dah"—*Hindu: "sun."* The Kalindas are a mountain range in Hindu mythology.

KALMIA, "KAHL-mee-ah" or "KAHL-myah" —*Latin: "laurel shrub."* Laurel leaves signified victory to the Greeks and Romans.

KAMA, "KAH-mah"—*Sanskrit: "love" or "desire."*

KAMAHINA, "kah-mah-HEE-nah"—*Hawaiian: "the moon goddess" or "strong or powerful girl."* **KAMAHINE.**

KAMALA, "kah-MAHL-ah"—*Hindu: "lotus"; Hawaiian: "garden."* M

KAMALI, "kuh-MAH-lee"—*Polynesian: "princess."*

KAMARIA, "kah-mah-REE-uh" or "kah-MAH-ree-ah"—*Swahili: "of the moon"; African: "like the lioness."* **MARA.**

KAMELE, "kuh-MAY-lay"—*Hawaiian: "song" or "melody."*

KAMI, "KAH-mee"—*Japanese: "deity."* M

KAMILA(H), "kah-MEEL-ah"—*Tunisian: "the perfect one."* M

KAMILLA, "kah-MIHL-ah" or "kah-MEE-lah"—*Greek: "ceremonial attendant."* **KAMILKA**—Polish. See also CAMILLE.

KANANE, "kuh-NAH-neh"—*Hawaiian:* "beauty." **KANANA.**

KANDIS, "KAHN-dihss"—*Ethiopian:* ancient title of Nubian queens. See also CANDACE/CANDICE.

KANI, "KAH-nee"—*Japanese:* "accomplished." **KANIKO.**

KANIELLE, "kah-nee-EHL"—*Arabic:* "bright spear" or "spear of the Lord." **KANIELLA.** M

KANIKA, "kuh-NEE-kah" or "KAH-nih-kah"—*African Mwera:* "black silk." **KANI(E), NIKA(H).**

KANOA, "kuh-NOH-ah"—*Polynesian:* "one who is free." M

KANYA, "KAHN-yah"—*Hindu:* "virginal" or "pure," and an equivalent to Virgo.

KAPALI, "kuh-PAW-lee"—*Hawaiian:* "cliff."

KARA, "KAH-rah"—*Norse:* "song of the swan." Kara was one of the Valkyries who took fallen battle heroes to their reward in Valhalla—you've heard the phrase "swan song" used to describe someone's last hurrah, haven't you? See also CARA.

KAREN, "KARE-en" or "KAH-rehn"—*traditionally lumped with Katherine, Greek:* "pure"; but more likely *Hebrew:* "horn"; also try *Latin/French:* "dear"; *Irish:* "little dark one"; *Burmese:* "mountain farmer." **CIARÁN** (KYAR-awn)—Irish Gaelic; **KARAN**—Danish; **KARIN, KARINE**—Nordic; **KEREN, KERYN**—Hebrew; **KIERAN** (KEER-un), **KIERON, KYRAN** (KEER-un), **QUERON** (KARE-on)—Scotch-Irish. The name of a few Christian saints can be found here. See also CIARAN, KATHARINE/KATHERINE, KIRAN, KIRIN.

KARIMAH, "kah-REE-mah"—*Arabic:*

"generous." **KAREEMAH.**

KARLA, "KAHRL-ah"—*version of Charlotte:* "strong and womanly." **KARCSI** (KAHR-chee)—Hungarian; **KARELLA, KA-RELLE; KARI** (KARE-ee or KAH-ree), **KAROL, KAROLINA; KAROLA, KAROLY, LINKA**—Eastern European. In 1993, some astronomers claimed to have found a tenth planet, beyond Pluto, and they tagged it Karla. **LINA.** See also CARLA, CHARLOTTE. M

KARME, "KAHR-may"—*Greek:* "brown sugar" or "warm sugar." In Greek mythology, Karme is one of the sweet maidens, probably a goddess of crops, after whom the chief god Zeus lusted. Thus, Karme is one of the moons of Jupiter (which is Zeus's Roman name).

KARMIA, "KAHR-myah" or "kahr-MEE-ah"—*Hebrew:* "vineyard of the Lord." **KAR-MIT** (kahr-MEET), **KARMELIT** (kahr-meh-LEET), **MARMEL, MARMELIT.**

KAROLA, "kare-OH-lah" or "KAH-rohl-ah"—*Eastern European version of Carol(e), French:* "joyous song," or *Gaelic:* "champion." **KAROLI**—Rumanian; **KAROLY**—Polish. See also CAROL(E). M

KARUNA, "kah-ROO-nah"—*Sanskrit:* "compassion." M

KATA, "KAH-tah"—*Japanese:* "worthy."

KATE. See KATHARINE/KATHERINE, KATHLEEN.

KATHARINE, KATHERINE, "KATH-uh-rihn" or "KAT-uh-rihn"—*traditionally Greek:* "pure"; but also *Hebrew:* "crown." **EKATERINA** (eh-kah-teh-REE-nah), **KATINKA, KATUSHKA, KATYA**—Russian; **KAATJE** (KAH-tyeh), **KATRIEN**—Dutch; **KATAKIN, KATERINA, KATI**—Eastern

European; **KATARIN** (kah-tah-reen)—Basque; **KATARINA** (kah-tah-REE-nah), **KATRINA**—Nordic; **KATARZYNA** (kah-tar-ZEE-nah), **KATINE, KATRINE, KATYA** (KAH-tyah)—Polish; **KATHRINE, KATHRYN**—English; **KATICA** (kah-TEE-chah), **KATOKA** (KAH-toh-kah), **KOTO**—Hungarian; **KATRIN.** Katherines have been saints, princesses, and queens. And then there is the memorable, outspoken actress Katherine Hepburn, winner of four Academy Awards, who is a true original. **KATE, KATEY, KATI(E), KATY; KATHEE, KATHEY, KATHI(E), KATHY.** See also CATHERINE, KAREN, KIT(TY).

KATHLEEN, "kath-LEEN"—*Greek: "pure."* **KATA, KATALIN, KATINKA**—Eastern European; **KATALIN(A)** (kah-tah-leen[-ah])—Basque; **KATINE**—Polish. **KATE, KATEY, KATI(E), KATY; KATHEE, KATHEY, KATHI(E), KATHY.** See also CATHLEEN.

KATHY. See KATHARINE/KATHERINE, KATHLEEN.

KATSU, "KAHT-soo"—*Japanese: "victorious."* M

KATY. See KATHARINE/KATHERINE, KATHLEEN.

KAVA, KAWA, "KAH-vah" and "KAH-wah"—*Maori: "bitter."* The kava or kawa is a pepper shrub, a pungent herb used for its calming and soothing psychological effects.

KAWA, "KAH-wah"—*Japanese: "river."*

KAY(E), "KAY"—*Gaelic: "attractive"; Greek: "rejoice"; Latin: "rejoiced in"; diminutive of Katherine, Greek: "pure" and Hebrew: "crown."* See also KATHARINE/KATHERINE.

KAYA, "kah-YAH"—*Japanese: "yew tree."*

KAYLA, "KAY-lah"—*Irish: "comely."* **CADHLA** (KYE-lah)—Irish Gaelic. This has been an enormously popular name in recent years. It is unusual in that there have been so few variations made in the spelling, unlike other much-used names.

KEA, "KAY-ah" or "KEE-ah"—*Maori.* The kea is a parrot, colored olive, brown, blue, and green, which is not only beautiful but formidable—it eats fruits, plants, and sheep!

KEBIBI, "keh-BEE-bee"—*Swahili: "little lady."* **KABIBI, KIBIBI. BIBI.**

KEE, "KEE"—*Irish: "one-eyed."*

KEELY, "KEE-lee"—*Gaelic: "little beauty."* **KEELEY.** See also KILLIAN. M

KEFIRA, "keh-FEE-rah"—*Hebrew: "young lioness."*

KEI, "keh-EE" or "KAY-ee"—*Japanese: "rapture."* **KEIKO.**

KELLY, "KEHL-ee"—*Welsh: "in the woods"; Gaelic: "warrior"; Native American Comanche/ Nimeneh: "sparrow hawk."* **KELE, KELLE, KELLEE, KELLEY, KELLI(E).** This name became popular in the 1970s through Jaclyn Smith's character on *Charlie's Angels.* M

KELSEY, "KEHL-see"—*Norse: "from the ship island,"* referring to a shape of a land mass, or *"from the ship's island,"* referring to a vessel or traveller's point of origination; *Cymric: "dweller in the woods by the sea"; German: "from the sea"* or *"near the sea."* **KELCEY, KELCI(E), KELCY; KELSI(E), KELSY.** This is a seaworthy name, at any rate. Actor Kelsey Grammer is largely responsible for the extraordinary popularity of Kelsey as a girls' name. See also CHELSEA. M

KEMBA, "KEHM-bah"—*English: "Saxon lady."* **KIMBA.**

KEMUELLE, "keh-myoo-EHL"—?, *probably Arabic.* **KEMU-EL.** Kemuelle is one of the great Seraphim of the angelic hierarchy, an angel who is in direct contact with God/Allah.

KENDAL(L), "KEHN-dul"—*Celtic: "ruler of the valley."* **KENDEL(L). KEN, KENN, KENNI(E), KENNY; KENDI(E), KENDY.** M

KENDRA, "KEHN-drah"—*Gaelic: "the knowing woman" or "the brave woman"; Anglo-Saxon: "queen" or "royal"; Irish: "one of the ancient ones"; Scottish: "to know how to" or "to be able to"*—do something special. **KENDIS. KENNA, KENNI(E).**

KENDRIKA, "KEHN-drihk-ah"—*Anglo-Saxon: "royal power."* **KENDIGA; KENDRA, KENDRI(E), KENDRY; KENDRICA, KENDRIKA, KENRICA. KENNI(E), KENNY, RICK(K)I(E), RICKY; RIKKI.** M

KENNA, "KEHN-ah"—*Scottish: "to make known" or "to know how, to be able."* **KENDA, KENDIS, KENDRA. KENNI(E), KENNY.** M

KENNI(E). This is a diminutive for all the names that begin with "Ken-."

KENYA, "KAY-nyah" or "KEE-nyah"—*Celtic: "fair-haired"; African: "antelope."* Kenya is the name of a country in eastern Africa. **KENNA, KENNI(E), KENNY.** M

KERANI, "kay-RAH-nee"—*Sanskrit: "sacred bells."*

KERRI(E). See CARRIE, KERRY.

KERRY, "KARE-ee"—*Irish: "dark."* This is a place name for southwest Ireland. **CARRI(E); KARRI(E); KERR, KERRI(E).** M

KERSEY, "KUR-see"—*English: "like cashmere."* **KERSI(E).**

KETIFA, "keh-TEE-fah"—*Arabic: "plucked flower."*

Kill-, -kill

This is a Dutch prefix or suffix that means "creek," "stream," or "channel." You may add it to any name.

KETURA, "keh-TOO-rah"—*Hebrew: "incense."* **KETTIE, KETTY.**

KHALIDA(H), "kah-LEE-dah"—*Arabic: "immortal."* **KHULUDA(H).**

KHEPRA, "KEHP-rah"—*Egyptian: "scarab beetle."* In Egyptian belief, Khepra was the scarab who laid the egg of the Sun and rolled it across the sky every day. To the Egyptians, the scarab is a symbol of eternal life.

KI, "KEE"—*Korean: "vigorous."* M

KIAH, "KEE-ah"—*African: "season's beginning."*

KIBBE, "KEEB-eh"— *Native American: "bird in the night."* **KIBBEE.** M

KIBIBI, "kee-BEE-bee"—*African Runyankore: "beautiful chubby girl."* **BIBI.** See also KEBIBI.

KICHI, "KEE-chee"—*Japanese: "fortunate."* **KICHIKO.**

KILLIAN, "KIHL-yahn"—*Gaelic: "little beauty" or "little fighter."* **CILLIAN** (KEE-lee-awn)—Irish Gaelic; **KEELAN, KEELY; KILIAN.** M

KILOHANA, "kee-loh-HAH-nah"—*Hawaiian: "apex."*

KIM, "KIHM"—*Vietnamese: "bird."* See also KIMBERLY. M

KIMBERLY, "KIHM-bur-lee"—*Welsh:*

"meadow near the fortress"; Afrikaans: "blue-ground." **KIMBELIN, KIMBELINA, KIMBELINE, KIMBELYN; KIMBERLEA, KIMBERLEE, KIMBERLEY, KIMBERLIE; KIMBERLIN, KIMBERLINA, KIMBERLINE; KIMBERLYN; KYBMERLEE, KYMBERLEY, KYMBERLIE, KYMBERLY.** The Afrikaans derivation refers to kimbelite, a mineral that produces a clay known as "blue-ground," and the "blue-ground" in southern Africa is the diamond-bearing region of Kimberley at the Cape of Good Hope. Kim Basinger is a leading lady who began her career in commercials. **KIM, KIMI(E), KIMMI(E), KIMMY, KYM, KYMEE; KIMBA, KYMBA, KIMBRA, KYMBRA.**

KIMI, "kee-MEE"—Japanese: "without peer." **KIMIKO, KIMIYO.** M

KINETA, "kih-NEHT-ah"—Greek: "active child." **KINETTE, KINNETTA; KYNETTE.**

KINU, "kee-NOO" or "KEE-noo"—Japanese: "silk." M

KIRA, "KEE-rah"—Russian: "light"; Persian: "the Sun."

KIRAN, "KEE-rahn"—Hindu: "ray." The ray refers to sunlight. **KIERAN.** See also KAREN, KIRIN.

KIRI, "KEE-ree"—Sanskrit: "amaranth." **KIRSI.**

KIRIMA, "kee-REE-mah"—Native American: "a hill."

KIRIN, "KEER-in" or "KEE-reen"—Japanese: "unicorn." This is a mythic animal, much like the Western unicorn, that appears in Japanese legend. See also KAREN, KIRAN.

KIRSTEN, "KUR-stehn"—version of Christine: "follower of Christ"; Scottish: "to christen." **KIRSTI(E), KIRSTY.** See also CHRISTIAN(E), CHRISTIN(E), KRISTA, KRISTIN(E).

KISHI, "KEE-shee"—Japanese: "beach." M

KIT(TY), "KIH-tee" or "KIHT"—diminutive of Katherine: "pure"; at face value: "kitten," "pussycat," or "young fox." **CHITA** (CHEE-tah)—Old English; **KISA** (KEE-sah)—Eastern European; **KISKA** (KEES-kah)—Russian. **KITTI(E), KITTEN.** See also CATHERINE, KATHARINE/KATHERINE. M

KITO, "KEE-toh"—Swahili: "jewel." M

KITRA, "KIHT-rah"—Hebrew: "crown."

KIYO, "kee-YOH" or "KEE-yoh"—Japanese: "happiness in our family."

KIZZY, "KIH-zee"—African Ashanti: "healthy child." **KESSIE, KESSY, KIZZIE.** This name was first seen (or heard) by most Americans in Alex Haley's masterpiece Roots, which was made into a miniseries—a perennial TV favorite. Kizzy was one of the most popular characters. M

KOHANA, "koh-HAH-nah"—Native American Sioux: "swift"; Japanese: "little blossom."

KOJAH, "KOH-jah"—Mongolian: "mink with long hair." **KOJAK.** M

KOKO, "KOH-koh"—Native American: "the night"; Japanese: "stork." Storks are a sign of good fortune in the house.

KONA, "KOH-nah"—Hindu: equivalent to Capricorn.

KONSTANTINA, "kon-stahn-TEE-nah" —Latin: "steadfast" or "constant." **KONSTANCJI** (kawn-STAHN-tsyee)—Polish; **KOSTYA, KOSTYUSHA** (koh-STYOO-shah)—Russian. See also CONSTANTINA. M

KORA, "KOH-rah"—Greek: "maiden." **KOREN.** In Greek mythology, Kora or Koren was the goddess-daughter of Zeus and Aphrodite. See also CORA.

-ko

This is a Japanese suffix that will feminize a masculine name, or it can be added as a term of endearment to an already feminine name, much like the French "ette."

KORUNA, "koh-ROO-nah"—*Czecho-slovakian: "crown."*

KOSMA, "KAWZ-mah"—*Latin: "the universe" and "order."* **KOSIMA, KOSMY.** See also COSMA.

KRISTA, "KRIHS-tah" or "KREES-tah"—*Nordic, from Greek: "the anointed one" or "the Light."* **KIRSTI(E), KIRSTY; KRISTI(E); KRISTY; KRYSIA, KRYSTA, KRYSTKA.** See also CHRISTIAN(E), CHRISTIN(E), KIRSTEN, KRISTIN(E). M

KRISTIN(E), "KRIHS-tihn" and "krees-TEEN"—*Nordic, from Greek: "follower of Jesus Christ."* **KARSTEN, KARSTI(E)**—Dutch; **KERSTIN**—Swedish; **KIRSTEN, KIRSTI(E); KJERSTI** (KYUR-stee)—Norwegian; **KRIS(H)-KA, KRISZTA, KRISZTINA** (kreezh-TEE-nah)—Hungarian; **KRISTI(E), KRISTINA; KRYSTYN**—Polish. See also CHRISTIAN(E), CHRISTIN(E), KIRSTEN, KRISTA.

KRYSTAL. See CRYSTAL.

KSENA, "k'SAY-nah"—*Polish: "praise to God."*

KUMA, "KOO-mah"—*Japanese: "bear."*

KUNI, "koo-NEE"—*Japanese: "born in the country."* As opposed to a child born in the city. M

KUPONA, "koo-POH-nah"—*Hawaiian: "honest" or "just."* M

KURA, "KOO-rah"—*Japanese: "house of treasure."* M

KURI, "KOO-ree"—*Japanese: "chestnut."* M

KYLA, "KYE-lah"—*Yiddish: "crowned with laurels"; Welsh: "chapel" or "narrow stream"; Irish: "comely."* **CADHLA** (KYE-lah)—Irish Gaelic; **KYLEY, KYLIE.** Kyla is one of the Christian saints. M

KYMBERLY. See KIMBERLY.

KYO, "KYOH"—*Pali: "golden light."*

KYRA, "KYE-rah" or "KEE-rah"—*version of Cyrus: "queen" or "lordly."* **KYRENE.** Kyra Sedgwick is an actress.

KYRIE, "KEER-ee-ay"—*Late Latin from Greek: "lord, master."* The "lord" in question is Jesus Christ.

THE TOP FIVE

LAUREN
LILITH/LILY
LAYLA/LEILA
LINDA
LETITIA

If the name you're looking for isn't here, see "Y."

LACE, "LAYCE"—*Old French from Latin: "noose" or "string."* **AGNEAU** (AHN-yoh)—French; **AGNELLO** (ahn-YEH-loh)—Italian; **BARANEK** (bah-RAH-nehk)—Polish; **BÁRÁNY** (bah-RAH-nee)—Hungarian; **CORDEIRA**—Portuguese; **CORDERA** (kohr-DARE-ah)—Spanish; **JAGNJE** (YAWN-yeh)—Slavic; **JEHNJE** (YEHN-yeh)—Czech and Slovakian; **LAMM** (LAHM)—German and Scandinavian; **YAGYONAK** (yahg-YOH-nahk)—Russian.

LACY, "LAY-see"—*Latin: "from Latius" or "an estate"; English: "like lace" or "covered with lace."* **LACE, LACEY, LACI(E).**

LADA, "LAH-dah"—*Russian.* In Russian folklore, Lada was a goddess of beauty.

LADINA, "lah-DEE-nah"—*Spanish: "wise, crafty, cunning."* M

LAILA, LEILA, "LAY-lah"—*Arabic: "born at night,"* and the angel of conception. **LAILI, LAILIE; LAILIT** (lay-LEET)—Hebrew; **LAYLA.**

LAKE, "LAYK"—*English: "lake."* **BAHRAT** (bah-RAWT), **HAWR**—Arabic; **CO, TSO**—Tibetan; **DARYACHEH** (DAHR-yah-cheh or dahr-YAH-cheh)—Persian; **EZERS** (EH-zehrz or AY-zayrz)—Latvian; **HU**—Chinese; **JARVI** (YAHR-vee)—Finnish; **JEZERA** (YEH-zeh-rah)—Albanian and Serbo-Croatian; **LACUL** (LAH-cool)—Romanian; **LOCH** (LAWK)—Scottish Gaelic; **LOUGH** (LAWKH—"KH" is guttural)—Irish Gaelic; **MIZUMI** (mee-ZOO-mee)—Japanese; **NUUR**—Mongolian; **OZERA** (OH-zeh-rah)—Russian; **SAGAR** (SAH-gahr or sah-GAHR)—Hindu; **SEE**—German; **SO**—Danish and Norwegian; **TELAGA**—Indonesian; **THALE** (THAH-leh or TAH-leh)—Thai; **TJARN** (TYARN), **VATTEN** (VAW-tehn)—Swedish; **TONLE** (TAWN-leh or DAWN-leh)—Khmer; **ZEE**—Dutch. M

LAKOTAH, "lah-KOH-tah"—*Native American Sioux: "friend to us."* Lakotah is the name for the Teton branch of the Great Sioux Nation. M

LALA, "LAH-lah"—*Czechoslovakian: "tulip."* See also LALIA.

LALE, LALO, "LAHL" or "LAH-loh"—*Latin: "to sing to sleep" or "lullabye."*

LALIA, "LAH-lee-ah"—*Latin: "fair speech."* **LAELIA, LALA, LALAH, LAYLIA; LELA, LELAR.**

LANA, "LAH-nah"—*Latin: "wool," "downy," or "soft."* **LANETTE, LENA.** Actress Lana Turner, the late 1940s and early 1950s "sweater girl," was supposedly discovered drinking a malted at the counter of a Hollywood drug store.

LANAKILA, "lah-nah-KEE-lah"—*Polynesian: "victory."*

LANE, "LAYN"—*English: "path."* **LAINE, LAINIE, LANEY, LAYNE.** M

LANETTE, "lah-NEHT"—*French: "from the little lane."*

LANI, "LAW-nee"—*Hawaiian: "sky" or "heaven."* M

LANTANA, "lan-TAN-ah"—*Latin: "viburnum."* The lantana bush produces little bouquets of little flowers in a variety of colors, even if it isn't carefully tended.

LARA, "LAH-rah"—*Irish: "a mare"; Russian: "famous"; Greek/Latin: "shining."* In Roman mythology, Lara is a river nymph. In Boris Pasternak's *Dr. Zhivago*, the heroine is named Lara. See also LARISA.

LARISA, "lah-REE-sah"—*Latin: "cheerful" or "laughter."* **LARA, LARYA; LARISSA** (lah-RIH-sah), **LAROCHKA.** Larissa is one of the moons of Neptune, named after a Roman water sprite.

LARK, "LAHRK"—*Anglo-Saxon: "the lark."* **LARKE, LARKIN.** Larks have very long and sweet songs. Also, a lark is a wonderful adventure undertaken on the spur of the moment.

LATEEFA(H), "lah-TEEF-ah"—*Moroccan: "gentle" or "pleasant."* **LATIF, LATIFAH**—*Arabic.* Rapper/songwriter/actress Queen Latifah has popularized this name. M

LATONIA, "lah-TOHN-yah" or "lah-TAWN-yah"—*Latin: "from Laton"; Eastern European: "the Fairy Queen."* **LATANIA, LATANYA, LATONYA.** See also TANYA, TATANIA, TATYANA, TITANIA.

LAULANI, "lah-oo-LAH-nee"—*Hawaiian: "heavenly offspring."*

LAURA, "LOH-rah"—*Latin: "the laurels."* **LAUREE, LAURI(E), LORA, LOREE, LORI(E); LORRI(E); LAURETTA, LAURETTE, LORETTA, LORETTE.** The ancient Romans thought laurel gave protection from lightning. See also LAUREL/LAUREN, LAURENCIA.

LAUREL, LAUREN, "LORE-ehl" and "LORE-ehn"—*Latin: "laurel tree" or "laurel leaves."* **LARAINE, LARENE, LAURAINE, LAURENE, LAURINE; LORENA, LORENE, LORINA, LORINE, LORRAINE.** A model and actress named Betty Bacall changed her name to Lauren and sparked the consistent popularity of this name. It has become even more popular in recent years because of its use as a TV character name. **LORI(E).** See also LAURA, LAURENCIA, LOREL/LORELEI.

LAURENCIA, "lore-ENHTS-ee-ah"—*Latin: "crown of laurel" or "of Laurentium."* **LARAINE, LARRAINE, LARRI(E); LAURENE, LAURETTA, LAURETTE; LORENE, LORETTA, LORINE, LORRAINE; LARENZA**—*Dutch;* **LAURINDA**—*Spanish;* **LAURENCA** (loh-REHN-kah), **LAURENCHA** (loh-REHN-chah) —*Portuguese;* **LAURENTIA**—*Swedish;* **LAURENTZI** (loh-rent-zee)—*Basque;* **LAURENZA** (loh-rent-ZAH), **LORENYA** (loh-REHN-yah), **LORETTA, RENZA**—*Italian;* **LAURICE**—*Norwegian;* **LAWRENCIA; LENCI** (LEHN-tsee), **LORECA** (loh-REH-tsah)—*Hungarian.* Loretta Young appeared in films, and later, on TV, and was noted for her grace and beauty. At fourteen, she answered a casting call meant for her sister, and didn't stop working for many decades. **LAURA, LAURIE, LAWRI(E); LORA, LORI(E), LORRI(E), LORRY, LORY.** See also LAUREL/LAUREN, LORRAINE. M

LAVEDA, "lah-VEE-dah"—*Latin: "purified."*

LAVENDAR, LAVENDER, "LAV-

La

"La" (pronounced "lah") is the feminine version of the article "the" in French, Spanish, Italian, and other languages. Therefore, the singular noun that follows it should end in an "a," "e," "i," or "y." You may add this yourself to a name; if going for the French sound, drop the "a" if "La" is to be followed by a vowel.

ehn-dur"—*Latin: "the lavender flower" or the color lavender.* Spicy lavender is used in many ways: perfumery, calming and antidepressant teas, insect repellants. It is beautiful, fragrant, and useful.

LAVERNE, "lah-VERN"—*French: "verdant."* **LAVERN.** See also VERNA.

LAVINIA, "lah-VIH-nee-ah"—*Latin: "woman of Rome."* In Roman mythology, Lavinia was the wife of Aeneas, the Trojan who led his people to Italy after the fall of Troy.

LAYLA, "LAY-lah"—*Swahili: "born in the night."*

LAYNE, "LAYN"—*Old English: "to conceal."* M

LEA, "LEE" or "LEE-ah"—*Anglo-Saxon: "grassy field."* See also LEAH, LEE, LI.

LEAF, "LEEF"—*English: "leaf."* **BLATT** (BLAHT)—German; **DAUN** (dah-OON)—Indonesian; **FEUILLE** (fooh-EEL)—French; **HOJA** (HOH-yah)—Spanish; **JANI** (JAH-nee)—Swahili; **YAPRAK** (YAHP-rahk)—Turkish. M

LEAH, "LEE-ah"—*Hebrew: "blear-eyed" or "weary"; English: "meadow or clearing."* In the Old Testament/Tanakh, Leah was the first wife of Jacob. **LEA, LIA, LIAH.** See also LEE.

LEANDRA, "lee-AHN-drah"—*Latin: "like a lioness"; English: "woman of the meadow."* **LEANTHRA.**

LEDA, "LEE-dah"—*Greek: "happy."* **LEDO, LIDA, LIDO; LIDOCHKA** (lee-DOCH-kah)—Russian. In Greek myth, Leda, queen of Sparta, was a great beauty who captured the ever-roaming eye of the god Zeus, who in turn transformed himself into a swan to be near her. The result of their union was Helen of Troy. With the king of Sparta, she mothered Castor, Pollux, and Clytemnestra. Leda is one of the moons of Jupiter.

LEE, "LEE"—*English: "meadow," "clearing," or "sheltered, covered"; Chinese: "pear."* **LEA, LEAH, LEIGH** (LEE or LAY). See also LI, YARDLEY/YEARDLEY. M

LEILANI, "LAY-ee-LAW-nee"—*Polynesian: "child from heaven" or "heavenly flower."*

LELA, "LEE-lah"—*French: "loyal" or "faithful."* **LEALA, LEALAH, LELAH.** See also LALIA, LILA, LILAH.

LENA, LINA, "LEE-nah"—*diminutives of Helen, Greek: "light"; Hebrew: "to sleep" or "to dwell."* Lina Basquette was an actress of the 1920s and 1930s whose private life got as much attention as her films—she was probably the first actress to

DEEP SOUTH GIRLS' NAMES

Girls born into the states along the Gulf Coast and the lower Mississippi River are most likely to have the following names:

1. Ashley	6. Sarah	11. Kayla	16. Amanda
2. Brittany	7. Amber	12. Victoria	17. Isabelle
3. Taylor	8. Courtney	13. Megan	18. Rachel
4. Jessica	9. Emily	14. Chelsea	19. Samantha
5. Jasmine	10. Alexis	15. Hannah	20. Elizabeth

go through six husbands. Lena Horne is an actress and singer who made her first popular appearances in the musicals *Cabin in the Sky* and *Stormy Weather*. See also HELEN, LANA, LENORA.

LENMANA, "len-MAH-nah"—*Native American Hopi: "girl playing flute."*

LENORA, "luh-NORE-uh"—*Greek: "luminous" or "light."* **LENORAH, LENORE; LEONORA, LEONORE; LIONOR(E); LYONOR(E).** Lenore is the object of the poet's obsession in Edgar Allan Poe's "The Raven." **LENA; NORA(H).** See also HELEN.

LEODA, "lee-OH-dah"—*German: "woman of the people."*

LEOMA, "lee-OH-mah"—*English: "brightness."*

LEONA, "lee-OH-nah" or "lay-OH-nah"—*Latin: "like a lioness."* **LEOLA, LEOLINA, LEOLINE, LEONELLE, LEONTINE, LEONTYNE; LÉONETTE, LÉONIE** (LAY-oh-nee)—*French;* **LEONIDA** (lay-oh-NEE-dah)—*Italian;* **LYONECHKA, LYONYA**—*Russian.* M

LEONARDA, "lay-oh-NAHR-dah"—*Teutonic: "courage of a lioness."* **LENARDA; LEONHARDE**(lay-oh-NAHR-deh)—*Danish.* M

LEORA, "lee-OHR-ah"—*Hebrew: "I have light" or "I am enlightened."* **LIORA.** See also ELIORA. M

LEOTI, "leh-oh-TEE"—*Native American: "prairie wildflower."*

LESLIE, "LEHZ-lee"—*Scottish: "low-lying meadow"; Celtic: "from the gray fortress."* **LESLEY. LES.** M

LETA, "LEE-tah"—*Latin: "glad."*

LETISHA. See LETITIA.

LETITIA, "leh-TEE-shah" or "leh-TISH-ah"—*Latin: "gladness" or "rejoicing."* **LETICIA, LETISHA, LETIZIA** (lay-TEET-zyah); **LETJE** (LEH-tyeh)—*Dutch;* **LETTICE, LETTI(E), LETTY** —*Irish.* Lettice was an Elizabethan era noblewoman who was the secret second wife of Robert Dudley, Earl of Leicester. He was one of the many lovers of Queen Elizabeth at the time, and the queen nearly had his head when she found out. But true love won—he chose Lettice, and Elizabeth decided not to have a public execution. The name Letisha has been popular in the African-American community. **TISH, TISHA.**

LEVANA, "leh-VAH-nah"—*Latin: "lifting*

up" or "rising sun." Levana was a Roman goddess of childbirth. **LEVANNA. VA(N)NA.**

LEWANA, "leh-WAH-nah"—*Hebrew: "beaming one" or "the Moon."* **LEWANNA.**

LEXY, "LEHKS-ee"—*Greek: "the word"; Latin: "the law."* **LEXIE.** See also ALEXANDRA. M

LEYA, "LAY-yah"—*Hindu: equivalent to Leo.*

LI, like "LEE" but shorter, closer to "LIH"—*Chinese: "plum."* See also LEA, LEE. M

LIA, "LEE-uh"—*Dutch: "dependence"; Greek: "announcer of good news."*

LIAN, "LEE-ahn"—*Chinese: "willow."* **LIANNE.**

LIANA, "lee-AH-nah"—*French: "climbing vine."* **LEANA, LEANNA, LIANNA.**

LIATRIS, "lee-AH-trihss" or "LEE-uh-trihss"—*Latin: "blazing star."* **LEATRICE, LEATRIS.** Liatris plants produce featherlike flowers in screaming colors.

LIBA, "LEE-bah"—*Greek: "the southwest wind."* M

LIBBE, "LEE-bee" or "LIH-bee"—*Yiddish: "loved one" or "beloved."* **LIBBI(E), LIBBY.**

LIBRA, "LEE-brah"—*Greek: "scales" or "balance."* The constellation Libra can be seen following the Sun at dusk from mid-June to mid-July. The Sun is "in" the Scales from late October through the month of November. To the early Christians, it was the sign of BARTHOLOMEW or NATHANIEL, the Knife. To the Egyptians, it was MAA, the Scales of Justice. To the Greeks, it was the sign of HEPHAESTUS, the Helmet. To the early Hebrews, it was MANASSEH the Palm Tree. To the Norse peoples, it was HODER, the Arrow or Dart. To the Romans, it was VULCAN, the Anvil. To the Aztecs, this was the sign of CHICHEN ITZA the Serpent. To the Babylonians, it was ZIBALACUNA the Claws. Heavenly Guides for the Sun at this time are IVY (with five days of the VINE) for the Celts and Druids, and the HERBS or GRASSES for the Japanese.

LIDA, "LEE-dah"—*Slavic: "loved by all."* See also LEDA.

LIDE, "lee-deh"—*Basque: "life."*

LIEN, "LEE-ehn"—*Chinese: "lotus."* **LIENNE.**

LILA, "LEE-lah"—*Hindu: "free will of God."* **LELA.** See also DELILAH, LILAH, MALILA.

LILAC, "LYE-lak"—*Arabic: "the lilac tree" or "the lilac bush,"* and the color lilac. **FLIEDER** (FLY-dur)—German and Yiddish; **LILAH; LILAS** (LEE-lahs)—French; **SIRYEN** (seer-YEHN)—Russian; **SYREN** (SEE-rehn), **SYRIN**—Scandinavian.

LILAH, "LEE-lah" (first derivation only) or "LYE-lah"—*Sanskrit: "play" or "sport"; Hebrew: "gentle, tender" or "the lilac."* **LELA, LELAH, LILA.** In the Hindu religion, the gods' activities in human life are explained as *lilah,* acts of spontaneity, without calculation. See also DELILAH.

LILITH, "LIHL-ihth"—*Assyrian: "of the night"; Babylonian: "night goddess"; Persian: "dark."* **LILICE, LILIS, LILITA, LILLIS, LILLITA; LILLITH.** The original Lilith was an Assyrian goddess who ruled over the night. In Jewish legend, Lilith is said to have been the first woman God made for Adam—beautiful, smart, and an equal of Adam in every way except physical. Adam couldn't handle it, and begged God to rework the design. The two of them came up with Eve, the more submissive version. Lilith is making quite a comeback, however, probably because of the character Lilith, Frasier's ex-wife, on the TV show *Cheers*. **LIL, LILLY, LILY.**

LILLIAN, "LIHL-ee-ahn"—*Greek: "graceful lily."* **LILIANE, LILLIANA, LILLIANNA, LILYAN, LILYANNA, LILYANNE.**

LILY, "LIHL-ee"—*Greek: "the lily."* **LILIAH; LILIKA**—*Greek;* **LILIKE** (lee-LEE-keh or LEE-leekeh)—*Slavic.* **LILI(E), LILLI(E), LILLY.** See also LILITH.

LINAH, "LEE-nah"—*Arabic: "tender."*

LINDA, "LIHN-dah"—*Spanish: "beautiful"; German: "snake"; Teutonic: "dragon" or "serpent."* **LINDE, LINDEE, LINDEL, LINDELLE; LYNDA, LYNDE.** Snakes are not always symbolic of evil; often, they are symbols of cleverness. **LINDY, LYNDI(E).** See also ADELINE, LINDY.

LINDSAY, "LIHND-zay"—*English: "island in the brook" or "brookside linden trees"; in a stretch, Anglo-Saxon: "island waterfall."* **LINDSEY. M**

LINDY, "LIHND-ee"—*Anglo-Saxon: "lime trees."* **LINDA. M**

LINNEA, "lih-NAY-ah" or "LIHN-yah"—*Norse: "a lime tree" and the blue national flower of Sweden.* **LYNNEA. LIORA.**

LIRON, "LEE-rawn" or "lee-RAWN"—*Hebrew: "my song."* **LIRONA, LIRONE. RONA.**

LISA, "LEE-sah"—*diminutive of Elisabeth: "consecrated to God"; African: "sun god(dess)" or "Jesus."* **ELIZE, LISE, LISETTE**—*French;* **LEESA, LIESJE** (LEE-syeh), **LISSA**—*Dutch;* **LIESEL** (LEEZ-ehl)—*German;* **LISE** (LEES-eh)—*Danish;* **LISZA** (LEE-zhah)—*Hunga-*rian. In Dahomey, Lisa is the male sun god whose twin is Mawu, the female moon goddess. With the coming of Christianity, Lisa became associated with Jesus, and Mawu became associated with God. See also ALYSSA, ELISABETH/ELIZABETH.

LITONYA, "lee-TONE-yah"—*Native American: "darting hummingbird."* **LITANYAH. TANYA, TONYA.**

LIV, "LEEV"—*Norse: "life."* **LIVE** (LEE-veh). **LIVIA.** See OLIVIA.

LIWA, "LEE-wah"—*Chinese: "princess."*

LIZA, "LEE-zah" or occasionally "LYE-zah"—*diminutive of Elizabeth: "consecrated to God."* **ELIZA, LEEZA, LIZETTE. LIZ.** See also ELISABETH/ELIZABETH.

LIZZIE, LIZZY. See ELISABETH/ELIZABETH.

LOIS, "LOH-ihss"—*Greek: "the better."* **ELOISE.** The "better" is not a gambler, but someone who is a better whatever than someone else.

LOKA, "LOH-kah"—*Sanskrit: "the world."* M

LOKI, "LOH-kee"—*Polynesian: "rose."* M

LOLA, "LOH-lah"—*Spanish: "strong woman."* **LOLITA.**

LOLLY, "LAW-lee"—*English: "candy"; Dutch: "to lie languidly."* This is often used as a diminutive of female "L" names.

LOLOA, "loh-LOH-uh"—*Polynesian: "tall."*

LOLOTEA, "loh-LOH-tay-ah"—*Native American Zuni: "a gift from the gods."* **LOLA, LOLO.**

LOMASI, "loh-MAH-see"—*Native American: "pretty flower."*

LORA, "LOH-rah"—*Latin: "grapes."*

LARAINE, LORAINE, LORRAINE. See also LAURA.

LORE, "loh-reh"—Basque: "flower."

LOREL(EI), "LOHR-ehl" and "LOH-reh-lye"—English: "to teach or instruct"; German: "alluring song." **LORAL, LORALEI, LORALIE.** In German legend, Lorelei is a siren, a beautiful seductress. **LOR, LORE, LOREE, LOR(R)EY, LORI(E), LORRI(E), LOR(R)Y.** See also LAUREL/ LAUREN.

LORETTA. See LAURA, LAURENCIA.

LORI(E). See LAURA, LAUREL/LAUREN, LAURENCIA, LOREL(EI), LORRAINE.

LORICE, LORIS, "loh-REESE" and "LOH-rihs"—first one, Latin: "thong" or "slender branch"; second one, Dutch: "clown." Lorice was the sash of Venus, the Roman goddess of love and beauty, a sash that contained the power of love.

LORNA, "LOHR-nah"—?, could be from Irish Gaelic, "Odharnait" (OY-ahr-nayt): "green" or "earth-colored." **LOREEN, LORENE.** Writer R.D. Blackmore created this name for his 1869 novel Lorna Doone.

LORRAINE, "loh-RAIN"—French: from the Lorraine region of France; Teutonic: "famous in battle." **LARAINE, LARRAINE, LARRAINNE; LORAINE, LORAINNE, LORRAINE. LORRA, LORRI(E).** See also LAURENCIA.

LOTTI(E), "LAW-tee"—diminutive of Charlotte: "strong and womanly." **LOTTA, LOTTE.** Lotte Lenya was an Austrian singer and actress who appeared in many musicals by her husband Kurt Weill. See also CHARLOTTE.

LOUISE, "loo-EEZ"—German: "famous warrior." **ELOISE, HELOISE** (HEH-loo-eez), **LOUISIANA, LOUISIANE**—French; **LOUISA;**

LOVISA (loh-VEE-sah)—Slavic; **LUISA**—Italian and Spanish; **LUJZA** (loo-EE-zah), **LUJZI, LUJZIKA**—Hungarian. Quite a few saint names are on this list. M

LUBA, "LOO-bah"—Slavic: "love" or "lover."

LUCENTA, "loo-SEHN-tah"—Latin: "shining" or "clear." M

LUCIA, "loo-CHEE-ah" or "LOO-syah"—Latin: "bringer of light" or "glittering." **LUCE, LUCIENNE** (loo-see-EN or loo-SYEN)—French; **LUCIA** (LOO-tsyah)—Eastern European; **LUCIANA** (loo-chee-AH-nah), **LUCILLE**—Italian; **LUCJA** (LOOTS-yah), **LUCYNA** (LOOT-see-nah)—Polish; **LUCZA** (LOO-tsah). Saint Lucy, or Santa Lucia, is the patroness of those with eye problems. A few other saints have borne names on this list. **LUCI(E), LUCY.** M

LUCILLE. See LUCIA.

LUCINA, "loo-SEE-nah"—Italian: "life (light) bringer." Lucina was a minor Italian goddess, associated with Juno, who held rulership over childbirth. **CINA; LUCE.** M

LUCY. See LUCIA.

LUDA, "LOO-dah"— Latin: "I play."

LUDMILLA, "lood-MEE-lah"— Russian: "loved by the people." **LUMILA, LYUBOCHKA, LYUDMILA, LYUDMILLA; LUDA, LYUDA, MILA, MILENA, MILENKA, MILLA.**

LUKA, "LOO-kah"—Latin: "bringer of light"; Greek: "from Lucania." **LUKENE** (loo-kehn-eh)—Basque. M

LUNA, "LOO-nah"—Latin: "the Moon" or "silver." Luna is what alchemists called silver. Don't use Lunette, because that means "eyeglasses" in French.

LUPE, "LOO-peh"—*Spanish from Latin: "she-wolf."* **LUPITA.** See also GUADALUPE.

LUTAH, "LOO-tuh"—*Native American Sioux: "red."*

LYDIA, "LIHD-ee-ah"—*Basque: "life"; English: "hillock"; Greek: "cultured" or "from Lidia."* Lidia is an ancient region once ruled by the spectacularly wealthy King Croesus. **LIDIA, LYDÍE** (LEE-dyeh)—Dutch; **LYDELL, LYDELLE; LYDIE** (LEE-dee or lee-DEE)—French. M

LYN(N), "LIHN"—*English: "a brook"; Anglo-Saxon: "a waterfall."* **LIN, LINN, LINNE, LINNETTE; LYNNA, LYNNE, LYNETTE.** See also MARILYN. M

LYNETTE, "lih-NET"—*French: "the lin- net bird"; Welsh: "idol."* **LINETT(E), LIN- NETT(E), LYNNETTE.** Lady Lynette and her sister Lyonesse were rescued by, and lovers of, Sir Gareth in Arthurian legend. **NETTIE.**

LYRA, "LEE-rah" or "LYE-rah"—*Latin: "lyre" or "harp."* **LYRIS.** The constellation Lyra can be seen following the Sun at dusk from late August through early September. The Sun is "in" the Lyre around Thanksgiving. Lyra is a little, delicate configuration, but it possesses one of the brightest stars in the heavens, Vega.

LYSANDRA, "lye-SAND-rah" or "lih-SAHN- drah"—*Greek: "liberator of humankind."* **LIS- SANDRA, LISSANDRE, LISSANDRO**—French. **LYS, LYSS; SANDI(E), SANDRA, SANDY, SON- DRA, SONNI(E)** (SAW-nee), **SONNY.**

THE TOP FIVE

MEGAN
MORGAN
MARY
MARGARET
MARIE

If the name you're looking for isn't here, perhaps it is a variant or a diminutive of another primary name.

MABEL, "MAY-behl"—*Latin: "lovable"; Gaelic: "mirthful."* **MABELLE, MAYBELL(E), MAYBELLINE; MABILIA** (mah-BEE-lee-ah)— Italian; **MAIBLE** (MAY-behl or MY-behl)—Irish; **MOIBEAL** (MOY-bale or MOY-behl)—Scottish.

MADDI(E). See MADELINE, MADISON, MAIDA.

MADELINE, "MAD-eh-lihn," "MAD-eh-lyne," or "mahd-LEEN"—*Hebrew: "from the high towers"; Greek: "from Magdala," a town on the Sea of Galilee.* **MADAILEIN** (mah-dye-LEEN)—Irish Gaelic; **MADALENE** (mah-dah-LAY-neh), **MADDALENE, MAGDALINA**—Italian; **MADALINE, MADOLYN; MADDALINA** (mah-dah-LEE-nah), **MADDE** (MAH-deh)—Polish; **MADE-LAINE** (MAD-eh-layn), **MADELEINE** (mahd-LAYN)—French; **MADELLA, MADELLE** (mah-DEHL)— French; **MAGDA, MAGDALA** (MAHG-dah-lah)—Hungarian; **MAGDALEN** (mahg-dah-lehn), **MATXALEN** (maht-shah-lehn)—Basque; **MAGDALENA** (mahg-dah-LAY-nah)—Scandinavian, Dutch, Spanish, and Portuguese; **MAGLI** (MAHG-lee), **MALENA, MALIN** (mah-LEEN)—Scandinavian and Dutch; **MAIGHDLIN** (my-LEEN)—Scottish; **MARLENE**—German and English. There are a few saint names

on this list. In the New Testament, Mary Magdalene was a follower of Jesus. **MADDI(E), MADGE, MAGGI(E).** See also MALINA.

MADGE. See MADELINE, MARGARET.

MADIHAH, "mah-DEE-hah"—*Arabic: "praiseworthy."*

MADISON, "MAD-ih-sun"—*English: "son of a soldier."* Like many female names, this started out as a male name, so you may want to think of it as "daughter of a soldier." **MADDI(E), MADDY; SONNI(E), SONNY.** M

MADONNA, "mah-DAW-nah"—*Old Italian: "my lady."* **MADOÑA** (mah-DOHN-yah)—Spanish and Portuguese. This is the archaic way of referring to the Virgin Mary, now primarily designated by the words "our lady" instead of "my lady," while "madonna" continues to refer to artistic representations of her. Madonna— who was born Madonna Ciccone—is a singer and actress.

MAGDA, "MAHG-dah"—*Hebrew: "high tower"; Greek: "woman of Magdala."* See also MADELINE.

MAGENA, "mah-GAY-nuh" or "mah-JAY-nuh"—*Native American Omaha: "the coming moon."* Give this name to a child born on first-crescent-moon or first-half-moon nights, that is the first crescent moon or first half moon of the lunar cycle—check a calendar. See also MIGINA.

MAGENTA, "mah-JEHN-tah"—*French: deep violet or purple-red.*

MAGGIE. See MADELINE, MAGNOLIA, MARGARET.

MAGHA, "MAHG-hah"—*Hindu: equivalent to Aquarius.*

MAGNA, "MAHG-nah"—*Norse: "strength"; Latin: "great."* MAGNE.

MAGNOLIA, "mag-NOHL-yah"—*Latin: "magnolia flower or magnolia tree."* MAGNOLA, MAGNOLIA (mag-NYOH-lyah), MAGNOLIE—*French.* This fragrant, flowering tree is named after Pierre Magnol, the French botanist who identifed and categorized it. MAGGI(E).

MAHA(T), "mah-HAH" or "mah-HAHT"—*Sanskrit: "great or high."* MAHAL(A). Mumtaz Mahal was the cherished wife of a seventeenth-century Indian emperor, and the emperor built the breathtaking Taj Mahal, located in Agra, in her honor. M

MAHALA, "MAH-hall-ah" or "mah-HALL-ah"—*Native American: "woman"; Hebrew: "tenderness."* MAHALAH, MAHALIA, MAHALIE; MUK'ALA, MUK'ELA—*Native American.* See also MAHA(T).

MAHICA, "mah-HEE-kah"—*Native American Algonquin: "clan of the wolf."* M

MAHILA, "mah-HEE-lah"—*Hindu: "woman."*

MAHINA, "mah-HEE-nah"—*Hawaiian: "the Moon."*

MAHIRA, "mah-HEER-ah"—*Arabic: "skilled," "speed," or "horse of Arabia."* M

MAHOE, "mah-HOH-eh"—*Hawaiian: "a twin."*

MAI, "MAH-ee"—*Native American: "coyote"; Japanese: "bright."* See also MARGARET, MAY/MAE. M

MAIA, MAYA, "MY-ah" or "MAY-ah" for either—*Greek: "mother" or "nurse"; Roman: "growing"; Sanskrit: "creative power."* In Greek myth, Maia was one of the early seven great goddess-daughters of Atlas—the Seven Sisters, or Pleiades—and the mother of Hermes. In Roman myth, she is a goddess of fertility and springtime, and consort of the fire god Vulcan. She also gives her name to the month of May. See also MAYA.

MAIDA, "MAY-dah"—*English: "maiden."* MADDI(E), MADDY; MAIDI(E), MAIDEL, MAIDEY.

MAJESTA, "mah-JEHS-tah"—*Latin: "with majesty" or "regal."* MAJESTICA.

MAKA(H), "MAH-kah"—*Native American: "earth."* This is a tribe name for a group of people who used to inhabit the Olympic Peninsula in the state of Washington. They used large seagoing canoes and yew-tree spears to hunt whales. The Makah performed potlatch ceremonies, in which guests at gatherings were given gifts in accordance with their social status. M

MAKALA, "mah-KAH-lah"—*Hawaiian: "myrtle tree."*

MAKALANI, "mah-kah-LAH-nee"—*African Mwera: "the writer."*

MAKANA, "muh-KAH-nuh"—*Polynesian: "gift."*

MAKANI, "muh-KAH-nee"—*Tahitian: "the wind."* M

MAKARA, "mah-KAH-rah"—*Hindu: equivalent to Capricorn.*

MAKOA, "mah-KOH-uh"—*Hawaiian: "brave."*

MALAMA, "muh-LAH-muh"—*Hawaiian: "torchlight."*

MALILA, "mah-LEE-lah"—*Native American Salish: "salmon swimming fast through rippling waters."* **MALELAH. LELAH, LILA.**

MALINA, "mah-LEE-nah"—*Greek: "from the high tower."* See also MADELINE.

MALORY, "MAL-oh-ree"—*German: "army counselor"; French: "covered with mail."* **MALLORUS, MALLORY.** The French derivation doesn't refer to the kind of mail that comes from the post office, but to the coat of mail, made of metal chain links, worn by knights. M

MALUHIA, "mah-loo-HEE-uh"—*Hawaiian: "peaceful" or "peace."*

MALVA, "MAHL-vah"—*Latin: "mallow plant"; Italian: "malmsey wine."* **MALVASIA.** Marshmallow and hollyhock plants are malvas. All sections of these lightly sweet plants are used in herbal and folk medicine.

MALVINA, "mahl-VEE-nah"—*Gaelic: "handmaiden(?)" or possibly "smooth brow,"* indicating youth. This is a name invented by James MacPherson for his *Ossianic Poems* (1765), in which Malvina is the lover of legendary Irish hero Finn MacCool's grandson.

MAME, "MAYM"—*?, possibly a version of Mary: "bitter"; or cockeyed French: "my sweetheart."* This could also possibly be a reference to the tropical mamey tree, which produces yellow mamey "apples." M.G. "Mamie" Eisenhower was First Lady from 1953 to 1960. **MAMIE, MAMEY.**

MANA, "MAH-nah"—*Polynesian: "universal grace" or "universal virtue."* In Polynesian religions, *mana* is the force, present in all things, upon which one can call for help in special undertakings or challenges.

MANASA, "mah-nah-SAH," "mah-NAH-sah," or "MAH-nah-sah" (did I miss one?)—*Hindu: "the mind."* Manasa is intellect and capacity for learning.

MANDA, "MAHN-dah"—*Hindu: "goddess of the occult."*

MANDALA, "mahn-dah-LAH" or "MAHN-dah-lah"—*Sanskrit: "circle" or "round."* This usually refers to the stars and planets, or to groups of people, but the circle has always been a mystical symbol in all cultures because it has no beginning or end. In Eastern religious art, the mandala is a pattern of circles within circles. See also MANDEL(L)A.

MANDARA, "mahn-DAH-rah"—*Hindu: "the counselor or counseling tree."* **DARA.** In Hinduism, this is a mythological tree.

MANDEANA, MANDA, "man-dee-AH-nah" and "MAHN-dah"—*Aramaic: "knowing" or "having knowledge."* **MANDEA, MANDIANA.** The Mandeans are a religious group, still found in the Middle East in small numbers. They claim to be descendants of John the Baptist, and believe in the God of Abraham—like the Christians, Jews, and Muslims. Their main religious goal is to achieve *Manda da Hayye,* Knowledge of Life, which will bring them closer to God. **DEANA, DIANA.** M

MANDEL(L)A, "man-DELL-uh" or "MAN-duh-luh"—*French: "almond"; Native American: "ceremonial shield or banner."* **MANDALA.** The Native American mandella is the decorative shield or banner used in a variety of ceremonies. Some mandellas are quite elaborate, decorated with leather, gems, feathers, fabric, and carved ornaments. **MANDY.** M

MANDY. See AMANDA, MANDEL(L)A.

MANSI, "MAHN-see"—*Native American Hopi: "plucked flower."*

MANTISSA, "man-TIHS-sah"—*Etruscan: "a trifle."*

MANUELLA. See EMMANUELLE, IMMANUELLE.

MANUKA, "muh-NOO-kah"—*Polynesian: "dove."*

MARAIIN, "mah-RYE-ihn"—*Australian Aborigine: "sacred."* **MARAIA(H); MAREIIN** (mah-RAY-ihn). Among the aborigines, *maraiin* are the rituals performed for and to the Earth Mother. M

MARAM, "mah-RAHM"—*Arabic: "aspiration."*

MARASCA, "mah-RAHS-kah"—*Italian: "black cherry."* The marasca is a dark cherry grown in Dalmatia that is used to produce the liqueur maraschino.

MARCA, "MARK-ah"—*Celtic: "mare," or version of Markie: "of Mars."* See also MARKIE. M

MARCELLA. See MARKIE.

MARCIA, MARCY. See MARKIE.

MARDELL(E), "mahr-DEHL"—*English: "little valley by the sea."* **MARTELL(E).** M

MARGARET, "MAHR-gah-reht"—*traditionally Greek: "pearl"; but also French: "daisy" and Avestan: "child of the light."* Now dive for the pearl of your choice (or pluck the best daisy): **GITTA, MARGIT, RITTA**—Eastern European; **GRETCHEN** (GREHT-chehn)—German; **MAG** (MAHG), **MARGA, MARGARETA, META**—Swedish; **MAGRIT** (mah-GREET), **MARGIT** (mahr-GHEET or mahr-ZHEET)—Finnish; **MAI,** **MAJ** (MAH-ee or MY), **MAJA** (MAH-ee-ah or MY-ah)—Danish; **MAIRÉAD** (mah-EER-ahd)—Irish Gaelic; **MAIRGHREAD** (MYRE-grehd or MARE-grade)—Scottish Gaelic; **MAISIE** (MAY-zee), **MARJORIE**—Scottish; **MALGORZATA** (mahl-gohr-ZHAT-ah)—Polish; **MARETE** (mah-REH-teh), **MARIT** (mah-REET), **METTE** (MEH-teh), **RITA**—Norwegian; **MARGALIT** (mahr-gah-LEET)—Israeli; **MARGARIDA**—Portuguese; **MARGARIQUE** (mahr-gah-REEK)—French; **MARGUERITE** (mahr-gheh-REET)—French; **MARGHERITA** (mahr-gare-EE-tah)—Italian; **MARGHETTA, MARGHETTE** (mahr-GEHT)—German; **MARGO, MARGOSHA**—Russian; **MARGRET; MARGRETHE** (mahr-GREH-teh)—Dutch; **MARGUERITA** (mahr-gay-REE-tah), **MARIQUITA** (mah-rih-KEE-tah)—Spanish; **MARJARITA, MARJETTA**—Slavic; **MEG, MEGAN** (MAY-gun)—Irish; **MEGGI(E), MEGHAN** (MAY-gahn)—Welsh. The names of many saints, queens, and princesses are on this list. **MADGE; MAGGI(E), MAGGY, MARGEE, MARGI(E), MARGY, MARJEE, MARJI(E), MARJY; MIDGE; PEGGY; RITA.** See also GRETA.

MARGAY, "MAHR-gay"—*Native American Tupi: "wild cat."*

MARGO, "MAHR-goh"—*Russian version of Margaret: "pearl."* **MARGA, MARGALO**—Swedish; **MARGAUX** (MAHR-goh), **MARGOT** (MAHR-goh)—French; **MARGOLA**—Italian. See also MARGARET.

MARIA, MARIE. See MARY/MARI.

MARIAH. See MORIA(H).

MARIANNE. See MARION.

MARILYN, "MARE-ih-lihn"—*English compound of Marie and Lynne: "waterfall by the sea," "bitter stream," or "stream flowing to the ocean."* **MARILYNNE.** Marilyn Monroe was born Norma Jean Baker, but she took the name "Marilyn" as a redheaded teen model because it was the name of one of her mother's favorite actresses. Marilyn became a platinum blonde actress and icon. She once said, "A sex symbol becomes a thing; I hate being a thing." See also LYN(N).

MARINA, "mah-REE-nah"—*Latin: "sea maiden" or "sea nymph."* **MAREN, MARENA, MARNEE, MARNIE; MARINE**—French and Nordic; **MARINOCHKA** (mah-ree-NOTCH-kah)—Russian. Marina is one of the Christian saints. Marina Sirtis is a petite, sloe-eyed actress, best known for playing Deanna Troi in the TV series *Star Trek: The Next Generation.* **RINA.**

MARINI, "mah-REE-nee"—*Swahili: "healthy" or "fresh."* **MARNI(E).**

MARION, "MARE-ee-on" or "MAHR-ee-on"—*sideways from Markie, Latin: "warlike" or "rebellious," or "of Mary."* **MARIAN, MARIANNA, MARIANNE; MARIEN, MARIENNE; MARIONNE.** See also MARY/MARI.

MARISA, "mah-REE-sah" or "mah-REE-zah"—*Latin: "laughter of the ocean" or "sea star"; Greek: "mermaid."* **MARIS, MARYS, MARYSA, MERIS, MERISA; MARISHA**—Russian; **MARISSA** (mah-RISS-ah). This is the name of one of the Christian saints. Marisa Tomei is an Academy award-winning actress.

MARIT, "MAH-riht" or "mah-REET"—*Aramaic: "lady" or "mistress."*

MARITA, "mah-REE-tah" or "MAH-ree-tah"—*German: combination of Mary and Rita.* Please see those individual names for the great variety of combined meanings.

MARJANI, "mar-JAH-nee"—*Swahili: "coral."*

MARJORIE. See MARGARET.

MARKIE, "MARK-ee"—*Latin: "of Mars (the god of war and power)" or "belonging to Mars"; Greek: "tender"; Celtic: "mare."* **MARCA, MARCEE, MARCI(E), MARCY; MARCELINA** (mahr-sheh-LEE-nah), **MARGISIA** (mahr-GHIH-see-ah), **MARZENA**—Polish; **MARCELINE** (mahr-seh-LEEN or mahr-cheh-LEEN), **MARCEL(L)INA, MARCEL(L)INE**—Italian and Portuguese; **MARCELLA** (mahr-SEHL-ah or mahr-CHEH-lah)—Italian and Latin; **MARCELLE**—French; **MARCELY** (mahr-SHEH-lee); **MARCIA, MARSHA; MARKEE, MARKEY, MARKY.** This name has three very different words that could serve as an origin. Pick one! See MARTINE. M

MARLA. See MARLENE.

MARLENE, "mahr-LEEN"—*German and English version of Madeline: "high tower" or "woman of Magdala."* **MARILYN, MARLYN; MARLA, MARLEE, MARLEEN, MARLEY; MARLENA, MARLIE, MARLINA, MARLINE.** Marlene Dietrich was a one-of-a-kind German actress and singer who got her first Hollywood break in the 1930s. It was rumored that she even participated in espionage for the United States during World War II. See also MADELINE.

MARLEY, "MAHR-lee"—*English: "seaside meadow or clearing."* **MARLEA, MARLEE, MARLEIGH.** Reggae singer Bob Marley was a strong supporter of human rights. See also MARLENE. M

MARLO, "MAHR-loh"—*Latin/German: "sea lion"; Latin/Norse: "lover of the sea"; English: "hills near the ocean."* **MARLIS.** Marlo Thomas is an actress known for her work in television.

MARMARA, "mahr-MAHR-ah"—*Greek: "flashing" or "glittering."* The Sea of

Marmara is between Europe and Asia.

MARMIONNE, "MAHR-mee-ahn" or "mahr-mee-AHN"—*Bretagne: "tiny one."* **MARMIENNE.** M

MARNI(E). See MARINA, MARINI, MARNINA.

MARNINA, "mahr-NEE-nah"—*Hebrew: "rejoice"; Latin: "daughter of the sea."* **MARNI(E), NINA(H).**

MARQUETTE, "mahr-KEHT"—*French: as a noun, "emblem," "flag," "banner"; as a verb, "to inlay with precious stone" or "to inlay with decorative (or contrasting) material."* M

MARRAM, "MAHR-am"—*Norse: "beach grass" or "grassy dune."* **MARAM.** M

MARSHA. See MARKIE.

MARTHA, "MAHR-thah"—*Aramaic: "noblewoman."* **MARCSA** (MAHR-chah), **MARTUS(H)KA** (mahr-TOOS[H]-kah)—Hungarian; **MARTA, MARTE** (MAHR-teh)—Norwegian; **MÄRTE**—Swedish; **MARTELLA, MARTELLE** (mahr-TEHL)—German and Slavic; **MARTHE** (MAHRT[-eh])—French; **MARTHENA, MARTHENE, MARTHINI, MARITHA**—Western/Southern European; **MARTILA** (mahr-TEE-lah), **MARTITA**—Eastern/Northern European. The Martha of the New Testament was a friend of Jesus' who spent a lot of time worrying about the household chores. Jesus told her there were more important things in life than that fresh lemon scent. She is patron saint of housewives and domestic workers.

MARTINE, "mahr-TEEN"—*Latin: "of Mars"; Celtic: "mare"; English: "the martin bird" or "a marten."* **MARCI** (MAHR-tsee), **MARCILKA** (mahr-TSEEL-kah)—Hungarian; **MARTEEN, MARTENE, MARTINA; MARTYNA**—Russian. Tennis player Martina Navratilova enjoyed unparalleled success and longevity in her athletic career. **MARTI(E), MARTY.** See also MARKIE. M

MARSH, "MARSH"—*English: "marsh."* **CHOTT**—Arabic; **ESTAING, ÊTANG, LANDE**—French; **HAMUN** (hah-MOON)—Persian; **UST**—Russian.

MARY, MARI, "MARE-ee" and "MAH-ree"—*traditionally, Hebrew: "bitter"; but also Latin: "sea"; Aramaic: "wished-for child"; Sanskrit: "protection from illness" or "keeper of health."* **MACIA** (MAH-tsee-ah), **MARYSIA** (mah-REE-see-ah)—Greek; **MAIR** (MARE), **MAIRE** (MAY-reh)—Scottish; **MÁIRE** (MAH-eer-eh), **MAIRONA**—Irish; **MANETTE, MANON** (mah-NOHN—put the "NOHN" in your nose), **MARIETTE** (mah-ree-EHT), **MARYETTE**—French; **MANIA** (MAH-nyah), **MANKA**—Polish; **MANYA, MARA** (MAH-rah), **MARUSYA** (mah-ROO-shyah), **MASHA** (MAH-shah), **MASHENKA** (mah-SHEN-kah), **MURA**—Russian; **MARA, MAREA** (mah-RAY-ah), **MARIANA** (mah-ree-AH-nah), **MARIETTA** (mah-ree-EH-tah)—Italian; **MARA, MARIA, MARIE; MAREN**—Norwegian; **MARIEKE** (MAH-ree-ehk-eh), **MARYK** (MAH-reek), **MIES, MIETJE** (MEE-tyeh)—Dutch; **MARIKA** (mah-REE-kah or MAHR-ee-kah)—Eastern European; **MARIS(H)KA** (mah-REES(H)-kah)—Hungarian; **MARIYAMMAN** (MAH-ree-yah-mahn)—Tamil and Sanskrit; **MARJA** (MAHR-yah), **MARJETTE** (MAHR-yeht)—Swedish; **MARYAM**—Arabic; **MIREN** (mee-rehn)—Basque; **MIRIAM**—Israeli and Persian; **MOLLY**—Gaelic. The Mari in the Sanskrit derivation is a village goddess who protects against disease. The "bitterness" in the Hebrew derivation comes from the bitter herb *maror* used in the Jewish Seder ceremony, a reminder of the "bitterness" of the lives of the Hebrews in captivity before Moses led them from Egypt. Probably the most famous Mary is Mary, the mother of Jesus, and because of her, Mary and its variations have long been favorites of European nobles and rulers, and of those without any power at all. Several saints' names are also on this list. See also MARION.

MASA, "MAH-sah"—*Japanese: "straightforward."*

MASIKA, "mah-SEEK-ah"—*Swahili: "born in the rain."*

MATA, "MAH-tah"—*Hindu: "mother."*

MATANA, "mah-TAH-nah"—*Hebrew: "gift."* **TAN(N)A.**

MATILDA, "mah-TIHL-dah"—*Teutonic: "brave in battle."* **MATHILDA** (mah-TIHL-dah or mah-TEEL-dah), **MATHILDE** (mah-TEELD), **MATILDE** (mah-TEELD); **MATYIDY** (mah-TYEE-dee)—Polish. Matildas have been Tuscan countesses and English queens. **MATTIE, MATTY; TILDA.**

MATIN, "mah-TAN" ("AN" in your nose)—*French: "morning."* **MATINE** (mah-TEEN). M

MATTHEA, "MATH-ee-ah" or "mah-TAY-ah"—*Hebrew: "gift of God."* **MATHEA** (mah-TAY-ah), **MATTEA; MAT(H)ELLA, MAT(H)ELLE** (mah-TEHL), **MATT(H)ELLE**—French; **MATTHIA** (mah-TYE-ah or mah-THY-ah)—Greek; **MÁTYÁS** (MAH-tyahs)—Hungarian. **MATTI(E), MATTY.** M

MATTI(E), MATTY. See MATILDA, MATTHEA.

MAUDE, "MAWD"—*Teutonic: "heroine."* **MAUD.** Maude Adams is a Swedish-American actress and model. **MAUDIE.**

MAUNDY, "MAWN-dee"—*English: "commandment."*

MAUREEN. See MAURICIA.

MAURICIA, "MORE-eese-yah"—*Latin: "a Moor, Moorish" or "child of the black one"; Hebrew: "God is my teacher."* **MAURA**—Italian; **MAURA, MAUREEN, MAURENE**—Irish; **MAURIDSJE** (moh-RIHDS-yeh), **MAURITSJE** (moh-RIHTS-yeh)—Dutch; **MAURYCY** (moh-REE-see)—Polish; **MAVRA** (MAHV-rah)—Russian; **MOIRA** (MOY-rah)—Scottish and Welsh; **MORENA** (moh-RAY-nah)—Spanish; **MUIRA, MUIRIS** (myoo-EER-ees)—Irish Gaelic. The Moors, Arabs from northern Africa, had their heaviest initial contact with Europeans during the Crusades. Several saint names are on this list. Maureen O'Sullivan and Maureen O'Hara are both striking redheaded Irish actresses who did their most notable work in the middle of this century. M

MAVIS, "MAY-vihss"—*Celtic: "songbird"; French: "the singing thrush."* **MAEVE, MAVE.**

MAXINE, "MACKS-een"—*Latin: "greatest" or "most."* **MAKIMA**—Polish; **MASSIMA** (MAH-see-mah)—Italian; **MAXIME** (mahk-SEEM)—French; **MAXIMA**—Greek. M

MAY, MAE, "MAY"—*Latin: "the month of May"; Anglo-Saxon: "kinswoman."* **GOGWATSU** (goh-GWAHT-soo)—Japanese; **MAGGIA** (MAHJ-jee-ah)—Italian; **MAI** (MEH)—French, German, and Indonesian; **MAJ** (MAY)—Scandinavian. The traditional flower of this month is the lily of the valley, and the traditional birthstone is the emerald. May comes from Maia, a goddess in both Greek and Roman mythology.

MAYA, "MY-ah"—*Mayan: "my people, our people, us."* This is a tribe name for a group of people once inhabiting all of

Central America. They were an architecturally, artistically, and mathematically advanced race with a complex religious pantheon. Some of their descendants survive in southern Mexico, Guatemala, and Honduras. See also MAIA/MAYA.

MAZAL, "MAH-zahl"—*Hebrew: "luck" or "star."* **MAZALA.**

MBITA, "m'BEE-tah"—*Swahili: "born on a cold night."*

MEAD(E), "MEED"—*English: "meadow"; Celtic: "honey wine."* Mead is an old traditional Celtic and Anglo-Saxon alcoholic beverage made from spiced honey. M

MEAVE, "MEEV" or "MAVE"—*Irish: "joy."*

MEDA, "MAY-dah" or "MEH-dah"—*Native American: "prophetess."*

MEDEA, "meh-DEE-ah"—*Greek: "divine sorceress."* In Greek mythology, Medea was a renowned sorceress encountered by the hero Jason in his search for the Golden Fleece.

MEDINA, "meh-DEE-nah"—*Arabic: "the city."* **ALMADINAH, MADINAH, MEDINAH.** Medina is "the city" of the prophet Mohammed, and is sacred to Muslims.

MEE, "MEE"—*Korean: "pretty."* **MEE-MEE, MI-MI.** See also MEI.

MEGAN, "MAY-gun"—*Gaelic version of Margaret: "pearl."* **MEAGAN; MEGHAN**—Welsh. Actresses Meg Foster and Meg Ryan are probably responsible for the booming popularity of this old name. **MEG, MEGGI(E), MEGGY.** See also MARGARET.

MEGARA, "mee-GAH-rah" or "mee-GAYR-ah"—*Greek/Latin: "mighty or great dark one"; Greek: "grudge."* **MEGAERA, MEGAYRA.** Megara is one of the three

Furies in Greek and Roman myth who punished humans for their sins. **MEG, MEGGI(E), MEGGY.**

MEGGI(E). See MARGARET, MEGAN, MEGARA.

MEI, "MEH-ee"—*Chinese: "pretty."* **MEI-MEI.** See also MEE.

MEIRA, "meh-EER-ah"—*Hebrew: "light" or "enlightened"; Teutonic: "farmer."* M

MELANIE, "MEHL-uh-nee"—*Greek: "black one" or "dark one."* **MELA, MELKA**—Eastern European; **MELAIN(E)**—German; **MELANEE, MELANI, MELANY; MELANIA** (meh-LAH-nee-ah)—Greek; **MELINA** (meh-LEE-nah)—Italian and Spanish. The two saints named Melania were grandmother and granddaughter. Actress Melanie Griffith plays both drama and light comedy.

MELANTHA, "meh-LAHN-thah"—*Greek: "dark flower."*

MELINA, "meh-LEE-nah"—*Greek: "canary."* This word refers to both the bird and the color.

MELINDA, "meh-LIHN-dah" or "may-LEEN-dah"—*English/Spanish: "my beautiful one" or "gentle."* **MALINA, MALINDA, MELINA.** Melinda Dillon is an actress.

MELISSA, "meh-LIH-sah"—*Arabic/Hebrew: "servant of Jesus"; Greek: "honeybee."* **MAELISA**—Irish; **MALISE** (mah-LEESE)—Scottish; **MAOLÍOSA** (mao-LYOH-sah)—Irish Gaelic; **MELESSA, MELISA; MELITTA** (meh-LEE-tah), **MELOSA**—Spanish; **MELUSINE** (MEH-loo-seen)—French. Melissa is another name for lemon balm, the spicy-sour leaves of which are used in herbal and folk medicine. Melusina or Melusine is the name of a fairy who often shows up in French romance stories. **MEL, MELLI(E).** See also MILLICENT.

MELODY, "MEHL-oh-dee"—*Greek: "song."* **MELODI(E). MEL, MELLI(E).**

MELORA, "meh-LOH-rah"—*Greek: "golden apple."*

MENSA, "MEHN-sah"—*Latin: "table" or "mountain."* The constellation Mensa is a South Pole configuration that follows the Sun at dusk during February. When the Antarctic sun disappears at the solstice in June, Mensa is the table upon (or under) which it sits to wait out the winter.

MERCEDES, "mur-SED-eez" or "mur-SAY-deez"—*Latin: "merciful."* **MERCEDA; MERCEDALIA** (mur-seh-DAY-lia)—*Greek;* **MERCEDAS**—Dutch and Nordic; **MERCEDE** (mur-CHAY-deh)—Italian; **MERCILLE**—French. The luxury car Mercedes was named after the daughter of its developer. **MERCIA, MERCY.**

MEREDITH, "MARE-eh-dihth"—*Welsh: "guardian of the sea."* **MEREDYDD** (MEH-reh-dihth)—Welsh; **MERIDITH. M**

MERLE, "MURL"—*Latin: "blackbird"; English: "swirl (of color)."* **MERIL; MERLA, MERLENE, MERLINA, MERLINE, MERRILL, MERRYL, MERYL** (MARE-ihl). Actress Merle Oberon was a Briton, raised in India, probably best known for her appearances in *Wuthering Heights, The Divorce of Lady X,* and *The Private Life of Henry the Eighth,* and for the mystique she created about her background. Meryl Streep is an award-winning actress. **M**

MERRY, MERRIE, "MARE-ee"—*English: "pleasant, jolly."* **MERIE, MERRIELLA, MERRIELLE, MERRILEE, MERY.** This name is also used as a variant of the name Mary. See also MARY/MARI.

MERTICE, "mur-TEESE"—*English: "renowned for pleasantness."*

MESHA, "MAY-shah"—*Hindu: equivalent to Aries.*

MESSINA, "meh-SEE-nah"— *Latin: "a middle child."* **MESSINE. SINA.**

META, "MEH-tah" or "MAY-tah"—*Latin: "ambitious."* **METTA.**

METEA, "meh-TEE-ah"—*Greek: "gentle."*

METRA, "MEHT-rah"—*Ancient Persian: "goddess of the Moon."* Metra's love was said to penetrate everywhere.

METTA, "MEH-tah"—*Pali: "love for all."* See also META.

METTE, "MEHT"—*Old English: "dream" or "to dream."* See also MARGARET.

METTEYA, "MEH-teh-yah" or "meh-TAY-ah"—*Pali: "friendly."* **MAITREYA** (MAY-treh-yah or may-TRAY-ah)—Hindu; **MI LO FO** (MEE LOH FOH), **MILOFO**—Chinese; **MIROKO** (mee-ROH-koh), **MIROKU** (mee-ROH-koo)—Japanese. Metteya is supposed to be one of the coming incarnations of the late Siddhartha Gautama, the Great Buddha, who is also said to have lived other lives long in the past.

MHINA, "m'HEE-nah"—*Swahili: "delightful."*

MIA, "MEE-ah"—*Latin: "mine."* Actresses Mia Farrow and Mia Sara have boosted the recognition of this name.

MICHAELA, "MY-kah-lah" or "mih-KAY-lah"—*Hebrew: traditionally "who is like God?" but also "who is the Lord?" and "stream."* **MAHAIL, MAHAILA, MAHALIA, MAKIS**—Greek; **MICAELA** (mih-kay-LAH or mih-KAY-lah), **MICHA** (MEE-khah—"kh" like you're clearing your throat), **MICHLA**—Israeli; **MICHAEL** (MY-kahl)—Hebrew; **MICHAILYA** (mee-KAY-lyah), **MIKHAILYA, MISHENKA** (mee-SHEHN-kah)—Russian;

MICHALA (MEE-kahl-ah), **MICHALINA** (MEE-kah-leen-ah)—Polish; **MICHELINE** (mish-LEEN), **MICHELLE** (mee-SHELL)—French; **MICHELE** (mee-SHEH-ieh)—Italian; **MICHIELLE** (mih-CHYEHL)—Dutch; **MICI** (MEE-chee), **MIHÁLYA** (MEE-HAH-lyah), **MIKA**—Hungarian; **MIGUELA, MIGUELITA**—Spanish; **MIKAELA**—Swedish; **MIKEL(E)** (mee-kehl[-eh])—Basque; **MIKKELE** (mihk-KEH-leh)—Norwegian. The Archangel Micha-el, called "the Prince of Light" and associated with the Last Judgement, is seen as God's warrior, and is often represented with a sword and shield. Michaela, the female version of Michael, is growing in popularity, probably because of Michaela Quinn, the heroine on *Dr. Quinn: Medicine Woman*. **MICK, MICKEY, MICKI, MICKY, MIKKI; MIKE, MIKEY.** M

MICHAL, "mee-KHAHL" ("KH" like you're hocking up something noteworthy)—*Hebrew: "stream" or "brook."* **MICHALY.** M

MICHELLE. See MICHAELA.

MICHIKO, "MEE-chee-koh" or "mee-CHEE-koh"—*Japanese: "beauty and wisdom."* **MACHIKO.**

MICKI(E). See MICHAELA.

MIDORI, "mee-DOH-ree"—*Japanese: "green."* Japanese violinist Midori captured the United States by storm as a young prodigy in the 1980s.

MIGINA, "mee-GHEE-nuh" or "mee-JEE-nuh"—*Native American Omaha: "the returning moon."* Give this name to a child born on full-moon or second-half-moon nights, that is the full moon or second half moon of the lunar cycle—check a calendar. See also MAGENA.

MIGNON, "meen-YAWN"—*French: "darling" or "cute."* **MIGNONETTE, MIGNONNE.**

MIGUELA. See MICHAELA.

MIKA, "MEE-kah" (for the first derivation) or "MY-kah" (for the second derivation)—*Japanese: "new moon"; Native American Creek: "the clever raccoon."* See also MICHAELA. M

MIKASA, "mee-KAH-sah"—*Native American Omaha: "coyote."* **MIKI, MIKKI.**

MILENA, "mee-LAY-nah"—*German: "mild."* See also LUDMILLA.

MILI, "MEE-lee"—*Israeli: "who is for me."*

MILILANI, "mee-lee-LAW-nee"—*Hawaiian: "praise" or "worthy of praise."*

MILLI(E). See EMILY, MILLICENT.

MILLICENT, "MIHL-eh-sehnt"—*German: "strong worker."* **MELICENT, MELLICENT, MILICENT MILISENT, MILLISENT; MELISANDE** (may-lee-SAHND), **MELUSINE** (mehl-yoo-SEEN or meh-looh-SEEN)—French; **MELISENDA** (may-lee-SEHN-dah)—Spanish. Melusina or Melusine is the name of a fairy who shows up often in French romance stories. **MILLI, MILLI(E), MILLY.** See also MELISSA.

MIMI, "MEE-mee"—*Greek diminutive of Demetra/Demetrius: "of Demeter (the goddess of the harvest)"; French from Miriam(?): "wished-for child"; Australian Aborigine: "gentle or good spirit."* These names are also diminutives of a variety of names with the "MEE" sound prominent. See also MEE, MEI, MIRIAM.

MINA, "MEE-nah"—*Hindu: equivalent to Pisces.*

MINAL, "mee-NAHL"—*Native American: "fruit."* M

MINDEL, "MIHN-dehl" or "MEEN-dehl"—*Hebrew: "sea of bitterness."* **MINDELA, MINDI(E). MINDY, MINAH, MINNA, MINTZE(H).** See also MIRKA.

MINDY. See MINDEL, MINNA.

MINERVA, "mee-NUR-vah"—*Latin.* Minerva was the Roman goddess of wisdom, strategy, purity, invention, and martial arts. **MINNI(E), MINNY.**

MINKA, "MIHN-kah"—*Teutonic: "resolute."*

MINNA, "MIH-nah"—*German: "love."* **MINA, MINDI(E), MINDY, MINETTA, MINETTE; MINNI(E), MINNY.**

MINOA, "mih-NOH-ah"—*Greek.* The island of Minoa once had one of the most advanced civilizations of the pre-Christian era.

MIRA, "MEER-ah"—*Russian: "earth" or "peace."* **MYRA.** M

MIRABELLE, MIRABEAU, "MEE-rah-behl/boh"—*Latin: "wondrous beauty."* **MIRABEL, MIRABELLA**—Italian and Spanish.

MIRARI, "mee-rah-ree"—*Basque: "miracle."*

MIRCEA, "meer-SEE-ah"—*Latin: "astonishing."* **MIRCIA.** M

MIREILLE, "mee-RAY(-eh)"—*French: "miracle."* **MIRELLE.**

MIREMBE, "mih-REHM-beh"—*African Luganda: "peace."* **NAMIREMBE. MIREH.** M

MIRI, "MEE-ree"—*Gypsy: "mine."* See also MIRIAM.

MIRIAM, "MEE-ree-um"—*version of Mary, traditionally: "bitter"; but also Aramaic: "wished-for child."* **MARYAM** (MARE-yahm)—Arabic; **MIMI**—French; **MIRIT** (mih-REET), **MITZI**—Israeli. In the Old Testament/Tanakh, Miriam was the sister of Moses and Aaron.

MIRA, MIRI. See also MARY/MARI.

MIRKA, "MEER-kah"—*Hebrew: "sea of bitterness."* **MIRKA, MIRTZA, MIRTZE.** See also MINDEL.

MISTY, "MIHS-tee"—*English: "cloudy," "misty," or "moist."* **MISTIE.**

MITENA, "mee-TAY-nah"—*Native American Ojibwa: "born under a coming or new moon."* This name is given to children born on nights when the Moon is in the first third of its lunar cycle, from the time the Moon is new but before it becomes full. If you're not sure about the cycle, consult a calendar.

MITSU, "MEET-soo"—*Japanese: "light."* **MITSUKO.** M

MIWA, "MEE-wah"—*Japanese: "far-seeing."*

MIYO, "mee-YOH"—*Japanese: "beautiful child."* **MIYOKO.** M

MOANNA, "moh-AHN-nah"—*Polynesian: "the ocean."* **MOANA**—Hawaiian.

MOHALA, "moh-HAH-luh"—*Hawaiian: "in bloom" or "blossoming."*

MOINA, "MOY-nah"—*Celtic: "gentle" or "soft."* **MOYNA.**

MOIRA, "MOY-rah"—*Irish: "long-haired"; Celtic: "great"; Greek: "the Fates."* **MORRIN**—Irish; **MOYRA; MUIREANN**(moo-EE-rahn or MOO-ee-rahn)—Irish Gaelic. In Greek mythology, the Fates were three daughters of Zeus who determined the path of human lives. See also FOMORIA, MAURICIA.

MOLLY, "MAW-lee"—*Gaelic form of Mary: "wished-for child."* **MOLLIE.** Molly Ringwald is an actress. See also MARY/ MARI.

MOMI, "MOH-mee"—*Hawaiian: "pearl."*

MONA, "MOH-nah"—*Greek: "solitary";*

Arabic: "wish"; Irish: "angel." This is the name of a Christian saint who was noted for her patience.

MONDAY, "MUN-day"—*Teutonic: "the Moon's day."* **ADWOA** (ah-dwoh-AH)—African Fante; **GETSUYOOBI** (geht-soo-YOO-bee)—Japanese; **JUMATATU** (joo-mah-TAH-too)—Swahili; **LUNDI** (LUHN-dee)—French; **MONTAG** (MAWN-tog)—German. M

MONICA, "MAW-nee-kah"—*Latin: "advisor"; Greek: "merit"; Irish: "noble."* **MONIKA;** **MONIQUE** (moh-NEEK)—French.

MONIFA, "MOW-nee-fuh" or "moh-NEE-fah"—*African Yoruba: "she is lucky."*

MONIQUE. See MONICA.

MONTANA, "mawn-TAN-ah"—*Latin: "mountains."* **MONTAGNE** (mawn-TAN-yeh)—French; **MONTINA.**

MOON, "MOON"—*English: "moon."* **BULAN** (BOO-lahn)—Indonesian; **MÅNE** (MAWN-eh)—Scandinavian; **MWEZI** (MWAY-zee)—Swahili; **QAMAR** (KAH-mahr and kah-MAHR)—Arabic; **TSUKI** (TSOO-kee)—Japanese.

MORAGA, "moh-RAH-gah"—*Gaelic: "the Sun."*

MORASHA, "moh-RAH-shah"—*Hebrew: "inheritance."* **MORESHA.**

MORELA, "moh-RAY-lah"—*Polish: "apricot."* **MORELLA.**

MORGAN, "MORE-ghin/gan"—*Welsh: "dweller by the sea" or "the white ocean waters"; German: "morning."* **MORGANA, MORGANE, MORGANNE, MORGEN, MORGIN; MORGANCE** (mohr-GAHNTS)—French. In Arthurian legend, Morganne le Fay was the half-sister of King Arthur, and an enchantress whose powers rivalled those of Merlyn. TV diva Morgan Fairchild and actress Morgan Brittany have popularized this name. See also MORRIGAN. M

MORIA(H), "MOH-ree-ah"—*Hebrew: "God is my teacher."* **MARIAH** (MAHR-ee-ah or mah-RYE-ah); **MORICE, MORIEL, MORIT** (moh-REET)—Israeli. The hill Moriah in Jerusalem is said to be the burial site of King Solomon. Singer Mariah (mah-RYE-ah) Carey has popularized both that spelling and that pronunciation of the name.

MORIE, "mo-REE-ay"—*Japanese: "the bay."*

MORLA, "MOHR-lah"—*Hebrew: "chosen by the Lord."*

MORNA, "MOHR-nah"—*Hebrew: "tender and gentle."*

MORRIGAN, "MOHR-ih-gan"—*Celtic: "great war queen."* Morrigan was a powerful deity in Celtic mythology, although this name has often been confused with Morgan, a Welsh god. See also MORGAN.

MORVENNE, "mohr-VEHN"—*Irish Gaelic: "grand blonde."* **MORVENNA, MORVINA.**

MORWENNA, "mohr-WEH-nah"—*Welsh or Celtic: "waves on the sea."* **MORWENNE.**

MOSELLE, "moh-ZEHL"—*Hebrew: "drawn/saved from the water"; Egyptian: "child."* **MOSELLA.** The Moselle or Mosel is a river that runs through France, Luxembourg, and Germany. **MO, MOE, MOSE, MOZE.** M

MOTEGA, "moh-TAY-gah"—*Native American: "new arrow."*

MOULINE, "moo-LEEN"—*French: "the mill."* **MOLINA**—Spanish and Portuguese.

MUFFY, MUFFIN, "MUHF-ee" and "MUHF-ihn"—*French: "soft."*

MUFIDAH, "moo-FEE-dah" or "MOO-fee-dah"—*Arabic: "useful."*

MUGISHA, "moo-GHEE-shah"—*African: "luck."* **MUGISA.**

MUNA, "moo-NAH"—*Arabic: "wish" or "desire."*

MUNIRA(H), "moo-NEER-ah"—*Arabic: "illuminating."* M

MURA, "moo-RAH"—*Japanese: "village."*

MURIEL, MURIELLE, "MYOO-ree-ehl" and "myoo-ree-EHL"—*Hebrew: "bittersweet"; Arabic: "myrrh"; Gaelic: "bright sea."* **MERIAL, MERIEL, MUIRGHEAL** (MYOO-ree-ehl), **MURIAL**—Irish Gaelic. The angel Muriel is one of the Dominions of the Judeo-Christian and Muslim tradition, angels who regulate the duties of other angels.

MURPHY, "MUR-fee"—*Irish: "sea warrior."* Murphy Brown is the hard-charging journalist on the popular TV show of the same name. M

MWAKA, "m'WAH-kah"—*Swahili: "born in the Springtime."* M

MWITA, "m'WEE-tah"—*Swahili: "summoner."*

MYRA, "MY-rah"—*Latin: "wondrous"; Greek: "fragrant"; Hebrew: "my messenger"; Old French: "quiet song."* **MIRA.**

MYRNA, "MUR-nah"—*Irish: "affection"* and *"beloved"; Arabic: "myrrh."* **MERNA, MORNA**—Irish; **MUIRNE** (MWEER-neh)—Irish Gaelic. Myrrh is a much-valued, aromatic resin used in many ways, including the preparation of incense, perfume, and medicine.

THE TOP FIVE

NICOLE
NATALIE
NATASHA
NAOMI
NINA

If your "N" name isn't here, perhaps it is a variant or a diminutive of another primary name.

NABAASA, "nah-BAH-ah-sah"—*African Runyankore: "omnipotent."*

NABIHAH, "nah-BEE-hah"—*Arabic: "clever."*

NABILA, "NAHB-eel-ah"—*Arabic: "noble."* NABILAH. M

NACIENNE, "nah-SYEN"—*Old French: "iridescent" or "mother of pearl(?)."* M

NADIA, "NAH-dyah"—*Eastern European: "hope."* NADÉGE (nah-DEHZH)—French; NADENKA, NADIYA (nah-DEE-yah), NADYA, NADYENKA (nah-DYEHN-kah), NADYSHA, NADYUSKA—Russian; NADEZHDA (nah-DEZH-dah), NADZIA (NAHD-zyah)—Polish; NADINA, NADINE—German and Italian. Romanian Nadia Comaneci was the first Olympic gymnast ever to receive a perfect score of 10 in competition; she did it seven times in 1976.

NADINE, "nah-DEEN" or "nay-DEEN"—*French diminutive of Bernadette: "courage of a bear."* NADEEN, NADENA, NADENE, NADETTE. See also NADIA.

NADIRA, "nah-DEER-ah"—*Arabic: "rare."*

NAGESA, "nah-GAY-sah"—*African: "born during harvest."*

NAGISA, "nah-GHEE-sah"—*Japanese: "shore."*

NAHIMANA, "nah-hee-MAH-nah"—*Native American Sioux: "the mystic."*

NAI'IMAH, "NYE-ee-mah"—*African: "she will live a happy life."* NA'IMAH.

NAILAH, "NAH-ee-lah"—*Moroccan: "successful one."*

NAIRN(E), "NAYRN" or "NAH-eern"—*Scottish: "lime trees or alder trees by the river."* NAIRNE. Nairn is a region in the south of Scotland.

NAJA, "NAH-juh" or "NAH-huh"—*Native American Navajo: "silver hands" or "priceless hands."*

NAJIYAH, "nah-ZHEE-yah"—*Arabic: "safe."*

NAKOTAH, "nah-KOH-tah"—*Native American Sioux: "friend to all(?)."* This was one of the three tribes in the Great Sioux Nation. M

NALANI, "nah-LAH-nee"—*Hawaiian: "calm skies."*

NALUKEA, "nah-loo-KAY-uh"—*Hawaiian: "white wave."*

NAMDEVA, "nahm-DAY-vah"—*Sanskrit: "name of the deity."*

NAMI, "nah-MEE"—*Japanese: "wave."* **NAMIKO.** M

NAMIDA, "nah-MEED-ah"—*Native American Chippewa: "the star dancer."* Namid was a coyote who wanted to dance with the stars above. As it is, coyotes, through their howling, can only provide musical accompaniment to the cosmic ballet. M

NANCY, "NAN-see" or "NAHN-see"—*pet form of Anne: "grace"; also a French place name.* **NAINSÍ** (NINE-shee)—*Irish Gaelic;* **NANCSI(E)** (NAHN-chee)—*Hungarian;* **NANETTE, NANITA.** Nancy Davis made a few fair films in the 1950s, but is best known as the second wife of Ronald Reagan. **NAN, NANNA, NANNI(E), NANNY; NANCE, NANCEE, NANCI(E); NUSA, NUSI.** See also ANN(E).

NANDI, "NAHN-dee"—*African Zulu: "her father's child"; Sanskrit: "happy" or "satisfied."* **NANDA**—*Hindu.* The African Nandi was the ambitious and proud mother of Shaka, king of the Zulu Nation. She ruled in tandem with her son who honored her by making her a queen, something she deserved. The Nandi or Nanda of Hinduism was a mythical cowherd—in some tellings, a cow—who reared the baby god Krishna.

NANI, "NAH-nee"—*Polynesian: "beauty."*

NANTALE, "nahn-TAH-lay"—*African Luganda: "a girl from the clan with the Lion Totem."*

NAOKI, "nah-OH-kee"—*Japanese: "straight tree."*

NAOMI, "nay-OH-mee"—*Hebrew: "pleasure."* This name is a bad speller's dream! Anything goes: **NAOMA, NEOMA, NIOMA; NEOMI, NIOMI, NYOMI.** Redheaded country singer Naomi Judd has contributed to the rise in popularity of this old name. See also NOAMI.

NAPEA, "nah-PAY-ah"—*Latin: "valley nymph."*

NARA, "NAH-rah"—*Japanese: "oak tree"; Celtic: "happy."*

NARADA, "nah-RAH-dah"—*Sanskrit: "water-giver" or "water-bearer."* M

NARI, "NAH-ree"—*Japanese: "clap of thunder."* **NARIKO.** M

NARMADA, "nahr-MAH-dah"—*Hindu: "gives pleasure."* Narmada is also the name of a river in India that is sacred to Hindus.

NASCHA, "NAS-chah"—*Native American Navajo: "an owl."*

NASTASSIA, "nah-STAH-syah"—*version of Anastasia: "resurrection."* **NASTASIA, NASTAS(S)JA, NASTASSA, NASTAS(S)YA, NATASCHA, NATASHA.**

NATA, "NAH-tah"—*Native American: "speaker" or "creator"; Hindu: "dancer"; Polish: "hope."* **NATIA.**

NATALIE, "NAT-uh-lee" or "NAH-tah-lee"—*Old French: "birthday girl" or "born at Christmastime"; Hebrew: "wreath."* **NATALIA** (nah-TAHL-yah), **NATALYA, NATASHENKA** (nah-tah-SHEHN-kah)—*Russian;* **NATASCHA, NATASHA** (nah-TAW-shah)—*Eastern European;* **NATHALIE** (nah-TAH-lee)—*French.* Several saints and nobles have had these names, one of which was Saint Natalia, who converted her husband—a high-ranking Roman official—to Christianity in the second or third century. Natalie Wood was an actress noted for her "yearning youth" roles in several big films of the 1950s and 1960s. **NAT, NATTI(E); TASCHA,**

TASCHI(E), TASHA (TAW-shah), **TASHI(E).**

NATANIA, "nah-TAHN-yah"—*Hebrew: "the given" or "the gift."* **NATANIELLA, NA-TANIELLE, NATANYA; NATHANIELLA, NA-THANIELLE. NAT, NATTY; TANIA, TANYA.** M

NATASHA. See NATASSIA, NATALIE.

NATHA, "NAH-thah"—*Sanskrit: "refuge."*

NAZIHAH, "nah-ZEE-hah"—*Arabic: "honest."*

NAZIRAH, "nah-ZEE-rah"—*Arabic: "an equal."*

NECI, "NEH-tsee"—*Hungarian: "fiery."*

NED(D)A, "NEE-dah" and "NEHD-ah"—*Slavic: "born on Sunday"; English: "guardian."* **NEDRA. NEDDI(E).** M

NEDIVAH, "NEHD-ih-vah" or "neh-DEE-vah"—*Hebrew: "generous."*

NEEMA, "neh-EE-mah" or "NEE-mah"—*Swahili: "born in our prosperity."*

NELDA, "NEHL-dah"—*English: "elder tree."*

NELL, "NEHL"—*Scotch-Irish: "cloud"; Celtic: "brave champion"; Scotch-Irish version of Helen: "luminous" or "light."* **NEILA, NELA; NIALLA**—*Irish Gaelic.* Nell Gwyn was a seventeenth-century English actress who was the mistress of Charles II. **NELLY.** See also HELEN.

NEMA, "NEE-mah"—*Greek: "thread"; Hebrew: "hair."* **NEMEA** (NEE-mee-ah or nee-MEE-ah). Nemea was a famous valley in ancient Greece, noted for the festival of the Nemean Games.

NEPHELE, "NEHF-eh-lee"—*Greek: "cloud."*

NEREA, "neh-ray-ah"—*Basque: "she is mine."*

NERISSA, "neh-RIH-sah" or "neh-REE-sah"—*Greek: "from the sea."* **NEREID** (NEH-ree-ihd), **NERICE, NERINE, NERISSE, NISSA.** In Greek myth, the Nereids are the fifty daughters of the god of the sea. Nereid is one of the moons of Neptune.

NEROLI, "NEE-roh-lee" and "nee-ROH-lee"—*Latin: "black" or "dark."* Neroli is the essential oil of orange blossoms, named after an Italian princess who is said to have been the first to discover this substance and use it in perfumery. **NERA.**

NESSA, "NEH-sah"—*Scandinavian: "the headlands" or "the promontory."* This is also a diminutive of names ending in "-esse" or "-essa," which usually have

---

NEW ENGLAND GIRLS' NAMES

Girls born in New England are likely to have the following names:

1. Jessica	6. Nicole	11. Brittany	16. Alexandra
2. Ashley	7. Emily	12. Lauren	17. Rebecca
3. Sarah	8. Stephanie	13. Kayla	18. Danielle
4. Samantha	9. Jennifer	14. Rachel	19. Victoria
5. Amanda	10. Elizabeth	15. Katherine	20. Melissa

something to do with gentleness, purity, sweetness. **NESHA, NESSI(E), NETIA.** See also AGNES.

NETSUKE, "neht-SOO-keh" or "NEHTS-keh"—*Japanese: "keeper of legend" or "keeper of magic."* Netsukes are special trinkets representing the lore and myth of Japan. They also serve to hold little pouches of magic herbs or stones in one's clothing.

NEVA, "NEE-vah" or "NEH-vah"—*Spanish: "bright and white or fair."*

NEVADA, "neh-VAH-dah"—*Spanish: "snow white."* M

NIABI, "nee-AH-bee"—*Native American: "fawn."*

NICKI(E). See NICOLE.

NICOLE, "nih-KOHL"—*Greek: "victory of the people."* **KOLENKA** (koh-LEHN-kah), **KOLYA, NIKITA** (nee-KEE-tah)—Russian; **NICCOLA** (NEE-koh-lah), **NICIA** (NEE-chee-ah)—Italian; **NICHELLE** (nee-SHEHL), **NICOLE** (nee-KOHL), **NICOLETTE**—French; **NICHOLA, NICHOLE, NICOL(L)A; NICKOL(L)A** (nih-KOH-lah or NEE-koh-lah), **NICKOLET-TA**—Eastern European; **NIKI, NIKOLA, NIKOLETA** (nee-koh-LEH-tah), **NIKOLIA** (nee-KOH-lee-ah)—Greek; **NIKOL(L)A**—Slavic. Several saints have borne the names on this list. **NICKI(E), NICKY; NIK, NIKI(E), NIKKI(E), NIKKY.** M

NIDA, "NEE-dah"—*Native American Omaha: "fairy."* **NIDAWI** ("little fairy" or "laughing fairy").

NIGESA, "nee-GEH-suh"—*African Lumasada: "born at harvest" or "born in the autumn."*

NILE, "NYLE"—*version of Neil: "champion or chief" or Egyptian: the great River Nile.* **NILA, NILES, NYLA, NYLES.** The Nile, which has supported and sustained Egypt for millennia, is one of the longest rivers in the world. M

NI'MAH, "NEE-mah" or "nee-MAH"—*Arabic: "a blessing."*

NIMUE, "NIH-myoo" or "NIHM-way"—*Phrygian: "the mists" or "the fog."* **NIMA.** In Arthurian legend, Nimue, the Lady of Broceliande, was a Breton enchantress and lover of Merlyn.

NINA, "NEE-nah"—*variant of Ann(e): "grace"; Italian: "girl"; Native American: "mighty one"; one of three goddesses.* **NEENAH, NENAH, NENEH, NINAH; NIÑA** (NEEN-yah)—Spanish; **NINÁCSKA** (nee-NACH-skah)—Hungarian; **NINON** (nee-NAWN)—French; **NINOTCHKA** (nee-NOHCH-kah or nee-NAWCH-kah)—Eastern European. Nina in Sumerian myth was a goddess of the ocean; Nina in Babylonian/Assyrian myth was a corn goddess; Nina in Incan myth was a goddess of fire. See also ANN(E), MARNINA, SHANE/SHANEEN.

NIPA, "NEE-pah"—*Sanskrit: "stream"; Malaysian: "great palm."* The Malaysian nipah provides food, clothing, and shelter from its several parts.

NIRELLE, "nee-REHL"—*Hebrew: "field of the Lord."* **NIRALIA. NIR.** M

NISHKALA, "neesh-KAH-lah"—*Hindu: "innocent."*

NISSA, "NIH-sah"—*Scandinavian: "friendly brownie or elf"; Hebrew: "symbol" or "emblem"; Greek: "beginning."* **ANISSA, NYSSA.** Nyssa is another name for the tupelo or gum tree. See also ANISA(H), NERISSA.

NITA(H), "NEE-tah"—*Native American*

Choctaw: "bear." **ANITA, ANITE** (ah-NEE-teh).

NITARA, "nee-TAH-rah"—*Hindu: "deeply rooted."*

NITYA, "NEET-yah"—*Sanskrit: "eternal"; Hindu: "forever."*

NIVEA, "NIHV-ee-ah" or "NEEV-ee-ah"—*Latin: "of the snow,"* and also *"life under the snow."* The second meaning refers to seeds or plants surviving the winter or thriving despite the cold. M

NIXIE, "NIHKS-ee"—*German: "water nymphs or "water sprite"; Latin: "snowy"; Greek: "night."* In Western European folklore, seeing the magical nixie on the night of the full moon meant you were in love with your companion of the evening.

NOAMI, "noh-AH-mee" or "noh-AY-mee"—*Hebrew: "pleasing."* **NAUMIT** (naw-MEET). See also NAOMI. M

NOELANI, "noh-eh-LAH-nee"—*Hawaiian: "heavenly girl."*

NOELLE, "noh-EHL"—*French: "Christmastime"; Latin: "new."* **NOËL; NOELLA, NOELLIA; NOVELIA** (noh-VAY-lee-ah)—Italian and Spanish. M

NOLA, "NOH-lah"—*Celtic: "famous."* **NOLI(E).** M

NONA, "NOH-nah"—*Latin: "ninth child."*

NORA(H), "NOH-rah"—*a diminutive of several names, but on its own, Nora(h) is a version of Helen: "light," "luminous," or "torch."* **NEORAH** (nay-OH-rah)—Israeli; **NOREEN** (noh-REEN)—Irish Gaelic; **NORLENE** (nohr-LEEN)—Scottish Gaelic. Nora is the newly enlightened feminist in Henrik Ibsen's 1879 play *A Doll's House.* See also HELEN, LENORA.

No-

No- is the Hawaiian prefix that means "of" or "from." You may use this with any name you choose.

NORDICA, "NOHR-dih-kah"—*French: "from the north."* **NORDIQUE** (nor-DEEK).

NOREEN. See NORA(H).

NORI, "NOH-ree"—*Japanese: "doctrine" or "principle."* **NORIKO.** M

NORMA, "NOHR-mah"—*English: "from the north"; Latin: "the T-square," "the example," or "the pattern."* The constellation Norma can be seen following the southern Sun at dusk from mid-July to the end of that month. The Sun is "in" Norma in November. M

NOVA(H), "NOH-vah"—*Native American Hopi: "chasing butterflies"; Latin: "new."* A new star is a nova.

NOYA(H), *Hebrew: "ornament."*

NUALA, "noo-AH-lah" or "NOO-ah-lah"—*Irish Gaelic: "white shoulders."* See also FINOLA.

NUI, "NOO-ee"—*Japanese: "tapestry."*

NURI, "NOO-ree"—*Hebrew: "my fire."* M

NUWA, "NOO-wah"—*Chinese: "great mother goddess."*

NYDIA, "NEE-dee-ah" or "NIH-dee-ah"—*Latin: "nest" or "home."* **NIDIA.**

NYSA, "NEE-sah"—*Latin: "the goal"; Greek: "beginning."* **NYSSA.**

THE TOP FIVE

OLIVIA
OPHELIA
ODETTE
OPAL
OLGA

If the name you're looking for isn't here, see the other vowels.

OBELIA, "oh-BEH-lee-ah"—*Greek: "tall monument."*

OCTAVIA, "awk-TAY-vee-ah"—*Latin: "eight" or "eighth."* Octavia was the wife of Roman Emperor Marc Antony. M

ODEDA, "oh-DEHD-ah" or "oh-DAYD-ah"—*Hebrew: "strong" or "encouragement."*

ODELE, "oh-DELL"—*Greek: "melody"; Danish: "otter"; Teutonic: "wealthy one."* **ODELIA, ODELIE, ODETTE; ODILA, ODILE, ODILIA.** M

ODESSA, "oh-DEH-sah"—*Greek: "long voyage" or "voyage of discovery."*

ODETTE. See ODILE.

ODINA, "oh-DEE-nah"—*Native American Algonquin: "the mountain."*

OGINA, "oh-GHEE-nah" or "oh-JEE-nah"—*Native American: "a wild rose."*

OIHANE, "oy-hah-neh"—*Basque: "forest."*

OKEKE, "oh-KEH-keh"—*African Ibo: "born on market day."*

OLA, "OH-lah"—*Norse: "reminder" or "from the ancestors."* **OLAVE**—*English.* This refers to a reincarnated ancestor, or someone who resembles an ancestor.

OLENA. See HELEN.

OLGA, "OHL-gah" or "ALL-gah"—*Russian: "holy."* **OLECHKA, OLENKA** (oh-LEHN-kah)**, OLEZKA, OLYA.** M

OLINDA, "oh-LIHN-dah"—*Latin: "fragrant."*

OLIVIA, "oh-LIHV-ee-ah" or "oh-LIHV-yah"—*Latin: "olive tree," and therefore, "peace" or "peaceful"; possibly also Norse: "from the ancestors"; Germanic: "army of the elves."* **OLIVETTE; OLIVERIA** (oh-lee-VAY-ree-ah)—*Portuguese.* The olive tree is a symbol of peace that appears across many, many cultures. The name Olivia was first used in Shakespeare's play *Twelfth Night.* Olivia de Havilland was a regal, redheaded actress who acted in several of the best swashbucklers filmed during Hollywood's golden age. Olivia Newton-John was a popular singer. **LIVIA, LIVVY, LIVY.** See also LIV. M

OLUJIMI, "oh-loo-JEE-mee"—*African Yoruba: "God gave us this."* M

OLWYNNE, "OHL-wihn"—*Welsh: "white footprint."* **OLWENNE.** In Welsh legend, Olwynne was the daughter of a giant who forced her suitor to complete many difficult tasks to win her hand.

OLYMPIA, "oh-LIHM-pee-ah"—*Greek: "mountain of the gods," thus "heavenly."* **OLYMPA, OLYMPE, OLYMPIAN, OLYMPIANNE; OLYMPA.** Olympus is a the mountain in Greece, which is also the mythic home of the Greek gods. Olympia Dukakis is an award-winning actress.

OMOROSE, "oh-moh-ROW-seh"—*African: "my beautiful child."* **OMAROSE.**

ONA, "OH-nah"—*Turkish: "prosperous"; Hebrew version of Ann(e): "graceful."* **ONIT** (oh-NEET). See also ANN(E), ONI, UNA.

ONAWA, "oh-NAH-wah"—*Native American: "one who does not sleep."* Every baby in the world, for example.

ONI, "oh-NEE"—*African: "desired."* **ONA, ONO.** M

OPA, "OH-pah"—*Native American Choctaw: "owl"; Greek: an exclamation of joy.*

OPAL, "OH-pahl"—*Sanskrit: "gemstone."* **OPALINA, OPALINE.**

OPHELIA, "oh-FEE-lee-ah"—*German: "help" or "wisdom"; Greek: "immortal" or from Theophilia, "divine love."* **OPHELIE**—French. Ophelia is the tragic heroine of Shakespeare's *Hamlet*. From this

Shakespearean character comes the name of one of Uranus's moons. See also THEOPHILIA.

OPHIRA, "oh-FEE-rah" or "OH-fih-rah"—*Hebrew: "gold."* **OPHIRAH.** The legendary land of Ophir is where King Solomon obtained all his gold and wealth. M

OPHRA(H), "OH-frah"—*Hebrew: "dust or dusty."* See also AFRA, OPHIRA.

OPRAH, "OH-prah"—*accidental variant of Orpah, Hebrew: "fresh" or "youthful."* **ORPAH** (OHR-pah). The Biblical Orpah, mentioned in the Book of Ruth, was the lovely daughter-in-law of Naomi. The name Oprah was created in the 1950s by a careless nurse who transposed letters when she filled out the birth certificate of newborn entertainment mogul Oprah Winfrey, who was supposed to be named "Orpah." Well, look what people did to the name Noami/Naomi . . . why not start playing with Orpah, too?

ORA, AURA, "OH-rah"—*Hebrew: "light."* **AURAH, ORAH.**

ORALEE, AURALEE, "OH-rah-lee"—*Hebrew: "my light."* **AURALI(E), AURLEE, AURLI(E), AURLY; ORALI(E), ORLEE, ORLI(E), ORLY.**

-ova, -ovna

"-ova" (pronounced "OH-vah") and "-ovna" (pronounced "OHV-nah") are Russian suffixes that mean "daughter of." You may use them with any female name you choose, using how the result sounds to determine which is best. In pronouncing a name with this suffix, the stressed syllable is the one before the suffix or the first syllable of the suffix itself. To be sure the name is pleasing to the ear, say it to yourself several times.

O'

"O'"—originally "Ui"—is the Irish prefix that means "of" or "from," and can be used with any name you choose.

ORCHID, "OR-kihd"—*Latin: "orchid"* or *"rosy-purple."* An orchid flower can blossom for months, so the long period of care needed to bring it into bloom is worth it. A nonblooming orchid has attractive foliage, which makes the wait easier.

ORELA, "oh-RAY-lah"—*Latin: "divine announcement."*

ORIANA, "oh-ree-AH-nah"—*Latin: "the east"* or *"golden."* M

ORLA, "OR-lah"—*Irish: "golden lady."* **AURLA**—Scottish; **ORFLAITH** (OR-flayth), **ORLAGH** (OR-lahg or OR-lay)—*Irish Gaelic;* **ORLEÉ** (OR-lee), **ORLY**—French.

ORLANDA. See ROLANDA.

ORLENDA, "or-LEHN-dah"—*Eastern European: "female eagle."* See also ORLANDA.

ORLENE, "or-LEEN"—*Latin: "golden."* **ORLENA, ORLINE, ORLYNNE. ORLY.** M

OSSIANNE, "AWS-ee-un" or "aws-ee-AHN"—*Irish: "fawn."* **OISÍN** (OY-seen)—*Irish Gaelic.* **OSSI(E), OSSY.**

OTTILIE, "AW-tih-lee"—*Teutonic: "prosperous"* or *"rich."* **OTTORINA** (aw-toh-REE-nah)—Spanish and Portuguese. See also OTELIA. M

OZORA, "oh-ZOH-rah"—*Hebrew: "strength of the Lord."*

THE TOP FIVE

PATRICIA
PAULA
PENELOPE
PAIGE
PAMELA

If the name you're looking for isn't here, see "F."

PAGE, "PAYJ"—*Greek: "child"; English: "a knight's attendant"; French: "royal servant."* **PAIGE, PAYGE.** M

PAKA, "PAH-kah"—*Swahili: "kitten."* See also PAKUNA.

PAKUNA, "pah-KOO-nah"—*Native American Miwok: "deer jumping as she runs down the hill."* **PAKA.**

PALBENE, "pahl-ben-eh"—*Basque: "blonde" or "yellow."*

PALILA, "pah-LEE-lah"—*Tahitian: "bird."*

PALLAS, "PAH-lahs"—*Greek: an alternate name for the goddess Athena.* "Pallas Athena" is often used in combination in referring to the Greek goddess. It's uncertain, but "Pallas" is probably in reference to Athena's virtue, of which she had tons compared to the rest of the crowd up Mount Olympus way. Incidentally, "pallas" is the root word for "palladium," theaters built to honor Athena's intelligence and grace with artistic offerings. Pallas is also one of the minor planets in the asteroid belt between Mars and Jupiter.

PALOMA, "pah-LOH-mah"—*Spanish: "dove."* **PALOMETA, PALOMITA.**

PALOMINA, "pal-oh-MEE-nah"—*Spanish: "dove-colored filly."*

PAMELA, "PAM-eh-lah"—*Greek: "all-honey" or "honeyed."* **PAMELYN, PAMLYN.** This name was invented by writer and bon vivant Sir Phillip Sidney in the sixteenth century for his book *Arcadia.* Samuel Richardson's novel Pamela (1740) is largely responsible for the spread of the name. **PAM, PAMMI(E).**

PANDITA, "pahn-DEE-tah"—*Hindu: "learned, scholarly."* **DITA.**

PANTHEA, "pahn-THEE-ah" or "PAN-thee-ah"—*Greek: "all the gods."* Why take a chance on making one of those guys/girls mad? Name the kid for *all* of them!

PANYA(H), "PAH-nyah"—*Swahili: "mouse" or "tiny one."*

PARASHA, "pah-RAH-shah"—*Russian: "born on Good Friday."*

PARTHENIA, "pahr-THEE-nee-ah"—*Greek: "virtuous."* **PARTHENIE; PARTHENOPE** (pahr-THEN-oh-pee)—Greek. In Greek myth, Parthenope was a siren who fell in love with the hero Odysseus.

PATI, PADI, "PAH-tee" or "PAH-dee"—*Persian: "great lady."* **PADDI, PADIA, PATIA,**

PATTI. See also PATRICE. For the male version see PADI.

PATIENCE, "PAY-shehnts"—*Latin: "patience."* This is another one of those Puritan virtue names.

PATRICE, "pah-TREECE"—*Latin: "noble."* **PÁDRAIGÍN** (pah-dry-GEEN)—Irish Gaelic; **PADRIKA**—Slavic; **PATRICIA**—Latin and Dutch; **PATRICKA** (pah-TREE-kah); **PATRIKA** (pah-TREE-kah)—Scandinavian; **PATRIZIA** (pah-TREET-zee-ah)—Italian; **PATRYKA**—Polish. The Latin word *patricius* was used to signify the aristocratic class in ancient Rome, the one that made all the laws (and all the money). Patricia Nixon was First Lady from 1969 to 1974. Patsy Cline was a country and western singer. **PADDI(E), PADDY; PAT, PATEE, PATI(E), PATTE, PATTY; PATSIE, PATSY; TRISH, TRISHA.** See also PATI/PADI. M

PATRICIA. See PATRICE.

PATTY, PATSY. See PATRICE.

PATZI, "PAHT-zee"—*Native American Omaha: "yellow bird."*

PAULA, "PAWL-ah"—*Latin: "little."* **PALIKE** (pah-LEE-keh)—Hungarian; **PAOLA** (pah-OH-lah), **PAOLETTA, PAOLINA**—Portuguese and Italian; **PASHA, PASHENKA, PAVLA, PAVLUSHA** (pahv-LOO-shah), **PAVLU-SHENKA** (pahv-loo-SHEHN-kah)—Russian; **PAULEEN; PAULETTE, PAULINE**—French; **PAULINA** (paw-LEE-nah)—Slavic; **PAWLA** (PAHV-lah)—Polish; **POLA**—Swedish; **PÓLÍN** (paw-LEEN)—Irish Gaelic; **POLLIE** (PAW-lee)—Scottish Gaelic. Several saints have these names. **PAULI(E); POLLI(E), POLLY.** M

PAULINE. See PAULA.

PAUSHA, "POH-shah" or "POW-shah"—*Hindu: equivalent to Capricorn.*

PAVANA, "pah-VAH-nah"—*Sanskrit: "wind goddess"; Italian or Spanish: "peacock."*

PAYTAH, "PAY-tah"—*Native American Sioux: "fire."* M

PEACH, "PEECH"—*Persian: "the peach,"* or peach-colored; *American slang: "beautiful"* or *"excellent."* **PECHE** (PESH)—French; **PERSICA** (PUR-sih-kah)—Latin; **PERSIKOS** (PUR-sih-kohss)—Greek; **PESCHE** (PESH-eh)—Italian. **PEACHIE, PEACHY; PEACHES.**

PEARL, "PURL"—*Latin: "sea mussel"; English: "pearl."* **PERL, PERLA, PERLE. PEARLI(E), PEARLY.** See also PURL.

PEGGY, "PEHG-ee"—*Gaelic diminutive of Margaret: "a pearl."* **PEGEEN, PEGGI(E); PEIGI** (PAY-ghee)—Scottish Gaelic; **PÉIGÍN** (pay-GHEEN)—Irish Gaelic. See also MARGARET.

PELE, "PEH-leh"—*Polynesian: goddess of volcanoes.*

PELLINORE, "PELL-ih-nor"—*Bretagne: "dark pool," "dark pond,"* or *"dark still waters."*

PELLKITA, "pehl-kee-tah"—*Basque: "happy."*

PENELOPE, "peh-NEHL-oh-pee"—*Greek: "the weaver"; Hebrew: "pearl"; Latin/Greek: "voice of judgement."* **FENELLA, PENELLA**—Gaelic; **PELCIA** (pehl-SEE-ah)—Polish; **PENELOPA; PENIEL**—Hebrew; **PENIEL** (PEH-nee-ehl), **PENIELLE**—Latin. In Greek legend, Penelope was the wife of Odysseus, who had gone off to fight in the Trojan War. He was believed to have been killed, but she knew in her heart that he hadn't been, and waited many long years for him to return. As time went on, Penelope was pressured to marry, and held off her many suitors by promising to choose a mate after she finished weaving a mourning shroud for her "dead" husband. She would weave all day, then unravel all her work at night. Hubby finally showed up about twenty years after he'd left, and they were reunited at last. **PENNA, PENNI(E), PENNY.**

PENNA, "PEH-nah"—*Latin: "feather."* See also PENELOPE.

PENNY. See PENELOPE.

PEPITA. See JOSEPHA.

PEPPER, "PEH-pur"—*Sanskrit: "berry."* **BIBER** (BEE-bur)—Turkish; **KOSHOO** (koh-SHOO)—Japanese; **MERITJA** (meh-REET-jah)—Indonesian; **PEPPAR**—Swedish; **PILIP-ILI** (pee-lee-PEE-lee)—Swahili; **PIPER** (PEE-pur)—Rumanian; **PYERETS** (PYEH-rehts)—Russian. The acquisition of pepper was one of the prime reasons Europeans left Europe on their many sea voyages. M

PERDITA, "pur-DEE-tah"—*Latin: "lost."* William Shakespeare invented this name for an abandoned baby, reared by a kindly shepherd, who turns out to be a princess in *The Winter's Tale.* **DITA; PERDI(E), PERDY.**

PER(R)I(E), "PARE-ee"—*English: "pear tree."* **PERR; PERRY.** M

PERRINE, "peh-REEN," sometimes "peh-RYNE"—*French from Greek: "stone."* M

PERSIS, PARSIS, "PUR-sihs" or "PAHR-sihss"—*Hindu: "fire worshippers."* This is a somewhat inaccurate name for the Zoroastrians of India, since they don't worship fire itself, but use the imagery of fire in their ceremonies. Persis Khambatta is an Indian actress and former model who first came to American notice in *Star Trek: The Movie* and *Nighthawks.* M

PESSA, "PEH-sah" or "PAY-sah"—

Yiddish: "pearl." **PERRIL; PESHA, PESHE; PESSEL, PESSYE.**

PETA(H), "PAY-tah"—*Native American Blackfoot: "golden eagle."*

PETRA, "PEH-trah"—*Greek: "rock."* **PETEN-KA** (peh-TEHN-kah), **PETYA**—Russian; **PETERKE** (PEH-tur-kee), **PETI**—Slavic; **PET-RINA** (peh-TREE-nah), **PETRINI**—Greek; **PETRONELLA**—Swedish; **PIER, PIERRETTE** (pyeh-REHT)—French; **PIERA** (PYARE-ah), **PIETRA** (PYEH-trah)—Italian. **PEDI(E); PET, PETA, PETEE, PETEY, PETI(E), PETTA.** M

PETRINA, "peh-TREE-nah"—*Greek: "steadfast," since the root word means "rock."* **PATRINA, PATRINI. TRINA, TRINI.** See also PETRA. M

PETULA, "peh-TOO-lah"—*Latin: "saucy" or "bouncy"; Persian: "young girl."* **BETULA, BETULLA; PETULIA.** Singer Petula Clark had several hits in the 1960s. **BET; PET.**

PETUNIA, "peh-TOON-ee-ah"—*French: "petunia flower" or "tobacco plant."* This name also refers to the nicotiana plant, an ornamental member of the tobacco family that bears beautiful flowers in a wide range of colors. **PETTE, PETTI(E).**

PHAEDRA, "FAY-drah"—*Greek: "dusky."* **PHAIDRA, PHEDRA.** In Greek legend, Phaedra was the wife of the hero Theseus, and the daughter of minor goddess Pasyphae and major god Zeus.

PHIL(L)IP(P)A, "FIHL-ih-pah" or "fee-LEE-pah"—*Greek: "lover of horses."* **FELI-PA** (feh-LEE-pah), **FELIPITA** (fee-lee-PEE-tah)—Spanish; **FLIPPA, PIP, PIPPA**—Dutch; **PIPPI**—Nordic; **PILIBIN** (pee-lee-BEEN)—Irish Gaelic. **FILLY; PHILLI(E), PHILLY.** M

PHILOMENA, "fee-loh-MAY-nah"—

GREAT PLAINS GIRLS' NAMES

Girls born in the largely agricultural states of the Great Plains are most likely to have the following names:

1. Jessica	6. Sarah	11. Brittany	16. Hannah
2. Ashley	7. Megan	12. Elizabeth	17. Courtney
3. Amanda	8. Shelby	13. Rachel	18. Taylor
4. Emily	9. Kayla	14. Lauren	19. Chelsea
5. Samantha	10. Kelsey	15. Jennifer	20. Rebecca

Greek: "lover of the human race." **FILOMENA.** This is a Christian saint name.

PHILOTHEA, "fih-loh-THEE-ah" or "fee-loh-TAY-ah"—*Greek: "lover of God."* Philothea is one of the Christian saints.

PHOEBE, "FEE-bee"—*Greek: "the brightest one."* Phoebe is another name for Artemis, Greek goddess of the moon (among her other duties). Phoebe is also one of the moons of Saturn, and is believed to have formed elsewhere in the universe before joining our solar system.

PHYLLIS, "FIHL-iss"—*Greek: "verdant" or "leafy."* **PHYL(L)ICIA** (fee-LEE-see-ah or fee-LEE-shah).

PIA, "PEE-ah"—*Latin: "pious," "soft," or "gentle."* Pia Zadora is an actress/singer who moved from films to plays and large stage revues.

PILAR, "pee-LAHR"—*Spanish: "a fountain or pillar."*

PILI, "PEE-lee"—*Swahili: "second born."*

PIPER, "PIE-pur"—*English: "pipe player."* Piper Laurie is an actress. See also PEPPER. M

PIPPI, "PIH-pee"—*Nordic version of Philipa: "lover of horses."* Pippi Longstockings is the cheerful, optimistic, plucky, magical little girl in the series of books by Astrid Lindgren. See also PHIL(L)IP(P)A.

PIROSKA, "pih-ROHSH-kah"—*Hungarian: "the ancients."* **PIRA, PIRI.**

PLACIDA, "PLAH-sihd-ah" or "plah-SEED-ah"—*Latin: "serene."* **PALACIDA** (pah-lah-SEE-dah)—Spanish; **PLACIDE. PLACI(E).** M

PO'ELE, "poh-AY-lay"—*Hawaiian: "dark one."*

POLLY. See PAULA.

POLOMA, "poh-LOW-mah"—*Native American Choctaw: "bows,"* as in bow and arrow.

POMONA, "poh-MOH-nah"—*Latin: "bearing fruit."* Pomona was the Roman goddess of fruit trees.

PORTIA, "POHR-shah"—*?: uncertain, possibly Latin: "doorway."* Portia is a wise female judge in Shakespeare's *Merchant of Venice.* Portia is also a moon of Uranus.

PRASADA, "prah-SAH-dah"—*Sanskrit: "gracious."*

PRISCILLA, "prih-SIHL-ah"—*Latin:* *"ancient."* **PRISCA** (PREES-kah)—*French.* **CILLA; PRIS, PRISSI(E), PRISSY.**

PRUDENCE, "PROO-dehnts"—*Latin:* *"foresight."* This is a Puritan virtue name. **PRUDENCIA, PRUDENTIA. PRU(E), PRUDI(E), PRUDY.**

PURL, "PURL"—*Norwegian: "to bubble up, to swirl"; Celtic: "twisting golden (or silver) strands"; French: "decorated or bedecked."* **PURLE, PURLI(E), PURLY.** To purl in the natural world is to whirl, to spin, or to flow with a bubbly sound. It is usually used to describe certain ways in which water behaves. To purl also means to edge with some type of decoration, such as braid or lace. See also PEARL.

PURLIN, PURLYN, "PUR-lihn"—*English: "by the brook," "by the waterfall," or "the support."* Purlins are the cross-beams in ceilings which support the rafters, attic, and roof. M

PYRENA, "pye-REE-nah"—*Greek: "fiery."*

THE TOP FIVE

QUINN
QUEEN
QUERIDA
QAMARA(H)
QUILLIAN

If the name you're looking for isn't here, see "K."

QAMARA, "KAH-mahr-ah" or "kah-MAHR-ah"—*Arabic: "the moon."* **QUAMARA(H).** M

QANDI, "KAHN-dee"—*Arabic: "made of sugar" or "sweet."*

QIYAMA(H), "kee-YAH-mah"—*Arabic: "resurrection."*

QUEEN, "KWEEN"—*English: "ruler."* **QUEENA, QUEENIE; REINE (REHN)**—*French;* **RIOGHNACH** (ree-OH-nakh—"kh" in your throat)—Irish Gaelic; **RIONA**—Irish.

QUELLA, "KWEHL-ah"—*English: "to destroy or pacify."*

QUERIDA, "keh-REE-dah"—*Spanish:* *"beloved."* M

QUILLA, "KEE-lah" or "KWEE-lah"—*Inca: "Moon."* In Incan mythology, Mama-quilla was the great goddess of the moon, and battled celestial pumas and snakes during eclipses.

QUINN(E), "KWIHN"—*diminutive of Quinby, Scandinavian: "from the queen's estate" or "from the belly (womb) of a queen."* **QUINBY** (KWIHN-bee).

QUINTINA, "kwihn-TEE-nah"—*Latin: "the fifth."* **QUINNA, QUINTANA, QUINTILLA, QUINTINE; QUINTA.** M

QUIRITA, "kee-REE-tah" or "kwee-REE-tah"—*Latin: "citizen."*

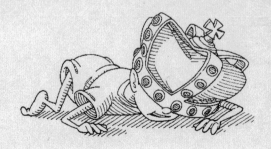

A SOAPY SAMPLER

Women's character names in both daytime and prime-time serials:

Alex	Emily	Kendall	Rebecca
Alexandra	Erica	Kimberley	Robin
Alice	Esther	Kristen	Rosanna
Alison	Felicia*	Laura	Samantha*
Amanda	Gina	Laurel	Sarah
Angela	Gloria	Lauren	Sharly
Billie	Hayley	Lesley	Sharon
Bobbie	Hillary	Lexie	Sheila
Brenda*	Hope	Linda	Skye
Bridget*	Iris	Lisa	Sofia
Cameron*	Jamie	Lorna	Steffi
Carly	Jane	Lois	Susan
Caroline	Janet	Lucy*	Tangie
Carrie*	Janice	Luna	Taylor
Casey	Janie	Macy	Tess
Celeste	Jennifer	Maggie*	Tina
Charlie	Jessica	Mari Jo	Tracy
Darla	Jocelyn	Marlena	Vanessa
Deborah	Julie	Monica	Victoria*
Dinah Lee	Kate*	Nadine	Vicki
Dixie	Katherine	Nikki	Vivian
Emily	Keesha	Paulina	Zoey
Eleni			

* more than one character   SOURCE: *TV Guide, Television Times*

THE TOP FIVE

RACH(A)EL
REBECCA
ROBERTA
RUTH
RENÉE

If the name you're looking for isn't here, perhaps it is a variant or diminutive of another primary name.

RABI, "RAH-bee"—*Arabic: "breeze."* **RABIA, RABIN.** M

RACH(A)EL, "RAY-chul"—*Hebrew: "innocent," "lamb," or "ewe."* **RACHEAL, RACHELL, RAECHEL, RAECHELLE; RACHELE** (rah-CHEH-leh)—Italian; **RAHEL** (RAY-hehl)—Polish; **RAHIL** (RAY-hihl), **RAHILKA**—Russian; **RÁICHÉAL** (RYE-khyahl or RAY-khyahl—"kh" in your throat)—Irish Gaelic; **RAKEL** (rah-KEHL)—Swedish; **RAONAID** (RAIN-aid or ROWN-aid)—Scottish Gaelic; **RAQUEL** (rah-KEHL)—French and Spanish; **RASHKA** (RAWSH-kah), **RASHKE, RECHELL**—Israeli. In the Old Testament/Tanakh, Rachel was the wife of Jacob. Rachel's father made Jacob work for him for fourteen years in order to take her as his wife. She was the mother of Joseph, who became a powerful ruler. Raquel Welch is an actress. **RACHE, RAE.**

RADA, "RAH-dah"—*Yiddish: "rose."* **RADE** (RAH-deh).

RADELLA, "rah-DEHL-ah"—*English: "elfin advisor."* **RADELLE.**

RADEYAH, "rah-DAY-ah"—*Arabic: "contented."*

RADHIYA(H), "rahd-HEE-yah"—*Swahili: "agreeable."* **RAZIYA(H).**

RADICE, "RAY-deese" or "rah-DEESE"—*Latin: "original" or "the source."*

RADINKA, "rah-DIHN-kah"—*Slavic: "active."*

RADMILLA, "rahd-MEE-lah"—*Slavic: "worker for the people."*

RAFA, "rah-FAH"—*Arabic: "prosperity."*

RAFAELA. See RAPHAELA.

RAIN, "RAYN"—*English: "rain."* **AME** (AH-may)—Japanese; **CHUVA**—Portuguese; **DOZHT** (DOHZHT)—Russian; **HUDJAN** (HUDE-jahn)—Indonesian; **MATAR** (mah-TAHR)—Arabic; **MVUA** (m'VOO-ah)—Swahili; **PIOGGIA** (pee-OH-jee-ah)—Italian; **SADE** (SAH-day)—Finnish; **YAGMUR** (yahg-MOOR)—Turkish. M

RAISA, "rah-EE-sah" or "RAY-sah"—*French: "thinker"; Yiddish: "rose."* **RAISSA, RAYSEL.** Stylish Raisa Gorbachev, wife of Mikhail, the Soviet president who broke down socialism, caused quite a stir by being the first presidential wife of that country who actually looked better than her husband.

RAJNI, "RAHZH-nee"—*Hindu: "night."*

RAMIELLE, "rah-mee-EHL"—*?, proba-

bly Babylonian: angel of thunder. **RAMI-EL.**
M

RAMONA, "rah-MOH-nah"—*Hebrew:*
"pomegranate"; Old German: "wise protec-
tor." **RAMONDA** (rah-MAWN-dah), **RAY-**
MONDA—English and German; **RAMONDE:**
(rah-MAWND)—French, (rah-MAWN-deh)—
Scandinavian; **RIMONA**—Israeli; **ROMONA**—
Eastern European and Slavic.

RAMYA, "RAWM-yah"—*Hindu: "pleasant."*

RANA, "rah-NAH" or "RAH-nah"—*Arabic:*
"to gaze upon"; Sanskrit: "royalty"; Latin:
"frog." **RANEE, RANIA, RANI(E)**—Sanskrit.

RANDI, "RAN-dee" or "RAHN-dee"—
English: "shield." **RANDA, RANDIE.**

RANGI, "RAHN-jee"—*Maori: "sky god-*
dess."

RANIYAH, "rah-NEE-yah"—*Arabic:*
"gazing."

RAPHAELA, "rah-fah-EHL-ah"—*He-*
brew: "God heals" or "healed by God."
RAFAELA, RAFAELLA, RAPHAELLE; RAFAËLA,
RAFAËLLA, RAPHAËLA, RAPHAËLLE; RAFALY
(RAH-faw-lee or rah-FAWL-ee)—Polish;
RAPHAËA; RAPHA-EL. Raphael is one of the
Archangels in the Judeo-Christian and Islamic
angelic domain. His strengths are science and
medicine. **RAFI(E), RAFFI(E), RAPHI(E).** M

RAQUEL. See RACH(A)EL.

RASHA, "RAH-shah" or "rah-SHAH"—
Arabic: "young gazelle."

RASHIDA(H), "rah-SHEED-ah"—*Arabic:*
"wise or mature" or Swahili: "righteous."
RASHEDA.

RAVEN, "RAY-vehn"—*English: "the raven."*
The Vikings used the raven on their banners and flags; to them, it symbolized the
warrior. M

RAVI, "RAH-vee"—*Hindu: "the sun god."*
The river Ravi runs through India and
Pakistan. M

RAYA, "RAH-yah" or "RAY-ah"—*Hebrew:*
"friend." **RAIA.**

RAYMONDA, "ray-MOHN-dah"—*Teu-*
tonic: "wise guardian" or "wise protector."
RAEMONIA—Greek; **RAIMONA, RAIMONDA**
—Italian; **RAJMUNDA** (RAH-ee-moond-ah),
RAJMUNDY—Eastern European and
Danish; **RAMONA**—Spanish, French, and
Italian; **RÉAMONNIE** (RAY-ah-moh-nee)—
Irish Gaelic. The names of several saints
are on this list. **RAE, RAYA, RAYE.** See also
RAMONA. M

RAYNA, "RAY-nah"—*Yiddish: "pure."*
REYNA.

RAZI, "rah-ZEE"—*Aramaic: "a secret."*
RAZIA, RAZIAH, RAZIEL, RAZIELLE, RAZIL,
RAZILLE, RAZIYE. RAZ. M

REAGAN, REGAN, "RAY-gun" or
"REE-gin" for either—*Irish Gaelic: "little*
queen"; Scandinavian and German: "rain."
REAGIN, REGIN, REGYN. Regan is a
princess, daughter of the title character in
King Lear.

REBBA," REH-bah"—*Hebrew: "fourth*
born." **REBA, REBBAH, REBBI(E).** See also
REBECCA

REBECCA, "reh-BEHK-ah"—*Hebrew:*
traditionally "servant of God," but more
accurately "binding"; Semitic: "to ensnare
or entrap." **RÉBA** (RAY-bah), **RÉBECCA**
(ray-beh-KAH or RAYB-kah)—French; **RE-**
BECKA, REBEKA—Nordic; **RIVA(H), RIVE,**
RIVKA(H) (REEV-kah)—Israeli. In the Old
Testament/Tanakh, Rebecca was the wife
of Isaac, and the mother of fraternal twins
Jacob and Esau. Rebeccas in literature

abound, including ones in *Ivanhoe, Vanity Fair,* and *Rebecca of Sunnybrook Farm,* and in the book entitled *Rebecca.* **BECCA, BECKA, BECKIE, BECKY; REBA.**

REEF, "REEF"—*Old Norse(?): "ridge."* **ARRECIFE** (ah-reh-SEEF)—Spanish; **ÉCUEIL** (ay-KWEEL), **RÉCIF** (ray-SEEF)—French; **RECIFE** (ray-SEEF)—Portuguese. M

REGINA, "reh-JEE-nah"—*Latin: "queen."* **RÉGINE** (ray-JEEN or ray-ZHEEN), **REINA, REINE** (RAIN)—French; **REINA, REYNA**—Spanish; **REINHILDA, REINHILDE** (rine-HIHL-deh)—German. **REGGI(E), REGGY.** M

REINA, "REH-ee-nah"—*Yiddish: "clean."* See also REGINA.

REMIELLE, "reh-mee-EHL"—*Assyrian: "whom God sets up" or "mercy of God."*

RE(E)NA, RINA, "REE-nah"—*Hebrew: "song of joy"; Old English: "to run together."* **RINA(H), RINNA(H).**

RENATA, "ray-NAH-tah" or "ruh-NAH-tuh"—*Latin: "reborn."* **RENATIA, RENATYA.** This is a Christian saint name. M

RENÉE, "reh-NAY"—*French from Latin: "reborn."* M

RESEDA, "ree-SEE-dah"—*Latin: "nignonette or mignonette flower" or "assuage or soothe."*

REUELLE, "roo-EHL"—*Hebrew: "friend of God."* **RUEL, RUELLE.** M

REVA, "REE-vah"—*Latin: "to gain strength."*

RHEA, "REE-ah"—*Greek: "the earth," "stream," or "poppy."* **REA.** In Greek mythology, Rhea was one of the "old ones"—gods and goddesses that were of the universe, not just of our planet. She was the mother of all the gods and goddesses we think of when we think of Greek mythology,

including Zeus, the chief god. Rhea is one of the moons of Saturn.

RHET(T)A, "REE-tah" or "REH-tah"—*Greek: "well-spoken."*

RHIANNON, "ree-AN-awn"—*Welsh: "great queen."* **RHIANNA, RIANNA, RIAN-NON.** In Welsh legend, Queen Rhiannon was the wife of King Pwyll, god of the underworld, among other things. She was associated with fertility and was a skilled sorceress. This name had a resurgence in the mid-1970s because of a popular song by Fleetwood Mac.

RHODA, "ROH-dah"—*Greek: "rose" or "red."* Saint Rhoda helped Saint Peter escape from prison, and thus is a patroness of those confined.

RHONDA, "RAWN-dah"—*Old Welsh: "noisy one," "strong river," and a place name (Rhondda); Old French: "round."* **RHONDDA** (RAWN-dah or RAWN-thah). The Rhondda Valley is near Cardiff in Wales. The name was given a boost in popularity by actress Rhonda Fleming in the 1940s and 1950s, and another boost by the Beach Boys' song "Help Me Rhonda" in the 1960s. **RHONDI(E), RHONDY; RONNA, RONNI(E).**

RIALTA, "ree-AWL-tah" or "ree-AL-tah"—*Italian: "deep brook" or "deep channel."* M

RICHARDA, "ree-SHAR-dah"—*Teutonic: "mighty ruler."* **RICARDA** (ree-KAHR-dah)—Spanish and Portuguese; **RICCIARDA** (ree-chee-AR-dah)—Italian; **RICKARDA** (rih-KAHR-dah)—Scandinavian; **RIKÁRDY** (ree-KAHR-dee)—Hungarian; **RYSZARDY** (rih-ZHAHR-dee)—Polish. **RIC, RICA, RICCI** (REE-chee); **RICH, RICHI(E), RICHY; RICKI(E), RICKY; RIKI, RIKKI(E), RIKKY.** M

RICKI, RIKKI. See BARIKA, ERICA,

HOMES ON THE RANGE GIRLS' NAMES

Girls born in the states near the Rocky Mountains are most likely to have the following names:

1. Ashley	6. Stephanie	11. Taylor	16. Danielle
2. Jessica	7. Samantha	12. Chelsea	17. Alexis
3. Amanda	8. Elizabeth	13. Courtney	18. Brianne(-a)
4. Brittany	9. Lauren	14. Jasmine	19. Maria
5. Sarah	10. Jennifer	15. Amber	20. Crystal

FREDERICA, KENDRIKA, RICHARDA.

RILIAN, "REE-lee-un" or "ree-LEE-un"—?, *perhaps German: "small stream" or "brook."* This is the name of a character in *The Chronicles of Narnia* by C.S. Lewis. **RILLA, RILLIE.**

RIMA, "REEM-ah"—*Arabic: "white antelope."*

RISA, "REE-sah"—*Latin: "laughing."*

RISHI, "REE-shee"—*Sanskrit: "one who sees" or "the seer."* M

RISHONA, "ree-SHOH-nah"—*Hebrew: "first."*

RITA, "REE-tah"—*a diminutive of Margaret: "pearl"; Hindu: "brave, strong," Sanskrit: "right" or "law"; Greek: "well-spoken."* **RETA; RHETA; RHITA**—Italian and German; **RIDA**—Portuguese; **RITTA.** See also AMRITA, CARITA, MARGARET.

RIVA, "REE-vah"—*French: "riverbank."* **RIVE.** See also REBECCA.

ROANNA, "roh-AN-ah"—*Latin: "sweet."* **ROANA, ROANNE.**

ROBERTA, "roh-BUR-tah" or "roh-BEAR-tah" ("r" in your throat for "real" French)—

English: "shining with fame," "shining in fame," or "illustrious." **ROBIA** (roh-BEE-ah or ROH-byah), **ROBI(E), ROBYA**—Eastern European. **BERTI(E); BOBBE, BOBBI(E), BOBETTE; ROBBI(E); ROBBY, ROBETTE, ROBI, ROBIN.** M

ROBIN, "RAW-bihn"—*English: "the robin,"* and another name for the black locust tree (*robinia*). **ROBBIN, ROBBINA, ROBBINE, ROBBYN, ROBINA, ROBINE, ROBINET, ROBINETTE, ROBYN, ROBZIA.** Robin is also considered a pet form of the name Roberta. See also ROBERTA. M

ROCHELLE, "roh-SHEHL"—*French: "little rock."* **ROCHELLA, ROCHETTE. SHELL, SHELLI(E), SHELLY.**

ROHANA, "roh-HAHN-ah"—*Hindu: "sandalwood."* M

ROHITA, "roh-HEE-tah"—*Sanskrit: "red."* In Hindu legend, the Sun is sometimes referred to as a great red horse, Rohita.

ROLANDA, "roh-LAHN-dah" or "roh-LAWN-dah"—*German: "famous throughout the land."* **ORLANDA** (ohr-LAHN-dah)—Spanish; **ROLEEN**—Scottish; **ROLLANDA, ROLLINA, ROLLINE, ROLLONDA, ROLONDA. ROLLI, ROLLIE, ROLLY.** M

ROMANA, "roh-MAH-nah"—*Latin: a Roman.* **ROMA; ROMAINE**—Slavic; **ROMANADE** (roh-mah-NAHD), **ROMANADIA, ROMANADYA; ROMANCE, ROMANCIA, ROMANETTE**—French and Italian; **ROMANTZA**—German and Eastern European; **ROME, ROMI; ROMOCHKA** (roh-MOTCH-kah)—Russian. A couple of Christian saint names are on this list. **ROMIE, ROMY.** M

ROMIA, "roh-MEE-ah"—*Hebrew: "exalted" or "high."* **ROMA, ROMIT.** Irish actress Roma Downey is a favorite on American TV. M

RONA, "ROH-nah"—*Norwegian: "might" as in power, not as in "maybe."* Rona is the name of a Scottish island. **RHONA.** See also LIRON.

RONALDA, "roh-NAHL-dah"—*Scottish form of Regina: "powerful ruler."* **RANALTA, RANALTE**—Irish Gaelic; **RINALDA** (ree-NAHL-dah)—Spanish, Italian, and Portuguese; **RONALDETTE, RONALDINA, RONALDINE**—French and Spanish. Ranalte was a queen of Connacht in Ireland. **RONI, RONNE, RONNI(E), RONNY.** M

RONDELLE, "ron-DELL"—*Old French: "round."* **RHONDELLA, RHONDELLE, RONDELLA.** A rondel is a type of French poem. **RON, RONDA, RONNA, RONNI(E), RONNY.** M

RONLI, "RAWN-lee" or "ROHN-lee"—*Hebrew: "joy is mine."* **RONA, RONIA, RONIT** (ROH-neet or roh-NEET)—Israeli.

RONNI(E). See RHONDA, RONALDA, RONDELLE.

RORY, "ROH-ree"—*Scotch-Irish: "red" or "ruddy."* **RORIE; RUAIDRI** (ROO-eye-dree), **RUAIRÍ** (roo-EYE-ree)—Irish Gaelic; **RUARAIDH** (ROO-ah-rye)—Scottish Gaelic. See also AURORA. M

ROSA. See ROSE/ROSA.

ROSALIE, "ROSE-ah-lee"—*Latin: "festival of roses"; English: "field of roses."* **ROSALEA, ROSALEE, ROSALEIGH; ROSALEEN, ROSALIA** (rose-ah-LEE-ah or rose-AH-lee-ah). There are some saint names on this list.

ROSALIND, "RAWZ-ah-lihnd" or "ROHS-ah-leend"—*Spanish: "beautiful rose"; German: "red dragon."* **ROSALINDA, ROSALYN, ROSAMOND, ROSAMUND, ROSELIN, ROSELINE** (rohs-LEEN), **ROSLIN, ROSLYN.** In many cultures, the dragon is a symbol of magic and wisdom, and not a terrible beast. Sir Edmund Spenser, an English poet, was the originator of this name, and Shakespeare used it in *As You Like It.* Rosalind is a moon of Uranus. **ROSA, ROZ.**

ROS(E)ANNE, "roh-ZAN"—*combination of Rose + Anne: "graceful rose."* **ROSANA, ROSANNA, ROZAN, ROZANNE.** Rosana is one of the Christian saints. Roseanne is the Emmy-winning queen of TV, challenging other imitators to match the quality, depth, and truth of the characters and situations in her sitcom. See also ANN(E), ROSE/ROSA.

ROSARIA, "roh-SAH-ree-ah"—*Spanish: "the Rosary."* **ROSARITA.**

ROSE, ROSA, "ROHZ(-ah)" or "ROH-sah"—*Latin: "the rose" or "dew."* **ARROSA** (ah-roh-seh)—Basque; **RASINE** (rah-SEE-neh)—Polish; **ROZYCZKA** (roh-ZEESH-kah)—Polish; **ROÍSÍN** (roy-SEEN), **ROÍS** (ROYSE)—Irish Gaelic; **ROSALEEN**—Irish; **ROSANA, ROSETA, ROSINA**—Italian; **ROSELLE** (roh-ZEHL), **ROSETTE** (roh-ZET), **ROSINE**—French; **ROSITA** (roh-SEE-tah)—Spanish; **ROSZA** (ROH-zhah), **ROSZI**—Hungarian; **ROZA**—Yiddish. There are several saint names on this list.

ROSIE, ROSEY. See also ROS(E)ANNE.

ROSEMARY, "ROSE-mare-ee"—*Latin: "ocean dew" and/or the rosemary plant.* **ROSEMARIE.** The herb rosemary, a symbol of remembrance, is a spicy herb used in cooking, particularly in Greek and other Mediterranean cuisines, and in herbal and folk medicine.

ROSLYN, ROSLIN, "RAWZ-lihn"—*French: "little redhead"; Celtic: "meadowbrook" or "meadow waterfall."* Roslyn Carter was First Lady from 1977 to 1980. Since then, she and her husband, Jimmy, have been very active in humanitarian causes. See also ROSALIND.

ROXANNE, "rocks-AN"—*Persian: "dawn" or "brilliance."* **ROXANA, ROXANE, ROXANN, ROXANNA.** Roxanne is the love interest in the story of Cyrano de Bergerac. **ROXI(E), ROXY.**

RUBY, "ROO-bee"—*Latin: "the ruby."* Ruby Dee is an actress whose career has spanned more than four decades.

RUFEN, "roo-FEHN"—*Chinese: "fragrant."*

RUFINA, "roo-FEE-nah"—*Latin: "red haired."* **RUFIA.**

RUKAN, "roo-KAHN"—*Arabic: "steady" or "confident."*

RUKIYA(H), "roo-KEE-yuh"—*Swahili: "goddess" or "angel."*

RULA, "ROO-lah"—*Latin: "model" or "example"; English: "precise" or "obedient."*

RUNA, "ROO-nah"—*Old German: "mystery" or "secret."* Runes are the mystic alphabet of the Celts and Druids, usually carved in wood plaques or on rock.

RURI, "ROO-ree"—*Japanese: "emerald."* **RURIKO.**

RUSA, "ROO-sah"—*Micronesian: "deer."*

RUSSI, "RUHSS-ee"—*French: "red"; Anglo-Saxon: "like a fox."* **RUSTY.** M

RUTH, "ROOTH"—*traditionally, Hebrew: "compassion"; but also Scottish: "abundant or abundance."* **ROUTH; RÚT** (ROOT)— Gaelic; **RUTHANNE** ("compassion and grace"), **RUTHIA.** In the Old Testament/ Tanakh, Ruth is a devoted wife and daughter-in-law. **RUTHIE.**

RYU, "REE-yoo"—*Japanese: "lofty."*

THE TOP FIVE

SARAH
SAMANTHA
SHELBY
STEPHANIE
SUSAN(NAH)/SHOSHANA

If the name you're looking for isn't here, see "C."

SAAMI, "SAH-mee"—*Finnish: "a Lapp."* M

SABA, "SAH-bah"—*Greek: "woman of Sheba."*

SABAH, "sah-BAH"—*Tunisian: "morning."*

SABLE, "SAY-bul"—*Slavic(?): "sable."* In heraldry, "sable" refers to the color black. In the animal world, "sable" refers to either an otterlike animal with a lush dark brown pelt or to a black or dark brown antelope that roams eastern and southern Africa.

SABRA, "SAH-brah" (or "SAY-brah")—*French: "a sword"; Hebrew and Arabic: "thorny cactus."* **ZABRA.**

SABRINA, "sah-BREE-nah"—*Latin: "from the border"; Hebrew: "little thorny cactus"; Celtic: the goddess of the River Severn; Anglo-Saxon: "princess."* **SABRINE; ZABRINA, ZABRINE.**

SACHA, "SAH-chah"—*Greek: "helpmate."*

SACHI, "SAH-chee"—*Japanese: "bliss."* **SACHIKO.** M

SADA, "SAH-dah"—*Japanese: "chaste."* **SADAKO.**

SADIE, "SAY-dee"—*English: "seed"; version of Sara(h): "princess."* **SADA, SADEY,** SADYE. See also SARA(H).

SADIRA, "sah-DEE-rah"—*Persian: "lotus plant."*

SAFARA, "sah-FAH-rah"—*Kiswahili: "a trip" or "born on a trip"; Swahili: "to travel or journey" or "the traveller."*

SAFFRON, "SAH-frawn"—*Arabic: "crocus plant."* Saffron, one of the most expensive of all spices, is made from the dried centers of the crocus plant.

SAGARA, "sah-GAH-rah"—*Hindu: "ocean."*

SAGI, "sah-GHEE" or "sah-JEE"—*Aramaic: "mighty."*

SAGIRAH, "SAH-jee-rah"—*Moroccan: "little one."*

SAIDA(H), "sah-EE-dah"—*African: "happy" or "fortunate."* **SAYIDA(H).** Saida is a port city in Lebanon.

SAKARI, "sah-KAH-ree"—*Sanskrit: "sweet."* **SAKARA.**

SAKI, "SAH-kee"—*Japanese: "cape,"* as in a warm, protecting garment. M

SAKINAH, "SAH-kee-nah"—*Tunisian: "tranquility with God."*

SAKURA, "sah-KOO-rah"—*Japanese:*

"cherry blossom"; Chinese: "educated." The Japanese derivation signifies wealth and prosperity, and the month of March.

SALLY, "SAL-ee—*traditionally, a version of Sara(h): "princess," but also Ancient Italian: "war dancer" and Latin: "to leap."* **SALAIDH** (sah-LYE)—*Gaelic;* **SALIAN(NE), SALII** (sah-LEE)—*Latin;* **SALLIE, SALLYE.** In ancient Italy, the Salii were priests of Mars, and performed rituals to open and close the time when war could be made—from mid-March to mid-October. **SAL.** See also SARA(H).

SALMA, "SAHL-mah"—*Swahili: "safe."*

SAMANA, "sah-MAH-nah"—*Pali: "ascetic one."* **SAMANERA** (sah-MAH-neh-rah)—*Hindu;* **SHRAMANA** (shrah-MAH-nah)—*Sanskrit.*

SAMANTHA, "sah-MAN-thah"—*Aramaic: "listener."* **SAMANTHÉE** (sah-mahn-THAY/TAY)—*French;* **SAMANTHY.** The character Samantha on the 1960s TV series *Bewitched* brought this ancient name into the popular imagination again. **SAM, SAMMI(E), SAMMY.**

SAMAR, "SAH-mahr" or "sah-MAHR"—*Arabic: "conversations at twilight."*

SAMARA, "sah-MAH-rah" or "SAH-mah-rah"—*Latin: "the seed of the elm" or "the fruit of the elm"; Hebrew: "watchful" or "cautious."* **SAMAR, SAMARIA.** Samar is an island in the Philippines. Samaria, a capital of ancient Israel, is now located in west Jordan.

SAMIA, "SAH-mee-ah"—*Arabic: "exalted."* **SAAMI, SAAMIE.** M

SAMIRAH, "sah-MEER-ah"—*Arabic: "entertaining companion."* **MIRAH.** M

SAMMA, "SAH-mah"—*Pali: "right" or "perfect."* **SAM, SAMMI(E), SAMMY.**

SAMMI(E). See SAMANTHA, SAMMA, SAMUELA.

SAMUELA, "sam-yoo-EHL-ah" or "sahm-WEHL-ah"—*Hebrew: traditionally "God listens," but sometimes given as "in the name of the Lord."* **SAAMI(E)** (SAH-mee)—*Native American;* **SAMIE** (SHAH-mee), **SAMUKA** (SHAH-moo-kah)—*Hungarian, Eastern European, and Slavic;* **SAMIELLA** (sahm-YEHL-ah), **SAMIELLE** (SAH-mee-ehl)—*French, German, and Scandinavian.* **SAM, SAMMI(E), SAMMY.** M

SANCHA, "SAHN-chah"—*Spanish from Latin: "holy or sincere."* **SANCHE, SANCHIA.** M

SANDHI, "SAND-ee" or "SAHND-hee"—*Sanskrit: "placed together" and "put together."* M

SANDRA, "SAN-druh" or "SAWN-druh"—*the half of Alexandra, Lysandra, etc., meaning: "of humankind."* **SANDRINE** (sahn-DREEN)—*French;* **SAUNDRA, SAUNEE, SAUNI(E), SAUNY; SONDRA, SONNEE, SONNI(E)** (SAW-nee), **SONNY.** Sandra Dee was an actress. **SANDEE, SANDI(E), SANDY.** See also ALEXANDRA, CASSANDRA, LYSANDRA. M

SANTINA, "sahn-TEE-nah"—*Latin: "holy or pure."* **SANTINE.** M

SANURA, "sah-NOO-rah"—*Swahili: "kitten."*

SAPPHIRE, "SAF-ire"—*Greek: "the sapphire stone"; Sanskrit: "precious to (the planet) Saturn."* **SAFFIRA, SAFIRE; SAPIRA, SAPPHA, SAPPHIRA.**

SAQARA, "suh-KAH-ruh"—*Egyptian: "of the falcon."* **SAQARRA, SAQQARA.** Saqara was a religious center in ancient Egypt where many Pharaohs were interred.

SARA(H), "SAH-rah"—*Hebrew: "princess"; Persian: "of the Mysteries."* **SADIE;**

SALLY; SARITA (sah-REE-tah)—Israeli; **SARA** (SHAH-rah), **SARI, SARIKA** (SHAH-ree-kah), **SASA** (SHAH-shah), **ZSAZSA** (ZHAH-zhah)—Eastern European; **SARAQA** (SAH-rah-kah)—Persian; **SARETTA**—Italian; **SARETTE** (sah-REHT)—French; **SARICE**—Swiss. In the Old Testament/ Tanakh and the Qur'an, Sarah was the favorite wife of Abraham, and she was the mother of Isaac very late in her life and after many years of infertility. A few saints have these names, one of which is said to have been Sara, the handmaiden of Mary Magdalene.

SARIELLE, "sah-ree-EHL"—Hebrew: "God's command." **SARI-EL, SURI-EL**—Hebrew; **SURIYEL**—Arabic. Sari-el is said to be an Archangel and a Seraph in the angelic scheme of things.

SARITA, "sah-REE-tah"—Hindu: "stream" or "river." **SERITA, SYREETA, SYRITA.**

SARIYAH, "sah-REE-yah"—Arabic: "clouds at night." **SARIYYAH.**

SASHA, "SAH-shah"—Russian diminutive of Alexandra, thus: "defender of humankind." **SACHA, SANYA, SASHENKA** (sah-SHEHN-kah), **SHURA, SHURIK, SHU-ROCHKA.** See also ALEXANDRA. M

SATINKA, "sah-TEEN-kah"—Native American: "magic dancer." **TINK.**

SATORI, "sah-TOH-ree"—Japanese: "enlightenment" or "comprehension." **TORI(E).** Satori is the sudden attainment of understanding for which Zen Buddhists strive. M

SAVANNAH, "sah-VAH-nah" or "sah-VAN-ah"—Caribbean: "fertile plain."

SCARLET(T), "SKAHR-leht"—French: "brilliant red"; English: "deep red." A main character in Margaret Mitchell's Gone With the Wind is named Scarlett O'Hara.

SCHEHEREZADE, "sheh-HEH-reh-zahd"—?. Scheherezade is the narrator of all the stories of the classic A Thousand and One Arabian Nights. She was a captive taken for a wife by a sultan who killed all his brides after the wedding night. She was able to stay her execution by relating wondrous stories to her rich and powerful captors, one story a night; in the morning, she would reveal the end. The name has the obvious storyteller association, but there are also connotations of courageousness, creativity, and cleverness.

SEAN(A), "SHAWN" and "SHAW-nah"—Gaelic version of Johnna: "God's gracious gift"; Gaelic: "old." **SHANNA, SHAUN(A), SHAWN(A).** Sean Young is a dark-haired, sultry actress known for her tempestuousness on screen and off. See also JOHNNA. M

SEBASTIANNE, "seh-BAHS-tyahn" and "seh-bahs-tee-AHN"—Greek: "venerable"; Latin: "from Sebastia." **SEBASTENE** (seh-bah-stehn-eh)—Basque; **SEBASTIANA, SEBASTIANI, SEBASTIANNA; SEBASTIENNE** (seh-bahs-TYENN)—French. **BASTA, BASTI(E)** (BAHS-tee), **BASTY; SEBA** (SAY-bah). M

SELA, "SEE-lah" or "SAY-lah"—Hebrew: "rock." **SALEET, SELETA**—Israeli. Sela Ward is an award-winning actress.

SELENA, "seh-LEE-nah" or "say-LAY-nah"—Greek: "the moon." **SELENE, SELI-NA.** See also CELINA, CELINE.

SELIMA, "seh-LEE-mah"—Arabic: "healthy." **SELIMAH.**

SELMA, "SEHL-mah"—Norse: "divine protection"; Celtic: "fair." **ZELMA.**

SEMELE, "seh-MEL-ee" or "SEH-meh-lee"—Greek: "honey-laden" or "fruitful." In Greek myth, Semele was a goddess who gave birth to Dionysus, son of Zeus. She was quite a beauty and a delight.

SEN, "SEHN"—*Japanese: "woodland fairy or elf."* M

SENDAL, "SEN-dahl"—*Old English: "fine cloth"* or *"fine linen."* M

SERAFINA, "seh-rah-FEE-nah"—*Hebrew: "a Seraph"* or *"the Seraphim"; Greek: "fiery."* **SERAPHIMA, SERAPHINA, SERAPHINE.** In Judeo-Christian and Muslim angelology, the Seraphim are the group of angels in direct contact with God. They are said to roar like lions and to be composed of fire. Saint Seraphina was a fifteenth-century martyr.

SERENA, "seh-RAY-nah" or "see-REE-nah"—*Latin: "serene."* **SERENE, SERRANA** (seh-RAH-nah).

SERI, "SEH-ree"—*Native American: "my family."* This is a tribe name for nomadic hunter-gatherers who inhabit Mexico and the extreme southwest United States. M

SETA, "SAY-tah"—*Latin: "silk."*

SETAI, "seh-TYE"—*African Zulu: "sorceress."* Setai was a legendary seer who foretold the rise and fall of the Zulu Nation under Shaka.

SHADA, "SHAH-dah"—*Native American Salish: "pelican."*

SHADE, "shah-DEH"—*African Yoruba: "confer the crown."* **SAADE** (shah-ah-DEH). M

SHADI, "shah-DEE"—*Arabic: "singer."* **SHADIYAH.**

SHAKTI, "SHAHK-tee"—*Sanskrit: "energy"* or *"power."* **SAKTI** (to be proper, put a dot under the "S"), **SHAKTA.** In Hinduism, Shakti is the divine female force.

SHAMIRA, "shah-MEER-ah"—*Hebrew: "diamond."* M

SHA(I)NA, "SHAY-nah"—*Yiddish: "beautiful."* **JANE, SHAINE, SHANE, SHAYNA.**

SHANDY, "SHAN-dee"—*English: "little boisterous one."* **SHANDEE, SHANDI(E).**

SHANE, SHANEEN, "SHAYN" and "shah-NEEN"—*version of Johnna: "God's gracious gift"; Gaelic: "magical hill"* (usually the kind of hill where one can find leprechauns). **SHANEENA, SHANINA, SHANINE, SHANYNA, SHANYNE; SHANYGNE** (shah-NEEN-yeh)—French. **NINA.** See also JAMIE, JOHNNA, SHA(I)NA, SHANNON.

SHANI, "SHAH-nee"—*Swahili: "marvelous."*

SHANNA, "SHAN-nah"—*Hebrew: "lily."* **SHANA, SHANNAH.**

SHANNON, "SHAN-nun"—*Irish: "smooth water"; Gaelic diminutive of Johnna: "God's gracious gift."* **CHANNEN, CHANYN; SEANAN** (SHAWN-un), **SHANNEN; SHANEEN.** See also JOHNNA.

SHANTHA, "SHAWN-thah"—*Hindu: "peaceful."* **SHANA, SHANATA.**

SHARAN, "SHAH-rawn"—*Hindu: "protection."*

SHARI(E). See SHARON.

SHARIFAH, "shah-REEF-ah"—*Tunisian: "honest"* or *"noblewoman"; Swahili: "distinguished."* M

SHARLENE, "shar-LEEN"—*version of the French Charlene: "strong and womanly."* **SHAR** (SHAHR), **SHARA, SHARI(E)** (SHAHR-ee or SHARE-ee), **SHARLEEN, SHARLINE, SHARLOTTE.**

SHARON, "SHARE-un" or "shah-RONE"—

SOUTHWEST GIRLS' NAMES

Girls born in the Southwest are most likely to have the following names:

1. Ashley	6. Brittany	11. Mariah	16. Vanessa
2. Jessica	7. Sarah	12. Victoria	17. Rebecca
3. Samantha	8. Amber	13. Megan	18. Melissa
4. Amanda	9. Nicole	14. Andrea	19. Crystal
5. Stephanie	10. Chelsea	15. Danielle	20. Michelle

Hebrew: a fertile plain in western Palestine; Arabic: "watering place." **SHARIA** (SHAH-ree-ah)—*Arabic;* **SHARONA**. In the Old Testament/Tanakh, the *Song of Solomon* describes the Plain of Sharon. The variant Sharona owes its popularity to a hook-laden 1980s song by a group called The Knack entitled "My Sharona." **SHARA, SHARI(E)**.

SHASHI, "SHAH-shee"—*Hindu: "moonbeams."*

SHASTA, "SHASS-tah"—*Native American Hokan: "forest people."* A mountain and a people found in northern California share this name. The Shasta Indians hunted and traded with their neighbors, providing deerskin products, obsidian, and sugar pine nuts. M

SHAWNA, "SHAW-nah"—*Gaelic version of Johnna: "God's gracious gift"; Gaelic: "the fairy hill."* **SHAUNA**. See also JOHNNA, SEAN(A), SHAWNEE. M

SHAWNEE, "shaw-NEE" or "SHAW-nee"—*Native American Algonquin: "my people, our people, us."* **SHAWNA, SHAWNIE**. This is a tribe name for a group of people who originally inhabited Ohio and Tennessee. M

SHEA, "SHAY"—*Gaelic: "fairy/leprechaun hill," "fairy/leprechaun fort," or just a fairy or leprechaun.* **SHAHAN, SHANE, SHAY, SHAYNE; SHEAN, SHEE, SHEEHAN, SHEEN.**

SHEBA, "SHEE-bah"—*Swahili: "oath" or "promise."* **SABA**—*Arabic.*

SHEILA, "SHEE-lah"—*Gaelic version of Cecilia: "gray eyes" or "blind"; Australian slang: "girl."* **SHAYLA**—*Australian;* **SHEELA, SHEELAH, SHEILAH; SHEELAGH** (SHEE-lay or SHEE-lah), **SHELAGH** (SHEH-lay or SHEH-lah)—*Gaelic.* The Australian usage popularized this name.

SHEKINAH, "SHEH-kee-nah"—*Hebrew: the female principle of the universe.*

SHELBY, "shel-BEE"—*Anglo-Saxon: "from the shelly farm"; Teutonic: "the manor farmhouse."*

SHELLEY, "SHEH-lee"—*English: "seaside ledge," "seaside meadow," "sloping meadow," "rocky hilltop field," or "covered with seashells."* **SHELLEIGH, SHELLI(E), SHELLY**. Shelley is a place name for several towns in Essex, Suffolk, and Yorkshire. Shelley Fabares and Shelley Duvall are both actresses; Duvall has gone into directing and producing as well. See also ROCHELLE.

SHERRIL(L), "SHEH-rihl"—*English: "a country hill."* **CHERILL, CHERRILL, CHERYL; SHERILL, SHERYL. SHERRI(E), SHERRY.**

SHERRY, "SHARE-ee"—*Spanish: "sweet wine"; French: "darling."* **SHEREE, SHERI(E), SHERIL(L), SHERILYN, SHERRI, SHERYL.**

SHIKA, "SHEE-kah"—*Japanese: "deer."* **SHIKAKO.**

SHINNA, "SHIH-nah" or "SHEE-nah"—*Gaelic: "vixen (female fox)."* **SHEENA, SHEENAGH**—Scottish Gaelic; **SHINNA, SHIN-NY**—Irish Gaelic. Sheena Easton is a Scottish singer.

SHIRA, "SHEE-rah"—*Hebrew: "song."*

SHIRLEY, "SHUR-lee"—*English: "the shire meadow" or "the white meadow."* **SHEREE, SHIRLEE, SHIRLEEN, SHIRLENE, SHERLI, SHERYL.** Shirley Temple was a child star of the 1930s, and every parent wanted an adorable moppet just like her.

SHOSHONA, "shoh-SHAH-nah"—*Hebrew: "lily," the original version of Susannah.* **SHOSHA,** (SHOH-shah)—Yiddish; **SHOSHANNA(H), SHUSHA** (SHOO-shah); **XUXA** (SHOO-shah)—Portuguese. See also SUSAN.

SHOSHONI, "shoh-SHOH-nee"—*Native American: "my people, our people, us."* This is a tribe name for a people who originated in the Great Basin in the western United States, and who eventually moved out onto the Great Plains to hunt buffalo.

SIDNEY. See SYDNEY.

SIDRA, "SIHD-rah"—*Latin: "a constellation."* **SIDRI; YSIDRA** (ee-SIHD-rah)—Portuguese, Basque, and Spanish. **SID, SIDDA.**

SIENNA, "see-EHN-ah"—*Italian.* Sienna is an orange- or yellow-brown earth tone that takes its name from the Italian city of Siena.

SIER(R)A, "see-AIR-ah"—*Spanish: "saw's edge."* The jagged mountain range called the Sierras in northern California resemble a saw's edge.

SIGOURNEY, "sih-GOOR-nee"—*French: "daring ruler."* This old and obscure name became popular in 1980 with the arrival of the thriller *Alien,* and its tough heroine, Ripley, who was played by Sigourney Weaver.

SIGRID, "SIHG-rihd"—*Norse: "victorious guardian."*

SILKA, "SEEL-kah"—*Yiddish: "princess."*

SIMA(H), "SEE-mah"—*Yiddish: "incense"; Aramaic: "treasure."* **ZIMA, ZIMAH.**

SIMBA, "SEEM-bah" or "SIHM-bah"—*Kiswahili: "lioness."*

SIMCHA, "SEEM-khah" ("kh" is from the back of your throat)—*Hebrew: "joy."* **SIMKA.**

SIMONE, "see-MOHN"—*Hebrew: "be heard," "God has heard," or "with acceptance"; Greek: "snub-nosed."* **CHIMONA; JIMENA** (hee-MAY-nah)—Spanish; **SHIMONIT** (shee-MOHN-eet or shee-moh-NEET)—Israeli; **SIMONA, SIMONIA, SYMONA; SIMON-ETTE** (see-moh-NEHT)—French; **XIMENA** (zee-mehn-ah or shee-mehn-nah), **XIMENE, XIMENIA**—Basque. Several Christian saint names are on this list. M

SINA. See ADESINA, ALCINA, HASINA, JEAN(NE), MESSINA.

SIRENA, "sih-REE-nah" or "sye-REE-nah"—*Greek: "to bind" or "to attract."* In Greek legend, and in many other cultures, Sirens were sea goddesses whose seductive calling, singing, etc., either drove sailors mad or lured them to their deaths on rocky shores.

SIRIA, "SEE-ree-ah"—*Latin: "hot" or "scorching."* **SYRIA.** Syria is a Middle Eastern country.

SISIKA, "see-SEE-kah"—*Native American: "thrush" or "swallow."* **SISI.**

SITA, "SEE-tah"—*Sanskrit: "furrow."* Sita is a Hindu earth goddess.

SITARA, "see-TAH-rah"—*Hindu: "Morning Star."*

SKY, "SKY"—*Old Norse: "cloud."* **CIÉL** (see-EHL)—French; **CIELA** (see-EHL-ah)—Italian and Spanish; **LANGIT** (LAWN-giht)—Indonesian; **MBINGU** (m'BIHN-goo)—Swahili; **RAKIA** (RAH-kee-ah)—Hebrew; **SAMA**—Arabic; **SORA**—Japanese. M

SLANIE, "SLAY-nee" or "SLAH-nee"—*French from Gaelic: "healthy."* **SIANY** (SHAH-nee)—Irish Gaelic; **SLÁINE** (SLY-neh)—Scottish Gaelic; **SLANEE, SLANIA.** M

SNOW, "SNOH"—*English: "snow."* **GALID** (gah-LEED)—Arabic; **KAR**—Turkish; **NEIGE** (NEHZH)—French; **NEVE** (NEH-veh)—Portuguese and Italian; **NIEVE** (nee-YEH-veh)—Spanish; **SCHNEE** (SHNAY or SHNEE)—German; **SNEEUWE** (SNEW-eh)—Dutch; **SNÖ, SNØ** (SNAW)—Scandinavian; **THELUJI** (theh-LOO-jee)—Swahili; **YUKI**—Japanese; **ZAPADA**—Rumanian. M

SOBEL, "SOH-behl"—*Yiddish: "sustenance."*

SOFIA, SOPHIA, "SOH-fee-ah" or "soh-FEE-ah"—*traditionally, Greek: "wisdom"; but also Hebrew: "looking toward" and Persian: "royal one."* **SAFA, SAFIYAH**—Arabic and Swahili; **SAFA** (SAH-fah); **SAFIYYAH** (sah-FEE-yah)—Tunisian; **SOFIE,**

SOPHIE; SOPHI, SOPHY—Persian; **SONYA** (SONE-yah), **SONYURU, SONYUSHA**—Russian; **SOPHRON** (soh-FROHN), **SOPHRONIA**—Greek; **TZOPHIAH** (TZOH-fee-ah)—Hebrew; **ZOFIA**—Polish; **ZSOFIA** (zhoh-FEE-ah), **ZSOFIE, ZSOFIKA**—Hungarian. The name's connection to royalty is strong. Third-century martyr Saint Sophia shares her name with several Arabic, Turkish, and Russian royals. Sophy was the title of kings and queens of ancient Persia. And in the seventeenth century, Sophia of Russia was regent while her younger brother, the future tzar, grew up. While she had power, she brought an era of artistic and philosophical enlightenment to the realm. See also SOFIEL(LE).

SOFIEL(LE), "soh-fee-EHL"—*?, Egyptian or Persian: angel of vegetation, plants.* See also SOFIA.

SOLITA, "soh-LEE-tah"—*Latin: "solitary."*

SONA(H), "SOH-nah"—*African: "elephant."* The elephant is seen as a powerful and noble animal by African tribes. M

SONDRA. See CASSANDRA, LYSANDRA, SANDRA.

SONNET, "SAWN-eht"—*Italian: a type of fourteen-line poem.* M

SONYA, "SONE-yah"—*Russian version of Sophia: "wisdom."* **SONIA, SONJA** (SONE-yah)—Slavic and Danish. Sonja Henie was a Norwegian Olympic skater who went to Hollywood in the 1930s. See also SOFIA/SOPHIA.

SOUBRETTE, "soo-BREHT"—*French: "coquette," "flirt," or "little maiden."*

SPICE, "SPYSS"—*Old French from Latin: "wares" or "spices."* **BACHARIKO** (bah-KAHR-ee-koh)—Greek; **BAHAR** (bah-

---

-sten

"-sten" (pronounced "-STEHN") is the old Teutonic word for "stone," which has connotations of steadfastness and strength. It is not the same as "-sen." You may add "-sten" to any name you choose.

HAHR)—Turkish; **BUMBU** (BOOM-boo), **REMPAH** (REHM-pah)—Indonesian; **ÉPICE** (eh-PEESE)—French; **ESPECIA** (ehs-PEH-see-ah)—Spanish; **ESPECIARIA** (ehs-peh-see-AHR-ee-ah)—Portuguese; **GEWÜRZE** (geh-VOORZ-eh)—German; **KRYDDA** (KREE-dah)—Swedish; **KRYDDEKE** (KREE-dehk-eh)—Norwegian; **KRYDDERI** (kree-DARE-ee)—Danish; **PRYANOSTI(Y)** (pree-YAH-nohs-tee[-yeh])—Russian; **SPEZIE** (SPEH-zee or SPEHTZ-ee)—Italian; **YAKU-MI**—Japanese.

SPRING, "SPRING"—*English: "spring."* **HARU** (hah-ROO)—Japanese; **PRIMAVERA** (pree-mah-VAY-rah)—Italian, Spanish, and Portuguese; **PRINTEMPS** (PRAN-tom—"R" in the back of your throat)—French; **TAVASZ** (tah-VAZH)—Hungarian; **VESNA** (vehz-NAH)—Russian; **VOORJAAR** (VOOR-yah-ahr)—Dutch.

STAC(E)Y. See ANASTASIA, EUSTACIA.

STAR(R), "STAR"—*English: "star."* **ASTRU** (AHZ-troo)—Rumanian; **BINTANG** (BIHN-tong)—Indonesian; **CSILLAG** (TSEEL-ahg)—Hungarian; **ESTREL(L)A** (ehz-TRALE-ah or ehz-TRAY-ah)—Spanish and Portuguese; **ÉTOILE** (ay-TWAHL)—French; **HOSHI**—Japanese; **KOCHAVA** (koh-KHAV-ah—"KH" like you're clearing your throat)—Hebrew; **NYOTA** (NYOH-tah)—Swahili; **STELLA**—Italian and Greek; **STJERNE** (STYERN)—Danish and Norwegian; **TAHTI** (TAH-tee)—Finnish; **ZVEZDA** (zvehz-DAH)—Russian.

See also ESTELLE, HOKU, IZARRA. M

STEFANIE. See STEPHANIE.

STELA, "STAY-luh"—*Sumerian: "keeper of wisdom."* Stela were fancy, carved tablets written in Sumerian cuneiform. See also ESTELLE.

STELLA, "STEHL-ah"—*Greek: "star."* The word was always in use, but its first use as a name came in the sixteenth century, when Sir Philip Sidney published a collection of his poems, sonnets, and songs entitled *Astrophel and Stella.* "Stel-LAAH!" is the long-suffering wife of Stanley Kowlaski in Tennessee Williams's *A Streetcar Named Desire.* See also ESTELLE, STAR(R).

STEPHANIE, "STEHF-ah-nee"—*Greek: "crowned with laurel."* **ÉTIENNE** (ay-TYEN), **FANETTE** (fah-NEHT)—French; **PANYA**, **STEPHANYA** (stehp-AWN-yah), **STESHA**—Russian; **STAFFANJE** (STAH-fah-nyeh)—Swedish; **STEFANIA** (steh-FAHN-ee-ah)—Italian; **STEFANIA** (steh-FAHN-yah), **STAVRA** (STAHV-rah)—Greek; **STEFANIE; STIOFÁSNIN** (STYOH-fah-neen)—Gaelic; **SZCZEPANIKE** (s'cheh-PAHN-ee-keh)—Polish. The Romans used to think that laurel provided protection from lightning. Stefanie Zimbalist and Stefanie Powers are actresses known for their television work. Steffi Graf was a gawky teenager when she first hit the pro tennis circuit, but she is now a respected champion. **STEF, STEFFI(E); STEPH, STEPHIE; STEVIE.** M

STEVIE. See STEPHANIE.

STORM, "STORM"—*English: "tempestuous."* **ARASHI** (AH-rah-shee)—*Japanese;* **ASIFA** (AH-see-fah or ah-SEE-fah)—*Arabic;* **BURYA** (BOOR-yah)—*Russian;* **DHORUBA** (d'hoh-ROO-bah)—*Swahili;* **FIRTINA** (feer-TEE-nah)—*Turkish;* **ORAGE** (oh-RAZH)—*French;* **SAAR** (SAHR)—*Hebrew;* **VIHAR** (vee-HAHR)—*Hungarian.* **STORMY.** M

SUBIRA, "soo-BEE-rah"—*Swahili: "our patience has been rewarded."*

SUDI, SUDY, "SOO-dee"—*Swahili: "lucky"; English: "southerly wind."*

SUE. See SUSAN.

SUGI, "SOO-jee"—*Japanese: "cedar."* M

SUKE, "SOO-keh"—*Hawaiian: "lily."*

SUKHA, "SOOK-hah"—*Sanskrit: "happiness" or "bliss."* M

SUKI, "SOO-kee"—*Japanese: "beloved."* M

SUMI, "SOO-mee"—*Japanese: "refined."* M

SUMMER, "SUM-mur"—*English: "summer."* **KAYITS** (kah-YEETS or KAH-yeets)—*Hebrew;* **LATO** (LAH-toh)—*Polish;* **LYETO** (LYAY-toh)—*Russian;* **NATSU** (NAHT-soo)—*Japanese;* **SAYF** (SYFE)—*Arabic;* **SOMMAR, SOMMER**—*German and Scandinavian;* **VERANA** (veh-RAH-nah)—*Spanish;* **VERÃO** (veh-RAH-oh)—*Portuguese;* **YAZ** (YAHZ)—*Turkish.* M

SUN, "SUN"—*Korean: "goodness."* M

SUNNY, "SUHN-ee"—*English: "of the Sun," "bright and warm," or "cheerful."* **SUNSHINE.**

SURYA, "SOOR-yah"—*Hindu: "sun goddess" or "sunshine" (equivalent to the constellation/astrological sign Leo); Sanskrit: "the sun."* **SURYAH.**

SUSAN, "SOO-sahn"—*Hebrew: "lily"; Japanese: "valiant, swift (and impetuous)," a Shinto god.* **SAWSAN** (SAW-sahn), **SOSSAN**—*Arabic;* **SHOSHANA(H)** (shoh-SHAH-nah)—*Hebrew;* **SIÚSAIDH** (SHOO-say or SHOO-sye)—*Scottish Gaelic;* **SIUSAN** (SYOO-sahn)—*Scottish;* **SIUSHÍN** (SHOO-sheen)—*Irish Gaelic;* **SOSANNA**—*Irish;* **SUSANNA**—*Swedish;* **SUSANNE, SUSETTE, SUZANNE, SUZETTE, SUZON**—*French;* **SUSANA-OH** (soo-SAH-nah-oh), **SUSANAWO**—*Japanese;* **SUSIANA**—*Semitic;* **SUZANNAH, SUZETTA**—*Italian;* **ZOZI** (ZOH-zee), **ZUZANNAH, ZUZI, ZUZU**—*Swiss;* **ZSA ZSA** (ZHAH-zhah), **ZSUSHKA** (ZHOOSH-kah), **ZSUSZA, ZSUZSANNA** (zhoo-ZHAH-nah), **ZSUZSHKA** (ZHOOZH-kah), **ZSUZSI**—*Hungarian;* **ZSUSKA** (ZHOOS-kah), **ZSUZSKA** (ZHOOZH-kah)—*Eastern European;* **ZUZANNI** (zoo-ZAHN-ee), **ZUZANNY**—*Polish.* In the apocryphal texts of the Bible, Susannah was a woman falsely accused of adultery, but was spared punishment because the prophet Daniel intervened. The Japanese deity Susanawo or Susana-oh ruled oceans and storms. Susiana, sometimes called Elam, was an ancient country in Asia Minor between the Persian Gulf and the Caspian Sea. Susianna might be considered to be a combination name meaning "graceful lily." **SUE, SUSIE; SUZIE, SUZY.**

SUZANNE. See SUSAN.

SUZU, "soo-ZOO"—*Japanese: "little bell."* **SUZUE** (soo-ZOO-ay—"branch of little bells").* M

SVANTE, "SVAHN-teh"—*Swedish: "swan."*

SVETLANA, "SVEHT-lah-nah"—*Russian: "bright star."* **SVETA, SVETOCHKA.**

SYBIL, SIBYL, "SIHB-ihl"—*Greek: "prophetess" or "wise woman."* **CYBELE**—

French; **SIBÉAL** (SHEE-bahl)—Irish Gaelic; **SIBYLLA** (sih-BIHL-ah), **SYBILLA**—Swedish; **SIBYLLE, SYBILLE**—French. Only a few women in ancient times were regarded as true Sybils, and those that had proved themselves became very powerful. The Sybil of Cumae sold a collection of predictions, her own and others, to a Roman king who consulted them regularly. When Christianity came into prominence, the Sibyls and their prophecies were still respected, because some of their prophecies had mentioned the coming of Christ.

SYDNEY, "SIHD-nee"—*Hebrew: "to lure" or "to entice"; Latin: "of Saint Denis"; from a combination of languages: "the Winding Sheet (shroud) of Christ."* **SIDAINE** (see-DEHN), **SIDOINE** (see-DWAHN)—French; **SIDONIA** (sih-DOH-nee-ah)—Dutch; **SIDNEY, SIDONIE; TZIDONI** (TSIH-doh-nee)—Israeli. **SID, SYD.** For the male version, see SIDNEY.

SYLPHIDE, "sihl-FEED"—*Latin: "wispy spirit."* **SYLPH.**

SYLVIA, "SIHL-vee-ah"—*Latin: "forest."* **SILVA, SYLVA, ZILVIA, ZYLVIA; SILVANA, SYLVANA** (sihl-VAH-nah); **SILVIA, SILVIE**—Nordic and Eastern European; **SILWIA** (SEEL-vee-ah)—Polish; **SYLVETTE, SYLVIE, SYLVIANNE**—French. Silvanae were the Roman wood nymphs and forest fairies. M

SYNA, "SYE-nah" or "SEE-nah"—*Greek: "together."*

SYSHA, "see-SHAH" or "sye-SHAH"—*German: "sweet."*

THE TOP FIVE

TAYLOR
TIA/TÉA
TABITHA
THERESA
TESS

If the name you're looking for isn't here, perhaps it is a variant or diminutive of another primary name.

TABIA, "tah-BEE-uh"—*Swahili: "talented."*

TABITHA, "TAB-ih-thah"—*Aramaic: "gazelle."* This beautiful, ancient name came into vogue in the 1960s after domestic witch Samantha gave birth to a sweet little sorceress named Tabitha on the TV series *Bewitched.* **TAB, TABBI(E), TABBY.**

TACHINE, "TAH-cheen," "TAHK-een-eh," or "tah-KEE-neh"—*Greek: "swift."*

TAFFY, "TAF-ee"—*Welsh version of Davida: "beloved"; Old English: "river."* **TAAFE, TAFFI, TAFFIE; TAVI.** See also DAVIDA.

TAHIRAH, "tah-HEER-ah"—*Arabic: "pure, chaste."* M

TAJA, "TAHZH-ah"—*Arabic: "crown."* M

TAKA, "TAH-kah"—*Japanese: "falcon."* M

TAKARA, "tah-KAH-rah"—*Japanese: "treasure" or "precious."*

TAKI, "TAH-kee"—*Japanese: "waterfall."* M

TAKIYAH, "tuh-KEE-yah"—*African: "pious, righteous."* **TAKEYAH, TEKEYAH, TEKIYAH.** T'keyah Keyma is a comedic actress.

TALA(H), "TAH-lah"—*Native American:* "wolf."

TALIA, TALYA, "TAHL-yah," "TAH-lee-ah," and rarely, "tah-LYE-ah"—*Aramaic: "lamb"; Hebrew: "dewdrop from heaven"; Greek: "abundance."* **TALIAH, TALYAH, THALIA** (TAHL-yah). In Greek mythology, Talia is one of the three Graces, and also one of the nine Muses, the one concerned with laughter and comedy. See also ATALIA.

TALMOR(H), "TAHL-mohr"—*Arabic: "a mound of myrrh."* **TALMORIT** (TAHL-mohreet or tahl-moh-REET). This is much like saying "worth her weight in gold," as myrrh was and is very expensive.

TAMA, "TAH-mah"—*Japanese: "jewel"; Native American: "thunderbolt."*

TAMARA, "tah-MAHR-ah" or "TAM-ahrah"—*Hebrew and Arabic: "date palm tree."* **TAMAR, TAMARAH; TAMARY** (tah-MAHRee)—Russian. Tamara Dobson is an actress. **TAMMI, TAMMY.**

TAMARINDA, "tah-mah-RIHN-dah"—*Arabic: "fruit-bearing tree of India" or "date tree of India."* **TAMAREND, TAMARENDA; TAMAR.** The wood of this tropical tree is used in furniture and carving art. **TAM, TAMMI(E), TAMMY.**

TAMIKA, "tah-MEE-kah" or "TAHM-ee-kah"—*Japanese: "people."* This name is popular in the African-American community.

TAMILA, "TAH-meel-ah" or "tah-MEE-lah"—*Sanskrit(?): "southern(?)."* M

TAMMA, "TAH-mah"—*Hebrew: "perfection."*

TAMMY. See TAMARA, TAMARINDA, THOMASINA.

TAN(N)A, "TAH-nah"—*Pali: "desire."* **TANHA**—Pali. Tana is a river that arises in Kenya and runs to the Indian Ocean. See also MATANA.

TANE, "tah-NAY" or "TAH-nay"—*Japanese: "seed."*

TANGINA, "tan-JEE-nah"—*?.* This was a name created for a very good and powerful, yet physically small, psychic in the series of *Poltergeist* movies in the 1980s. A possible meaning could come from the Latin word tangere, which means "to touch" (the Other Side, in the psychic's case).

TANI, "TAH-nee"—*Japanese: "valley."* M

TANISHA, "tah-NEE-shah" or "TAH-nee-shah"—*Japanese: "born on Monday."* **TANEISHA** (tah-NAY-shah), **TANESHA, TANISHIA; TENEISHA** (teh-NAY-shah), **TENISHA, TENISHIA.** These are popular names in the African-American community.

TANITH, "TAH-nihth"—*Irish: "heiress."* **TANITHA.**

TANYA, "TAH-nyah"—*Greek: "great one"; Eastern/Northern Europe: the Fairy Queen.* **TANJA** (tah-NYAH), **TONJA, TONYA.** The latter derivation comes from the folklore and fairy tales of these regions, in which she is also called Titania. See also LATONIA, LITONYA, NATANIA, TATANIA, TATYANA, TITANIA.

TASIDA(H), "tah-SEE-dah"—*Native American Sarcee: "rider."*

TATANIA, "tah-TAHN-yah"—*version of Titania: "the great one."* This is the Fairy Queen in European folklore. **TANIA, TANYA; TATIANA.** See also LATONIA, TATYANA, TITANIA.

TATARA, "tah-TAHR-ah"—*Turkish(?): "of the rugged mountains"; Persian: "hellion."*

TATUM, "TAY-tum"—*English: "cheerful"; Native American Algonquin: "windy" or "great talker."* Tatum O'Neal was one of the youngest Oscar recipients in the Best Actress category—she was ten years old when she won for *Paper Moon.* M

TATYANA, "tah-TYAH-nah"—*version of Titania in Eastern/Northern Europe: "great one."* **TATANIA, TATIANA, TATJANA** (tah-TYAH-nah); **TITANIA** (tih-TAHN-yah), **TITANJA, TITANYA.** In these regions' folklore and fairy tales, Titania is the Fairy Queen. Tatiana is also one of the Christian saints. See also LATONIA, TANYA.

TAWNY, "TAW-nee"—*French: "bronzed"; Gypsy: "small."* **TAWNEE, TAWNI(E).**

TAYLOR, "TAY-lur"—*English: "tailor, clothesmaker."* Songstress Taylor Dane is largely responsible for the skyrocketing popularity of what was an exclusively male trade name on the baby-girl name charts. M

TE, "TEH"—*Chinese: "virtue" or "power."* M

TEDDI(E). See THEODORA.

TEGAN, "TEE-ghen" or "TAY-ghen"—*Celtic: "doe."* **TEG, TEGGIE, TEGGY.**

TEMA, "TAY-mah"—*African Akan: "queen."*

TEMIMA(H), "teh-MYE-mah" or "teh-MEE-mah"—*Arabic and Hebrew: "honesty."*

TEMIRA(H), "teh-MEE-rah"—*Hebrew: "tall."* TIMORA(H).

TEMPEST, "TEHM-pehst"—*French: "stormy."*

TERENCIA, "tare-ent-SEE-ah" or "teh-REHN-syah"—*Latin: "tender"; Greek: "guardian"; Teutonic: "people's ruler."* TERANCIA, TERANTIA, TERENTA (tare-ENT-ah), TERENTIA, TERENTILA (tare-ehn-TEE-lah), TERENTINA; TEROCENCIA (tare-oh-SEHN-see-ah); TERRANCIA, TERRANTIA, TERRENCIA, TERRENTIA. TERI(E), TERRI(E). M

TERESA, THERESA, "teh-REE-sah" or "teh-REH-sah" for both—*Greek: "corn carrying"; Latin: "reaper"; Irish: "strength."* RESI, TERESSA (teh-REHS-sah), TRESSA—Greek; REZI, RIZA, TECA, TEREZ, TERÉZA (teh-REH-zah)—Eastern European; TERCSA (TUR-zhah), TERIKE (teh-REE-keh), TERUS (teh-ROOSH), TRESZKA—Hungarian and Slavic; TERESIA (teh-REH-see-ah)—Swedish; TERESSA (teh-REHS-sah), THÉRÈSE (tay-RAISE)—French; TEREZINHA (teh-reh-ZEEN-hah)—Portuguese; TOIRÉASA (tye-RAY-ah-sah), TRÉASA (TRAY-sah), TREISE (TREESE)—Irish Gaelic. Three saints have borne this name. The best known is probably Saint Teresa of Avila, who founded several convents, and did a lot of writing and missionary work. Several European queens and princesses have had names on this list. TERI, TERIE, TERRI(E), TERRY.

TERRI(E). See TERENCIA, TERESA/THERESA.

TERTIA, "TUR-shah"—*Latin: "third."*

TERUMA, "teh-ROO-mah"—*Hebrew: "offering."*

TESSA, "TEH-sah"—*Greek: "the fourth."* TESS. English novelist Thomas Hardy wrote *Tess of the d'Urbervilles* (1891).

TESZIA, "TESH-yah"—*Hungarian/Polish: "loved by God."* TESHA.

TEYA(H), "TAY-yah"—*Native American: "precious."*

THALASSA, "thah-LASS-ah" or "tah-LASS-ah"—*Greek: "the sea."* Thalassa is a moon of Neptune.

THALIA, "TAHL-yah" or "THAHL-yah"—*Greek: "to flourish" and "joy."* In Greek mythology, Thalia is one of the nine Muses; her area of influence is comedy. Thalia is also one of the three Graces, the one of joy. See also TALIA/TALYA.

THAN(N)A, "THAH-nah"—*Arabic: "thankful."*

THAR(R)A, "THAH-rah"—*Arabic: "wealth."*

THEA, "THEE-ah"—*Greek: "goddess."* See also ALTHEA, THEODORA, THEOPHILIA.

THEANA, "thee-AN-ah"—*Greek: "divine name."*

THEDA, "THAY-dah" or "THEE-dah"—*Greek: "divine."* See also THEODORA.

THELMA, "THEHL-mah" or "TEHL-mah"—*Greek: "nursing child," or "will" (in a stretch).* TELMA. The name was made up by Marie Corelli, a novelist in the nineteenth century, for her book *Thelma, a Norwegian Princess.*

THEODORA, "thee-oh-DOH-rah"—*Greek: "divine gift."* FEODORA (fay-oh-DOHR-ah)—Spanish; TEODORA (tay-oh-DOH-rah)—Swedish; TEODOZJI (tay-uh-DOH-zhee)—Polish; THEDA, THEODOSIA (tay-oh-DOH-see-ah)—Russian. Theodora was a Byzantine empress. DORA, DORI(E), DORY; TEA, TEDDI(E), TEDDY; THEA. M

THEOPHILIA, "thee-oh-FEE-lee-ah" or "tay-oh-FEE-lee-ah"—*Greek: "divine love."* **TEOFILIA, THEOFILIA. TEA, THEA.**

THERA, "THARE-ah"—*Greek: "untamed."*

THOMASINA, "taw-mah-SEE-nah"—*traditionally, Aramaic: "twin"; also Sanskrit: "darkness"; Sumerian: "true child"; Greek: "cutting"; a Mesopotamian crop god.* **TAM, TAMERLANE, TAMLANE, TAMMI(E), TAMMY**—Scottish; **TAMÁSA** (tah-MAWSH-ah)—Eastern European; **THOMASETTE** (toh-mah-SEHT)—French; **TOMA, TOMASSA** (toh-MAH-sah)—Italian; **TOMASINE, TOMASINHA**—Spanish and Portuguese; **TOMCIA** (TAWM-chyah)—Polish. **TOMMA, TOMMI(E), TOMMY.** M

THORA, "THOHR-ah"—*Norse: "the thunderer."* **THORDIS, TORA.** M

THURSDAY, "THURZ-day"—*Teutonic: "Thor's day."* **ABA** (ah-BAH)—African Fante; **CHETVERK** (cheht-VAYRK)—Russian; **DONNERSTAG** (DAWN-urz-tog)—German; **HAMISI** (hah-MEE-see), **MWANAHAMISI** (m'WAH-nah-hah-MEE-see)—Swahili; **JEUDI** (ZHUH-dee)—French; **JOVEDI** (joh-VAY-dee)—Italian; **JUEVES** (ZHWAY-vehz)—Spanish; **KEMIS** (KEH-mihss)—Indonesian; **LAKYA** (LOCK-yah)—India; **MOKUYUBI** (moh-koo-YOO-bee or moh-KOO-yoo-bee)—Japanese; **PERSEMBE** (pare-SEHM-beh)—Turkish; **TORSDAG** (TOHRZ-dog)—Scandinavian; **YAA** (YAH-ah)—African Ewe. Thor was a Norse god.

TIA, "TEE-ah"—*Egyptian: "princess."* **TEA, TÉA.** See also TIAMAT.

TIAMAT, "TYAH-maht"—*Babylonian: "chaos," "primeval," or "first one."* In Babylonian mythology, Tiamat is the first creature of the universe. **TIA.**

TIBERIA, "tee-BEAR-ee-ah" or "tie-

BEE-ree-ah"—*Latin.* The Tiber River runs from the Apennines in Tuscany to the Tyrrhen Sea, passing through Rome on the way.

TIERNEY, "TEER-nee"—*Irish: "lordly" or "noble."* **TIARNA**—Irish Gaelic. M

TIFFANY, "TIHF-ah-nee"—*Greek: "divine manifestation."* **THEOPANIA** (thee-oh-FAN-ee-ah)—Greek and Latin; **TIPHANIE**—French. Louis Comfort Tiffany was a leader of the aesthetic art movement in the last half of the nineteenth century, and worked mainly in glass. Tiffany's finest pieces are like gentle watercolor naturescapes in the hard medium of glass, more exquisite and lifelike than the stained glasswork being done up to that time.

TILDA, "TIHL-dah"—*Teutonic: "heroine."* See also MATILDA.

TIMOTHEA, "tihm-oh-THEE-ah"—*Greek: "honoring the gods" or "honoring God."* **TEEMOFA** (TEE-moh-fah), **TIMIRA** (tee-MEE-rah), **TIMIRIA**—Russian; **TIMOTHÉA** (tee-moh-TAY-ah), **TIMOTHÉE** (TEE-moh-tay)—French. **TIMI, TIMMI(E), TIMMY.** M

TINA, "TEE-nah." This is a diminutive for all names that end in "-tine" or "-tina." **TE(E)NA.** See also FATINAH, JUSTINE, VALENTINE.

TIPPER, TIPRA, "TIH-pur" and "TIH-prah" or more rarely "TEE-pur" and "TEE-prah"—*version of Zipporah: "bird"; Irish: "the well."* Tipper Gore is the wife of Vice President Albert Gore. Tippi Hedren is a former model who came to the big screen in the late 1950s. Her best-known roles are both under the direction of the legendary Sir Alfred Hitchcock: *The Birds* and *Marnie.* **TIP, TIPPI(E), TIPPY.**

TIRZA, "TUR-zah"—*Hebrew: "cypress tree"*

or "desirable." **THIRZA, THYRZAH, TIRZAH.** M

TISHA(H), "tih-SHAH" or "TIH-shah"—*Hebrew: "the ninth."* This refers to the ninth day, hour, month, child, etc. See also LETITIA.

TITANIA, "tih-TAHN-yah"—*Greek: "great one."* **TANIA, TANYA, TATIANA** (tah-TYAH-nah). Titania, the Fairy Queen in much of European folklore, makes an appearance in Shakespeare's *A Midsummer Night's Dream.* Saint Tatiana or Titania was a miracle-working young virgin who was martyred in the second or third century. Titania is one of the moons of Uranus. See also LATONIA, TANYA, TATANIA, TATYANA. M

TI(I)U, "tee-OOH"—*Norse: "goddess of war."* Tuesday is named in honor of Tiu.

TIVONA(H), "tee-VONE-ah"—*Hebrew: "lover of nature."*

TOBI, "TOH-bee"—*Hebrew: "God is good."* **TOBA, TOBE, TOBELLE, TOBIE, TOBIT. TOBY.** M

TOHONA, "toh-HOH-nah"—*Native American: "river."* **TOHONEE.**

TOMI, "TOH-mee"—*Japanese: "riches."* M

TONI(E). See ANTONIA.

TONYA. See ANTONIA, TANYA.

TOPAZ, "TOH-paz"—*Greek: "topaz stone."* **TOPAZA.**

TORA, "TOH-rah"—*Japanese: "tigress."* See also THORA.

TORI, "TOH-ree"—*Japanese: "bird"; Irish: "bandit" and "outlaw."* **TORII** (toh-ree-EE, Japanese for "bird's perch" or "bird's perching"); **TOREY, TORIE, TORY.** A torii is the gateway to many Shinto shrines and meditation spots, and consists of two vertical poles crossed by a pair of horizontal posts. Tori Amos is a singer/songwriter, and Tori Spelling is an actress. See also ETTARE/ETTORE.

TORUN, "TOR-un"—*Norwegian: "beloved of Thor/Tor."* **TOR(R)IN.**

TOVA(H), "TOH-vah"—*Hebrew: "good."* **TOVE(H).** Tovah Feldshuh is an actress. M

TOYA(H), "TOY-ah"—*English: "dalliance" or "trifle."* **LATOYA(H).**

TRAC(E)Y, "TRAY-see"—*Latin: "to lead" or "to investigate"; Anglo-Saxon: "defender."* **TRASEY, TRAYCE(E).** Swimmer Tracy Caulkins was just fifteen when she won six medals in the 1978 Olympics. Tracy Scoggins is a willowy actress. Tracey Ullman is an actress and comedienne. **TRACE, TRACI(E), TRASE.** M

TRINA, TRINI, "TREE-nah/nee"—*Latin: "the Trinity"; Greek: "pure"; Hindu: "sharp points" ("Trina" only).* **TRIND, TRINDE** (TREEN-deh)—Swedish; **TRINDADE** (TREEN-dahd); **TRINE** (TREE-neh)—Norwegian; **TRINIDAD** (TREE-nee-dahd)—Spanish; **TRYN, TRYNJE** (TREE-nyeh)—Dutch. The Trinity refers to

---

TRIBAL TRADITIONS

In many African and South American regions, one of a child's names must identify the clan totem or protecting animal, or it must identify his or her individual guardian spirit.

the Father, the Son, and the Holy Ghost in Christian tradition. The Hindu derivation refers to the "sharp points" of the Kusa Grass, an object sacred to Hindus. See also PETRINA.

TRISHA, "TREE-shah" or "TRIH-shah"—*Hindu: "the thirst of love."* **TRISH.** See also PATRICE.

TRUDY, "TROO-dee"—*German/Norse: "strength."* **TRUDE, TRUDI(E).**

TSILLA, "TSEE-lah"—*Hebrew: "protection."*

TUESDAY, "TOOZ-day"—*Celtic: "Tyw's day."* **ABENA** (ah-beh-NAH), **BABA** (BAH-bah)—African Fante; **ABLA** (AH-blah)—African; **DIENSTAG** (DEENZ-tog)—German; **DINSDAG** (DEENZ-dog)—Dutch; **KWAYUBI** (KWAH-yoo-bee)—Japanese; **MARDI** (MAHR-dee)—French; **MARTEDI** (mahr-TEH-dee)—Italian; **MARTES** (MAHR-tehz)—Spanish; **SALI** (SAH-lee)—Turkish; **SELASA** (seh-LAH-zah)—Indonesian; **TIRSDAG** (TEERZ-dog)—Norwegian and Danish; **TISDAG** (TIHZ-dog)—Swedish. Tyw—spelled a number of ways—is a war god or goddess in Europe mythology. Tiw is brother of Thor and a son of Odin in Norse mythology. Actress Tuesday Weld had her heyday in the 1960s, and made naming your children after days of the week fashionable.

TULA, "TOO-lah"—*Hindu: equivalent to Libra;* Native American Nahuatl: "bullrushes." **TULE** (TOOL or TOO-leh).

TULLA, "TUH-lah" or "TOO-lah"—*Gaelic: "a little hill"; Irish: "mighty people"; Latin: "a title."* **TULA, TULLEY.**

TULLIA, "TOO-lee-ah" or "TOO-lyah"—*Gaelic: "peaceful" or "quiet."* M

TUPI, "TOO-pee"—*Native South American: "comrade."* The Tupi are a large group of South American Indians, found primarily in the Amazon, Tapajos, and Xingu Valleys.

TUSA(H), "TOO-sah"—*Native American Zuni: "prairie dog."*

TWYLA, "TWY-lah"—*English: "double threaded."* **TWILA.** Twyla Tharpe is a revolutionary dancer and choreographer.

TYCHE, "TYE-kee"—*Greek: the goddess of chance.* M

TYNA(H), "TYE-nah"—*Gaelic: "dark" or "gray."* M

TYNE, "TINE"—*English: "river."* Tyne Daly is an actress.

THE TOP FIVE

URSULA
UNDINE
UMA
UNA
ULEMA

If the name you're looking for isn't here, see the other vowels.

UALANI, "oo/yoo-ah-LAH-nee"—*Hawaiian: "heavenly rain."*

UDELLE, "yoo-DEHL"—*English: "small valley of yew trees."* M

UHURA, "oo-HOO-rah"—*Swahili: "free" or "freedom."* Uhura was the African-American woman on board the U.S.S. Enterprise in the original TV series *Star Trek*. It was a revolutionary role, since the character was a strong, educated officer—quite a departure from the usual roles played by black women on television at the time. See also AHURA. M

UL(L)A, "OO-lah" or "YOO-lah"—*Nordic: "magnificent"; Celtic: "gift from the sea"; French: "to fill up"; Hebrew: "burdened"; Swedish: "will"* (the kind you have, not the kind you make out). **ULI.** In Norse mythlogy,

Ull was a skilled hunting god, well liked by all.

ULEMA(H), "yoo-LAY-mah" or "oo-LAY-mah"—*Arabic: "wise."* **ULAMA, ULIMA(H).**

ULRICA, "UHL-rihk-ah"—*German: "ruler of all."* **ALRIKA, ULRIKA.** M

UMA, "OO-mah"—*Hindu: "mother goddess" or "bestower of blessings."* Uma Thurman is an actress.

UMBRIELLE, "UHM-bree-ehl"—*Latin: "one in the shade" or "one in the shadows"; Latin/Hebrew: "in the shadow of the Lord."*

UMEKO, "oo-MAY-koh"—*Japanese: "plum blossom."* **UMEKI.** The plum blossom symbolizes patience and perseverance.

UNA, "YOO-nah" or "OO-nah"—*Latin: "one" or "together"; Irish: "lamb."* **ONA, OONA; OONAGH** (OO-nah)—*Irish.*

UNDINE, "un-DEEN" or "UN-deen"—*Greek: "of the waves."* **ONDINE; UNDINA.**

-lin, -lyn

"-lin" and "-lyn" (both pronounced "LIHN") are suffixes—and sometimes prefixes—that mean "a brook" in English and "a waterfall" in the older Anglo-Saxon. You may add them to any name.

Undine is a water sprite in Greek myth who longs for a soul; she achieves this by marrying a mortal and bearing a child. **DINA.**

UPALA, "oo-PAH-lah"—*Hindu: "opal stone."*

URBI, "OOR-bee"—*African: "princess."*

URSULA, "UR-soo-lah" or "OOR-soo-lah"—*Latin: "little bear" or "she-bear."* **ORSEL, ORSELINE**—Dutch; **URSA; URSOLA** —Russian; **URSULINA** (ur-soo-LEE-nah)— Spanish and Italian; **URSZULI** (oor-SHOO-lee)—Polish. The very large constellation Ursa Major ("great bear" or "big bear") can be seen chasing the Sun at dusk from late April to late June. The distinctive section called the Big Dipper is prominent from May to June. Ursa Minor ("little bear" or "bear cub") chases the Sun in early August at extreme northern latitudes. Saint Ursula, who was martyred as a young girl is the patroness of young women. Ursula Andress is a Swiss actress who first appeared in the 1965 movie *She.*

USHA, "OO-shah"—*Hindu: "sunrise."*

USOA, "oo-soh-ah"—*Basque: "dove."*

THE TOP FIVE

VICTORIA
VANESSA
VERONICA
VALERIE
VADA/VEDA

If the name you're looking for isn't here, see "B," "F," and "W."

VACHELLE, "vah-SHEHL"—*French: "keeper of cattle."* M

VADA, "VAY-dah"—*Latin: "the one going" or "to go."* **VAYDA, VAYDRA.** Vada is the main character in the 1992 movie *My Girl,* and is responsible for this name's current popularity.

VALA, "VAH-lah"—*Eastern European: "chosen."*

VALDA, "VAHL-dah"—*Teutonic: "battle heroine."*

VALENCIA, "vah-LENS-ee-ah"—*Italian and Spanish: "glorious ruler."* **VALESKA** (vah-LESS-kah)—Russian; **VELASCA, VELASKA; WALESKA** (vah-LESS-kah). For the male version, see VALESKO.

VALENTINE, "vahl-ehn-TINE," "vahl-ehn-TEEN," or "vahl-ehn-TEEN-eh"—*Latin: "strong and courageous"* and *"healthy."* **BÁLINTKA** (BAH-leent-kah or bah-LEENT-kah)—Eastern European; **VALENCIA** (vah-LEHN-see-ah or vah-LEHN-chah)—Spanish, Portuguese, Basque, and French; **VALENTIA** (vah-LEHN-tee-ah or vah-LEHN-tyah)—Italian, Swiss, and French; **VALENTIJNE** (vah-lehn-tee-YEHN-eh)—Dutch; **VALENTINA** (vah-lehn-TEE-nah). **TINA; VAL, VALLI(E), VALLY.** M

VALERIA, "vah-LARE-ee-ah" or "vah-LARE-yah"—*Latin: "strong"* or *"healthy."* **VALAREE, VALERI(E)** (VAH-lah-ree), **VALERY, VALLERI(E).** M

VALERI(E). See VALERIA.

VAN(N)A. See LEVANA, VANESSA.

VANESSA, "vah-NEHS-sah"—*some say Greek: "butterfly,"* but closer to: *"to vanish";* with Dutch and Scandinavian you can create: *"child of/from the headlands";* but more likely of Irish origin. **VANESHA, VENESSA.** This is a name invented by writer Jonathan Swift (d. 1745) for his lady love, Esther Vanhomrigh. As was the custom then, writers would often disguise their lovers' true names or use euphemisms—see how the "Van" and "Esther" (pet name: Essa) are mixed? **VANIA, VANNA, VANNI(E), VANNY, VANYA.**

VANORA, "vah-NOHR-ah"—*Slavic: "white wave."*

VANYA, VANIA. See ANN(E), VANESSA.

VARIANNE, "vare-ee-AN"—*Latin: "clever"* or *"capricious."*

VARUN(N)A, "vah-ROON-ah"—*Tamil: "rain goddess"; Sanskrit: "to bind"* or *"to envelop"; Norse: "love of truth."* The Varuna

Vel-, -veld, -vel(d)t

"Vel-," "-veld," and "-vel(d)t" (pronounced "VEHL," "VEHLD," and "VEHLT") are Afrikaans and Dutch prefixes and suffixes meaning "field" or "pasture." You may add them yourself to any name. The names by themselves, in the south of Africa, also mean a wide open space, such as a grassland or a low-lying wooded area, not owned by anyone.

in ancient India was a supreme deity associated with the skies, and had many functions. Later beliefs had several gods and goddesses doing the work of the one. It's either the intrusion of bureaucracy into divinity, or they just don't make deities like they used to. M

VASHTI, "VAHSH-tee"—*Persian: "beautiful one."* The Vashti mentioned in the Old Testament/Tanakh was a Persian queen who was divorced by her husband because she got tired of taking orders from him.

VEDA, "VAY-dah"—*Sanskrit: "knowledge."* The Hindu sacred writings are called the *Rig-Veda.*

VEDETTE, VIDETTE, "veh/vih-DEHT" —*Italian/Spanish: "the vigilant one."* See also VIDA, VITA.

VELA, "VAY-lah"—*Latin: "sail."* Vela is a Southern Hemisphere constellation. It can be seen sailing after the Sun at dusk from mid-March through early May. The Sun is "in" the Sails from July to the end of August.

VELIKA, "VEH-lee-kah"—*Russian: "great."*

VELVET, "VEHL-veht"—*English: "soft fabric"; Latin: "shaggy hair."* **BARKHAT** (BAHR-kaht)—Russian; **BÁRSONY** (BAHR-soh-nee)—Polish; **CATIFEA** (kah-TEE-fay-

ah)—Rumanian; **FLØJL** (FLAW-eel)—Scandinavian; **KADIFE** (kah-DEE-feh)—Turkish; **KETIFAH** (keh-TEE-fah)—Hebrew; **MAHAMELI** (mah-hah-MEH-lee)—Swahili; **QATIFA** (kah-TEE-fah)—Arabic; **SAMMET(TE)**—Swedish; **VELLUTA**—Italian; **VELOUR** (veh-LOOR)—French; **VELUDA**—Portuguese; **VELVINA.**

VENECIA, VENETIA, "veh-NEE-see-ah" and "veh-NEE-shah"—*Latin: "merciful" or "forgiveness."* **VENICE; VENTANA** (vehn-TAH-nah)—Spanish; **VINICIA** (vih-NEE-see-ah or vih-NEE-chee-ah)—Italian and Eastern European; **VENITA, VINITA.** M

VENUS, "VEE-nuhss"—*Old Italian: "charmer" or "charming"; Latin: "come" or "forgive, forgiveness."* Venus began as a very early native Italian goddess before being taken over by the Romans. She was associated with love, beauty, art, fertility, and the feminine in nature.

VERA, "VEE-rah"—*Latin: "true"; Russian: "faith"; Sanskrit: "great hero."* **VEREEN** (veh-REEN)—Scotch/Irish; **VERENA** (veh-REH-nah or vay-RAY-nah)—Spanish, Portuguese, and Italian; **VERINA** (veh-REE-nah), **VER-INE**—French; **VERILEA(H), VERILEE, VERILY, VERITY, VERLE, VIRLE**—English; **VERLINA** (vuhr-LEE-nah)—German; **VERLONNA**—Swiss; **VEROCHKA**—Russian; **VIRA**—Sanskrit. M

VERANA, "veh-RAH-nah"—*Spanish: "summer."* M

VERENA, "veh-REE-nah" or "vay-RAY-nah"—*Latin: "integrity."* **VERADIS** (veh-RAH-dihss)—Dutch; **VEREEN, VERENE, VERINA, VERINE; VERINKA** (veh-RIHN-kah), **VEROCHKA** (veh-ROHCH-kah)—Russian.

VERNA, "VUR-nah"—*Latin: "springtime."* **LAVERN(E); VARNEY, VERNÉE** (vur-NAY), **VERNEY. VERNI(E), VERNY.** M

VERONICA, "veh-RAWN-ih-kah"—*Greek: "bringer of victory"; Latin: "true," "true image or reflection," or "from Verona."* **VERONIKA**—Scandinavian; **VERONIKE** (veh-roh-NY-kee)—Greek (see also **BERNICE**); **VÉRONIQUE** (vare-oh-NEEK)—French; **WERONIKIA** (veh-roh-NEE-kyah)—Polish. According to legend, Saint Veronica was a woman who wiped the sweating, bleeding face of Christ as he carried his cross to Calgary. The image of Jesus' face was, supposedly, left in the fabric. She is the patroness of photographers. Veronica is another name for the speedwell plant, which bears spikes of flowers in a variety of colors and is valuable in herbal medicine. Veronica Lake was a slinky blonde actress of the 1930s and 1940s, most noted for her peek-a-boo hairstyle. Veronica Cartwright was a child actress who has continued to make films as an adult.

VERRILL, "VARE-ihl"—*French: "true one."* **VERYL.**

VESPERA, "VEHS-pur-ah" or "vehs-PEH-rah"—*Greek: "Evening Star."* **VESPERIA.** This refers to either Jupiter or Venus.

VESTA, "VEHS-tah"—*Greek: "goddess of the hearth"; Latin: "pure" or "virginal."* **HEST(I)A**—Greek. Vesta was the Roman goddess of the hearth, the center of the

home, and in her temples a perpetual flame burned. This is one of the minor planets of the asteroid belt between Mars and Jupiter.

VEVINA, "veh-VEE-nah" or "VEH-vee-nah"—*Gaelic: "sweet lady."* See also **BEVIN.**

VICKI(E). See VICTORIA.

VICTORIA, "vihk-TOH-ree-ah"—*Latin: "victorious."* **BITTORE** (bee-tohr-reh), **BIXENTA** (bee-shen-tah)—Basque; **VICTEOIRIA** (veek-TOY-ree-ah)—Irish; **VIDORA** (VEE-dohr-ah or vee-DOHR-ah)—Eastern European; **VIKTORIA**—Swedish; **VITENKA** (vee-TEHN-kah), **VITYA** (VEET-yah)—Russian; **VITTORIA** (vee-TOH-ree-ah)—Italian; **WICIA** (VEECH-yah), **WIKITORIA, WIKTA, WIKTORJA** (veek-TOR-yah), **WISIA** (VEE-syah)—Polish. There are several saints' names on this list, but the name Victoria is best known from England's Queen Victoria, who ascended to the throne as a young woman and had one of the longest reigns in history. Her name was given to an age, in England and all over, and Victorian-era accoutrements are enjoying a resurgence of popularity. **VIC, VICK, VICKI(E); VIK, VIKKI(E); VITA.** M

VIDA, "VEE-dah"—*Hebrew: "beloved"; Latin: "behold!" or "see."* **VIDETTA, VIDETTE.** See VITA.

VIJAYA, "vee-JAY-ah"—*Hindu: "victory."* M

VIMALA, "VEE-mah-lah"—*Sanskrit: "stainless" or "pure."*

VINCA, "VING-kah"—*Latin: "periwinkle."* Vinca shrubs bear a variety of different-colored blooms above lustrous foliage.

VINCENTA, "vihn-SEHN-tah"—*Latin: "the conqueror."* **UINSEANNIN** (ween-shaw-NEEN)—Gaelic; **VICENTA** (vih-CHEHN-tah)—Italian and Portuguese; **VINCENTIA** (vihn-SEHN-tee-ah)—Dutch; **VINCENTINHA** (veen-sehn-TEEN-hah)—Portuguese; **VINCENZA** (veen-CHEHN-zah), **VINCENZIA**—Italian. **VINCI(E), VINCY; VINNA.** M

VIOLET, "VYE-oh-leht" or "vee-oh-LEHT"—*Latin: the violet flower or the color violet.* **FIALKA** (fee-AHL-kah)—Nordic and Gaelic; **VIOLA** (vee-OH-lah or vye-OH-lah); **VIOLETTA** (vee-oh-LEHT-ah)—Italian and French; **VIOLETTE** (vee-oh-LEHT)—French; **WIOLETTE** (vee-oh-LEHT-eh)—Polish. The violet is a symbol of modesty, and is used in herbal and folk medicine. **VI, VY.**

VIRGA, "VUHR-gah"—*Latin: "the pure," "virgin," "wispy or misty clouds," "streaks in the sky," or "twig."* The constellation of Virgo can be seen chasing the Sun at dusk from mid-May through the end of June. The Sun is "in" the sign from September to late October. To the Assyrians, it was the sign of MYLITTA the Harvest or "bringing forth." To the early Christians, it was PHILIP the Serpent. To the Egyptians, it was NUT/ NUUT the Cow Goddess. To the Greeks, it was the sign of DEMETER. To the early Hebrews, it was ASHUR, the Olive Branch. To the Norse peoples, it was the sign of VIDAR the Forests. To the Romans, it was CERES the Crop Goddess. The Aztecs called this sign QUETZPALIN the Lizard. To the Babylonians, it was SIRU the Ear of Corn. Earthly rulers at this time are the VINES (seven days of the HAZEL TREE) for Celts and Druids, and the LOTUS for the Japanese.

VIRGINIA, "vuhr-JIH-nee-ah"—*Latin: "pure," "unspoiled," or "virginal."* **VIRGINIE** (VEER-zhee-nee or veer-ZHEE-nee)—

French, Swiss, and Dutch. The state of Virginia was named in honor of the English monarch seated at the time of its initial colonization, Queen Elizabeth I, the so-called Virgin Queen because she never married. The first child born in the British colonies was named Virginia (Dare) to honor the queen. **GINGER, GINNI(E), GINNY; VIRGI(E).**

VITA, "VEE-tah"—*Italian diminutive of Victoria: "conqueror"; Latin: "life."* **DA VIDA, VIDA; DE VITA**—Spanish, Italian, and Portuguese; **VIDETTA, VIDETTE; VITALIA** (vye-TAL-yah or vee-TAHL-yah)—French, German, and Dutch. See also VEDETTE/ VIDETTE, VICTORIA, VIDA. M

VIVACE, "vee-VAH-cheh"—*Italian: "lively, vibrant."*

VIVEKA, "VIH-veh-kah" or "vih-VEH-kah"—*Scandinavian: "living voice."* **VIVECA, VIVECKA.**

VIVIAN, VIVIEN, "VIHV-yen"—*Latin: "life" or "lively".* **BIBIANA** (bee-bee-AHN-ah)—Portuguese; **VIBIANA, VIBIANE** (vee-bee-AHN)—Spanish and Portuguese; **VIVIANNA, VIVIANNE, VIVIENNE.** In Arthurian legend, Vivienne is the seductive, smart woman who captures Merlyn's heart and mind and steals him away from Camelot. Vivien Leigh was the British actress whose greatest coup was landing the role of Southern belle Scarlett O'Hara in the epic film *Gone With the Wind.* **VIB, VIV, VIVI.**

VOLANTE, "voh-LAHNT(-eh)"—*Latin: "to fly."* **VOLANTA** (voh-LAWN-tah)—French; **VOLARA** (voh-LAH-rah)—Italian. M

VOLETA, "voh-LEH-tah" or "voh-LAY-tah"—*French: "flowing veil."*

THE TOP FIVE

**WENDY
WINONA
WHITNEY
WEDNESDAY
WILLA/WILLOW**

If the name you're looking for isn't here, see "B" and "V," and the vowels.

WAKANA, "wuh-KAH-nah"—*Native American Sioux: "holy woman."* M

WAKANDA, "wah-KAHN-dah"—*Native American Sioux: "power of the spirit."*

WALDA, "WAHL-dah" or "VAHL-dah"—*German: "ruler."* M

WALLIS, "WAHL-ihss"—*English: "Welsh"; Teutonic: "stranger"; Norse: "choice"; Celtic: "to gush forth" or "to boil."* **WALLACE**—*British;* **WALLACHE**—*German.* Wallis Warfield Simpson was a twentieth-century American who fell in love with Britain's King Edward. Marriage to commoners is not allowed for a monarch or a potential monarch, so rather than live a loveless life, the king abdicated his throne to marry her. **WALLI(E), WALLY.** M

WANDA, "WAHN-dah" or "VAHN-dah"—*Slavic: "shepherdess"; German: "wanderer"; Old English: "supple or nimble."* **VANDA, VONDA; WANDY** (VAHN-dee)—*Polish.*

WANETTA, "wah-NEHT-ah"—*English: "dark."* **WANETTA, WANNETTA, WANNETTE. NETTIE, NETTY.**

WAPITI, "wah-PEE-tee"—*Native American Shawnee: "pale" or "white."*

WAUNA, "wah-OO-nah"—*Native American Miwok: "snow geese calling as they fly overhead."*

WEATHERLY, "WHEH-thur-lee"—*English: "able to keep a straight course."* This refers to a ship, but is metaphorically applied to a person. See also WETHERLY.

WEDNESDAY, "WED'NZ-day"—*Anglo-Saxon: "Woden's day."* **AKUA** (ah-KOO-uh)—African Ewe; **KUKUA** (koo-KOO-uh)—African Fante; **MERCOLEDI** (mare-KOH-leh-dee)—Italian; **MERCREDI** (MARE-creh-dee)—French; **MIERCOLES** (mee-AYR-koh-lehz)—Spanish; **MITTWOCH** (MIHT-vawk)—German; **ONSDAG** (OHNZ-dog)—Scandinavian; **REBO** (RAY-boh)—Indonesian; **SREDA** (sreh-DAH)—Russian; **SRODA** (SHROH-dah)—Polish; **SUIYUBI** (soo-ee-YOO-bee)—Japanese. The mythic Woden of Europe is equated with the god Mercury of Rome.

WENDA, "WEHN-dah"—*English: "winding valley"; Teutonic: "to wander"; Norse: "to change course" or "to move forward."* **VEND, VENDA, VENDEL, VENDELLA** (vehn-DEH-lah or VEHN-deh-lah), **VENDELLE** (vehn-DEHL)—Scandinavian; **WENDA, WENDE** (VEHND), **WENDELA** (VEHN-deh-lah or vehn-DEH-lah)—German. See also WENDY. M

NORTHWEST GIRLS' NAMES

Girls born into the Pacific Northwest are most likely to have the following names:

1. Jessica	6. Amanda	11. Megan	16. Nicole
2. Ashley	7. Elizabeth	12. Rachel	17. Stephanie
3. Emily	8. Taylor	13. Brittany	18. Chelsea
4. Sarah	9. Hannah	14. Kelsey	19. Courtney
5. Samantha	10. Kayla	15. Jennifer	20. Haley

WENDY, "WEHN-dee"—*English: from Wynn—"friend(?)"; Celtic: from Gwen—"fair or white(?)"; German: from Wanda—"wanderer(?)"; Prussian: "Wend woman(?)."* This is a name made up by Sir James Barrie for the heroine of his Peter Pan stories. There is no record of it as a given name before 1904. The Wends were a group of people who inhabited what are now modern-day Slavic countries. See also WENDA.

WENON(N)A, "weh-NOH-nah"—*Native American: "first born daughter"; German: "joy and bliss."* **WINON(N)A, WYNON(N)A.** Country singer/songwriter Wynonna Judd and actress Winona Ryder are largely responsible for the modern popularity of these names. **NON(N)A; WENN, WINN, WYNN.**

WETHERLY, "WEH-thur-lee"—*English: "white wether sheep meadow."* **WETHERLEA, WETHERLEE, WETHERLEIGH, WHETHERLEY.** See also WEATHERLY.

WHITNEY, "WHIHT-nee"—*English: "white island."* Singer/actress Whitney Houston is responsible for the rise in popularity among girls of this traditionally male name. M

WIJDAN, "wihj-DAHN"—*Arabic: "ecstasy."*

WILDA, "WYLE-dah" or "WIHL-dah"—*English: "untamed," or the older "strong army."*

WILLA, "WIHL-ah"—*Anglo-Saxon: "desirable."* Willa Cather (d. 1947) was an American novelist who wrote of pioneer life. See also WIL(L)ONA.

WILLETTE, "wih-LEHT"—*American: a shore bird.* M

WILLOW, "WIH-loh," *English: the willow tree.* The Celts throught the willow was imbued with magical qualities. A woman is said to be "willowy" if she is slender and graceful.

WILMA, "WIHL-mah"—*German: "determined."* **VILMA.** A redheaded babe from Bedrock is probably the best-known Wilma. Track star Wilma Rudolph overcame polio to become an Olympic gold medalist. M

WIL(L)ONA, "wih-LOH-nah"—*English: "desired."* See also WILLA.

WINEMA, "WIH-neh-mah" or "wih-NEE-mah"—*Native American: "woman chief."*

WIN(N)IFRED, "WIHN-ih-frehd"—*Celtic: "gentle friend."* **WENNAFRED, WYNETTE, WYNNEFRED.** The legend of Saint Winifred is wild. Seems a pushy suitor tried to force her into marrying him, and when she resisted, he killed her. The ground opened up to swallow him, and her uncle Bueno—who also became a saint, by the way—brought her back to life. She lived out her life as a nun, and water that sprang from the earth where the earth swallowed the obnoxious ex-suitor was said to have curative powers. **FREDDI(E), FREDDY; WINNIE, WINNY, WYNN(E).**

WINNIE, "WIHN-ee"—*Celtic: "friend";* *Old English: "joy."* **WYNNE, WYNNIE.** See also GWENDOLYN, WIN(N)IFRED. M

WINONA. See WENON(N)A.

WISTERIA, "wih-STEE-ree-ah" or "wih-STEH-ree-ah"—*English: "wistful."* **WISTARIA.** Wisteria is a rapidly growing vine that bears drooping clusters of blue-to-purple flowers amidst luscious, green, fernlike leaves.

WOKA, "WOH-kah"—*Native American Klamath: "yellow water-lily."* **WOKAS.**

WYANET, "why-uh-NET"—*Native American: "beautiful."* **WYANETTA, WYANETTE; WYNETTE. NETTIE.** M

THE TOP FIVE

XAVIERA
XANTHE(E)
XIA
XIMENA
XIMARA

If the name you're looking for isn't here, see "Z."

XANTHE(E), "ZAHN-theh"—*Greek: "yellow or golden."* **XANTHA, XANTHIA.** M

XAVIERA, "zah-vee-AIR-ah" or "hah-vee-AIR-ah"—*Basque: "owner of the new house"; Arabic: " bright"; Latin: "to save" or "savior."* **JAVIERA** (hah-vee-AIR-ah)—*Spanish;* **XABIERA**—*Basque;* **XAVIÉRE**—*French.* M

XENA, "ZEE-nah"—*Greek: "guest."* See also XENIA. M

XENIA, "ZEE-nee-ah"—*Greek: "hospitality."* **XENA.** This is one of the Christian saints.

XIA, "ZEE-uh" or "zee-AH"—*Chinese: ?*

Xia is the first recorded dynasty of ancient China. See also XIAMARA.

XIAMARA, "zee-ah-MAH-rah"—*Aramaic: "rejoicing deer" or "joyful doe."* **TZIAMARA**—*Eastern European;* **TZIAMARNIT** (tzee-ah-MAHR-neet or tzee-ah-mahr-NEET)—*Hebrew.* **TZIA, XIA.** See also ZAMARRA.

XIMENA. See CHIMENA, SIMONE.

XIPHIA, "ZEE-fee-ah"—*Greek: "the sword."* **XIPHA. XIP** (ZEEP or ZIP), **XIPH** (ZEEF).

XOXA, "SHOH-shah"—*Spanish from the Yiddish Shosha: "lily."* **XIUXIA, XUXA.**

THE TOP FIVE

YOLANDA
YVETTE
YVONNE
YOKO
YURIKO

If the name you're looking for isn't here, see the vowels.

YAEL, "YALE" or "YAY-el"—*Hebrew: "mountain deer."* **YALE.** See also JAELLA.

YAHIMBA, "yah-heem-BAH"—*African: "there's no place like home."* Toto, I don't think we're in Kansas.

YAKIRA, "yah-KEER-ah"—*Hebrew: "beloved and honored."* M

YAPHA, "YAH-fah"—*Hebrew: "beautiful."* **JAFFA** (YAH-fah); **YAFFA.** M

YARDLEY, YEARDLEY, "YAHRD-lee" for both, or "YEERD-lee" for the second—*English: "enclosed property" or "pastureland."* **YARDLEA, YARDLEIGH; YEARDLEA, YEARDLEIGH.** Yeardley Smith is an actress with a distinct look and a distinct sound; she gives her natural voice to Lisa Simpson on TV's *The Simpsons.* **LEE, LEIGH; YARD.** M

YARKONA, "YAHR-koh-nah" or "yahr-KOH-nah"—*Hebrew: "the color green."* **YARKONAH.** The yarkonah bird is found in the Middle East. M

YASU, "yah-SOO"—*Japanese: "peaceful."* **YASUKO.**

YATVA, "YAHT-vah"—*Hebrew: "goodness."* **YATVAH.**

YAVNIELLE, "yahv-nee-EHL"—*Hebrew: "God will build."*

YAZATA, "yah-ZAH-tah"—*Persian/Avestan: "worthy of praise."*

YEDIDAH, "yeh-DEED-ah"—*Hebrew: "friend."* **YADIDAH; YEDIDYAH.** M

YEIRA, "YAY-rah"—*Hebrew: "light."*

YELENA, "yeh-LAY-nah" or "yeh-LEH-nah"—*Russian from Latin: "lily flower."*

YETTA, "YEH-tah"—*Teutonic: "mistress of the house/home"; Yiddish: "light"; or try on Scottish: "gate."* **JETJE** (YEHT-yeh)—Dutch; **YETTE** (YEH-teh). **ETTA, ETTE; ITTA, ITTE.**

YETUNDE, "yeh-TOON-deh"—*African Yoruba: "mother comes back."* This could take a variety of meanings; it may refer to the belief that the female child is a reincarnated ancestral matriarch.

YIN, "YEEN"—*Chinese: "goddess."*

YOKI, "YOH-kee"—*Native American: "rain"; Hopi: "bluebird on the mesa."* M

YOKO, "YOH-koh" or "yoh-KOH"—*Japanese: "positive," "one," or "female."* Yoko Ono is the widow of Beatle, John Lennon, known for her avant-garde artistic endeavors and political views.

PAIRING SURNAMES

This is a long-standing practice, usually done by bestowing upon a child a hyphenated (and sometimes very long!) last name. Now, the idea is to assign one of the surnames as a middle name. You can do it as a first name, but only once—unless you want to have children with the same name (presumably followed by a number).

YOLANDA, IOLANDA, "yoh-LAWN-dah"—*Greek: "violet blossoms"; Latin: "modest, shy"; also German: "country."* **IOLANDA** (yoh-LAHN-dah), **IOLANDE**—Greek; **IOLANTHE** (yoh-LAHN-teh)—French; **JOLÁN** (yoh-LAWN), **JOLANKA, JOLI** (YOH-lee)—Eastern European; **JOLANDA** (yoh-LAWN-dah)—Danish; **JOLANDE** (yoh-LAWN-deh), **YOLANDE**—Swedish; **JOLANTA** (yoh-LAWN-tah)—Polish; **JOLANTE** (yoh-LAWN-teh)—Norwegian.

YON, "YAWN"—*Korean: "lotus blossom."*

YOSHI, "YOH-shee"—*Japanese: "good" or "respectful."* **YOSHIKO.** M

YOVELA, "yoh-VEH-lah"—*Hebrew: "ram's horn"; Latin: "joyful celebration."* In ancient times, the ram's horn was blown to announce special occasions.

YUCELLA, "yoo-SEHL-ah"—*Turkish: "sublime."* **YUCELINA, YUCELINE.** M

YUKIKO, "YOO-kee-koh"—*Japanese: "snow daughter."* This name is for a girl born in December.

YUNG, "YUNG"—*Korean: "flower."*

YURIKO, "YOO-ree-koh"—*Japanese: "lily."* M

YVETTE, "ee-VET"—*French from Hebrew: "life"; French: "yew tree" or "archer."* **EVETTE.** The yew tree provided excellent wood for bowmaking, thus the association with archers. Yvette Mimieux is an actress who, fresh from college, was given a major role in *The Time Machine.* She has continued to work in features and TV movies. M

YVONNE, "ee-VAWN"—*French version of Johnna: "God's gracious gift"; Greek: "tranquility" and "flower."* **IBANE** (ee-bahn-eh), **IBONA** (ee-bohn-ah)—Basque; **IWONA** (ee-VOH-nah)—Polish; **YVAINNA** (ee-VEHN-ah or ee-VAY-nah)—Bretagne. Yvonne DeCarlo is a Canadian actress who will always be remembered for playing Lily Munster on TV's campy and outrageous *The Munsters,* and not for the campy and sometimes outrageous movies she did over the span of five decades. **VON, VONNI(E), VONNY.** See also EVANIA, EVANTHE. M

THE TOP FIVE

ZOE/ZOEY
ZIPPORAH
ZULEIKA
ZARA/ZAIRA
ZAINA/ZAYNA

If the name you're looking for isn't here, see "S" and "X."

ZADA, "ZAH-dah"—*Syrian: "lucky one."*

ZAFFRA, "ZAHF-rah"—*Italian: "sapphire blue"; Arabic: "copper."* **ZAFFARA, ZAFFERA, ZAFFERY, ZAFFIRA, ZAFFRE. ZAF(F).**

ZAHARA, "zah-HAH-rah"—*Swahili: "flower."* **ZA(H)RA.**

ZAHIRA(H), "zah-HEER-ah"—*Arabic: "luminous" or "shining."* **ZAIRAH; ZAIRE. M**

ZAHRA(H), "zah-RAH"—*Arabic: "white."* **ZARA.**

ZAIDA, "zah-EED-ah"—*Arabic: "increase" or "growth."* **ZAHIDA, ZAYDA, ZIY(Y)ADA. M**

ZAINA, ZAYNA, "zay-nah"—*variants of Zainabu, Swahili: "beautiful."* Zainabu was the eldest daughter of Mohammed. **ZAINABU** (zah-ee-NAH-boo), **ZAYNABU.**

ZAIRA, "ZYE-rah" or "zah-EE-rah"—*Irish: possibly version of Sarah, "princess."* This is a name invented by writer C.R. Maturin for his novel *Women (1818)*, which is subtitled *Pour & Contre*—*"for and against."* **ZARA** (ZAH-rah). See also SARA(H), ZAHIRA(H), ZEHIRA(H).

ZAKIYA, "zah-KEE-yah" or "ZAH-kee-yah"—*Swahili: "intelligent"; Tunisian: "pure."* **ZAKIYYAH.**

ZALIKA, "zah-LEE-kah"—*Swahili: "born to a good family" or "born to a wealthy family."* **ZALEIKA, ZULEIKA, ZULLKA. LEIKA, LIKA.**

ZAMARRA, "zah-MAH-rah"—*Spanish: "shepherd's coat."* See also XIAMARA.

ZANDRA, "ZAHN-drah"—*Greek: "friend" or "helper."* **M**

ZARA(H), "ZAH-rah"—*Arabic: "dawn."* See also ZAHRA(H).

ZAREBA, "zah-REE-bah"—*Arabic-African: "in the fold."* "In the fold" as in sheepfold or cattlefold—as in "protected." **ZAREEBA, ZARIBA(H).**

ZARIZA, "zah-REE-zah"—*Hebrew: "industrious."*

ZAYNA(H), "ZAY-nah"—*Arabic: "beautiful."* **ZAINA.**

ZEHIRA, "zeh-HEE-rah"—*Hebrew: "guarded."* **ZAIRA** (zah-EE-rah), **ZIRA.**

ZEIRA, "ZAY-rah" or "ZEE-rah"—*Aramaic: "small."* **ZIRA.**

ZELDA, "ZEHL-dah"—*Yiddish: "rare."* **ZELZAH.** See also GRISELDA.

ZELIA, "ZEH-lee-ah" or "ZEHL-yah"—*Hebrew: "zealous."*

ZELKOVA, "ZEHL-koh-vah"—*?: the Japanese elm tree.* The Japanese elm grows faster and is more hardy than other members of the elm family.

ZEMELA, "ZEH-meh-lah" or "zeh-MEH-lah"—*Phyrigian/Early Greek: "heavy with honey"* or *"honey-laden."* This was an earth goddess of Phyrigia and Thrace.

ZEMIRAH, "zeh-MEE-rah"—*Hebrew: "song of joy."* **ZAMORA, ZEMORA.**

ZENA, "ZEE-nah"—*Greek: "hospitable."* **ZENIA.**

ZENDA, "ZEHN-dah"—*Persian: "sacred"* or *"fire worshipper"; Arabic: "atheist," or more specifically, a Zoroastrian.* M

ZERLINA, "zare-LEE-nah"—*Teutonic: "beautiful and serene."* **ZERLINE; ZERLA.**

ZETA, "ZAY-tah"—*Hebrew: "olive"; Greek: "six"* or *"sixth."* **ZETTA.** M

ZIA, ZEA, "ZEE-ah"—*Hebrew: "to tremble"; Greek: "corn goddess"; Latin: "rosemary."* Corn gods and goddesses were important deities in many cultures, as they signified abundance and health.

ZIGANA, "zee-GAH-nah"—*Hungarian: "gypsy."* **TZIGANE.**

ZILA, "ZEE-lah"—*Hebrew: "shade"* or *"shadow."* **ZILLA(H), ZILLI(A), ZILLYAH.**

ZINAH, "ZIH-nah," "ZEE-nah," or "ZY-nah"—*Hebrew: "abundance."* **ZINA.**

ZIPPORAH. See CEPHORAH.

ZITA, ZYTA, "ZEE-tah"—*Polish: "harvester"; Persian: "mistress"; Spanish: "little rose"; Old French: "bedroom."* Saint Zita is the patroness of domestic servants.

ZIVA(H), "ZEEV-ah"—*Hebrew: "splendor"* or *"brightness."* **ZIVIT** (zee-VEET). M

ZIZI, "ZEE-zee"—*Hungarian from Hebrew: "consecrated to God."*

ZOE(Y), "ZOH" and "ZOH-ee"—*Greek: "life."* **ZOË** (ZOH-ee); **ZOÉ** (zoh-AY), **ZOËLIE, ZOELLE**—French; **ZOYA, ZOYSA, ZOYSHA, ZOYSIA** (ZOY-shah or ZOY-see-ah)—Eastern European; **ZOYECHKA, ZOYENKA** (zoy-EHNK-ah)—Russian; **ZOIA.**

ZOHARA, "zoh-HAHR-ah"—*Hebrew: "splendor."* M

ZOLA, "ZOH-lah"—*German: "payment."* **ZOLLA, ZOLLI(E), ZOLLO, ZOLLY.**

ZONTA(H), "ZAWN-tah"—*Native American Sioux: "trustworthy."*

ZORA, "ZOH-rah"—*Slavic: "dawn."* **ZORAH, ZOREEN, ZORENE, ZORINA, ZORINE.**

ZORILLE, "ZOH-rihl"—*Greek/Spanish: "little fire"; French/African: "striped muishond."* **ZORILA.** A muishond is like a mischievous weasel or otter. M

ZUDORA, "zoo-DORE-ah"—*Sanskrit: "hard worker."* **ZADORA.**

ZULEIKA. See ZALIKA.

ZULEMA, "zoo-LAY-mah"—*Arabic: "peaceful."* **ZULENA.**

THE TOP FIVE

ANDREW
AUSTIN
ALEXANDER
ANTHONY
ALBERT

If the name you're looking for isn't here, see the other vowels.

AARON, "AH-rohn" or "AIR-un"—*Hebrew: "enlightened one" or teacher"; Arabic: "mountain."* **AARÃO** (ah-RAH-oh)—Portuguese; **AHARON**—Hebrew; **ARON**—Eastern European and Scandinavian; **ÁRÓN**—Irish Gaelic; **AROUN, HAROUN** (hah-ROON)—Arabic. The Aaron of the Old Testament/Tanakh was the older brother of Moses and the first high priest of the Hebrews. Aaron Burr, vice president from 1801 to 1809, fought a famous duel with Alexander Hamilton, a former secretary of the treasury, as the result of a long-standing quarrel between the two men.

AARU, "ah-AH-roo"—*Egyptian: "peaceful fields."* In Egyptian mythology, these fields were where the sun god, Ra, had his throne, and where deities and souls of the blessed were located.

ABBAS, "ah-BAHS"—*Arabic: "lion."* **ABBA** (AH-bah)—Ethiopian. Abbas was an uncle of Mohammed and the ancestor of the Abbassid dynasty, which ruled the Islamic world from the mid-sixth to the thirteenth centuries.

ABBOTT, "AH-buht" or "AB-uht"—*Aramaic: "father."* **ABAD**—Spanish; **ABBOID** (AH-

boyd)—Gaelic; **ABBOT; ABT**—German.

ABBUD, "ah-BOOD"—*Arabic: "worshipper."*

ABD AL BARI, "AHBD AHL ba-REE/BAH-ree"—*Arabic: "servant of the Creator."*

ABD AL HAKIM, "AHBD AHL hah-KEEM"—*Arabic: "servant of the Wise."*

ABD AL QADIR, "AHBD AHL kah-DEER"—*Arabic: "servant of the Capable."* Abd al Qadir Jilani was a Muslim Sufi, or mystic, who was a well-known preacher and teacher of the twelveth century. He founded the Madrasa school of thought and the Tariqa religious order, and there are Tariqa branches in every Islamic country.

ABDALLA, "ahb-DOLL-uh"—*Swahili: "servant of God."*

ABDIEL, "ahb-dee-EHL" or "AHB-dyehl"—*Hebrew: "servant of God."* **ABDE-EL** (AHB-deh-ehl)—Hebrew; **ABDEL, ABDUL**—Arabic. See also ABID. F

ABDU, "ahb-DOO"—*Swahili: "worshipper (of God)."*

ABEGIDE, ABEJIDE, "ah-beh-JEE-deh"—*African Yoruba: "born in winter."* **GIDE, GIDEH; JIDE, JIDEH.**

ABEL, "AY-bell" or "AH-bell"—*Hebrew: "breath" or "meadow"; Assyrian: "son."* In

Abd al

This is an Arabic prefix in many masculine and family names that means "the servant of." You may use it with any name you choose. Capitalize only the "A" in "Abd," never the "a" in "al." The noun that follows is rarely capitalized, unless it is one of the Ninety-nine Beautiful Names of God in Islamic tradition.

the Old Testament/Tanakh, Abel is the second son of Adam and Eve. He well understands the sacrifice ritual, and pleases God. F

ABID, "ah-BEED"—*Arabic: "worshipful."* **ABDI, ABDIEL.**

ABIEL, "ah-bee-EHL" or "AH-bee-ehl"—*Hebrew: "father of strength."*

ABIOLA, "ah-BYOH-lah"—*African Yoruba: "born in honor."*

ABNER, "AB-nur"—*Hebrew: "father of light" or "divine brightness."* **AVNER**—Israeli. The Abner of the Old Testament/Tanakh was a Hebrew general. Abner Doubleday was a nineteenth-century Army officer who supposedly invented the game of baseball—it isn't true, but the myth persists. He did write a book about it, though, and America's passion for baseball in its early days led to the popularity of Abner as a name.

ABRAHAM, "ABE-rah-ham"—*Hebrew: "father of multitudes" or "father of a nation"; Arabic: "exalted father."* **ABARRAN** (ah-bah-rahn)—Basque; **ABRACHAM** (ah-brah-KHAHM"—"KH" in the back of your throat)—Irish Gaelic; **ABRAHAMO** (ah-brah-HAH-moh)—Spanish; **ABRAHAN** (AH-brah-hahn), **ABRAN**—Eastern European; **ABRAM; ABRAMO** (ah-BRAH-moh)—

Italian; **AVRAHAM** (AHV-rah-hahm),**AVRAM, AVROM**—Hebrew; **IBRAHIM** (EE-brah-heem)—Arabic. Abraham (Ibrahim in the Qur'an) is the common "father" of the Jewish, Islamic, and Christian faiths. He married late and had trouble having children by his favorite wife, Sarah. So God made him this promise: that Abraham would have more children than he would ever be able to count. Indeed, his "children" pretty much cover the globe. God tests Abraham's faith by telling him to sacrifice his son, Isaac (Ismail, in the Qur'an), but God intervenes at the last minute, and is satisfied that Abraham is most obedient and righteous. In the Qur'an, Ibrahim and Ismail together construct the Ka'ba, the shrine in Mecca towards which Moslems turn to pray. Abraham Lincoln was president during the Civil War. Because Lincoln freed the slaves, Abraham became a popular name among African-Americans. **ABE, ABIE; BRAM.**

ABSALOM, "AHB-sah-lawm"—*Hebrew: "father of peace."* **AVSHALOM** (AHV-shah-lawm)—Hebrew. In the Old Testament/Tanakh, Absalom is, despite his rebelliousness, the best-loved son of King David.

ABU BAKR, "AH-boo BAHK-ur"—*Swahili: "possessor of nobility" or "nobleman."* **ABUBAKAR.** Abu Bakr was the first

Muslim caliph, or political successor, to Mohammed. He believed very strongly in the visions and dreams of the Prophet, no matter how fantastic they might have seemed to others, and so he is also called As-Siddiq—"Witness to the Truth." During his tenure as caliph, he devoted his energies to spreading Islam among the Arabs. **ABU.**

ABU TALIB, "ah-BOO tah-LEEB"—*Arabic: "possessor of knowledge."* This is the nickname of the uncle of Muhommed, Abd Manaf ibn Adb al Muttalib, who, although he did not convert to Islam, nevertheless protected and stood by his nephew. Thus, the name is associated with family unity and love.

ACARAHO, "uh-KAR-uh-hoh"—*Native American Crow/Apsarukeh: "mountain."*

ACE, "AYS"—*Latin: "one" or "unity."* Ace is also a slang term for someone who is the best at what he does. During World War I, pilots who downed more than three planes were called Ace.

ACHILLES, "ah-KILL-eez"—*Greek: "strength."* **ACHILIOS, ACHILLEUS**—*Greek;* **ACHILL, AKHYLLE, AKILLES**—Eastern European and Russian; **AQUILLES** (ah-KEEL-ehz)—Spanish and Portuguese. When the legendary Greek hero, Achilles, was a baby, his mother, Thetis, dipped him into a sacred river under instruction from a deity in order that he would be invulnerable to death and disease. Holding him by one ankle, she dunked him into the river; the arrow that finally killed this great warrior hero entered that heel—the small little spot that was not protected. This is where the expression "Achilles' heel" originates. Achilles is also the name of a river, one of the Christian saints, and a pair of tendons.

ACKERLEY, "AK-ur-lee"—*English: "the acre meadow."* **ACKERLEA, ACKERLEE, ACKERLEIGH.** An "acre" also meant a small meadow, so it may also be understood as "the clearing."

ACKLEY, "AK-lee"—*English: "meadow of acorns."* This refers to fertile oak trees. **ACKLEA, ACKLEE, ACKLEIGH.**

ACTON, "ACK-tun"—*English: "village by the oaks."*

ADAD, "ah-DAHD"—*Babylonian/Assyrian: "god of storms."* Adad is also associated with the sign Taurus, as his sacred animal was the bull.

ADAHY, "ah-DAH-hee"—*Native American Cherokee: "in the woods."*

ADAIR, "uh-DARE"—*Scottish: "the oak ford."* See also ADAR.

ADAM, "AD-um" or "ah-DAHM"—*Hebrew: "of the Earth" or "red earth."* **ADAMNAN**—Irish; **ADAMO** (ah-DAH-moh)—Spanish and Italian; **ADAO** (ah-DAH-oh)—Portuguese; **ADHAMH** (AH-yahv or AH-yaw)—Irish Gaelic. One of the Judeo-Christian stories of humanity's creation has Adam being formed from the clay or soil of the Earth. Saint Adamnan of Ireland was the first writer to ever mention the existence of a monster in Scotland's Loch Ness, circa A.D. 650. See also ADOM. F

ADAR, "ah-DAHR"—*Hebrew: "dark noble"; Arabic: "pure"; Greek: "beauty."* **ADAIR, ADIR.** F

ADDISON, "AD-ih-sun"—*Anglo-Saxon: "son of Adam" or "son of Adelaide."*

ADE, "ah-DEH" or "AH-deh"—*African Yoruba: "crown."*

ADEAGBO, "ah-deh-AG-bow"—*African*

Yoruba: "crown of honor."

ADEBAYO, "ah-DEH-bah-yoh"—*African Yoruba: "crowning joy."* **AKELEKE.**

ADELPHUS, "ah-DEHL-fah/fuhs"—*Greek: "brotherly."* **ADELFUS.**

ADEWOLE, "ah-DEH-woh-leh"—*African Yoruba: "a prince enters our house."*

ADI, "ah-DEE"—*Sanskrit: "first."*

ADIEL, "ah-dee-EHL"—*Hebrew: "ornament of God."* F.

ADIGUN, "ah-dee-GOON" or "ah-DEE-goon"—*African Yoruba: "righteousness."*

ADIL, "ah-DEEL"—*Arabic: "equal" or "just."* F

ADIO, "ah-DEE-oh"—*African Yoruba: "he is righteous."*

ADOM, "ah-DOHM"—*African Akan: "God's help."* See also ADAM.

ADON, "ah-DOHN" or "ah-DAWN"—*Phoenician: "lord."* **ADONAI** (ah-doh-NAH-ee or ah-doh-NEE)—*Semitic.* F

ADONIS, "ah-DOH-neese" or "uh-DAW-niss"—*Greek: "beautiful young one."* This is lifted from the earlier Phoenician words for gods and goddesses. Adonis was the incredibly attractive male god of agriculture. Some Greek myths say Aphrodite, goddess of love, and Persephone, goddess of Spring, both competed for his hand, and Zeus decided on shared custody, six months spent with each woman. This accounts for the changing seasons and for much planting folklore. Adonis is one of the minor planets of the asteroid belt between Mars and Jupiter, extraordinary in that its orbit takes it in very close to the Sun as well. F

ADRI, "AH-dree"—*Hindu: "rock."*

ADRIAN, "AY-dree-un"—*Greek: "rich" or "of the (Adriatic) sea"; Latin: "of the Adriatic" or "dark-haired."* **ADRIANO** (ah-dree-AH-noh)—Italian; **AIDRIAN** (eye-dree-AHN)—Irish Gaelic. The Adriatic seaport of Adria was renowned for its dark water and dark sand, and this is how the name's derivations came about. Several saints have names on this list. One of them was Saint Adrian, a Roman official who, with his wife, Natalia, was converted to Christianity and martyred. Another Saint Adrian was an African who helped to create a scholarly monastery. **ADRY.** See also HADRIAN. F

ADRIEL, "AH-dree-ehl"—*Hebrew: "God's majesty" or "of God's congregation."* F

ADROA, "ah-DROH-ah"—*African Luganda: "God's will."*

AGA, "AH-gah"—*Turkish: "great."*

AGU, "ah-GOO"—*African Ibo: "leopard."*

AHAB, "AY-hab" or "AH-hahb"—*Hebrew: "father's brother."* A king of Israel who defended his kingdom against Syrians and Assyrians was named Ahab. He was married to the schemer Jezebel, so you can see, he had his hands *full.* Another Ahab, the captain of Herman Melville's *Moby Dick,* also had his hands full.

AHANU, "ah-HAH-noo"—*Native American: "he laughs."*

AHD, "AHD"—*Arabic: "knowledge."*

AHMAD, "ah-MAHD" or "AH-mahd"—*Arabic: "commendable."* Ahmad al Badawi was a renowned thirteenth-century Sufi, or Moslem mystic, and saint who lived in Egypt.

AHMED, "ah-MEHD" or "AH-mehd"—*Arabic: "highly adored."* **ACHMED** (akh-

MEHD—"kh" in the back of your throat); **ACHMET; AHMET.**

AIDAN, "AY-dehn"—*Latin: "to help"; Gaelic: "little fire."* **AODHAN** (ah-OH-yahn—first two syllables as one)—Irish Gaelic. Saint Aidan was an Irish missionary of the seventh century. See also EDAN.

AINSLEY, "AYNZ-lee"—*Scottish: "my own meadow"; English: "nearby meadow."* **AINSLEIGH.**

AJANI, "ah-JAH-nee"—*African Yoruba: "the victor."*

AKA, "AH-kuh"—*Hawaiian: "laughter."* F

AKAL, "ah-KAHL"—*Hindu: "timeless."*

AKAU, "uh-KAH-oo"—*Polynesian: "from the North."*

AKBAR, "AHK-bahr"—*Arabic: "praised."* Akbar was a sixteenth-century Islamic emperor of northern India who practiced religious tolerance after having several moving visions. He encouraged the debate of religious differences and similarities, and ended up founding a new sect called Din Ilahi ("Divine Faith") that attempted to mix a variety of religious beliefs into a workable whole.

AKEMI, "ah-KEH-mee"—*Japanese: "beauty of dawn."*

AKEN, AKIN, "AY-kun"—*Irish: "horse lord"; Scottish: "holding fast."* **EACHAN**—Irish Gaelic.

AKER, "AH-kur"—*Egyptian: "guardian of the horizons."* In Egypt, Aker was depicted as a two-headed lion, with one head on either end of the body, or as two twin lions facing in opposite directions.

AKI, "ah-KEE"—*Japanese: "born in the autumn."* F

AKIA, "ah-KEE-ah"—*African Ateso: "first son."*

AKIB(A), "ah-KEEB" and "ah-KEE-bah"—*Hebrew: "to protect" or "the supplanter."* Akiba ben Joseph was a Hebrew sage who helped to shape the early Talmud. He was politically active and participated in a rebellion against the Roman Empire in the second century. See also AKIV, JACOB.

AKIL, "ah-KEEL"—*Moroccan: "one who reasons well" or "thoughtful."* F

AKIN, "ah-KEEN"—*African Yoruba: "hero, strong."*

AKIRA, "ah-KEE-rah"—*Japanese: "bright boy."* **AKIO.**

AKIV, "ah-KEEV"—*Hebrew: "to protect."* **AKIB**—Israeli. See also JACOB. F

AKULE, "ah-KOO-leh"—*Native American: "he looks up."*

AL. See AL(L)AN, ALASTAIR, ALBERT, ALFONSO.

AL(L)AN, "AL-un"—*Irish: "noble"; Celtic: "harmony" or "handsome."* **AILÍN** (EYE-leen)—Irish Gaelic; **ALAIN** (ah-LAWN)—French; **ALANO**—Spanish; **ALANUS; ALEN; ALYN; ALLEN, ALLYN. AL.** F

ALARD, "AL-ard"—*German: "noble and enduring."* **ALLARD, ALART.**

ALASTAIR, "AL-ih-stare" or "AL-ih-stur"—*Gaelic version of Alexander: "defender of mankind."* **ALASDAIR, ALASTER, ALISDAIR, ALISTAIR. AL.** See also ALEXANDER.

ALBERN, "AHL-burn"—*English: "noble knight."*

ALBERT, "AL-burt" or "ahl-BEAR"—*German: "noble and bright."* **AILBE** (EYE-L-beh), **AILBHE** (EYE-L-veh)—Irish Gaelic; **ALBERTKO**—Slavic; **ALBERTO**—Italian; **ALBERTOK**—Eastern European; **ALBRECHT** (AHL-breckt or ahl-BRECKT)—Nordic. Several Christian saint names are on this list. Albert Einstein was a famous twentieth-century physicist who revolutionized our way of viewing the universe, and whose name has become a synonym for "intelligence." Nineteenth-century British Prince Albert was the prince consort and great love of Queen Victoria's long life. A lot of British boys were named Albert in his honor. **AL; BERT, BERTIE, BERTOK, BERTY.** F

ALBIN, "AHL-bihn"—*Latin: "white" or "blond."* **ALBAN, ALBANY, ALBEN.** Saint Alban was a Roman living in Britain in the third century who gave shelter to persecuted Christians. F

ALCANDER, "al-KAN-dur" or "ahl-KAHN-dur"—*Greek: "strong-minded."* **ALCAN.** F

ALDEN, "AHL-dehn" or "AL-dehn"—*English: "old friend."* **ALDIN.**

ALDO, "AHL-doh"—*Italian: "antiquity" or "the ancestors"; Teutonic: "wealthy."* See also ALDOUS.

ALDOUS, "AHL-doh-us," "AL-doh-us," or "AL-duhs"—*German: "old" or "wise."* **ALDIS, ALDOS, ALDUS.** Aldus Manutius was a Venetian printer who, soon after printing presses were in use, revived interest in classical Greek and Roman writers with his editions of their works. **ALDO.**

ALDRICH, "ALL-drich"—*Teutonic: "wise old ruler."* **ALDRICK, AUDRIC.**

ALEC. See ALEXANDER.

ALERON, "AL-eh-rawn"—*Latin: "on the wing."* The "wing" originally referred to the wing of an army, and thus to an ally in battle.

ALEXANDER, "al-ex-AN-dur" or "ah-lehk-ZAHN-der"—*Greek: "defender or protector of humankind."* Okay, here we go: **ALEJANDRO** (ah-leh-HAHN-dro)—Spanish; **ALEKOS, ALEXIOS**—Greek; **ALEKSANDR, ALEKSY**—Polish; **ALESANDESE** (ah-leh-sahn-deh-seh)—Basque; **ALESSANDR, ALESSANDRO**—Italian; **ALEXANDR, ALEX-IS; ALEXANDRE** (ah-lehk-ZAHN-dreh), **ALIX**—French; **ALEXEI** (ah-LEHK-say), **ALEXEYEV, ALYOSHA** (ahl-YOH-shah), **LYAKSANDR** (LYAHK-sahn-dur)—Russian; **ALEXIO**—Portuguese; **ELEK, ELEKSANDER** (eh-leck-SHAHN-dur), **ELI, SÁNDOR**—Eastern European; **ZINDEL** (ZEEN-dehl or zeen-DEHL), **ZINDIL, ZUNDE**—Yiddish. Alexander the Great was just in his twenties by the time he had conquered Asia, the Middle East, and much of Europe in the fourth century B.C. The name has been associated with rulers since then. Several Christian saints' and popes' names can also be found on this list. **ALEC, ALECK, ALEX, LEX; SASHA.** See also ALASTAIR, SANDER. F

ALFONSO, "ahl-FAWN-soh"—*Teutonic: "eager or ready soldier."* **ALFONZO, AL-PHONSO; ALONSO, ALONZO; ALPHONSE.** Alfonso or Alphonso has a long and royal Spanish history—several kings have borne these names. **AL, ALF, ALFIE, ALFY; FONZ, FONZIE, FONZO.** F

ALFRED, "AHL-freh" or "AHL-fred"—*Nordic: "king of the elves"; English: wise counsellor"; Anglo-Saxon: "elfin counsel."* **AILFRID** (EYE-l-freed)—Irish Gaelic; **ALFR**—Norwegian; **ALFREC(K); ALFRID**—German and Eastern European. The Anglo-Saxon derivation doesn't refer to a teeny-tiny house of representatives, but to someone who receives magical assistance and guidance. Alfred the Great was an early English king who united most of the island, drove out the Norsemen, and founded the navy, while creating a set of laws and educational guidelines. Alfred Nobel was a nineteenth-century inventor who began the Nobel Prize awards for persons making discoveries or other breakthroughs that contribute to the peace, harmony, and well-being of the world. He did so in reaction to the use of his inventions dynamite and nitroglycerin in warfare, which was not his intent. **ALFI(E), ALFY; FRED, FREDDI(E), FREDDY.** F

ALGER, "AL-jer"—*English: "clever warrior" or "elfin spear."*

ALI, "ah-LEE"—*Swahili: "exalted."* Ali was the cousin and son-in-law of Mohammed, one of the first converts to Islam. In *A Thousand and One Arabian Nights*, Ali Baba is the simple woodcutter who gains entrance to a cave storing the forty thieves' haul by uttering the words "Open sesame."

ALLAH, "AH-lah"—*Semitic(?) or Persian(?): "god" or "deity."* It is only since the Prophet Mohammed that the Arabic world has generally adopted the notion of God as one being—Allah. Before Islam, Allah was one of the principle deities in the Middle Eastern pantheon, considered to be a creative force and the power that determined weather. The Jinn—genies and other magical beings—were said to be celestial cousins who assisted Allah in his work.

ALLEN. See AL(L)AN.

ALON, "ah-LAWN"—*Hebrew: "oak tree."* F

ALONZO, "ah-LAWN-zoh"—*version of Alfonso: "eager or ready soldier."* **ALONSO.** Alonso de Ercilla y Zuniga was a sixteenth-century Spanish epic poet. He was an adventurer in the New World, in what is modern-day South America.

ALPHONSO. See ALFONSO.

ALROY, "AHL-roy"—*Irish Gaelic: "red-haired boy."*

ALSTON, "AHL-stun"—*English: "from the old manor house" or "old village."* **HALSTON.**

ALTAIR, "ahl-TARE"—*Arabic: "bird."* Altair is one of the so-called fixed stars used for centuries by navigators and astrologers because of their apparent constance. Astrologically, bright Altair is in Capricorn, but the actual star is part of the constellation Aquila. Altair is associated in folklore with heroism and tenacity.

ALTON, "AHL-tun" or "AL-tun"—*English: "the old town."* **ALDEN, ALTEN.**

ALVAR, "AHL-vahr"—*Hindu: "immersed one"; German: "elf army"; Latin: "fair, white."* The Alvars were twelve Hindu poet-saints from the seventh to the tenth centuries who were completely and fanatically devoted to the worship of the god Vishnu. Their writings are immediate, passionate, personal. One or more were female.

ALVARO, "ahl-VAH-roh"—*Portuguese: "white."* F

ALVIN, "AHL-vihn" or "AL-vihn"—*English: "noble friend" or "elfin friend."* **ALUINO** (ahl-WEE-noh)—Spanish; **ALVINO** (ahl-VEE-noh)—Italian; **ALWIN**—German; **ALWYN, AYLWIN, ELVIN, ELWIN**—Scottish and Irish.

AMA(H)L, "ah-MAHL"—*Arabic: "hope."*

AMAN, "ah-MAHN"—*Arabic: "aspiration."*

AMASA, "ah-MAH-sah" or "AH-mah-sah"—*Hebrew: "bearer of a burden."*

AMIEL, "ah-mee-EHL"—*Hebrew: "the God of my people."* F

AMIN, "ah-MEEN"—*Arabic: "trusted" or "faithful."*

AMIR, "ah-MEER"—*Arabic: "prince"; Yiddish: "grain."* **AMEER**—Afghani. F

AMIRAM, "AH-mee-rahm"—*Hebrew: "lofty people" or "mighty nation."* **AMRAM.** Amram and Yoshebel were the natural parents of Moses, who set him on the waters of the Nile in a basket in the hope that he would be spared the Pharaoh's death sentence on all Hebrew males under the age of three. Their son was saved, and he returned to them in a *big* way.

AMMAR, "ah-MAHR"—*Arabic: "the builder."*

AMNON, "AHM-nawn"—*Hebrew: "faithful."*

AMOR, "ah-MOHR" or "AH-mohr"—*Latin: "love."* This is one of the minor planets of the asteroid belt between Mars and Jupiter, one of the rare ones that actually passes between Earth and Mars as well.

AMORY, "AY-moh-ree"—*Latin: "loved."* **AMARY, AMERY, EMBREY.**

AMOS, "AH-mohss" or "AY-mohs"—*Hebrew: "burdened."*

AMUN, "AH-mun"—*Egyptian: "what is hidden" or "eternal."* **AMAN, AMIN, AMMON.** The Egyptian god Amun began his existence as god of air and wind, but was elevated to sun god and even greater status later on. Amun has associations with the astrological sign Aries, as his animal and symbol were the ram and the ram's horns.

ANASTASIO, "ahn-ah-STAH-see-oh," "ahn-ah-STAY-see-oh," "ahn-ah-STAH-syoh," or "ah-nah-STAY-syoh"—*Latin: "resurrection."* **ANASTAGIO**—Italian; **ANASZTÁZ** (AHN-ush-tahz)—Hungarian; **ANSTÁS** (AHN-stos[h] or ahn-STOS[H])—Irish Gaelic. Anastasio is one of the Christian saints. **STACY, STASSIE, STASSY.** F

ANATOL, "AN-uh-toll" or "AWN-uh-toll"—*Greek: "from the East" or "rising sun."* **ANATOLE, ANATOLI, ANATOLY; ANATOLIO**—Italian; **ANATOLIOS**—Greek; **TOLYA, TOLENKA**—Russian. Anatol is one of the Christian saints.

ANDRAS, "AHN-drahs"—*Norse: "breath."* F

ANDREW, "AN-drew"—*Greek: "strong and manly."* **AINDRÉAS** (eye-n-DRAYas[h])—Irish Gaelic; **ANDERE** (ahn-deh-reh)—Basque; **ANDERS**—Norwegian; **ANDI, ANDOR, ANDRAS, ANDRIS**—Eastern European; **ANDRAS, ANDREAS, ANDRIAN, ANDROS**—Greek; **ANDRÉ** (AWN-dray—"r" deep in your throat)—French; **ANDREAN**—Italian; **ANDRED**—Old English; **ANDREI, ANDREYEV**—Russian; **ANDRES**—Portuguese; **ANDRIES**—Dutch; **ANDRO; ANDRZEJ** (AHND-r-zheh)—Polish; **ANDZS** (AHNDZ)—Latvian. The names of several Christian saints can be found on this list. One of them is Andrew, the first disciple of Jesus, and another is the patron saint of Scotland. Andrew Jackson, president from 1829 to 1836, duelled and killed a Nashville lawyer in 1806 over remarks made about Mrs. Jackson (cool!). **ANDY; DREW.** F

ANDY. See ANDREW.

ANGELO, "AN-jeh-loh" or "AHN-jeh-loh"—*Latin: "messenger"; Greek: "an angel."* **AINGEAL** (EYE-n-ghal)—Irish Gaelic; **ANGAROS** (AHN-gah-rohss)—Persian; **ANGE** (ONZHE)—French; **ANGELO** (anh-YEH-loh)—Greek; **ANGELOV, ANZHEL** (AHN-zhehl)—Eastern European; **ANGERES** (AHN-jeh-rehz)—Sanskrit; **ANIOL** (AHN-

CHANGING MALE NAMES TO FEMALE NAMES

If you like a particular male name, but are expecting a girl, no problem! Many male names are acceptable for girls, and many names are shared by both genders. Or you can use a male name as a girl's middle name. If, however, you have to feminize a selection, it's as easy as removing the final consonants until you reach an "a," "e," "i," or "y" and/or adding any one of these endings: "a," "ay," "e," "ey," "i," "ia," "ie," or "y," or "anne," "anna," "elle," "el(l)a," "enne," en(n)a," "ette," "et(t)a," "il(l)a," "ille," "in(n)a," "in(n)e," "is(s)e," "is(s)a," "it(t)a," or "itte," to list just a few possibilities.

Jonathan—JONATHA
Kenneth—KENNETTE
Daniel—DANIELLE, DANIEL(L)A

Juan—JUANITA
Thomas—THOMASINA
Mark—MARKIE

---

yohl)—Polish. **ANGEL, ANGIO, GELO.** F

ANGUO, "AHNG-whoh"—*Chinese: "protector."*

ANGUS, "ANG-guhss"—*Scottish: "vigor"; Celtic: "exceptional"; Greek: "first choice" or "unique choice."* **AONGHUS** (AH-ohn-yus[h]—first two syllables as one)—Irish Gaelic. Angus was a chief god in Gaelic myth who looked out for the prosperity of his people.

ANKH, "AHNK"—*Egyptian: "life."* **ANKHA.**

ANNAN, "AN-un"—*Celtic: "from the stream."*

ANOKI, "ah-noh-KEE"—*Native American Apache: "actor" or "performer."*

ANSAR, "ahn-SAHR"—*Arabic: "helper."* The Arabs of Medina who were converted to Islam by Mohammed were called Ansar, since they helped Mohammed in his exploits. F

ANSEL, "AHN-sehl"—*English from Yiddish: "blessed, happy"; German: "god."* **ANCEL, ANCELIN**—German; **ANSHEL** (AHN-shehl),

ANSHIL—Yiddish.

ANSELM, "AHN-sehlm"—*Teutonic: "helmet of the gods" or "protector."* **ANZELM, ANZELMY**—Polish.

ANSGAR, "AHNS-gahr"—*Dutch: "warrior."*

ANSON, "AN-sun"—*English: "son of Anne."*

ANTHONY, "AN-thoh-nee"—*English from Latin: "inestimable."* **TONY.** See also ANTONIO.

ANTONIO, "an/ahn-TOHN-ee-oh"—*Latin: "of infinite value" or "inestimable"; Greek: "beyond praise."* **ANDONE, ANDONI, ANDONIÑE** (ahn-do-nee-nyeh)—Basque; **ANDONIOS, ANTONIOS**—Greek; **ANTAINE** (ahn-TYE-n), **UAITHNE** (WHYTH-nay)—Irish Gaelic; **ANTAL** (ahn-TALL)—Eastern European; **ANTEK, ANTONIY** (ahn-toh-NEE-yeh), **TOLA, TOSIA**—Polish; **ANTHONY, ANTONY, ANTINKO**—Russian; **ANTOINE** (ahn-TWAHN)—French; **ANTON**—Scandinavian; **HEWNEY**—Irish; **TONCSE** (ton-CHEH)—Hungarian. Marc Antony, a Roman soldier, was a lover of Cleopatra, and this affair brought about a major upheaval in Rome during the time of Julius Caesar. Several Christian saints' names can be found on this list. Antony of Egypt was a very early Christian who gave away all his possessions to live in the desert as a hermit as one of the early church's Desert Fathers. He came out though, quite often, to encourage others in the new faith. Saint Antony of Padua was the first official professor of theology in the Franciscan order and is said to have performed many miracles in his travelling ministry. He is the patron of things that are lost. **TONY.** F

ANU, "AH-noo"—*Sumerian: "heaven."* Anu was the supreme god of the Sumerian pantheon. He was the patron god of kings, who, when inscribing monuments to themselves, called themselves "the beloved of Anu." Anu was also the Babylonian sky god.

ANWAR, "AHN-wahr"—*Arabic: "ray of light."* Anwar Sadat was a twentieth-century Egyptian president who won a Nobel Peace Prize for making the first peace with Israel in the millennia of the two peoples' animosity. He was assassinated for his trouble.

ANWELL, "AN-wehl"—*Cymric (Old Welsh): "beloved one."*

APIATAN, "ah-PYAH-tahn"—*Native American Kiowa: "wooden lance."* **PIATA(H).**

APOLLO, "ah-PAW-loh"—*Greek: "the God of the Sun."* **APOLLINAIRE** (ah-paw-lih-NARE)—French; **APOLON; APOLONIUSZ** (ah-pah-LOW-nee-ush)—Polish; **APPOLON, APOLLONIUS.** Apollo was not only the Greek god of the Sun, he had rulership over the day, light, manliness, hunting, flocks, herds, medicine, music, prophecy,

etc. He was a busy god. Saint Appolonius or Appolon had all his teeth pulled out before he was martyred in the third century. Thus, he is called upon to ward off toothaches, and is the patron saint of dentists. F

ARA, "AH-rah"—*Latin: "altar."* In the southern skies, the constellation Ara can be seen chasing the Sun at dusk from late July through mid-August. The Sun is "in" the Altar near Thanksgiving—appropriate to give thanks at an altar, isn't it?

ARABIS, "AH-rah-bihss" or "AIR-ah-bihss"—*Latin: "of Arabia."* Arabis is another name for the rock cress flower.

ARCHARD, "AR-churd"—*Anglo-Saxon: "sacred" or "powerful."* **ARCHERD.**

ARCHER, "AR-chur"—*English: "bowman" or "archer."*

ARDEN, "AR-dehn"—*Latin: "to blaze," "to sparkle," or "to dazzle."* **ARDIN.**

ARDLEY, "AHRD-lee"—*English: "meadow of our homestead."* **ARDLEIGH.**

ARDON, "AHR-dun" or "AHR-dohn"—*Hebrew: "subduer" or "bronze."* In the Old Testament/Tanakh, Ardon was Moses' reconnaissance man who went ahead of the Israelites into Canaan. Thus, the name is associated with scouting and bravery.

AREN, "AH-ren"—*African: "eagle."*

AREND, "AH-rend"—*German: "eagle" or "power."*

ARES, "AH-reez"—*Greek: "god of war."* Ares was the son of Zeus and Hera, king and queen of the Greek gods. He also represents the masculine element in nature.

ARGENT, "AHR-ghent" or "ahr-GHENT," or "AHR-jehnt" or "ahr-JEHNT"—*Latin: "silver."* **ARGENTUM.**

ARGES, "AHR-gheez"—*Greek: "silver-smith."* This is a name of one of the giant Cyclops in Greek mythology. They were known as fine craftsmen.

ARGUS, "ARE-guss"—*Greek: "watchful or vigilant."* The Argus of Greek myth couldn't help but be watchful, what with having a hundred eyes and all.

ARI, "AH-ree—*Hebrew: "lion."* **ARYEH.**

ARIEL, "AH-ree-ehl" or "ah-ree-EHL," or "AIR-ee-ehl" or "air-ee-EHL"—*Hebrew: "lion of God."* In the Tanakh/Old Testament, Ariel is another name used poetically for Jerusalem. Ariel is the brightest moon of Uranus. F

ARIES, "AIR-eez"—*Greek: "ram."* The constellation Aries can be seen chasing the Sun at dusk from mid-December through early January. The Sun is "in" Aries from late March throughout April. It has been seen as a symbol by many different peoples. To the Assyrians, this was the sign of SAN, the Lamb. To the early Christian church, this was the sign of PETER, or the Two Keys. To the Egyptians, it was the sign of SOBEK, the Crocodile. To the Greeks, it was the sign of ATHENA, or the Owl. To the early Hebrews, it was the sign of GAD, or the Tents. To the Norse peoples, it was the sign of ODIN, or the Ravens. To the Romans, it was the sign of MINERVA, or the Aegis. To the Babylonians, it was the sign of AGGARU the Messenger. Earthly rulers at this time are the ALDER TREE (six days of the WILLOW TREE) for the Celts and Druids, and the PEACH BLOSSOM for the Japanese.

ARILD, "ARE-ihld"—*Norse: "war chief."*

ARIO, "AH-ree-oh"—*Latin: "melody."* F

ARION, "AH-ree-ohn"—*Hebrew: "melodious."*

ARISTO, "ah-RIHS-toh"—*Greek: "the best."* **ARISTOKLES** (ah-RIHS-tuh-kleez or air-is-TAWK-lees)—Greek. One of the Christian saints is named Aristokles. F

ARLEGE, "AHR-lehj"—*English: "rabbits by the lake."* **ARLEDGE.**

ARLO, "AHR-loh"—*English: "fortified hill."*

ARMAND, "ahr-MAWND"—*Teutonic: "soldier" or "army man"; or Hebrew: "castle" or "palace."* **ARMAN, ARMIN, ARMON, ARMONI**—Israeli; **ARMANDO**—Spanish; **ARMANO, ARMANI, ARMINO**—Italian.

ARNET, "AHR-neht"—*German/French: "little eagle."*

ARNO, "ARE-noh"—*Teutonic/German: "eagle."* **ARE, ARNDT, ARNT**—German; **AREN** (AH-rehn)—Norwegian; **ARNE**—Nordic; **ARNE, ARNOT** (ARE-noh)—French; **ERNÖ**—Eastern European. **ARNI(E), ARNY.** F

ARNOLD, "ARE-nohld"—*Teutonic: "he who frightens the eagle"; German: "strong as an eagle"; Irish: "great valor."* **ARDÁL** (ahr-DOLL)—Irish Gaelic; **ARNALDO**—Portuguese; **ARNAUD** (ahr-NOH—"r" in the back of your throat), **ARNAUT** (ahr-NOH—"r" in the back of your throat)—French; **ARNELD, ARNLJOT** (ARN-lyot)—Norwegian. Certainly award-winning muscleman turned actor Arnold Schwarzenegger meets these descriptions. **ARNI(E), ARNY.**

ARNON, "ahr-NAWN"—*Hebrew: "roaring waters."*

ARNY. See ARNO, ARNOLD.

ARSENIO, "ahr-SEH-nee-oh"—*Greek: "strong," as in "intense."* **ARSÈNE** (ahr-SEHN—with the "r" in your throat)—French. **ARSEN, SENIO.**

ART. See ARTHUR.

ARTEMAS, "AHR-teh-mahs"—*Greek: "belonging to Artemis."* **ARTEMUS; ARTIMAS, ARTIMUS.** Artemis was the Greek goddess of the Moon, the hunt, and animals, among other things. F

ARTHUR, "ARE-thur"—*Celtic: "noble" or "bear"; Irish: "stone."* **ARTAIR**—Scottish; **ARTHURO** (ahr-TOO-roh)—Italian; **ARTUR** (ahr-TOOR—with the "r" sounds in your throat)—French; **ARTUREK** (AHR-too-rehk or ahr-TOO-rehk)—Polish; **ARTURO** (ahr-TOO-roh)—Spanish and Portuguese. The legendary English king Arthur and the events around his life have so captured the imagination that there are countless references to him and to his court in classic and modern literature, in films, and in plays. Historically, the Arthur in question probably really did exist as a Celtic tribal chieftain who united several groups. **ART, ARTE, ARTIE, ARTY.**

ARUN, "ah-ROON"—*Hindu: "radiant as the sun."* **ARUNI.** F

ARUNDEL, "AIR-un-dehl"—*English: "the eagle dell."* F

ARVAD, "AHR-vahd"—*Hebrew: "wanderer."*

ASA, "AH-sah" or "AY-sah"—*Japanese: "born in the morning"; Hebrew: "physician" or "healer."* Asa, king of Judah, was the grandson of King David in the Old Testament/Tanakh.

ASAD, "AH-sahd"—*Sanskrit: "lion."*

ASADEL, "AH-sah-del"—*Arabic: "most prosperous."*

ASGARD, "AZ-gahrd"—*Norse: "hall of the gods."* Asgard was the citadel of the Scandinavian gods.

ASHBY, "ASH-bee"—*English: "farm by the ash trees."*

ASHER, "AH-shur" or "ASH-er"—*Hebrew: "blessed."*

ASHFORD, "ASH-furd"—*English: "river-crossing by the ash trees"* or *"the ford near the ash trees."*

ASHTON, "ASH-tun"—*English: "the town near the ash trees."* **ASHTIN, ASTIN, ASTON.**

ASHWIN, "AHSH-win"—*Hindu.* Ashwin is the name of a star.

ASTLEY, "AST-lee"—*Greek/Celtic: "star-lit meadow."* **ASTLEIGH, ASTLY.** F

ASTOR, "AS-tohr"—*Irish Gaelic: "loved one."* **ASTHOR** (as-TORE), **ASTHORE**—French and Nordic; **ASTOIR** (ah-STOW-eer)—Irish Gaelic. F

ATHERTON, "ATH-ur-tun"—*English: "the town at the spring"* or *"the farm at the spring."*

ATLAS, "AT-luhs"—*Greek: "holding or bearing the world."* Atlas was one of the Titans, the great early Greek gods. He was said to support the pillars of heaven. Atlas is also one of the moons of Saturn.

ATLEY, "AT-lee"—*English: "at the meadow"* or *"at the clearing."* **ATLEIGH.**

ATU, "AH-too"—*Maori: "god."*

ATWELL, "AT-wehl"—*English: "the well."* **ATWILL.**

ATWOOD, "AT-wood"—*English: "in the woods"* or *"in the forest."*

AUBIN, "AW-bihn"—*Latin: "fair"* or *"pale."* **ALBION.**

AUBREY, "AW-bree"—*French: "blond king"; Teutonic: "ruler of the elves."* **BRE, BREY.**

AUDUN, "AWD-uhn"—*Norwegian: "friendship and prosperity."* **AUDI(E).**

AUGUST, "AWG-ust"—*Latin: "venerable," "majestic,"* and *"born in August."* **AGAISTIN** (ah-GUY-steen)—Irish Gaelic; **AGOSTINO** (ah-goh-STEE-noh)—Portuguese, Italian, and Spanish; **ÁGOSTON** (ah-GOSH-tun), **AGUSZTAV** (ah-GOOSH-tahv)—Hungarian; **AOÛT** (AHOO or AHOOT)—French; **AUGUSTIN** (aw-GOO-stan)—French; **AUGUSTIN, AUGUSTINO(S)**—Greek; **AUGUSTUS; AUGUSTYN**—Slavic; **AVGUST** (AHV-goost)—Russian; **HACHIGWATSU**—Japanese. Our month of August got its name by being the month in which Augustus Caesar was born. I don't know what people called the eighth month before; in some cultures, August isn't even what they consider to be the eighth month. The names of several Christian saints, one of whom became the first archbishop of Canterbury, are on this list. **AUGGI(E), AUGI(E); GUS, GUSSI(E).** F

AURELIUS, "oh-RAY-lee-us"—*Latin: "golden."* **ARANYU**—Hungarian; **AUREK** (OR-ek)—Polish; **AUREL, AURELIAN; AURÈLIEN** (aw-REH-lyen)—French; **AURELNE** (oh-rehl-neh)—Basque. F

AUSTIN, "AW-stihn" or "OH-stan"—*Scottish/French form of Augustin: "venerable"* or *"majestic."* **OISTIN** (OY-steen)—Irish Gaelic.

AUTUMN, "AWT-um"—*Latin: "autumn!"* **AKI**—Japanese; **AUTOMNE** (aw-TUN), **AUTONNE**—French; **AUTUNNO** (aw-TOO-noh)—Italian; **CHARIF** (KHAH-reef—the "KH" in your throat)—Arabic; **HERBST**—German; **HØST** (HAWST), **HÖST**—Scandinavian; **JESIEN** (yeh-see-EHN)—Polish; **OSEN** (OH-sehn)—Russian; **OTOÑO** (oh-TOHN-yoh)—Spanish; **SONBAHAR** (SAWN-bah-hahr or sawn-BAH-hahr)—Turkish. F

AVERIL, "AH-veh-rihl"—*Latin: "open to the sun"; Celtic: "boar warrior."* **ABRIL** (AH-breel)—Spanish, Portuguese, and Arabic; **APRYEL** (ah-pree-EHL)—Russian; **AVERELL, AVERILL; AVRIL** (ahv-REEL)—French; **SHIGWATSU**—Japanese. These two meanings make a very odd pair!

AVERY, "AY-veh-ree"—*Anglo-Saxon: "elfin ruler."*

AVI, "ah-VEE"—*Hebrew: "father."*

AVIDAN, "ah-vee-DAHN"—*Hebrew: "God (the Father) is just."* **AVEDAN, AVEDON.**

AVIDOR, "ah-vee-DOHR"—*Hebrew: "father of a generation."*

AVIEL, "AH-vee-ehl"—*Hebrew: "God is my father."* F

AVIV, "ah-VEEV"—*Hebrew: "springtime"* or *"fresh."* F

AVNIEL, "AHV-nee-ehl"—*Hebrew: "my father is my rock."*

AVOCET, "AH-voh-seht"—*French: a long-legged shore bird with a slightly upturned beak.* **AVOCETTO** (ah-voh-CHEH-toh)—Italian. F

AXTON, "ACKS-tun"—*English: "swordstone"* or *"ax-stone."* An ax-stone is used to sharpen the ax's blade.

AYINDE, "ah-yeen-DEH"—*African Yoruba: "we gave praise and he came."*

AYLWARD, "AIL-wurd"—*English: "awe-inspiring guardian."*

AYO, "AH-yoh"—*African Yoruba: "joy."*

AYODELE, "ah-yoh-DEH-leh"—*African Yoruba: "joy in our home."* **AYO.**

AZA, "ah-ZAH"—*Arabic: "comfort."*

AZI, "ah-ZEE"—*African: "youth" or "energy."*

AZIM, "ah-ZEEM"—*Arabic: "powerful."*

AZRIEL, "ahz-ree-EHL"—*Hebrew: "God is my help."* **AZRA-EL.**

AZUR(E), "ah-ZOOR" or "AZ-yoor"—*Persian: "lapis-lazuli stone."* Lapis lazuli was ground up to make deep blue dyes the color of the sky, thus leading to the meaning most of us know: "clear blue." F

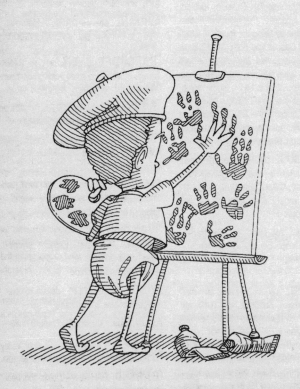

THE TOP FIVE

B BRANDON
BRETT
BOBBY
BILLY
BRIAN

If the name you're looking for isn't here, see "V."

BAE, "BAH-ee"—*Korean: "inspiration."*

BAILEY, "BAY-lee"—*English: "meadow where berries grow"; Teutonic: "able-bodied."* BAILEIGH, BAILIE, BAILLIE, BAILLEY, BAILY, BAYLEY; BEGLEIGH, BEGLEY, BEGLIE, BEGLY.

BAINBRIDGE, "BANE-brihj"—*English: "bridge over white water."*

BAION, "bye-YOHN"—*Portuguese.* The baion is a slow, sensual dance. **BAYON.**

BAIRD, "BAYRD"—*Scottish: "minstrel."* **BARD.**

BAL, "BAHL"—*Gypsy from Sanskrit: "hair."* So how did we come up with *bald* to mean hairless?

BALA, "BAH-lah"—*Sanskrit: "strong arms."*

BALAN, "bah-LAN"—*Old English: "one with much hair."* In Arthurian legend, Sir Balan was a Knight of the Round Table, brother of Balin.

BALDWIN, "BAHLD-wihn"—*German: "courageous friend."* **BAUDOIN** (BOWD-wan—"BOW" as in "wow")—*French and Arabic;* **BALDEWIN, BALDWYN.**

BALIN, "bah-LIN"—*Old English: "valiant."* In Arthurian legend, Sir Balin was a Knight of

the Round Table, brother of Balan. He was also called the Knight of Two Swords.

BALLARD, "BAL-ahrd"—*Latin: "to dance"; German: "strong."*

BANCROFT, "BAHN-krawft" or "BANK-rawft"—*English: "a small holding" or "bean-field."*

BANDELE, "bawn-DEH-leh"—*African Yoruba: "born away from our home."*

BANNING, "BAN-ihng"—*Gaelic: "little blondie."*

BAPTISTE, "bawp-TEEST"—*Greek: "baptizer" or "one who is baptized."* **BATTISTE** (bah-TEEST), **BAUTISTE** (boh-TEEST)—*Italian.*

BARAK, "bah-RAHK" or "BAH-rahk"—*Arabic: "white one"; Hebrew: "blessing" or "lightning."* In the Old Testament/Tanakh, Barak was a warrior who fought under the direction of the Hebrew queen Deborah. See also BURAQ. F

BARCLAY, "BAHR-klay"—*Anglo-Saxon: "boatsman's meadow" or "ship-builder's meadow."*

BARDEN, "BAHR-dehn"—*English: "valley of barley."* **BARDON, BARTON. BARD, BARDO.**

BAREND, "BAH-rend"—*Dutch: "firm bear."* **BARENDT, BARENT.**

BARKER, "BAR-kur"—*English: "birch tree logger"; French: "vessel."* The vessel referred to is a three-masted ship.

BARLOW, "BAR-loh"—*English: "the bare hill."* **BARLOWE.**

BARNABY, BARNABAS, "BAHR-nah-bee" and "BAHR-nah-buhss"—*Aramaic: "son of ecouragement" or "plowman."* **BARNABA** (bahr-NAH-bah), **BERNABA**—Italian and Portuguese; **BARNABE** (bahr-NAWB[-eh]), **BERNABE**—French and Spanish; **BARNABÉ** (bahr-nah-BAY—"r" to clear your throat)—French; **BARNABUS; BARNAIB** (BAR-nah-eeb)—Irish Gaelic. Barnabus is one of the Christian saints. **BARNEY, BARNI(E), BARNO.**

BARNARD, "BAHR-nahrd" or "bahr-NAHRD"—*German: "brave bear."* **BARNARDO, BARN, BARNI(E), BARNEY.**

BARNETT, "BAR-neht" or "bar-NEHT"—*English: "leader."*

BARNEY. See BARNABY, BARNARD.

BARNUM, "BAR-num"—*English: "barley storehouse."*

BARON, "BARE-un"—*German: "free man."* Baron is also a title for a class of nobility. **BARONET, BARRON; BARRONE** (bah-ROHN), **BARONNES** (bah-ROH-nehz)—Spanish and Portuguese.

BARR, "BAHR"—*Irish: "the topmost point"; English: "a gateway."*

BARRAN, "BAH-rahn"—*Irish: "little top."* This is the name of a Christian saint.

BARRET, "BEAR-eht"—*Teutonic: "mighty bear."* **BARRETT.** See also BARRY.

BARRY, "BARE-ee"—*Irish and Welsh: "spear."* **BARRET, BARRETT, BARRIS; BEAR-**

ACH (BAH-rahkh—"kh" in your throat)—Irish Gaelic. F

BART. See BARTHOLOMEW, BARTON, BURTON.

BARTHOLOMEW, "bahr-THOH-loh-myoo" or "bahr-TOH-loh-myoo"—*Hebrew: "from the small hill" or "son of a plowman."* **BARTEL**—Dutch; **BARTHELMY** (bahr-TEHL-mee—"r" in your throat)—French; **BARTOLOMEO** (bahr-toh-loh-MAY-oh)—Spanish and Portuguese; **PARTHOLON** (PAR-thoh-lone)—Irish. Bartholomew is listed as one of the disciples of Christ. There is a book called the *Gospel of Bartholomew*, but it was not allowed into the Scriptures by the mainstream church. Saint Bartholomew is said to have done missionary work in India and Armenia, where he was crucified upside down. Talk about a tough crowd. **BART.**

BARTON, "BAHR-tun"—*English: "village of barley farms," "broad town," or "Boudica's town."* Pick a definition. Boudica was an ancient Celtic queen who fought the Roman invasion of Britain. **BART.** See also BURTON.

BARUCH, "bah-ROOHK" or "ba-ROOGH" ("GH" that sounds like you're going to bring up some phlegm!)—*Greek: "doer of good"; Hebrew: "blessed."* **BARRUCH, BAR(R)USH; BARRUCIO** (bah-ROO-chee-oh)—Italian; **BERAKHIAH** (beh-RAH-khee-ah—"kh" at the back of the throat)—Israeli. Barush was the companion of the prophet Jeremiah in the Old Testament/Tanakh.

BASIL, "BAZ-ihl" or "BAY-sihl"—*Greek: "royal" or "regal."* **BASILE** (bah-SEEL or bah-ZEEL)—French; **BASILIO**—Italian; **BASUL**—Arabic; **BAZEL**—Persian; **BAZYLI**—Polish. Fourth-century Saint Basil the Great had a

Bar-, Ben-

These are Hebrew prefixes that mean "son of" and "the family of." You may add them to any name.

lot of family pressure: his mother, father, grandmother, older sister, and two younger brothers were all saints, too. The herb basil is used in many cultures' cusines. See also VASILI(I). F

BASIM, "bah-SEEM"—*Arabic: "smiling."* **BASSAM.**

BAVOL, "BAH-vohl"—*Gypsy: "moving air" or "wind."* **BAVEL, BEVAL, BEVOL.**

BAXTER, "BACKS-tur"—*Teutonic: "the baker."*

BAY, "BAY"—*Vietnamese: "seventh child" or "seventh month (July)"; a body of water.* **BAHIA** (bay-YAH)—Spanish; **ESTERO** (EH-steh-roh)—Spanish; **BAIE, BAYE**—French; **BANDAR** (bawn-DAHR)—Persian; **BODDEN** (BOW-dehn), **BUCHT** (BOO-kht—"kh" is gutteral), **BUSEN** (BOO-sehn)—German; **BOKA** (boh-KAH or BOH-kah)—Serbo-Croatian; **BUGT, BUKT**—Scandinavian; **FLOI**—Icelandic; **GHUBBAT** (goo-BAWT), **KHALIJ** (khah-LEEJ), **SAWQIRAH** (saw-KEE-rah or SAW-kee-rah)—Arabic; **GUBA** (GOO-bah), **LIMAN** (LEE-mawn), **ZALIV** (zah-LEEV)—Russian; **HAVE** (HAH-veh)—Swedish; **KENET** (keh-NEHT)—Albanian; **KOLPOS, ORMOS**—Greek; **KORFEZI** (kohr-feh-ZEE or kohr-FEH-zee)—Turkish; **OKI** (OH-kee)—Japanese; **SELKA**—Finnish; **TELUK** (teh-LOOK)—Indonesian; **VINH**—Vietnamese; **WAN**—Chinese; **ZALEW** (zah-LEHV), **ZATOKA** (ZAH-toh-kah)—Polish. F

BAYARD, "BYE-yahr" ("r" rustles in the back of your throat) or "BYE-yahrd"—*French: "fiery-haired" or "bay-colored."* Medieval legend says that Bayard was a magical horse given by Charlemagne to one of his allies, Rinaldo.

BEAGAN, "BEE-ghan" or "BAY-ghan"—*Irish Gaelic: "little one."*

BEAMAN, BEEMAN, "BEE-mun"—*English: "beekeeper."* This is an easy one to figure out.

BEAR, "BARE"—*the king of the forest.* **BERUANG** (BARE-wong)—Indonesian; **DOUB** (DOOB)—Arabic; **DOV** (DOHV)—Hebrew; **DUBU**—Swahili; **KUMA** (KOO-mah)—Japanese; **MEDVED**—Slavic; **MEDVYED** (mehd-vee-EHD)—Russian; **ORSO** (OHR-soh)—Italian; **OSO** (OH-soh)—Spanish; **OURO**—French. See also HONON, ORSON.

BEAU, "BOH"—*French: "handsome."* See also BO.

BEAUMONT, "BOH-mawnt"—*French: "beautiful mountain."* **MONTEBELLO** (mawn-teh-BEH-loh)—Italian. **BEAU, BO, MONTE, MONTY.**

BECK(E), "BEHK"—*Swedish: "brook"; Irish: "small."* **BEK**—Danish.

BEDAGI, "beh-DAH-jee"—*Native American Abenaki: "big thunderstorm."*

BEJIDE, "beh-JEE-deh"—*African Yoruba: "born in the rain."*

BEL, "BEHL"—*Babylonian: "god of the earth."*

BELDEN, "BEHL-dehn"—*English: "the beautiful glen."*

BEN, "BEN"—*Scottish: "peak."* See also BENEDICT, BENJAMIN.

BEN-AMI, "BEHN AH-mee"—*Hebrew: "son of my people."*

BEN-ZION, "BEHN ZYE-awn"—*Hebrew: "son of Zion."* **BEN-TZYION.** Zion refers both to the God of Jewish tradition, and to the nation and people of Israel.

BENEDETTO, "beh-neh-DEHT-oh"—*Italian: "he blesses" or "blessings."* **BENITO.** F

BENEDICT, "BEHN-eh-dikt"—*Latin: "blessed."* **BENCE** (BEN-tseh)—Hungarian; **BENDIK**—Norwegian; **BENDIT** (BEHN-deet)—Yiddish; **BENDIX**—Dutch; **BENEDEK, BENEDIK, BENKE**—Eastern European; **BÉNÉDICTE** (bay-nay-DEEKT), **BENÔIT** (behn-WAH)—French; **BENEDICTO** (beh-neh-DEEK-toh)—Spanish and Portuguese; **BENGT**—Swedish; **VENEDICT** (VEH-neh-deekt)—Greek. Several saints and popes have borne this name, including Benedict of Nursia, who founded the Benedictine order of monks. **BEN, BENNY, BENITO, BETTO; DIX.** F

BENJAMIN, "BEHN-jah-mihn" or "BEHN-yah-meen"—*Hebrew: "son of the right hand" or "son of the south."* **BANNERJEE**—Gaelic; **BEINISH** (BEH-ih-nish or BAY-ee-neesh)—Yiddish; **BENIAMIN** (BEHN-yah-mihn)—Slavic; **BENIAMINO** (behn-yah-MEE-noh)—Italian; **BENKAMIN** (behn-kah-meen)—Basque; **BINYAMIN**—Israeli; **VENIAMIN** (vehn-YAH-mihn)—Greek. Benjamin is one of the Christian saints. In the Old Testament/Tanakh, Benjamin is the son of Jacob and Rachel. Benjamin Franklin was a famous playboy, humorist, writer, philosopher, inventor, ambassador, bon vivant, and participant in the emergence of the United States of America. One of the more unique collections of his writings is entitled *Fart Proudly*. An interesting guy. **BEN, BENJI(E), BENJY, BENNI(E), BENNY.** F

BENO, "BEH-noh"—*African Mwera: "one of our band."*

BENTLEY, "BEHNT-lee"—*English: "bent-grass meadow."* **BENTLEIGH.** Either the grass is long and bent or flattened from animal or human feet, or the grass bends in the breeze. Then again, bent grass could indicate one of those weird crop-circle sites, where people say UFOs land.

BENTON, "BEHN-tun"—*Anglo-Saxon: "the moors" or "the marshlands."*

BERKELEY, "BERK-lee"—*English: "birch tree meadow."* **BARCLAY, BERKLEY, BERKLY.** See also BIRKLEY.

BERNARD, "bur-NAHRD" or "BEAR-nahrd"—*Old German: "heart of a bear" or "courage of a bear."* **BERNAL** (bear-NAHL), **BERNALDINO, BERNARDIN** (baer-nahr-DAN), **BERNON** (bear-NON), **BERNOT** (bear-NOH)—French; **BERNARDINO** (bare-nahr-DEE-noh), **BERNARDO**—Spanish; **BEÑAT** (behn-yaht)—Basque; **BERNHARD, BERNHARDT, BERNHART**—German and Austrian. Several Christian saints have names on this list. One, Saint Bernard of Montjoux, did his missionary work in the Alps—two mountain passes bear his name—and he developed a breed of dog that rescues people lost in the snow. **BERN, BERNI(E), BERNY.** F

BERT, "BURT"—*German: "bright" or "glorious."* **BERD, BERDY**—Russian; **BERTIL** (BARE-teel or bare-TEEL)—Swedish; **BERTRAND** (bear-TRAWN—"r" in your throat)—French; **BERTUS**—Hungarian. **BURT.** See also ALBERT, BERTRAM, BURTON, GILBERT, HERBERT, HUBERT, ROBERT. F

BERTRAM, "BUR-trum"—*German: "bright raven."* **BARTRAM, BELTRAN, BERTRAND. BERT(IE), BERTY.**

BILL(Y). See WILLIAM.

BING, "BING"—*Welsh: "crib" or "wicker basket"; German: "kettle-shaped hollow."* F

BINGHAM, "BING-ahm"—*English: "maker of wicker" or "maker of cribs"; German: "from the kettle-shaped hollow."*

BIRCH, "BURCH"—*English: "the birch tree."* BURCH.

BIRGER, "BIHR-gher"—*Norwegian: "rescue."* BIRGEN, BIRGIN.

BIRKETT, "BUR-keht" or "bur-KEHT"—*English: "the birch tree headlands."*

BIRKLEY, "BURK-lee"—*English: "birch tree meadow."* BIRCHLEY, BIRKLEA, BIRKLEIGH. See also BERKELEY.

BIRNEY, "BUR-nee"—*English: "island in the brook."*

BIRUNGI, "bih-ROON-jee"—*African Luganda: "something nice" or "something perfect."*

BISHOP, "BISH-uhp"—*Greek: "overseer."*

BLADE, "BLAYD"—*Celtic: "glory."* BLAIDE, BLAYDE.

BLAINE, "BLAYN"—*Celtic: "slender"; English: "fire."* BLAAN, BLAIN, BLANE, BLAYNE. A Scottish saint bears the name Blane. F

BLAIR, "BLARE"—*Celtic: "place" or "plains"; German: "field of battle."* F

BLAISE, "BLAZE"—*Celtic: "firebrand."* BLAZE, BLEISE. Bleise is said to have been Merlyn the Magician's tutor and a chronicler of King Arthur's reign. Also, two Christian saints have names on this list: one is called upon for protection of the throat, the other is patron of those who work with wool. F

BLAKE, "BLAYK"—*Irish: "black"; English: "pale" or "shining white."* Look at those definitions and go figure.

BLANC, properly "BLAWNK" but also "BLANK"—*French: "white."* F

BO, "BOH"—*Chinese: "precious"; Vietnamese: "black."* See also BEAU, BEAUMONT, BOGART, BOTAN. F

BOB(BY). See ROBERT.

BODAWAY, "boh-DAH-way"—*Native American: "fire maker."*

BODEN, "BOH-dehn"—*French: "herald."*

BODI, "BOH-dee"—*Hungarian: "God protect the king."*

BODIL, "BOH-dihl"—*Norwegian: "commanding."*

BOGART, "BOH-gahrt"—*Gaelic: "soft" or "marshlands"; German: "strong bow."* BOGARDE. Actor Humphrey Bogart often played the likeable, or at least honorable, tough guy in several of *the* classic films of all time. BO, BOGEY, BOGIE.

BOGDAN, "BOHG-dan"—*Polish: "God's gift."* BOHDAN—*Ukrainian.* DANYA.

BOMANI, "boh-MAH-nee"—*African Ngoni, Zulu, Malawi: "warrior."* NBOMANI.

BOND, "BAWND"—*Norse: "fasten together."* BONDEN, BONDON. James Bond is the hero of a series of books on espionage and science fiction by Ian Fleming. What were once imaginary gadgets in his spy capers are very often reality today.

BOOKER, "BOOK-ur"—*English: "maker of books," "beechwood," or "beech tree."* The ancient runes, or magical alphabetlike characters, of the Celts and Druids were carved on beechwood slabs.

BOONE, "BOON"—*Norse: "favor" or "blessing."* Daniel Boone was a man, he was a big man; he had a knife like an eagle and tall as a mountain was he . . . But seriously, folks, Daniel Boone was a nineteenth-century American frontiersman whose exploits are a part of history and folklore.

BOOTH, "BOOTH"—*Teutonic: "from the marketplace" or "home-loving."* **BOOTHE.**

BORDEN, "BOHR-dehn"—*English: "from the boar's den" or "near the boar's den."*

BORIS, "BOH-rihss"—*Slavic: "to fight."* **BORKA, BORYENKA, BORYS.** Saint Boris is the patron saint of Moscow. He is buried in Saint Basil's church, and miracles were supposed to occur at his gravesite.

BORRES, BORS, "BORZ"—*German: "to be indebted" or "to protect"; Gypsy: "hedges"; Hungarian: "pepper."* **BORREY.** In Arthurian legend, Sir Bors was a Knight of the Round Table.

BOSLEY, "BAWZ-lee"—*English: "thicket."*

BOSWELL, "BAWZ-wehl"—*French: "well in the woods."*

BOSWORTH, "BAWZ-wurth"—*English: "near the cattle enclosure."*

BOTAN, "bow-TAHN"—*Japanese: "peony."* In Japan, this name is given to a child born in June. **BO.** F

BOURNE, "BORN" or "BOORN"—*English: "the brook."* See also BURNE.

BOWER, "BAU-ur"—*Dutch: "farmer" or "farm"; Anglo-Saxon: "shady place," "arbor," or "rustic retreat"; English: "anchor"; German: "peasant" or "knave."* **BAUER**—German; **BOUWER**—Dutch.

BOWIE, "BOH-wee"—*Gaelic: "yellow-haired."*

BOWLES, "BOHLZ"—*Gypsy: "snail."*

BOYAR, "BOY-ahr" or "boy-AHR"—*Russian: "aristocrat, aristocratic."* **BOYARD; BOYARDI**—Italian; **BOYARIN** (boy-AHR-ihn)—Russian; **BOYER** (bwah-YAY)—French. Charles Boyer was considered one of the silver screen's great romantic leading men.

BOYCE, "BOYSS"—*English from French: "the forest."*

BOYD, "BOYD"—*Celtic: "yellow."* Yellow as in hair color. Or, if you're a Tweety Boyd, yellow as in feathers.

BOYNE, "BOYN"—*Irish: "white bull."*

BOYNTON, "BOIN-ton"—*English: "of the river Boyne" or "town of the white cattle."*

BRAD. See all names with "Brad-" as the first syllable.

BRADBURN, "BRAD-burn"—*English: "the broad brook."* **BRADBOURN, BRADBOURNE. BRAD.**

BRADEN, "BRAD-un" or "BRAY-dehn"—*English: "broad little valley."* **BRADDEN, BRADDON, BRAYDEN. BRAD.**

BRADFORD, "BRAD-furd"—*English: "broad ford."* **BRAD.**

BRADLEY, "BRAD-lee"—*English: "broad meadow."* **BRADLEE, BRADLEIGH; BRAD.**

BRADY, "BRAY-dee"—*Irish: "spirited one."* This is an example of a name that has been popularized by its use in a soap opera.

BRAM. See ABRAHAM, BRAMWELL.

BRAMWELL, "BRAM-wehl"—*English: "from Abraham's well."* **BRAM.**

BRAND, "BRAND"—*English: "firebrand" or "our mark."*

BRANDON, "BRAN-dun"—*English: "fla-*

ming torch"; Irish: "raven." **BRAN**—Irish. Bran was a deity in Celtic lore who shows up in the legends of the British Isles. Irish tellings of his adventures include *The Voyage of Bran, Son of Febal*. In the Welsh *Mabinogion*, a collection of medieval romances, he shows up as Bendigeidfran ("blessed Bran"). Legendary Irish hero Finn MacCool's dog was even named Bran. Brandon is one of the Christian saints. F

BRANT, "BRANT"—*Teutonic: "fiery"; Danish: a wild arctic goose.* **BRANDT; BRANTLEIGH, BRANTLEY** (both mean "a meadow where geese congregate.")

BRAUD, "BROWD"—*Irish: "throat" or "gorge."* **BRAUDE, BRAUDY.**

BRAWLEY, "BRAW-lee"—*English: "meadow on the hill slopes."*

BRAXTON, "BRAX-tun"—*Anglo-Saxon: "Brock's town."*

BRAZE, "BRAYZ"—*French: to make brass or to have a brass color.* It also means to combine metals with fire. Don't make it Braise unless you want a chef in the family.

BREDE, "BREH-deh"—*Norwegian: "broad" or "glacier."*

BRENCIS, "BREHN-tsis"—*Latvian: "crowned with laurel."*

BRENDAN, "BREHN-dun"—*Irish: "prince"; Celtic: "fiery hill."* **BREANDAN** (BRAWN-dun)—Irish Gaelic; **BRENDON, BRENNAN, BRENNON.** This is the name of several Christian saints, one of which is the sixth-century Irishman Brendan the Navigator, who may have sailed as far as North America.

BRENT, "BREHNT"—*Irish: "raven" or "burnt"; English: "steep hill."* **BRENTANO.**

BRES, "BREHSS"—*Irish Gaelic: ancient Irish god of fertility.* This god was in charge of keeping livestock and the land itself fertile.

BRETT, "BREHT"—*Celtic: "from Bretagne" or "from Brittany."* **BRET.** This is a very popular name for both boys and girls. F

BRIAN, "BRY-ahn"—*Celtic: "from the hills"; Greek: "strong."* **BRAREUS** (BRARE-ee-us)—Latin and Slavic; **BRIANO; BRIAROS** (BREE-ah-rohss or bree-AH-rohss)—Greek; **BRIEN, BRION, BRYAN, BRYANT, BRYON.** The Briaros in Greek mythology was a protective creature with many heads and arms. Brian Boru was one of the greatest Irish kings. He put an end to any hopes the Norsemen may have had for conquering the island in the early eleventh century. F

BRICE, "BRYCE"—*German: "son of the ruler," "son of wealth," or "son of power"; Celtic: "ambitious" or "alert."* **BRICK, BRYCE.** This is a Christian saint name.

BRIGHAM, "BRIHG-ahm"—*Italian: "home of the contentious"; English: "dweller by the bridge."* **BRIGMAN.** Brigham Young is the nineteenth-century American founder of the Church of Jesus Christ of Latter-day Saints, also known as the Mormon Church. Many Mormon men use Brigham as a middle name.

BRINDLEY, "BRIHND-lee"—*Norse: "glowing embers."* **BRINLEY.**

BRISHAN, "BRIH-shahn"—*Gypsy: "rainstorm."*

BROCK, "BRAWK"—*Celtic: "badger."*

BRODERICK, "BRAWD-eh-rihk"—*German: "famed ruler."* **BRODY, RICK.**

BRODIE, "BROH-dee"—*Irish Gaelic: "ditch."* **BRODY.**

BROMLEY, "BRAWM-lee"—*English: "meadow of broom shrubs."* **BROMLEE, BROMLEIGH, BROMLY.** The broom shrub is a tough little plant with sunny yellow flowers.

BRONISLAV, BRONISLAW, "BRAW-nih-slahv"—*Slavic: "weapon of glory."*

BROOK, "BRUK"—*English: "a brook or small stream."* **BAHR**—*Arabic;* **BROOKS, BROOKES; CAYI** (KAH-yee)—*Turkish;* **LAM** (LAWM)—*Thai.* F

BROUGHTON, "BROW-tun" ("BROW" like "wow") or "BROH-tun"—*English: "the fortress town."* **BRAUTON, BROWTON.**

BRUCE, "BROOS"—*French: "the woods" or "the thicket."* **BRUIS** (BROO-ee)—*French.* Robert the Bruce, a Scottish king, won Scotland's independence from England in a battle during 1314; the arrangement took fourteen years to be ratified. **BRUCEY, BRU-CIE, BRUCY.**

BRUNO, "BROO-noh"—*German: "brown."* **BRUNON.** Saint Bruno of Cologne was a professor of theology and philosophy who founded a monastic order in Grenoble. F

BUCK, "BUHK"—*English: "stag" or "billy-goat."* **BUCKNER, BUCKY.**

BUCKLEY, "BUHK-lee"—*English: "deer meadow."*

BUD(D), "BUHD"—*Gaelic: "winner"; English: "offshoot."* **BUDDY.**

BUNYORO, "bun-YOH-roh"—*African: "my people, our people, us."* This is a tribe name for a group of people inhabiting east and central Africa around what is now called Lake Victoria. **BUNYORA.**

BUR(R), "BUR"—*Scandinavian: "youth";*
English: "rough edge."* A bur was a broad ring on a medieval spear that protected the hand during the joust or the combat, and it is likely that the name evolved from this usage.

BURAQ, "boo-RAHK"—*Arabic: "white one"; Hebrew: "lightning."* There are two stories that go with this name. *Either* Buraq is the mountain upon which Mohammed is said to have begun his Night Journey from Mecca, through Jerusalem, and then through the Seven Heavens, *or* Buraq is the creature upon which Mohammed is supposed to have made his Night Journey, a winged mare with a peacock's tail and a woman's head. See also BARAK. F

BURDETT, "bur-DEHT"—*French: "little shield."*

BURDON, "BUR-dun"—*Celtic: "castle hill."*

BURFORD, "BUR-furd"—*Celtic: "river-crossing at the castle."*

BURGESS, "BUR-jehss"—*Latin: "fortified place."* **BURGISS.** A burgess is also a political representative.

BURHAN, "bur-HAHN"—*Arabic: "proof."*

BURKE, "BURK"—*Teutonic: "the strong-hold."*

BURL, "BURL"—*French: "coarse wool"; English: "cup bearer."*

BURLEY, "BUR-lee"—*English: "the meadow by the fortress," "the meadow by the town," or "rough-edged clearing."* **BUR-LEIGH.**

BURNABY, "BUR-nah-bee"—*Norse: "warrior's estate"; English: "brookside homestead."*

BURNE, "BURN"—*English: "brook"; Nor-*

dic: "warrior." **BURNS.** See also BOURNE.

BURNELL, "bur-NEHL"—*Celtic: "brunet."*

BURNETT, "bur-NEHT"—*Celtic: "brown one."*

BURNEY, "BUR-nee"—*English: "island in the brook."*

BURRELL, "bur-EHL"—*French: "reddish-brown."* **BURELL.**

BURTON, "BUR-tun"—*English: "from the fortress."* **BARTON, BERTON.** Dr. Burton White wrote a baby-care book, *The First Three Years of Life,* that has been used by thousands of parents. **BART, BERT, BURT.** See also BARTON.

BWIRE, "BWEE-reh"—*African: "born at night."*

BYRON, "BY-run"—*English: "hut" or "bear cub."* Nineteenth-century writer Lord Byron wrote poetry and novels. His works included *Don Juan,* an epic satire about the famous womanizer. It caused sensation and outrage then, but is PG by modern standards. See also BRIAN.

THE TOP FIVE

CHRISTOPHER
CHARLES
CARL
CRAIG
CLINT

If the name you're looking for isn't here, see "K" or "S."

CADAO, "kah-DAH-oh"—*Vietnamese: "song."*

CADBY, "KAD-bee"—*English/Norse: "warrior's settlement."*

CADDELL, "kah-DEHL"—*Welsh: "battle spirit."*

CADDOCK, "KAD-ohk"—*Welsh: "keen in battle."*

CADMAN, "KAD-man"—*Celtic: "brave warrior."*

CADY, "KAY-dee"—*Irish: "hillock."* **KEADY.** F

CAESAR, "SEE-sur"—*Latin: "dark haired," "long haired,"* or *"to cut open."* **CESARE** (say-SAHR), **CESAREO**—*Italian;* **CÉZAR**—*Eastern European;* **KAISER** (KYE-zur)—*German;* **KESAR** (keh-sahr)—*Basque.* The last meaning refers to the way Julius Caesar was born, by cutting into the womb, and from which we get the term "cesarean section." Ruler of the Roman Empire, Caesar was a clever soldier who was interested in the amassing of knowledge—he established the first public library system. A few saints have borne this name as well: one, Saint Caesarius of Arles, founded the first convent.

CAHIL, "KAH-hihl" or "KAY-hihl"—*Turkish: "young"* or *"naive."* **CAHILL.**

CALDER, "KAHL-dur"—*Celtic: "stony river."*

CALDWELL, "KAHLD-wehl"—*English: "cold spring"* or *"cold well."* **COLDWELL.**

CALEB, "KAY-lehb"—*Arabic: "brave";* *Hebrew: "bold and impetuous."* In the Old Testament/Tanakh, Caleb led the Israelites, in tandem with Joshua, after the death of Moses. In some stories, it is Caleb's horn, and not Joshua's, that brings down the walls of Jericho.

CALEDON, "KAL-uh-dawn"—*Scottish.* Caledonia is the old name for Scotland. F

CALEY, "KAY-lee"—*Irish Gaelic: "thin."*

CALHOUN, "kal-HOON"—*Irish Gaelic: "the narrow forest."*

CALUM, "KAW-lum" or "KAL-um"—*Scottish Gaelic from Celtic: "dove."* **CALLUM.**

CALVERT, "KAL-vurt"—*English: "cowherd"* or just *"herdsman."*

CALVIN, "KAL-vihn"—*Latin: "bald"; English: "calf."* **CALVINO** (kahl-VEE-noh)—*Italian and Spanish.* J. Calvin Coolidge was president from 1923 to 1929. The "J." stood for John, and the John Calvin in question was a sixteenth-century French reformer, churchman, and theologian who led the way in the Protestant movement against the Catholic Church by founding Presbyterianism. **CAL; VINNIE, VINNY.**

CAM. See CAMERON, DECAMERON.

CAMBRIC, "KAM-brihk"—*Flemish: "fine white linen" or "fine white cloth."* **CAMBRAI** (KAHM-bray)—*French;* **KAMERYK** (KAH-meh-rihk)—*Flemish.*

CAMDEN, "KAM-dehn"—*Scottish Gaelic: "winding valley."*

CAMERON, "KAM-eh-rawn"—*Celtic: "crooked nose"; Latin: "from Cameris."* **CAMEREN, CAMARENO, CAMERIN, CAMERINO.** Cameris was a Sabine region of ancient Rome, in what is now central Italy. Two Scottish Camerons were religious men in the sixteenth and seventeenth centuries, of whom one founded the Cameronian (or Reformed) Presbyterian Church. **CAM.** F

CAMLO, "KAM-loh"—*Gypsy: "lovable."* **KAMLO.**

CAMPBELL, "KAM-behl"—*Latin/French: "beautiful field" or "beautiful plain."* **CAMPO-BELLO. CAMPI(E), CAMPY.**

CANAAN, "KANE-ah-an," usually rushed into "KANE-an"—*Hebrew: "the Promised Land."* This land, located between the Jordan River and the Mediterranean Sea, was where the Hebrews finally settled after their long trek from Egypt.

CA(I)NE, "KANE"—*Semitic: "stalk, stem, rod."*

CANTOR, "KAN-tur"—*Latin: "singer."* In Judaism, the cantor leads the synagogue in liturgical chant.

CANUTE, "kah-NOOT"—*Norse: "knot."*

CNUTE, KNUTE. Canute was an eleventh-century king of Denmark and England.

CARDEN, "KAHR-dehn"—*French: "to comb out" or "to untangle."* To carden wool is to straighten it out and prepare it for spinning.

CAREW, "kah-ROO"—*Latin: "beloved" or "loving"; Celtic: "from our fortress."*

CARL, "KAHRL—*Teutonic: "strong and manly,"* one of the many versions of Charles; *Scottish: "precocious."* **CAREL, CAROLUS**—*Dutch;* **CARLITO** (kahr-LEE-toh)—*Spanish and Portuguese;* **CARLO**—*Italian;* **CARLOS**—*Spanish;* **CAROLOS**—*Greek.* German engineer Carl F. Benz was one of the first men to invent an efficient gasoline-driven motor vehicle; the Mercedes Benz auto name came from his daughter. See also CHARLES, KARL. F

CARLIN, "KAHR-lihn"—*Irish Gaelic: "little champion"; but Scottish "old woman"!* Go figure how that happened.

CARLISLE, "KAHR-lyle"—*Latin: "fortress on the island."*

CARLOS. See CARL.

C(H)ARLTON, "KARL-tun" or "CHARL-tun"—*English: "town of free men" or "farmers' settlement."* **CARLETON.**

CARMICHAEL, "KAHR-my-kehl"—*Scottish Gaelic: "friend of (saint) Michael."*

CARMINE, "KAHR-myne"—*Latin: "vivid red."*

CARN, "KARN"—*Irish: "great heap of stones."* **KARN.**

CARNEY, "KAHR-nee"—*Irish: "victory."*

CARR, "CAHR"—*Irish: "rock" or "rocky land"; Scandinavian: "from the marsh."* **KARR, KERR.**

CARROLL, "KARE-ohl" or "KAH-rohl"—*French: "to sing" or "joyous song"; Gaelic: "champion."* See also KAROL. F

CARSWELL, "KAHRZ-wehl"—*English: "the spring where watercress grows."*

CARTER, "KAHR-tur"—*Anglo-Saxon: "maker of carts."* **CARTWRIGHT.**

CARVER, "KAHR-vur"—*Anglo-Saxon: "one who carves."*

CARVEY, "KAHR-vee"—*Gaelic: "athletic."*

CARY, "KARE-ee"—*Latin: "loved"; English: "castle"; Welsh: "stony island"; Irish: "Kerry,"* a place name. **CAREW, CAREY, CARREY; KERRY.** Actor Cary Grant was a gentleman's gentleman, and was equally at home in comedy or in drama. F

CASEY, "KAY-see"—*Gaelic: "brave."*

CASIMIR, "KAHZ-ee-meer"—*Polish: "announcing peace."* **KASIMIR, KAZIMIERZ** (KAH-zee-meersh)—Polish; **KAZMER** (KAHZ-mare)—Eastern European. Saint Casimir, the patron saint of Poland, rejected the Polish throne and all the goodies that went with it for a life of celibacy and worship.

CASPAR, "KAS-pahr"—*German: "imperial."* **CASPER, GASPAR, KASPAR, KASPER.** Casper is traditionally one of the Three Wise Men, the Magi, who visited the baby Jesus in Bethlehem.

CASSIDY, "KAS-ih-dee"—*Gaelic: "clever one."*

CASSIUS, "KAH-shuss" or "KASH-ee-us"—*Latin: "champion" or "blue-gray"; Greek: "cinammon bark."* Cassius M. Clay was an American abolitionist, and Olympic medalist and many-time champion boxer Cassius Clay was named after him. The latter Clay accepted Islam and honored the Prophet Mohammed and Mohammed's cousin, Ali, in the name he took for himself.

CASTOR, "KAS-tohr"—*Latin: "pious one" or "modest one"; Greek: "beaver" or "woodchuck."* Castor is one of the so-called fixed stars, used for centuries by navigators and astrologers because of their apparent constance. It has folkloric association with renown. Castor is one of the twins of Gemini.

CAULEY, CAWLEY, "KAW-lee"—*Pictish: "ancestral relic."*

CEDRIC, "SEHD-rihk"—*Welsh: "amiable"; but Celtic: "war chief."* **CERDIC.** This is another "go figure" translation. Cedric is the legendary founder of West Saxony in Great Britain; it is from a misspelling or misunderstanding of his name that we now have the name Cedric. **CED, CID; RIC(K), RICKIE, RICKY.**

CEDRO, "SEHD-roh" or "SAYD-roh"—*Spanish: "cedar" or "juniper."* **CEDROS, CEDRUS.** The cedar and juniper both produce fragrant woods.

CELADON, "SEH-lah-dawn"—*Bretagne(?).* Celadon is a soft or grayed green. F

CELESTIN, "seh-LESST-in"—*Latin: "the heavens."* **CELES, CELESTYN.** F

CERVIN, "SUR-vihn"—*Latin: "like a deer."* **CERVINUS; SERVIN, SERVINUS.**

CETUS, "SEE-tuhss"—*Latin: "the whale."* The celestial Whale can be seen swimming after the Sun at dusk from Thanksgiving through mid-January (appropriate for holiday eating). The Sun is "in" Cetus from mid-February through the end of April. F

CHAC, "CHAWK"—*Mayan: god of rain and plants.* Chac rode on a snake, which is the Mayan symbol of rain, while carrying water in a container, and he held the torches that make lightning.

CHAD, "CHAD"—*English: "warlike."* **CEADDA** (CHAH-dah)—*Irish Gaelic.* Saint Ceadda of Mercia was a British bishop of the seventh century. **CHADDY, CHADIE.**

CHADWICK, "CHAD-wihk"—*Celtic: "defender."* **CHADWICKE.**

CHAIM, "KHAYM" ("KH" in the back of your throat)—*Hebrew: "life."* **CHAYIM, CHAYYIM; HAIM, HAYM.**

CHALMER, "CHAHL-mur" or "KAHL-mur"—*Teutonic: "king of the house."*

CHAM, "JAHM"—*Vietnamese: "works hard."*

CH'AN, "ch'AHN"—*Chinese: "Zen."* F

CHANCE, "CHANSS"—*diminutive of Cha(u)nc(e)y, thus Latin: "chance" or "luck"; French: "official recordkeeper."*

CHANDER, "CHAHN-der"—*Hindu: "god of the moon."* F

CHANDLER, "CHAND-lur"—*French: "candlemaker."* Chandler is one of TV's *Friends.*

CHANE, "CHAH-neh"—*Kiswahili: "strong."*

CHANEY, "CHAIN-ee"—*Latin: "chancellor" or "secretary."* See also CHENEY.

CHANNING, "CHAN-ing"—*Anglo-Saxon: "regent"; Latin: "canal" or "strait."*

CHANSON, "shahn-SAWN"—*French: "song."* **CHANTICLEER.** F

CHAPIN, "CHAY-pihn" or "SHAY-pihn"—*French from Latin: "clergyman."* **CHAPEN.**

CHARLES, "CHARLZ" or "SHARLZ" (French)—*Teutonic: "manly"; Germanic: "free man."* **CARL; CARLO** (KAHR-loh)—Italian; **CARLOS** (KAHR-lohss)—Spanish and Portuguese; **KARL; SÉARLAS** (SHARE-loss)—Irish Gaelic; **XARLES** (zahr-lehz)—Basque. Charles has a long association with European royalty. In Britian, that royalty has included the seventeenth century's King Charles II, who reigned during the Restoration, and the twentieth century's Prince Charles. In this country, the fame of aviator Charles Lindbergh led to surge of popularity for the name. **CHARLI(E), CHARLEY, CHARLY, CHUCK.** F

CHARON, "KARE-awn"—*Greek: "ferryman," "conductor," or "guide."* Charon guided souls down the river Styx into the Greek afterworld. For a coin, he would deliver souls to their various destinations—but no matter how big a tipper you were, you didn't get taken anywhere you didn't deserve to be taken. Charon is the lone moon of Pluto, and is almost as big as its parent planet.

CHASE, "CHAYS"—*French: "to hunt."*

CHAUNCEY. See CHANCE.

CHAYTON, "CHAH-ee-tun" or "CHAY-tun"—*Native American Sioux: "the falcon."*

CHEN, "CHEHN"—*Chinese: "vast" or "great," or "orange" or "tangerine."* F

CHENET, "cheh-NEHT"—*Greek: "goose" or French: "oak tree."* F

CHENEY, "CHAY-nee" or "CHEE-nee"—*French: "dweller in the oaks."* See also CHANEY.

CHETWIN, "CHEHT-wihn"—*English: "home along a winding path."* **CHET.**

CHEYENNE, "shy-EN" or "shy-AN"—*French/Sioux: "people of a different language."* This is a tribe name for a group of people originally from what is now Minnesota.

SOUTHERN COLONIAL BOYS' NAMES

Boys born in Southern states along the Atlantic coast are most likely to have the following names:

1. Christopher	6. Brandon	11. Robert	16. Austin
2. Michael	7. Taylor	12. Tyler	17. Jacob
3. Joshua	8. Matthew	13. Andrew	18. Nicholas
4. William	9. Justin	14. David	19. Joseph
5. James	10. John	15. Zachary	20. Jonathan

The Sioux forced the Cheyenne out onto the Great Plains by the mid-eighteenth century, where they became the typical Plains Indians—nomadic hunters. The Cheyenne were among the most deeply religious of the Native American tribes. In addition to publicly practicing the Sun Dance and other ceremonies, prayers were a part of every person's daily private life, and personal, supernatural visions were expected. F

CHI, "CHEE"—*African: "guardian angel" or "guardian spirit."* F

CH'I, "CHEE"—*Chinese: "breath" or "vapor."* Ch'i is one of the fundamental elements of the cosmos in Taoist and Confucianist thought. In Confucianism, Ch'i brings order and focus to matter and energy. F

CHICO, "CHEE-koh"—*Native American Nahuatl: "poppy"; Spanish: "greasewood tree,"* or from Spanish *"chicote": "whip."*

CHIKE, "CHEE-keh"—*African Ibo: "power of God."*

CHILTON, "CHIHL-tun"—*Anglo-Saxon: "town by the coldwater spring."*

CHIN, "CHIN"—*Korean: "precious."*

CHINELO, "CHEE-neh-low"—*African Ibo: "thought of God."*

CHIRON, "KY-rawn"—*Greek: "hands(?)."* **CHEIRON.** Chiron is a planetoid in orbit between Uranus and Saturn. It is named for Chiron, who in Greek mythology was a centaur—half-man and half-horse. He was also a gifted medicine man; he was said to have tutored Achilles and Asclepius in the healing arts, among other subjects. Astrologers attribute the areas of learning, teaching, and healing to Chiron's influence.

CHIUMBO, "chih-OOM-boh"—*African Mwera: "small creation" or "small miracle."*

CHRIS. See CHRISTIAN, CHRISTOPHER.

CHRISTIAN, "KRIHS-tyahn"—*Greek: "of the (golden) Light."* **CHRÉSTIEN, CHRÉTIEN** (kreh-TYEN—"r" back in your throat)— French; **CHRISTIAAN**—Dutch; **CHRISTION; CHRISTOS**—Greek; **KRISTIAN**—Nordic. Jesus of Nazareth is the light in question. There are several Christian saints' names on this list. **CHRIS, CHRISTI(E), CHRISTY.** See also CHRISTOPHER, KRIST. F

CHRISTOPHER, "KRIHS-toh-fer"—*Latin: "Christ-bearer" (apostle or disciple)* or *"shield of Christ."* **CHRISTOF(F), CHRISTOPHE** (kree-STOFE)—French; **CHRISTOF(F)ER, CRISTOFORO** (kree-STOH-foh-roh or kree-stoh-FOH-roh)—Italian; **CHRISTOFFEL, CHRIS-**

TOPHEL, CRISTOF(F)EL—*Dutch;* **CRIS-TOPHOROS** (kree-STOH-foh-rohs)—*Greek;* **CRIOSTOIR** (KREE-uh-stoh-eer)—*Irish Gaelic;* **CRISTOBAL**—*Portuguese;* **KRISTOF(F)ER**—*Nordic.* The legend of Saint Christopher goes as follows: Christopher was a huge, physically powerful man who was a wandering day laborer and troublemaker. One day, a small boy asked Christopher to carry him across a fast-moving river. Of course, this was a cinch—he thought. But as Christopher went further and further into the water, he felt the child getting heavier, and heavier . . . so heavy, in fact, that Christopher felt he would drown and his back would break from the burden. The little child then revealed himself as the Christ child who bore the weight of the world. Saint Christopher is the patron saint of travellers and all those who bear others to their destinations. Cristobal Colon—Christopher Columbus to you, unless you're one of his fellow Italians, then it's Cristoforo Columbo—sailed the ocean blue in fourteen-hundred-ninety-two . . . and ran into America. **CHRIS, CHRISTY** (common in Scotland and Ireland); **CHRISTO, CRISTO; KIT.** See also CHRISTIAN, KRIST.

CHUCK. See CHARLES.

CHUL, "CHOOL"—*Korean: "firm."*

CHUMANI, "choo-MAH-nee"—*Native American Sioux: "dewdrops."*

CHUN, "CHUN"—*Korean: "justice."*

CIAN, "KYAHN" or "KEE-ahn"—*Irish Gaelic: "ancient."* **KEAN** (KEE-ahn), **KIAN.** F

CICERO, "SIHS-eh-roh"—*Latin: "chickpea."*

CLANCY, "KLAN-see"—*Gaelic: "offspring."* Aye, a member of the clan, see?

CLARENCE, "CLARE-ents" or "KLAH-rents"—*Anglo-Saxon: "illustrious";* *Latin:* "clear"; *Yiddish: "clean."* **CLARENT, CLARUS.** Several saint names are on this list. F

CLARK(E), "KLAHRK"—*English: "clerk" or "scholar"; Latin: "a cleric or clergyman"; Greek: "of the inheritance."* "The Inheritance of the Levites" is the Word of God and the Scriptures, and those who keep the inheritance—that is, those who can read the sacred writings—for the people are clerks or clerics.

CLAUDE, "KLAWD"—*Latin: "lame."* **CLAUD, CLAUDIAN** (KLOH-dyan)—*French;* **CLAUDIO; CLAUDIOS**—*Greek;* **CLAUDIUS**—Latin. A first-century Roman noble named Claudius was so named because he was disabled, and so, it was thought, he was "simple." However, when Emperor Caligula was murdered, Claudius became emperor, and proved himself to be as sound or more sound than any of his predecessors. Claude Monet (d. 1926) is the best known of the Impressionists; he was one of the first painters to actually work outside of a studio, in the midst of his subjects. He pioneered the unusual use of color spots that seem strange up close, but at a distance, blend and give the impression of the subject. Later, his paintings used sweeping brush strokes. William Claude is what the "W.C." in W.C. Fields stands for; an inimitable comic actor, there could never be another like him. He skewered the taboos of his age, and never worried about being politically correct. Sample quote: "If at first you don't succeed, try, try again. Then quit. No use being a damn fool about it." There are also several Christian saints' names on this list. **CLAUDI(E).** F

CLAUS, "KLOWSS"—*from Nic(h)olas: "victory of the people."* See also KLAUS, NIC(H)OLAS.

CLAY, "KLAY"—*Old English: "clay" or "earth."* See also CLAYMORE.

CLAYMORE, "KLAY-mohr"—*Scottish.* The claymore was the double-edged sword of the Highlanders. CLAY.

CLAYTON, "KLAY-tun"—*Old English: "mortal man (men)."* CLAYBORN, CLAYBORNE; CLAIBORN, CLAIBORNE.

CLEARY, "KLEE-ree"—*Irish Gaelic: "scholar."*

CLEMENT, "KLEH-mehnt"—*Latin: "merciful."* CLÉIMEANS (clay-MEE-unz)—Irish Gaelic; CLÉMENCE (kleh-MONSS), CLÉMENT (kleh-MAWN)—French; CLEMENS, CLEMMENS; CLEMENTE (kleh-MEHN-teh)—Spanish. A whole lot of saints' and popes' names appear on this list, one of which was the third pope of the Catholic Church, baptized by Saint Peter, who was martyred by Roman Emperor Trajan for preaching the gospel. Clement was thrown into the sea, and thus is the patron saint of sailors and all who come in contact with water. F

CLEON, "KLEE-awn"—*Greek: "glory" or "glorious."*

CLETE, "KLEET"—*Greek: "summoned."* CLETUS. F

CLIFFORD, "KLIHF-furd"—*English: "ford near the cliffs."* CLIFF.

CLIFTON, "KLIHF-tun"—*Anglo-Saxon: "village near the cliffs."*

CLINTON, "KLIHN-tun"—*Nordic: "hill town"; Anglo-Saxon: "from the farm at the headlands."* Award-winning actor/director Clint Eastwood, known for playing fast-shooting tough guys, showed a gentler side in *The Bridges of Madison County.* CLINT.

CLIVE, "KLYV"—*English: "cliff."* Robert Clive conquered and colonized India for Great Britain. He was such a powerful and admired man that all sorts of variants of his name popped up: CLEAVANT, CLEAVON, CLEVE, CLEVEY, CLEVIE, CLEVY.

CLURE, "KLOOR"—*Latin: "of good reputation."* MAcCLURE, McCLURE.

COBURN, "KOH-burn"—*English: "where the streams meet."*

CODY, "KOH-dee"—*Greek: "poppies"; Latin: "of books"; Anglo-Saxon: "(saddle)bags"—that is, a messenger or courier.* Cody is one of the most popular names for boys, probably because, with its cowboy association, it sounds simple and masculine. The fact that talk-show host Kathy Lee Gifford talks about her son, Cody, has also helped popularize the name.

COLBERT, "KOHL-burt" or "KOHL-bare" ("r" in the back of your throat)—*French concoction from German and Latin: "a clear mountain pass"; Anglo-Saxon: "seafarer."* COLVERT, CULBERT.

COLBY, "KOHL-bee"—*English: "coal mining town."*

COLIN, "KAWL-in" or, rarely nowadays, "COLE-ihn"—*Scottish: "pup" or "cub"; Welsh: "young, strong."* CAILEAN (KYE-lahn)—Scottish Gaelic; CÓILEAN (KOY-lahn)—Irish Gaelic; COLINS, COLLIN, COLLINS. COL, COLAN, COLE.

COLLIER, "KAWL-yer"—*Welsh: "miner."*

COL(E)MAN, "KOHL-man"—*Irish: "little dove" or "dove keeper"; English: "coal miner."*

COLTER, "KOHL-tur"—*English: "breeder of horses."* COULTER.

COLTON, "KOHL-tun"—*English: "coal mining town" or "horse-breeding town."*

COLUMBO, "koh-LUHM-boh"—*Latin: "dove" or the columbine plant.* **COLM**—Irish; **COLOMBO**—Spanish; **COLUMBAN, COLUMBANUS.** F

COMAN, "koh-MAHN"—*Arabic: "a nobleman."*

CONAN, "KOH-nun"—*Irish: "little hound"; Celtic: "intelligent."* **CONANT.** Conan is a Christian saint name.

CONCORD, "KAWN-kord"—*Latin: "agreement" or "peace."*

CONLAN, "KAWN-lahn"—*Irish Gaelic: "hero."*

CONN, "KAWN"—*Gaelic: "fierce hound."* **CONNY.**

CONNELL, "KAW-nehl"—*Irish Gaelic: "church."* **CONAL, CONNAL, CONNALLY, CONNALY; CONEL, CONNEL, CONNELLY, CONNELY.**

CONNOR, "KAW-nur"—*Scotch-Irish: "hound lover" or "from the heights."* **CONCOBHAR** (KONE-koh-vahr)—*Irish Gaelic;* **CONNER, CONNERY; CONNORY, CONOR.** Conor mac Nessa was a legendary king of Ulster in what is now Northern Ireland.

CONRAD, "KAWN-rad"—*German: "bold counsellor."* **CORRADO** (koh-RAH-doh)—Italian; **KONRAD**—Eastern European. F

CONROY, "KAWN-roy"—*Celtic: "wise."*

CONSTANTIN, "KAWN-stan-tihn"—*Latin: "constant or steadfast."* **CONSTANTINE, CONSTANTIOS, COSTAS**—Greek; **CONSTANZO** (kawn-STAHN-zoh)—Italian; **KONSTANCJI** (kawn-STAHN-chee), **KONSTANTY**—Polish. Several Christian saints are on this list. Constantine the Great was a fourth-century Roman emperor who converted to Christianity and ceased the persecution of Christians. Present-day Istanbul was his capital city, Constantinople. Several Scottish and Pictish rulers have had this name as well. **CON, CONNI(E), CONNY, CONSTANT.** See also KONSTANTIN. F

CONWAY, "KAWN-way"—*Celtic: "dweller on the plains."*

CORBET, "KOHR-beht"—*Latin: "raven."* **CORBETT.**

CORBIN, "KOR-bin"—*Latin: "raven" or a place name.* **CARBONEK, CARNEK.** The castle Corbin is where the Holy Grail was said to be hidden.

CORIN, "KOH-rihn"—*Irish: "spear."* **CORY.** Corin Nemec is an actor.

CORMAC(K), "KORE-mak"—*Irish: "son of the raven(?)"; Scottish Gaelic: "charioteer"; Greek: "tree trunk."* **CORMIC, CORMICK.** Cormac mac Art is a legendary Irish king.

CORNEL, "kore-NELL"—*Latin: "horn" and "cornell tree."* **CORNELIUS; KEES** (KAYS), **KRELIS**—Dutch; **KORNEL, KORNELIUS.** Cornel is one of the Christian saints. F

CORSAIR, "kohr-SARE"—*French.* A corsair was a pirate from the Barbary Coast, the northern coast of Africa.

CORT, "KORT"—*Scandinavian: "short."* **CORTIE, KORT.**

CORWIN, "KOHR-wihn"—*Latin and Welsh: "friendly raven."* **CORWAN, CORWYN.**

CORY, "KOH-ree"—*Irish: "spear"; Greek: "helmet."* **COREY, CORIE.** See also CORIN.

CORYDON, "KORE-ih-dawn"—*Greek: "crested one" or "helmeted one," that is, a guard or soldier.* **CORIDEN, CORIDON, KORUDON.**

COVE, "KOHV"—*English: a sheltered inlet, or "my fellow," "my man," or "my boy."* Cove is a term for one's circle of male friends.

COVEY, "KOH-vee"—*Irish: "hound of Meath."* **COOVAY, COOVEY; CÚMHÉ** (KOO-vay)—Irish Gaelic. The covey is a beast that figures in Gaelic folklore.

COWAN, "COW-un"—*English: "hooded robe," that is, a monk; Irish: "hillside plain."* **COE, COWIE.**

COYLE, "KOYL"—*Irish Gaelic: "follower of battle."*

CRAIG, "KRAYG"—*Irish Gaelic: "rock."*

CRANE, "KRAYN"—*English: "to stretch out" and the crane bird.* **CRANDALL, CRANDELL** (a dell where the birds are found); **DARU** (DAH-roo)—Hungarian; **GRU**—Italian; **GRUA** (GROO-ah)—Spanish; **GRUE** (GROO)—French; **KRAN** (KRAHN)—Scandinavian, German, Polish, and Russian; **YASHTAHI** (yahsh-TAH-hee)—Arabic; **YERANOS** (yeh-RAH-nohss)—Greek. The crane, a long-necked bird, is a symbol of luck in many cultures. The constellation of the Crane seems to be flying after the southern Sun at dusk from October through the first week of November. The Sun is "in" the Crane in late February through most of March.

CRANSTON, "KRANZ-tun"—*English: "the crane town."*

CRAWFORD, "KRAW-furd"—*English: "ford where crows gather."*

CRAWLEY, "KRAW-lee"—*English: "meadow of crows."* **CRAWLEA, CRAWLEE, CRAWLEIGH; CROWLEA, CROWLEE, CROWLEIGH, CROWLEY.**

CRICHTON, "KRY-ton"—*Welsh: "from the hilltop town"; English: "town by the creek."* **CREIGHTON, CRIGHTON.**

CRISPIN, "KRIHS-pihn" and "krihs-PEE-nah"—*Latin: "curled or crimped hair."* **CRISPIAN, CRISPUS.** Brothers Crispin and Crispian were shoemakers martyred for their Christian beliefs in the third century. They're patron saints of . . . shoemakers, right! Crispus Attucks was an African-American who was the first to die for American independence in the Boston Massacre.

CROFT, "KRAWFT"—*English: "small pasture"; Scottish: "a small land holding."* A croft is a field that belongs to someone in particular, as opposed to a common holding that belongs to a village.

CRONAN, "KROW-nan"—*Irish: "dark brown."* **CRONIN, CRONYN.**

CRONIN, "KROW-nihn"—*Greek: "companion."* **CRONAN.**

CROSLEY, "KRAWZ-lee"—*English: "from across the clearing."* **CROSLEA, CROSLEE, CROSLEIGH.**

CROSS, "KRAWSS"—*American diminutive of Croccifixio, Italian: "crucifix."*

CULLEN, "KUL-ehn"—*Irish: "holly"; Celtic: "cub"; English: "to gather or choose."* **CULLIN.**

CULLEY, "KUH-lee"—*Irish: "the holly meadow."* F

CULVER, "KUHL-vur"—*Anglo-Saxon: "gentle" or "peaceful."* **COLVER.**

CURRAN, "KUR-ahn"—*English: "to churn up"; Irish: "heroic."* See also CURRY/CURRIE.

CURRY, CURRIE, "KUR-ee"—*Irish: "a marsh."*

CURTIS, "KUR-tihss"—*Latin: "courtyard"; Bretagne: "courteous."* **CURT, KURT.**

CUTLER, "KUHT-lur"—*English: "the knife maker."*

CYRIL, "SEER-ul"—*Greek: "lordly"* or *"masterly."* **CIRO**—Spanish, Portuguese, and Italian; **COIREALL** (KOY-rahl)—Irish Gaelic; **CYRILLIO; CYREK, CYRYL**—Eastern European; **KIRIL.** Several Christian saints have had this name, including one who ministered to the early Slavic peoples and invented the Cyrillic alphabet used by Russian-speaking and some Slavic-speaking countries. F

CYRUS, "SYE-ruhss"—*Persian: "throne"; Greek: "sun."* The great King Cyrus mentioned in the Old Testament/Tanakh had visions of the future. He also allowed the Israelites to establish a homeland. **CIRO, CY, CYRO.**

THE TOP FIVE

DYLAN
DANIEL
DAVID
DEREK
DRAKE

If the name you're looking for isn't here, perhaps it is a variant or a diminutive of another primary name.

DACEY, "DAY-see"—*Irish: "southerner."* **DACE.**

DAE, "DAH-ee"—*Korean: "great" or "renowned."*

DAG, "DAHG"—*Norwegian: "day"; Norse: "bright," as in daylight.* This is not to say the name's bearer can't also be bright as in brainpower. Dag Hammarskjöld was a Swedish statesman who was secretary-general of the United Nations during the 1950s, a very tense period in world politics, and died in a 1961 plane crash while on a peace mission to Africa. He was awarded a posthumous Nobel Peace Prize. F

DAGAN, "DAY-gahn"—*Phoenician: "grain,"* usually corn; *Assyrian: "king of the land."* **DEGAN.** In Phoenician myth, Dagan was a deity of fertility, among other things. He was represented as half-man, half-fish—sort of a mer-man. This is the same "Dagon" mentioned in the Old Testament/Tanakh as the god of the Philistines.

DAI, "DAH-ee"—*Japanese: "great."* F

DAISHI, "DYE-shee" or "dye-SHEE"—*Japanese: "great teacher."*

DAKOTA(H), "dah-KOH-tah"—*Native American Sioux: "friendly one(s)."* This is one of the three tribes of the Great Sioux Nation. F

DALE, "DAYL"—*English: "valley"; Norse: "hollow," as in the topographical feature.* **DAEL, DAILE, DAYLE.** F

DALLAS, "DAL-us"—*Celtic: "skilled" or "spirited."* The Texas city was named after George M. Dallas, who was vice president under James Polk in the 1840s.

DALTON, "DAHL-tun"—*English: "town in the valley."* **DALLTON.**

DALY, "DAY-lee"—*Gaelic: "counsellor."* **DALEY.**

DAMEK, "DAH-mehk" or "dah-MEHK"—*Slavic: "man of the earth."*

DAMIAN, "DAY-mee-un" or "DAH-mee-ahn"—*Greek: "to tame," "to domesticate," or "to calm."* **DAMIANO; DAMIEN.** There is already one Christian saint with this name, the patron saint of surgeons. But there is another who has been beatified—the step prior to sainthood: Belgian Damien de Veuster (d. 1889). De Veuster was a missionary to the Hawaiian islands, where he worked closely with lepers. F

DAMON, "DAY-mon"—*Greek: "deity," "spirit," or "fate"; Latin: "evil spirit."* **DAEMON**—Latin and English; **DAIMON**—Greek; **DAMONE** (dah-MOAN)—Italian. Go as Greek as possible with this one, unless you *like* the other versions, and be aware that the "spirit" the Greeks had in mind is the one that acts as a go-between for gods and humans. When the Christian era took hold, anything that wasn't Christian was considered evil, so "daimons," "daemons," and "demons" were all "Satanic." Damon is traditionally the name of a character used in poems and novels with a pastoral setting, owing to the ancient epic poet Virgil's *Ecologues*, in which Damon is a shepherd.

DANBY, "DAN-bee"—*English: "the Danish town."*

DANE, "DAYN"—*Norse: "man of Denmark."* **DAINE, DAYNE; DANIR** (Old Norse name for the people of Denmark).

DANIEL, "DAN-yul" or "DAH-nyel"—*Hebrew: "God is my judge."* **DAINÉAL** (DINE-yal)—Irish Gaelic; **DANEIL** (dah-NEEL)—Eastern European; **DANELE** (dah-neh-leh)—Basque; **DANIEL(L)I**—Italian; **DANIYEL**—Israeli. In the Old Testament/Tanakh, Daniel refuses an order of the king of Persia on religious grounds, and is sentenced to die in a den of hungry lions. God calms the lions, and Daniel stays down there for days until a kindly Ethiopian pays to be allowed to release the old man. Several Christian saint names are on this list, and Dan is the name of one of the twelve tribes of Israel, named after the fifth son of Jacob. **DAN, DANNY.** F

DANNY. See DANIEL.

DANTE, "DAHN-tay"—*Italian: "lasting" or "patience."* **DURAN; DURANTE** (doo-RAHN-teh)—Italian. Dante Alighieri was an Italian poet (d. 1321) whose creative gifts were offered in remembrance of his childhood sweetheart, Beatrice, who was the center of his universe. After she died, his passion turned to knowledge, politics, and philosophy. His masterwork is *La Commedia (The Divine Comedy)*, which is a three-book series: *Inferno, Purgatorio,* and *Paradiso.* In it, he journeys from the depths of hell to the highest heaven, where he is granted visions of God. Beatrice is his guide through heaven, by the way. Dante Gabriel Rossetti (d. 1882) was a pre-Raphaelite artist who used romantic subjects and rich color. (I can always tell if it's a Rossetti by the way he drew lips, although not every one of his works is drawn that way. You'll see what I mean if you look him up.) F

DAR, "DAHR"—*Hebrew: "pearl"; Irish: "oak tree."* F

DARBY, "DAHR-bee"—*Gaelic: "free man."* An early eighteenth-century ballad about a John Darby and his wife, Joan, was a very popular story-song. Therefore, "Darby and Joan" refers to married bliss and the types of happiness couples share. F

DARDANOS, "dahr-DAH-nohss"—*Hungarian: "a dart"; Hebrew: "pearl of wisdom"; Greek: Troy and the Trojan people.* **DARDAN, DARDEN.** Greek legend says that Dardanos, who founded Troy, was the son of the gods Zeus and Electra.

DAREN, "DAH-rehn"—*African: "born at night."*

DARIUS, "DARE-ee-us"—*Persian: "many possessions"; Latin: "dark king."* **DARIC; DARIO.** There were several Persian kings named Darius, one of whom divided his empire into provinces and set about expanding the territory. He even led an invasion into Greece. F

DARRELL, "DARE-ihl"—*English: "dear" or "darling."* **DAREL, DARELL, DARREL, DARRYL, DARYL; DERELL, DERRELL, DERRY.** F

DARREN, "DARE-un"—*Irish(?): "little great one(?)."* **DAREN, DARIN, DARRIN, DARRON.**

DARROW, "DARE-oh"—*English: "spear."* But not arrow, though! Go figure.

DARTON, "DAHR-tun"—*Celtic: "village near the water"; English: "deer park."* **DARDEN.**

DARWIN, "DAHR-wihn"—*Celtic: "friend of the sea" or "lover of water."* **DARWYN, DERWYN, DURWYN; DERWIN.** One Darwin, first name Charles, was a lover of the sea, and it was on one of those voyages in the nineteenth century that he formed his theory of evolution; which caused a lot of controversy back then, and—well, it's still controversial in some areas today.

DAR(R)YL. See DARRELL.

DASAN, "DAH-sahn"—*Native American Pomo: "bird clan leader."*

DASH, "DASH"—*English: "quick" or "masculine charm."* **DASHELL, DASHING.**

DATTO, "DAH-toh"—*Tagalog: "Moslem chief" or "head man."* **DATOQ**—Tagalog.

DAUPHIN, "doh-FAN"—*French: "prince" or "dolphin."* See also DELPHINO, DELVIN. F

DAVE. See DAVID.

DAVID, "DAY-vihd" or "dah-VEED"—*traditionally, Hebrew: "beloved" or "adored";* but also *Scandinavian: "two rivers."* **DABID** (dah-beed)—Basque; **DAFFYD** (DAH-fihd), **TAFFY**—Welsh; **DAIBHIDH** (DYE-vee)—Scottish Gaelic; **DÁIVI** (DYE-vee)—Irish Gaelic; **DAOUD** (DAH-ood), **DAVED, DAVEN**—Scandinavian; **DAVI**—Israeli; **DAWUD** (DAH-wood)—Arabic; **TEVEL** (TEH-vehl)—Yiddish. In the Old Testament/Tanakh, David was a shepherd who became the second king of Israel. He wrote much of the sacred book of Psalms. While just a boy, and with his people at war, he killed the Philistine's most effective weapon, the giant Goliath, with his slingshot and a rock, and the Hebrews were eventually victors. The names of two Scottish kings and several saints can be found in this list; one Saint David is the patron saint of Wales. In sailors' lore, Davy Jones is the spirit of the sea. **DAVE.** See also DEWEY. F

DAVIN, "DAH-vihn" or "dah-VEEN"—*Norse: "Finnish."* F

DAVIS, "DAY-vihss"—*English: "son of David."* **DAVIES.**

DAY, "DAY"—*English: "day" (duh!).* **DIAS** (DEE-ahss)—Spanish; **JOUR** (ZHOOR)—French; **TAGE** (TAH-geh)—Teutonic.

DEACON, "DEE-kun"—*Greek: "servant."* A church deacon ranks just below a priest.

DEAN, "DEEN"—*English: "from the forest."* **DEANE; DENBY, DENTON; DINO** (DEE-noh)—Italian. F

DECAMERON, "dee-KAM-eh-rawn"—*Italian: "ten days."* In the city of Florence there was a great plague in the fourteenth century, and ten of its citizens secluded themselves in a home for ten days and kept themselves entertained by telling stories. Italian writer Giovanni Boccaccio recorded the 100 stories and published them in 1353; the collection is called *Decameron*. **CAM, CAMMI(E), CAMMY.**

DEE, "DEE"—*Welsh: "holy one" or "black."* F

DEEMS, "DEEMZ"—*English: "son of a judge."*

DEEPAK, "DEE-pahk"—*Hindu: "lamp" or "light."* This is a common name in India, similar to John in this country.

DEER(E), "DEER"—*English: "deer."* Pretty easy to figure out.

DEION. See DION.

DEKEL, "DEH-kehl"—*Hebrew: "date palm tree."*

DELANEY, "deh-LAY-nee"—*Irish: "challenger."*

DELL. See DELLING, UDELL.

DELLING, "DEHL-ing"—*Norse: "resplendent" or "dazzling."* **DEL, DELL.**

DELMAR, "dehl-MAHR" or "DEHL-mahr"—*Latin: "from the sea."* **DEL MAR, DELMER, DELMORE. DEL.** F

DELPHI, "DEHL-fye"—*Greek: "sacred" and "love."* Delphi is the site of sacred temples of the Greek gods of Olympus, a place where mortals could learn the will of the gods. It is located on Mount Parnassus at the Gulf of Corinth. The most famous structure here is the temple of Apollo, where his oracles, always women, would prophesy. A sacred stone is at Delphi, the Omphalos or "navel stone," said to mark the center of the Earth. As the center of the Earth, this place was a gathering spot for governments, and was an important place to sack if you were taking over Greece. There is even a shrine to John the Baptist at the sacred stream of Delphi. F

DELPHINO, "dehl-FEE-noh"—*Greek: "a dolphin" or "serenity."* **DELPIN** (dehl-PIHN), **DELPINO.** The constellation Delphinus can be seen chasing the Sun at dusk in the last half of September. The Sun is "in" the Little Dolphin at Christmastime. See also DAUPHIN, DELVIN. F

DELVIN, "DEHL-vihn" or "dehl-VIHN"—*English from Greek: "dolphin."* **DELFIN.** See also DAUPHIN, DELPHINO. F

DELWIN, "DEHL-wihn"—*Celtic: "proud friend."* **DELWYN.**

DEMAS, "DAY-mahs" or "day-MAHS"—*Greek: "popular."*

DEMBE, "DEHM-beh"—*African Luganda: "peace."* F

DEMETROS, "deh-MEE-trohss"—*Greek: "of Demeter,"* the Greek goddess of plenty. **DEMETRIOS, DEMETRIUS, DEMITRIUS; DHIMITRIOS** (dee-MEE-tree-ohss), **MITROS, MITSOS**—Greek; **DIMA, DIMITRI** (dee-MEE-tree), **DMITRI, MITYA**—Russian; **DYMITR** (DYEH-mee-ter)—Polish.

DEMOS, "DAY-mohss"—*Greek: "of the people."* This is the root of the word "democracy."

DEMPSEY, "DEHMP-see"—*English: "absence of merit."* **DEMPSTER. DEMP.**

DEN, "DEHN"—*Japanese: "gift from the ancestors."*

DENBY, "DEHN-bee"—*English: "near the Danish town."*

DENIS, "DEH-nihss" or "deh-NEE"—*French: "Dionysius,"* Greek god of wine; *Greek: "of Nysa,"* a Greek mountain. **DENES, DENNES** — Eastern European; **DENISKOV** (DEH-nihs-kov)—Russian; **DENNIS** (DEHN-iss), **DENYS**—English; **DINIS**

de, d', de la, de l', du, des

These are French name prefixes, and they are *not* usually capitalized. "De" means "of" or "from"; use "d" instead of "de" when the noun to follow begins with an "a," "e," "i," "o," "u," or "y," since the "d" sound links up with the vowel sound—for example, "d'Arcy" is pronounced "DAR-see." "De la" means "of the" or "from the," and must be followed by a name considered to be a singular, feminine noun—no final "o." "De l" is used the same as "de la" or "du," but only when the noun you choose begins with "a," "e," "i," "o," "u," or "y"—the "l" sound links up to the vowel sound. For example: "de l'Eau" is pronounced "duh-LOW." "Du"—pronounced "dew" or "dyew"—means "of the" or "from the" and must be followed by a name considered to be a singular, masculine noun—no final "a." "Des," pronounced "day," means "of the" or "from the" and must be followed by plural nouns. You may add these yourself to any name.

(DEE-nees)—Portuguese; **DUNIXI** (doo-nee-shee)—Basque. One of the saints named Denis is the patron saint of France. F

DENTON, "DEHN-tun"—*English: "valley town."*

DENVER, "DEHN-vur"—*Anglo-French: "verdant little valley."*

DENZIL, "DEHN-zihl"—*Celtic: "from the high stronghold."* **DENZEL.** Actor Denzel Washington has brought this old name back into public awareness.

DERBY, "DUR-bee"—*English: "near the deer" or "near the water."* **DARBY, DORSEY; DARLAND, DERLAND.**

DEREK, "DARE-ehk"—*Irish: "red"; German: "wealthy ruler"; Persian: "gold coin."* **DARIC**—Persian; **DARRICK, DERRICK; DERRIG, DERRIK**—Irish. **DIRK; RICK, RIK.**

DERMOT, "DUR-mut" or "DARE-muht"—*Irish: "free of envy."* **DERMIT, DERMOD, DIARMID.**

DERON, "DEH-rohn"—*Hebrew: "bird" or "freedom."* **DERRON.**

DERRY, "DARE-ee"—*Irish: "oak grove."* **DERRI(E).** See also DARRELL. F

DES, DIS, "DEHZ" or "DEEZ"—*Celtic.* **DEES, DESPATER, DISPATER.** This is the Celtic god of the night and the afterworld. **DYS.**

DESHI, "DEH-shee"—*Chinese: "man of virtue."*

DESI, "DAY-see" or "DEH-zee"—*French via Latin: "desire" or "desired."* **DESIDERIO** (deh-see-DEH-ree-oh)—Spanish. Desi Arnaz was the male star of early TV's megahit *I Love Lucy.* F

DESMOND, "DEHZ-mund"—*Latin: "a part of all creation"; Greek: "a bond or pledge."* **DES.** F

DEVERELL, "DEHV-ur-ehl"—*Cymric: "from the riverbank."* **DEVEREAUX** (DEHV-eh-roh)—French; **DEVEREUX** (DEHV-eh-roh)—Bretagne.

DEVIN, "DEHV-ihn"—*Celtic: "poet."* F

DEVON, "DEHV-un"—*Celtic: a place name.* **DEVIN.**

DEWEY, "DOO-ee"—*English: "covered with dew."* Dew indicates newness, freshness, or innocence. Dewey is also a Welsh alternative to the name David. See also DAVID.

DEWITT, DE WITT, "deh-WIHT"—*Flemish: "blond one."*

DEXTER, "DECKS-tur"—*Latin: "right-handed" or "skillful."* **DEX, DEXEY, DEXY.**

DHANI, "d'HAH-nee"—*Sanskrit: "wealthy."* F

DHARM, "d'HARM"—*Sanskrit: "right-eousness."*

DICK, DIK, "DIHK"—*diminutive of Richard; for the second spelling, African: "little antelope."* **DIK-DIK.** See also RICHARD.

DIEGO, "dee-AY-goh"—*Spanish: version of James, "the supplanter."* Diego Velazquez was a Spanish Baroque painter who avoided the artificial ornamentation and clutter found in much of the Baroque style of art. He was quite a realist, and his use of color dabs, and of light, fluid brush strokes, lead many to conclude he was a father of the Impressionist movement 225 years ahead of his time. See also JACOB, JAMES.

DIETER, "DEE-tur"—*Dutch: "ruler of the people."* **DIEDRICH** (DEED-rihk), **DIETRICH** (DEET-rihk), **DIEDRICK, DIETRICK.**

DILLIAN, "DIHL-ee-an"—*Latin: "image of worship."* **DILLO, DILLY.** F

DILLON, "DIHL-un"—*Celtic: "faithful."* See also DYLAN.

DINO. See DEAN.

DION, "dee-AWN" or "dee-OHN"—*Greek: "child of heaven and earth" or "sky god."* **DEION, DEON; DIONIS.** Dion was a student of Plato who became ruler of the Greek city of Syracuse in the first century B.C. Deion Sanders is a multisport superstar who has popularized the name. F

DIRK, "DEERK" or "DURK"—*Teutonic: "a dagger"; Irish: "a cave."* See also DEREK.

DIXON, "DIHKS-un"—*Latin: "tenth"; Norse: "busy sprite."* **DIX.** F

DOAN, "DOH-ahn" or "DOHN"—*Celtic: "sand dunes."* F

DOBRY, "DOH-bree"—*Russian: "good."*

DOHOSAN, "doh-HOH-sahn"—*Native American: "the small bluff."*

DOLAN, "DOH-lun"—*Gaelic: "black-haired."* **DOLAND, DOLANS, DOLANT; DOLEN, DOLEND, DOLENS, DOLENT, DOLENZ.**

DOMINIC, "DAWM-ih-nihk"—*Latin: "of the Lord."* **DEDO, DOME, DOMINIK, DOMO, DOMOKOS** (DOH-moh-kohss), **DOMONKOS**—Eastern European; **DOMENIC, DOMINICK; DOMENICO**—Italian, Spanish, and Portuguese; **DOMENIKOS** (doh-MEHN-ee-kohss)—Greek; **DOMINGO** (doh-MEEN-goh), **DOMINGUEZ**—Spanish; **DOMINICO** (doh-MEE-nee-koh)—Italian; **DOMINIQUE** (doh-mee-NEEK)—French. Dominic, one of the Christian saints, founded the Dominican order. **DOM.** F

DON, "DAWN"—*Italian: "lord"; Spanish: "landowner" or "esquire."* See also DONALD, DONNELL.

DONALD, "DAW-nahld"—*Celtic: "proud chief."* **DOMHNALL** (DOY-nahl)—*Gaelic;* **DONAL**—Irish. This is a Christian saint name, and the name of six Scottish kings. **DON, DONNIE, DONNY.**

DONAR, "DAWN-ahr"—*German: the ancient "thunder god."* **DONNER.**

DONATO, "doh-NAH-toh"—*Latin: "gift" or "to give."* **DONAT, DONATUS; DONATEL** (daw-nah-TEHL), **DONATELLI, DONATELLO**—Italian; **DONATIEN** (doh-NAH-tyen or doh-nah-TYEN)—French. Donaut map Papo was a Welshman of power and influence in Arthurian lore. Saint Donatus was an Irish saint who became an Italian bishop. Donato di Betto Bardi, better known as Donatello, was an early Renaissance master who revolutionized sculpture by recreating the classical Roman and Greek styles. Donatello, who worked in stone and bronze, returned realism and the depiction of natural movement to sculpture.

DONEGAL, "DAWN-eh-gahl"—*Irish: "fort of the foreigners."* **DÚNNANGALL** (DOO-nahn-gahl)—Irish Gaelic.

DONNEL(L), "DAWN-ehl"—*Irish Gaelic: "hill fort."* **DONELLY, DONNAN.** Irish saint Donnan was martyred in Scotland in the seventh century. **DON, DONNI(E), DONNY.**

DOOLEY, "DOO-lee"—*Gaelic: "dark hero."*

DORADO, "doh-RAH-doh"—*Latin: "gold."* The constellation Dorado, the Goldfish, can be seen chasing the Sun at the end of January. The Sun is "in" Dorado in May.

DORAN, "DOH-run" or "DOH-ran"—*Greek: "gift"; French: "golden."* See also DORON. F

DORIAN, "DOH-ree-ahn"—*Greek: "gift"; Latin/French: "golden."* **DORIEN; DORJÁN** (dor-YAHN)—Hungarian; **DOREN, DORAN, DORAL.** In Oscar Wilde's *Picture of Dorian Gray*, a vain man makes a deal with a demon for immortality; he does not age, but a portrait of him does. **DOR.** F

DORON, "DOH-rawn"—*Hebrew: "gift."* America's first test-tube baby boy, born from an elite sperm bank—Nobel Prize winners, professors, etc.—was named Doron. See also DORAN.

DORREN, DURRAN, "DOH-rehn" or "DUR-un"—*English: "to encourage" or "to stir up."*

DOTAN, "DOH-tahn"—*Hebrew: "law."* **DOTHAN.**

DOUG. See DOUGLAS.

DOUGAL, "DOO-gul"—*Scottish: "dark foreigner."* **DÚGHALL**—Scottish Gaelic.

DOUGLAS, "DUG-less" (totally without dug?)—*Scottish: "black stream" or "black-blue."* **DOUGLASS; DÚGHLAS**—Scottish Gaelic. **DOOGIE, DOOGY; DOUG, DOUGEY, DOUGIE.**

DOV, "DOHV"—*Yiddish: "little bear."* See also BEAR.

DOW, rhymes with "HOW"—*Gaelic: "black or dark haired."*

DOYLE, "DOIL"—*Irish: "assembling" or "gathering"; Celtic: "dark newcomer."*

DRAKE, "DRAYK"—*French: "male duck"; English: "dragon."*

DREW, "DROO"—*Greek, diminutive of Andrew: "strong"; German: "carry" or "trust."* **DRU.** See also ANDREW. F

DRISCOLL, "DRIHS-kohl"—*Celtic: "sad"; English: "speaker" or "interpreter."*

DRUCE, "DROOSE"—*Celtic: "capable."* F

DRURY, "DROO-ree"—*Bretagne: "sweetheart."*

DRYDEN, "DRY-dehn"—*English: "dry or secluded valley."*

DUANE, "DWAYN" or "doo-WAYN"—*Irish: "little dark one"; Celtic: "singing."* **DUWAYNE; DWAIN(E), DWAYNE.** F

DUFFY, "DUHF-ee"—*Irish: "black-haired" or "dark-haired."* **DUFF, DUFFI(E).**

DUGAN, "DOO-gan"—*Gaelic: "dark-skinned."*

DUKE, "DOOK"—*Latin: "leader."* **DUC** (DOOK)—*French;* **DUX**—*Latin.*

DUKHAN, "dook-HAHN"—*Arabic: "smoke."* **DUK(E), DUKH.**

DUKKER, "DOOK-ur" or "DUCK-er"—*Gypsy: "to bewitch."* **DUKKAN, DUKKIN, DURIKKEN.**

DUNCAN, "DUN-kihn"—*Gaelic: "dark warrior" or "brunet."* **DONNCHADH** (DAWN-kheye—"kh" in your throat)—*Scottish Gaelic;* **DUNKAN, DUNKANAN, DUNKANAS.** This name has a long history among Scottish kings and Icelandic rulers.

DUNN, "DUHN"—*English: "brown" or "dark."*

DUNSTAN, "DUHNZ-tun"—*English: "dark stone" or "brown stone."* **DONESTAN; DUNN, DUNNE.**

DURAN, "doo-RAN"—*English: "to stir up."*

DURIEL, "DOO-ree-ehl"—*Hebrew: "my house belongs to the Lord."* **DURIAL, DURYEA** (DOO-ree-yah/yay).

DURRIL(L), "DUR-ihl"—*Gypsy: "berry."*

DURWALD, "DUR-wahld"—*English/German: "the deer woods."* **DURWALT, DURWARD, DURWOOD.**

DUSTIN, "DUHS-tihn"—*Teutonic: "strong-hearted."* Dustin Hoffman has popularized this uncommon name. He, in turn, was named after a silent film star his mom liked. **DUSTY.**

DUTTON, "DUHT-uhn"—*Celtic: "fortified hill."*

DWAYNE. See DUANE.

DWIGHT, "DWITE"—*German: "white"; Dutch: "fair."* General Dwight Eisenhower was commander of the European theater of operations in World War II, and was supreme commander of the Allied forces before the war ended. His popularity led to his election as president in 1954.

DYANI, "dee-YAH-nee" or "dye-AH-nee"—*Native American: "a deer."* **DYAN.** F

DYLAN, "DIH-lahn"—*Celtic: "son of the wave," Celtic god of the sea.* **DILLON.** Dylan Eil Ton was heard in the waves, and the place where water and earth reach for one another was sacred to the Celts, since it was a place where mortals can touch gods and vice versa. Dylan Thomas was a twentieth-century Welsh writer whose works were filled with emotion. A midwestern American folksinger changed his name from Bob Zimmerman to Bob Dylan in honor of the Welsh poet. The name's current popularity comes from the popularity of the character Dylan on *Beverly Hills 90210.* **DILLIE, DILLY.**

DYRE, "DEE-reh"—*Norse: "deer" or "dear."*

DYSIS, "DY-sihss"—*Greek: "musical interlude" or "sunset."* **DIESIS, DYESIS. DICE, DIES, DYS.** F

THE TOP FIVE

EDWARD
EVAN
ERIC
ELIJAH
EMMET/EMMIT

If the name you're looking for isn't here, see "Y" and the other vowels.

EACHAN, "AY-kahn" or "EE-kahn"—*Irish Gaelic: "little horse."* **AIKEN, AKEN.**

EAMON, "AY-mun"—*Irish: "rich protector."* **AIMON, IAMON.**

EARL, "URL"—*English: "nobleman" or "warrior."* **EARLE, ERLE; ERROL, ERROLL.**

EARVIN. See IRVIN(G).

EATON, "AY-tun" or "EE-ton"—*Anglo-Saxon: "riverside."* **ETON.**

EDAN, "EE-dahn"—*Irish Gaelic: "little fiery one."* **ED, EDDY.** See also AIDAN. F

EDDY, "EH-dee"—*Swedish: "unresting"; Norse: "whirlpool."* This is also a diminutive for all names beginning with "Ed-." F

EDEL, "EHD-ehl"—*German: "noble."* **ED, EDDY.**

EDELMAR, "EHD-ehl-mahr"—*German: "noble sea(farer)."* **ED, EDDY.**

EDEN, "EE-dehn"—*Hebrew: "delight."* The legendary Garden of Eden was a paradise on Earth until Adam and Eve goofed. **ED.** F

EDGAR, "EHD-gur"—*English: "lucky warrior."* **EDGARD; EDGARDO** (ehd-GAHR-do)— Italian and Spanish. Edgar Dégas was an Impressionist painter most known for his portraits of motion frozen in time. He never centered his subjects, adding to the illusion of a random moment. **ED, EDDY.**

EDMOND, EDMUND, "EHD-mund"— *English: "propserous protector."* **EAMON** (AY-mun)—Irish; **EDMONDO** (ehd-MAWN-doh)—Spanish and Italian. Several kings and saints have used these names. Among them is Saint Edmund, a ninth-century king of East Anglia who was martyred for refusing to denounce Christianity when the Danish took over. **ED, EDDIE, EDDY; MONDO.**

EDOM, "EE-dohm" or "AY-dohm"—*Hebrew: "red."* Edom is sometimes an alternate name for the Esau of the Old Testament/Tanakh, and is the name of the ancient country in which his descendants settled—present-day Jordan and Israel. **ED, EDDY.**

EDRIC, "EHD-rihk"—*Hebrew: "mighty"; Anglo-Saxon: "wealthy or happy ruler."* **EDERIC, EDREA, EDRICK, EDRIK. ED, EDDI(E), EDDY; RICK.** F

EDWARD, "EHD-wurd"—*English: "happy or wealthy guardian."* **DUARTE** (doo-AHR-teh)—Portuguese; **EDOARDO** (eh-doh-WAHR-doh)—Italian; **EDUARDO** (eh-doo-AHR-doh)—Spanish; **EDVARD** (ehd-VAHRD)—Swedish and Eastern European;

EIDEARD (AYD-yard)—Scottish Gaelic. Edward has been the name of many European saints and kings. One of them was both: Edward the Confessor, an eleventh-century Briton, who founded the monastery at Westminster and performed miracles. Twentieth-century King Edward VIII abdicated his throne rather than spend his life without the woman he loved, an American divorcée. Edouard Manet was a nineteenth-century French painter who scandalized European society by presenting female nudes as contemporary women. Until then, nudity was acceptable only if it was shown in the context of a goddess or other pagan female . . . and what was *worse* was that these contemporary, naked women in the portraits were looking directly at the spectator! (Pass the smelling salts!) He also painted uncompromising portraits of modern society. **ED, EDDI(E), EDDY.** F

EDWIN, "EHD-wihn"—*English: "happy or wealthy friend."* **EDUIN** (EHD-oo-ihn), **EDUINO**—Spanish and Portuguese; **EDVIN, EDVINO**—Eastern European; **EDWYN**—Welsh. Saint Edwin was a seventh-century king of Northumbria in England who converted to Christianity. **ED, EDDI(E), EDDY.** F

EFRAM, EPHRAM, "EHF-rahm"—*Hebrew: "fruitful."* **EFRAIM, EPHRAIM; EFRAYIM.**

EGAN, "EE-ghin" or "AY-ghin"—*Teutonic: "formidable"; Irish: "little fire."* **AODHGAN** (AY-oh-ghin)—Irish Gaelic; **EGEN, EGON, KEEGAN, MAC EGAN.**

EGIL, "EH-ghihl"—*Norse: "awe-inspiring."* **EIGIL** (AY-ghihl).

EHREN, "EH-rehn"—*German: "honorable."*

EHUD, "eh-HOOD"—*Hebrew: "union."*

EIDER, "AY-dur" or "EYE-dur"—*Icelandic: "sea duck."* The eider parent plucks its own down to keep its eggs or little ones warm in the bitter winters. Thus, the name has a connotation of loving devotion and self-sacrifice.

EINAR, "EYE-nahr"—*Norse: "warrior."* **AINAR, EHNAR.**

EIR(E), "AIR"—*Norse: "peaceful."* Eire is another name for the island of Ireland.

EKUNDAYO, "eh-KOON-dah-yoh" or "eh-koon-DAH-yoh"—*African Yoruba: "our sorrow becomes joy."*

ELAM, "EE-lam"—*Hebrew.* Elam was an ancient country in Asia Minor between the Caspian Sea and the Persian Gulf. It is sometimes called Susiana.

ELAN, "ay-LAHN"—*Latin: "spirited"; French: "ardor" or "vivaciousness."* **ELA, ELAH, ELAI, ELON.** F

ELAND, "EE-land"—*African: "antelope-ox with twisted horns"; Dutch: "great elk."*

ELDON, "EHL-dun"—*English: "the alder-tree hill" or "old age."* **ELDIN, ELTON.** The association with age may be that he is the child of a couple having children late in life.

ELDRIDGE, "EHL-drihj"—*Teutonic: "wise advisor."*

ELDWIN, "EHLD-wihn"—*English: "old friend."*

ELGIN, "EHL-jihn"—*English: "white noble" or "pure noble."*

ELI, "EE-lye" or "EHL-ee"—*Hebrew: "height" or "the highest."* See also ALEXANDER.

ELIAS, "ee-LYE-us"—*Hebrew: "Jehovah is my God."* **ILIAS**—Greek. See also ELIJAH, ELISHA, ELLIS. F

ELIHU, "EHL-ee-hoo"—*Hebrew: "Jehovah, the Lord."*

El

This is the Spanish prefix that means "the." You may add it yourself to any name, provided it is considered masculine and singular (does not end in "a" or "s").

ELIJAH, "ee-LYE-zhah/jah" or "eh-LEE-zhah"—*Hebrew: "God is my salvation" and "Jehovah is God."* **ELIAS, ELIHU, ELISHA.** The prophet Elijah in the Old Testament/Tanakh was a powerful orator and miracle worker of the ninth century B.C. He did not die, but was taken into heaven by God when his time came. Customarily, Jews set a place for him at Passover and at a bris. In the New Testament, Jesus refers to John the Baptist as the reincarnated Elijah. In the Qur'an, Elijah is considered to be a major prophet who tried to turn his people from paganism to monotheism.

ELIOT, "EHL-ee-uht"—*Hebrew: "close to God."* **ELIOTT, ELLIOT, ELLIOTT.**

ELISHA, "eh-LIH-shah," sometimes "eh-LYE-shah"—*Hebrew: "God is generous."* **ELIAS** (EH-lee-ahs or ee-LYE-ahs), **ELLIS**—English; **ELISEO** (eh-lee-SAY-oh)—Spanish; **ELIZUR**—Eastern European. In the Old Testament/Tanakh, Elisha was a holy man who was the companion of the prophet Elijah, and who succeeded Elijah when the prophet was taken up by God. See also ELIJAH.

ELLARD, "EHL-urd"—*Teutonic: "noble and brave."*

ELLERY, "EHL-eh-ree"—*German: "alder tree."* **ELLARD; ELEREY, ELERY, ELLERRY; ELLSDEN, ELLSDON, ELLSTON.** Ellery Queen was a fictional detective who was involved in hundreds of cases, beginning in comics, going through books and magazines, and then on to TV and film. **EL, ELLIE, ELLY.**

ELLIS, "EHL-ihss"—*Hebrew: "the Lord is God."* **ELIAS.** See also ELISHA. F

ELLSWORTH, "EHLZ-wurth"—*Anglo-Saxon: "lover of the earth" or "farmer"; English: "nobleman's estate."* **ELSWORTH.**

ELMORE, "EHL-mohr"—*English: "elm trees by the moors."*

ELRAD, "EHL-rahd"—*Hebrew: "God rules."*

ELROY, "EHL-roy"—*French and Spanish: "the king."*

ELTON. See ELDON.

ELVIN, "EHL-vihn"—*German: "elfin friend" or "spritely friend."* **ELVERT; ELVYN, ELWIN, ELWYN.** See also ALVIN.

ELVIS, "EHL-vihss"—*Gaelic: "leader of the elves"; Nordic: "wise elf."* The little magical beings are certainly bright, but the whole crowd of them can't outshine the memory of Elvis Presley, a singer, actor, and entertainer who revolutionized popular music and popular culture. F

ELVY, "EHL-vee"—*English: "elfin warrior."*

ELWOOD, "EHL-wood"—*English: "old forest"; German: "alder tree wood."* **ELLWOOD. WOOD, WOODY.**

EMERSON, "EHM-ur-sun"—*German: "son of the chief."*

EMERY, "EM-uh-ree" or "EM-ree"—*German: "ruler or chief."* **EMERICK, EMORY, EMRYS.** In Arthurian lore, the wise sorcerer

Merlyn is sometimes given the second name Emrys. **EM.** See also MERLIN/MERLYN.

EMIL, "EH/AY-meel"—*Latin: "industrious"; Teutonic: "energetic."* **EMELINHO** (ay-meh-LEEN-hoh), **EMILINHO**—Portuguese; **EMILANO** (ay-mee-lee-AH-noh)—Spanish, Portuguese, and Italian; **EMILIAN**—Slavic; **EMILIO**—Spanish and Scandinavian; **MILO** (MY-loh or MEE-loh)—*Latin.* F

EMMANUEL, "ay-MAHN-yoo-ehl"—*Hebrew: "God is with us."* **MANUEL.** This is another name for Jesus Christ, and is also the name of a Christian saint. **MANNI(E), MANNY.** See also IMMANUEL. F

EMMET, "EHM-eht"—*Hebrew: "truth"; Anglo-Saxon: "industrious like the ant."* **EMMETT, EMMIT, EMMITT.** Football star Emmitt Smith has popularized this name. **EM.**

ENKAIN, "ehn-KAYN"—*Greek: "renewal."* **ENCAEN, ENCAIN, ENCAYN, ENKAYN.**

ENKI, "EHN-kee"—*Babylonian: "god of the waters."* Enki was one of the Big Three in the Babylonian triumvirate of gods. His waters of life fertilized the lands, quenched thirst, and delivered people from disease and demons.

ENNEAS, "EHN-ee-us"—*Greek: "nine."*

ENNIS, "EHN-ihs"—*Irish: "one choice."* Ennis is also a place name.

ENOS, "EE-nawss"—*Hebrew: "mortal man."* Enos was a grandson of Adam and Eve.

ENRICO, "ehn-REE-koh"—*Spanish version of Henry: "lord of the estate."* **ENRIQUE** (ehn-REEK-eh)—Portuguese. **RICO.** See also HENRY. F

EPHRAM. See EFRAM/EPHRAM.

Al, El

These are Arabic prefixes that mean "the," and sometimes for "of" or "from." You may add them to any name.

ERASMUS, "eh-RASS-mus"—*Greek: "lovable" or "lovely."* **ERASMO, ERASTUS.** Desiderius Erasmus was a Dutch Renaissance philosopher who reacted against the pomp and ceremony of the Catholic Church by encouraging people to read the Bible themselves and to practice a more personal faith; he even provided understandable translations of the Bible and other writings of antiquity. **RAS, RASTUS.**

EREK, "EH-rehk"—*Polish: "lovable."* F

ERIC, "EH-rik"—*traditionally Teutonic: "king"; Norse: "ever powerful"; but try Turkish: "plum" or Russian: "appointed by God."* **ERICH** (AIR-ihk)—German; **ERIK**—Scandinavian; **ERYK**—Polish. Scandinavian chieftains and Viking explorers have borne these names. **RICK, RICKY; RIK, RIKKY.** F

ERLEND, "EHR-lehnd"—*Norse: "to the chief"; Teutonic: "eagle."* **ERLAND.**

ERLING, "EHR-lihng"—*Norse: "descendant of the chief."* **ERLICH** (EHR-lihk).

ERNEST, "UR-nehst"—*German: "vigor"; Teutonic: "intense."* **EARNEST; ERNEK, ERNT**—Estonian, Latvian, and Lithuanian; **ERNESTO** (ur-NEHS-toh)—Spanish and Italian; **ERNST**—German, Eastern European, and Nordic; **ESTEK**—Polish. Oscar Wilde's last play was the very funny (and punny) *The*

Importance of Being Earnest, about the misadventures of two English college men. Ernest Hemingway was an American writer as famous for his real-life adventures as for his short stories and novels. F

ERROLL. See EARL.

ERSKINE, "EHR-skihn"—*Gaelic: "from the high cliffs."* KIN, KINNY.

ESAI, "EE-sye" or "ee-SAH-ee"—*Hebrew: "wealthy" or "gift."* YSAI (EE-sye), YSAIS (EE-size)—Spanish and Portuguese. This is a version of Jesse. See also JESSE.

ESTEBAN, "EHS-teh-bahn" or "ehs-teh-BAHN"—*Spanish version of Stephan: "crowned with laurel."* ESTEBE (ehs-teh-beh)—Basque; ESTEVAO (eh-steh-VAH-oh)—Portuguese; ISTVÁN (ihst-VAHN)—Hungarian. See also STEPHAN.

ESTES, "EHS-teez"—*Italian: "from the East"; Latin: "of a famous ruling house."* F

ETHAN, "EE-thun"—*Hebrew: "strength" or "permanence."* AITAN (EYE-tahn or EE-tahn)—Israeli.

ETSU, "EHT-soo"—*Japanese: "delight."*

ETU, "eh-TOO"—*Native American: "the sun."*

EUGENE, "yoo-JEEN" or "yoo-HAYN"—*Greek: "nobly born" or "well-born."* EUGEN (yoo-JEHN)—Swedish; EUGÉNE (yoo-ZHANE)—French; EVGENI(I) (ehv-GAY-nee), YEVGENI(I)—Russian; EWEN (YOO-ehn)—Scottish; JENÖ (YEH-noh)—Hungarian; OWEN—Welsh. Several saints and popes have had names on this list. GENE, GINO. F

EVAN, "EH-vun"—*Welsh: "youth"; Gaelic version of John: "God's gracious gift"; Irish:* "fair form," "fit," or "attractive"; *Celtic: "young warrior."* AOIBHEANN (ah-OY-vahn)—Irish Gaelic; EAVAN, EVIN; EYVIN (EH-vihn, AY-vihn, or EYE-vihn), EYVIND. Evan was an early Welsh ruler who decreed that all women in the kingdom belonged to the king. It took a thousand years for a queen to get her husband to repeal that law, and then only if men paid a tax. See also IVAN, JOHN.

EVANDER, "ee-VAN-dur" or "EHV-uhn-dur"—*Greek: "good man."* In the *Aeneid,* Evander is a Greek prince who gives shelter and aid to Aeneas and his men. A second Evander was a son of the god Hermes. A third Evander is first-rate boxer Evander Holyfield. F

EVANGELO, "eh-vahn-JEH/JAY-loh" or "eh-vahn-HEH-loh"—*Greek: "brings good news."* EVANGELIN, EVANGELIST. EVANO. F

EVERETT, "EHV-ur-eht"—*German: "strong as a boar"; English: "strong as a bear."* EVERHARD, EVERHARDT, EVERHART—German; EVERT—Swedish.

EZEKIEL, "ee-ZEE-kyehl" or "ee-ZEE-kee-ehl"—*Hebrew: "may God strengthen."* ÉZÉCHIEL (ay-ZAY-kee-ehl)—French; EZEQUIEL (ay-ZAY-kee-ehl)—Spanish; HESEKIEL. Ezekiel was a prophet in the Old Testament/Tanakh. ZEKE.

EZRA, "EHZ-rah"—*Hebrew: "help" or "helper."* ESDRA, ESDRAS, ESRA, EZER, EZZRET; ÚZAIR (ooh-zah-EER or ooh-ZAH-eer)—Arabic. Ezra is an Old Testament/Tanakh prophet who is also mentioned in the Qur'an.

THE TOP FIVE

FREDERICK
FRANK
FORREST
FRASIER
FOSTER

If the name you're looking for isn't here, see "P" and "V."

FABIAN, "FAY-bee-un" or "FAH-bee-ahn"—*Latin: literally "bean grower," but traditionally translated as "prosperous farmer."* **FABI, FABIYAN; FABIEN** (fah-bee-AHN)—French; **FABIO, FABIUS**—Italian. This was the name of a saint and a pope, as well as a Roman emperor. Quintus Fabius Maximus Verucosus was a second-century Roman general who used to win battles by annoying his enemies with delays and diddling around. Fabian was a popular singer-actor-heartthrob of the 1950s and 60s. **FAB.** F

FABRICE, "fah-BREESE" or "fah-BREE-cheh"—*Latin: "skilled crafter."* **FABRICIO** (fah-BREE-see-oh), **FABRICO** (fah-BREE-chee-oh); **FABRIZIO** (fah-BREE-tsee-oh)—Italian. **FAB, FABBIE, FABBY.** F

FABRON, "fah-BROHN" (hock up the "R")—*French: "blacksmith" or "metal worker."* **FAB, FABRAY, FABRIE, FABRY, FABBY.** F

FADIL, "fah-DEEL"—*Arabic: "generous."*

FAHD, "FAHD"—*Arabic: "lynx."*

FAIR, "FARE"—*English: "attractive," "light-colored," or "equitable."* **FAIRE.** Pick a definition (or two or three). F

FAIRLEY, "FARE-lee"—*English: "fair or beautiful meadow."* **FAIRLEA, FAIRLEE, FAIRLEIGH.**

FAISAL, "FYE-sahl" or "fah-ee-SAHL"—*Arabic: "decisive."* **FAYSAL.** Saudi kings have borne this name.

FALCHION, "FAWL-chawn"—*French.* This was a sword used in the Middle Ages that had a slightly curved blade. F

FALLOW, "FAL-oh"—*Old English: "tawny"; Modern English: "pale yellow" or "pale red"; both: "the fallow deer."* The fallow deer is a small deer that develops a white-spotted coat in the summer. F

FANCHON, "FAN-chon"—*French: "liberated."* **FANCHE, FANN.** F

FARADAY, "FARE-ah-day"—*Anglo-Saxon: "a day's journey," "travel day," "day traveller," etc.* Michael Faraday was a nineteenth-century English physicist who worked with electromagnetism. He gave his name to measuring units of certain types of electromagnetic and electric activity.

FARAMOND, "FAH-rah-mund"—*German: "guardian on the journey" or "protected traveller."* **FARAMAN, FARMAN, FARRIMAN.** Some legends say a man named Faramond was the first king of France. **FARR.**

FARAND, "FAH-rahnd" or "FARE-und"—Teutonic: *"attractive"* or *"pleasant."* **FARANT, FARRAND, FARRANT. RAN, RAND.**

FARANDO, "FARE-an-doh"—*Bretagne: "spinning"* or *"whirling."* **FARANDOLO** (FARE-an-doh-loh). "Farando" comes from "farandole," a type of fast dance with partners spinning one another in and out around the edge of a circle of dancers. F

FARID, "fah-REED"—*Arabic: "unique."* F

FARIS, "fah-REES" or "FARE-ihss"—*Arabic: "knight."* **FARRIS, FERIS, FERRIS.**

FARLEY, "FAHR-lee"—*English: "the far meadow."* **FARLEA, FARLEE, FARLEIGH.**

FARNELL, "fahr-NEHL" or "FAHR-nuhl"—*English: "from the ferny slope."* **FERNELD, FERNELL; FURNELD, FURNELL.**

FAROLD, "FARE-old"—*English/German: "mighty traveller."*

FARR, "FAHR"—*English: "traveller."*

FARRAR, "FAH-rahr" or "fah-RAHR"—*Latin: "blacksmith"* or *"iron."* **FERRER, FERRIER.** See also FARRIER.

FARRELL, "FARE-uhl"—*Celtic: "valorous."* **FARRIS, FERRIS.**

FARRIER, "FARE-ee-ur"—*English: "blacksmith (who shoes horses)."* **FARRER.** See also FARRAR.

FARUQ, "fah-ROOHK"—*Arabic: "he distinguishes truth from lies."* **FAHRUK, FAIRUK, FAROUK.** Saudi kings have borne this name.

FASTE, "FAH-steh"—*Norwegian: "firm."*

FAVIAN, "FAY-vee-an"—*Latin: "man of understanding."* **FAVIEN. FAVE.** F

FAXON, "FACKS-un"—*Teutonic: "famed for his hair."*

FEIVEL, "FAY-vehl" or "FYE-vehl"—*Yiddish: "God aids."*

FELIPE, "feh-LEE-peh"—*Spanish version of Phil(l)ip(p): "lover of horses."* **FILIPPO**—Italian. **LIPPO; PIP, PIPPO.** See also PHIL(L)IP(P). F

FELIX, "FEE-lix" or "fay-LEEKS"—*Latin: "happy"* or *"lucky."* **FELCHER**—German; **FELCIO** (FEHL-chyoh), **FELIKS** (FEHL-ihks)—Polish; **FELICIO** (feh-LEE-chee-oh or feh-LEE-see-oh)—Spanish and Italian; **FELICJAN** (feh-LEETS-yahn)—Slavic; **FELIZ** (fay-LEEZ)—Spanish and Portuguese. Felix is the Latin name for the cat family—large and small, wild and domestic. A *ton* of Christian saints have had these names, as have four popes. F

FELTON, "FEHL-tun"—*Norse: "from the hill town"; English: "from the field estate."*

FENTON, "FEHN-tun"—*English: "from the village by the marsh."*

FEODOR, "FAY-uh-dohr"—*from Theodore, Greek: "gift of God."* **FEDER, FEDOR, FYODOR, PHEODORE.** See also THEODORE. F

FERDINAND, "FUR-dih-nand" and "fur-dih-NAHND"—*Teutonic: "adventurous"; German: "horse"; Latin: "wild, headstrong."* **FERDYNAND, FERDYNANDY**—Slavic; **FERNAND, FERNANDO**—Spanish and Portuguese; **FERRAND** (feh-RAHN—make the "R" in your throat)—French; **FERRANDO** (feh-RAWN-doh)—Italian. Almost two dozen European kings have had the name Ferdinand, and it is a name that shows up frequently in Shakespeare's plays and English literature. Probably the best-known King Ferdinand was the one married to Queen Isabella: they funded Christopher Columbus's journeys. **FERD, FERDI(E), FERDY.**

FERGUS, "FUR-gus"—*Gaelic: "strong man."* **FARGUS, FARKUS; FEARGHUS** (FAR-yuss)—*Scottish Gaelic;* **FEARGUS** (FAR-gus)—*Irish Gaelic.*

FERRIS, "FARE-ihss"—*Latin: "iron"; Celtic: "rock."* **FARRIS.**

FESS, "FEHSS"—*French: "band."* In heraldry, the fesse was a horizontal band on the shield or coat of arms, usually in the center, covering one third of the surface.

FIDEL, "fee-DEHL"—*Latin: "faithful."* **FIDELIO** (fee-DAY-lee-oh)—*Italian;* **FIDELIUS.** F

FINLAY, "FIHN-lay"—*Gaelic: "fair-haired fighter."* **FINDLAY, FINDLEY, FINLEY.**

FINN, "FIHN"—*Irish: "fair"; Norse: "from Lapland" or "from Finland."* **FINGAL, FINGAR, FINIAN, FINNE, FYNN, FYNNE.** Several Christian saint names are on this list. F

FINTAN, "FIHN-tahn"—*Irish: "little fair one."* **FENTAN, FENTON, FINTON.**

FISHER, "FISH-ur"—*English: "one who fishes."* The legendary Fisher Kings are the descendants of Joseph of Arimathea, who brought the Holy Grail—a cup that was used, as legend had it, by Jesus at the Last Supper—out of the Holy Land and into Europe.

FISK(E), "FIHSK(-eh)"—*Swedish: "fisher."* **FISCUS**—Dutch; **FISKUS**—Norwegian, Finnish, and Danish.

FITCH, "FIHTCH"—*English: "ermine" and "marten."* Ermine and marten is not a comedy team; these are sweet little mammals once valued for their soft fur, which was so expensive it was generally used to line or accent only royal robes.

FITZGERALD, "fihts-JARE-ahld"—*Irish: "son of the spearman."* **FITZ GERALD.**

John Fitzgerald Kennedy's modern, revolutionary vision for America never wavered during his presidency.

FLETCHER, "FLEHCH-ur"—*French: "maker of arrows."* Fletcher Christian was an eighteenth-century English naval hero, or he was a mutineer, depending on whose stories you believe about the voyage of the HMS *Bounty* under the harsh Captain Bligh. **FLETCH.**

FLINT, "FLIHNT"—*English: "rock."*

FLOYD, "FLOYD"—*Welsh: "gray."* See also LLOYD.

FLYNN, "FLIHN"—*Gaelic: "son of the redhead."* **FLINN.**

FOLADE, "fohl-ah-DEH" or "fohl-AH-deh"—*African Yoruba: "honor is my crown."* F

FOLEY, "FOH-lee"—*Norse: "colt, foal."* **FÖLI** (FAW-lee)—*Finnish and Norwegian.*

FORBES, "FOHRBS"—*Irish Gaelic: "man of wealth."* This name was certainly true for twentieth-century American billionaire publisher Malcolm Forbes.

FORD, "FORD"—*English.* A ford is a shallow river or stream crossing.

FORREST, "FOR-est"—*English: "forest" or "forester."* **DE FOREST; FOREST, FORESTER, FORRESTER.** This is one of the most popular nature-based names for boys.

FOSTER, "FAWS-tur"—*Latin: "keeper of the forest."* **FORSTER. FOSS.**

FOWLER, "FOW-lur" ("FOW" like in "cow")—*English: "keeper or trainer of birds."*

FOX, "FAWKS"—*English: the fox.* **FOXE, FOXX.** Foxes are fabled for their speed and smarts. Ever since the debut of the TV series *The X Files*, this name has squeaked its way onto the popular name lists, since one of the main characters is FBI Special Agent Fox "Spooky" Mulder.

FRANCESCO, "frahn-CHEHS-koh"— *version of Francis: "free" or "a Frank."* FRANCESKAN, FRANCISKAN—Eastern European; FRANCISCUS—Dutch; FRANCISZKO (frahn-TSEESH-koh)—Polish; FRANSJEN (FRAWN-syen)—Scandinavian. FRANK. F

FRANCIS, "FRANT-sihs—*Teutonic: "free man" or "a Frank," a member of a European tribe.* FERENC, FERKO—Eastern European; FRANC (FRONK), FRANCO (FRONK-oh, FRANK-oh)—Italian and French; FRANCESCO (frahn-CHEHS-koh); FRANCHOT (FRAWN-shoh), FRANÇOIS (frawn-SWAH)—French; FRANCISCO (frahn-SEES-koh)—Spanish; FRANCISCUS (fran-SIHS-kuhss)—Dutch; FRANCISZK (frahn-TSEESH)—Slavic; FRANKEN, FRANTZ, FRANZ (FRANZ, FRAWNZ), FRANZEN—German; FRANS, FRANSEN—Scandinavian; PROINSIAS (PROYN-shee-ahss)—Irish Gaelic. Several saints have had names on this list. They include Saint Francis of Assisi, the patron saint of animals and ecology. He founded the Franciscan order, which stresses a simple faith and a simple life. There was also Saint Francis Xavier, cofounder of the Jesuit order, which stresses education, logic, and the practical applications of faith. FRANK, FRANKI(E), FRANKO. F

FRANK, "FRANGK"—*Germanic: "lance" or "spear."* FRANCUS—Latin. The Franks were a European tribe that arose around the Rhine River and caused a ruckus with the neighbors when they started to spread out or when anyone else tried to spread in. See also all the names beginning with "Fran-."

FRANKLIN, "FRANG-klihn"—*German:*

Fitz-

This is the Irish prefix that means "son of" or "child of" and can be used with any name you choose.

"free man" or "little Frank." In medieval Britain a franklin was a landlord who was a free man but not of noble birth. That is why in Geoffrey Chaucer's *Canterbury Tales,* the character named Franklin is a landowner. FRANK.

FRASIER, FRAZIER, "FRAY-shur" or "FRAY-zhur"—*French: "charcoal," "fresh," "curly haired," or "strawberry."* FRAISER, FRAIZER; FRASER, FRAZER. This is quite a variety of translations, depending upon which era of French vocabulary you choose, and which version you select of the six spelling possibilities offered here. Like most names, people don't know the actual meaning because the names have been in use for so long; pick the word-translation pair you like and enjoy it—that's all that matters. The TV character Frasier, who first appeared on *Cheers* before getting his own show, has made that spelling popular. FRASE, FRAZE.

FRED. See ALFRED, FREDERIC(K), MANFRED.

FREDERIC(K), "FREHD-eh-rihk"— *Teutonic: "peaceful ruler."* FEDERICO (feh-deh-REE-koh)—Italian; FREDEK (FREH-dehk)—Eastern European; FRÉDÉRIC (FRAY-day-reek)—French; FREDERICO (freh-deh-REE-koh)—Spanish; FREDERIK—Nordic; FREDRIC—Swiss; FREDRIK—

German; **FRYDERYK** (FRIHD-eh-rihk)—Polish. Many Germanic and Danish kings and nobles have had this name, as have many emperors and saints. Fred Astaire was a much-loved actor, dancer, choreographer, director, and producer, most remembered for the class and style he brought to a production, and for his breezy elegance in his dance routines. It is said that the idiot who did Astaire's first screen test commented, "Can't act. Can't sing. Slightly bald. Can dance a little." **FRED, FREDDI(E), FREDDY; RICK, RICKY, RIK, RIKKY.** F

FREEMAN, "FREE-mun"—*English: "one born free"* or *"one freed."* **FREEDMAN, FREEMON.**

FREEMONT, "FREE-mawnt"—*German: "freedom protector."*

FREWIN, "FREE-wihn," "FREH-wihn," or "FROO-wihn"—*English: "free friend"* or *"friend of freedom."* **FREEWER, FREEWIN, FREEWYN; FREWER, FREWYN.**

FRITZ, "FREETZ" or "FRIHTZ"—*Teutonic: "peaceful."* **FRID, FRIDS, FRITS.**

FULANI, "foo-LAH-nee"—*African Ibo: "my people, our people, us."* **FALANI.** This is a tribe name for a northern African people, who, because they more closely resemble Arabs than do the southern Africans, may have largely escaped the tragedy of slavery. F

FULLER, "FULL-er"—*Latin: "a fuller."* A fuller was someone who shrunk, thickened, pleated, and gathered cloth to give it body and fullness.

FULTON, "FUHL-tun"—*English: "fields of the village."*

THE TOP FIVE

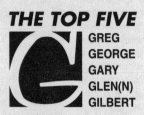

GREG
GEORGE
GARY
GLEN(N)
GILBERT

If the name you're looking for isn't here, see "J" and "Q."

GABE. See GABRIEL.

GABLE, "GAY-behl"—*English: a triangular feature in architecture; French: "little Gabriel."*

GABRIEL, "GAY-breel"—*Hebrew: traditionally "God is my strength," but also "servant of God."* **GABIREL** (gah-bih-rel)—Basque; **GÁBOR** (GAH-bor or gah-BOR)—Hungarian; **GABRI-EL**—Hebrew and Persian; **GAVIREL, GAVRIEL** (GAH-vree-ehl)—Hebrew; **GAVREL**—Russian; **JIBRIL**—Arabic. Gabriel is one of the four Archangels in Judeo-Christian and Islamic tradition. **GABBIE, GABBY; GABE, GABI(E).** F

GAD, "GAHD" or "GAWD"—*Arabic/Hebrew: "good fortune."* In the Old Testament/Tanakh, Gad is a son of Joseph. **GADMAN, GADMON.**

GAEL, "GALE"—*Welsh: "wild"; Scottish: "a highlander."* This is the collective term for Gaelic speakers in Scotland, Ireland, and the Isle of Man. See also GALE. F

GAETANE, "GAY-tun" or "guy-TAHN"—*Italian: "from central Italy."* **GAETANO.** F

GALE, "GAYL"—*Norse: "to sing"; Danish: "crow"; Icelandic: "fury" or "furious"; Irish: "vapor"; French: "gallant" or "brave."*

GAYLE. See also GAEL. F

GALEN, "GAY-lehn"—*Greek: "calm" or "healer"; English: "happy lands."* **GALAND, GALON, GALYN, GAYLON.** Galen was a second-century Greek physician who wrote the book on medicine—his guidelines were followed for the next seventeen centuries.

GALLET, "GAL-eht"—*French: "pebble" or "chip of stone."* **GALLETT.** This is a good name for your chip off the old block.

GALT, "GAWLT"—*Norse: "high ground."*

GALTON, "GAWLT-un"—*Norse: "highland village"; English: "a rented estate."*

GALVIN, "GAL-vihn"—*Gaelic: "sparrow."* **GALVAN, GALVEN. GAL.**

GALWAY, "GAHL-way"—*Irish: "stony."* **GALLOWAY.** County Galway is a district in Ireland.

GANNON, "GAN-un"—*Gaelic: "fair-complected."*

GARDINER, "GAHR-dih-nur"—*Latin: "keeper of the garden."* **GARDNER.**

GARETH, "GARE-eth"—*Welsh: "gentle."* **GEAORAITH** (GAY-oh-ryth), **GIORAITH** (GYOH-ryth)—Gaelic; **GWAREDD** (GWAH-rehth)—Welsh. In Arthurian legend, Sir Gareth was a young Scottish Knight of the

Round Table who remained faithful to Arthur when the rest of Gareth's clan plotted rebellion. His tender age when he came to Arthur's court led the elders of the Round Table to believe that he could not possibly be ready for knighthood. He begged to work in the kitchen, hoping for a chance to prove himself, and it wasn't long before he left the kitchen.

GARFIELD, "GAHR-feeld"—*English: "triangular field."*

GARMAN, "GAHR-man"—*English: "spearman."* **GARMON.**

GARNER, "GAHR-nur"—*Teutonic: "the defender."*

GARRETT, "GARE-eht"—*English: "hard spear."* **GARETT, GARRET, JARETT, JARRETT; GEAROID** (GARE-oit), **GIOROID** (GYOH-roit)—Irish Gaelic; **GERLAD**—Scottish. **GAR(R)Y.**

GARRICK, "GARE-ihk"—*Teutonic: "mighty warrior."* **GAR(R)Y; RICK.**

GARRISON. See GARSON.

GARSON, "GAHR-suhn" or "gahr-SAWN"—*French: "to protect" or "boy."* **GARÇON** (gahr-SOHN)—French; **GARRISON** (GAHR-eh-suhn). Writer and broadcaster Garrison Keillor is known for his stories from Lake Woebegon.

GARTH, "GARTH"—*Norse: "groundskeeper" or "garden."* Garth Brooks is a country singer.

GARTON, "GAHR-tun"—*English: "the triangular farmstead" or "the town near the firs."*

GARVEY, "GAHR-vee"—*Gaelic: "rough peace."*

GARVIN, "GAHR-vihn"—*English: "ally in battle."* **GARWIN.**

GARWOOD, "GAHR-wood"—*English: "the fir forest."*

GAR(R)Y, "GARE-ee"—*Old English: "triangle" or "spear."* The two meanings are related because spearheads are triangular. Actor Gary Cooper helped popularize this name. See also GARRETT, GARRICK.

GASPAR, "GAHS-pahr"—*Persian: "bringer of treasure."* **CASPAR, CASPER, KASPAR, KASPER; GAZSI** (GAH-zhee)—Hungarian. By tradition, one of the Three Wise Men from the East who visited the infant Christ in Bethlehem is called Gaspar.

GAVIN, "GAV-ihn"—*Welsh: "little hawk"; Teutonic: "a district officer."* **GAUVIN, GAVEN, GAWEN, GAWIN; GOWEN, GOWIN.** See also GAWAINE.

GAWAINE, "guh-WAYN"—*Welsh: "May hawk."* **GAVAIN, GAVIN, GAWAIN.** Sir Gawaine was a Knight of the Round Table.

GAYNOR, "GAY-nohr"—*Irish Gaelic: "son of the fair."*

GEDDES, "GEH-dehz"—*Norse: "spear" or "rod."*

GEE, "GHEE"—*Korean: "bravery."*

GEIR, "GARE" or "GHEER"—*Norse: "spear."*

GEN, "GHEN"—*Japanese: "spring."* "Spring" as in water, not as in the season.

GENE. See EUGENE.

GENTIAN, "JEN-shen"—*Latin.* The gentian is a mountain plant with tubular blue or purple flowers. King Gentius, an Ilyrian king of the second century B.C., was said to have discovered the medicinal applications of this plant.

GEOFFREY, "JEHF-ree"—*Teutonic: "peaceful district"; French: "pledge of* peace." **GEOFFROI** (ZHOH-frwah—hock up the "r" in your throat), **JEFFROI** (ZHEH-frwah—hock up the "r" in your throat)—French; **JAFFREZ** (ZHAH-fray)—Breton; **JEFFREY; JOFFREY** (JOF-ree or YOF-ree)—Northern and Eastern European; **SÉAFRA** (SHAY-frah), **SIOFRAI** (SHOH-fry)—Irish Gaelic; **SEAFRAID** (SHAY-frayd), **SEARTHRA** (SHARE-thrah)—Scottish Gaelic. Geoffrey Chaucer is the author of many classics, but is best known for *The Canterbury Tales,* a collection of stories told among a group of travellers on a pilgrimage to Canterbury. **GEOFF, JEFF.**

GEORGE, "JORJ" and "JOR-jah"—*Greek: "farmer."* **GEORDI, GEORDIE** (JOHR-dee)—Scottish; **GEORG** (GYORG)—Swedish; **GEORG** (geh-YORG), **JOREN** (YOH-rehn)—Danish; **GEORGES** (ZHORZH)—French; **GEORGI(I)** (geh-OHR-ghee/zhee), **GORYA**—Russian; **GEORGIOS** (JOR-jyohss), **IORGOS** (YOR-gohss)—Greek; **GEORGIUS**—Dutch; **GIORGIO** (JYOHR-jee-oh)—Italian; **GYÖRGY** (DTHOR-ghee or DTHOR-dthee), **GYURI** (DTHYOO-ree)—Hungarian; **JERZY** (YEHR-zee)—Polish; **JOJI**—Japanese; **JORAN** (YOH-rahn)—Scandinavian; **JORGE** (ZHOR-hay)—Portuguese; **JORGEN** (YOHR-ghen)—Scandinavian; **SEOIRSE** (SHORE-sheh or SHORSH), **SÉORAS** (SHOW-rawss)—Irish Gaelic. Saint George, the one who slew a dragon, is the patron saint of England (and Boy Scouts and soldiers), and his cult came into prominence with the returning crusaders. Several English kings have been named George. George Washington was the first president of the United States, from 1789 to 1796, and as a result, George became a very popular name in this country. Georges Seurat was a nineteenth-century painter who created pointillism, the painstakingly precise application of dots of color on a canvas, which created a wondrous and peculiar graininess. George Gershwin was a twentieth-century popular music composer. George Washington Carver was an educator and inventor. F

GERALD, "JEH-rahld" or "GHEH-rahld"—*Teutonic: "mighty with the spear."* **GARALD** (gah-RAHLD), **GAROLD**—Russian; **GEARÁRD** (GARE-ard), **GEARÓIDIN** (gare-oy-DEEN)—Irish Gaelic; **GÉRALD** (zhay-RAHL), **GÉRAUD** (zhay-ROH), **GIRAUD** (zhee-ROH)—French; **GERALDO** (heh-RAHL-doh)—Spanish; **GERROLD.** See also JERALD. F

GERARD, "jeh-RARD"—*Teutonic: "hard spear."* **GERARDO, GHERARDO**—Italian; **GERARDUS**—Latin; **GERART**—Old French; **GERHARD; GERRARD. GERRY.**

GERIK, "GARE-ihk"—*Polish: "spearman."*

G(U)ERIN, "ZHARE-an" or "GARE-an"—*French: "warrior."* **GARRA, JARRA, JERRIN.** Gerin of Chartres was a French nobleman who honored King Arthur.

GERMAINE, JERMAINE, "jur-MAYN" or "jare-MAYN"—*Latin: "full of buds"; Celtic: "of (the area of and around present-day) Germany."* **GERMAIN, JERMAIN.** F

GERMUND, "GARE-mund"—*Norse: "protect the world."*

GERONIMO, JERONIMO, "juh-RON-ih-mo"—*Native American Apache and Greek: "exalted name."* Geronimo, a great Native American leader and mystic, one of the Chiricahua Apaches who resisted the European-Americans' territorial claims for over forty years. See also JEROME.

GERRY. See GERARD, JEROME.

GERSHOM, "GHER-shum" or "gher-SHOM"—*Yiddish: "a stranger (t)here."*

GIDEON, "GIH-dee-on"—*Hebrew: "indomitable spirit."* The Gideon of Old Testament/Tanakh fame was a Hebrew judge and soldier.

GIFFORD, "GHIH-furd"—*German: "boldly given"* or *"bold gift."* **GIFFERD.**

GIL, "GHIL" or "GHEEL"—*Hebrew: "happiness."* See also GILBERT, GILBY, GILES, GILMER, GILMORE.

GILBERT, "GHIHL-burt"—*German: "bright pledge"* or *"bright promise."* **GILBERTO** (jeel-BARE-to)—Italian; **GILIBEIRT** (GHEEL-eh-bayrt)—Irish Gaelic; **GUILBERT** (GHEEL-bear—"r" in your throat)—French. Gilbert is the name of a saint. **BERT; GIL, GILI, GILLI(E), GILLY.**

GILBY, "GHIHL-bee"—*Norse/English: "estate of the hostage"; English: "estate near the ravine."* **GIL.**

GILEAD, "GHIH-lee-ahd"—*Arabic: "camel hump(s)."* **GILAD(I).** This is a place name for a favorite oasis on the Middle Eastern desert trade routes.

GILES, "JYLES," "JEELS," "GHYLES," or "GHEELS" (did I miss one?)—*Scottish: "servant"; Greek: "shield-bearer"; Latin: "kidlike."* **ÉIGID** (AY-gheed)—Irish Gaelic; **GILLE** (GHIHL-eh)—Scottish Gaelic; **GILLES:** (GHIL-us)—Dutch, (ZHEEL)—French; **GILETTE, GILLETTE.** The "kid" in the Latin derivation refers to a frisky goat baby, not to the modern term for children. Saint Giles was a Greek monk in the seventh century who left his Aegean home because of the ruckus his miracles supposedly caused. He went to France to become a hermit, but wasn't successful at that, especially after he performed miracles for Emperor Charlemagne. He is the patron saint of beggars and cripples, since he was both of these at one time

himself, and the patron saint of Edinburgh, Scotland. **GIL, GILLIS.**

GILFORD, "GHIHL-furd"—*English: "river-crossing (ford) at the ravine."*

GILMER, "GHIHL-mur"—*Norse/English: "famous hostage."* **GIL.**

GILMORE, "GHIHL-mohr"—*English: "ravine near the moors."* **GIL.**

GILON, "ghee-LAWN"—*Hebrew: "circle."*

GILROY, "GHIHL-roy"—*Gaelic/French: "servant of the king."*

GINGAN, "GHIN-ghan"—*Malaysian: "striped."* **GINGANG.**

GINO. See EUGENE.

GIOVANNI, "joh-VAH-nee"—*Italian version of Roman Jove: "of the god Jupiter."* Jupiter was the supreme male Roman god, the ruler of learning, good fortune, increase, prosperity, etc. See also JOVE. F

GIVON, "ghee-VAWN"—*Hebrew: "the hills"* or *"the heights."*

GLAS, "GLOSS"—*Irish: "grass."*

GLEN, "GLEHN"—*Scottish: "a glen or small valley."* **GLAN, GLENN, GLIN, GLYN.** John Glenn was the first American astronaut to orbit the Earth.

GODDARD, "GAWD-urd"—*Teutonic: "firm-natured."* **GOTARD, GOTHARD** (GAWTH-urd or GAWT-hurd). This name means firm as in one's approach to things, not as in one's muscle tone.

GODFREY, "GAWD-free"—*Teutonic: "God's peace."* **GODFRIED** (GAWD-freed)—Dutch; **GODOFREDO** (goh-doh-FRAY-doh)—Portuguese and Italian; **GOFFREDO** (goh-FRAY-doh), **GIOTTO** (JYOH-toh)—Italian; **GOFRAIDH** (GOH-fry)—Irish Gaelic; **GOT-**

SAINT NAMES

Catholic and Anglican tradition dictates that one of a child's names must be that of a saint or angel. In some European countries, it is traditional to name the child for the saint on whose feast day he or she was born, regardless of gender.

TFRID (GAWT-frihd)—Hungarian and Swedish; **GOT(T)FRIED**—German. King Godfrey de Bouillon was the French leader of the First Crusade.

GOLDWIN, "GOHLD-wihn"—*English: "golden friend."* **GOLDWYN.**

GORDON, "GORE-dun"—*Anglo-Saxon: "from the cornered-hill"; Scottish: "wooded dell"; Greek: "complex" or "intricate."* **GORDAN, GORDEN, GORDION, GORDIUS, GORTON.** The Gordian knot in Greek mythology was an extremely complicated knot tied by a king of Phrygia. It was rumored that whoever could untie the knot would be ruler of not only Phrygia, but the entire world. **GORDIE, GORDY, GORE.**

GORMAN, "GOHR-mun"—*Gaelic: "blue-eyed one."*

GOWAN, "GOW-un" ("GOW" like "cow")—*Irish: "calf or goat" or "a smith"; Cymric: "pure"; Norse: "golden."* **GOWALL, GOWER, GOWIN.**

GRADY, "GRAY-dee"—*Latin: "incline"; Gaelic: "illustrious."*

GRAHAM, "GRAY-am" or "GRAM"—*English: "from the gray hamlet/village," "from the village near gravel," or "bestowal of a home."* **GRAM, GRAEME, GRAENUM, GRANTHAM, GRANUM.**

GRAIG, "GRAYG"—*Irish: "a village."* **GRAIGUE. GREG.**

GRANGER, "GRAYN-jur"—*English: "farmer of grain"; Latin: "worker at the granary."* **GRANGE.**

GRANT, "GRANT"—*French: "to agree, bestow, or allow."* **GRANTLAND, GRANTLEN, GRANTLEY.** Ulysses S. Grant was President of the United States after a successful Union army career in the Civil War.

GREG. See GRAIG, GREGORY.

GREGORY, "GREH-goh-ree"—*traditionally, Greek: "vigilant"; but can also come from Irish: "village."* **GERGELY** (GARE-gheh-lee), **GERGO** (GARE-goh)—Hungarian; **GREAGÓIR** (GRAW-goyr)—Irish Gaelic; **GREGER**—Swedish; **GRÉGOIRE** (gray-GWAHR—"R" in the throat)—French; **GREGOOR** (greh-GOH-or)—Dutch; **GREGOR** (GREH-gohr)—Norwegian and Scottish Gaelic; **GREGORIO** (greh-GOH-ree-oh)—Portuguese and Italian; **GREGORIOS**—Greek; **GREGOS**—Danish; **GRIGOR, GRIGORI(I)** (gree-GOH-ree), **GRISHA**—Russian; **GRZEGORZ** (gr-ZHAY-gorzh)—Polish. More than a dozen popes and several saints have borne this name. The most influential was probably Gregory the First (d. 604), who reformed church administration, clarified the church's duties and goals, developed the Gregorian chant, and established the Gregorian calendar under which most of the world now operates. Gregory Peck is an award-winning stage and screen actor who always plays noble and powerful characters: check out *To Kill a Mockingbird, Gentlemen's Agreement,* and *The Omen.* **GREG, GREGG.**

GRESHAM, "GREHSH-um"—*Anglo-Saxon: "from the grazing land."*

GRIFFIN, "GRIH-fihn"—*Greek.* **GRIFFON, GRYFFON, GRYPHON.** In Greek mythology, the griffin was a beast that was said to have the body of a lion, signifying strength and nobility, the wings of an eagle, signifying swiftness, and sometimes an eagle's head, signifying intelligence.

GRIFFITH, "GRIHF-ihth"—*Welsh: "lord of the griffins"; Celtic: "red-head."* **GRIFFETH, GRYFETH, GRYFITH; GRYFUDD** (GRIHF-uth)—*Welsh.*

GUILLERME, "ghih-LAYRM" or "ghee-YAYRM"—*version of William: "resolute protector."* **GUGLIELMO** (goo-lee-EHL-moh)—Italian; **GUILHERME** (ghee-LAYRM)—Portuguese; **GUILLAUME** (ghee-LAWM/YAWM)—French; **GUILLERMO.** See also WILLIAM.

GUNNAR, "GUH-nahr"—*Teutonic: "bold warrior."*

GUNT(H)ER, "GUN-tur" and "GOON-tur" or "GUN-thur" and "GOON-ther"—*Norse/Gaelic: "bold knight" or "brave warrior."* In Arthurian legend, Gumphar is the king of the Orkneys, a group of islands off of Scotland.

GURI, "GOO-ree" or "goo-REE"—*Hebrew: "little lion cub."*

GURION, "GOO-ree-awn"—*Hebrew: "young lion."*

GUS. See AUGUST, GUSTAV.

GUSTAV, "GOO-stahv"—*Teutonic: "staff of the gods."* **GUSTAOF** (goo-STAWF)—Danish; **GUSTAVE, GUSTAVO; GUSZTÁV** (GOO-shtav)—Polish. **GUS, GUSTO.**

GUTHRIE, "GUHTH-ree"—*Celtic: "war hero" or "serpent."* Guthrum, king of East Anglia in the late ninth century, made treaties with Alfred the Great and converted to Christianity. Woody Guthrie and his son, Arlo, had separate careers as folksingers/songwriters.

GUY, "GHY" or "GHEE"—*French: "guide"; Hebrew: "valley."* Saint Guy is patron saint of comedians and dancers. *Guy Mannering,* a novel by Sir Walter Scott, introduced the contemporary meaning of "a guy," as in "one of the guys."

GWYN, "GWIHN"—*Celtic: "blessing."* **GUINN, GWIN, GWYNN(E).** F

THE TOP FIVE

HA(Y)DEN
HARRISON
HARLEY
HAMILTON
HAKIM

If the name you're looking for isn't here, see the vowels and "J."

HABIB, "hah-BEEB"—*Tunisian and Kiswahili: "beloved."*

HADAR, "hah-DAHR"—*Hebrew: "ornament" or "glory."* F

HADDAD, "hah-DAHD"—*Arabic: "the smith."*

HADDEN, "HAD-ehn"—*English: "of the moors."* **HADEN, HAYDEN.**

HADDIN, "HAD-ihn"—*Scottish: "dwelling" or "a holding."* **HADIN.**

HADDON, "HAD-ohn"—*Scottish: "heathland."* **HADDEN.**

HADEN. See HADDEN.

HADI, "HAH-dee"—*Arabic: "guide to righteousness."* F

HADID, "hah-DEED"—*Arabic: "iron."*

HADLEY, "HAD-lee"—*Scottish: "heather meadow."* **HADLEA, HADLEE, HADLEIGH.**

HADRIAN, "HAY-dree-un"—*from Adrian: "of the Adriatic" or "dark-haired."* **HADRIEN.** Hadrian's Wall is a landmark in Britain, placed there by the Roman Emperor Hadrian to mark the northernmost boundary of his territory in A.D. 122. See also ADRIAN.

HADWIN, "HAD-wihn"—*English: "ally in war."* **HADEWIN, HADEWYN; HADWYN.**

HAGEN, "HAH-ghehn," occasionally "HAY-ghen"—*Irish: "little one" or "young one."* **HAGMAN.**

HAI, "HAH-ee" as one syllable—*Vietnamese: "sea."*

HAIDAR, "HYE-dahr"—*Sanskrit: "lion."*

HAIDUK, "HY-dook"—*Hungarian: "the drover."* **HAJDUK.** A drover is either a small fishing boat with a drift net or someone who moves flocks of animals to market.

HAIG, "HAYG"—*English: "the hedged place."*

HAINES, "HAYNZ"—*Teutonic: "the vined cottage."* **HAINEY, HANES, HANEY, HAYNES.**

HAJI, "HAH-jee"—*Swahili: "born during the pilgrimage to Mecca."*

HAKAN, "hah-KAHN"—*Native American: "fiery."*

HAKEEM, HAKIM, "hah-KEEM"—*Arabic: "the wise one."* Hakeem Olajuwon is a basketball superstar.

HALBERT, "HAL-burt"—*English/German: "brilliant hero."* **HALBARD(E), HALBERD.**

HALE, "HAYL"—*English: "safe and sound" or "healthy"; Norse: "hero."* **HALEY.**

HALFORD, "HAHL-furd" or "HAL-furd"—English: "hill slope river-crossing." **HALLIFORD.**

HALIL, "hah-LEEL"—Hebrew: "flute." **HALLIL, HALLILL.**

HALIM, "hah-LEEM"—Arabic: "gentle" or "patient"; Swahili: "tender." F

HALL, "HAHL"—English: "the master's house."

HALLEY, "HAH-lee"—Norse: "heroic"; English: "covered" or "the meadow by the manor." **HALLEIGH, HALLY.** Sir Edmund Halley is the discoverer of the famous comet that returns every seventy-five years and bears his widely mispronounced name. F

HALOKE, "hah-LOW-keh"—Native American Navajo: "shimmering salmon." F

HALSE, "HAHLS"—Old English: "embrace." **HALSEY.**

HALSTEAD, "HAHL-stehd"—English: "of the manor farm" or "of the manor cottage." **HALSBY.**

HALSTON, "HAHL-stun"—English: "hill-slope estate," "village near (or by) the manor," or "hallowed stone." **HALSTEN.** See also ALSTON.

HALSY, "HAHL-see"—English: "the hallowed island." **HALDSEY.**

HALTON, "HAHL-tun"—English: "hill-slope town."

HALVOR, "HAHL-vor"—Norse: "strong as a rock." **HALVARD.**

HAMADI, "huh-MAH-dee"—Swahili: "praise." **HAMIDI.**

HAMAL, "hah-MAHL"—Arabic: "lamb."

HAMAR, "HAH-mahr"—Norse: "ingenuity."

HAMID, "hah-MEED"—Arabic: "praise-worthy." F

HAMIEL, "HAH-mee-ehl"—Sumerian: "bronze angel(?)." **HAMI-EL.** Traditionally, Hami-el is the angel who took the Old Testament/Tanakh prophet Enoch to heaven.

HAMILTON, "HAM-ihl-tun"—English: "home town" or "mountain hamlet." **HAMIL(L).** Alexander Hamilton was a flamboyant American revolutionary, philosopher, and writer who organized and ran the United States treasury.

HAMLET, "HAM-leht"—German: "little home"; Scandinavian-Gaelic: "descendant of the ancestors." **HAMNET** (HAM/HAHM-neht)—Anglo-Saxon; **HAMO** (HAH-moh), **HAMON**—German. The tragic life of Hamlet, prince of Denmark, was made into a play by William Shakespeare—who, by the way, named his own son Hamnet.

HAMLIN, "HAM-lihn"—English: "home by the brook." **HAMBLEN, HAMBLIN, HAMBLING, HAMBLYN; HAMLYN, HAMMELIN.**

HAMMOND, "HAM-und"—English: "mountain home"; Hebrew: "warm" or "swarthy."

HAMPTON, "HAMP-tun"—English: "home in the valley" or "home in the clearing." **HAMPDEN, HAMPDON.**

HANAN, "HAH-nahn"—Hebrew: "grace."

HANANEL, "HAH-nah-nehl"—Hebrew: "God is gracious." F

HANFORD, "HAN-furd"—Anglo-Saxon: "high river-crossing."

HANIF, "hah-NEEF"—Kiswahili and Moroccan: "true believer." In Islam, a Hanif is a true believer in the god of Abraham and Ismail, even if the person is not a Muslim. F

HANK. See HENRY.

HANLEY, "HAN-lee"—*Anglo-Saxon: "the high meadow."* **HANLEA, HANLEE, HAN-LEIGH; HENLEIGH, HENLEY.**

HANNIBAL, "HAN-ih-bul"—*Assyrian: "gift of Baal,"* a god of fertility and fortune. **HANBEL, HANIBAL.** Hannibal was a Carthaginian general who gave the Roman Empire heck in the third century B.C. You've probably heard the stories about him and his army crossing the Alps with elephants—talk about packing big trunks for a trip! **HAN.**

HANS. See JOHN.

HANTAY, "HAHN-tay"—*Native American Sioux: "cedar trees."*

HARDEN, "HAHR-dehn"—*English: "the hare's den" or "the hare's hollow."* **HARDIN. HARRY.**

HARDING, "HAHR-ding"—*English: "brave man's son."* **HARRY.**

HARDWIN, "HAHR-wihn"—*Celtic: "courageous friend."* **HARDWYN. HARRY.**

HARDY, "HAHR-dee"—*French: "to become bold"; English: "robust, strong."* **HARRY.**

HAREL, "HAIR-ehl"—*Hebrew: "mountain of God."* **HARRELL.**

HARFORD, "HAHR-furd"—*English: "hares at the river-crossing."* **HARRY.**

HARGROVE, "HAHR-grohv"—*English: "hare's grove."* **HARRY.**

HARI, "HAH-ree"—*Hindu: "dark" or "tawny."* F

HARIM, "hah-REEM"—*Hebrew: "flat-nosed."* **HAREEM.**

HARITH, "HAH-reeth"—*Moroccan: "farmer."*

HARKER, "HAHR-kur"—*Scottish: "listener."* **HARRY.**

HARLAN, "HAHR-lahn"—*Teutonic: "from the battle lands."* **HARLAND. HARRY.** See also HARLEY.

HARLEY, "HAR-lee"—*English: "hare's meadow"; German: "field of flax or hemp."* **HARLAN, HARLEA, HARLEIGH. HARRY.** F

HARLOW, "HAHR-loh"—*Celtic: "fortified hill."* **HARLOWE.** Actress Jean Harlow was the first platinum blonde; her line from *Hell's Angels*—"Excuse me while I slip into something more comfortable . . ."—became an instant classic. **HARRY.**

HARMATAN, "HAHR-mah-tan" or "hahr-mah-TAN"—*African: "winter's west wind."* This is a dry, sandy wind that blows from the interior to the West African coast in December, January, and February.

HARMON, "HAHR-mun"—*Greek: "agreement, concord."* **HARMONIOUS, HARMONIUS.** F

HAROLD, "HAIR-old"—*Norse: "war chief"; Anglo-Saxon: "army commander"*—all in all, a take-charge type. **ARALT**—*Irish;* **HARALD, HARRALD, HARROLD; HERALDO** (heh-RAHL-doh)—*Portuguese.* Two kings of the Saxons were named Harold—the last one fought at the Battle of Hastings against the Norman invaders in 1066. Norwegian kings have also borne this name, and the Norwegian Harold III even fought the English Harold II. **HARRY.** F

HARPER, "HAHR-pur"—*English: "the harp player"; Latin: "sickle-wielding."* **HARRY.**

HARRIS, "HARE-ihss"—*Welsh: "son of Harry."* **HARRY.**

HARRISON, "HARE-ihss-sun"—*Welsh: "son of Harry's son(!)."* Harrison Ford was an American leading man in silent pictures. Oh, yeah, and there's another Harrison Ford who exploded onto the big screen in the 1970s and hasn't stopped making blockbusters since. **HARRY.** See also HARRIS.

HARRY, "HARE-ee"—*English: "to lay waste to"* or *"to ravage."* This is also a diminutive of European names beginning with "Har-."

HART, "HART"—*English: "hart deer"* or *"stag."* A hart deer is a mature male deer more than five years old. Thus, his antlers are quite stunning. **HARRY.**

HARTFORD, "HART-furd"—*English: "hart deer at the river-crossing."* **HARRY.**

HARTLEY, "HART-lee"—*English: "hart deer meadow."* **HARTLEA, HARTLEE, HARTLEIGH. HARRY.**

HARTMAN, "HAHRT-man"—*German: "strong man."* **HARRY.**

HARTWELL, "HAHRT-wehl"—*English: "the deer's spring."* **HARWELL, HARWILL. HARRY.**

HARTWOOD, "HART-wood"—*English: "hart deer forest."* **HARRY.**

HARU, "HAH-roo"—*Japanese: "born in Spring."*

HAR(O)UN, "hah-ROON"—*Arabic: "exalted."* See also AARON.

HARVEY, "HAHR-vee"—*French: "bitter"; Bretagne: "battle-worthy."* **HERVÉ** (air-VAY—"r" in the back of the throat)— French; **HERVEY.** Saint Harvey was a blind sixth-century monk. He is the patron saint of sight and the sightless. **HARRY; HARVE, HERVE.**

HAS(S)AD, "hah-SAHD"—*Turkish: "harvest."*

HAS(S)AN, "hah-SAHN"—*Arabic: "handsome."* **HASANI**—Swahili; **HUSAIN, HUSAYN, HUSSAIN; HUSANI**—Kiswahili; **HUSSEIN**— Arabic/Middle Eastern.

HASHEM, "HAH-shem"—*Algerian: "destroyer of evil."* **HASHIM.**

HASIN, "HAH-seen"—*Hindu: "laughter."*

HASKELL, "HASK-ehl"—*French: "ashkettle."* **ASCHILL, ASKELL; HASCHILL, HASKEL.** Ash was used in soapmaking. Thus, a haskell is a maker of cosmetics.

HASNI, "HAHS-nee"—*Arabic: "beautiful."* **HOSNI.** F

HATIM, "hah-TEEM"—*Arabic: "judge."*

HATSU, "HAHT-soo"—*Japanese: "first born."*

HAVASU, "HAH-vah-soo"—*Native American Hokan: "willow trees."* Havasu is a tribe name for a group of farming people in northwestern Arizona.

HAWLEY, "HAW-lee"—*English: "hawk's clearing."* **HAWLEA, HAWLEE, HAWLEIGH; HAWKLEIGH, HAWKLEY.**

HAYDEN, "HAY-dehn" or "HYE-dehn"— *English: "hay meadow"* or *"grassland."* **HAYDN** (HYE-dehn)—German; **HAYWOOD.** Franz Josef Haydn was a classical composer best known for his symphonies. **HAY, HAYES.** See also HADDEN.

HAYES, "HAYZ"—*English: "from the grasslands"* or *"hunter."* See also HADDEN.

HAYWOOD, "HAY-wood"—*English: "surrounded by forest."* **HEYWOOD.**

HEATH, "HEETH"—*Scottish: the heather flower or heather plant.* F

HECTOR, "HEHK-tur"—*Greek: "to hold*

fast" or *"anchor."* **EACHANN** (AYKH-awn— "KH" in your throat)—Scottish Gaelic; **EACHTAR** (AYKH-tahr—"KH" in your throat)—Irish Gaelic; **ECTOR**. In Homer's epic poem the *Iliad,* Hector was the Trojan soldier who was killed by Achilles. In Arthurian legend, the foster father of King Arthur was Sir Ector, and there was also a knight at Arthur's Round Table named Ector.

HEDLEY, "HEHD-lee"—*English: "meadow of young sheep."* **HEDLEA, HEDLEE, HEDLEIGH.**

HELAKU, "heh-LAH-koo"—*Native American: "a sunny day."*

HELIOS, "HE-lee-ohss"—*Greek: "the Sun."*

HELMUT, "HEHL-mut"—*Teutonic: "warrior's fury."* **HELMER.**

HENRY, "HEHN-ree"—*Teutonic: "owner of the estate" or "lord of the estate."* **ANRÁI** (ahn-RAH-ee)—Irish Gaelic; **ENRICO** (ehn-REE-koh)—Italian and Spanish; **HEINRICH** (HINE-rihk), **HEINRICK**—German; **HEINRIK** (HINE-rihk); **HENDRIK** (HEHN-drihk)— Dutch; **HENERIK** (HEH-neh-rihk)—Danish; **HENNING; HENRI** (on-REE)—French; **HENRYK**—Polish. French, English, and German kings have all been named Henry. The most famous of them is probably Henry VIII of England who, in his obsession with producing a male heir, broke from the Catholic Church and founded the Anglican Church so that he could divorce wives who "failed to produce." **HANK; HEN, HENNI(E), HENNY.** F

HERBERT, "HUR-burt"—*Teutonic: "bright warrior" or "illustrious warrior."* **EBER, EBERT, EBERTO**—Spanish and Portuguese; **HARBERT; HEBER** (ee-BARE), **HEBERT**— French; **HERBERTO, HERIBERTO**—Italian;

HOIREABARD (HOY-rah-bahrt)—Irish Gaelic. Several Christian saints are named Herbert. **BERT, BERTIE, BERTY; HERB, HERBIE, HERBY.**

HERMAN, "HUR-mun" or "HARE-mahn"— *Teutonic: "warrior" or "soldier."* **ERMAN** (AIR-mahn), **ERMANNO, ERMANO** (air-MAH-noh), **ERMANOS**—Portuguese, Italian, and Basque; **HEREMON, HERMON**—Irish; **HERMANN, HERMON; HERMANO** (air-MAH-noh), **HERMANOS**—Spanish. **HERM, HERMIE, HERMY.**

HERMES, "HUR-meez"—*Greek: "messenger of/from the gods," "swift," or "the marker."* Hermes was the Greek god who handled Olympian communication. He was fleet of foot, quick of wit, very creative and intelligent, and somewhat of an Olympian mischief-maker. Hermes is associated with the planet Mercury, the accumulation of information, and travel.

HERRICK, "HARE-ihk"—*German: "army leader."* **HARRICK.**

HERSCHEL, "HUR-shell"—*German: "deer."* **HERSHEL, HERSHEY.** As a chocolate lover, I must honor the Hershey family of Pennsylvania, who brought us the first American chocolate factory.

HERSH, "HURSH"—*Yiddish: "buck."* **HERSCH, HIRSCH, HIRSH.** This means buck as in male deer, not as in dollars.

HERWIN, "HER-wihn"—*Teutonic: "lover of battle."* **ERWIN.**

HESPERUS, "HEHS-pur-uhss"—*Greek: "Evening Star" or "western star."* **HESPERIO, HESPERIUS.** Hesperus was a Greek deity represented as a boy with a torch to watch over a world in darkness. He was said to be the father of the Hesperides, the nymphs of the west. F

HEWETT, "HYOO-eht"—*French: "little Hugh."* See also HUGH.

HI, HY, "HEE"—*Vietnamese: "hope."* See also HIRAM/HYRAM.

HIDALGO, "hee-DAHL-goh" or "ee-DAHL-goh"—*Spanish: "son of something."* The "something" in question is a parent who holds some kind of rank above that of a common citizen. Hidalgo is one of the minor planets in orbit between Mars and Jupiter, but quite extraordinary in that its orbit can stretch out to Saturn and back.

HIDEAKI, "hee-day-AH-kee"—*Japanese: "wise" or "clever."*

HIERONYMOS, "hye-ROH-nee-muhs"—*Latin: "exalted or sacred name."* **GERONIMO**—Native American; **HIERONIM**—Polish. Hieronymus Bosch was a Dutch Renaissance painter whose works were satirical, bizarre, and grotesque, really grotesque—like a train wreck: it's horrible, but you can't stop looking at it. He is often copied merely for the shock value, but imitators miss the moral in his art. See also HIRAM/HYRAM, JEROME.

HIL(L)EL, "hee-LEHL"—*Arabic: "the new moon"; Hebrew: "renowned."*

HILL, "HILL"—*English: "hill."* **BARQA, KEREB** (KEH-rehb), **TALL, TALLAT** (taw-LAHT), **TARAQ**—Arabic; **CERRO** (SEH-roh), **COLINAS** (koh-LEE-nahs), **CUCHILLAS** (koo-CHEE-yahs)—Spanish; **CHAPADA** (chah-PAH-dah)—Portuguese; **COTEAU** (koh-TOH)—French; **GHAT** (GAWT)—Hindu; **SLIEVE** (SLEEVE, SLIVE)—Gaelic; **VOZVYSHENNOST** (voze-VEE-sheh-nawst)—Russian.

HILLAIRE, HILLARY, "hih-LARE" or "ee-LARE" and "HIH-lah-ree"—*Latin: "cheerful."* **HILAIRE, HILARI(E), HILLARI(E), HILARY; ILARI** (ee-lah-ree)—Basque. Hilary was a fifth-century saint. F

HILLIARD, "HIHL-yurd"—*Teutonic: "protector in war."*

HILTON, "HIHL-tun"—*English: "the hilltop town."*

HINTO, "HIHN-toh"—*Native American Sioux: "blue."*

HINUN, "hee-NOON"—*Native American: "clouds and rain."*

HIRANY, "hee-RAH-nee"—*Sanskrit: "golden."* **RANY.** F

HIRAM, HYRAM, "HYE-rum"—*version of Jeremiah: "exalted brother" or "God will uplift."* **HIEREMIAS** (hye-eh-REHM-ee-ahs)—Greek. In the Old Testament/ Tanakh, King Hiram of Tyre, in what is now Lebanon, was friendly to both King David and to David's son and successor, Solomon. Hiram provided cedar wood for their homes and palaces. **HY.** See also JEREMIAH, HIERONYMOS.

HIROSHI, "hee-ROH-shee"—*Japanese: "generous."*

HISHAM, "hee-SHAHM"—*Arabic: "generosity."*

HO'ANO, "HOH AH-noh"—*Hawaiian: "divine one."*

HOBART, "HOH-bahrt"—*Anglo-Saxon combination of Hugh + Bert: "bright heart," "bright soul," or "bright mind."* See also HUGH, HUBERT.

HOD, "HAWD" or "HODE"—*Hebrew: "vigorous" or "splendid."*

HOGAN, "HOH-ghan"—*Native American Navajo: "dwelling" or "home"; Native American: "Morning Star"; Irish Gaelic: "youth."*

HOKU, "HOH-koo"—*Hawaiian: "star."* See also STAR. F

HOLBROOK, "HOHL-brook"—*English: "stream in the valley" or "sheltered stream."*

HOLDEN, HOLDIN, "HOLE-dun"—*English: "deep valley"; Teutonic: "kindly."* Holdin was king of a Celtic tribe. The central character in J.D. Salinger's classic novel *Catcher in the Rye* is named Holden Caulfield, who in turn got his name from actors William Holden and Joan Caulfield—two names on a theater marquee in Salinger's neighborhood!

HOLLAND, "HAWL-end"—*Dutch: an old name for the Netherlands.*

HOLLEB, "HOH-lehb" or "HAW-lehb"—*Polish: "like a dove."*

HOLLIS, "HAW-lihss"—*English: "holly tree" or "holly shrub."* **HOLLEN, HOLLIN, HOLLING, HOLLINGER** (HAW-lihn-jur); **HOLLEY.** F

HOLM, "HOHLM"—*English: "the holm oak tree."*

HOLMES, "HOHLMZ"—*Norse: "meadow"; Anglo-Saxon: "little island(s)."* **HUME.**

HOLST, "HOHLST"—*English: "hidden."*

HOLT, "HOHLT"—*English: "wooded hill" or "otter's den."*

HONON, "hoh-NOHN"—*Native American Miwok: "bear."* See also BEAR. F

HONOR, "AWN-er"—*Latin: "honor" (what'd ya think?).* **HONORÉ.** This name refers to honor either in the sense of personal integrity or in the sense of a reward or recognition. It is another one of those Puritan virtue names. F

HONOVI, "hoh-NOH-vee"—*Native American Hopi: "the strong deer."* F

-holm

"-holm" is a Nordic suffix that means "meadow" or "field." It can be attached to the end of any name.

HORACE, "HOR-us"—*Latin: "timekeeper"; Egyptian: the god Horus.* **HORACIO** (oh-RAH-see-oh)—*Spanish;* **HORATIO; HORATIUS**—*German;* **HORATS** (oh-RAHTS or hoh-RAHTS)—*Dutch;* **ORACIO, ORAZIO**—*Italian.* A great Roman poet was named Horace (Horatius). See also HORUS.

HORST, "HOHRST"—*German: "leap."*

HORTON, "HOHR-tun"—*English: "from the gray manor."*

HORUS, "HOR-us"—*Egyptian: "sun god."* **HORIS.** Horus, the child of Isis and Osiris, was the Egyptian god of the Sun. He was shown as having the head of a hawk and the body of a human. See also HORACE.

HOSEA, "HOH-say-ah" or rarely "HOH-say"—*Hebrew: "salvation."* **HOSHEA**—*Israeli;* **JOSÉ** (HOH-say)—*Spanish and Portuguese.* Hosea is one of the prophets of the Old Testament/Tanakh.

HOSHI, "HOH-shee"—*Japanese: "star."* See also STAR. F

HOUGHTON, "HOH-tun" or "HOW-tun"—*English: "town on the bluffs."*

HOUSTON, "HYOO-stun"—*Teutonic/English: "spirited or spiritual town" or "stone of knowledge"; Celtic: "brimstone, firestone," or "inspirational place"; Anglo-Saxon: "mountain town."* **UISDEAN** (YOOSdyahn)—Scottish Gaelic. The town in Texas is named for General Sam Houston, who was president of the independent Republic of Texas in the mid-nineteenth century.

HOWAKAN, "hoh-wah-KAHN"—*Native American Sioux: "voice of mystery(-ies)."* **HOWAH, WAKAN.** This means that he speaks of things a holy man would know.

HOWARD, "HOW-urd"—*English: "guardian of the soul/heart" or "keeper/warden of hogs"; Teutonic: "chief guardian."* **HOVARD.** Howard Hughes was a twentieth-century actor, director, producer, inventor, adventurer, and magnate who ended up the wealthiest and weirdest recluse in the world. Oliver Otis Howard was a Union army general during the Civil War. After the war, he founded Howard University in Washington, D.C., a school of higher learning for the newly freed slaves. **HOWE, HOWES, HOWIE.**

HOWE, "HOW"—*German: "eminence."* **HOWES.** See also HOWARD.

HOWEL(L), "HOW-el" or "HOH-ehl"—*English: "hill where boars roam" or "hill where hogs graze"; Cymric: "alert one"; German: "to smooth."* In Arthurian legend, King Howel ruled over the Armorican Britons, a Celtic tribe that had conquered modern-day Brittany/Bretagne.

HOWI, "HOH-wee"—*Native American Miwok: "the turtle dove."*

HOYT, "HOYT"—*Irish: "spirit" (as in soul, not as in ghost); Scottish: "to limp."* **HOYTE.**

HUBERT, "HYOO-burt"—*German: "bright heart"; Teutonic: "bright mind."* **HOBARD, HOBART; HOIBEARD** (HOY-bahrt)—Irish Gaelic; **HUBER, UBER; HUBERTO**—Spanish;

UBERT, UBERTO—Italian. Saint Hubert is the patron saint of hunters. Hubert Van Eyck was one of the Flemish Renaissance greats. He is credited with the invention of oil painting, for which his right arm was preserved as a holy relic. Yuk! **BERT, HUBE, HUBIE, HUGH.**

HUGH, "HYOO"—*German: "heart" or "soul"; Teutonic: "mind" or "intelligence."* **AODH** (AH-oy)—Irish Gaelic; **HUGHES.** An English saint and a French ruler share the name Hugh. Irish rebels Aodh (Hugh) O'Neill and Aodh Rua (Red Hugh) O'Donnell started an insurrection during Queen Elizabeth I's reign, and Aodh has been the name of several regional Irish chieftains. **HUGHIE, HUEY.** See also HEWETT, HUBERT.

HUGO, "HYOO-goh" or "OO-goh"—*Teutonic: "intelligent" or "spirited."* **HUGUE(S)** (OOG)—French.

HUMAM, "HOO-mam"—*Arabic: "courageous."*

HUMBERT, "HUHM-burt"—*Teutonic: "bright or shining home"; Germanic: "bright or shining giant."* **HUMBERTO** (huhm-BARE-toh), **UMBERTO.** At least two kings of Italy have borne this name. **HUM.**

HUME, "HYOOM"—*Teutonic: "lover of home."*

HUMPHREY, "HUM-free"—*French/German mix: "peace through power," or vice-versa.* **HUMFREDO** (hum-FRAY-do)—Portuguese; **HUMFREY, HUMFRY; ONFREDO, ONOFRE** (oh-NOH-fray)—Spanish; **UNFRAI** (OON-fry)—Irish Gaelic. Several Christian saint names are on this list. Actor Humphrey Bogart often played the likeable, or at least honorable, tough guy in several of *the* classic films of all time.

HUNT, "HUHNT"—*English: "to hunt" (duh).* **HUNTER.**

HUNTLEY, "HUHNT-lee"—*English: "hunter's clearing."* **HUNTLEA, HUNTLEE, HUNTLEIGH.**

HURACAN, "HUH-rah-kahn"—*Mayan: "Triple Heart of the Universe."* Huracan was the supreme Mayan deity. This is the root for our present-day word "hurricane."

HURLEY, "HER-lee"—*Gaelic: "sea tides."*

HURST, "HURST" (like "burst")—*Anglo-Saxon: "forest dweller."*

HUSAM, "HOO-sahm" or "hoo-SAHM"—*Arabic: "sword."*

HUSSEIN, "hoo-SAYN"—*Arabic: "good."* **HOSEIN, HOSSEIN, HUSAIN, HUSSAIN.** In the Muslim world, this is a common name, like John and Christopher are in the United States. See also HAS(S)AN.

HUTTON, "HUH-ton"—*English: "estate on the ridge."*

HUXLEY, "HUCKS-lee"—*English: "meadow of ash trees" or "hawk's meadow or clearing."* **HUXLEA, HUXLEIGH.**

HYATT, "HYE-uht"—*English: "the high gate."*

HYDE, "HIDE"—*English: "a measure of land" or "tanner."*

THE TOP FIVE

**IAN
ISAAC
IVAN
ISAIAH
ISLAM**

If the name you're looking for isn't here, see "Y" and the other vowels.

IAN, "EE-un"—*Gaelic version of John: "God's gracious gift."* **IAIAN** (EE-yane), **IAIN** (EE-ahn). Ian Fleming was a writer whose credits are as diverse as the delightful *Chitty-Chitty-Bang-Bang* and the James Bond spy novels. It's amazing that Baron von Bomburst and Pussy Galore can come from the same mind. . . See also JOHN.

IBO, "ee-BOW"—*African: "my people, our people, us."* This is a tribe name for a group of herding and farming people who inhabit western and central Africa.

IBRAHIM. See ABRAHAM.

IDI, "EE-dee"—*Swahili: "born during the Idd Festival."*

IGNATIUS, "ihg-NA-shee-us"—*Latin: "fiery": Irish Gaelic: "forceful person."* **ÉIGNEACHÁN** (egg-NAKH-on—"KH" back in your throat)—Irish Gaelic; **IGNAC** (EEG-notch)—Hungarian; **IGNAT; IGNATI**—Irish; **IGNATIO**—Spanish and Portuguese; **IGNA-TIOS**—Greek; **IGNAZIO** (ee-NYAH-tsee-oh)—Italian. Several saints have this name, including Saint Ignatius of Antioch, who was martyred in the Roman arena, and Saint Ignatius Loyola, founder of the Jesuit order.

In the 1980s, this was among the hundred most popular names, probably as the Italian and Spanish versions. **IGGY.** F

IKU, "EE-koo"—*Japanese: "nourishing."* F

IMAD, "ee-MAHD"—*Arabic: "support" or "pillar."*

IMMANUEL, "ee-MAN-yoo-ehl" or "ee-MAN-well"—*Hebrew: "God is with us."* **IMANOL** (ee-mah-nohl)—Basque; **MANUEL.** This is another name for Jesus Christ. See also EMMANUEL. F

IMRE, "IHM-ree"—*Teutonic: "industrious"; Hebrew: "tall."* **IMRIC, IMRIE; OMRI.**

INDUS, "IHN-duhss"—*Latin: "Indian."* The constellation Indus can be seen chasing the Sun in the Southern Hemisphere at dusk from late September through mid-October. The Sun is "in" the Indian at Christmas and New Year.

ING(E)MAR, "ING-eh-mahr" and "ING-mahr" (softened "G")—*Norse: "child of the sea" or "famous child."* Ingmar Bergman is a Swedish director noted for his stylistic direction and "high-concept" films.

INNES, INNIS, "IH-nehs"—*Celtic: "(from the) island."*

INTI, "EEN-tee"—*Inca: "sun god."*

IRA, "EYE-rah—*Aramaic: "stallion"; Hebrew: "watcher"; Latin: "anger."*

IRVIN(G), "UR-vihn" or "UR-vihng—*Gaelic: "handsome, fair of face."* **EARVIN, EARVING; ERVIN, ERWIN; IRWIN.** Earvin "Magic" Johnson is perhaps one of the all-time favorite (and best) basketball players.

IRWIN. See IRVIN(G).

ISAAC, "EYE/EE-sack" or "EYE/EE-zack"—*Hebrew: "laughter."* **EISIG** (EYE-zihg)—German; **ICEK** (ee-SEHK)—Polish; **IZAK** (ee-ZAHK)—Polish; **IOSÓG** (YOH-zawg)—Irish Gaelic; **IRAK; ISAAK**—Dutch; **ISAAKIOS**—Greek; **ISHAQ** (EE-shock), **SHAQIL**—Arabic; **ITZAK** (EET-zahk), **ITZHAK**—Israeli; **IXAKA** (ee-shah-kah)—Basque; **IZAAK, IZAK**—Swedish and French; **IZSÁK** (EE-zhahk)—Hungarian. In the Old Testament/Tanakh and the Qur'an, Isaac is one of the sons of Abraham. Born to Abraham's favorite wife, Sarah (who was thought to be barren, as it was very late in her life), Isaac was a cherished baby. Isaac is also one of the Christian saints. Sir Isaac Newton was the physicist who first came up with the modern theory of gravitation, and you can thank him for also devising calculus (yeah, thanks a *lot*, Newt). See also SHAQUIL.

ISAIAH, "eye-SAY/ZAY-ah" or "ee-SYE/ZYE-ah"—*Hebrew: "God lends" or "God is salvation."* **ESAIAS** (ee-SYE-ahss)—Latin; **IKAIA** (ee-KYE-ah or ee-KAY-ah)—Greek; **ISA** (EE-sah)—Persian; **ISIAH** (ee-SYE-ah); **ISSA** (IH-sah)—Arabic; **YESHAYA** (yeh-SHAH-yah)—Hebrew; **YSAI** (EE-sye), **YSAIS**—Spanish and Portuguese. Isaiah is a prophet of the Old Testament/Tanakh. Isiah Thomas is a basketball player turned team owner and executive.

Il

"Il" is the Italian article that means "the" and must be followed by a masculine noun (if it ends in an "o," chances are you're correct). You may add this yourself to a name.

I(H)SAN, "ee-SAHN" or "IH-sahn"—*Arabic: "beneficent."*

ISAS, "ee-SAHS"—*Japanese: "worthy."*

ISHAM, "IHSH-um"—*English: "from the Iron One's estate."* Who exactly the "Iron One" was isn't specified, but it was likely a valorous knight.

ISHMAEL, ISMA'IL, "ISH-mah-ehl" and "IHZ-mah IHL," or "ish-mah-EHL" and "IHSS-mah IHL"—*Hebrew: "God hears"; Arabic: "outcast."* In the Old Testament/Tanakh and the Qur'an, Sarah thought she was barren, and gave her handmaiden, Hagar, to her husband, Abraham, to produce children from their union (in a surrogate kind of way). Ishmael (Isma'il, in the Qur'an) was the result. Soon thereafter, Abraham and Sarah found out that Sarah was pregnant by Abraham, and Hagar and Ishmael/Isma'il left the home. But God promised Abraham, Hagar, and Ishmael/Isma'il that the child would not be forgotten, and Isma'il became the father of the Arabic nations.

ISI, "EE-see"—*Native American Choctaw: "deer."* F

ISIDOR(E), "IHZ-ih-dohr" or "EEZ-ee-dohr"—*Greek: "a gift of ideas"; Latin: "gift of*

Isis." **ISDRO** (EES-droh)—*Portuguese;* **IXIDOR** (ee-shee-dohr)—*Basque;* **IZIDOR(E)**—Eastern European; **IZYDOR**—Polish. This is the name of a Christian saint. F

ISLAM, "ihs-LAHM"—*Arabic: "submission" or "surrender."*

ISRAEL, "eez-RAH-ehl" or "IHZ-rail"—*Hebrew: "he who struggles with God," "the Lord's warrior," or "may God prevail,"* and of course, the country Israel. **IZRAEL, YISRAEL.** In the Old Testament/Tanakh, This is a name given to Jacob who, one dark, lonely night, after being kicked out of his home for stealing the birthright of his older twin, fought with an angel of the Lord, who had brought him a message of comfort. Jacob, from then on called Isra-el or Yisra-el, went on to found the kingdom of Israel.

ISTAS, "EES-tahs"—*Native American: "snow on the ground."*

ISTU, "EES-too"—*Native American: "sugar from the sugar-pine."*

ITO, "ee-TOH"—*Japanese: "thread."*

ITUHA, "ee-TOO-hah"—*Native American: "a sturdy oak."* F

IVAN, "ee-VAHN" or, incorrectly, "EYE-vahn"—*Eastern European version of John: "God's gracious gift."* **EYVAN** (EYE-vahn), **EYVIND**—Gaelic; **VANYA**—Russian; **YVAN** (ee-VAHN)—Bretagne. Ivan the Terrible was a heck of a boss to have when he ruled Russia in the sixteenth century. See also EVAN, JOHN, YVON. F

IVAR, "EE-vahr" or rarely "EYE-vahr"—*Teutonic: "yew tree" or "archer"; Welsh: "lord."* **IBHAR** (EE-vahr), **ÍOMHAR** (YOH-vahr)—Irish Gaelic; **IVARR**—Norse; **IVO**—Irish; **IVOR.** The Teutonic derivations may seem unrelated, but the yew tree produced a wood desirable for bowmaking, and thus was associated with archery. Ivarr was the name of several kings of Dublin, and Ibhar is an Irish saint. F

IVES, "EEVZ" or (incorrectly, if you're a purist) "EYVS"—*Teutonic: "yew tree" and "archer."* This is the name of a Catholic saint and several European cities. See note at IVAR.

IWA, "EE-wah"—*Japanese: "rock."*

IZAR, "ee-zar"—*Basque: "star."* See also STAR. F

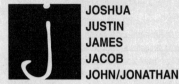

THE TOP FIVE

JOSHUA
JUSTIN
JAMES
JACOB
JOHN/JONATHAN

If the name you're looking for isn't here, see "G", "H", and "Y", and the vowels.

JA, "JAH"—*Korean: "magnetism" and "fertile."*

JAB(B)ARI, "jah-BAR-ee"—*Swahili: "brave."* JABAR, JABBAR.

JACK, "JAK"—*diminutive of Jacob: "the supplanter," but also: "assistant," "knave," "a fish," "to increase, to advance," "breadfruit tree," "blond or yellow wood," or "coat of mail (mostly leather)."* CHAK(K)A—Polynesian and Malaysian; JACA—Portuguese; JACO—Spanish; JACQUES (ZHAWK)—French; JOCK, JOCKO—Scottish; SHAK(K)—Arabic. Now a name in its own right, Jack is actually a nickname for Jacob, via the French version Jacques, but it has come to be used for James and John as well. See also JACOB. F

JACKSON, "JAK-sun"—*"son of Jack" or "son of Jacob."* Populist Andrew Jackson became president in 1829 after a military career that included a victory over British forces in the War of 1812. Thomas "Stonewall" Jackson was a Confederate general in the Civil War. See also JACK, JACOB.

JACOB, "JAY-kub"—*Hebrew: traditional-ly "the supplanter," but more likely "protector" or "guardian."* AKIB (ah-KEEB), AKIV—Persian and Arabic; AKKUB (AH-koob), AKKUBIAN (ah-KOO-bee-ahn), AKOUB, AKOUBIAN—Latvian, Lithuanian, and Armenian; AKOOBJEE (ah-KOOB-jee)—Hindu; DIEGO (dee-AY-goh), TIAGO (tee-AH-goh)—Spanish; GIACO, GIACOBBE (JAH-koh-beh), GIACOBO, GIACOMO (JAH-koh-moh), GIACOPO—Italian; IAKOVOS (yah-KOH-vohss or YAH-koh-vohss)—Greek; JACOPO (yah-KOH-poh or YAH-koh-poh), JAGO (YAH-goh)—Portuguese; JAKOB (YAH-kohb)—Scandinavian; JAKUB (YAH-koob)—Polish; JAMES (JAYMZ)—European; YAKOBE (yah-koh-beh)—Basque. The traditional "supplanter" meaning comes from the folklore that accompanied the Old Testament/Tanakh Jacob's birth. It is said that Jacob, the second-born of twins, came out of the womb grasping his brother Esau's heel. This story foreshadows what happens later, when Jacob tricks Esau into giving up his inheritance and tricks his blind father into giving Jacob the first blessing. JACK, JACKI(E), JACKY; JAKE; JOCK, JOCKO. See also JACQUES, YAKOFF/ YAKOV. F

JACQUES, "ZHAHK"—*French version of Jacob: "the supplanter."* JACK—English; JACKOLINO (YAH-koh-lihn-oh or JAH-koh-lihn-oh)—Eastern European; **JACQUE**; **JACQUETTO** (zhah-KEH-toh)—Italian; **JOCK**, **JOCKO**—Scottish. Jacques-Yves Cousteau is a French inventor and oceanographer who has done much to educate the world about the environment, and who has always actively pressed for legislation that would restore and preserve the health of our world. This name is rising in popularity within the African-American community. See also JACOB. F

JACY, "JAH-see" or "JAY-see"—*Native American Kiowa: "the powers of the moon."* **JACE**. F

JAEGER, "JAY-ghur" or "YAY-ghur"—*Norse: "sea hawk"; German: "hunter."* **JÄGER**; **YAEGER, YEAGER**.

JAEL, "yah-EHL" or "YALE"—*Hebrew: "mountain billy goat" or "climber."* **F**

JAFAR, "JAH-fahr" or "jah-FAHR"—*Hindu, Swahili, and Arabic: "a little stream."* **JA'FAR**—Arabic; **JAFARI, JAFFARI** (jah-FAH-ree)—Swahili; **JAFFAR**.

JAHAN, "JAH-hahn" or "jah-HAHN"—*Swahili: "dignity."* **JAHI**. Shah Jahan was the Mogul emperor of India who, to preserve the memory of his beloved wife, built the breathtaking Taj Mahal in the mid-seventeenth century.

JAI, "HYE"—*Basque: "festival."*

JAIME. See also JAMES.

JAIR, "YAY-ir"—*Hebrew: "God enlightens."*

JAKE. See JACOB.

JAMAL, "jah-MAHL"—*Arabic: "handsome."*

JAMES, "JAYMZ"—*popular European variation on Jacob, traditionally "the supplanter" but more likely "protector" or "guardian."* **DIEGO** (dee-AY-goh)—Spanish;

HAMISH (HAH-mish or HAY-mish)—Scottish Gaelic; **JAAP** (YAHP), **JIM** (YIHM)—Dutch; **JAIME** (HY-may)—Spanish and Portuguese; **HAMISH** (HAY-mish), **SÉAMUS** (SHAY-moose)—Irish Gaelic; **SHAMUS** (SHAY-muhss), **SHANE** (SHAYN)—Scotch-Irish. Several saint names are listed here, including James, an apostle who was the brother of Jesus and the first bishop of Jerusalem. Another James was the brother of the apostle John and the first Christian martyr. Confusing enough? Several English kings have been named James, as have several presidents. And if you want a change of James pace, try 1950s actor turned icon James Dean and fictional character Bond, James Bond. **JAIME, JAIMEY, JAMEY, JAMI; JIM, JIMI, JIMMI(E), JIMMY; JOCK, JOCKO.** See also JACOB. F

JAN, Nordic: "YAHN"; others: "JAN"—*Dutch and Nordic spin on John.* **JANEK** (YAH-nehk or JAH-nehk); **JANSEN** (YAHN-sehn or JAN-sehn); **JANUS** (YAH-noose). This is a popular name in families of Nordic ancestry. See also JENSIN, JOHN.

JAREB, "JARE-ehb"—*Hebrew: "he will maintain."* **JARIB**.

JARED, "JARE-ehd"—*Greek: "rose" or "bud"; Hebrew: "descendant."* **JARRED**; **JARETT, JARRET, JARRETT; JAROD, JARROD.** This is becoming a popular name.

JARETT. See GARRETT, JARED.

JARVIS, "JAHR-vihs"—*Teutonic: "spear-wielding."* **GERVAIS** (jur-VAYZ), **GERVASE**, **JERVIS**.

JASON, "JAY-sun"—*Greek: "healer."* **IASAN** (YAW-sawn)—Irish Gaelic; **JAYSON**. In Greek legend, Jason led a group of men in search of the magical Golden Fleece; they sailed on a ship called the Argo and had many enchanted adventures. He married a sorceress named Medea to help him further his goal, but paid an awful price later when he dumped her. Jason is also one of the Christian saints, and another Jason was a prophet credited with writing the Old Testament/Tanakh book of Ecclesiastes.

JASPER, "JASS-pur"—*version of Gaspar: "bringer of treasure"; Arabic: the semiprecious stone jasper.* By tradition, Gaspar is one of the Three Wise Men from the East who visited the infant Christ in Bethlehem. See also GASPAR.

JAVAS, "JAH-vahss"—*Hindu: "swift."*

JAY, "JAY"—*Latin: "rejoice"; Anglo-Saxon: "little crow" or "lively."* Jay also refers to the colorful, noisy blue jay. F

JED, "JEHD"—*Arabic: "hand."*

JEDRIK, "YEH-drik"—*Polish: "manly."*

JEFFERSON. See JEFFREY.

JEFFREY, "JEHF-ree"—*Teutonic: "peaceful district"; French: "pledge of peace"; Hebrew: "he will open the way."* **GEOFFREY; GEOFFROI** (ZHOH-frwah—hock up the "r" in your throat), **JEFFROI** (ZHEH-frwah), **JEOFFROI**—French; **JAFFREZ** (ZHAH-fray—hock up the "r" in your throat)—Breton; **JEFFERS, JEFFERSON, JEFFERY, JEFFRY; JOFFREY** (JOF-ree or YOF-ree)—Scottish, and Northern and Eastern European; **SÉAFRA** (SHAY-frah), **SIOFRAI** (SHOH-fry)—Irish Gaelic; **SEAFRAID** (SHAY-frade), **SEARTHRA** (SHARE-thrah)—Scottish Gaelic. The Hebrew derivation means that this child "will open the way" for other children to follow. Thus, this refers to a first son or a son born after miscarriages or long periods of infertility. Thomas Jefferson was president of

the United States from 1801 to 1808. **GEOFF, JEFF.**

JEGAR, "JEH-gahr"—*Hebrew: "witness our love."* **JEGGAR, JEGGER; YEGAR**—Hebrew.

JELANI, "jeh-LAH-nee"—*Swahili: "mighty."* **JELAN.**

JENSIN, "YEHN-sihn"—*Scandinavian: "God is gracious."* **JENSEN.** See also JAN. F

JERALD, "JEH-rahld" or "YEH-rahld"—*Teutonic: "mighty with the spear."* **JERROLD.** See also GERALD. F

JEREMIAH, "jare-eh-ME/MY-ah" or "yare-eh-ME/MY-ah"—*Hebrew: God will uplift"; Greek: "exalted brother."* **GEREMIA** (jeh-reh-MEE-ah)—Italian; **HIEREMIAS** (hye-eh-REHM-ee-ahs)—Greek; **HIRAM** (HYE-rum); **IRIMIAS** (eer-ee-MEE-ahs)—Irish Gaelic; **JERAMIE, JERAMY, JEREMIE, JEREMY; JERMIJA** (yehr-MEE-ah)—Russian. In the Old Testament/Tanakh, Jeremiah was a prophet credited with writing the book of Lamentations. Jerhme-el is one of the Archangels in Hebrew and Christian legend.

JEREMY. See JEREMIAH.

JERMAINE. See GERMAINE/JERMAINE.

JEROME, "jeh-ROME"—*Greek: "exalted name."* **GEROME, GERONE; HIERONYMOS** (hye-ROH-nih-muhss)—German and Greek; **IAROM** (yah-ROME)—Irish Gaelic. Saint Jerome translated the Hebrew and Greek biblical texts into the Latin version, called the Vulgate. **GERRY, JERRY.** See also GERONIMO, HIERONYMOS.

JERRY. See JEROME.

JESSE, "JEH-see"—*Hebrew: "God is (exists)," "riches," or "wealthy."* There is quite a range of Jesses. Jesse was the father of King David of Israel. Jesse Jackson was the first African-American man to run for the presidency of the United States. Jesse Owens, "the Ebony Express," was a groundbreaking Olympic track star who embarrassed Adolf Hitler, host of the 1936 Games, by *creaming* the "superior Aryan" German team. **JESSIE, JESSY.** See also ESAI. F

JESUS, "JEE-zuhs" or "HEH-soos"—*Egyptian/Arabic version of Jason, from Hebrew: "the healer"; a variation on Joshua: "God is salvation."* **JESITO, JESUSITO**—Spanish; **JÉSU** (JAY-soo or YAY-soo)—European. Jesus of Nazareth was a Jewish rabbi who rebelled against the entangled and overly complicated way in which people were expected to worship God, and against the ever-increasing distance (created by politics and bureaucracy) between humankind and the Lord. He stressed simple, personal interaction directly with God, and the equal worth of all people in the eyes of a loving and involved Creator. F

JET, "JEHT" or "YEHT"—*diminutive of Jethro, "abundance"; Danish: "coal black"; Greek: "black stone."* The Greek derivation refers specifically to the Great Stone of Gagai in ancient Lycia, which was like a black diamond. F

JIBBEN, "JIH-behn"—*Gypsy: "life."*

JIM. See JAMES.

JIN, "JIHN"—*Chinese: "gold" or "golden"; Korean: "truth."*

JINN, "JIHN"—*Arabic: "spirits."* These spirits are usually associated with air or fire. This is another version of the English word "genie." F

JIRO, "jee-ROH"—*Japanese: "second son."*

JIVIN, "JEE-veen"—*Hindu: "giver of life."* **JIBBEN, JIBBIL; JIVIL.** F

JOCK. See JACK, JACOB, JACQUES, JAMES.

JOE. See JOSEPH.

JOEL, "JOLE" or "YOLE"—*Hebrew: "Jehovah is God."* In the Old Testament/Tanakh, Joel is one of the prophets. F

JOHANNAN, "yoh-HAHN-un" or rarely "joh-HAHN-un"—*Hebrew: "the grace of God."* **IOANNES** (yoh-AH-nehz), **IOANNIKIOS** (yoh-AHN-ee-kyohss)—Greek; **JOANNY** (yoh-AWN-ee)—Polish; **JOHANN, JOHANNE** (yoh-HAHN-eh), **JOHANNES**—German and Scandinavian; **YOCHANNAN** (yoh-KHAHN-nahn—"KH" in the throat)—Hebrew. Johann Sebastian Bach was one of the most gifted composers in history—his work pretty much ushered in the Baroque period and set the standard for the musical accompaniment of the time. Several names of the Christian saints can be found on this list as well. See also JOHN. F

JOHN, "JAWN"—*Hebrew: there are several translations: "God's gracious gift," "God has favored," "the Lord is favored," "the Lord is gracious," "the Lord is merciful," "God is kind."* Here are a few versions, but by no means all, I'm sure! **EOIN** (ay-OYN), **SÉAN** (SHAWN)—Irish Gaelic; **GIAN** (JYAHN)—Italian; **HANS, HANDSEL, HANSEL**—German; **HANS, JAN** (YAWN)—Dutch and Danish; **IAIN, IAN** (EE-un), **SEON** (SHONE)—Scottish Gaelic; **IVAN** (ee-VAHN), **JÁNOS** (YAH-nos), **JANKO**—Eastern European; **JAN** (JAN)—Scotch-Irish; **JAN** (YAN), **JANEK** (YAN-ehk), **ZANE**—Polish; **JAN** (YAHN), **JENS** (YEHNZ), **JONAM** (YOH-nahm)—Swedish; **JAN** (YAHN), **JOEN** (YOH-

"JUNIOR" OR "II"

How does it sound? "The Second" may be too high-falutin' for your taste, but it is often the option for a girl named after her mother. Numbers are always represented by Roman numerals: "II," "III," "IV," "V," "MCLVIIDX." The numbers and the words "Senior" and "Junior" are always preceded by a comma—"Curlington J. Howard, III."

ehn)—Danish; **JANCSI** (YAHN-tsee)—Hungarian; **JANNES, YANNI**—Greek; **JEAN** (ZHAWN)—French; **JENS** (YEHNS)—Norwegian; **JOÃO** (ZH-WOW—like one syllable)—Portuguese; **JONAM** (YOH-nahm)—Swedish; **JUAN** (HWAHN), **JUANITO** (HWAH-nee-toh or hwah-NEE-toh)—Spanish; **SEAN** (SHAWN), **SHAWN**—Scottish; **HAUN**—Irish; **SIAN** (SHAHN)—Welsh. The names of two dozen popes and over eighty saints are on this list. Probably the most important Christian Johns were John the Baptist, cousin of Jesus, and Saint John (the Divine), a disciple of Jesus—the John whom Christ, while on the cross, asked to take care of his mother, Mary, and the one who wrote of some of the books of the New Testament. The four English Johns—Donne, Dryden, Keats, and Milton—are classic examples of literary genius in their poems and prose. Lots of Johns have been great actors of stage and screen, lots of Johns have held political office (four presidents), and lots and lots of Johns wake up every morning and do the things regular people do. John has been one of the most popular boy's names for three hundred years and counting. **JOHNNI(E), JOHNNY; JON, JONNY.** See also EVAN, JOHANNAN, JONATHAN, YVON. F

JONAH, "JOH-nah" or "YOH-nah"—*Hebrew: "dove" or "God gives."* **IÓNA** (YOH-nah), **JONAS**—Irish Gaelic. In the Old Testament/Tanakh and the Qur'an, Jonah is a reluctant prophet who attempts to head in the opposite direction from which God has pointed him, away from the city Nineveh. Jonah flees by ship, but God causes a storm to throw Jonah overboard and the runaway is swallowed by a whale. Needless to say, during some quiet time in the belly of the whale, Jonah decides that a trip to Nineveh might not be so bad after all.

JONATHAN, "JON-uh-thin"—*Hebrew: combination of John and Nathan, "beloved gift" or "God has graciously given."* **IONATÁN** (yoh-nah-TAWN)—Irish Gaelic; **JONATHEL, JONATHEN.** The Jonathan of the Old Testament/Tanakh was a son of King Saul and a beloved friend of King David. Jonathan Swift was a late seventeenth- and early eighteenth-century Irish writer of satire, best known for *Gulliver's Travels.* **JON, JONNY; NATE.** See also JOHN, NATHAN. F

JORDAN, "JORE-den" or "YORE-den"—*Hebrew: name of a river in the Middle East, meaning "to flow down" or "to descend."* **GIORDANO** (johr-DAH-noh)—Italian; **JAR-**

DEN—Hebrew; **JORDAAN** (yore-DAHN)—Dutch; **JORDÃO** (YAHR-da-oh)—Portuguese. The River Jordan plays a major role in the religion and folklore of the Middle East. As a personal name, "Jordan" has been popularized both by the superstardom of basketball player Michael Jordan and by the soap operas. F

JOREN, "YOH-rehn"—*Scandinavian: "love of the chief."* **JORUNN**—Norwegian. See also GEORGE. F

JORGE. See GEORGE.

JOSÉ. See HOSEA, JOSEPH.

JOSEPH, "JOH-sehf" or "YOH-sehf"—*Hebrew: "God will add" or "he will add."* **CHE** (CHAY)—Spanish and Portuguese; **GIUSEPPE** (joo-SEHP-eh)—Italian; **JOÃO** (ZH-WOW), **JOOP** (YOHP or JOHP)—Dutch; **JOSÉ:** (ZHOH-zeh)—Portuguese, (HOH-zay or JOH-zay)—Spanish and French; **JOSEF**—German and Scandinavian; **JOSEP** (YOH-sehp)—Polish; **JOSKA** (YOHSH-kah), **JÓSZEF** (YOH-zhehf), **JÓZSEF** (YOH-sehf)—Hungarian; **JOXEP** (yoh-shep), **YOSEB** (yoh-seb)—Basque; **JOZSA, JOZSEF** (YOH-zhef), **JOZSI, JOZSKA**—Eastern European; **PEPE** (PEH-peh), **PEPITO, PEPPO**—Spanish, Portuguese, Basque, and Italian; **SEOSAMH** (SHOH-sahv), **SEOSAPH** (SHOH-sahf)—Irish Gaelic; **YOUSSEF, YUSUF** (yuh-SUHF)—Arabic and Swahili. The Joseph of the Old Testament/Tanakh and the Qur'an was his father Jacob's favorite son, and he was sold into slavery by his twelve jealous brothers. A responsible and drop-dead gorgeous guy, he became a trusted servant of a high Egyptian official until he was thrown in prison after refusing the amorous advances of his boss's wife. There Joseph stayed until he successfully interpreted the troubling dreams of the Pharaoh. Joseph became the Pharaoh's trusted aide, a free man with a major title and lots of power, which he used to relax most of the oppression of his people. If living well is the best revenge, Joseph did a bang-up job. The New Testament Joseph was the loving earthly father of Jesus. Joseph of Arimathea was a wealthy Israelite who had been converted by Jesus. When Christ was taken from the cross, Joseph provided a tomb and proper accoutrements for Christ's burial. Several Christian saint names are on this list. **JOE.** F

JOSHA, "JOH-shah"—*Hindu: "satisfied."*

JOSHUA, "JOSH-oo-ah"—*Hebrew: "God is my salvation" or "whom God has saved."* **GIOSUE** (JOH-soo-eh or joh-SOO-eh)—Italian; **JOSUA** (YOH-soo-ah), **JOZUA**—Dutch; **JOZSUA** (YOH-zhua)—Hungarian; **YEHOSHUA** (yeh-HOH-shoo-ah)—Israeli; **YUSHUA** (YUH-shoo-ah)—Arabic. The Joshua of the Old Testament/Tanakh was Moses' right-hand man in the Exodus of the Hebrews from Egypt to the Promised Land. He became a great manager of people and a good military man under Moses' tutelage. He also authored one of the books in the Old Testament/Tanakh. Joshua is a very popular name for boys these days. **JOSH.**

JOSIAH, "joh-SYE-ah"—*Hebrew: "may the Lord heal and protect."* In the Old Testament/Tanakh, Josiah is a king of Judah who ascended the throne at the age of eight.

JOSS, "JAWSS" or "JOHSS"—*Chinese misunderstood by the Portuguese, or vice-versa: "idol" or "god."*

JOTHAM, "JOH-thum" or "YOH-thahm"—*Hebrew: "God is perfect."*

JOVE, "JOHV"—*Roman: "of Jupiter," the Roman supreme male god.* **GIOVANNI** (joh-VAH-nee)—Italian; **JOVAN** (joh-VAHN). Jupiter is a planet associated with happiness, good fortune, and learning. F

JUAN. See JOHN, JUANITO.

JUANITO, "wah-NEE-toh" or "hwah-NEE-toh"—*Spanish: "little John."* **JUAN, JUANO.** F

JUBAL, "JOO-bahl"—*Latin: "joyous celebration"; Hebrew: "ram's horn,"* which was used to announce a joyful celebration. **YOVEL** (YOH-vehl)—Hebrew. In the Tanakh/Old Testament, Jubal is said to be a son of Cain who invented many musical instruments. Jubal Early was a Confederate army general noted for his many successful raids in the Shenandoah Valley and near Washington, D.C., and his fame made Jubal a popular name in the South.

JUDAH, "JOO-dah" or "YOO-dah"—*Hebrew: "praised."* **JUDAS.** Judah was the name of the ancient kingdom of the Hebrews in southern Palestine. **JUDD, JUDE.** F

JUDD, "JUHD"—*Hebrew: "descendant."* See also JUDAH.

JUDE. See JUDAH.

JULES, "JOOLS" or "YOOLS"—*Latin: "youthful"; Greek: "soft" or "downy."* **GIULIANO, GIULIO** (JYOO-lee-oh)—Italian; **JULE, JULIAN, JULIUS; JULES** (YOOLS)—Dutch; **JULI** (YOO-lee)—Hungarian; **JULIO** (ZHOOL-yoh)—Portuguese; **JULIUSZ** (YOO-lee-oosh)—Polish. A couple of popes and a comedian named Groucho Marx have borne the name Julius, along with a Caesar. There are several saint names on this list. F

JULIUS. See JULES.

JUN, "JOON"—*Japanese: "obedient."*

JUNG, "JUNG"—*Korean: "righteous."*

JURRIEN, "YOO-ree-en"—*Dutch from Hebrew: "God will uplift."*

JUSTIN, "JUSS-tihn"—*Latin: "the just."* **GIUSTINO** (joo-STEE-noh)—Italian; **JUSTIN** (yoo-STEEN)—Greek; **JUSTINIAN** (juhs-STIHN-ee-un); **JUSTUS**—Scandinavian; **JUSTYN** (yoo-STEEN)—Polish. Justinian was the name of a Byzantine emperor who united his kingdom in Christianity (for a nanosecond) and revised the old Roman code of laws. Several saints have had names on this list. F

JUTE, "JOOT" or rarely, "YOOT"—*Germanic: "of the lindens."* This is a tribe name for a group of Germanic peoples originating along the Rhine River. They eventually moved into the island of Britain and the Isle of Wight. The bark of the herb jute yields a soft yet strong fiber.

THE TOP FIVE

KEVIN
KEITH
KENNETH
KAREEM
KYLE

If the name you're looking for isn't here, see "C" and "Q."

KADAR, "kah-DAHR"—*Arabic: "powerful."* **KEDAR.**

KADIR, "kah-DEER"—*Arabic: "verdant."*

KAGA, "KAH-gah"—*Native American: "writer" or "chronicler."* F

KAHANU, "kuh-HAH-noo"—*Hawaiian: "breath of life."*

KAI, "kah-EE"—*Polynesian: "sea."* F

KAIGANI, "KYE-gah-nee" or "kye-GAH-nee"—*Native American: "of the willow trees."* This is a tribe name for a group of people living in modern-day British Columbia and Alaska. They are skilled carvers of ivory, wood, and argillite, and they participate in potlatch ceremonies—in which the host gives his possessions to his guests—and in ritual tattooing.

KALA, "kuh-LAW"—*Hawaiian: "the Sun."*

KALANI, "kuh-LAW-nee"—*Hawaiian: "the heavens."* F

KALFANI, "kahl-FAH-nee"—*Swahili: "destined to rule."*

KALIL, "kah-LEEL"—*Arabic: "good friend" or "beloved friend"; Greek: "handsome."* **KAHIL, KAHILLE, KAHLIL, KHALIL.** Kahlil

Gibran is a celebrated Persian poet who rejoiced in all things, from the tiniest plant to the wonder of God. A collection of his works is called *The Prophet.* F

KALINO, "kuh-LEE-noh"—*Hawaiian: "golden."*

KALIQ, "kah-LEEK"—*Arabic: "creative."*

KALLE, "KAH-leh"—*Scandinavian: "masculine."* **KAL.**

KAMAL, "KAH-mahl" or "kah-MAHL"—*Arabic: "perfection"; Hindu: "lotus."* **KAMIL.** F

KAMI, "KAH-mee"—*Japanese: "deity."* F

KAMIL, "kah-MEEL"—*Tunisian: "the perfect one."* F

KANE, "KAYNE"—*Latin: "tribute"; Gaelic: "bright."* **KAIN, KAINE, KAYNE.**

KANIEL, "KAH-nee-ehl"—*Arabic: "bright spear" or "spear of the Lord."* **KANI.** F

KANOA, "kuh-NOH-ah"—*Polynesian: "one who is free."* F

KANTU, "KAHN-too"—*Hindu: "happy."* **CANTU.**

KAREEM, "kah-REEM"—*Arabic: "noble."* **KARIM, KARIME, KARIO, KHARIM.** Kareem Abdul-Jabbar was one of the all-time greatest basketball players.

KARIF, "kah-REEF"—*Arabic: "born in autumn."* **KAREEF.**

KARL, "KAHRL"—*version of Charles: "strong and manly."* **KARCSI** (KAHR-chee)—Hungarian; **KAREL** (KARE-ehl or KAH-rehl); **KAROL** (KARE-ohl or KAH-rohl); **KAROLY**—Eastern European; **KAROLEK, KAROLIN.** See also CHARLES, CARL. F

KAROL, "KARE-ohl" or "KAH-rohl"—*Eastern European version of Carroll, French: "joyous song"; Gaelic: "champion."* **KAROLEK**—Russian; **KAROLI**—Rumanian; **KAROLY**—Polish. Karol Wojtyla was an artistically talented young Polish boy who grew up to be the first non-Italian Pope of the Catholic church in centuries, John Paul II. See also CARROLL, KARL. F

KARUN, "kah-ROON" or "KAH-roon"—*Sanskrit: "compassion."* F

KASIB, "kah-SEEB"—*Arabic: "fertile."*

KASIM, "kah-SEEM"—*Arabic: "divided."* **KASEEM, KASEM, QASIM.**

KASPAR, "KAHS-pahr"—*Persian: "bringer of treasure."* **CASPAR, CASPER, GASPAR, KASPER.** Kaspar is one of the Three Wise Men from the east, Magi of the Zoroastrian faith, who are traditionally thought to have visited Jesus in Bethlehem.

KATSU, "KAHT-soo"—*Japanese: "victorious."* F

KAYIN, "kah-YEEN"—*African Ibo: "celebrated."*

KEAN(E), "KEEN" or "KEE-un"—*English: "wise and brave"; Irish: "ancient."* **CIAN** (KEE-un), **KIAN**—Irish Gaelic; **KEAN, KEENAN, KIENAN**—Scottish; **KEENE, KEYNE**—English; **KENE**—Irish.

KEANU, "kee-AH-nu" or "KEE-ah-nu"—*Hawaiian: "sky warrior(?)" or "god of the sky(?)."* Keanu Reeves is an actor.

KEAU, "KAY-ah-ooh"—*Hawaiian: "movement" or "motion."*

KEDAR, "KAY-dahr" or "keh-DAHR"—*Hindu: "mountain lord"; Arabic: "powerful."*

KEDEM, "KEH-dehm"—*Hebrew: "facing east."*

KEEFE, "KEEF"—*Irish: "handsome" or "gentle"; Arabic: "enjoyment."* **KAIF** (KAYF), **KEF**—Arabic; **KEEFER, KEEVER, KIEFE, KIEFER, O'KEEFE.** Kiefer Sutherland is an actor.

KEEGAN, "KEE-gun"—*Irish Gaelic: "little fire."* See also EGAN.

KEELAN, "KEE-luhn"—*Irish Gaelic: "little slender one."* See also KILLIAN.

KEELER, "KEEL-ur"—*English: "one who cools."* A keeler cools things such as metals in a shallow tub of water.

KEELY, "KEE-lee"—*Gaelic: "little beauty."* **KEELEY.** See also KILLIAN. F

KEENAN, "KEE-nuhn"—*Irish Gaelic: "little ancient one" or "little old one."* **KEENEN, KEENON.** This is a leprechaun's name in some Irish folktales.

KEITH, "KEETH"—*Scottish: a place name and "the forest"; Gaelic: "the wind."*

KELL, "KEHL"—*Nordic: "from the spring."*

KELLER, "KEHL-ur"—*Irish Gaelic: "little companion."* **KELLAR.**

KELLY, "KEHL-ee"—*Welsh: "in the woods"; Gaelic: "warrior"; Native American Comanche/Nimeneh: "sparrow hawk."* **KELE, KELLE, KELLEE, KELLEY KELLI(E).** F

KELSEY, "KEHL-see"—*Norse: "from the*

ship island," referring to a shape of a land mass, or "from the ship's island," referring to a vessel or traveller's point of origination; Cymric: "dweller in the woods by the sea"; German: "from the sea" or "near the sea." **KELCEY, KELCI(E), KELCY; KELSI(E), KELSY.** This is a seaworthy name, at any rate. F

KELVIN, "KEHL-vihn"—English: "fond of ships," "seafarer," or "sailor"; Irish Gaelic: "from the narrow river." **KELVIN.** William Thomson, First Baron Kelvin of Largs, devised the alternate and more scientifically useful means of measuring temperature that now bears his name.

KEMEN, "keh-men"—Basque: "strength."

KEMP, "KEMP"—Celtic: "warrior" or "chief"; English: "champion."

KEN. This is a diminutive of all the names that begin with "Ken-."

KENDAL(L), "KEHN-dul"—Celtic: "ruler of the valley." **KENDEL(L). KEN, KENN, KENNIE, KENNY; KENDIE, KENDY.** F

KENDRICK, "KEHN-drihk"—Anglo-Saxon: "royal power." **KENDIG, KENDIGO; KENDRIC, KENDRIK, KENRIC; KENDRY. KEN, KENNIE, KENNY; RICK, RICKY.** F

KENLEY, "KEHN-lee"—English: "the king's meadow." **KENLEA, KENLEE, KENLEIGH. KEN, KENNIE, KENNY.**

KENNAN, "KEHN-un"—Scottish: "to make known" or "to know how, to be able." **KEN, KENNIE, KENNY.** F

KENNARD, "KEH-nahrd"—English: "bold, strong." **KENNERD. KEN, KENNIE, KENNY.**

KENNETH, "KEHN-eth"—Celtic: "striking (as in appearance)" or "chief." **CAIONEACH** (KAY-oh-naykh—"kh" in your throat)—Scottish Gaelic; **CENNYDD** (KEHN-ihth), **CYNNEDD** (KIHN-ehth)—Welsh; **CIONAOD** (kee-OH-nowt), **COINNEACH** (koh-EE-nakh—"kh" in your throat)—Irish Gaelic; **KENNET, KINNET.** Kenneth MacAlpine was a ninth-century king, the first to rule over both the Picts and the Scots in Caledonia, which then, united, became Scotland. A seventh-century Irish saint was named Caioneach. **KEN, KENNIE, KENNY.**

KENT, "KENT"—Scottish Gaelic: "chief"; Celtic: "white." **KENTON.**

KENTON, "KEHN-tun"—English: "from the royal estate." **KEN, KENNIE, KENNY; KENT.**

KENYON, "KEHN-yuhn"—Celtic: "fair-haired." **KEN, KENNIE, KENNY.** F

KERN, "KURN"—Irish: "infantry man"; Gaelic: "little dark one." **KEARN, KEARNEY, KEARNY.**

KERRY, "KARE-ee"—Irish: "dark." This is also a place name for southwest Ireland. **CARRI(E); KARRI(E); KERR.** See also CARY. F

KERWIN, "KUHR-wihn"—Gaelic: "little black one"; Celtic: "dark friend."

KEVIN, "KEH-vihn"—Irish: "little handsome one." **CAOIMHÍN** (COW-veen or cow-VEEN), **CAOMHÁN** (COW-vahn)—Irish Gaelic; **KEVAN, KEVEN.** Saint Kevin is one of the patron saints of Dublin, Ireland. **KEV.**

KEY, "KEE"—Irish Gaelic: "son of fire"; English: "key." **KEE, KIE.**

KHAN, "KAHN"—Chinese: "king"; Turkish: "chief" or "lord"; Hindu: "master" or "ruler"; Arabic: "an inn."

KI, "KEE"—Korean: "vigorous." F

KIBBE, "KEEB-eh"—Native American: "bird in the night." **KIBBEE.** F

KIEFER. See KEEFE.

KIER, KEIR, "KEER" for both, "KARE" for the second—*Norse: "tub" or "tank."* A kier is a cylindrical vat in which fabric is bleached or cleaned, or a person who performs this work. Keir Dullea is an actor probably best known through *2001: A Space Odyssey.* See also KIERAN.

KIERAN, "KEER-un"—*Irish: "little dark one."* **CIARÁN** (KYAR-awn)—Irish Gaelic; **KIER; KIERON, KYRAN, QUERON.** This is the name of a Christian saint.

KIHO, "kee-HOH"—*African Rutooro: "fog" or "born in the fog."*

KIKUNO, "kee-KOO-noh"—*Japanese: "field of chrysanthemums."*

KILLIAN, "KIHL-yahn"—*Gaelic: "little beauty" or "little fighter."* **CILLIAN** (KEE-lee-awn)—Irish Gaelic; **KEELAN, KEELY; KILIAN, KILMER.** F

KIM, "KIHM"—*Vietnamese: "bird."* See also KIMBALL. F

KIMBALL, "KIHM-bahl"—*Greek: "vessel"; Anglo-Saxon: "royally brave."* **KEMBLE, KIMBELIN, KIMBELL, KIMBLE, KYMBELINE. KIM.**

KIMI, "kee-MEE"—*Japanese: "without peer."* F

KIN, "KIHN"—*Japanese: "gold."* Kin Shriner is a television actor. See also ERSKINE.

KINCHLOE, "KINTCH-loh"—*English/ Dutch: "salt hills"; Scandinavian: "the family lands."*

KINGSLEY, "KINGS-lee"—*English: "the king's meadow."* **KINGSLEA, KINGSLEE, KINGSLEIGH; KINSLEA, KINSLEE, KINSLEIGH, KINSLEY. KING.**

KINGSTON, "KINGS-tun"—*English: "the king's town."* The port city of Kingston is the capital of Jamaica.

KINNARD, "KIHN-ahrd"—*Irish: "from the highlands."*

KINSEY, "KIHN-see"—*English: "royal victory."*

KINU, "kee-NOO" or "KEE-noo"—*Japanese: "silk."* F

KIP, "KIHP"—*Anglo-Saxon or Dutch: "the tanner."* See also KIPP.

KIPP, "KIHP"—*English: "peak or pointed hill."* **KIP, KIPPIE, KIPPY.**

KIRBY, "KUR-bee"—*English: "near or in the village church."* **KERBY.**

KIRITAN, "kee-ree-TAHN"—*Hindu: "crowned."*

KIRK, "KURK"—*Scottish Gaelic and Scandinavian: "church."* **KIRKLAND.** Kirk Douglas is an award-winning actor, producer, and writer. One of his greatest achievements is the epic *Spartacus.* See also KIRKLEY, KIRKWOOD.

KIRKLEY, "KURK-lee"—*English/Scottish: "from the church meadow."* **KIRKLEA, KIRKLEE, KIRKLEIGH. KIRK.**

KIRKWOOD, "KURK-wood"—*English/ Scottish: "the woods by the church."* **KIRK.**

KIRN, "KURN" or "KEERN"—*Scottish: "last sheaf of harvest" or "to churn."*

KISHI, "KEE-shee"—*Japanese: "beach."* F

KIT, "KIHT"—*diminutive of Christopher: "Christ-bearer;" or at face value: "young fox."* **KISA** (KEE-sah)—Eastern European; **KISKA** (KEES-kah)—Russian. See also CHRISTOPHER. F

KITO, "KEE-toh"—*Swahili: "jewel."* F

NO MORE SAINTS & PROPHETS, NOW IT'S SPORTS & STARS

Before the rise of film and TV, most people got their names from the religious group to which they belonged. Nowadays, most people admire celebrities in entertainment and sports. Character names and star names come and go with the popularity of the story or the person. The name JORDAN has speared a top spot in name lists for both sexes since basketball star Michael Jordan made the scene. TV talk-show hostess Kathy Lee Gifford named her baby Cody a few years ago, and CODY has soared in popularity. Other examples of this can be taken from the TV show *Cheers:* the wonderful old names REBECCA and SAMUEL—the latter in the form of just "Sam"—crept back up the popularity ladder, since they belonged to well-loved characters. Quite unusual, however, is the instance of the show's classically trained actor Kelsey Grammer: after his character dumped the character Diane and he became just one of the guys, the name FRASIER popped onto the top-twenty name list. Even more mystifying is that the name KELSEY, a long-forgotten, fine old boy's name, made a *wild* comeback . . . for girls! The fame of songstresses Taylor Dane and Mariah Carey have caused a rise in popularity for those once-thought-unusual names.

KIYOSHI, "kee-YOH-shee"—*Japanese: "quiet," "clear," or "bright."*

KIZZE, "KIH-zeh"—*African Ashanti: "healthy child."* **KESSE.** F

KLAUS, "KLOWSS"—*from Nic(h)olas: "victory of the people."* **KLAAS** (KLAHSS)—Danish; **KLAS**—Polish. See also CLAUS, NIC(H)OLAS.

KNOX, "NAWKS"—*English: "from the hills."* It is Henry Knox, a general in the Revolutionary War, who gave his name to Fort Knox, where the government keeps its precious metals.

KOJAH, "KOH-jah"—*Mongolian: "mink with long hair."* **KOJAK.** F

KONO, "KOH-noh"—*Native American Miwok: "tree squirrel with pine nut."*

KONSTANTIN, "kon-STAHN-tihn"—*Latin: "steadfast" or "constant."* **KONSTANCJI** (kawn-STAHN-tsyee)—Polish; **KOSTAS**—Greek; **KOSTYUSHA, KOTIK** (KOH-teek)—Russian. Konstantin is one of the Christian saints. See also CONSTANTIN. F

KOSUMI, "koh-SOO-mee"—*Native American Salish: "fishes for salmon with spear."*

KOTO, "KOH-toh"—*Japanese: "harp."*

KOUROS, "KOO-rohss"—*Greek: "young man."*

KRAFT, "KRAFT" or "KRAWFT"—*German: "strength."*

KRIST, "KRIHST" or "KREEST"—*Nordic, from Greek: "the anointed one"* or *"the Light."* **KRISTOS. KRISTY.** See also CHRISTIAN, CHRISTOPHER. F

KRISTIAN. See CHRISTIAN.

KRISTOFER. See CHRISTOPHER.

KUMAR, "KOO-mahr"—*Hindu: "youth"* or *"prince."*

KUNI, "koo-NEE"—*Japanese: "born in the country."* As opposed to a child born in the city. F

KUPONO, "koo-POH-noh"—*Hawaiian: "honest"* or *"just."* F

KURA, "KOO-rah"—*Japanese: "house of treasure."* F

KURI, "KOO-ree"—*Japanese: "chestnut."* F

KURT. See CURTIS.

KWAN, "KWAHN"—*Korean: "strong."*

KYDOS, "KYE-dohss" or "KEE-dohss"—*Greek: "glory."* This is the root word for "kudos."

KYLE, "KILE"—*Yiddish: "crowned with laurels"; Welsh: "chapel"* or *"narrow stream"; Irish: "comely."* **KILEY, KYLEY.** Kyle is one of the Christian saints. F

KYLO, "KYE-loh"—*Celtic: "grazing cattle"* or *"cows in the pasture."* **KYLEAU** (KYE-loh), **KYLOE.**

KYN, "KYNE" or "KIHN"—*Irish Gaelic: "intelligent"; Norse: "related to us"; English: "royalty."* If you're lucky, maybe he's all three.

KYU, "kee-YOO"—*Korean: "the standard."* This means the standard by which all to follow will be judged.

THE TOP FIVE

LAWRENCE
LEO
LEONARD
LEWIS/LOUIS
LEE/LI

If the name you're looking for isn't here, see "Y."

LABAN, "LAH-bahn" or "LAY-bun"—*Hebrew: "white."* **LAVAN.** In the Old Testament/Tanakh, Laban was the father of Rachel.

LADINO, "lah-DEE-noh"—*Spanish: "wise, crafty, cunning."* Ladino horses are wild and untamable. F

LADRON, "lah-DRAWN"—*Spanish: "mercenary"* or *"rascal."*

LAIBROOK, "LAY-brook"—*English: "pathway along the brook."* **LAYBROOK.**

LAIRD, "LAYRD"—*Scottish: "lord"; Celtic: "proprietor."*

LAKE, "LAYK"—*English: "lake."* **BAHRAT** (bah-RAWT), **HAWR**—Arabic; **CO, TSO**—Tibetan; **DARYACHEH** (DAHR-yah-cheh or dahr-YAH-cheh)—Persian; **EZERS** (EH-zehrz or AY-zayrz)—Latvian; **GOLU** (GOH-loo)—Turkish; **HU**—Chinese; **JARVI** (YAHR-vee)—Finnish; **JEZERO** (YEH-zeh-roh)—Albanian and Serbo-Croatian; **LAC** (LOCK)—French; **LACUL** (LAH-cool)—Romanian; **LAGO** (LAH-goh)—Spanish, Portuguese, and Italian; **LOCH** (LAWK)—Scottish Gaelic; **LOUGH** (LAWKH—"KH" is guttural)—Irish Gaelic; **MIZUMI** (mee-ZOO-mee)—Japanese; **NUUR**—Mongolian; **OZERO** (OH-zeh-roh)—Russian; **SAGAR** (SAH-gahr or sah-GAHR)—Hindu; **SEE**—German; **SO**—Danish and Norwegian; **TELAGA**—Indonesian; **THALE** (THAH-leh or TAH-leh)—Thai; **TJARN** (TYARN), **VATTEN** (VAW-tehn)—Swedish; **TONLE** (TAWN-leh or DAWN-leh)—Khmer; **ZEE**—Dutch. F

LAKOTAH, "lah-KOH-tah"—*Native American Sioux: "friend to us."* Lakotah is the name for the Teton branch of the Great Sioux Nation. F

LAL, "LAHL"—*Hindu: "beloved."*

LAMAR, "lah-MAHR"—*Portuguese: "the ocean"; German: "land-wealthy."* **LAMARR.**

LAMBERT, "LAM-burt"—*German: "bright land"; Teutonic: "rich in land."*

LAMONT, "lah-MONT"—*Norse: "lawyer"; French: "the mountain."* **LEMONT.** Lamont Cranston is the true identity of the comic book, radio, and film antihero called the Shadow. **MONTE, MONTY.**

LANCE, "LANCE"—*diminutive of Lancelot, thus Latin: "battle spear"; German: "demigod."* **LANCELOT** (LANCE-lot or LAN-suhlot), **LAUNCELOT; LANCING, LANSING.** Sir Lancelot was the most skilled of the Arthurian Knights of the Round Table; he fought bravely and fiercely, but he also had a fragile and sensitive psyche. Despite his troubles, he was adored by Queen Guinevere and many other women, and King Arthur dearly loved him . . . enough to look the other way when the knight and the queen got involved.

LANDON, "LAN-dun"—*German: "territory."* **LANDAN, LANDER, LANDERS, LANDIS, LANDRY.**

LANE, "LAYN"—*English: "path."* **LAINE, LAINIE, LANEY, LAYNE.** F

LANG, "LAHNG"—*Norse: "tall."* **LANGE.**

LANGDON, "LANG-dun"—*English: "long hill" or "long town."*

LANGFORD, "LANG-furd"—*English: "the long river-crossing."* **LANFORD.**

LANGSTON, "LANG-stun"—*English: "long town" or Celtic: "long stone."* **LANGSTEN, LANSTEN, LANSTON.**

LANI, "LAW-nee"—*Hawaiian: "sky" or "heaven."* F

LARES, "LAH-rehz"—*Etruscan: "guardian."* In ancient Italian folklore, there were many lares for many places and things.

LARRY. See LAURENCE/LAWRENCE.

LARS, "LAHRSS"—*Scandinavian from Latin: "laurel tree."* **LARSE, LARSEN.**

LASLO, "LAHS-low"—*Slavic: "famous ruler."* **LACI** (LAH-chee), **LACKO; LASZLO** (LAH-shlow), **LAZLO.**

LATEEF, "lah-TEEF"—*Moroccan: "gentle" or "pleasant."* **LATIF.** F

LATHAM, "LAY-thum"—*English: "owned lands"; Norse: "the barnstable."*

LAUGHTON, "LAW-tun" or "LAO-tun"—*Anglo-Saxon: "man of refinement."* LAWTON sounds the same, but has an entirely different meaning. Have a look.

LAURENCE, LAWRENCE, "LORE-ehnts"—*Latin: "crown of laurel" or "of Laurentium."* **LABHRÁS** (LAHV-rahs)—Irish Gaelic; **LARENZ**—Dutch; **LAURANS, LAURITS, LAVRANS**—Norwegian; **LAURENCHO** (loh-REHN-choh), **LORENCO** (loh-REHN-coh)—Portuguese; **LAURENTIJ** (loh-REHN-tee-ee)—Russian; **LAURENTIOS** (loh-REHN-tee-ohss)—Greek; **LAURENTIUS** (loh-REHN-chus or loh-REHN-tee-us)—Swedish; **LAURENTZI** (loh-rent-zee)—Basque; **LAURENZO** (lohrent-ZOH), **LOREN, LORETTO, RENZO**—Italian; **LORÁNT, LÖRENC, LORINC**—Eastern European; **LORENCZ** (loh-RENCH)—Hungarian; **LORENS, LORITZ**—Danish; **LORNE**—American. Several saint names are on this list, three of which are Lawrences. D.H. Lawrence was an early-twentieth century novelist. T.E. Lawrence was a British soldier and adventurer of the early twentieth century, better known as the flamboyant Lawrence of Arabia. **LARRI(E), LARRY; LAWRI(E), LAWRY.** F

LAVI, "LAH-vee"—*Hebrew: "lion."* See also LEO, LEON, LION, LYON, NAPOLEON.

LAWFORD, "LAW-ford"—*English: "ford in the hills."*

LAWLER, "LAW-lur"—*Gaelic: "mumbler."*

LAWTON, "LAW-tun"—*English: "village on the hill."* **LAUDON, LAUTON; LAWDON.**

LAYNE, "LAYN"—*Old English: "to conceal."* See also LANE. F

LEAF, "LEEF"—*English: "leaf."* **BLATT** (BLAHT)—German; **DAUN** (dah-OON)—Indonesian; **FEUILLE** (fooh-EEL)—French; **HOJA** (HOH-yah)—Spanish; **JANI** (JAH-nee)—Swahili; **YAPRAK** (YAHP-rahk)—Turkish. F

LEAL, "LEEL" or "LEE-ahl"—*Anglo-Saxon: "loyal."*

LEBEN, "LEH-behn"—*Yiddish: "life."*

LEE, "LEE"—*English: "meadow," "clearing," or "sheltered, covered"; Chinese: "pear."* **LEA, LEIGH** (LEE or LAY). See also LEO, YARDLEY/YEARDLEY. F

LEGRAND, "luh-GRAND"—*French: "the great," "the tall," or "the big."* **LE GRAND.**

LEIF, "LAYF"—*Norse: "descendant" or "the one who remains."*

LEIGHTON, "LAY-tun"—*English: "the farmsteads near the meadow."*

LELAND, "LEE-land"—*English: "meadowland"; Anglo-Saxon: "low lands."*

LEMUEL, "LEM-yoo-ehl"—*Hebrew: "dedicated to God."* Some Tanakh/Biblical scholars credit a prophet Lemuel with writing the book of Proverbs. Lemuel is the first name of the main character in Jonathan Swift's classic *Gulliver's Travels,* about a goodhearted seaman who gets lost on a voyage and finds himself in a variety of strange and wondrous lands, in which his common sense and kindness teach lessons to all.

LEN, "LEHN"—*Native American Hopi: "flute"; English: "tenant house."* **LENDON, LENNON, LENNOX.** See also LEONARD.

LENNON, "LEH-nuhn"—*Irish Gaelic: "little cloak."* **LENAN, LENIN, LENNAN, LENNIN, LENON.** John Lennon was one of the Beatles, a band that changed almost everything about popular music, culture, and fame. See also LEN.

LENNOR, "LEHN-or"—*Gypsy: "spring" or "summer."*

LEO, "LEE-oh" or "LAY-oh"—*traditionally, Latin: "the lion"; but also Cymric: "dear"; Anglo-Saxon: "loyal."* **LEE; LEU**—*Rumanian;*

LOEB (LOBE)—*German;* **LOWE**—*Scandinavian.* Over a dozen popes have been named Leo, including one who kept the Huns from destroying Rome. Quite a few kings of Constantinople bore this name. A Russian noble, Count Leo Tolstoy, is one of the great writers of the nineteenth century; his works include *War and Peace* and *Anna Karenina.* The constellation Leo can be seen chasing the Sun at dusk in April and May. The Sun is "in" Leo in August. To the Assyrians, it was the sign of NABU the Sent One or Sent Forth. To the early Christians, it was the sign of JOHN, the Eagle. To the Egyptians, it was TEFNUT, the Lioness. To the Greeks it was ZEUS, the Eagle or Thunderbolt. To the early Hebrews, it was the sign of EPHRAIM, the Bull or Ox. To the Norse, it was the sign of BRAGI, the Harp. To the Romans, it was the sign of JUPITER or Lightning. The Aztecs called this the sign of TZAKMUL the Jaguar. To the Babylonians, it was ARU RABU the Great Lion. Natural rulers at this time are the HOLLY TREE and HAZEL TREE for the Druids and Celts, and the MORNING GLORY for the Japanese. See also LAVI, LEON, LIO, LION, LYON, NAPOLEON.

LEON, "LEE-on" or "LAY-on"—*Latin: "like a lion."* **LÉON** (lay-AWN), **LÉONCE**—*French;* **LEONE** (lay-OH-neh), **LEONIDAS** (lay-oh-NEE-dahs)—*Italian;* **LEONID** (lay-oh-NIHD), **LEV**—*Russian;* **LEONTINOS, LEONTIOS.** See also LAVI, LEO, LION, LYON, NAPOLEON. F

LEONARD, "LEH-nahrd" or "LAY-oh-nahrd"—*Teutonic: "courage of a lion."* **LAUNART** (lawn-AR—"R" in the back of your throat, no "t"), **LIENARD** (lee-NAR—"R" in the back of your throat, no "d")—

French; **LENARD, LENHARDT; LENNART**—Swedish; **LEONARDO**—Italian and Spanish; **LEONHARD, LEONHARDE** (lay-oh-NAHR-deh)—Danish; **LOWENHARD**—German and Nordic. Saint Leonard was a sixth-century saint who converted a European king to Christianity, thus taking a giant step towards spreading the religion. Leonardo da Vinci is *the* Renaissance Man: artist, sculptor, architect, anatomist, engineer, astronomer, mathematician, musician, mountain climber, naturalist. He developed medical theories centuries before anyone else, developed flying machines, tanks, and diving equipment centuries before anyone else . . . all written in notebooks upside down and backwards, lest they be discovered. **LEN, LENNY.** F

LEOR, "LEE-ohr"—*Hebrew: "I have light" or "I am enlightened."* **LIOR.** F

LERON, "luh-RAWN"—*French: "the circle."* **LERIN, LERON, LEROND.**

LES, "LES"—*diminutive of Lester, English: "meadow near or in the city;" Anglo-Saxon: "from the army encampment."* See also LESLIE.

LESLIE, "LEHZ-lee"—*Scottish: "low-lying meadow"; Celtic: "from the gray fortress."* **LESLEY. LES.** F

LEV, "LEHV"—*Hebrew: "heart"; Russian version of Leon: "like a lion."* **LEB; LEVKA, LEVUSHKA.** See also LEON.

LEVANT, "leh-VANT" or "LEH-vant"—*French: "from the sunrise."* **LEVANTIN.** Levant refers to someone from the Eastern Mediterranean, especially Syria or Lebanon.

LEVI, "LEE-vye," "LEH-vee," or "leh-VEE"—*Hebrew: the Levites were one of the twelve tribes of Israel, and Levi means "joined in harmony."* **LEVEY, LEVY.** In the nineteenth century, Levi Strauss designed a utilitarian pair of pants using a hardy cloth first made in Nîmes, France, and his company hasn't stopped since. "Levi's pants" are now known as just Levis. **LEV.**

LEWIS, "LOO-wihss"—*version of Louis: "famous warrior."* **LEWES.** The Isle of Lewis is a northern Scottish outpost in the New Hebrides chain. The weather was often brutal, and the early inhabitants developed a lot of interesting board games to pass time indoors, so the association may be made with gamesmanship. See also LOUIS.

LEX, "LEHKS"—*Greek: "the word"; Latin: "the law."* **LEXING, LEXTON, LEXUS.** See also ALEXANDER. F

LI, like "LEE" but shorter, closer to "LIH"—*Chinese: "plum."* **LE**—Vietnamese. F

LIAM, "LEE-ahm"—*Irish version of William, Gaelic: "fox."* This name has begun to pop up more often, probably because of the popularity of Irish actor Liam Neeson. See also WILLIAM.

LIANG, "lee-AHNG"—*Chinese: "excellent."*

LIBERIO, "lee-BARE-ee-oh"—*Portuguese: "free."*

LIBOS, "LEE-bohss"—*Greek: "the southwest wind."* **LIBECCIO** (lee-BETCH-yoh), **LIBECCHIO** (lee-BECK-yoh)—Italian. F

LIKO, "LEE-koh"—*Chinese: "protected by the Buddha."*

LINCOLN, "LIHN-kuhn"—*Celtic: "the hollow by the clear pool"; English: "brookside hollow"; Anglo-Saxon: "waterfall in the hollow."* Abraham Lincoln, president during the Civil War, is considered to be one of America's greatest leaders. If George

Washington was the heart of America, Abraham Lincoln was its soul. Many newly freed slaves who found themselves without a last name declared Lincoln to be their new family name, and it became popular as a first name as well. **LINK.**

LIND, "LIHND"—*Anglo-Saxon: "lime trees."* **LINDO.** F

LINDELL, "LINH-dehl"—*English: "linden-tree dell or hollow."* **LINDL, LINDLE. LINDY.** See also LYNDON.

LINDEN, "LIHN-dehn"—*English: "lithe,"* and the linden tree. **LIND, LINDON, LYNDON.** Linden flowers are used in herbal and folk medicine. **LINDY.**

LINDSAY, "LIHND-zay"—*English: "island in the brook"* or *"brookside linden trees"; in a stretch, Anglo-Saxon: "island waterfall."* **LINDSEY.** F

LINK, "LIHNK"—*English: "from the banks."* The banks referred to are those of a river or stream. **LINC.** See also LINCOLN.

LIO, "LEE-oh"—*Hawaiian: "seahorse."* See also LEO.

LION, "LI-on"—*Latin from Greek: "lion."*

ASAD, ASSAD—*Arabic;* **LEEUW** (lee-OOH or lay-OOH)—*Dutch;* **LEJON** (LAY-ohn)—Swedish; **LEONE** (lay-OWN)—*Italian;* **LÖOWE**—*German;* **SINGA**—*Indonesian;* **RAION** (RYE-awn)—*Japanese;* **SIMBA** (SEEM-bah)—*Swahili.* See also LAVI, LEO, LEON, LYON, NAPOLEON.

LISLE, "LYLE" or "LEEL"—*French: "from the island."* **L'ÎLE**—*French.* See also LYLE.

LITTON, "LIHT-un"—*Celtic: "hillside village."*

LIWANU, "lee-WAH-noo"—*Native American Wakash: "growling bear."*

LLEWELLYN, "loo-WEHL-lihn"—*Welsh: "lightning"* or *"lion."* **LEWELYN, LLEWELYN; LLYWELLYN, LLYWELYN.** Several kings and tribal chieftains of Wales have had this name. **LEW.**

LLOYD, "LOYD"—*Welsh: "gray"* or *"dark."* **FLOYD, LOYD.**

LOCKE, "LAWK"—*Norse: "conclusion"* or *"closure."* **LOCK.**

LOGAN, "LOH-gahn"—*Scottish Gaelic: "little hollow (tiny valley)"; English: "record"* or *"log."*

DEEP SOUTH BOYS' NAMES

Boys born into the states along the Gulf Coast and the lower Mississippi River are most likely to have the following names:

1. Christopher
2. Michael
3. Brandon, Joshua
4. Tyler
5. Justin
6. James
7. Matthew
8. Jacob
9. Nicholas
10. John
11. Ryan
12. Joseph
13. Zachary
14. William
15. David
16. Jeffrey
17. Cody
18. Robert
19. Austin
20. Dylan

LOGGAN, "LOH-gun" or "LAW-gun"—*English: "rocking."* This doesn't mean rocking as in rock'n'roll, but as in moving to and fro.

LOKA, "LOH-kah"—*Sanskrit: "the world."* F

LOKI, "LOH-kee"—*Norse: "mischievous."* The Norse god Loki was anything but low key, as he was a bit of a troublemaker for gods and mortals alike. He was said to be able to change shape and to fly, and was associated with fire and earthquakes. F

LOMBARD, "LAWM-bahrd"—*German: "long beard."* **BARDO, LOMBARDO** (lohm-BAHR-doh)—Italian, Spanish, and French; **LOMBARK**—Norse. The Lombards were a Germanic people who established a kingdom in northern Italy from the 560s to the 770s.

LONAN, "LOW-nahn"—*Native American Zuni: "cloud."*

LONO, "LOW-noh"—*Polynesian. Lono is the Polynesian god of agriculture, prosperity, and peace.*

LORCAN, "LOHR-kahn"—*Irish: "little fiery one."* This is the name of one of the Christian saints.

LORNE, "LORN"—*American version of Laurence: "crowned with laurels."* **LORIN.** Actor Lorne Greene was known for his roles as the noble cowboy, noble rancher, noble whatever, forever remembered in reruns as Ben Cartwright on TV's *Bonanza.* See also LAURENCE/LAWRENCE.

LOUIS, "LOO-iss" or "loo-EE"—*German: "famous warrior."* **LEWIS; LOVISO** (loh-VEE-soh)—Slavic; **LUIGI** (loo-EE-jee)—Italian; **LUIS** (loo-EESE)—Spanish; **LUJZ** (loo-EEZ)—Hungarian. Eighteen French kings have been named Louis. Louis IX was made a saint for his efforts on behalf of the Crusades, while Louises XIV and XV built

most of the grand palaces we associate with France and Paris. Quite a few saint names are on this list, too. F

LOWELL, "LOW-ehl"—*English: "low hills" or "wolf cub"; Scandinavian: "lion cub."* **LOWE, LOWEL.**

LUCAS. See LUCIO, LUKE.

LUCENT, "LOO-sent"—*Latin: "shining" or "clear."* F

LUCIO, "loo-SEE-oh," "loo-CHEE-oh," or "LOO-syoh"—*Latin: "bringer of light" or "glittering."* **LUCAS** (LOO-kuhs)—American and English; **LUCIANO** (loo-chee-AH-noh)—Italian; **LUCIEN** (loo-see-EN or loo-SYEN)—French; **LUCIO** (LOO-tsyoh)—Eastern European; **LUCIUS** (LOO-shuhss); **LUCJAN** (LOOTS-yahn)—Polish; **LUCZO** (LOO-tsoh)—Hungarian. A few saints have borne names on this list. Lucius Licinius Lucullus (I'm serious!) was a Roman general in the first century B.C. best known for the great food served at the great parties he hosted. F

LUCKY, "LUHK-ee"—*Greek: "fortunate."* Lucky Vanous is a model who gained fame in a Diet Coke commercial . . . so much fame that he became yet another model turned actor.

LUDLOW(E), "LUHD-loh"—*English: "the prince's hill."*

LUGOS, "LOO-gohss"—*Celtic: god of prophecy, wisdom, medicine.* **LUGUS.** Lugos was said to be a tall, fair-haired warrior. He shows up in Irish legend as the father of great heroes and in Gaul (ancient France) as the patron of Lugus or Lugudunum—modern-day Lyons. In some regions of the British Isles, he was associated with the sun. Lugos healed by gently singing the

Le

"Le" (pronounced "luh") is the French version of the article "the" for masculine names only. Generally, the singular noun that follows will end in a consonant. You may add this yourself to a name; drop the "e" if "le" is to be followed by a vowel.

wounded to sleep and mixing up magical herbs. The slang term "big lug" comes from this good-hearted strongman.

LUIS. See LOUIS.

LUKE, "LOOHK"—*Latin: "bringer of light"; Greek: "from Lucania."* **LOUKAS**—Greek; **LUC** (LOOHK)—French; **LUCAS, LUKAS; LÚKÁCS** (LOO-katch)—Hungarian; **LUKASZ** (LOO-kahsh)—Polish; **LUKEN** (loo-kehn)—Basque; **LUKYAN**—Russian. Saint Luke was a Greek physician and artist who wrote the book that bears his name in the New Testament, and possibly the book of Acts. He is the patron saint of physicians and painters. Luc Robitaille is a hockey player. F

LUKI, "loo-kee"—*Basque: "warrior."*

LUNN, "LUHN"—*Irish Gaelic: "fierce."*

LUO, "LOO-oh"—*African Nilotic: "of the lake."* This is a tribe name for a group of people who farm and fish in the area around present-day Lake Victoria.

LUTAH, "LOO-tuh"—*Native American Sioux: "red."* F

LUTHER, "LOO-thur"—*German: "battle."* **LOTAIRIO** (loh-TARE-ee-oh), **LUTHERIO** (loo-TARE-ee-oh)—Italian; **LOTHAIRE** (loh-TARE—"R" back in the throat)—French; **LOTHARIO** (loh-THAH-ree-oh), **LOWTHER**—English; **LUTERIS** (loo-TARE-ihss), **LUTERIUS** (loo-TARE-ee-uhss), **LUTHERIUS** (loo-TARE-ihss), **LUTHERUS** (loo-TARE-ihss)—Latin and Nordic; **LUTERO** (loo-TARE-oh)—Spanish. This was a name of several Holy Roman Emperors, as well as the man who initiated the big break with Catholicism, Martin Luther, the founder of the Protestant movement.

LYDIO, "LIHD-ee-oh"—*Basque: "life"; English: "hillock"; Greek: "cultured" or "from Lidia."* **LIDIO; LYDELL.** Lidia is a region once ruled by the spectacularly wealthy King Croesus. F

LYLE, "LILE" or "LEEL" (French)—*French: "fine thread, quality thread."* **LILLE, LYALL, LYELL.** The thread can be either the thread to carry on the family, or the thread made in the French city of Lille. Lyle Lovett is a singer/songwriter and bandleader. See also LISLE.

LYMAN, "LYE-muhn"—*English: "man of the valley or plains."*

LYN(N), "LIHN"—*English: "a brook"; Anglo-Saxon: "a waterfall."* **LIN, LINN, LINNE; LYNNE.** Lynn Swan was a fleet-of-foot football player, and his fame popularized Lynn as a name for boys. F

LYNDON, "LIHN-duhn"—*English: "the linden tree" or "lake."* **LINDEL, LINDEN, LINDON.** Lyndon Johnson was president from 1963 to 1968. His most notable contributions were in domestic policy, including his appointment of the first African-American Supreme Court justice.

LYNX, "LINKS"—*Latin: "lynx."* The constellation Lynx can be seen stalking the Sun at dusk from mid-February to mid-April. The Lynx "catches" the Sun from late May to late July.

LYON, "lee-YON"—*French: "a lion."* It is also a place name for the city and region in France. See also LAVI, LEO, LEON, LION, NAPOLEON.

LYULF, "LYE-uhlf"—*Scottish: "fiery wolf."* **LIULF, LYOLF.**

THE TOP FIVE

MICHAEL
MATTHEW
MARK
MARCUS
MUHAMMAD

If the name you're looking for isn't here, perhaps it is a variant or a diminutive of another primary name.

MABRY, "MAH-bree"—*Cornish: "mirth."*

MACE, "MAYSS"—*French: the spiked globe-on-a-chain weapon; Latin: the aromatic spice.* **MACEO** (mah-SAY-oh)—*Italian and Spanish;* **MACEY, MACY**—*English;* **MACK, MACKEY**—*Scottish.* See also MASON.

MACK, "MAK"—*Scottish: "son of" or "son."* See also MACE.

MACKENZIE, MAC KENZIE, "mah-KEHN-zee"—*Gaelic: "child of the wise leader."* **MC KENZIE.** MacKenzie is a region in Canada's Northwest Territories, and it is also the name of a Canadian river.

MACON, "MAY-kun"—*English: "to create or perform."*

MADDOCK, "MAD-awk"—*Welsh: "fortunate"; Celtic: "fire" or "beneficent."* **MADDOC**—*Irish;* **MAD(D)OX; MADOC**—*Welsh;* **MADOCH** (MAD-awkh—"kh" in your throat)—*Scottish.*

MADISON, "MAD-ih-sun"—*English: "son of a soldier."* **MADDI(E), MADDY; SONNI(E), SONNY.** F

MAGEE, "mah-GHEE"—*Irish Gaelic:* "son of the flame." **MAC GEE, MC GEE.**

MAGEN, "MAH-ghehn"—*Hebrew: "shield."* **MOGEN.**

MAGI, "MAH-jye"—*Avestan/Ancient Persian: "gifted" or "with riches"; Greek: "priest."* **MAGOI** (MAH-goy), **MAGOS** (MAH-gohss)—*Greek;* **MAGOO**—*English from French pronunciation of MAGUS;* **MAGU** (MAH-joo or MAH-goo), **MAGUS** (MAH-guhss or MAH-juhss)—*the proper singular of Magi.* The Magi are the priestly class of the Zoroastrian faith, an old monotheistic religion from Persia. The Three Wise Men, or Magi, who visited the infant Jesus were not named in the Bible. The names assigned to them—Balthasar, Gaspar, and Melchior—first appeared in Longfellow's "The Adoration of the Magi."

MAGUIRE, "mah-GWIRE"—*Irish: "child of the dark(-haired, -skinned) one."* **MAC UIDHIR** (mahk-WHIRE)—*Irish Gaelic.*

MAGUS, "MAH-guhss"—*Ancient Persian/ Avestan: "priest"; Latin: "magician or wizard."* One of the Christian saints is named Magus. See also MAGI.

MAHAL, MAHAT, "mah-HAHL" and "mah-HAHT"—*Sanskrit: "great or high."* The title "mahatma" means "great man" or "high soul"; a famous mahatma was Mohandas K. Gandhi. F

MAHICAN, "mah-HEE-kun"—*Native American Algonquin: "clan of the wolf."* This is a tribe name for a group of people who once lived in the Northeast United States. It is the preferred name for a people immortalized by James Fenimore Cooper's novel *The Last of the Mohicans*. If you are seeking an "Indian" name, it might be nice to consider this one, along with names of other tribes that are no longer in existence. F

MAHIR, "mah-HEER"—*Arabic: "skilled," "speed," or "horse of Arabia."* F

MAHMUD, "mah-MOOD"—*Arabic: "praised."*

MAHON, "MAH-un" or "MAY-un"—*Irish: "bear."* **MAHONEY; MATHGHAMHAIN** (mahth-YAH-vah-een)—*Irish Gaelic.* Mahon, king of Munster in the tenth century, was the brother of fabled Irish hero Brian Boru.

MAI, "MAH-ee"—*Native American: "coyote"; Japanese: "bright."* F

MAKA(H), "MAH-kah"—*Native American: "earth."* This is a tribe name for a group of people who used to inhabit the Olympic Peninsula in the state of Washington. They used large seagoing canoes and yew-tree spears to hunt whale. The Makah performed potlatch ceremonies, in which the host would give his possessions to his guests. F

MAKANI, "muh-KAH-nee"—*Tahitian: "the wind."* F

MAKIN, "MAH-keen"—*Arabic: "strong."*

MAKOTO, "mah-KOH-toh"—*Japanese: "sincerity."* Sincerity is one of the great virtues of Shintoism, a native Japanese religion. **MAKATO.**

MALCOLM, "MAHL-kum" or "MAL-kum"—*Scotch-Irish: "servant of Saint Columba"; Celtic: "dove."* **MALKOLM.** One of the Christian saints was named Malcolm, as were several Scottish kings. Malcolm Little (d. 1965) was a habitual criminal who educated himself in prison and rose above his past. As Malcolm X, he went on to become one of the most controversial and effective advocates for the civil rights movement.

MALDEN, "MAHL-dehn"—*English: "meeting place."* **MALDON, MALTON.**

MALIK, "mah-LEEK"—*Arabic: "master" or "king"; Latin: "apples."*

MALIN, "MAH-lihn" or "MAL-ihn"—*English: "war-mighty."*

MALONE, "mah-LONE"—*traditionally, Irish: "servant of Saint John"; but also old Italian: "of the apple trees."* **MALONEY.**

MALORY, "MAL-oh-ree"—*German: "army counsellor"; French: "covered with mail."* **MALLORUS, MALLORY.** The French derivation doesn't refer to the kind of mail that comes from the post office, but to the coat of mail, made of metal chain links, worn by knights. Sir Thomas Mallory wrote of the legends of King Arthur and the Knights of the Round Table in *Le Morte d'Arthur.* F

MANAR, "mah-NAHR"—*Arabic: "beacon" or "lighthouse."*

MANCHU, "MAHN-choo"—*Chinese: "pure."* Manchu is one of the provinces of China.

MANDEAN, "MAN-dee-un"—*Aramaic: "knowing" or "having knowledge."* **MANDIAN.** The Mandeans are a religious group, still found in the Middle East in small numbers. They claim to be descendants of

Mac-, Mc-

These are Scottish prefixes that mean "child of-" and can be used with any name you choose.

John the Baptist, and believe in the God of Abraham, like the Christians, Jews, and Muslims. Their main religious goal is to achieve *Manda da Hayye,* Knowledge of Life, which they believe will bring them closer to God. F

MANDEL(L)A, "man-DELL-uh" or "MAN-duh-luh"—*French: "almond"; Native American: "ceremonial shield or banner."* **MANDAL, MANDALA, MANDEL, MANDELL.** Nelson Mandela is one of the founders of the African National Congress, a fighter against South Africa's apartheid system. After twenty-five years in jail, he was released and his continuing work brought about an all-race government, of which he became president. The Native American mandela is the decorative shield or banner used in a variety of ceremonies. Some are quite elaborate, decorated with leather, gems, feathers, fabric, and carved ornaments. **MANDY.** F

MANFRED, "MAN-frehd"—*German: "man of peace."* **MANNFRED. FRED, FREDDY; MANNY.**

MANI, "MAH-nee"—*Norse: "moon god"; Babylonian: "son of light."* One of the few mythologies that give the Moon over to the masculine force is the Norse. Mani fights with the wolves Skoll and Hati as he flies around the world, the skirmishes accounting for the waxing and waning of the Moon,

and for lunar eclipses. The Babylonian Mani was a prophet who founded the belief system called Manicheism, in which sparkles of light are trapped in the realm of darkness, to be gradually released by prophets or children of the Father of Light—like Zarathustra, Buddha, Jesus, Mani, etc.

MANNING, "MAN-ing"—*English: "to guard" or "to operate."* **MANNY.**

MANNY. See EMMANUEL, MANFRED, MANNING.

MANSUR, "mahn-SOOR"—*Arabic: "divinely aided."*

MANU, "MAH-noo"—*Sanskrit: "thinking" or "thoughtful."* The Indian Manu mythology has a few versions: there were either seven Manus in the early ages before mankind who wrote codes, laws, etc., or Manu was the mate of the first woman and the father of all humans.

MANUEL. See EMMANUEL, IMMANUEL.

MARAIIN, "mah-RYE-ihn"—*Australian Aborigine: "sacred."* **MARAIA(H); MAREIIN** (mah-RAY-ihn). Among the aborigines, *maraiin* are the rituals performed for and to the Earth Mother. F

MARC, "MARK"—*Celtic: "stallion," or version of Mark: "of Mars."* See also MARK. F

MARCEL. See MARCH, MARK.

MARCH, "MARCH"—*Latin: "of Mars," and the month March; Germanic: "borderland."* **MACHI** (MAH-chee)—*Swahili;* **MARCEL** (mar-SEL)—*French;* **MARET** (MAH-reht)—*Indonesian;* **MARS**—*French, Swedish, and Norwegian;* **MÄRZ**—*German;* **MARZO** (MAHR-zoh)—*Spanish and Italian;* **SANGWATSU** (SONG-waht-soo)—*Japanese.* The traditional flower for this month is the jonquil, while the traditional birthstone is the aquamarine. The god Mars is the Roman god of war, among other things; March was so named because it was the first month in which winter's frost had begun to melt enough for soldiers to effectively *march* to wherever. Mars rules Aries, which is the March astrological sign, and Ares, appropriately enough, is the Greek god of war. The German derivation comes from the word "marchlands," which is used to describe a border area between estates or countries.

MARCUS. See MARK.

MARDELL, "mahr-DEHL"—*English: "little valley by the sea."* **MARTEL(L).** F

MARDEN, "MAHR-dehn"—*English: "seaside cove."* **MARSDEN, MARSTEN** (a rocky cove).

MARDUK, "MAHR-dook"—*Babylonian: "warrior god" or "mighty god."* In Babylonian mythology, Marduk defeated chaos and overcame the infighting within the heavenly pantheon, setting order on the universe. He also arranged the calendar and made humankind.

MAREN, "mah-rihn"—*Basque: "the sea."*

MARID, "mah-REED"—*Arabic: "rebellious."*

MARIN, "MARE-ihn"—*Latin: "of the sea" or "sailor."* **MARINER, MARRINER; MARINO** (mah-REE-noh)—Spanish and Italian; **MARINOVICH** (mah-RIHN-oh-vitch), "son of a sailor" or "son of the sea"—Russian.

MARIO. See MARK, MARTIN.

MARK, "MARK"—*Latin: "of Mars"—the god of war and power—or "belonging to Mars"; Greek: "tender"; Celtic: "stallion."* **LEMAREK** (luh-MAH-rehk—"r" in your throat), **MAREK** (MAH-rehk)—Old French;

Ap, Map

These are Welsh prefixes that mean "of," "from," or "child of." You may add them to any name.

MARC; MARCAS—Irish; **MARCEAU** (mahr-SOH), **MARCEL** (mahr-SEHL—"r" back in your throat)—French; **MARCELIN** (mahr-seh-LEEN or mahr-cheh-LEEN), **MARCEL(L)INO, MARCO, MARCOS**—Italian and Portuguese; **MARCELLO** (mahr-SEHL-oh or mahr-CHEH-loh); **MARCELY** (mahr-SHEH-lee), **MARCIN, MARCINEK**—Slavic; **MARCO, MARKO, MARKOS**—Greek; **MARCUS**—Latin; **MARIO, MARTIAL** (mahr-SHAWL)—Spanish; **MARX**—German; **MARSHAL(L); MASHA** (mah-SHAH)—Israeli. Marcus was a name often used by Roman nobles for their sons. Saint Mark wrote the book of the New Testament that bears his name. Marco Polo was a Venetian explorer and adventurer who opened up trade and diplomatic routes between Europe and Asia. Mark Twain was the pseudonym of American writer and wit Samuel Clemens. Marc Chagall was a famous French artist. Mario Andretti is a race car driver. Swimmer Mark Spitz won seven gold medals in the 1972 Summer Olympics. **MARKEY, MARKY.** See also MARQUIS, MARTIN. F

MARLEY, "MAHR-lee"—*English: "seaside meadow or clearing."* **MARLEA, MARLEE, MARLEIGH.** Reggae singer Bob Marley was a strong supporter of human rights. F

MARLIN, "MAHR-lihn"—*English: "seafarer" or the marlin fish.* **MARLON, MARNIN.**

Marlon Brando is a charismatic, eccentric actor—much imitated but never surpassed—who rose to fame in the 1950s playing emotionally tortured, troubled antiheroes. **MAR, MARN.**

MARLON. See MARLIN.

MARQUES, "MAR-kehz" or "mar-KEHZ"—*French: "emblem," "flag," or "banner."* F

MARQUIS, "mahr-KEE" or "mahr-KEEZ"—*Latin: "commander of the marches"; French: "nobleman" and "canopy."* **MARQUITO** (mahr-KEE-toh)—Spanish and Portuguese. The second French derivation comes from the fact that commoners weren't toted about and protected by a covered conveyance. **MARK, MARKIE, MARQ.**

MARRAM, "MAHR-am"—*Norse: "beach grass" or "grassy dune."* **MARAM.** F

MARSDEN, "MAHRZ-dehn"—*Anglo-Saxon: "little clearing by the marshes."*

MARSH, "MARSH"—*English: "the wetlands" or "marsh."* **CHOTT**—*Arabic;* **ESTAING, ÊTANG, LANDE**—*French;* **HAMUN** (hah-MOON)—*Persian;* **UST**—*Russian.* See also MARSTON, SEYMOUR.

MARSHALL, "MAR-shahl"—*French: "horse groomer."* **MARSHAL.** In the United States, a marshall is also a law-enforcement officer.

MARSTON, "MAHRZ-tun"—*Anglo-Saxon: "town by the marshes."* See also MARSH.

MARTIN, "MAHR-tihn"—*Latin: "of Mars" (see the note at Mark); Celtic: "stallion" or "mare"; English: "the martin bird" or "a marten."* **MAARTEN, MARTIJN** (mahr-TEE-en)—Dutch; **MARIO** (MAH-ree-oh)—Italian and Spanish; **MARTEEN, MARTEN, MARTENE, MARTON; MARTINO** (mahr-TEE-noh)—Italian; **MARTINOS**—Greek; **MARTON**—Hungarian; **MARTYN**—Russian; **MORTEN**—Norwegian. Several popes and saints have had this name; one, Saint Martin, is the patron saint of France. Martin Luther was the initiator of the Protestant Christian movement. Martin Luther King, Jr. was a twentieth-century preacher who was a passionate and philosophical hero of the American civil rights movement. **MART, MARTI(E), MARTY.** F

MARTY. See MARTIN.

MASATO, "mah-SAH-toh"—*Japanese: "justice."*

MASIKO, "mah-SEE-koh"—*African Runyankore: "invincible."*

MASON, "MAY-sun"—*French: "to make or create" or "stone cutter"; Arabic: "beautiful face."* **MAÇON** (may-SAWN), **MASSON** (mah-SAWN)—French. **MACE, MAC(E)Y, MASE, MAS(E)Y.**

MASUD, "mah-SOOD"—*Arabic: "fortunate."*

MATIN, "mah-TEEN"—*Arabic: "strong" or "firm."* F

MATO, "MAH-toh"—*Native American: "brave" (adjective).*

MATSU, "MAHT-soo"—*Japanese: "pine tree."*

MATTHEW, "MATH-you"—*Hebrew: "gift of God."* **MÁTÉ** (MAH-teh)—Hungarian; **MATEUS** (mah-TAY-oos), **MATTEUS, MATTHIUS** (mah-THY-us)—Italian and Latin; **MATHEW; MATHIS** (MATH-ihss), **MATHUS**—Dutch; **MATISYAHU** (mah-tihs-YAH-hoo)—Israeli; **MATS** (MAHTS)—Swedish; **MATTHEU** (mah-TYUH), **MATTHIEU** (mah-tee-YUH)—French; **MATTHIAS** (mah-THY-ahss)—Greek; **MATVEY** (MAHT-vay)—Russian; **MAYHEW** (MAY-hyoo). Saint Matthew was a tax collecter for the

Roman government in Judea until he met an ex-carpenter from Nazareth. He became a disciple of Jesus, and the writer of one of the books in the New Testament. Matthias was chosen by lot to be the twelfth disciple after Judas turned Jesus in to the authorities. **MATT, MATTI(E).** F

MAURI, "MOH-ree" or "MAW-ree"—*Phoenician: "western."* This is what the Romans called northwestern Africans.

MAURICE, "MORE-eese" or "more-EESE"—*Latin: "a Moor, Moorish" or "son of the black one"; Hebrew: "God is my teacher."* **MAURIDS, MAURIDSJE** (moh-RIHDS-yeh), **MAURITS, MAURITSJE** (moh-RIHTS-yeh)—Dutch; **MAURIZIO** (moh-REE-tsee-oh)—Italian; **MAURY**—Irish; **MAURY, MAURYCY** (moh-REE-see)—Polish; **MORENO** (moh-RAY-noh)—Spanish; **MORICZ** (MORE-each)—Hungarian; **MUIRIS** (myoo-EER-ees)—Irish Gaelic. The Moors, Arabs from north Africa, had their heaviest initial contact with Europeans during the Crusades. Several saint names are on this list. See also MORRIS. F

MAX, "MACKS" or "MAWKS"—*Latin: "greatest" or "most."* **MAKIMUS**—Polish; **MAKS, MAKSIM, MAXIM** (mahk-SEEM)—Russian; **MAKSYM** (mahk-SEEM), **MAKSY-MILIAN** (mahk-see-MIHL-yahn)—Eastern European; **MASSIMO** (MAH-see-mo)—Italian; **MAXIM, MAXIMO** — French; **MAXIMOS**—Greek; **MAXIMILIAN, MAXMILIAN, MAXMIL-LIAN.** Maximus was a title bestowed on the greatest of the Roman warriors—like a rank, but an actual name added to their own. F

MAXWELL, "MACKS-wehl"—*Scottish: "great spring" or "large spring"; could be taken to mean: "great and good" if you're expanding on Max.* See also MAX.

MAYNARD, "MAY-nurd"—*German: "strong and powerful."*

MAZI, "MAH-zee"—*African Ibo: "sir."*

MEAD(E), "MEED"—*English: "mead-ow"; Celtic: "honey wine."* Mead is an old traditional Celtic and Anglo-Saxon alcoholic beverage made from spiced honey. F

MEGED, "MEH-ghehd"—*Hebrew: "sweet" or "good."*

MEHTAR, "MEH-tahr"—*Hindu: "prince."*

MEIR, "meh-EER"—*Hebrew: "light" or "enlightened"; Teutonic: "farmer."* **MAYIR, MEYER.** F

MELVIN, "MEHL-vihn"—*English: "friend on/of the council" or "friend at/of the mill"; Celtic: "chief."* **MELVYN.**

MENACHEM, "meh-NAH-khem" ("kh" in your throat)—*Hebrew: "the comforter."*

MENASSAH, "meh-NAH-sah"—*Hebrew: "causing to forget."* This could be a child who would cause one to forget past sorrows.

MENDEL, "MEHN-dehl"—*Yiddish: "comforter"; Persian: "knowledge."*

MENDELEY, "mehn-deh-LEE/LAY"—*Yiddish: "comforter"; Latin: "of the mind."*

MENES, "MEH-nez"—*Egyptian: "glorious."* Menes was the king who united various regions of the Lower Nile and Nile Delta into one kingdom in the fifth century B.C. He is traditionally called the first Egyptian king.

MERCURY, "MUR-kyur-ee"—*Roman: "messenger/communicator of the gods" or "quicksilver."* Mercury was a fleet-footed, fast-witted, lively Roman god. He was the god of commerce, skill, and travel. He was also the "coordinator" of the Muses, kind of an Olympian traffic cop, letting them know where they should go—an expediter, if you will. The planet Mercury is the closest to the Sun, and zips through our skies faster than any other heavenly body except the Moon.

MEREDITH, "MARE-eh-dihth"—*Welsh: "guardian of the sea."* **MEREDYDD** (MEH-reh-dihth)—Welsh; **MERIDITH.** F

MERLE, "MURL"—*Latin: "blackbird"; English: "swirl (of color)."* **MERIL, MERL; MERRYL, MERYL** (MARE-ihl). See also MERLIN/MERLYN. F

MERLIN, MERLYN, "MUR-lin"—*Cymric/ Welsh: "sea brook" or "seaside fortress"; Latin: "blackbird"; Anglo-Saxon: "(a small) hawk or falcon."* **MARLON, MERLON; MYRDDIN** (MEER-thehn)—Welsh. Merlyn, sometimes called Myrddin Emrys in Welsh, was a mystical Druid who was known as tutor and advisor to the legendary King Arthur throughout the king's life. Most of the knights feared him because his magical power was, apparently, unlimited. However, women didn't seem to avoid him, and he was quite vulnerable in love. **MERL, MERLE.** See also EMERY.

MERRICK, "MARE-ihk"—*English/German: "ruler of the sea"; Teutonic: "ambitious."* **EMERICK, MERRIK. RICK, RIK.**

MERRITT, "MARE-iht"—*Latin: "deserving" or "valuable."* **MERRIT.**

MERTON, "MUR-tun"—*Anglo-Saxon: "the village by the sea."*

MICHAEL, "MY-kahl"—*Hebrew: traditionally "who is like God?" but also "who is the Lord?" and "stream."* **MAHAIL, MIKHOS, MAKIS**—Greek; **MICHA** (MEE-khah—"kh" like you're clearing your throat), **MICHA-EL** (mee-khah-EHL—do the "kh" thing), **MICH-LA**—Israeli; **MICHAIL** (mee-kah-EHL or mee-KAH-ehl), **MIKHAIL** (mee-kah-EHL or mee-KAH-ehl), **MISHA**—Russian; **MICHAL** (MEE-kahl), **MICHALIN** (MEE-kah-leen)—Polish; **MICHÉAL** (meekh-YAHL—"kh" down in your throat)—Irish Gaelic; **MICHEIL** (meekh-YALE—"kh" down in your throat)—Scottish Gaelic; **MICHEL** (mee-SHELL), **MICHELIN** (MISH-lihn)—French; **MICHIEL** (mih-CHYEHL)—Dutch; **MICI** (MEE-chee), **MIHÁLY** (mee-HAH-lee), **MIKA, MIS(H)KA**—Hungarian; **MIGUEL** (mee-GHEL), **MIGUELITO**—Spanish; **MIKAEL**—Swedish; **MIKEL(E)** (mee-kehl[-eh])—Basque; **MIKKEL**—Norwegian; **MITCHELL, MITCH.** The Archangel Micha-el, called "the Prince of Light," is seen as God's warrior, and is often represented with a sword and shield. Michael also shows up as one of the Virtues in the heavenly hierarchy, and supervises the guardian angels. In Muslim tradition, the tears Michael sheds over the sins of the faithful form the cherubs. He is associated with the Last Judgement, being God's enforcer. His loyalty is never in question, he always stands with God and acts for Him. The Essenes, a Jewish sect, consider Michael to be the Angel of Earth and give him rulership over Sunday. A few saints, and many kings, tsars, and emperors worldwide have borne the names on this list. Michelangelo (name meaning "the angel Micha-el") Buonarotti was born into a well-to-do family and raised by a nanny whose husband was a stonecutter. From a very young age he was absorbed in creative expression, compelled to create even as his family beat him regularly to force him to give up all that nonsense and get a "respectable" job. At age 15, a local nobleman took him from his family, recognizing a genius when he saw one, and thus, one of the world's greatest artists was finally free to do what he was born to do. His first publicly shown work was the Pieta, and no one could believe that a young "novice" had done such a work. Upon hearing these comments, Michelangelo chiselled his name into the ribbon across Mary's chest, making this piece the only work he ever signed. Thirteen popes kept his work in demand, and his painted, carved, and architectural pieces are among the most grand in history. **MICK, MICKEY, MICKY; MIKE, MIKEY.** See also MICHAN. F

MICHAL, "mee-KHAHL" ("KH" like you're hocking up something noteworthy)—*Hebrew: "stream" or "brook."* **MICHALY.** F

MICHAN, "mee-CHAWN" or "mee-KHAN" ("KH" is guttural)—*Irish pet form of Michael: "who is like God?"* Michan is one of the Christian saints. See also MICHAEL.

MICKY, "MIH-kee"—*Scottish version of Michael: "who is like God?"* **MICKEY, MICKI(E), MIKKI(E).** Mick Jagger is the singer/musician/composer who leads the long-lived British group The Rolling Stones. Yankee Hall-of-Famer Mickey Mantle was a hero to small boys and grown men alike. **MICK.** See also MICHAEL.

MIGUEL. See MICHAEL.

MIKA, "MEE-kah" or "MY-kah"—*Native American Creek: "the clever raccoon."* See also MICHAEL. F

MIKE. See MICHAEL.

MIKSA, "MEEK-shah"—*Hungarian: "the greatest."* **MIKCZA** (MEEK-shah).

MILES, "MYLZ"—*German/Slavic: "merciful"; Teutonic: "warrior"; Latin: "soldier."*

MILAN, MILLS, MILO, MILOS (MY-lohss or MEE-lohss), **MYLES.** This name shows how derivations can be quite different from one another. The word for distance, "mile," comes from the Latin phrase *mille passum,* or "a thousand paces." Trumpeter Miles Davis was an innovator who mastered every style of jazz, from bebop to fusion.

MILLER, "MIHL-ur"—*English: "one who works in a mill" or "grinder of grains."* **MILLARD.** Millard Fillmore was president from 1850 to 1853. He is perhaps best known for having a name like Millard Fillmore. **MILO.**

MILOS, "MEE-lohss" or "MY-lohss"—*Slavic: "pleasant."* **MILO.** Milos is one of the Christian saints. See also MILES.

MILTON, "MIHL-tun"—*English: "mill town."* John Milton was one of the greatest English writers of poetry and prose; his works include *Paradise Lost* and *Paradise Regained.* Milton Hershey (d. 1945) is the Hershey in Hershey's chocolate. He and his wife gave most of their profits to a home for orphaned boys. Because he was a good guy—and because he *did* make that wonderful food—I will refrain from any humorous comment on his middle name: Snavely. **MILT.**

MIN, "MIHN"—*Egyptian.* This is the Egyptian god of fertility, masculine sexual power, and storms.

MINAL, "mee-NAHL"—*Native American: "fruit."* F

MING, "MING"—*Chinese: "luminous."*

MIR, "MEER"—*Russian: "earth" or "peace."* F

MIRCEO, "meer-SEE-oh" or "meer-say-oh"—*Latin: "astonishing."* **MIRCIO; MIROSLAV**

(mee-roh-SLAHV)—Slavic. **MIRO, MIRRO.** F

MIREMBE, "mih-REHM-beh"—*African Luganda: "peace."* **NAMIREMBE. MIREH.** F

MISTRAL, "MIHZ-trawl"—*French: "master of winds."* The mistral is a hard, cold, dry northwest wind that blows through the Alps.

MISU, "MEE-soo"—*Native American Miwok: "rippling water."*

MITCHELL. See MICHAEL.

MITSU, "MEET-soo"—*Japanese: "light."* F

MIYO, "mee-YOH"—*Japanese: "beautiful child."* F

MOHAMMED, "moo-HAH-mahd" or "muh-HAH-mahd"—*Arabic: "the praised one."* **MAHMOUD, MAHMUD; MAHOMET, MEHMET; MAHOUND**—Gaelic; **MOHAMMAD, MUHAMMAD, MUHAMMED; MUSTAFA**—Turkish. Mohammed, the founder of Islam, was a rich Arab merchant who rejected the beliefs of his ancestors after much time spent meditating. Instead, he said that God, through the angel Gabriel, gave him a new faith, one based on submission to Allah. He tried to spread this idea around, but ran into opposition and had to flee from his hometown of Mecca to Medina in A.D. 622. Eventually, Mohammed succeeded, and at one point the Islamic empire he started stretched from Spain to India. Today, his followers number more than a billion.

MOHAN, "moh-HAHN"—*Hindu: "delightful."* **MOHANDAS.** Mohandas K. Gandhi (d. 1948), was a very great Hindu leader who worked tirelessly for human rights by engaging in nonviolent protest. His religious beliefs were an amalgam of several ideologies, and some view him as a modern avatar, or a god incarnated as a living being.

MOHICAN. See MAHICAN.

MONDAY, "MUN-day"—*Teutonic: "the Moon's day."* **COJO** (koh-JOH)—African Ewe and Akan; **GETSUYOOBI** (geht-soo-YOO-bee)—Japanese; **JOJO** (joh-joh)—African Fante; **JUMATATU** (joo-mah-TAH-too)—Swahili; **KODWO** (koh-DWOH)—African Twi; **LUNDI** (LUHN-dee)—French; **MONTAG** (MAWN-tog)—German. F

MONROE, "muhn-ROH"—*Gaelic: "near the River Roe" in Ireland; Celtic: "from the red swamp."* **MONRO, MUNROE, MUNROW.**

MONTANA, "mawn-TAN-ah"—*Latin: "mountains."* **MONTAGNE** (mawn-TAN-yeh)—French. F

MONTEL(L). See MONTGOMERY.

MONTGOMERY, "mawnt-GUH-meh-ree"—*French: "the pointed hill."* **MONTAGUE** (MAWN-tah-gyoo)—French. **MONTE, MONTEL(L)** (mawn-TEL), **MONTY.**

MONTY. See BEAUMONT, LAMONT, MONTGOMERY.

MOORE, "MORE" or "MOOR"—*French: "a Moor" or "dark-skinned."* The Moors were from northern Africa.

MORGAN, "MORE-gin/gan"—*Welsh: "dweller by the sea" or "the white ocean waters"; German: "morning."* **MORGEN, MORGIN.** F

MORLEY, "MOHR-lee"—*English: "meadow or clearing by the moors."* **MORLEA, MORLEIGH.**

MORRIS, "MORE-iss"—*Latin: "a Moor, Moorish" or "son of the black one"; English: "from the marshlands."* **MORIS**—Greek; **MORITZ**—German; **MORIZ**—Russian; **MORSE.**

MORRIE, MORRY. See also MAURICE, SEYMOUR.

MORTON, "MORE-tun"—*English: "village of the Moors" (North Africans) or "the town on the moors" (or marshlands).* **MORTEN. MORT, MORTIE.**

MOSES, "MOH-zehz"—*Hebrew: "drawn/ saved from the water"; Egyptian: child."* **MOISES** (MOY-sehs)—*Portuguese;* **MOISHE, MOSHE** (MOH-sheh), **MOSHEH, MOYSHE**—*Hebrew;* **MÓIZES**—*Slavic;* **MOYSES**—*Greek;* **MOUSA** (MOO-sah)—*Arabic.* The Moses of Judeo-Christian tradition ("Mousa" in Islamic tradition) was set upon the Nile in a reed basket by his mother with the prayer that he would be spared the death sentence the Egyptian Pharaoh had decreed for all Hebrew males under three years of age. Moses was drawn from the water at the Pharaoh's palace by Pharaoh's childless wife (or daughter) Bithia, and she raised him as her own. After reaching the height of Egyptian power and wealth, Moses discovered his true origins. He grew to intimately know the God of the Hebrews, and made it his life's goal to free the Hebrews from Egyptian slavery and lead them into a Promised Land. In the nineteenth century, Moses Fleetwood Walker was another leader of sorts: he was the first black man to play major league baseball. **MO, MOE, MOKE, MOSE, MOZE.** F

MOSI, "MOH-see"—*Swahili: "first born."*

MUBIRU, "moo-BEER-ooh"—*African Luganda: "a boy from the clan with the Eel Totem."*

MUGABA, "moo-GAH-bah"—*African Runyoro: "God's gift."*

MUHAMMAD. See MOHAMMED.

MUHANNAD, "moo-HAHN-nahd"—*Arabic: "sword."*

MUIR, "MYOOR"—*Celtic: "the sea"; Scottish: "the moor" or "heath."*

MULLEN, "MUHL-ehn"—*Irish: "a mill."* **MULLIN. MULL, MULLY.**

MUNI, "MOO-nee" or "MEW-nee"—*Sanskrit: "sage."* **MOONI.**

MUNIR, "moo-NEER"—*Arabic: "illuminating."* F

MURACO, "MOO-rah-koh"—*Native American Hokan: "white moon."*

MURDOCK, MURDOCH, "MURdawk"—*Gaelic: "experienced sailor"; Celtic: "prosperity from the sea."* **MUIREADHACH** (MYOOR-reh-dawkh—hock up that "kh"!)— *Gaelic;* **MURDAGH** (MUR-dawg), **MURDO**— *Scottish;* **MURTAGH** (MUR-tawg or MURtaw), **MURTAUGH**—*Irish.*

MURPHY, "MUR-fee"—*Irish: "sea warrior."* F

MURRAY, MURREY, "MUHR-ee"— *Celtic: "man of/from the sea"; French: "mulberry-colored."* **MAURY, MURRY.**

MURROW, "MUR-oh"—*Irish: "sea warrior."* **MURROUGH.**

MUSCAT, "MUHSS-kat"—*French and Arabic: "musk"; French and Creole: "fox grape."* **MASQAT**—*Arabic;* **MUSCADEL, MUSCATEL.** Muscat is a sweet white wine made from European muscat grapes. Muscat and Oman is a sultanate on the Gulf of Oman.

MUSTAFA, "moo-STAH-fah"—*Turkish from Arabic: "chosen one."* **MUSTAFAH.** This is the Turkish version of Mohammed. It is the name borne by several sultans of the Ottoman Empire. See also MOHAMMED.

MWAKA, "m'WAH-kah"—*Swahili: "born in the Springtime."* F

MYUNG, "mee-YUNG"—*Korean: "brightness."*

THE TOP FIVE

NIC(H)OLAS
NATHANIEL
NEIL/NEAL/NILES
NOAH
NOLAN

If the name you're looking for isn't here, perhaps it is a variant or a diminutive of another primary name.

NABIL, "NAHB-eel"—*Arabic: "noble."* F

NACHMAN, "NAHKH-mahn"—*Hebrew: "compassion."* **NAHUM.**

NACIEN, "NAH-syen"—*Old French: "iridescent"* or *"mother of pearl(?)."* Nacien was a descendant of Joseph of Arimathea, who, legend has it, took the cup from which Christ drank at the Last Supper and saved it. Nacien is said to have brought that cup, the Holy Grail, to either the British Isles or France. F

NADAV, "NAH-dahv"—*Hebrew: "giver."*

NADIM, "nah-DEEM"—*Arabic: "friend."*

NADIV, "NAH-deev"—*Hebrew: "noble."*

NAEEM, "nah-EEM"—*Moroccan: "benevolent."* **NAIM.**

NAJI, "nah-ZHEE"—*Arabic: "safety."* F

NAJIB, "nah-ZHEEB"—*Arabic: "nobleman."*

NAKOS, "NAH-kohs"—*Native American Arapaho: "sagebrush."*

NAKOTAH, "nah-KOH-tah"—*Native American Sioux: "friend to all(?)."* This was one of the three tribes in the Great Sioux Nation. F

NAMI, "nah-MEE"—*Japanese: "wave."* F

NAMID, "nah-MEED"—*Native American Chippewa: "the star dancer."* Namid is a coyote who wanted to dance with the stars above; as it is, coyotes, through their howling, can only provide musical accompaniment to the cosmic ballet. F

NAMIR, "nah-MEER"—*Hebrew and Arabic: "leopard."*

NANNAR, "nah-NAHR"—*Babylonian: "moon god."*

NAOKO, "nah-OH-koh"—*Japanese: "straight"* or *"honest."*

NAPOLEON, "nah-POH-lee-ahn"—*Greek: "from the new city"; Latin/Greek: "new lion."* Napoleon Bonaparte was a military genius and skilled politician who rose to be emperor of most of Western Europe by 1804. He was defeated and exiled once, but came back again. **LEON; NAP, NAPPY.** See also LAVI, LEO, LION, LYON.

NARADA, "nah-RAH-dah"—*Sanskrit: "water-giver"* or *"water-bearer."* F

NARI, "NAH-ree"—*Japanese: "clap of thunder."* F

NASH, NESH, "NASH" or "NESH"—*Old English: "soft."*

NASIM, "nah-SEEM—*Arabic: "fresh air."*

NAT(E). See JONATHAN, NATHAN.

NATHAN, "NAY-then—*Hebrew: "the given" or "the gift."* **NATAN, NATHANIEL; NATANAEL** (nah-TAHN-ah-el)—*Swedish.* In the Old Testament/Tanakh, Nathan was the only friend of King David who was brave enough to tell the king that David had committed a grave set of sins to obtain the woman Bathsheba. In the New Testament, Nathaniel, sometimes called Bartholomew, is one of the twelve disciples. Nathan Hale was one of the fires that lit the American Revolutionary War. Nat "King" Cole was an African-American musician who broke the color barrier of television when he had his own show in the 1950s. **NAT, NATE, NATTY.** See also JONATHAN. F

NATSU, "NAHT-soo—*Japanese: "born in summer."*

NAVARRO, "nah-vahr-oh—*Basque.* This is the name of the Basque kingdom in what is now northern Spain. The Basques were able to resist conquest by many tribes and groups of people in Europe, holding fast when domains all around them were falling.

NAWAR, "nah-WAHR—*Arabic: "flower."*

NEAL, "NEEL—*Scotch-Irish: "cloud"; Celtic: "brave champion"; Gaelic: "the chief."* **NEALL, NEIL, NEILL; NIALL** (NEEL or NY-ahl)—*Irish Gaelic;* **NILE.** Niall of the Nine Hostages was one of the most famous kings of Tara, and the founder of the Ui Neill (O'Neill) dynasty of Irish kings. Neil Armstrong was the first human to set foot on the Moon. See also NELS.

NED, "NEHD—*Slavic: "born on Sunday";* *English: "guardian."* Somehow, Ned has also become a nickname for Theodore. **NEDDIE, NEDDY.** See also THEODORE. F

NEHRU, "NEH-roo—*Hindu: "canal."* Jawaharlal Nehru helped India to make many reforms in her change from a British possession to an independent state.

NEIL. See NEAL.

NELS, "NEHLS—*Celtic: "chief."* **NILS.** See also NEAL.

NELSON, "NEHL-sun—*English: "son of the chief."* **NIELSEN, NIELSON.**

NEMO, "NEE-moh—*Greek: "from the glen"; Latin: "no one."* Captain Nemo was the strange, ingenious scientist with the passionate-yet-mysterious past who appeared in many of the books of H.G. Wells.

NEPTUNE, "NEHP-toon—*Old Italian: "sea god."* Neptune was the Roman god of the waters, and of the deep places in the world and in the human soul.

NEVADA, "neh-VAH-dah—*Spanish: "snow white."* F

NEVAN, "NEH-vahn—*Irish: "little saint"; Anglo-Saxon: "nephew."* **NAOMHAN** (NOW-vahn)—*Irish Gaelic;* **NEVANS, NEVIN, NEVINS.**

NEVILLE, "NEH-vihl" or "neh-VEEL—*French: "from the new town."* **NEVIL, NEVILL. NEV.**

NEWELL, "NOO-ehl—*Latin: "young or new."* **NOVELL, NOWELL.** See also NOEL.

NEWTON, "NOO-tun—*Anglo-Saxon: "from the new estate" or "from the new village."* **NEWT.**

NIBAL, "nee-BAHL—*Arabic: "arrows."*

NICK. See NIC(H)OLAS.

NIC(H)OLAS, "NIHK-oh-luhs—*Greek:*

NEW ENGLAND BOYS' NAMES

Boys born in New England are most likely to have the following names:

1. Michael	6. Joseph	11. Joshua	16. Tyler
2. Matthew	7. Ryan	12. David	17. Robert
3. Christopher	8. John	13. Alexander	18. Zachary
4. Nicholas	9. Andrew	14. Jonathan	19. Kyle
5. Daniel	10. James	15. Kevin	20. William

"victory of the people." **KOLYA, NICOLAI** (NEE-koh-lye), **NIKITA** (nee-KEE-tah), **NIKO-LAI**—Russian; **NICCOLO** (NEE-koh-loh)—Italian; **NICHOL(S)**; **NICKLAUS, NICKOLAUS, NICLAUS, NICOLAUS, NIKLAUS, NIKO-LAUS**—Scandinavian; **NICKOLAS**—Eastern European; **NICOL** (NEE-kohl)—French; **NICOLAO**—Portuguese; **NICOLAUS** (nih-koh-LOUSE — "LOUSE" like "house"), **NIKLAAS** (nih-KLAHSS)—Dutch; **NIKI, NIKO, NIKOLAOS** (nee-koh-LAY-ohss), **NIKOLOS** (NEE-koh-lohss), **NIKOS, NILOS**—Greek; **NIK(K)O, NIKOLAS**—Slavic. Several saints have borne the names on this list, not the least of which is the man in the red suit who breaks into houses once a year, just when they're loaded with presents, looking for food. Actually, Saint Nicholas was a bishop who saved young girls from prostitution, children from hunger, wrongfully convicted people from the gallows, and sailors from crashing on the rocks. **NICK, NICKY; NIK, NIKKY.** F

NIGEL, "NYE-jihl"—Latin: "black" or "dark." **NYE.**

NILE, "NYLE"—version of Neil: "champion or chief" or Egyptian: the great River Nile. **NILES, NYLES.** The Nile, which has supported and sustained Egypt for millennia, is one of the longest rivers in the world. See also NEAL, NYE. F

NINOVAN, "nee-NOH-vahn"—Native American Cheyenne: "our home."

NIREL, "nee-REHL"—Hebrew: "field of the Lord." **NIRAL. NIR.** F

NISSIM, "nee-SEEM"—Hebrew: "wonders" or "miracles."

NIVAL, "NIHV-ahl" or "NEEV-ahl"—Latin: "of the snow" or "life under the snow." The second meaning refers to seeds or plants surviving the winter or thriving despite the cold. F

NIZAM, "nee-ZAHM"—Algerian: "disciplined."

NOAH, "NOH-ah"—Hebrew: "wandering" or "rest," sometimes "long-lived." **NOACH** (NOH-akh—"kh" to hock something up)—Israeli; **NOAK, NOE, NOÉ; NUH** (NOOH)—Arabic. In the Judeo-Christian tradition, Noah was told by God to build a giant ark to save the seeds of a new world from a Great Flood God was sending to purge the earth of the evil that was running rampant at the time. Though ridiculed by the neighborhood, Noah complied. The neighbors were singing a different tune after the rains came, and Noah, his family, and a mated pair of every creature on earth sailed off.

NOAM, "NO-ahm" or "NOME"—*Hebrew:* *"pleasant."* **NAUM.** F

NOBLE, "NOH-buhl"—*Latin: "aristocratic" or "honorable."* This is a Puritan virtue name. Noble Winningham is an actor.

NOEL, "NOLE"—*French: "Christmastime"; Latin: "new."* **NOËL** (noh-EHL); **NOLLAIG** (noh-LYG)—Irish Gaelic; **NOVELO** (noh-VAY-loh)—Italian and Spanish. Noel Coward was a playwright. See also NEWELL. F

NOLAN, "NOH-luhn"—*Celtic: "famous."* **NOLAND.** Nolan Ryan was a baseball pitcher "famous" for his wicked fastball and incredibly durable arm. **NOLI(E).** F

NOLTY, NULTY, "NOHL-tee" or "NUHL-tee"—*Danish: "knotted" or "kind."* **NOLTE, NOLTEY; NULTE, NULTEY.**

NORI, "NOH-ree—*Japanese: "doctrine" or "principle."* F

NORMAN, "NOHR-mun"—*English: "from the north"; Latin: "the T-square," "the example," or "the pattern."* **NORMAND, NORRIS.** The Normans were a tribe of people from the north of France and Germany, and the Norman Conquest of Great Britain was achieved after the Battle of Hastings in 1066. **NORM, NORMI(E), NORMY.** F

NORVAL, "NOHR-vahl"—*English: "from a northern valley."* **NORDELL, NORDEN.**

NORWOOD, "NOHR-wood"—*English: "from the northern wood or forest."*

NURI, "NOO-ree"—*Hebrew: "my fire."* F

NURU, "NOO-roo"—*Swahili: "of light" or "born in the daytime."*

NUZKU, "NOOZ-koo"—*Sumerian/Akkadian: "Evening Star."*

NYE, "NYE"—*English: "islander."* **NILE, NYLE.** See also NIGEL.

THE TOP FIVE

OLIVER
OWEN
OSCAR
OMAR
OGDEN

If the name you're looking for isn't here, see the other vowels.

OCHEN, "oh-CHEHN"—*African: "one of the twins."*

OCTAVIO, "awk-TAY-vee-oh"—*Latin: "eight"* or *"eighth."* **OCTAVIUS; OTTAVIO.** Octavian is another name for Augustus Caesar, a Roman emperor in the first century B.C. F

ODE, "oh-DEH"—*African: "born along the road."*

ODELL, "oh-DELL"—*Greek: "melody";* *Danish: "otter"; Teutonic: "wealthy one."* See also ODILO. F

ODILO, "oh-DEEL-oh"—*French version of Otto: "rich."* **ODILIO.** Saint Odilo was an abbot in the Middle Ages who began the celebration of All Souls' Day, a special day of prayer for the deceased. See also OTTO.

ODIN, "OH-dihn"—*Norse.* Odin was the supreme male deity in Norse mythology. He had a special interest in law, war, art, sex . . . all the three-letter words. **ODIE.**

ODOM, "oh-DOHM"—*African: "oak tree."*

OGDEN, "AWG-dehn"—*English: "little oak tree valley."* Ogden Nash was an insightful, amusing, and sometimes incredibly concise poet of the twentieth century.

OGUN, "oh-GOON"—*African Yoruba: "the god of war."*

OIDU, "oh-EE-doo"—*African Ateso: "sharp-eyed."*

OJAI, "OH-hye"—*Native American Chumash: "nest."*

OKPARA, "oak-PAH-rah"—*African Ibo: "first son."*

OLEG, "OH-lehg"—*Russian: "holy."* **OLEN-KA** (oh-LEHN-kah), **OLEZKA. OLYA.** F

OLIVER, "AW-lihv-ur"—*Latin: "olive tree,"* and therefore, *"peace"* or *"peaceful";* possibly also Norse: *"from the ancestors";* Germanic: *"army of the elves."* **OILIBHÉAR** (OY-lee-vare or oy-lee-VARE)—Irish Gaelic; **OLIVERIO** (oh-lee-VAY-ree-oh)—Portuguese; **OLIVIER** (oh-lee-vee-AY)—French. The olive tree is a symbol of peace that crosses many, many cultures. F

OLNEY, "OHL-nee" or "AWL-nee"—*English: "the old island."*

OLUJIMI, "oh-loo-JEE-mee"—*African Yoruba: "God gave us this."* F

OMAHA, "OH-muh-hah"—*Native American Sioux: "people who go upstream."* This is both a place name and a tribe name for a very warlike group of people who had a rigidly structured warrior society.

OMAR(R), "OH-mahr" or "oh-MAHR"—*Arabic: "the highest" or "long-lived"; Hebrew: "talkative."* The Rubaiyat is a collection of works by a wonderful Persian poet—and astronomer-mathematician, by the way—named Omar Khayyam, whose work covers everything from religion to lust. Many Middle Eastern and African princes and sultans have also borne this name. See also OMARI.

OMARI, "oh-MAH-ree"—*Swahili: "God is highest."* OMAR(R).

OMOTO, "oh-MOH-toh"—*Japanese: "great source" or "powerful source."*

OMRI, "OHM-ree" or "AHM-ree"—*Arabic: "long life."* IMRI—Hungarian.

ONI, "OH-nee"—*African Yoruba: "born in God's house."* ONA, ONO, ONU. F

OPHIR, "OH-feer"—*Hebrew: "gold."* The legendary land of Ophir is where King Solomon obtained all his gold and wealth. F

ORAL, "OH-rahl"—*Latin: "mouth" or "endowed with speech."* Oral Roberts is a famous evangelist. Both Oral and Orel are names that are generally encountered in the South. See also OREL.

ORAM, "ORE-ehm"—*English: "riverbank."* OREM.

ORAN, "OH-rawn"—*Gaelic: "coldwater spring."* ARAN, URAN.

OREL, "oh-REHL"—*Latin: "to listen" or "listener."* Orel Hershiser is a baseball player. This name, like Oral, is generally encountered in the South. See also ORAL.

OREN, "OH-ruhn"—*Hebrew: "pine tree"; Gaelic: "pale."* ORIN, ORREN, ORRIN.

ORESTES, "oh-REHS-teez"—*Greek:* "of the mountains." In Greek legend and history, Prince Orestes was the fiercely loyal son of King Agamemnon.

ORIAN, "OH-ree-ahn"—*Latin: "the east" or "golden."* F

ORION, "oh-RYE-un"—*Greek: "son of fire" or "son of light"; Latin: "giant" or "hunter."* The constellation of Orion the Hunter is among the biggest and brightest, and easiest to find. It can be seen following the Sun at dusk from mid-January through late February. The Sun is "in" Orion throughout the month of May. One of the largest and most gorgeous nebulae can be seen with the naked eye or binoculars in Orion; the Hunter has a lovely star cloud hanging from his belt. The Native American name of the hunter who became the constellation is PINON.

ORLANDO, "ohr-LAHN-doh"—*Spanish version of Roland: "famous throughout the land."* ORLOV—Russian. See also ROLAND.

ORLEN, "OR-lehn"—*Latin: "golden."* ORLIN, ORLY, ORLYN. F

ORMAND, "OHR-mund"—*Scandinavian: "shipmate."* ORMANDY; ORMON, ORMOND.

ORO, "OH-roh"—*Spanish: "gold."*

ORSON, "OR-sun"—*Latin: "bear."* ORSEN; ORSINI, ORSINO (or-SEE-no)—Spanish, Portuguese, and Italian. Orson Welles was a boy genius who revolutionized radio and film with his unique ideas. His works have become the standards by which many who have followed have been judged. See also BEAR.

ORVAL, "OHR-vahl"—*English: "mighty with the spear."*

OSBORN, "AWZ-born"—*English: "man of God" or "God's man."* OSBORNE. OZ, OZZIE.

-ovich, -vich

These are Russian suffixes that mean "son of." You may use them with any name you choose. You may need to add or remove a letter, as there is always a vowel sound preceding "vich." The syllable prior to that vowel sound is the stressed syllable of the name.

OSCAR, "AWZ-kahr"—*Norse: "God's spear"; Irish: "champion warrior" or "jewel."* **OSKAR; OSZKÁR** (OSH-kahr)—Hungarian. Oscar was the name of legendary Irishman Finn MacCool's grandson. Oscar Wilde was a controversial novelist, essayist, playwright, and wit of the nineteenth century. Among his more notable quotes are "I can resist everything except temptation" and "Experience is the name everyone gives to their mistakes."

OSGOOD, "AWZ-good"—*English: "benevolence of the gods."* **OZ, OZZIE.**

OSMAN, "AHZ-mun"—*English: "servant of God"; Arabic: "soft as a new chick" or "tender as a chicken."* **OSMAND, OSMANT; OSMIN, OSMIND; OSMON, OSMOND.** Osman was the founding emperor of the Ottoman Empire, based in present-day Turkey. In Britian, Saint Osmand was chancellor for William the Conqueror, and he is largely responsible for the Domesday Book, the first-ever census. **OZ, OZZIE.**

OSMOND, "AWZ-mawnd"—*Teutonic: "protected by God."* **OSMAND, OSMONT, OSMUND.** An osmund is a type of fern.

OSRIC, "AWZ-rihk"—*English: "divine ruler."* **OZ, OZZIE; RIC, RICK, RIK.**

OTIS, "OH-tihss"—*Greek: "keen hearing."* **ODIS, ODIE, OTIE.**

OTTAWA, "AW-tuh-wah"—*Native American Cree: "trader."* This is a tribe name for a group of people who used to inhabit the Great Lakes region.

OTTO, "AW-toh"—*Teutonic: "prosperous" or "rich."* **ODILO** (oh-DEEL-oh), **OTTON** (oh-TON)—French; **OTELLO** (oh-TEHL-oh)—Italian; **OTHELLO** (oh-THEHL-oh or oh-TEHL-oh)—English and Nordic; **OTHO** (oh-TOH)—German; **OTTORINO** (oh-toh-REE-noh)—Spanish and Portuguese; **OTTMAR, OTTOMAR**—Slavic and Turkish. Germanic and Teutonic tribal chieftans and kings bore this name. F

OTU, "OH-too"—*Native American Hokan: "seashells in a basket."*

OWEN, "OH-when"—*Celtic: "young warrior"; Gaelic: "a river"; Welsh version of Eugene: "well-born."* **EWEN** (YOO-wehn)—Scottish; **OWAIN, OWAYNE; YWAIN** (ee-WANE)—Celtic. Owen of Gwynedd was a twelfth-century Welsh soldier, and Owen Glendower was a fifteenth-century crusader for an independent Wales. See also EUGENE.

OZI, "OH-zee"—*Hebrew: "strong."* **OZ.**

OZNI, "OHZ-nee"—*Hebrew: "good hearing."*

OZZIE. See OSBORN, OSGOOD, OSMAN, OSRIC.

THE TOP FIVE

PETER
PAUL
PATRIC(K)
PHIL(L)IP
PARKER

If the name you're looking for isn't here, see "F."

PABLO. See PAUL.

PADDY, "PAD-ee"—*English: the ruddy duck, Malaysian: "rice in the straw."* See also PADI, PATRIC(K).

PADI, "PAH-dee"—*Persian: "master."* **PADDI, PADDY.** See also PATRIC(K). For the female version, see PATI/PADI.

PAGE, "PAYJ"—*Greek: "child"; English: "a knight's attendant"; French: "royal servant."* **PAIGE, PAYGE.** F

PAINTON, "PAYN-tun"—*Latin: "country town."* **PAGANEL, PAINE, PAYNTON.**

PALADIN, "PAL-uh-dihn"—*French: "of the palace" or "the princely one."* **PALADINE, PAL(L)ATIN, PAL(L)ATINE, PALLDIN(E).** This was a title of honor given to Charlemagne's twelve best knights. See also PALLATON.

PALLATON, "PAH-lah-tun"—*Native American Iroquois: "fighter."* **PALADIN, PALATIN, PALATON, PALLADIN, PALLATIN.**

PALMER, "PAWL-mur"—*Latin: "pilgrim."* This derivation came about because medieval European pilgrims to the Holy Land often brought back palm branches.

PAN, "PAN"—*Greek: "all"; Hindu: "leaf" or "feather"; Italian: "bread."* Pan was the half-man, half-goat Greek god of forests, flocks, and shepherds, noted for his merriment and mischievous nature. A moon of Saturn is named Pan—it is a little moon in the midst of the rings, "shepherding" them around the planet.

PANCHO, "PAWN-choh"—*Spanish from Latin: "plume."* **PANCHITO, PANCHOLO, PANZO.**

PARIS, "PARE-ihss"—*Greek.* This is a place name for the city in France, and the name of the Trojan who started the Trojan War by abducting (or relocating with her permission) Helen, the wife of King Menelaus, from Greece.

PARKER, "PAHR-kur"—*English: "gamekeeper" or "groundskeeper."* **PARK.**

PARNELL, "pahr-NEHL"—*French from Greek: "little Peter," that is, "little rock."* **PERNELL.** See also PETER.

PARR, "PAHR"—*Scottish: "young salmon."*

PARRY, "PARE-ee"—*French: "guard" or "protect."* See also PERRY.

PARVIS, PURVIS, "PAHR-vihss" or "PUR-vihss"—*Latin: "courtyard."* This refers to the courtyard of a church or large building.

PASCAL, "pahs-KAHL"—*French from Hebrew: "of the Passover"; English: "Easter."*

PASCALE—French; **PASCHALIS, PASHA, PASKAL; PASCHALL, PASCHELL, PASCO, PASKO, PASQUAL, PASQUALE.** This name is given to children born on Good Friday.

PAT, "PAHT"—*Native American: "fish."* See also PATRIC(K).

PATRIC(K), "PAH-trihk"—*Latin: "noble."* **PÁDRAIG** (PAH-drayg)—Irish Gaelic; **PADRIK**—Slavic; **PATRICIUS**—Latin and Dutch; **PATRIK; PATRICIO** (pah-TREE-see-oh)—Spanish and Portuguese; **PATRIZIO** (pah-TREET-zee-oh)—Italian; **PATRYK**—Polish; **PAYTON**—Pictish. The Latin word *patricius* was used to signify the aristocratic class in ancient Rome, the one that made all the laws (and all the money). Patrick is generally thought to be such a completely Irish name because several very early saints who made the Emerald Isle their home had such a huge impact on the inhabitants. **PADDY, PAT.** F

PATTON, "PAT-un"—*English: "the combatant's estate."*

PATWIN, "PAHT-win"—*Native American Penute: "man."* This is a tribe name for a group of people who used to inhabit northern California. If you're looking for a Native American name, it would be nice to use the name of a tribe, such as the Patwin, that no longer exists.

PAUL, "PAWL"—*Latin: "little."* **PABLO** (PAHB-loh)—Spanish; **PAL** (PAHL)—Norwegian; **PALI** (PAH-lee)—Hungarian; **PAOLO** (pah-OH-loh)—Portuguese and Italian; **PASHA, PASHENKA, PAVEL** (PAH-vehl), **PAVLUSHA** (pahv-LOO-shah)—Russian; **PAULIN**—Slavic; **PAULIN** (poh-LAN)—French; **PAVLOS** (PAHV-lohss)—Greek; **PAWEL** (PAH-vehl), **PAWELEK**—Polish; **POL**—Swedish; **PÓL**—Irish Gaelic; **POLL**

(PAWL)—Scottish Gaelic. This name originated as an adjective applied to members of the Aemilian tribe in one of Rome's territories; they were "little" because they were of less-than-Roman-average height. Several saints and popes have had these names. The most notable of them was the apostle Paul, who began as a persecutor of Christians and wound up spreading Christianity throughout the eastern half of the Roman Empire. Paul Revere was a participant in the Revolutionary War who called the colonists to arms, when he wasn't busy crafting fine silver objects at his day job. Paul McCartney dumped his first name, James, and opted for his middle name to present to the world when he and his friends formed the Beatles, a band that would change the face of popular music forever. Artists such as Cezanne, Gauguin, and Klee, have borne this name, and one who bore a variant—Pablo Picasso—was an innovator thought by some to have been the greatest artist of the twentieth century. **PAULEY, PAULY.** F

PAVEL. See PAUL.

PAXTON, "PAKS-tun"—*Latin: "peaceful town"; Teutonic: "traveller from a far land."* **PAYTON. PAX.**

PAYTAH, "PAY-tah"—*Native American Sioux: "fire."* F

PAYTON, "PAY-tun" or "PAYT-n"—*Pictish version of Patric(k): "noble"; Anglo-Saxon: "the fighter's estate."* **PATTON, PEYTON.** See also PATRIC(K), PAXTON.

PAZ, "PAHZ"—*Hebrew: "golden."*

PEDRO. See PETER.

PELHAM, "PEHL-ahm"—*English: "hamlet with the tannery."*

GREAT PLAINS BOYS' NAMES

Boys born in the largely agricultural states of the Great Plains are most likely to have the following names:

1. Michael
2. Matthew
3. Tyler
4. Joshua
5. Jacob
6. Kyle
7. Cody
8. Andrew
9. Brandon
10. Zachary
11. Jordan
12. Ryan
13. John
14. Nicholas
15. Christopher
16. Joseph
17. James
18. Daniel
19. David, Robert
20. Austin

PELL, "PEHL"—*Anglo-Saxon: "scarf" or "mantle (hooded cloak)"; English: "tannery."*

PELTON, "PEHL-tun"—*English: "estate by the pool."*

PEMBROKE, "PEHM-broke"—*Celtic: "from the headlands."*

PENLEY, "PEHN-lee"—*English: "enclosed pasture" or "swan meadow."* PEN, PENN.

PEPE. See JOSEPH, PEPPER.

PEPIN, "PEH-pihn"—*German: "petitioner."*

PEPPER, "PEH-pur"—*Sanskrit: "berry."* BIBER (BEE-bur)—Turkish; KOSHOO (koh-SHOO)—Japanese; MERITJA (meh-REET-jah)—Indonesian; PEPE (PEH-peh)—Italian; PEPPAR—Swedish; PFEFFER (p'FEHF-ur)—German; PILIPILI (pee-lee-PEE-lee)—Swahili; PIPER (PEE-pur)—Rumanian; PYERETS (PYEH-rehts)—Russian. The acquisition of pepper was one of the prime reasons Europeans left Europe on their many sea voyages. F

PEREZ, "peh-REHZ"—*Hebrew: "to blossom" or "to burst forth."* PERETZ—Hebrew.

PERON, "PARE-awn"—*Old English: "block of stone."* PERRI(E), PERRY.

PERRIN, "PEH-rihn" and "peh-REEN," sometimes "peh-RYNE"—*French from Greek: "stone."* F

PERRY, "PARE-ee"—*English: "pear tree."* Far and away the most famous and beloved Perry is Perry Mason, the ever-vigilant, ever-confident defender of the wronged, knight of justice . . . what everyone wishes a lawyer would be. PERR; PERRIE. See also PARRY, PERON. F

PERSHING, "PUR-shing"—*German: "under or near the peach tree."*

PERSIS, PARSIS, "PUR-sihs" or "PAHR-sihss"—*Hindu: "fire worshippers."* This is a somewhat inaccurate name for the Zoroastrians of India, since they don't worship fire itself, but use the imagery of fire in their ceremonies. F

PETER, "PEE-tur"—*Greek: "rock."* PANOS, PETRINI (peh-TREE-nee), PETRINO—Greek; PEADAIR (PAY-dare)—Scottish Gaelic; PEADAR (PAY-dahr)—Irish Gaelic; PEDER, PETTER—Norwegian; PEDRO (PAY-droh)—Portuguese and Spanish; PETENKA (peh-TEHN-kah), PETYA, PYOTR (PYOH-tr)—Russian; PETERKE, PETI—Slavic; PIERO (PYARE-oh), PIETRO (PYEH-troh)—Italian;

PIERRE (pee-AIR)—*French;* **PIET, PIETER, PIETR**—*Dutch;* **PIOTR** (PYOH-tr), **PIOTRY, PIOTREK**—*Eastern European.* The apostle Simon was renamed Cephus, which means "rock" in the Aramaic tongue, by Jesus. When the New Testament was being written in its original Greek form, the non-Greek names were changed, too. Since the word for "rock" in Greek is a feminine word, *petra,* a masculinization was contrived: "Petros," which has come down to us as Peter in all its forms. Several saints and popes, and three Russian tsars, have borne names on this list. Peter and its variants have also been borne by artists: Pieter Brueghel, Pierre August Renoir, and Peter Paul Rubens, to name just three. Pietr Ilyich Tchaikovsky made a big noise in the world of classical music. His most-performed work is probably *The Nutcracker Suite,* a Christmas story that is entertaining enough for kids, but has some very adult metaphor. **PEDI(E); PET, PETA, PETE, PETEE, PETEY.** See also PARNELL. F

PETRINO, "peh-TREE-noh"—*Greek: "steadfast" (since the root word means "rock").* **PATRINI, PATRINO, PETRINI. TRINI, TRINO.** See also PETER. F

PEVERELL, "PEH-veh-rehl" or "peh-veh-REHL"—*French: "piper."* **PEVIE, PEVEY.**

PHELAN, "FAY-lahn"—*Irish: "wolf."* **PALAN, PALIN, PHAELAN.** This is a wolf with special powers: it actually means "charmed wolf," but I can't find any specifications on exactly what kind of charms surrounded the wolf in question.

PHIL(L)IP(P), "FIHL-ihp" or "fee-LEEP"—*Greek: "lover of horses."* **FELIPE** (feh-LEE-peh)—*Spanish;* **FILIP**—*Norwegian;* **FLIP, PIP**—*Dutch;* **FÜLÖP** (FUH-luhp)—*Hungarian;* **PHILBIN, PILBIN**—*Scottish;*

PHILIPPE (fee-LEEP)—*French;* **PILIB** (PEE-leeb)—*Irish Gaelic.* Philip was a name borne by several kings of Macedonia, one of whom raised a fine boy called Alexander the Great, Ruler of the World as We Know It by his contemporaries. Saints, and Spanish and French kings, have borne this name. **PHIL, PHILLY.** F

PHOENIX, "FEE-nihks"—*Greek: "the Phoenix," "deep purple," "crimson," and even "of Phoenicia."* The Phoenix—which appears in the beliefs of several cultures—is also sometimes called the Firebird. Once or twice a millennium, the exquisite creature would consume itself in fire, but then rise, renewed, from the ashes of its own destruction. If someone tried to kill it between those times, it would still rise again. It is a symbol of rebirth and hope. The Phoenix constellation can be seen chasing the Sun at dusk in late November to mid-December. The Sun is "in" the Firebird in February and March.

PIAF, "pee-AHF"—*French: "slow trot."* A piaf is a slow trot in place, such as by a horse posing and prancing for show.

PICARD(Y), "pee-CARD" and "pee-CARD-ee" or "pee-car-DEE"—*French from Basque: "to prick" the bull with lances in bullfighting.* **PECARD, PECARDO; PICARDO.** Picardy is a region in northern France. Jean-Luc Picard will be born in the twenty-fifth century and will grow up to be the captain of the starship U.S.S. *Enterprise,* the pride of Star Fleet.

PIERCE, "PEERSS"—*English: "to pierce" or "to break through."* Pierce Brosnan is an Irish actor who is the latest to take over the role of James Bond in the series of movies based on the Ian Fleming character.

PIERRE. See PETER.

PIPER, "PIE-pur"—*English: "pipe player."* See also PEPPER. F

PITNEY, "PIHT-nee"—*English: "island preserve."*

PLACIDO, "PLAH-sihd-oh" or "plah-SEED-oh"—*Latin: "serene."* **PLACID; PALACIDO** (pah-lah-SEE-doh)—*Spanish;* **PLACYD** (plah-TSEED)—*Slavic.* Placido Domingo is a world-famous opera singer. **PLACI(E).** F

PORTER, "POHR-tur"—*French: "to carry"; Latin: "doorkeeper" or "gatekeeper."*

POTTER, "PAW-tur"—*Anglo-Saxon: "maker of pottery."* Duh.

POWELL, "POW-ehl" ("POW" like "how")—*Celtic: "alert, watchful."*

POWERS, "POW-urs"—*Latin: "strengths" or "forces."* The Powers are part of the heavenly hierarchy of angels who seem to waver back and forth between virtue and temptation, probably due to their intense interaction with us on the material plane. It is their job to balance and reconcile.

PRAJNA, "PRAHJ-nah" or "prahj-NAH"—*Sanskrit: "wisdom, knowledge."* **PRAJNYA, PRANNYA; PRANNA** (prah-NAH or PRAH-nah)—*Pali.*

PRENTICE, "PREHN-tihss"—*English: "an apprentice."* **PRENTISS.**

PRESCOTT, "PREHS-kawt"—*English: "the priest's/preacher's cottage."*

PRESLEY, "PREHS-lee"—*English: "the priest's/preacher's pastureland."* **PRESLEA, PRESLEE, PRESLEIGH.** Elvis Presley was an entertainer who revolutionized popular culture.

PRESTON, "PREHSS-tun"—*English: "priest's town."*

PURLIN, PURLYN, "PUR-lihn"—*English: "by the brook," "by the waterfall," or "the support."* Purlins are the crossbeams in ceilings which support the rafters, attic, and roof. F

PUTNAM, "PUHT-num"—*Latin: "to prune" or "to shape"; Anglo-Saxon: "dwells by the pond."*

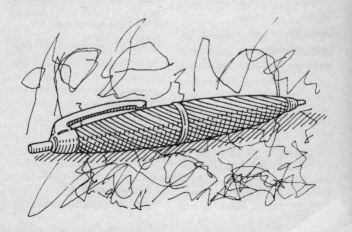

THE TOP FIVE

QUENTIN
QUINN
QUINCY
QUIRT
QADIR

If the name you're looking for isn't here, see "K."

QADAR, "kah-DAHR"—*Arabic: "decree" or "determination" (meaning destiny).*

QADIR, "kah-DEER"—*Arabic: "capable."*

QAMAR, "KAH-mahr" or "kah-MAHR"—*Arabic: "the moon."* F

QUENTIN, "KWEHN-tihn"—*Latin: "the fifth son," or just "the fifth."* **QUENTAN, QUENTON, QUINTIN, QUINTON, QUINTUS.** Saint Quentin was a fifth-century martyr. **QUINN, QUINT.**

QUERIDO, "keh-REE-doh"—*Spanish: "beloved."* F

QUILLAN, "KIHL-an"—*Irish Gaelic: "cub."*

QUILLON, "KIHL-un," "kih-LAWN," or "KWIHL-un"—*Latin: "sword."* **QUILL, QUILLO.**

QUINCY, "KWIHN-see"—*Latin: "in the fifth . . ." whatever.* **QUINN.**

QUINN. See QUENTIN, QUINCY.

QUINNAT, "KWIHN-at"—*Native American Chinook: "great salmon."*

QUINT. See QUENTIN, QUINTUS.

QUINTUS, "KWIN-tus"—*Latin: "the fifth."* Quintus Ennius was one of the very earliest Roman poets. He was held in the highest regard by subsequent writers, but unfortunately, only tiny fragments of his writings remain for study. Quintus Arias is the honorable, generous Roman general who takes the exiled Judah Ben-Hur as his own son in the story *Ben-Hur*. **QUINT.** F

QUIRT, "KWURT"—*Spanish/Indian: "whip."*

A SOAPY SAMPLER

Men's character names in both daytime and prime-time serials:

Adam	Cooper	James	Omar
Alan-Michael	Cord	Jared	Paul*
Alden	Cory	Jason	Peter*
Alec	Craig	Jeremy	Phillip
Alex	Curtis	John*	Rafael
Anthony*	Damian	Jonah	Ridge
Antonio	Danny	Keemo	Roger
Asa	David*	Kevin	Ryan
Austin	Derek	Kyle*	Shawn
Avery	Dillon	Lucas	Shawn-Douglas
Barry	Dorian	Luke	Sonny
Bill	Douglas	Mac(k)*	Soto
Blade	Dylan*	Malcolm	Stefano
Blair	Edmund	Marty	Stone
Bo	Eduardo	Mark	Stuart
Brady	Eric*	Mateo	Tad
Brandon	Evan	Matt	Taylor
Brett	Franco	Max	Thorne
Brook*	Frank	Micky	Todd
Buck*	Grant	Miguel	Tomas
Buzz	Gregory	Mike*	Tony*
Cabot	Hart	Ned*	Trent
Cal	Ivan	Neil	Trevor
Carl*	Jack	Nicholas	Trucker
Clay	Jake	Nick*	Victor*
Connor			

* more than one character   SOURCE: *TV Guide, Television Times*

THE TOP FIVE

RYAN
ROBERT
RICHARD
RAND/RANDY
RAFAEL/RAPHAEL

If the name you're looking for isn't here, perhaps it is a variant or diminutive of another primary name.

RABI, "RAH-bee"—*Arabic: "breeze."* **RABIN.** F

RACHAMIN, "RAKH-ah-mihn" ("KH" in the back of your throat)—*Hebrew: "compassion"* or *"kindness."*

RADBURN, "RAD-burn"—*English: "red stream."* This derivation is a reference to the color of the clay or stones in the water. **RADBOURN(E).**

RADCLIFF, "RAD-clihf"—*English: "red cliffs."* **RADCLIFFE, RADCLYFF, RADCLYFFE.**

RADFORD, "RAD-furd"—*English: "the red river-crossing."*

RADLEY, "RAD-lee"—*English: "red clearing"* or *"red meadow."* **RADLEIGH.**

RAFAEL. See RAPHAEL.

RAF(F)I, "rah-FEE"—*Arabic: "exalting."* See also RAPHAEL.

RAGHIB, "rah-GHEEB"—*Arabic: "desirous."*

RAGUEL, "RAH-goo-ehl" or "rah-GHEHL"—*Latin/Hebrew: "friend of God."* **AKRASIEL, RUFAEL; RAGU-EL; RASUIL** (RAH-soo-ihl)—Arabic. According to the Old Testament/Tanakh prophet Enoch, Ragu-el is the Archangel who is the stern watchman over the other angels' behavior, punishing those who break the rules.

RAHMAN, "rah-MAHN"—*Arabic: "merciful"* or *"gracious."*

RAI, "RAH-ee"—*Japanese: "trust."*

RAIDEN, "RYE-dehn" or "rah-EE-dehn"—*Japanese: "god of thunder."*

RAIN, "RAYN"—*English: "rain."* **AME** (AH-may)—Japanese; **DOZHT** (DOHZHT)—Russian; **HUDJAN** (HUDE-jahn)—Indonesian; **MATAR** (mah-TAHR)—Arabic; **MVUA** (m'VOO-ah)—Swahili; **SADE** (SAH-day)—Finnish; **YAGMUR** (yahg-MOOR)—Turkish. F

RAJA, "rah-JAH" or "RAH-jah"—*Arabic: "hope";* Sanskrit: *"king"* or *"prince."* **RAJAH. RAJ.**

RAKIN, "rah-KEEN"—*Arabic: "respectful."*

RALEIGH, "RAH-lee"—*English: "roe deer meadow."* **RAWLEY, RAWLING(S), RAWLY.**

RALPH, "RALF"—*German: "praised wolf"* or *"swift wolf."* **RÁDHULBH** (RAY-ulf)—Irish Gaelic; **RADISLAW** (RAH-dih-slahv)—Polish; **RADOSLAV** (RAH-doh-slawv); **RALF, ROLF; RAOUL** (rah-OOL)—Spanish and French; **RAUL** (RAWL)—Eastern European; **RAULO** (rah-OO-loh)—Italian; **REZSO** (REHZ-shoh)—Hungarian.

RAMADAN, "RAH-mah-dawn"—*Arabic.* Ramadan is the ninth month of the Muslim year.

RAMAT, "RAH-maht" or "rah-MAHT"—*Ainu: "soul" or "spirit."* In the ancient Japanese religion of the Ainu, *ramat* has no beginning or end and is present in all creation. One's own personal part of *ramat* can leave the body in sleep.

RAMIEL, "RAH-mee-ehl"—*?, probably Babylonian: "angel of thunder."* **RAMI-EL.** F

RAMIRO, "rah-MEE-roh"—*Spanish: "great judge."* **RAMIREZ, ROMERO.**

RAMSDEN, "RAMZ-dehn"—*Celtic: "raven's clearing"; Scottish: "ram's grotto."*

RAMSEY, "RAM-zee"—*English: "island of wild-garlic"; Celtic: "raven island"; Scottish: "rams on the island."* **RAMSAY.**

RAMSON, "RAM-sun"—*English: "wild garlic."*

RAN, "RAHN"—*Japanese: "water lily."*

RANCE, "RANS" or "RANTS"—*Flemish: "red marble."* This Belgian marble has some white and blue markings as well.

RAND, "RAND"—*Scottish: "reedy riverbank" or "border."* The rand is the unplowed border at the edge of a field. **RANDEY, RANDIE, RANDY.** See also FARAND, RANDOLF/RANDOPH.

RANDOLF, RANDOLPH, "RANdawlf"—*English: "shield of the wolf."* **RANDALL, RANDELL, RANDLE. RAND, RANDEY, RANDI(E), RANDY.**

RANDY. See RAND, RANDOLF/RANDOLPH.

RANEN, "RAH-nehn"—*Hebrew: "song of joy."* **RANNEN, RANNON, RANON.**

RANSLEY, "RANZ-lee"—*English: "the raven meadow."* **RANSLEA, RANSLEE, RANSLEIGH.**

RA(O)UL. See RALPH.

RAPHAEL, "rah-fah-EHL"—*Hebrew: "God heals" or "healed by God."* **RAFAEL, RAFAELLO, RAFAELO; RAFAËL, RAFAËLLO, RAFAËLO, RAPHAËL; RAPHA-EL; RAFAL** (RAH-fawl or rah-FAWL)—Polish. Raphael is one of the Archangels in the Judeo-Christian and Islamic angelic domain. Raphael also shows up as one of the Virtues in the heavenly hierarchy of angels, and is called the Angel of the Sun, of Science, and of Knowledge. The Essenes give him rulership over Monday. In the aprocryphal Old Testament *Book of Tobit*, Rapha-el gives instruction on medicine and health to Tobias; he heals the pain of circumcision for Abraham; resets the disjointed hip of Jacob; and helps Noah to prepare for and survive the Great Flood. Legends portray him as a warm, friendly, talkative sort, fond of travelling with unsuspecting mortals. Raphael Sanzio was one of the great Renaissance masters; unlike the others, he was also able to have a social life, and, oh *boy*, what a social life. He was very handsome, rich, and quite the ladies' man, the life of any party. **RAFFI(E), RAFI(E), RAPHI(E).** F

RASHAD, "rah-SHAHD"—*Arabic: "integrity."*

RASHIDI, "rah-SHEE-dee"—*Swahili: "good advice."* **RASHID.**

RASUL, "rah-SOOL"—*Arabic: "messenger."* Such a messenger is a minor prophet or person who possesses great understanding of religion.

RAVEN, "RAY-vehn"—*English: "the raven."*

The Vikings used the raven on their banners and flags; to them, it symbolized the warrior. F

RAVI, "RAH-vee"—*Hindu: "the sun god."* The river Ravi runs through India and Pakistan. F

RAY. See RAYBURN, RAYMOND, REYNARD.

RAYBURN, "RAY-burn"—*English: "roe deer at the stream."* **RAIFORD, RAYFORD; RAYBOURN(E). BURN, BURNIE; RAY.**

RAYMOND, "RAY-muhnd"—*Teutonic: "wise guardian" or "wise protector."* **RAEMON** (ray-MAWN)—Greek; **RAIMON, RAIMONDO**—Italian; **RAJMUND** (RAH-eemoond), **RAJMUNDY**—Eastern European and Danish; **RAMON** (rah-MON), **RAMONES** (rah-MOH-nez)—Spanish, French, and Italian; **RÉAMONN** (RAY-ah-mohn)—Irish Gaelic. Several saints' names are in this list. **RAY.** F

RAZI, "rah-ZEE"—*Aramaic: "a secret."* **RAZIA, RAZIAH, RAZIEL, RAZIELLE, RAZIL, RAZILLE, RAZIYE. RAZ.** F

REDD, "REHD"—*Old English: "to put in order," "to make ready," or "to rescue."* Redd Foxx was a comedian who moved into TV and film in the last part of his career.

REDFORD, "REHD-furd"—*English: "ford of red stones" or "red (stones at the) river crossing."*

REDMOND, "REHD-mund"—*English: "red guardian."* **REDMOND, REDMUND.**

REED, "REED"—*English: the reed plant.* **REID.**

REEF, "REEF"—*Old Norse(?): "ridge."* **ARRECIFE** (ah-reh-SEEF)—Spanish; **ÉCUEIL** (ay-KWEEL), **RÉCIF** (ray-SEEF)—French; **RECIFE** (ray-SEEF)—Portuguese. F

REESE, "REES"—*Welsh: "impetuous."* **RACE, RASE, REECE.**

REEVE, "REEV"—*English: "assembly" or "steward"; Old(er) English: "to plunder" or "to take away or deprive."* **REEVES.** The "assembly" refers to an Anglo-Saxon governmental body, a reeve being one of the men who served there.

REGGIE. See REGIS.

REGINALD. See REGIS.

REGIS, "REE-jihs"—*Latin: "king."* **RAYNOLD** (ray-NOH), **REGNAULD** (rain-YOH), **REGNAULT** (rain-YOH), **RENAULT** (rayNOH)—French; **REGINALD, REYNOLD**—English; **REINALD** (RAY-nahld or RYEnahld)—German; **REINALDO, REYNALDO** (ray-NAHL-doh)—Spanish. Reggie Jackson was a big home-run hitter in his baseball-playing days. **REEGE, REG, REGE, REGGI(E), REGGY.** See also RONALD. F

REI, "reh-EE"—*Japanese: "gratitude."*

REID, "REED"—*English: "advisor"; Anglo-Saxon: "redhead."* **READ, READING, REED, REEDE; RED, REDD, REDDING; REIDAR** (RAY-dahr)—Scandinavian; **RHOTEN** (RHOHtun)—German.

REMI, "reh-MEE"—*French: "from Reims,"* a region in France; *Latin: "as swiftly as possible."* **REMER, REMY.** Saint Remi was a bishop who later became a king of the Franks.

REMINGTON, "REHM-ing-tun"—*English: "town near the border."* Eli Remington was a nineteenth-century gunsmith. **RIMINGTON.**

RENATO, "ray-NAH-toh"—*Latin: "reborn."* **RENAUS.** This is a Christian saint name. F

RENÉ, "reh-NAY"—*French from Latin: "reborn."* René Descartes was a seventeenth-century French philosopher, physicist, and mathematician. He developed analytical geometry and also formulated a lot of modern metaphysical thinking. His best known, and most often misquoted, statement is *dubito ergo cogito; cogito ergo sum,* which, to us normal people, means "I doubt, therefore I think; I think, therefore I am." F

RENFREW, "REHN-froo"—*Welsh: "from the channel"; Cymric: "from the still river."*

RENNY, "REH-nee"—*Irish: "little prosperous one."* **RENI(E), RENNI(E).**

RENO, "REE-noh"—*Hebrew: "song of joy"; French: "to make (one's name) famous."*

RENTON, "REHN-tun"—*English: "estate where roe bucks run."*

RESHEF, "REH-shehf"—*Phoenician: "god of lightning."* **RESHEPH.** Reshef was also worshipped in Egypt, where images of him survive, showing a headdress with gazelle horns or a human body with the head of a gazelle.

REUBEN, "ROO-behn"—*Hebrew: "behold, a son!"* **REUVEN; ROUBEN**—Eastern European; **ROUVIN**—Greek; **RUBEN, RUBIN.** The Old Testament/Tanakh Reuben was the first son of Jacob and Leah. Leah was less attractive and less favored by Jacob than her sister Rachel, but Leah gave birth to the first son, the heir. **RUBY.**

REUEL, "roo-EHL"—*Hebrew: "friend of God."* **RUEL.** F

REX, "REHKS"—*Latin: "king."* **REY, REYES** (RAY-ehz)—Spanish; **ROI** (RWAH—"R" at back of your throat)—French; **ROY.**

REYNARD, "ray-NAHRD"—*German: "wise and brave."* **RAINARDO** (ray-NAHR-

doh), **RAYNARDO**—Spanish, Portuguese, and Italian; **RAYNARD, RENARD, REYNOLD, REYNOLDS; REGNARD** (REHG-nahrd), **REGNART**—Scandinavian; **REINHARD** (RINE-hard), **REINHART, RENART**—German; **RENAUD** (reh-NOH), **RENAULT** (reh-NOH), **REYNAUD** (ray-NOH), **REYNAULD**—French. **RAY, REY.**

RHETT, "RHET"—*Welsh: "rash."* **RHETT, RHYENCE, RHYS.** The Welsh noble family Rhys stopped the Norman invasion at their borders. Rhett Butler is the hero in Margaret Mitchell's *Gone With the Wind.* See also RIANCE/RIENCE.

RIALTO, "ree-AWL-toh" or "ree-AL-toh"—*Italian: "deep brook" or "deep channel."* Rialto is the island on which the city of Venice was founded. F

RIANCE, RIENCE, "RYE-ins" or "REE-ehnts"—*Celtic: "little chieftain" or "rashness"; French: "laughing."* **RIAN, RYAN.** See also RHETT.

RICHARD, "RICH-erd" or "ree-SHARD"—*Teutonic: "mighty ruler."* **RICARDO** (ree-KAHR-do)—Spanish and Portuguese; **RICCIARDO** (ree-chee-AR-doh)—Italian; **RICKARD** (RIH-kard)—Scandinavian; **RIKÁRD**—Hungarian; **RIOCARD** (REE-oh-card)—Scottish Gaelic; **RISTEARD** (REES-tard)—Irish Gaelic; **RYSZARD** (RIH-zhard)—Polish. Several Christian saints have names on this list. Richard is the name of several English kings, including one, Richard I, called "Coeur du Lion" or "Lion-hearted." Sir Richard Burton was a nineteenth-century writer and adventurer who wrote books as diverse as *Book of the Sword,* a study of the history of hilt weapons, and the English translation of the erotic Indian handbook the *Kama Sutra.* A twentieth-century Richard Burton was a Welsh stage and screen actor, as famous for his personal life as for his professional life. **DICK, DICKI(E), DICKY; RIC, RICCI (REE-chee), RICO; RICH, RICHI(E), RICHY; RICK, RICKIE, RICKY; RIK, RIKKY.** F

RICHMOND, "RICH-mund"—*Teutonic:* "mighty protector." **RICHMUND.**

RICK. See BRODERICK, CEDRIC, DEREK, EDRIC, ERIC, FREDERICK, GARRICK, KENDRICK, MERRICK, OSRIC, RICHARD, ULRIC.

RIDDOCK, "RIHD-awk"—*Irish Gaelic:* "from the smooth field" or "from the cleared field." **RIDDICK.** Riddick Bowe is a world-class boxer.

RIDER, "RYE-dur"—*Anglo-Saxon:* "knight" or "horseman." **RYDER.**

RIDGE, "RIDJ"—*English:* "ridge." **RIG(G).** See also RIDGELEY.

RIDGLEY, "RIDJ-lee"—*English:* "the edge of the meadow." **RIDGELEIGH; RIDGELEY, RIDGLEIGH. RIDGE.**

RIDLEY, "RIHD-lee"—*English:* "the red meadow." **RIDLEA, RIDLEIGH.**

RIFF, "RIF"—*Moroccan:* "a Berber"; *English:* "(musical) motif."

RIGEL, "RYE-jehl"—*Egyptian:* "the foot." This is one of the so-called fixed stars used for centuries by navigators and astrologers because of their apparent constance. Rigel is the bright left foot of the constellation Orion, the Hunter. It has superstitious association with energy, power, and good fortune. Blue-white Rigel is one of the brightest and most distant objects in the sky; if it were as close to us as our nearest star-neighbor, Proxima Centauri, nighttime would be rich, royal blue instead of black, and you could read outside at night without a flashlight.

RILEY, "RYE-lee"—*German:* "small stream" or "brook"; *English:* "field of rye." **REILLY; RILEA, RILEIGH; RYLEA, RYLEIGH, RYLEY.**

RIMMON, "RIH-mawn"—*Persian:* "the roarer." In Persian mythology, this was the sometimes good, sometimes bad Angel of Lightning and Storms.

RINGO, "RIHN-goh"—*English:* "a ring"; *Japanese:* "apple" or "peace be with you." Ringo Starr, the Beatle—whose nickname referred to his rings—went to Japan with this name, and the kids there thought it was really cool.

RIO, "REE-oh"—*Spanish and Portuguese:* "river."

RIORDAN, "REE-ohr-dahn"—*Gaelic:* "bard" or "poet." **REARDON, RIORDON.**

RIP, "RIP"—*Scottish:* "handful of grain (or hay)"; *Flemish:* "rip."

RIPLEY, "RIHP-lee"—*Old English:* "meadow of the screamers" (really, I'm serious). **RIPLEIGH.**

RISHI, "REE-shee"—*Sanskrit:* "one who sees" or "the seer." F

RISTON, "RIHZ-tun"—*English:* "the brushwood estate."

RIVER, "RIH-vur"—*Latin:* "river," silly! **ALVE (AWLV), ALVEN**—Swedish; **BRATUL** (brah-TOOL)—Romanian; **CHIANG** (CHEE-awng), **HO, JIANG, KIANG**—Chinese; **ELVE** (EHL-veh)—Norwegian; **FLEUVE** (FLUHV)—French; **RIVIÈRE** (ree-vee-AIR)—French; **FLUSS** (FLOOSE)—German; **IRMAK** (err-MAHK), **NEHIR** (neh-HEER)—Turkish; **JOKI** (YOH-kee)—Finnish; **KAL** (KAHL), **SUNGAI** (SOON-guy)—Indonesian; **KAWA** (KAH-wah)—Japanese; **MAE NAM** (MAY NAWM)—Thai; **MTO** (m'TOH)—Swahili; **NAHAR, NAHR**—

Arabic and Hebrew; **REKA** (ray-KAH)—Russian; **RIBERO, RIBIERO**—Portuguese and Basque; **RIJEKA** (REE-yeh-kah)—Serbo-Croatian; **RIO, RIVERA** (ree-VAY-rah)—Spanish; **RZEKA** (r'ZHEH-kah)—Polish; **SONG**—Vietnamese.

ROALD, "ROH-ald"—*German: "praised ruler."* Roald Dahl was a Norwegian writer whose subjects ranged from children's fantasy to adult horror.

ROARKE, "RORK"—*Gaelic: "famous ruler."* **ROURKE.**

ROBERT, "RAW-burt" or "roh-BEAR" (both "r"s in your throat [French])—*English: "shining with fame," "shining in fame," or "illustrious."* **RAIBEART** (RAY-bayrt or RY-bayrt), **RAIBEARTAG** (ray-BEAR-tawg or ry-BEAR-tawg)—Scottish Gaelic; **ROBERTO** (roh-BEAR-toh)—Italian, Spanish, and Portuguese; **ROBI** (roh-BEE or ROH-bee)—Eastern European; **ROIBEÁRD** (ROY-bay-ahrd)—Irish Gaelic; **RUPERT**—German. Robert was the name of two Norman kings. Robert the Bruce, a legendary national hero of Scotland, and Scottish poet Robert Burns are another pair of Robs/Bobs. This name has a fine literary tradition: Robert Louis Stevenson wrote the exciting novels *Treasure Island* and *Kidnapped,* Robert Frost was a poet, and Robert E. Sherwood was a playwright. Robert Schumann was a nineteenth-century composer best known for his solo piano works, which are tender, intimate, and understated. **BERT, BERTI(E); BOB, BOBBY; ROB, ROBBI(E), ROBBY; ROBIN.** F

ROBIN, "RAW-bihn"—*English: "the robin," and another name for the black locust tree (robinia).* **ROBBIN, ROBBYN, ROBINET, ROBYN.** Robin is also considered a pet

form of the name Robert. The very-probably-real Robin Hood of English legend was probably Sir Robert (or Robin) of Locksley, or Sir Robert (or Robin) Hode, Earl of Huntingdon. Robin is Batman's youthful sidekick, probably because Robert Kane was Batman's creator. See also ROBERT. F

ROC, "RAWK" or "ROHK"—*Arabic.* **ROKH**—Arabic; **RUKH**—Persian. The roc was a massive, powerful bird of prey in Persian legend. See also ROCK.

ROCK, "RAWK"—*English: "rock," of course.* **ROCCO, ROCKY.** This name is strongly tied to the world of boxing: Rocky Marciano was the only undefeated heavyweight champ, and the *Rocky* movies propelled Sylvester Stallone to stardom. See also ROC.

ROCKWELL, "RAWK-wehl"—*English: "well in the rocks" or "rocky spring"; Celtic: "to cradle."*

ROD. See RODERICK, RODNEY.

RODERICK, "RAWD-rihk"—*German: "famous ruler."* **RODERIC, RODRICK; RODERICH**—German; **RODERIGO**—Italian; **RODRIGO** (roh-DREE-goh)—Spanish; **RODRIGUE** (roh-DREEG—both "r"s in the back of your throat)—French; **RORY**—Irish. Roderick was a king of the Visigoths. **ROD, RODDY.**

RODHAM, "RAWD-hum"—*Scottish: "house/home near the reeds"; English: "hamlet with/near the crucifix,"* a little town with a Catholic church.

RODNEY, "RAWD-nee"—*Teutonic: "renown"; Scottish: "reedy island"; English: "Isle of Hroda."* The Isle of Hroth, or Hroda, is a mysterious island that shows up in some old Celtic and Nordic legends. **ROD, RODDY.**

ROGER, "RAW-jur—*English: "famous spearman."* **RODGER, RODGERS, ROGERS; ROGELIO, ROGERIO** (roh-YARE-ee-oh or roh-HARE-ee-oh)—Spanish, Portuguese, and Basque; **ROGER, ROGET** (both "roh-ZHAY")—French; **ROGUERIO** (roh-GARE-ee-oh), **ROJELIO** (roh-JAY-lee-oh)—German; **RUDIGER** (RUHD-ih-ghur), **RUTGER** (RUHT-ghur)—Nordic; **RUGGERO** (roo-GARE-oh), **RUGGIERO** (roo-jee-AIR-oh)—Italian. Rogers have been noblemen and princes of Sicily. Roger Williams was the founder of the state of Rhode Island, one of the most liberal-minded leaders of the colonies. Roger Maris was a baseball player; he hit sixty-one home runs in 1961. **RAJ** (RAWJ).

ROHAN, "roh-HAHN"—*Hindu: "sandalwood."* F

ROHIN, "ROH-heen" or "roh-HEEN"—*Hindu: "the upward path."*

ROLAND, "ROH-land"—*German: "famous throughout the land."* **ORLANDO**—Spanish; **RALDAN, ROLDANN**—Scottish; **RODHLANN** (ROY-lahn)—Irish Gaelic; **ROELAND**—Dutch; **ROLANDO** (roh-LAWN-doh)—Spanish and Portuguese; **RÓLANN**—Irish; **ROLDAN, ROLLAN**—Scandinavian; **ROLLAND, ROLLIN, ROLLINS, ROWLAND.** Roland was the greatest warrior-knight of Emperor Charlemagne, and his exploits are told in the French epic poem *Chanson de Roland.* Rollo was a Viking who led in the Norman invasion of Britain. **ROLLI, ROLLIE, ROLLO, ROLLY.** F

ROLF, "ROHLF"—*Teutonic: "praised wolf" or "swift wolf."* **RODHULBH** (ROY-ulf)—Irish Gaelic; **ROLPH.** See also RALPH.

ROLT, "ROHLT"—*German: "power."*

ROMEO, "roh-MAY-oh" or "ROH-mee-oh"—*Latin: "a Roman."* **RAMEO, ROMARICO, ROMINO.** F

ROMI, "ROH-mee"—*Hebrew: "exalted" or "high."* F

ROMNEY, "RAWM-nee"—*Welsh: "curving river"; Scottish: "curved or round island"; Eastern European: "gypsy."* **ROM.**

RON, "ROHN" or "RAWN"—*Hebrew: "to sing."* This is also a diminutive of names beginning with "Ron-" or "Rhon."

RONALD, "RAW-nahld" or "roh-NAHLD"—*Scottish form of Reginald: "powerful ruler."* **RAGNALL** (RAW-nyal)—Scottish Gaelic; **RANALT**—Irish Gaelic; **RAONULL** (RAH-oh-nool)—Scottish Gaelic; **RINALDO** (ree-NAHL-doh)—Spanish, Italian, and Portuguese; **RONALDO** (roh-NAHL-doh)—French and Spanish. Ronald Reagan was president from 1981 to 1988. His tenure saw the breakdown of worldwide communism, a rise in offensives against worldwide terrorism, and the first female United States Supreme Court Justice. **RON, RONNI(E), RONNY.** See also REGIS. F

RONAN, "ROH-nahn"—*Gaelic: "little seal"; Norwegian: "mighty."* **RON.**

RONDEL(L), "ron-DELL"—*Old French: "round."* **RHONEL(L).** Rondell Sheridan is a comedian and TV actor. **RON, RONNIE, RONNY.** F

ROONE, "ROON"—*Celtic: "secret sign" or "mystical symbol."* **ROONEY.** Runes are magical symbols of the Druids and Celts that were carved into rocks or wooden plaques.

ROOSEVELT, "ROSE-eh-vehlt"—*Dutch: "field of roses."* Theodore Roosevelt was president from 1901 to 1909. Although known for his belligerence—he formed the Rough Riders cavalry unit to fight in the Spanish-American War—Roosevelt won the Nobel Peace Prize in 1906 for mediating an end to the Russo-Japanese War. A dedicated outdoorsman, Roosevelt also raised the nation's consciousness about the need for wilderness preservation. Franklin Delano Roosevelt, younger cousin of Theodore, was president from 1933 to 1945. He saw the country through recovery from the Great Depression and through World War II. His First Lady, Eleanor, was respected and honored in her own right. **NED; ROSE, ROSEY, ROSI(E).**

RORY, "ROH-ree"—*Scotch-Irish: "red" or "ruddy."* **RUAIDRI** (ROO-eye-dree), **RUAIRÍ** (roo-EYE-ree)—*Irish Gaelic;* **RUARAIDH** (ROO-ah-rye)—*Scottish Gaelic.* The last high king of Ireland was Rory O'Conor, and Rory O'More was a famous Irish chieftain. See also RODERICK. F

ROSCOE, "RAWS-koh"—*Teutonic: "from the deer forest."*

ROSS, "RAWS"—*Teutonic: "swift horse"; Celtic: "meadow"; Norse: "a headland."* **ROSSIE, ROSSY.**

ROWELL, "ROH-ehl"—*English: "the deer spring."*

ROWEN, "ROH-wehn"—*Scottish: "little red one"; Celtic: "white mane"; Teutonic: "mountain ash."* **ROWAN.** This is certainly a colorful name.

ROWLAND, "ROW-land" ("ROW" like "how") or "ROH-land"—*English: "rugged land."* See also ROLAND.

ROY, "ROY"—*French: "king"; Scottish Gaelic: "red."* **ROI; RUAY** (ROO-ay)—*Scottish Gaelic.* Rob Roy was a Scot who led a rebellion against the English. See also REX.

ROYAL, "ROY-uhl"—*Latin: "superior" or "majestic."*

ROYCE, "ROYSS"—*French: "son of the king"; Latin: "rose."*

ROYDON, "ROY-dun"—*English: "the rye hill."*

RUDOLF, "ROO-dohlf"—*Teutonic: "famous wolf."* **REZSÓ** (REH-zhoh)—*Hungarian;* **RODOLFO** (roh-DOHL-foh)—*Italian;* **RODOLPHE** (roh-DOHLF—"r" rolls in your throat, not on your tongue)—*French;* **RUDOLFO, RUDOLPH.** Besides belonging to a reindeer, this had been the name of several noble Austrians. Rudolf Valentino was the very first male sex symbol in entertainment, lighting a million fires in the hearts of female American moviegoers in the 1920s. **RUDY.**

RUDY. See RUDOLF, RUDYARD.

RUDYARD, "RUHD-yurd"—*English: "red yard"; Anglo-Saxon: "red pole."* Rudyard Kipling was a novelist and poet of the British Empire who wrote material as diverse as stories for little children and rousing, passionate adventures for adults. **RUDD, RUDDY, RUDY.**

RUPERT, "ROO-purt"—*German version of Robert: "shining fame."* **RUPRECHT** (ROO-prehkt). Rupert was a seventeenth-century Bavarian prince and general in the English Civil War. See also ROBERT.

RUSK, "RUHSK"—*Gaelic: "a marsh."*

RUSKIN, "RUSS-kihn"—*German: "red-haired child."*

RUSSEL(L), "RUHSS-ehl"—*French: "red"; Anglo-Saxon: "like a fox."* **RUSH, RUSS, RUSSIE, RUSTY.** F

HOMES ON THE RANGE BOYS' NAMES

Boys born in the states near the Rocky Mountains are most likely to have the following names:

1. Christopher
2. Michael
3. Joshua
4. Matthew
5. David
6. John
7. Justin
8. James
9. Daniel
10. Jonathan
11. William
12. Jacob
13. Cody
14. Brandon
15. Anthony
16. Jordan
17. Robert
18. Darius
19. Xavier
20. Jose

RUSTY, "RUST-ee—*Bretagne: "reddish" or "orange."* See also RUSSEL(L).

RUTGER, "ROOT-gur"—*Teutonic: "famous warrior."* Rutger Hauer is a Dutch actor who plays a great bad guy. See also ROGER.

RUTLAND, "RUT-land"—*Norse: "the cleared forest" or "stump land."* **RUTLEIGH, RUTLEY.**

RYAN, "RYE-un"—*Scottish Gaelic: "little king" or "strong one"; Latin: "to laugh."* **RIAN** (but not RIEN, which means "nothing" in French), **RYEN.** See also RIANCE/RIENCE.

RYKER, "RY-kur"—*Scottish: "one who reaches" or "one who strives."* **RIKER. RIKE, RYKE.**

RYLAN, "RYE-lan"—*English: "rye lands."*

RYLE, "RYL"—*English: "rye hill."*

RYLEY, "RYE-lee"—*Irish Gaelic: "valiant."* See also RILEY.

THE TOP FIVE

SAMUEL/SAM
STEVEN/STEPHEN
SCOTT
SEAN
STEFANO/STEPHAN

f the name you're looking for isn't here, ee "C."

SAAMI, "SAH-mee"—*Finnish: "a Lapp."* See also SAMI, SAMUEL. F

SABIN, "SAY-bihn" or "SAB-ihn"—*Latin: of the Sabines," a tribe of people who used o inhabit northern Italy; Arabic: one of the people of the Book."* **AL-SABI'A** (AHL sah-BEE-ah), **SABEAN, SABIAN** (sah-BEE-ahn)—rabic and Persian; **SABIN** (sah-been)—asque; **SABINY** (sah-BEE-nee)—Polish; **AIDHBHIN** (sye-yeh-VEEN)—Gaelic; **SAVIN**—astern European. The Sabians or al-Sabi'a re people listed in the Qur'an—along with luslims, Christians, and Jews—as "People f the Book," all members of the same xtended family of the God of Abraham, ound by their worship of the same one od. **BINO.**

SABIR, "sah-BEER"—*Arabic: "patient."*

SACHI, "SAH-chee"—*Japanese: "bliss."* F

SAFFORD, "SAF-furd"—*English: "from e willow tree river-crossing."*

SAGE, "SAYJ"—*Latin: "wise."* Sage is a hrub with lavender flowers, and leaves at have a warm, spicy flavor.

SAHEL, "SAH-hehl"—*Arabic: "from the wlands."*

SAKI, "SAH-kee"—*Japanese: "cape,"* as in a warm, protecting garment. F

SAL. This is a diminutive of all the "Sal-" names, but is mostly used as a diminutive of Salvador and Salvatore.

SALADIN, "SAHL-ah-deen"—*Arabic: "peace through faith" or "perfection through faith."* Saladin was a celebrated sultan of Egypt and Syria, best known in the West as Richard I's adversary in the Crusades. **SAL.**

SALIM, "sah-LEEM"—*Arabic: "flawless."* **SELIM. SAL.**

SALVADOR, "sahl-vah-DOR"—*Spanish: "savior" or "saved."* **SALBATORE** (sahl-bah-toh-reh), **XALBADOR** (zahl-bah-dor)—Basque; **SALVADORE** (sahl-vah-DOR-eh), **SALVATOR, SALVATORE** (sahl-vah-TORE-eh). **SAL.**

SALVATORE. See SALVADOR.

SALVIO, "SAHL-vee-oh"—*Latin: "sage."* **SAL.**

SAM, "SAHM"—*Korean: "achievement"; diminutive of Samuel.* This name has been gaining popularity over the past ten years as a diminutive of Samuel. See also SAM-SAR, SAMUEL.

SAMAD, "sah-MAHD"—*Arabic: "immortal."*

SAMBAR, "SAHM-bahr" or "sahm-

BAHR"—*Hindu: "deer with strong antlers."* **SAMBARA**—*Sanskrit;* **SAMBUR.**

SAMI, "SAH-mee"—*Arabic: "exalted."* **SAAMI.** F

SAMIR, "sah-MEER"—*Arabic: "entertaining companion."* F

SAMSAR, "sahm-SAHR"—*Pali and Sanskrit: "a reincarnation."* **SAM, SAMMI(E), SAMMY, SAM(M)S, SAMSA, SAMSI(E), SAMSO, SAMSY.**

SAMSON, "SAM-suhn"—*Hebrew: "like the Sun."* **SAMPSON; SHIMSHON**—*Hebrew;* **SIMPSON.** Samson was a legendary Hebrew strongman and judge who ran into trouble when his wife cut his hair, which is what he believed to be the source of his strength. Sampson is also the name of a Christian saint.

SAMUEL, "SAM-yoo-ehl" or "SAM-yool"—*Hebrew: traditionally "God listens," but sometimes given as "in the name of the Lord."* **SAAMI(E)** (SAH-mee)—*Native American;* **SAMIEL** (SAH-mee-ehl)—*French, German, and Scandinavian;* **SAMU** (SHAH-moo), **SÁMUEL** (SHAH-myoo-el)—*Hungarian, Eastern European, and Slavic;* **SHMUEL** (shmoo-EHL)—*Hebrew.* The Samuel of the Old Testament/Tanakh was a Hebrew judge with very far-reaching powers. **SAM, SAMMI(E), SAMMY.** F

SANBORN, "SAN-born"—*English: "born on the sand."* Makes sense, doesn't it?

SANCHO, "SAHN-choh"—*Spanish from Latin: "holy or sincere."* **SANCHE, SANCHEZ, SANCHIO.** Sancho Panza is the long-suffering, gentle, and smart squire of a slightly off-kilter nobleman who fancies himself a knight in Cervantes's *Don Quixote.* F

SANDER, "SAN-dur" or "SAHN-dur"—*the half of Alexander, Lysander, etc., meaning: "of humankind."* **SANDER, SANDERS, SANDRO; SAUNDER, SAUNDERS. SANDY.** See also ALEXANDER. F

SANDHI, "SAND-ee" or "SAHND-hee"—*Sanskrit: "placed together" and "put together."* F

SANDY. See SANDER, SANFORD.

SANFORD, "SAN-furd"—*English: "sandy ford" or "sandy river-crossing."* **SANDY.**

SANTINO, "sahn-TEE-noh"—*Latin: "holy or pure."* **SANTINI, SANTO.** F

SANYU, "sahn-YOO"—*African Luganda: "happiness."*

S(H)ARAD, "shah-RAHD"—*Hindu: "born in the autumn."* To be proper, if you choose to spell it "Sarad," a dot must appear under the "S."

SASHA, "SAH-shah"—*Russian diminutive of Alexander, thus: "defender of humankind."* **SACHA, SANYA, SASHENKA** (sah-SHEHN-kah), **SHURA, SHURIK.** See also ALEXANDER. F

SATO, "SAH-toh"—*Japanese: "sugar."*

SATORI, "sah-TOH-ree"—*Japanese: "enlightenment" or "comprehension."* **TORI(E)** Satori is the sudden attainment of understanding for which Zen Buddhists strive. F

SAUL, "SAWL"—*Hebrew: "longed for" or "asked for."* The Old Testament/Tanakh Saul was the first king of the Israelites. The New Testament Saul was a persecutor of Christians who underwent a conversion and changed his name to Paul. **SOL SOLLY; ZOLLIE, ZOLLY.**

SAVERIO, "sah-VER-ee-oh"—*Italian "version of Severin(?), "of the Sabines."*

SAVILLE, "sah-VEEL" or "SAV-ihl"—*Bretagne: "estate with willow trees."*

SAVIN, "SAV-ihn"—*French: "juniper bush."* This European bush bears blue-green berries. In folk medicine, the foliage is used in medicinal oils. See also SABIN.

SAWYER, "SAW-yur" or "SOY-yur"—*French: "maker of planks"; Celtic: "woodsman"; English: "one who saws"* or *"one who works at the sawmill."* Tom Sawyer is one of the delightful books and characters created by Mark Twain. See also SAYER.

SAYER, "SAY-ur"—*Welsh: "carpenter"; contracted German: "my people are victorious."* **SAYERS, SAYRE, SAYRES. SAY.** See also SAWYER.

SAY(Y)ID, "sah-YEED"—*Arabic: "lord."*

SCHUYLER, "SKY-lur"—*Dutch: "shelter"* or *"wise man."* **SKYLER. SCHUY, SKYE.**

SCOT(T), "SCOT"—*Greek: "darkness"; Norse: "payment"* or *"assessment"; Gaelic: "Scottish"* or *"Irish."* **SCOTCH.** Did I make a mistake? Nope! Scota, wife of Niul, and Scota, wife of Milesius, are two of the mythical first women from whom sprang the whole Gaelic race. Ireland was called Scotia as late as the Middle Ages, and Irish persons who crossed the sea to settle in Caledonia, or northern England, were called "Scots" by the native inhabitants of Caledonia, the Picts. Pretty soon all inhabitants of Caledonia were called Scots, Scottish, or Scotch. As always happens, separation produces a divergence in culture, and the Scots, who began as the Irish, aren't so Irish any more. **SCOTCHI(E), SCOTCHY; SCOTTI(E), SCOTTY.**

SCULLY, "SKULL-ee"—*Scottish: a type of large wicker basket; French: "kitchen";*

Danish: "long oars"; or Gaelic: "town crier." The Gaelic derivation refers to the ancient version of a news anchorman.

SEABROOK, "SEE-brook"—*English: "brook flowing into the sea."*

SEAN, "SHAWN"—*Gaelic version of John: "God's gracious gift"; Gaelic: "old."* **SEANAN, SHAN.** This name has long been popular in Ireland, but the fame of Oscar-winning Scottish actor Sean Connery has helped make it popular in the United States. "Old" or not, Connery is still considered a sexy man. In 1992, at the age of sixty-two, he was named "The Sexiest Man Alive" by *People* magazine. He gets my vote every year. See also JOHN, SHAWN. F

SEBASTIAN, "seh-BAHS-tyahn"—*Greek: "venerable"; Latin: "from Sebastia."* **BASTE** (BAH-steh)—Norwegian; **BASTIAAN** (bahs-TYAHN)—Dutch; **SEBASTEN** (seh-bah-stehn)—Basque; **SEBASTIANI, SEBASTIANO**—Italian; **SEBASTIEN** (seh-bahs-TYEN)—French; **SEBESTYÉN** (sheh-BESH-tyen)—Hungarian. This is the name of a Christian saint who rose to the rank of Officer of the Imperial Guard in the Roman army before his faith was found out, and he was martyred. **BASTE, BASTI(E)** (BAHS-tee). F

SEDGEWICK, "SEHJ-wihk"—*Anglo-Saxon: "from the village of victory"; English: "swordsman's village."* **SEDGEVILLE** (SEHJ-vihl), **SEDGEWINN; SEDGWICK, SEDGVILLE, SEDGWIN.**

SEELY, "SEE-lee"—*English: "blessed"* or *"happy."* **SEELEY.**

SEGEV, "SEH-gehv"—*Hebrew: "majestic."*

SELBY, "SEHL-bee"—*Teutonic: "the manor farmhouse."* **SHELBY.**

SELDEN, "SEHL-dehn"—*English: "wonderful" or "rare."* **SELDAN, SELDON.**

SELWIN, "SEHL-wihn"—*English: "friend of the family."* **SELWYN.**

SEN, "SEHN"—*Japanese: "woodland elf."* F

SENDAL, "SEN-dahl"—*Old English: "fine cloth" or "fine linen."* F

SENNETT, "SEHN-eht"—*French: "old wise one."*

SERGIO, "SARE-jee-oh"—*Latin: "the attendant"; Greek: "silk."* **SERGEI** (SEHR-gay or sehr-GAY), **SERIOZHA** (sehr-ee-OH-zhah), **SERIOZHENKA** (sehr-ee-oh-ZHEHN-kah)—*Russian;* **SERGEOH, SERGIOH; SERGIOS** (SARE-yohss)—*Greek;* **SERGIUSZ** (SARE-gyoosz)—*Polish.* This is one of the Christian saints. **SERGE.**

SERI, "SEH-ree"—*Native American: "my family."* This is a tribe name for nomadic hunter-gatherers who inhabit Mexico and the extreme southwest United States. F

SERLE, "SURL"—*German: "armor or armored."* **SARILO** (sah-RIH-loh)—*German;* **SEARLE, SERILL; SERILO** (seh-REE-loh)—*Italian and French.*

SETH, "SEHTH"—*Hebrew: "appointed";* also an Arabic name for the Evening Star. In the Old Testament/Tanakh, Seth is the third son of Adam and Eve.

SETON, "SEE-tun"—*English: "village by the sea."* **SEATON** (SEE-tun or SHAY-tun).

SETSU, "SEHT-soo"—*Japanese: "fidelity."*

SEWELL, "SOO-ehl," also "SEH-wehl" and "SOO-wehl"—*English: "strong victory"; Teutonic: "sea victory."* **SEWAL, SEWEL.**

SEXTON, "SEHKS-tun"—*English: "the sexton."*

SEYMOUR, "SEE-more"—*Englis*[?] "marshes near the sea," "salt marshes,"[?] "marine wetlands."* **MORRI(E), MORRI**[?] **MORRY.** See also MARSH.

SHADE, "shah-DEH"—*African Yoruba*[?] "confer the crown."* **SAADE.** F

SHAKA, "SHAH-kah"—*African Elanger*[?] *Zulu: "beetle"; Sanskrit: "branch."* Shak[?] was king of the Zulu Nation, a huge, unite[?] front of various tribes from the central an[?] southern part of Africa who almost kept th[?] English from taking over. Shaka was a br[?] liant ruler and a military genius: he bu[?] alliances, redesigned weaponry and wa[?] fare, and completely annihilated oppo[?] nents, thus becoming an irresistible forc[?] He was interested in the European ways-[?] as he felt all knowledge was power—an[?] allowed a small band of representative[?] from George III, King of England, to stay [?] his Royal Kraal for several years a[?] "ambassadors."

SHAMAN, "SHAH-mun" and "SHA[?] mun"—*Sanskrit: "ascetic" or "magician*[?] *Native American: "medicine man"; O*[?] *Russian: "wizard."*

SHAMIR, "shah-MEER"—*Hebrew: "dia*[?] mond."* In Jewish folklore, the shamir wa[?] a little creature who could cut diamond[?] and he was enlisted to do the work on Kin[?] Solomon's temple. F

SHAMUS, "SHAY-muhss"—*Scotch-Iris*[?] version of James: "the supplanter"; Gaeli[?] "fox."* **SÉAMUS** (SHAY-moose)—*Irish Gaeli*[?] **SEUMAS** (SHOO-muhss)—*Scottish Gaeli*[?] See also JAMES.

SHANDY, "SHAN-dee"—*English: "litt*[?] *boisterous one."* **SHANDEE, SHANDI(E**[?] *Tristram Shandy* is a novel by eighteent[?] century writer Laurence Sterne. F

SHANE. See JAMES.

SHANLEY, "SHAN-lee"—*Irish Gaelic:* "old hero."

SHAQUIL, "SHAH-kihl" or "shah-KIHL"—*Arabic version of Isaac:* "laughter." **SHAQUILLE** (shah-KEEL)—*American invention.* Seven-foot-two Shaquille O'Neal is a well-known and well-liked basketball player and product pitchman. **SHAQ.** See also ISAAC.

SHARIF, "shah-REEF"—*Tunisian:* "honest" or "nobleman"; *Swahili:* "distinguished." Omar Sharif is a dashing Arabic actor, best known for his roles in blockbusters of the 1960s like *Lawrence of Arabia, Dr. Zhivago,* and *Funny Girl.* F

SHASTA, "SHASS-tah"—*Native American Hokan:* "forest people." A mountain and a people found in northern California share this name. The Shasta Indians hunted and traded with their neighbors, providing deerskin products, obsidian, and sugar pine nuts. F

SHAW, "SHAW"—*Old English:* "thicket"; *Anglo-Saxon:* "grove."

SHAWN, "SHAWN"—*Gaelic version of John:* "God's gracious gift" or "the fairy hill." **SHAUN; SHEAUN** (SHAY-un). See also JOHN, SEAN. F

SHAWNEE, "shaw-NEE" or "SHAW-nee"—*Native American Algonquin:* "my people, our people, us." This is a tribe name for a group of people who originally inhabited Ohio and Tennessee. F

SHEFFIELD, "SHEHF-feeld"—*English:* "the crooked field."

SHELDON, "SHEHL-dun"—*English:* "low, sloping hills." **SHELTON. SHEL, SHELLEY, SHELLY.**

SHELL(E)Y. See SHELDON, SHELTON.

SHELTON, "SHEHL-tun"—*English:* "village near the slopes" or "village of shells." **SHEL, SHELLEY, SHELLY.**

SHEPHERD, "SHEHP-hurd"—*English:* "herder of sheep." **SHEPARD, SHEPERD, SHEPPARD, SHEPPERD; SHEP.**

SHERARD, "SHEH-rurd" or "sheh-RAWRD"—*Anglo-Saxon:* "brave soldier."

SHERIDAN, "SHARE-ih-dun"—*Gaelic and Celtic:* "satyr" or "wild." **SHERATON.**

SHERMAN, "SHUHR-mun"—*English:* "sheep-shearer." **SHERM, SHERMI(E), SHERMY.**

SHERWIN, "SHUHR-wihn"—*English:* "bright friend." **SHERWYN.**

SHERWOOD, "SHUHR-wood"—*Anglo-Saxon:* "bright forest." Sherwood Forest is where Robin Hood did most of his hooding.

SHILIN, "shee-LEEN"—*Chinese:* "intellectual."

SHIPLEY, "SHIHP-lee"—*English:* "the sheep meadow." **SHIPLEA, SHIPLEE, SHIPLEIGH.**

SHIRO, "SHEE-roh"—*Japanese:* "fourth son."

SHOKI, "SHOH-kee"—*Japanese:* "the demon queller." In Japanese legend, the magical Shoki catches demons and takes them away, and as such, he often is a symbol of the New Year.

SHOMARI, "sho-MAH-ree"—*Swahili:* "forceful" or "stubborn."

SIDNEY, "SIHD-nee"—*Hebrew:* "to lure" or "to entice"; *Latin:* "of Saint Denis"; from a combination of languages: "the Winding Sheet (shroud) of Christ." **SIDAINE** (see-DEHN), **SIDOINE** (see-DWAHN)—*French;*

SIDONIA (sih-DOH-nee-ah)—*Dutch;* **SIDONIE, SYDNEY; TZIDONI** (TSIH-doh-nee)—*Israeli.* "Sidonie" is what the English heard when the French said "Saint Denis." Sidney Poitier was the first black man to be accepted (somewhat) in a romantic role opposite a white woman in the wonderful *Guess Who's Coming to Dinner?* **SID, SYD; SY.** For the female version, see SYDNEY.

SIGMOND, "SIHG-mond"—*German: "victorious protector."* **SIEGMOND** (SEEG-mawnd); **SIGISMONDO** (see-jees-MAWN-doh)—*Italian;* **SIGISMUNDO** (see-ghees-MOON-doh)—*Spanish;* **SIGISMUNDUS** (sihg- ihs-MUN-duhs)—*Dutch;* **ZIGMUND; ZSIGMOND** (ZHEEG-mond)—*Hungarian.* Sigmund Freud is considered to be the father of psychoanalysis, and one of the first doctors to give credibility to the examination of one's soul as a means of regaining health. **SIG, SIGGI(E), SIGGY, SIGII; ZIG, ZIGGI(E), ZIGGY.**

SIMEON, SYMEON, "SIH-mee-awn"—*Greek: "a sign"; Hebrew: "obedient."* This *is not* the same name as Simon, though the two are often carelessly thrown together in name books. One of the Christian saints was named Simeon of Stylites. He lived on top of a pillar for forty years, symbolically doing a heck of a good job at relinquishing the earthly realm for the heavenly realm.

SIMHA, "SEEM-hah"—*Hindu: "lion."* Simha is one of the avatars, or earthly forms, of Vishnu.

SIMON, "SYE-mun" or "see-MOHN"—*Hebrew: "be heard," "God has heard," or "with acceptance"; Greek: "snub-nosed."* **CHIMON; JIMENES** (hee-MEH-nehz), **JIMENO** (hee-MAY-noh)—*Spanish;* **SHIMÓN** (shee-MOHN)—*Israeli;* **SIMEN**—*Dutch;* **SÍMON** (SHEE-mohn)—*Eastern European;* **SÍOMÓN** (SHEE-oh-mon), **SUIMON** (SWEE-mon)— Irish Gaelic; **SZYMON** (SHIH-mon)—*Polish;* **XIMEN** (shee-mehn), **XIMON** (shee-mohn), **XIMUN** (shee-moon)—*Basque.* Simonides of Keos was a Greek poet of the sixth and fifth centuries B.C. Several Christian saint names are on this list. F

SINCLAIR, "sihn-CLARE"—*French: "of Saint Clair" or "saintly shine."* **SYNCLAIRE.** Sinclair Lewis was a Nobel Prize-winning novelist.

SINDBAD, "SIHND-bahd"—*Persian/Hindu or Persian/Latin(?): "city of lions" or "city of mustard"; Latin/Turkish(?): "city of Pakistan."* **SINBAD.** Sindbad the Sailor is a character from *A Thousand and One Arabian Nights;* he is a merchant seaman who shows up in Baghdad and relates stories of his seven voyages.

SINGH, "SING(-eh)" (the "eh" is almost an afterthought)—*Sanskrit: "lion."* **SINHA** (SIHN-hah or SEEN-hah)—*Sanskrit.* Every adherent of Sikhism—a religion that combines elements of Hinduism and Islam—must have Singh somewhere in his or her name. **SINA.**

SKAH, "SKAH"—*Native American Sioux: "white."*

SKANDA, "SKAHN-dah"—*Hindu.* In Hindu legend, Skanda is the god of war and the ruler of the planet Mars.

SKEETER, "SKEE-tur"—*Norwegian: "shooter"; English: "mosquito."*

SKELLY, "SKEH-lee"—*Gaelic: "the storyteller."*

SKERRIT(T), "SKARE-it"—*Old English: "to move rapidly"; the skerrit plant.* **SKIR-RET(T).** Skerrit is a European herb with white, edible tubers. See also SKERRY.

-son

"-son" (pronounced "-SUN") is the Anglo-Saxon suffix that means "child of." You may add this to any name you choose.

SKERRY, "SKARE-ee"—*Gaelic: "jagged stone"* or *"sharp rock."* **SKERRIG.** See also SKERRIT(T).

SKIFT, "SKIHFT"—*Old English: "fate."* **SKIFF.**

SKIVE, "SKYV(-eh)"—*Norse: "leatherworker"* or *"tanner"; Dutch: "gem cutter."* **SCHŶF, SCHYFE**—Dutch; **SKIFA, SKIFE**—Norse.

SKY, "SKY"—*Old Norse: "cloud."* **CIÉL** (see-EHL)—French; **CIELO** (see-EHL-oh)—Italian and Spanish; **HIMMEL**—German and Scandinavian; **LANGIT** (LAWN-giht)—Indonesian; **MBINGU** (m'BIHN-goo)—Swahili; **NIEBO** (NEE-boh)—Polish; **NYEBO** (NYAY-boh)—Russian; **RAKIA** (RAH-kee-ah)—Hebrew; **SAMA**—Arabic; **SORA**—Japanese. F

SLADE, "SLAYED"—*Old English: "valley."* **SLAYDE.**

SLAKE, "SLAYK"—*Old English: "ravine."* **SLAYKE.**

SLANEY, "SLAY-nee" or "SLAH-nee"—*French from Gaelic: "healthy."* **SIANY** (SHAH-nee)—Irish Gaelic; **SLÁINE** (SLY-neh)—Scottish Gaelic; **SLANEE.** F

SLEE, "SLEE"—*Scottish: "sly"* or *"dextrous."*

SLY. See SYLVESTER.

SNOW, "SNOH"—*English: "snow."* **GALID**

(gah-LEED)—Arabic; **KAR**—Turkish; **NEIGE** (NEHZH)—French; **NEVE** (NEH-veh)—Portuguese and Italian; **NIEVE** (nee-YEH-veh)—Spanish; **SCHNEE** (SHNAY or SHNEE)—German; **SNEEUW** (SNEW)—Dutch; **SNÖ, SNØ** (SNAW)—Scandinavian; **SNYEK** (SNYEHK)—Russian; **THELUJI** (theh-LOO-jee)—Swahili; **YUKI**—Japanese; **ZAPADA**—Rumanian. F

SOL, "SOHL"—*Latin: "the Sun."* See also SAUL.

SOLOMON, "SAWL-uh-muhn"—*Hebrew: "peaceful"; Latin: "of the Sun."* **SALAMON** (SHAH-lah-mon)—Hungarian; **SALMAN, SALOMAN**—Eastern European and Turkish; **SHELOMON** (SHEH-loh-mohn)—Israeli; **SHELOMON**—Arabic; **SULAIMAN** (SOO-lay-mawn), **SULEIMAN**—North African; **ZALMAN, ZALMON, ZELMO**—Slavic. In the Old Testament/Tanakh, Solomon was the son of King David and Bathsheba, and was about the wisest and most sensitive king anyone could ask for. Solomon wrote the sexy love poem *Song of Solomon,* which is found in the sacred scriptures, and was an example to all who would follow in his capacity as a leader.

SOLON, "SOH-lun"—*Greek: "wise man."*

SOMERSET, "SAW-mur-seht"—*English: "place of the summer settlers."* Somerset Maugham was an English writer of the late nineteenth and early twentieth centuries who often wrote about the fallen members of society.

SONGKOI, "SONG-koy"—*Vietnamese: "red river."*

SONNET, "SAWN-eht"—*Italian: a type of fourteen-line poem.* F

SONO, "SOH-noh"—*African: "elephant."* The elephant is seen as a powerful and noble animal by African tribes. Shaka, king of the Zulu Nation, was known as The Great Elephant. F

SORLEY, "SOHR-lee"—*Gaelic from Norse: "viking."* **SOMERLED** (SOH-mehr-lehd)—Scottish Gaelic; **SOMHAIRLE** (SOH-ire-leh)—Irish Gaelic. The Vikings who moved down into the British Isles referred to themselves as the southern tribe, the southern frontier, *sumerlidi.* In Irish history, Sorley MacDonnell the Yellow (as in hair color, not cowardice), a Viking from what is now Scotland, was grandfather of rebel Red Hugh O'Donnell. Sounds like a colorful family.

SORRELL, "SORE-ehl"—*Scandinavian: "Viking"; French: "chestnut-colored"; English: the sorrel plant, sorrel tree, or a three-year-old male deer.* **SÖREN** (SORE-uhn or SAHR-un)—Swedish; **SØREN** (SAHR-un)—Norwegian.

SOSHAN, "SOH-shahn"—*Ancient Persian: "savior" or "benefit."* **SOSHYAN; SAOSHYAN** (sah-OH-shee-ahn)—Avestan. Saoshyan is the Zoroastrian messiah, yet to come. Zoroastrianism is one of the world's major monotheistic faiths, and is primarily found nowadays in parts of Persia and India.

SOUTER, "SOO-tur"—*Scottish: "shoemaker."* **SOWTER.**

SPALDING, "SPAWL-dihng"—*English: "divided or split clearing."* **SPAULDING.**

SPARTAN, "SPAR-tun"—*Greek.* The Spartans were an ancient Greek people, noted for their hardiness and "no frills" approach to life.

SPENCER, "SPEHN-sur"—*English: "steward" or "shopkeeper,"* a contraction of "dispenser of provisions." **SPENSER.** Spencer Tracy was a much-beloved actor. **SPENCE, SPENSE.**

SPOFFORD, "SPAW-ford"—*English: "place near the ford."* **SPOFFERT, SPOFFIRTH, SPOFFORTH. SPOFFER, SPOFFOR.**

SQUIRE, "SKWIRE"—*French: "an esquire" or "attendant."* In the Middle Ages, a squire was a young noble who wished to become a knight.

STACY. See ANASTASIO.

STAFFORD, "STAFF-urd"—*English: "the landing by the river-crossing."*

STAN, "STAN"—*Nordic/Teutonic: "stone";* diminutive of all "Stan-" names. **STEN.**

STANBURY, "STAN-buh-ree"—*English: "the stone fortress" or "the tin mining region."* **STAN.**

STANFORD, "STAN-furd"—*English: "stony ford (river-crossing)."* **STAN.**

STANIEL, "STAN-yehl"—*English: the kestrel bird.* **STAN.**

STANLEY, "STAN-lee"—*English: "stony meadow or clearing"; Slavic: "pride of the camp."* **STANLEA, STANLEIGH, STANLY.** Baseball legend Stan "The Man" Musial popularized this name in the 1950s. **STAN.**

STANTON, "STAN-tun"—*English: "stony town or place" or "tin-mining town."* **STAN.**

STANWICK, "STAN-wihk"—*English: "the rocky village."* **STANWYCK, STANWYK. STAN.**

STAR, "STAR"—*English: "star."* **ASTRU** (AHZ-troo)—Rumanian; **BINTANG** (BIHN-tong)—Indonesian; **CSILLAG** (TSEEL-ahg)—Hungarian; **ÉTOILE** (ay-TWAHL)—French; **HOSHI**—Japanese; **KOCHAV** (koh-KHAV—"KH" like you're clearing your

Sen-

"Sen-" is the ancient Egyptian prefix that means "son of." You may add this to any name you choose.

-sen

"-sen" is the Scandinavian suffix that means "child of." You may add this to any name you choose.

-sin

This a very ancient suffix in early Mesopotamian languages that means "king."

---

throat)—Hebrew; **NYOTA** (NYOH-tah)—Swahili; **STERN**—German; **STJERNE** (STY-ERN)—Danish and Norwegian; **TAHTI** (TAH-tee)—Finnish; **ZVEZDA** (zvehz-DAH)—Russian. See also HOKU, IZAR. F

STEDMAN, "STEHD-mun"—*English: "owner of a farm."*

STEN, "STEHN"—*Teutonic: "stone."*

STENTOR, "STEHN-tohr"—*Greek: "he of the strong voice."* Stentor is a character in the *Iliad*, a herald and a singer noted for the volume he could produce. He was good to have around in stormy weather or noisy situations, since he provided encouragement above the din.

STEPHAN, "STEHF-an"—*Greek: "crowned with laurel."* **ÉTIEN(NE)** (ay-TYEN)—French; **PANYA, STEPHAN** (STEHP-awn),

STESHA—Russian; **STAFFAN**—Swedish; **STAVROS** (STAHV-rohss), **STEFANOS** (STEHF-ah-nohss)—Greek; **STEFAN; STE-FANO** (STEHF-ah-noh)—Italian; **STEPHEN** (STEE-fehn); **STEVEN; STIOFÁN** (STYOH-fawn)—Gaelic; **SZCZEPAN** (S'CHEH-pahn)—Polish. The Romans used to think that laurel provided protection from lightning. Saint Stephen is the very first Christian martyr. His stoning is related in the New Testament book of Acts. Some popes and some saints also have names on this list; including a saint who was a king of Hungary. English and Polish kings have also taken the names Stephen or Stephan. **STEVE, STEVIE.** See also ESTEBAN. F

STERLING, "STIR-ling"—*English: "without blemish or stain,"* or the starling bird. **STIRLING.**

STEVEN, "STEE-vun"—*Old English: "occasion"* or *"voice";* French: *"derrick," "spar,"* or *"to stow (or unload) cargo";* American version of Stephan: *"crowned with laurel."* **STEVAN.** Stevan was the name of several Serbian kings in the Middle Ages. **STEVE, STEVIE.** See also STEPHAN.

STEWART, "STOO-wurt"—*English: "steward"* or *"caretaker."* **STUART, STEWARD. STU, STEW, STEWEY.**

STIAN, "STEE-ahn"—*Norwegian: "quick on his feet."*

STIG, "STIHG"—*Swedish: "mount(ain)."*

STINSON, "STIHN-sun"—*Anglo-Saxon: "son of stone."*

STOCKLEY, "STAWK-lee"—*English: "meadow of felled trees."* **STOCKLEA, STOCK-LEE, STOCKLEIGH.**

STOCKTON, "STAWK-tun"—*English:*

"town near felled trees." **STOCKDALE, STOCK-DON.**

STODDARD, "STAWD-urd"—*Anglo-Saxon: "owner of horses."* Specifically, this refers to the owner of stud horses.

STOKE, "STOHK"—*English: "village."*

STONE, "STOHN"—*English: a stone.* **STONES, STONEY, STONY.**

STORM, "STORM"—*English: "tempestuous."* **ARASHI** (AH-rah-shee)—Japanese; **ASIFA** (AH-see-fah or ah-SEE-fah)—Arabic; **BURYA** (BOOR-yah)—Russian; **DHORUBA** (d'hoh-ROO-bah)—Swahili; **FIRTINA** (feer-TEE-nah)—Turkish; **ORAGE** (oh-RAZH)—French; **SAAR** (SAHR)—Hebrew; **VIHAR** (vee-HAHR)—Hungarian. **STORMY.** F

STORR, "STOHR"—*Nordic: "great."* **STØR** (STAWR or STUHR)—Swedish and Norwegian.

STRATH, "STRATH"—*Scottish: "wide valley" or "river course."* **STRATHMORE** ("wide valley marsh" or "riverside marsh.")

STROM, "STRAWM"—*Greek: "bed."*

STROUD, "STROWD"—*English: "from the thicket."*

STRUTHER, "STRUH-thur"—*Scottish: "stream."* **STROTHER, STROTHERS, STRU-THERS.**

STUART. See STEWART.

SUFFIELD, "SUHF-eeld"—*English: "southern field."*

SUGI, "SOO-jee"—*Japanese: "cedar."* F

SUKHA, "SOOK-hah"—*Sanskrit: "happiness" or "bliss."* F

SUKI, "SOO-kee"—*Japanese: "beloved."* F

SULLIVAN, "SUHL-ih-vahn"—*English: "plowing the highfields"; Irish Gaelic: "black-eyed one."* **SULLAVAN. SULLIE, SULLY.**

SULTAN, "sool-TAHN"—*Swahili: "ruler."*

SUMI, "SOO-mee"—*Japanese: "refined."* F

SUMMER, "SUM-mer"—*English: "summer."* **KAYITS** (kah-YEETS or KAH-yeets)—Hebrew; **LATO** (LAY-toh)—Polish; **LYETO** (LYAY-toh)—Russian; **NATSU** (NAHT-soo)—Japanese; **SAYF** (SYF)—Arabic; **SOMMAR, SOMMER**—German and Scandinavian; **VERANO** (veh-RAH-noh)—Spanish; **VERÃO** (veh-RAH-oh)—Portuguese; **YAZ** (YAHZ)—Turkish. F

SUN, "SUN"—*Korean: "goodness."* F

SUTTON, "SUHT-un"—*English: "southern town."*

SUZU, "soo-ZOO"—*Japanese: "little bell."*

SVEN, "SVEHN"—*Scandinavian: "young man."* **SVAIN**—Norwegian; **SVEND**—Swedish; **SVENS; SWAIN**—English.

SWEENEY, "SWEE-nee"—*Scottish: "little hero"; Irish: "well-going."* **SIVNEY** (SHEEV-nee), **SUIBHNE** (SWEEV-neh)—Irish; **SUIDHNE** (SWEE-nee)—Scottish Gaelic.

SYLVAN, "SIHL-vahn"—*Latin: "forest."* **SILVAN, SILVANO** (sihl-VAH-noh)—Italian and Spanish; **SILVANUS** (sihl-VAH-nuhss)—Dutch; **SILWAN** (SIHL-vahn)—Polish; **ZIL-VAN, ZYLVAN.** Silvanus was the Roman god of the forests. F

SYLVESTER, "sihl-VEST-er"—*Latin: "from the forest."* **SAILBHÉASTAR** (sile-VAY-stahr)—Irish Gaelic; **SILVESTRO, SIL-VESTRI.** Actor/writer/director Sylvester Stallone is best known for blockbuster action-adventure movies. **SYL, SLY.**

THE TOP FIVE

TAYLOR
TYLER
TIMOTHY
TANNER
THOMAS

If the name you're looking for isn't here, perhaps it is a variant or diminutive of another primary name.

TAB, "TAHB"—German: "popular." Tab Hunter was a blond teen idol of the 1950s and 1960s. See also TABOR.

TABIB, "tah-BEEB"—Turkish: "doctor." Talk about putting career pressure on a kid!

TABOR, "TAY-bur," "TAH-bohr," or "tah-BOHR"—Hungarian: "camp"; Irish: "well"; Persian: "drummer." **TABER, TOBAR**—Irish. Mount Tabor is near Nazareth in Galilee. **TAB, TABBY.**

TAD, "TAD"—diminutive of Thaddeus, Hebrew: "praising Jehovah"; Aramaic: "praise"; Greek: "courageous one." **TADEO** (tah-DAY-oh), **TADDEO**—Spanish; **THADDEO** (tah-DAY-oh)—Italian; **THADDEUS** (THAD-ee-us or TAD-ee-us). Thaddeus was one of the twelve disciples of Jesus; he is sometimes identified with Saint Jude. **TADDY; THAD, THADDY.**

TADI, "TAH-dee"—Native American Omaha: "the winds."

TAFT, "TAFT"—English: "river."

TAGGART, "TAG-urt"—Irish Gaelic: "son of the prelate."

TAHIR, "tah-HEER"—Arabic: "pure, chaste." F

TAISHO, "TYE-shoh"—Japanese: righteousness."

TAIT, "TIGHT" or "TAYT"—Scandinavian: "cheerful." See also TATE.

TAJ, "TAHZH"—Arabic: "crown." F

TAKA, "TAH-kah"—Japanese: "falcon." F

TAKI, "TAH-kee"—Japanese: "waterfall." F

TAL, "TAHL"—Hebrew: "dew" or "rain."

TALBOT, "TAL-bawt" or "TAHL-bawt"—Anglo-Saxon: "bloodhound." **TALBERT, TALBOTT. TALLIE, TALLY.**

TALCOTT, "TAL-kawt" or "TAHL-kawt"—English: "lakeside cottage."

TALIB, "tah-LEEB"—African: "seeker of knowledge."

TALOR, "TAHL-ur"—Hebrew: "mountain dewdrop" or "mountain rain."

TAMBO, "TAM-boh"—Gypsy or Turkish: "drummer, percussionist." **TAMBEAU** (tahm-BOH); **TAMBU.** This makes a tambourine a little drummer.

TAMIL, "TAH-meel"—Sanskrit(?): "southern(?)." The Tamil language of southern India has been found written on a cave wall, and dated to the third century B.C. That makes it one of the oldest recorded languages still in use today. F

TAMIR, "tah-MEER"—*Arabic: "date palm trees."*

TANE, "TAH-neh"—*Maori: "god of trees."* Tane is a god who grew trees so huge, they separated Rangi (sky) from Papa (earth).

TANI, "TAH-nee"—*Japanese: "valley."* F

TANNER, "TAN-ur"—*English: "a tanner" or "maker of leather goods."* **TARVER.**

TANO, "tah-NOH"—*African: "river god."* Tano is the name of a river in western Africa.

TANTON, "TAN-tun"—*English: "the quiet river town."*

TAO, "TAU"—*Chinese: "peach."*

TAPA, "TAH-pah"—*Polynesian: "mulberry tree."* Polynesians have used all parts of the tapa tree for clothing, shelter, and ceremonial items.

TARG, "TARG"—*English: "watching the enemy"; Scottish: "to discipline"; Norse: "a shield"; Aramaic: "to interpret."* **TARGE** (TAR-geh or TARJ).

TARIQ, "tah-REEK"—*Arabic: "Evening Star."*

TARN, "TARN" like "barn"—*Norse: "lake in the mountains."* **TARNE.**

TARO, "TAH-roh"—*Japanese: "first son" or "big boy."*

TARRANT, "TARE-ant"—*Welsh: "thunderer."* **TARRAN.**

TATCH, "TATCH"—*Old English: "quality."*

TATE, "TAH-teh" or "TAYT"—*English:*

"cheerful"; Native American Algonquin: "windy," also means "great talker." See also TAIT. F

TATSU, "TAHT-soo"—*Japanese: "dragon."* This name is good for a child born in the Year of the Dragon. In Asian cultures, dragons are good beings.

TAU, "TAH-oo"—*African Tswana: "lion."*

TAVI, "TAH-vee"—*Aramaic: "good."* **TAV, TOOVI, TOVI.**

TAVIS, "TAV-ihs"—*Celtic: "son of David (or Daffydd),"* thus *"son of the beloved."*

TAVISH, "TAH-vihsh"—*Gaelic: "twin."*

TAYLOR, "TAY-lur"—*English: "tailor, clothesmaker."* **TAILOR.** F

TAZ, "TAZ" or "TAHZ"—*Persian: "goblet"; English: "heap."*

TE, "TEH"—*Chinese: "virtue" or "power."* F

TEAGUE, "TEEG"—*Scottish: "poet."* **TADGH** (TAHD-eh)—*Irish.*

TED, TEDDER, TEDDY, "TEHD," "TEHD-ur," and "TEHD-ee"—*English: "to separate," "to stir," or "to spread."* The derivations refer to the handling of grains, such as wheat. These names can also be diminutives of other names, usually derived from those beginning with "Theo." See also TEDMOND, THEODORE.

TEDMOND, "TEHD-mund"—*Anglo-Saxon: "protector of the nation."* **TED, TEDDIE, TEDDY.**

TEFF, "TEHF"—*African: "abyssinian flour" or "abyssinian grain."* Teff is an African grain used to make a fine, white flour.

TELFORD, "TEHL-fohrd"—*French: "ironworker."*

TERCET, "TUR-seht" or "tur-SEHT"—

Italian: "triplet" or "trio." **TIRCET.**

TERENCE, *"TARE-ents"—Latin: "tender"; Greek: "guardian"; Teutonic: "people's ruler."* **TARAN, TARANS, TARANT, TERANCE, TERANT, TERRANCE, TERRANT, TERRENCE, TERRENT; TERANCIO** (tare-ANTS-ee-oh), **TERENCIANO** (tare-ents-ee-AH-no), **TERENCIO**—Italian; **TERENTILO** (tare-ehn-TEE-loh or teh-REHN-tee-loh), **TARANTINO, TERENTINO**—Greek; **THIERRY** (TYEH-ree)—French. The great Roman playwright, Terence, began his life in the second century A.D. as a North African slave in the house of the region's Roman governor. He earned his freedom and produced plays that changed the ways Romans performed theater and the types of subjects they enjoyed. **TERREL, TERRIS, TERRY.** See also TORRENCE. F

TERRILL, *"TARE-ihl"—Teutonic: "of Thor."* **TERRIN.**

TERRY. See TERENCE.

TEVYE, *"tehv-YEH" or "TEHV-yeh"—Hebrew: "goodness of God."* **TUVYE, TUVYAHU** (toov-YAH-hoo).

TEW, *"TYEW"—Celtic: "warrior god."* **TEWES** (TYOOZ or tyoo-WEEZ)—English; **TYR** (TYEER)—Scandinavian; **TYW** (TEEW)—Anglo-Saxon. This same god was also known as Zio among the ancient Germanic tribes. Tuesday is named for him.

THADDEUS. See TAD.

THANE, *"THAYN"—Scottish: "warrior-lord."* A thane ruled a region of Scotland, and answered to the king. **THAIN, THAINE, THAYNE.**

THANOS, *"THAH-nohss"—Greek: "bear" or "noble."* **THANASIOS** (thah-NAH-syohs), **THANASIS.**

THAYER, *"THAY-ur"—Teutonic: "of the nation's army."*

THEODORE, *"THEE-oh-dohr"—Greek: "divine gift."* **FEODOR** (FAY-oh-dohr)—Spanish; **FYODOR** (FYOH-dohr or fee-OH-dohr)—Eastern European; **TEODOR** (TAY-oh-dohr)—Polish and Swedish; **THAO** (TAY-oh), **THEODOSIOS** (tay-oh-DOH-syohs or thay-oh-DOH-syohs)—Greek; **THEODREKR** (thee-OH-dreh-ker)—Norwegian; **TUDOR**—Welsh. About twoscore Christian saints have borne names on this list. Roman and Byzantine emperors were named Theodosius. Theodore Roosevelt, president from 1901 to 1909, was an advocate of what he called "the strenuous life" who raised the nation's consciousness about the need for wilderness preservation. Nineteenth-century novelist Fyodor Dostoyevsky is perhaps best known for *Crime and Punishment* and *The Brothers Karamazov.* **DORO; NED, NEDDY; TAD, TED, TEDDY; TEO, THEO.** F

THEON, *"THEE-awn"—Greek: "godly."* **THEO.**

THERON, *"THARE-awn" or "TARE-awn"—Greek: "hunter" or "wild animal."* **TARAN, TARON; TERON; THARAN, THARON.**

THEROS, *"THARE-ohss"—Greek: "summer."*

THOMAS, *"TAW-mahss"—traditionally, Aramaic: "twin"; also Sanskrit: "darkness"; Sumerian: "true son"; Greek: "cutting"; a Mesopotamian crop god.* **TAM, TAMMY, TAMLANE**—Scottish; **TAMAS**—Sanskrit; **TAMÁS** (TAH-mahsh), **TAMERLANE** (TAM-ur-layn)—Eastern European; **TAMMUZ**—Sumerian; **TOMA**—Russian; **TOMAS**—Spanish and Portuguese; **TOMAS, TOMASSO** (toh-MAH-soh)—Italian; **TOMASZ** (TOHmawsh), **TOMASZY**, **TOMCIO** (TAWM-choh), **TOMEK**, **TOMISLAV** (TOH-mee-slahv), **TOMIS-LAW** (TOH-mee-slahv)—Polish. Thomas was one of the apostles of Jesus. He had trouble believing that Christ had risen—even though Jesus was right there in front of him—and he insisted on inspecting the wounds on the body. This is where the expression "a doubting Thomas" got its start. Several Christian saints have borne the name Thomas, and several of them were important factors in British history. **TOM**, **TOMMY**. F

THOR, "THOHR"—*Norse: "the thunderer."* **THORDUS**, **TOR**, **TORIN**. In Norse mythology, Thor was the god of war, storms, and fire. He was a son of the supreme male god, Odin. Thor Heyerdahl was a twentieth-century Norwegian anthropologist and explorer. F

THORLEY, "THOHR-lee"—*Teutonic: "Thor's clearing."* **THORLEA**, **THORLEIGH**.

THORMOND, "THOHR-mund"—*English: "Thor's protection."* **THORMUND**, **THURMOND**, **THURMUND**.

THORNTON, "THORN-tun"—*English: "town near (or of) the hawthorn trees."* **THORNE**, **THORNY**.

THORPE, "THORP"—*English: "farmstead" or "hamlet."*

THURGOOD, "THUR-good"—*English: "Thor's goodness."* **THURGOODE**. Thurgood Marshall was the first African-American United States Supreme Court justice.

THURLOW, "THUR-loh"—*English: "Thor's mountain."* **THURLOWE**.

THURMAN, "THUR-mun"—*English: "man of Thor."* **THURMON**.

THURSTON, "THUR-stun"—*Danish:*

"stone of Thor"; Latin: "place of frankincense." **THORSTEIN**, **THORSTEN**, **THORSTON**; **THURSTAN**, **THURSTEN**.

TIBOR, "TEE-bor"—*Slavic: "holy place."*

TIBORG, "TEE-borg"—*Scandinavian: "holy castle" or "sacred castle."*

TIERNAN, "TEER-nan"—*Irish: "lordly" or "noble."* **TIARNACH** (TYAR-nakh—"kh" in your throat), **TIARNAN**—Irish Gaelic. F

TIGER, "TYE-gur"—*Latin and Greek: "tiger"; Avestan: "arrow."* **HARIMAU** (hah-ree-MAO)—Indonesian; **TIGHRI**—Avestan and Ancient Persian; **TIGR**, **TYGR** (TEE-gur)—German, Scandinavian, Slavic, and Russian; **TIGRE**: (TEE-gruh)—French, (TEE-gray)—Spanish, Portuguese, and Italian; **TIGRIS**, **TYGRYS** (TEE-greese or TY-grihs)—Polish, Greek, and Hungarian; **TORA**—Japanese. Tiger Woods has gone from young amateur golf champion to young pro.

TIKI, "TEE-kee"—*Maori: "creator."* In Maori legend, Tiki is the god who fashioned the first man.

TILDEN, "TIHL-dehn"—*English: "cultivated, protected field."*

TIMOTHY, "TIHM-oh-thee"—*Greek: "honoring the gods" or "honoring God."* **TEEMOFE** (TEE-mohf), **TIMIRO** (tee-MEE-roh)—Russian; **TIMON**; **TIMOTHÉ** (TEE-moh-tay)—French; **TYMON**, **TYMOTEUSZ** (tih-moh-TAY-oosh)—Polish. Timothy was one of Jesus' twelve disciples. *Timon of Athens* is one of Shakespeare's plays. **TIM**, **TIMMY**. F

TINO. See VALENTIN(E).

TIRZO, "TUR-zoh"—*Hebrew: "cypress tree" or "desirable."* F

TITAN, "TY-tun"—*Greek: "great one."*

The Titans of Greek mythology were a race of very powerful giants born when the world was brand new. Titan is the largest of Saturn's moons. It is one of the great mysteries of our solar system: it is the only moon with a dense atmosphere, and even the Voyager probes were unable to enlighten scientists as to what's down there. **TY, TAN.** F

TITO, "TEE-toh"—*Greek: "of the giants (the Titans)."* **TITOS.** This is one of the Christian saints. See also TITUS.

TITUS, "TYE-tuhss"—*Greek: "daylight" or "sunlight"; Latin: "safe" or "saved."* Titus was a name borne by two Roman emperors. Titus Maccius Plautus was a Roman playwright in the third and second centuries B.C. whose comedies kept people laughing out loud. **TITO, TY.**

TOBBAR, "TOH-bahr"—*Gypsy: "the road."* **TOBAR, TOBE, TOBY.**

TOBIAS, "toh-BY-ahs"—*Hebrew: "God is good."* **TOBIT, TOBBIT.** The Old Testament's apocryphal Book of Tobit tells the story of a Hebrew captive in Nineveh. **TOBE, TOBY.** F

TOBY. See TOBBAR, TOBIAS.

TODD, "TAWD"—*English: "a fox."* **TOD, TODDIE, TODDY.**

TODOR, "TOH-dor"—*Hungarian from Greek: "gift of God."* **TIVADAR.**

TOFT, "TAWFT"—*English: "small farm."*

TOLLER, "TOH-lur" or "TAWL-ur"—*Greek: "collector of payments."*

TOM. See THOMAS.

TOMI, "TOH-mee"—*Japanese: "riches."* F

TOMO, "TOH-moh"—*Japanese: "knowledge."*

TONY, "TOH-nee"—*diminutive of Anthony and Antonio: "inestimable"; in and of itself: "stylish," "high-class,"* and *"extravagant."* See also ANTHONY, ANTONIO.

TWINS OR MORE

In a University of Minnesota study done on twins with alliterative names—names with the same first letters—in the 1980s, approximately half of the pairs liked their names and half did not. So it's up to you, as parents, to decide if you want to encourage individuality, even in the basic naming ritual, or if you think the twin connection is a more important factor. Remember, if the names sound alike, it's easier than usual to call one by the other's name, and this may or may not be a sensitive area for your child. Personally, I have names for multiple births picked out. In the girls' case, I opted for an identical *last* syllable to tie the names together at the end—therefore, all the nicknames will be different. In the boys' case, I chose names of the Knights of the Round Table—names can be related without being similar.

TOR, "TOR"—*Norse: god of thunder and lightning; African: "king"; Irish: "a tower."*

TORC, TORK, "TORK"—*Irish: "boar"; Celtic: "gold neckring."* **TORQUE.** The Celtic torc or tork was made of braided or twisted strands of gold, silver, or copper, with two round finials that faced the front.

TORMEY, "TORE-mee"—*Irish Gaelic: "thunder spirit."* **TORMÉ, TORMO.**

TORRENCE, "TOHR-ehnts"—*Teutonic: "the people's ruler."* **TORRANCE. TORR, TORREY, TORRY, TORY.** See also TERENCE.

TORSTEN, "TOHR-stehn"—*Teutonic: "rock of Thor."* Torsten was the rock upon which the Norse blacksmith god Thor hammered out his swords.

TOVI, "TOH-vee"—*Hebrew: "good."* F

TOWNSEND, "TOWNS-end"—*English: "edge of town."* **TOWNSHEND.**

TRAC(E)Y, "TRAY-see"—*Latin: "to lead" or "to investigate"; Anglo-Saxon: "defender."* **TRASEY, TRA(Y)CE, TRAYCEE.** F

TRAHERN, "TRAY-hurn" or "TRAH-urn"—*Welsh: "strong as a lion."*

TRAVERS, "TRA-vurs"—*Latin: "from the crossroads."*

TRAVIS, "TRA-vihss"—*French: "to traverse" or "crossroads."* **TRAVERS.** Randy Travis is a country singer.

TREMAYNE, "treh-MAIN"—*Cymric: "the house by the rocks."* **TREMAIN(E).**

TRENT, "TREHNT"—*Latin: "swift."* Terence Trent Darby is a Caribbean singer/songwriter.

TREVOR, "TREH-vur"—*Celtic: "prudent"; Welsh: "great homestead."* **TREFOR**—Welsh. **TREV.**

TRIGG, "TRIHG"—*Norse: "trusted."*

TRISTAN, TRISTRAM, "TRIST-in" and "TRIST-rum," two names for the same Knight of the Round Table. *Tristan—Latin: "sorrow" and Tristram—Old French and Latin: "sorrowful labor"; either—Cymric: "tumult" or "loud noise."* Sir Tristan/Tristram—the name depends on whose version of the Arthurian legends you consult—was the second most skilled Knight of the Round Table after Lancelot. He was sent to ensure safe passage of the Princess Isolde on her way to her arranged marriage with King Mark, but instead fell in love with her himself. In addition to the stories told in Arthurian lore, Tristan's/Tristram's story is told in Wagner's opera *Tristan und Isolda.*

TROY, "TROY"—*Greek: "curly-haired."* **TROI, TROILUS, TROJ** (TROHJ or TROY), **TROJAN.** The ancient city of Troy was involved in a ten-year battle with the Greeks over a Greek woman named Helen. *Troilus and Cressida* is one of Shakespeare's plays. Troy Aikman is a Super Bowl-winning quarterback.

TRUMAN, "TROO-man"—*English: "faithful, loyal, honest."* Truman Capote was a wildly popular novelist, whose biggest selling works such as *Breakfast at Tiffany's* and *In Cold Blood,* always went to the screen. **TRU, TRUE.**

TUARI, "too-AH-ree"—*Native American Hokan: "young eagle."*

TUCKER, "TUCK-ur"—*English: "to stretch"—cloth, that is.* **TUCK.**

TUDOR, "TOO-dur"—*Welsh version of Theodore: "gift of God."* The Tudors are one of the families who have ruled over the British Isles. See also THEODORE.

TULLIO, "TOO-lee-oh" or "TOO-lyoh"—

Gaelic: "peaceful" or "quiet." F

TULLY, "TUH-lee" or "TOO-lee"—*Gaelic: "a little hill"; Irish: "mighty people"; Latin: "a title."* **TULLEY, TULLUS. TUL.** F

TURNER, "TURN-ur"—*Latin: "to turn" or "one who turns."* This refers to material on a lathe.

TUYEN, "t'WHEN"—*Vietnamese: "angel."*

TY. See TITAN, TITUS, TYLER, TYRONE, TYSON.

TYBALT, "TIH-bahlt"—*Teutonic: "the people's prince."* **THEOBALD; THIBAULT** (tee-BOW or tee-BOWL)—French; **TIBBIT**—English; **TIBBOT**—Scottish; **TIOBÓID** (TEE-oh-boyd)—Irish; **TYBALD**—German.

TYCHO, "TY-koh," "TYEH-koh" if you want a Scandinavian sound—*Greek: "of/from Tyche, the goddess of chance."* F

TYLER, "TYE-lur"—*Anglo-Saxon: "maker or crafter of tiles or bricks."* John Tyler was president from 1841 to 1844. He fathered fifteen children with two wives. No wonder he only lasted one term, he was *exhausted.* **TY.**

TYNAN, "TYE-nun"—*Gaelic: "dark" or "gray."* F

TYRONE, "ty-ROHN"—*Greek: "sovereign"; Latin: "recruit"; Norse: "chief"; Gaelic: "gray seal."* Tyrone is a county in Ireland. Tyrone Power was a stage actor who came to the screen in the 1910s and 1920s. And oh, yes, he had a son named Tyrone Power, Junior, who became a huge sensation as a romantic lead with dark good looks in many, many films from the 1930s to the 1950s—some of the best are *The Mark of Zorro, Blood and Sand, The Black Swan,* and *The Sun Also Rises.* **TY.**

TYSON, "TYE-sun"—*Old French: "fire-bird."* **TY.**

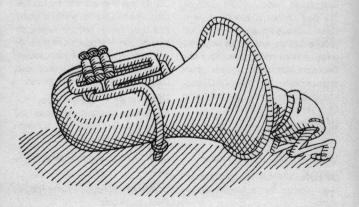

THE TOP FIVE

ULYSSES
ULRICH/ULRICK
UMBERTO
URBANO
UHURU

If the name you're looking for isn't here, see the other vowels.

UDELL, "yoo-DEHL"—*English: "small valley of yew trees."* **UDALE, UDALL. DELL.** F

UHURU, "oo-HOO-roo"—*Swahili: "free" or "freedom."* F

ULF, "UHLF"—*Teutonic: "wolf."*

ULRIC, "UHL-rihk"—*German: "ruler of all."* **ALRIK; ULRICH, ULRI(C)K.** Saint Ulric was a bishop in the tenth century. **RICK.** F

ULYSSES, "yoo-LIHS-sees"—*Roman version of Odysseus: "wounded in the thigh" or "angry one."* **ULIXES** (yoo-LICK-seez)—*Latin;* **ULUXE** (yoo-LUCKS-eh)—*Etruscan.* The here Ulysses (Odysseus, if you're Greek) had many fantastic experiences with gods, goddesses, and various wonderous creatures as he tried to return home from the Trojan War. Some of these stories appear in Homer's epic poem, the *Odyssey.* Ulysses S. Grant was the commander of the Union army during the Civil War.

UMBERTO, "UHM-burt-oh"—*Italian: "bright earth."* **UMBERT.** See also HUMBERT.

UNNI, "UH-nee"—*Hebrew: "modest."*

UPTON, "UHP-tun"—*English: "uptown."* Upton Sinclair was a twentieth-century author.

URBAN, "UR-ban"—*Latin: "of the city."* **URBAIN** (oor-BAN)—*French;* **URBANO** (oor-BAH-noh)—*Spanish and Italian;* **URBANUS** (oor-BAN-uss)—*German;* **URVAN**—*Russian.* Several popes took this name.

URI, "yoo-REE" or "YOO-ree"—*Hebrew: "lights" or "fire."*

URIAH, "YOO-rye-ah"—*version of Uriel, Hebrew: "fire of God."* **PENIEL, PHANIEL, PHANUEL, PHENIEL; URIEL** (YOO-ree-ehl or OOH-ree-ehl), **URI-EL.** Uriel is said to be one of the Archangels, primarily in Muslim tradition. He is the angel of judgement, and there is no leniency in him. The Uriah of the Old Testament/Tanakh was the first husband of the beautiful and sweet Bathsheba. King David desired her, and so sent her husband, one of his generals, off to a battle with instructions to lead the attack, insuring that he would be killed. With Uriah dead, David could take Bathsheba for his own.

USHI, "oo-SHEE"—*Chinese: "the ox."* "Ox" has Asian connotations of patience and determination, and is often given to children born in the Year of the Ox.

UTU, "OO-too"—*Sumerian: the god of the Sun.*

UZMATI, "ooz-MAH-tee"—*Native American Salish: "grizzly bear."*

-on, -won, -quon

These are African-American suffixes often found in the names of urban boys. They were invented after World War II as the African-American community began to assert its own identity. There was precious little native African scholarly work available to the average American, so a unique *sound* was created. Urban African-American names take the first syllable or two of a more traditional name and add the suffix that the parents think sounds best. The suffix is always a stressed syllable.

David—Davon
Adam—Adawon
Mark—Marquon

The suffix "-el(l)," seen in names such as Davell and Marquell, is also becoming popular. This suffix is also the stressed syllable.

THE TOP FIVE

VICTOR
VINCENT
VLADIMIR
VAL
VERNON

If the name you're looking for isn't here, see "B," "F," and "W."

VACHEL, "vah-SHEHL"—*French: "keeper of cattle."* F

VADIN, "VAH-deen"—*Hindu: "talker" or "speaker."*

VAIL, "VAYL"—*Latin: "a vale or valley."*

VAL, "VAHL"—*diminutive of Valdemar, Teutonic: "strength and fame" or "power and fame"; German: "famous ruler."* **BALDEMAR; VALDEMAR** (VAHL-deh-mahr); **WALDEMAR.** Three Danish kings were named Valdemar. Val Kilmer is an actor. See also VALENTIN(E), VALERIAN.

VALENTIN(E), "VAHL-ehn-tihn" and "vahl-ehn-TINE" or "vahl-ehn-TEEN" and "vahl-ehn-TEEN-eh"—*Latin: "strong and courageous" and "healthy."* **BÁLINT** (BAH-leent or bah-LEENT)—Eastern European; **VAILINTÍN** (vay-leen-TEEN)—Irish Gaelic; **VALENCIO** (vah-LEHN-see-oh or vah-LEHN-choh)—Spanish, Portuguese, Basque, and French; **VALENTIJN** (VAH-lehn-tee-yen or vah-lehn-tee-YEHN)—Dutch; **VALENTINO** (vah-lehn-TEE-noh); **VALENTIO** (vah-LEHN-tee-oh or vah-LEHN-tyoh)—Italian, Swiss, and French; **VALENTYN**—Eastern European. Saint Valentinus was martyred on February 14, which was near the time of the Roman fertility festival of Lupercalia. As often happened, old ideas merged with new ideas, and Saint Valentine is now associated with erotic love and mating rituals. Valentinian was the name of three popes. **TINO; VAL, VALLY.** F

VALERIAN, "vah-LARE-ee-ahn"—*Latin: "strong" or "brave."* **WALERIAN**—Polish. Spicy valerian rhizomes are used in herbal medicine. **VAL.**

VALERIO, "vah-LARE-ee-oh" or "vah-LARE-yoh"—*Latin: "strong" or "healthy."* **VALERIUS, VALERY.** F

VALESKO, "vah-LESS-koh"—*Russian: "glorious ruler."* **VALENCIO**—Italian and Spanish; **VELASCO; VELASKO; WALESKO** (vah-LESS-koh)—Polish. For the female version, see VALENCIA.

VANCE, "VANTS"—*Dutch: "son of Van"; Manx: "marsh."*

VANDER, "VAN-dur"—*Dutch: "from the . . ." or "belonging to . . . ".* "Belonging to us" is a translation if you wish to use Vander by itself, without any additions.

VARGAS, "VAHR-guss" or "VAHR-gahss"—*Gaelic: "strong man."* **FARGUS.**

VARUN, "vah-ROON"—*Tamil: "rain god";*

Von

This is the German, Austrian, and Eastern European prefix that means "child of" or "from," and can be placed before any name you choose. It is sometimes capitalized, sometimes not.

Van

This is the Dutch prefix that means "child of" or "from," and can be placed before any name you choose. It is sometimes capitalized, sometimes not. An alternate spelling is "Vanne."

Sanskrit: "to bind" or "to envelop"; Norse: "love of truth." F

VASILI(I), "VAH-see-lee" or "vah-SEE-lee"—Russian, from Basil, thus: "like a king" or "royal." **VASILIK, VASILY, VASYA, VASYENKA** (vahs-YEHN-kah)—Russian; **VASILIOS** (vah-SEE-lee-ohss), **VASOS**—Greek. See also BASIL.

VASIN, "vah-SEEN"—Hindu: "ruler."

VAUGHAN, "VAWN"—Celtic: "small." **VAUGHN, VAUN.**

VAYU, "VAH-yoo"—Sanskrit: "god of wind and warfare."

VEGARD, "VEE-gahrd"—Norse: "protection" or "sanctuary."

VENCEL, "VEHN-tsehl"—Hungarian: "wreath" or "garland."

VENECIO, VENETIO, "veh-NEE-shoh" or "veh-NEET-syoh"—Latin: "merciful" or "forgiveness." **VENTAN, VENTANO** (vehn-TAH-noh)—Spanish; **VINICIO** (vih-NEE-see-oh or vih-NEE-chee-oh)—Italian and Eastern European. F

VENN, "VEHN"—Gaelic: "fair."

VERANO, "veh-RAH-noh"—Spanish: "summer." F

VERDIN, "VUR-dihn" or "vur-DAN" (with the "r" stuck in your throat)—French: "yellow hammer." This is a type of bird native to the southern United States. **VERDAN, VERDUN.**

VERED, "VEH-rehd"—Hebrew: "rose."

VERNON, "VUR-nun"—Latin: "springtime." **VARNEY. VERN, VERNE, VERNEY, VERNI(E), VERNY.** F

VERO, "VEE-roh" or "VAY-roh"—Latin: "true"; Russian: "faith"; Sanskrit: "great hero." **VEREEN** (veh-REEN), **VEREN**—Scotch/Irish; **VERENO** (veh-REH-noh or vay-RAY-noh)—Spanish, Portuguese, and Italian; **VERINO** (veh-REE-noh)—French; **VERLE, VIRLE**—English; **VERLIN**—German; **VERLON**—Swiss; **VIRO**—Sanskrit. F

VICK. See VICTOR.

VICTOR, "VIHK-tor"—Latin: "victorious." **VICTOIRE** (veek-TWAHR)—French; **VIDOR** (VEE-dohr)—Eastern European; **VIKTOR** (VEEK-tohr)—Russian and Swedish; **VITTORIO** (vee-TOH-ree-oh)—Italian; **WICTOR**

(VEEK-tor)—Polish. There are several saints' names on this list. Victor Emmanuel II (d. 1878) was the first king of Italy; his father, Victor Emmanuel I, was only king of Sardinia. **VIC, VICK, VIK; VITO.** F

VIDAL, "vee-DAHL"—*Latin: "living" or "alive."* **VITALE.**

VIDAR, "vee-DAHR"—*Norse: "quiet god."* Vidar was a Norse forest or woodland deity who was the strong and silent type, one of the sons of the supreme god Odin. No one expected him to surpass his brothers in bravery and strength, but he did kill the great wolf Fenrir, a feat even his father wouldn't try.

VIHO, "VEE-hoh"—*Native American Cheyenne: "chief."*

VIJAY, "vee-JAY"—*Hindu: "victory."* F

VINCENT, "VIHN-sehnt"—*Latin: "the conqueror."* **UINSEANN** (WEEN-shawn)—Gaelic; **VICENTE** (vih-CHEHN-teh); **VINCENTE** (veen-SEHN-teh)—Portuguese; **VINCENTIUS** (vihn-SEHN-tee-uhss)—Dutch; **VINCENZO** (veen-CHEHN-zoh)—Italian; **VINCZE** (VEEN-tcheh)—Hungarian; **WICENT** (VEE-tsehnt), **WINCENTY, WIENCZYSLAV/ WIENCZYSLAW** (VEEN-sih-slahv)—Polish.

Saints have borne some of the names listed here. The best known is probably the most revered Spanish holy man, Saint Vincent of Sargossa, who was martyred very early in the fourth century. Vincent van Gogh was a Dutchman who lived a short and difficult life, but who had one of the most prolific careers of any artist, painting almost 1,000 paintings in ten years. Since then, van Gogh's emotionally charged, dazzling paintings have been sold for record prices at auctions the world over. **VIN, VINCE, VINCIE, VINCY; VINNI(E), VINNY.** F

VINNY. See CALVIN, VINCENT.

VIRGIL, "VUR-jihl"—*Latin: "chaste, pure."* **VERGIL, VIRGILIO.** Virgil is one of the ancient classic writers of Rome. His best-known masterpiece is the epic poem, the *Aeneid.* **VIRGE.**

VIRL, "VURL"—*Scottish: "ring" or "band."*

VISHNU, "VEE-shnoo"—*Hindu: "protector."* Vishnu is one of the three primary Hindu gods.

VITO, "VEE-toh"—*Italian diminutive of Victor: "conqueror"; Latin: "life."* **DA VITO, DE VITO**—Spanish, Italian, and Portuguese; **VIEL** (vee-EHL)—French; **VITALIS** (vye-

---

PURITAN VIRTUE NAMES

These names arose as the Puritan version of the Catholic and Anglican tradition of naming one's child after a saint. Rather than give a baby the name of a saint who was an example of a preferred moral and/or physical trait, the Puritans went straight for the trait itself. Thus, we have names like Chastity, Constance, True, Loyal, Hope, and Faith, and more unusual ones like Increase, Plenty, and Evangel.

TAL-ihss or vee-TAHL-ihss), **VITALY**—*French, German, and Dutch.* **VIDO.** See also VICTOR. F

VIZIER, "vih-ZEER" or "VIHZ-ee-air"—*Persian: "counselor."*

VLADIMIR, "VLAH-dee-meer" or "vlah-DEE-meer"—*Russian/Eastern European: "possesses peace" or "possesses the world" (imagine if someone possessed both).* **WLA-DIMIR** (VLAH-dee-TAHL-meer)—*Polish.* Vladimir the First was the first Christian ruler of Russia. In addition to being a great military man who expanded the territory; he was determined to treat all people fairly and generously. He was sainted by the Catholic Church. **DIMKA, VIMKA; VLAD, VLADI, VLADIK, VLADY, VLADYA; VOLODYA** (voh-LOH-dyah).

VOLANS, "VOH-lahnz"—*Latin: "flying (fish)."* This constellation flies through the South Pole skies, following the Sun at dusk from early February through March. The Sun is "in" Volans in June.

VOLANTE, "voh-LAHNT(-eh)"—*Latin: "to fly."* F

THE TOP FIVE

WILLIAM
WESLEY
WAYNE
WARREN
WILLEM

If the name you're looking for isn't here, see "B" and "V," and the vowels.

WABAN, "WAH-bahn"—*Native American: "the east wind."*

WADE, "WAYD"—*English: "to wade."* **WADDELL, WADELL, WAYDE.**

WAITE, "WAYT"—*English: "guard."*

WAKAN, "wuh-KAHN"—*Native American Sioux: "holy man."* See also HOWAKAN. F

WAKELEY, "WAYK-lee"—*English: "the wet meadow."* **WAKELEA, WAKELEE, WAKELIGH.**

WALDEN, "WAHL-dehn"—*English: "the forest valley."*

WALDO, "WAHL-doh" or "VAHL-doh"—*German: "ruler."* This old name has gained attention once more through the successful *Where's Waldo?* series of books for children. F

WALFORD, "WAHL-furd"—*English: "the Welshman's river-crossing."*

WALI, "wah-LEE"—*Arabic: "saint."*

WALKER, "WAH-kur"—*English: "a fuller" is the old meaning, in addition to "one who walks."* A fuller was someone who worked with cloth.

WALLACE, "WAHL-ihss"—*English: "Welsh";* *Teutonic: "stranger"; Norse: "choice"; Celtic: "to gush forth" or "to boil."* **VLACH** (VLAHK)—*Slavic;* **WALACHE** (VAH-lahk)—*Polish;* **WALLACH** (WAH-lahk), **WALLACHE**—*German;* **WALSH, WELCH, WELSH**—*American.* **WALLI(E), WALLY.** F

WALLY. See WALLACE, WALTER, WALTON.

WALT. See WALTER, WALTON.

WALTER, "WAHL-tur"—*German: "the people's ruler" or "rule of the people," thus, "democracy"; Welsh: "the hare."* **BHALTAIR** (VAHL-tare)—*Scottish Gaelic;* **GAULTHIER** (gawl-tee-AY), **GAULTIER** (gall-tee-AIR or gawl-tee-AY)—*French;* **GUALTIERO** (gawl-tee-AIR-oh or gwahl-TARE-oh)—*Italian;* **GUITTEIRO** (gwee-TYARE-oh)—*Spanish;* **UALTAIR** (WAHL-tare)—*Irish Gaelic;* **VALTER**—*Swedish;* **WALTHER** (WAHL-tur)—*German;* **WOUTER** (VOH/WOH-ter)—*Dutch.* Record-setting Walter "Sweetness" Payton was a fleet football player, and this star running back didn't even *play* football until his junior year in high school. **WALLI(E), WALLY, WALT, WAT.**

WALTON, "WAHL-tun"—*English: "walled town" or "fortified town."* **WALLY, WALT.**

WARD, "WOHRD"—*English: "guard."* **WARDEN.**

WARE, "WAYR"—*Anglo-Saxon: "careful."*

WARFORD, "WORE-furd"—*English: "ford at the small stream dam."*

WARLEY, "WOHR-lee" or "WAR-lee"—*English: "meadow with the small stream dam."* **WARLEA, WARLEIGH; WORLEA, WORLEIGH, WORLEY.**

WARNER, "WOHR-nur"—*Teutonic: "protective warrior."* **WARINER, WARRINER; WERNER** (WUR-nur or VUR-nur)—*German and Slavic.*

WARREN, "WOHR-un"—*German: "game warden"; English: "a game park."* **WERNER**—*German.*

WARRICK, "WOHR-ihk"—*Teutonic: "strong king."*

WARWICK, "WAR-wihk"—*English: "village hero."* **WARWICKE.**

WASHBURN, "WASH-burn"—*English: "the flooding brook."*

WASHINGTON, "WASH-ing-tun"—*English: "flooded town" or "flooded estate."* George Washington was the first American president, serving from 1789 to 1796. Some people wanted him to be emperor, but he stressed that this would not make the United States different from any other monarchy. The artist who painted George's portrait—the unfinished one that ended up on the dollar bill—didn't like Washington, and it shows. In other portraits, the Father of Our Country looks much nicer.

WAVERLEY, "WAY-vur-lee"—*English: "quaking aspen meadow."* **WAVERLEIGH.**

WAYLAND, "WAY-lend"—*English: "near the pathway."* **VIDLAND** (VEED-lahnd), **VIDLANDER**—*Nordic;* **WAYLEN, WAYLEND, WAYLON; WEYLAN, WEYLAND; WIELAND** (VEE-lahnd)—*Polish.* The Wayland of English and Teutonic mythology is a magical blacksmith, who has the power of invisibility.

WAYLON. See WAYLAND.

WAYNE, "WAYN"—*English: "wagon" or sometimes "meadow or clearing."* Wayne Gretzky is a high-scoring hockey player and highly paid product pitchman.

WEAVER, "WEE-vur"—*English: "one who weaves"; Welsh: "waterside path."*

WEBB, "WEHB"—*English: "weaver."* **WEBBE, WEBBER, WEBER, WEBSTER.**

WELFORD, "WEHL-furd"—*English: "river-crossing at the spring."*

WELL(E)S, "WEHLZ"—*English: "well or spring."* **ABAR** (ah-BAHR), **ABYAR, BIAR** (bee-AHR), **BIR** (BEER), **B'IR, BIRKAT** (beer-KAHT), **BIRKET, IDD, QALAMAT** (KAH-lah-maht), **QALIB** (kah-LEEB), **THAMAD** (tah-MAHD)—*African and Arabian sources.*

WENDEL(L), "WEHN-dul"—*English: "winding valley"; Teutonic: "to wander"; Norse: "to change course" or "to move forward."* **VEND, VENDEL**—*Scandinavian;* **WENDE** (VEHND)—*German.* Wendel Phillips was an American abolitionist. Oliver Wendell Holmes was a thoughtful, wise, far-sighted U.S. Supreme Court Chief Justice of the nineteenth century. F

WERNER, "WUR-nur"—*German version of Warren: "game park keeper"; Teutonic: "defending army."* **VERNER.** See also WARREN.

WES. See WESLEY, WESTON.

WESCOTT, "WEHS-kawt"—*English: "western cottage."*

WESH, "WEHSH"—*Gypsy: "the forest."*

NORTHWEST BOYS' NAMES

Boys born into the Pacific Northwest are most likely to have the following names:

1. Joshua	6. Tyler	11. Joseph	16. Alexander
2. Michael	7. Justin	12. Daniel	17. David
3. Matthew	8. Ryan	13. James	18. John
4. Christopher	9. Nicholas	14. Zachary	19. Jacob
5. Brandon	10. Jordan	15. Andrew	20. Cody

WESLEY, "WEHSS-lee"—*English: "the west meadow."* **WESLEA, WESLEE, WESLEIGH** (WEHSS-lee); **WESTLEA, WESTLEIGH, WESTLEY.** John Wesley was a charismatic Protestant reformer of the eighteenth century. His views emphasized the warmth, acceptance, and personal freedom in Jesus' teachings. He and his brother, Charles, travelled and preached much as Jesus did, in open fields, town halls, community parties, and private gatherings. After his death, the United Methodist Church was formed in his memory, and he is considered the founder. **WES.**

WEST, "WEST"—*English: "west."*

WESTON, "WEHSS-tun"—*English: "the west town."* **WES.**

WHEATLEY, "WEET-lee"—*English: "wheatfield."* **WHEATLEA, WHEATLEIGH.**

WHITFIELD, "WHIHT-feeld"—*English: "field of white" or "small field."* **WHITAKER, WHITTAKER; WHITLEA, WHITLEIGH, WHITLEY.**

WHITFORD, "WHIHT-furd"—*English: "the white river-crossing."*

WHITNEY, "WHIHT-nee"—*English: "white island."* F

WHITTAKER, "WHIHT-ah-kur"—*English: "the white acre" or "white park."* See also WHITFIELD.

WIES, "VEES"—*Teutonic: "renowned warrior."*

WIGHT, "WYTE"—*Norse: "prowess" or "valiant"; Old English: "stalwart creature"; Gaelic: a place name, The Isle of Wight.* **DWIGHT** (de + Wight).

WILBUR, "WIHL-bur"—*German: "bright willow."* **WILBER, WILBERT, WILBURT.**

WILL. See WILLARD, WILLIAM.

WILLARD, "WIHL-urd"—*German: "strong-willed."* **WIL, WILL, WILLIE, WILLY.**

WILLEM. See WILLIAM.

WILLET, "wih-LEHT"—*American: a shore bird.* F

WILLIAM, "WIHL-yahm"—*Teutonic: "resolute protector"; Gaelic: "fox."* **GIL(L)EN** (ghee-lehn)—Basque; **GUGIELMO** (goo-GEEL-moh or goo-GYEHL-moh), **GUGLIELMO** (goo-GLEEL-moh or goo-glee-EHL-moh)—Italian; **GUILLERME** (ghih-LAYRM or ghee-YAYRM); **GUILLERMO** (gwee-YARE-moh), **GULLERMO** (goo-YARE-moh), **HIERMO** (YARE-moh)—Spanish; **LIAM** (LEE-ahm), **UILLIAM** (WILL-ee-ahm)—Irish; **VIL-MOS** (VEEL-mohss)—Slavic; **WILLEM** (WIHL-lehm or VIHL-lehm), **WIM**—Dutch. Several kings, princes, presidents, and saints have had these names. William is a good name for a writer, as evidenced by William Shakespeare, William Faulkner, William Wordsworth, William Butler Yeats, and William Blake, to name but a few. William H. "Bill" Cosby is an African-American actor, educator, and activist who is most noted for his TV work. William Jefferson "Bill" Clinton is the first baby boomer president. **BILL, BILLY; WIL, WILL, WILLIE, WILLY.**

WILLIS, "WIHL-ihss"—Teutonic: "resolute"; Anglo-Saxon: "strong desire."

WILMOT, "WIHL-mawt"—German: "determined spirit."

WILTERN, "WIHL-turn"—Gaelic: "master of the wolves." **FAOILTIARN** (faw-WEEL-tee-arn)—Irish Gaelic; **WHILTIERN**—Scottish.

WILTON, "WIHL-tun"—Anglo-Saxon: "town of/near the wolves." Wilt Chamberlain, one of the only basketball players ever to score over 100 points in one game, is also credited with almost 24,000 rebounds. **WILT.**

WINDSOR, "WIHND-zur"—English: "boundary bank." The Windsor family rules the current Royal House of Britain.

WINN, "WIHN"—Celtic: "friend"; Old English: "joy." **WYNN, WYNNE.** F

WINNOCK, "WIHN-nawk"—Scottish: "window."

WINSLOW, "WIHNZ-loh"—Teutonic: "friendly hill" or "safe hill."

WINSTON, "WIHNS-tun"—English: "friendly town" or "friend's town." **WINSTEN, WINTON; WYNSTEN, WYNSTON, WYNTON.**

Winston Churchill was a great twentieth-century prime minister, writer, and motivator. He kept up Britian's—and the Allies'—spirits and resolve during World War II. **WIN, WYNN.**

WINTHROP, "WIHN-thruhp"—English: "friendly farm" or "friend's farm."

WINTON, "WIHN-tun"—Celtic: "a friend's town." **WYNTON.** Trumpeter Wynton Marsalis has mastered both classical music and jazz. See also WINSTON.

WIRT, "WURT" or "VURT"—German: "master." **WERT.**

WITAN, "WIHT-un"—Anglo-Saxon: "councilor." **WHITAN, WHITTEN, WITTEN.**

WITHE, "WYTHE"—English: "supple twig" or "willowy twig." **WYTHE.**

WOLF(F), "WUHLF[?]"—English: "the wolf." **WOLFE, WOLFGANG, WULF(F).** The fame of CNN newsman Wolf Blitzer has gained attention for this name. See also WOLFRAM.

WOLFRAM, "WUHLF-ram" or "VUHLF-rawm"—Teutonic: "respected wolf" or "feared wolf"; Germanic: "cream (colored) wolf" or "sooty wolf." **WULFRAM. WOLF, WULF.**

WOODROW, "WOOD-row"—English: "row of cottages near the wood." Thomas Woodrow Wilson was president from 1913 to 1920. He won the Nobel Peace Prize in 1919 for his work in establishing the League of Nations. **WOOD, WOODIE, WOODY.**

WOODY. See ELWOOD, WOODROW.

WYANET, "why-uh-NET"—Native American: "beautiful boy." F

WYATT, "WY-uht"—English: "watering

place"; French: "a guide or scout." **WYAT-TE, WYETH.** Wyatt Earp (d. 1929) was a gunfighter, gambler, and lawman of the American Old West who fought in a famous shootout at the O.K. Corral.

WYCLIFFE, "WIH-klihf" or "WYE-klif"—*Norse: "village near the cliffs."* John Wycliffe was a fourteenth-century religious philosopher who produced the first English translation of the Bible.

WYLIE, "WY-lee"—*Anglo-Saxon: "beguiling."* **WILEY.**

WYMAN, "WY-man"—*Anglo-Saxon: "fight-er."* **WYMER, WYMORE.**

WYNDHAM, "WIHND-hum"—*Anglo-Saxon: "hamlet with a winding path"* or *"from the windy hamlet."* **WINDHAM.**

WYNTON. See WINSTON, WINTON.

WYTHE, "WITHE"—*English: "willow tree."* **WYETH** (WY-ehth).

WYVERN, "WY-vurn"—*English from French: "flying dragon."* **WIVERN.** In European legend, the wyvern is a two-legged dragon with a barbed tail, bird's wings, and feet. It is often used in heraldry.

THE TOP FIVE

XAVIER
XERXES
XIMEN(ES)
XENOS
XANTHUS/OS

If the name you're looking for isn't here, see "Z."

XANTHOS, "ZAHN-thohs"—*Greek: "yellow or golden."* **XANTHIUS, XANTHUS.** Xanthus is one of the alternate names for the Greek god Apollo. Xanthos was one of the immortal horses that belonged to the god Poseidon. F

XAVIER, "ZAH-vee-air" or "HAH-vee-air"—*Basque: "owner of the new house"; Arabic: "bright"; Latin: "to save" or "savior."* **JAVIER** (HAH-vee-air)—Spanish; **XABIER**—Basque. Saint Francis Xavier cofounded the Jesuit order in the fourteenth century. Xavier Cugat was a jovial Spanish-American bandleader who appeared as a jovial Spanish-American bandleader in MGM musicals of the 1940s. F

XENOS, "ZEE-noss"—*Greek: "guest."* **XENO.** F

XERXES, "ZURK-zees" or "ZUR-zees"—*Persian: "king."* This was the name of several ancient Persian kings.

XIMEN(ES). See SIMON.

XULON, "ZOO-lawn"—*Greek: "the woods."* **XUTHOS.** Xuthos was the mythic son of Helene, the founder of the Ionian race.

XYLON, "ZEE-lawn"—*Greek: "the forest."*

THE TOP FIVE

YANCY
YUL(E)
YAPHET
YASIR
YORK

If the name you're looking for isn't here, see the vowels.

YAGGER, "YAG-ur"—*Scottish: "wanderer" or "ranger."*

YAHRIEL, "YAH-ree-ehl"—*Hebrew: "heavenly fire."* This is one of the Dominion angels in the heavenly hierarchy. **YAHRI-EL.**

YAIR, "YAH-eer"—*Hebrew: "he will enlighten."*

YAKIR, "yah-KEER"—*Hebrew: "beloved and honored."* F

YAKOFF, YAKOV, "YAH-kawf/kawv"—*Russian, from Jacob: "the supplanter."* See also JACOB.

YALE, "YALE"—*Scottish: "vigorous"; English: "old"; Teutonic: "one who pays" or "one who yields."*

YAN(G), "YAHN(G)"—*Chinese: "god" or "lord."*

YANCY, "YAN-see"—*French: "Englishman."* **YANCEY.**

YAPHET, "YAH-feht"—*Hebrew: "handsome."* **JAFFA** (YAH-fah), **YAFFA.** Yaphet Koto is a actor best known for action-adventure roles. F

YARB, "YAHRB"—*Gypsy: "fragrant herbs."*

YARDLEY, YEARDLEY, "YAHRD-lee" for both, or "YEERD-lee" for the second—*English: "enclosed property" or "pastureland."* **YARDLEA, YARDLEIGH; YEARDLEA, YEARDLEIGH. LEE, LEIGH; YARD.** F

YARKON, "YAHR-kawn"—*Hebrew: "the color green."* F

YARON, "YAH-rawn"—*Hebrew: "singing."*

YARROW, "YAH-roh" or "YARE-oh"—*English.* Yarrow blooms in a variety of colors and bears aromatic foliage that is used in herbal medicine.

YASHAR, "yah-SHAHR"—*Hebrew: "honest" or "moral."* **YESHER.**

YASIR, "YAH-sir"—*Arabic: "wealthy."* **YASSER** (YAH-sur), **YASSIR.** Yasir Arafat is the head of the Palestine Liberation Organization.

YEDID, "yeh-DEED"—*Hebrew: "friend."* **YADID.** F

YEMON, "YEH-mon"—*Japanese: "guarding the gate."*

YERIK, "YEH-rihk"—*Russian from Hebrew: "appointed by God."* **YAREMA, YAREMKA.**

YIGAL, "yee-GAHL"—*Hebrew: "God will redeem."* **YAGEL, YIGAEL.**

SOUTHWEST BOYS' NAMES

Boys born in the Southwest are most likely to have the following names:

1. Michael
2. Joshua
3. Christopher
4. Matthew
5. Daniel
6. Joseph
7. Anthony
8. Andrew
9. Ryan
10. David
11. Brandon
12. Jacob
13. Justin
14. James
15. Robert
16. Tyler
17. Aaron
18. John
19. Zachary
20. Jose

YMIR, "EE-mihr" or "UH-mihr"—*Norse: the father of giants.* In Norse mythology, Ymir was made of frost and fire. From his body, the gods of Valhalla created the world.

YNGVE, "ING-veh" (soft "G")—*Norse: "lord, master."* **INGVE.**

YOKI, "YOH-kee"—*Native American: "rain"; Hopi: "bluebird on the mesa."* F

YORAH, "YOH-rah"—*Hebrew: "to teach."*

YORI, "YOH-ree"—*Japanese: "worthy of trust."*

YORICK, "YOH-rihk"—*Danish version of George: "farmer"; Latin: "sacred tree."* **YORICH, YORIK, YORK, YORKE.** Yorick is a character in Shakespeare's *Hamlet.* See GEORGE.

YORK. See YORICK.

YOSHI, "YOH-shee"—*Japanese: "good" or "respectful."* F

YU, "YOO"—*Chinese: "jade."* Yu the Great founded China's first dynasty, the Xia. Legend says he was descended from a magical dragon-god, one who invented the art of divination, and devised nets for hunting and fishing. Yu tamed the great Yellow River and built a magnificent city called Erlitou.

YUCEL, "yoo-SEHL"—*Turkish: "sublime."* **YUCELO.** F

YUKIO, "yoo-KEE-oh" or "YOO-kee-oh"—*Japanese: "snowy boy."* This is a name for a boy born in December.

YUL(E), "YUHL" or "YOOL"—*Norse and Teutonic: "winter festival."* **EUELL, EWELL; YULLIS.** Yul was a central and northern European pagan celebration that was adapted by the Christians into a celebration of Jesus Christ's birth in order to ease the transition to the new faith. Yul Brynner was an actor noted for playing delicious villains, with the notable exception of his musical turn as the King of Siam in the film and play *The King and I.*

YUMA, "YOO-mah"—*Native American Navajo: "son of the chief."*

YURI, "YOO-ree"—*Japanese: "lily"; Russian, from George: "farmer."* **YURA, YURIK, YUROCHKA.** F

YVES, "EVE" or "EEVZ"—*French from*

Hebrew: "life"; French: "yew tree" or "archer." The yew tree provided excellent wood for bowmaking, thus the association with archers. Saint Yves was a fourteenth-century priest, lawyer, and judge from Brittany who was an all-'round good guy. Yves Montand was a French singer and actor who made American musicals in the 1950s and 1960s. Jacques-Yves Cousteau is a famed oceanographer and activist. F

YVON, "ee-VON" or "ee-VAWN"—French version of John: *"God's gracious gift"; Greek: "tranquility" and "flower."* **IBAN** (ee-bahn), **IBON** (ee-bohn)—Basque; **YVAN** (ee-VAN), **YVAIN**—Bretagne. In the Arthurian lore of Bretagne, Sir Yvain was a Knight of the Round Table driven mad by love. He wanders, wild and troubled, in the woods, and encounters a lion. The lion and he take a liking to one another, and they calm and restore one another. **VON, VONNY.** See also EVAN, IVAN, JOHN. F

THE TOP FIVE

ZACHARY
ZED
ZEV/ZIV
ZAIRE
ZEUS

If the name you're looking for isn't here, see "S" and "X."

ZABDI, "ZAHB-dee"—*Hebrew: "my gift."* **ZABEDEE, ZAVDI, ZEBEDEE.**

ZACHARY, "zah-kah-REE"—*version of Zachariah, Hebrew: "remembered by the Lord."* **ZACCARIA** (zah-kah-REE-ah or zah-KAH-ree-ah), **ZACCARIO**—Italian; **ZACCHA-RIE**—French; **ZACHARIAH** (zah-kah-REE-ah or zah-kah-RYE-uh); **ZACHARIAS** (zah-KAH-ree-ah)—Dutch; **ZACHARIAS** (zah-kah-REE/RYE-uhss)—Latin and Hebrew; **ZECHARUAH**. In the Old Testament/Tanakh, Zechariah was one of the minor prophets. In the New Testament, Zacharias was a rabbi and the father of John the Baptist. Zachary is one of the Christian saints. **ZACH, ZACK, ZAK.**

ZACK. See ZACHARIAH, ZAKKAI.

ZAHID, "zah-HEED"—*Arabic: "ascetic."*

ZAHIR, "zah-HEER"—*Arabic: "luminous" or "shining."* **ZAIRE.** F

ZAID, "zah-EED"—*Arabic: "increase" or "growth."* **ZAHID, ZAYD, ZIYAD, ZIYYAD.** F

ZAIDE, "ZAH-ee-dah"—*Yiddish: "elder."* **SAIDE.**

ZAIRE. See ZAHIR.

ZAKAT, "zah-KAHT"—*Arabic: "integrity."*

ZAKKAI, "ZAH-kye"—*Hebrew: "pure" or "innocent."* **ZA(C)K.**

ZAMIR, "zah-MEER"—*Hebrew: "bird song."*

ZANDRO, "ZAHN-droh"—*Greek: "friend" or "helper."* F

ZANE, "ZAYN"—*Polish version of John, "God's gift."* Zane Grey was a prolific American author who specialized in romantic tales of the Old West. See also JOHN.

ZAREK, "ZAH-rehk"—*Polish: "God protect the king."*

ZEB, "ZEHB"—*diminutive of Zebadiah: "God has bestowed."* **ZEBADIAH** (zeh-bah-DYE-ah), **ZEBEDEE**—Hebrew. In the New Testament, Zebedee is the father of two apostles, James and John.

ZED, "ZEHD"—*diminutive of Zedekiah: "God's justice."* **ZEDEK** (ZEH-dehk)—Polish; **ZEDEKIAH** (zeh-deh-KYE-ah)—Hebrew. In the Tanakh/Old Testament, Zedekiah was the last king of Judah.

ZEHAVI, "zeh-HAH-vee"—*Hebrew: "brilliant gold."*

ZEKE, "ZEEK"—*Arabic: "intelligent."* See also EZEKIEL.

ZEN, "ZEHN"—*Japanese: "meditation" or "peacefulness."* Adherents of Zen Buddhism believe that enlightenment can be found through intuition, self-contemplation, and meditation.

ZENAS, "ZEE-nahs"—*Greek: "Zeus' gift."*

ZENDIK, "ZEHN-dihk"—*Persian: "sacred" or "fire worshipper"; Arabic: "atheist," or more specifically, a Zoroastrian.* F

ZENO, "ZEE-noh"—*Greek: "sign" or "portent," and another name for the god Zeus.* **ZENAS, ZENON, ZENOS.** Zeno was a radical Greek philosopher of the fourth and third centuries B.C.

ZENON, "ZEE-non"—*Greek: "hospitality."*

ZETAN, "ZAY-tahn"—*Hebrew: "olive"; Greek: "six" or "sixth."* F

ZEUS, "ZOOSE"—*Greek: "brighter than all."* Zeus was the supreme Olympian god in Greek mythology.

ZEV, "ZEHV"—*Hebrew: "wolf."* **ZEEV, ZIF,**

ZIV. See also ZIVEN.

ZIGGY. See SIGMOND.

ZIKOMO, "zee-KOH-moh"—*African Ngoni: "thanks."*

ZISKIND, "ZIHS-kinned" or "ZEES-keend"—*Yiddish: "God aids."*

ZIV, "ZEEV"—*Hebrew: "splendor" or "brightness."* F

ZIVEN, "ZIH-ven" or "ZY-ven"—*Slavic: "vigorous."* **ZEVON, ZIVON. ZEV, ZIV.**

ZOHAR, "zoh-HAHR"—*Hebrew: "splendor."* F

ZORILL, "ZOH-rihl"—*Greek/Spanish: "little fire"; French/African: "striped muishond."* **ZORIL.** A muishond is like a mischievous weasel or otter. F

ZORION, "zoh-ree-ohn"—*Basque: "happy."*

ZUHAYR, "zoo-hah-EER"—*Arabic: "bright."*

ZURIEL, "ZOO-ree-ehl"—*Hebrew: "God is my rock."*

Afterword

I hope that you found the name or names for which you were looking within the pages of this book. I'm curious as to which ones you chose and why, so if you have the time and a stamp, or if you're online, send me a note at the address below. Also, if you encounter a new and unusual name, find out about it if you can, and let me know. The publisher and I hope to update this book periodically, and maybe the name you find or create will make it into the next edition!

Thanks again for selecting this book. I liked doing it, and I hope you found it informative and interesting.

Yvonne M. de La Paix
P.O. Box 1452
Burbank CA 91507
e-mail: ACoolCrab @ aol.com